FOLLOWING IN LINCOLN'S FOOTSTEPS

FOLLOWING IN LINCOLN'S FOOTSTEPS

A Complete Annotated
Reference to
Hundreds of
Historical Sites
Visited by
Abraham Lincoln

RALPH GARY

CARROLL & GRAF PUBLISHERS
NEW YORK

This is dedicated to my two best friends: my father, the best man I have known, whose exemplary life, Christian faith, wit, positive inspiration, and example into his ninth decade continue to inspire all; and my beloved wife whose love, patience, understanding, and support have been a treasure to me and made this book possible.

FOLLOWING IN LINCOLN'S FOOTSTEPS
*A Complete Annotated Reference to Hundreds of Historical Sites
Visited by Abraham Lincoln*

Carroll & Graf Publishers
A Division of Avalon Publishing Group Incorporated
161 William St., 16th Floor
New York, NY 10038

Copyright © 2001 by Ralph Gary

Interior and back cover maps © Jeffrey L. Ward

First Carroll & Graf edition 2001

Library of Congress Cataloging-in-Publication Data is available.

ISBN: 0-7867-0941-3

9 8 7 6 5 4 3 2 1

Designed by Kathleen Lake, Neuwirth & Associates, Inc.

Printed in the United States of America
Distributed by Publishers Group West

Acknowledgments

A work of this kind could not be done without the help of authors, historians, historical societies, libraries, and others in possession of local information, and also of a broader scope. Even though I have combed thousands of publications and sources all over the country, I could not have located many of these sites without the help of many including the following. So thanks go to:

Frank Williams and Jack Waugh for their knowledge and encouragement during the completion of this work.

Dr. Wayne C. Temple, with his incomparable knowledge of Lincoln and Springfield, Illinois. He reviewed that chapter and provided information and advice that were essential to its accuracy and completeness.

Richard E. Hart, also who possesses a great knowledge and interest in Lincoln's Springfield.

Norman Hellmers and Tim P. Townsend of the National Park Service in Springfield for their knowledge and direction in the Park Service records.

Thomas Schwartz, the Illinois State historian, for his direction and suggestions.

Kin Bauer, Kathryn M. Harris, George Herman, and others at the Illinois State Historical Library for their aid at that great library.

Ed Russo, Curtis Mann, and Linda Garvert at the Sangamon Collection of the Springfield Public Library.

Leigh A. Gavin and the many helpful specialists at the Chicago Historical Society.

Ron Keller and Paul Gleason at the Lincoln College Museum and library.

Steven J. Wright and Dr. Bradley R. Hoch for their knowledge of Pennsylvania sites.

Cindy VanHorn, registrar and library assistant at the Lincoln Museum in Fort Wayne.

Dr. Rodney Davis for his personally guided tour and direction in Galesburg.

Bridgewater College president Dr. Philip C. Stone for his personal Lincoln tour in the mountains of Virginia, and knowledge of the Virginia Lincoln connections.

Steven M. Wilson and the assistants at Lincoln Memorial University. Their publication, *The Lincoln Herald*, always contains useful and interesting material on Lincoln, including a great source aiding in site location and recognition.

Chris Calkins, historian at Petersburg National Battlefield.

Warren Winston for his knowledge and tour of Pittsfield and Griggsville, Illinois.

Kenneth Miller at Farmington Home in Louisville.

Carl Howell Jr., Jim Larue, and park historian Gary Tally in Hodgenville.

Steven Rogstad for his knowledge of Lincoln's Wisconsin connection.

Dr. Edward Steers and Michael Burlingame for their advice and direction.

Lincoln actors James Getty and B. F. McClerren for their insights and knowledge of their local areas.

Historical societies in Washington, D.C., Columbus, Ohio, Bloomington, Illinois, Quincy, Illinois, Alton, Illinois, Danville, Illinois, Worcester, Massachusetts, Gettysburg, among many others who were of help.

Gettysburg guide and author Gary Kross.

Historian and author Donald Pfanz of Fredericksburg National Historic Park. Several others have been helpful in my several trips to that area: Mac Wackoff and Beth Getz at the Fredericksburg National Historic Park; D. P. Newton at the White Oak Museum, a local expert on Lincoln's presence in that area; Mike Litterst, now at Yorktown, an expert on Lincoln in Richmond. These were among the many in Virginia National Park Service. I am indebted also to author and historian John Coski, historian and library director at the Museum of the Confederacy in Richmond.

Michael and Kathleen Crews of the Indiana State Park in Indiana, and others at the State and National Historic Parks. William B. Bartelt also provided many insights and valuable information about this area.

Historians Jim Patton and Charlie Starlin at New Salem, especially the latter for his personal tour of the area to little-known sites.

Historian, author, and guide John Schildt at Antietam for his insights and knowledge of that area.

And the many more unmentioned but not unappreciated.

Contents

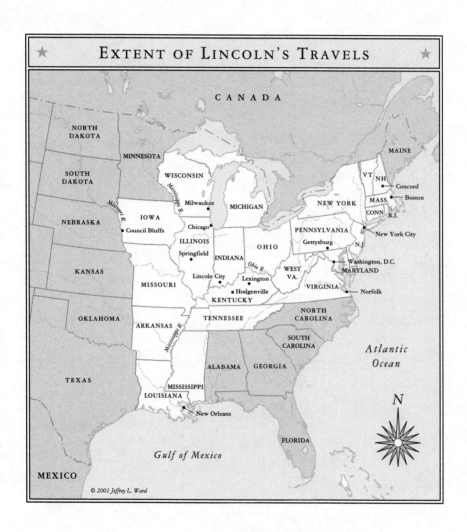

EXTENT OF LINCOLN'S TRAVELS

CANADA

NORTH DAKOTA

MINNESOTA

SOUTH DAKOTA

WISCONSIN

MAINE

VT
NH
Concord
Boston

Milwaukee

MICHIGAN

NEW YORK

MASS.
CONN.
R.I.

NEBRASKA

IOWA

Council Bluffs

Chicago

PENNSYLVANIA

New York City

ILLINOIS

Springfield

INDIANA

OHIO

Gettysburg

N.J.

KANSAS

MISSOURI

Lincoln City

Lexington

Hodgenville

KENTUCKY

WEST VA.

Washington, D.C.

MARYLAND

VIRGINIA

Norfolk

OKLAHOMA

ARKANSAS

TENNESSEE

NORTH CAROLINA

SOUTH CAROLINA

Atlantic Ocean

TEXAS

ALABAMA

GEORGIA

MISSISSIPPI

LOUISIANA

New Orleans

N

FLORIDA

MEXICO

Gulf of Mexico

© 2001 Jeffrey L. Ward

Mississippi R.
Missouri R.
Ohio R.
Mississippi R.

Note to Readers

Abraham Lincoln lived in places still in existence in our world today. This book will help readers identify these sites and better visualize, almost touch his life. It will allow us to reclaim real pieces of Lincoln's life from its otherwise mythic position by allowing us to better sense his presence and walk in his steps.

There are sixteen thousand publications on Lincoln, one of the two or three most written about individuals in world history. Every facet of his existence is covered repeatedly except for tracing and identifying specific locations and sites. We pass sites unaware that some identifiable event happened there. Many sites are now parking lots or groceries, ignored or unknown by authors and neighbors. Even so, many of those sites still exist. This subject that has never been fully documented and presented, and is thus unique and long overdue. Lincoln's reputation and fame continue to grow. With this our interest and fascination grow about places associated with him.

Lincoln is the most honored, respected, written about, and best loved (and among some, still the most hated) American. Even ex-Confederate General James Longstreet called him the "greatest man" of the times, "matchless among forty millions for the peculiar difficulties of the period." He has been called, "the supreme American in our history," "the Father of the Nation," and "First Citizen of America." There are Lincoln statues and monuments around the world, including in Austria, India, Japan, San Marino, Denmark, Norway, many South and Central America countries, and the British Isles. He is revered in Cuba.

There is a Lincoln statue near the coronation site of English kings in London. The specific places in his own country where his life occurred should be better recognized and remembered.

Many, even most of the sites listed here are not marked and are little known. Many local histories will mention a long-gone hotel, house, or other location without showing where it was. Unrelated historical markers showing more recent and arguably, more trivial events are sometimes readily found near or adjacent to unmarked Lincoln sites which, to many of us, may be the most significant or interesting episode in the town's history. If the "First Citizen," "supreme American," etc. was there, surely residents and visitors would like to know about it.

Tour guides, brochures in statehouses, and many large and small towns do not acknowledge that Lincoln was there. His associations with Boston, Indianapolis, Richmond, Philadelphia, Albany, New York City, Columbus, Council Bluffs, Woonsocket, and hundreds of other towns throughout America should be known. Surely most of the visitors to buildings not directly related to Lincoln would be interested to learn of a small Lincoln presence. Places visited by Henry Clay, Daniel Webster, or some local pioneer may be marked, but natives sometimes do not know that Lincoln was also there. Lincoln's presence should be known and marked, wherever it can reliably be established.

Historical and biographical background is provided here to help readers understand the significance of the sites. With the site descriptions are hundreds of insights and anecdotes revealing the human being. Many factual conflicts, obsolete addresses and other disagreements not evident from reading most biographical sources are also examined.

This book generally relates to sites, but also recognizes disagreements between reliable historians in identifying actual locations. I generally mention, but do not exhaustively analyze, factual variances about Lincoln's life. There are many "probably's," "some believe," and other statements here indicating lack of agreement. Actually, it is not so remarkable that we have so many differing opinions about every aspect of Lincoln's life and surrounding events. Almost all we know about his early life comes from recollections of those who knew him, but had no reason to document their memories and relationships for many years. Stories about his early years especially are questionable, as are many events and the analysis of all phases of his life. Most of these memories were not documented before contact with biographer William Herndon, Lincoln's law partner. About a month after Lincoln's death, he began collecting thousands of documents, and stories, some of which he probably colored. The reader should be aware of speculation, prejudices, wishful thinking, embellishments, inventions, and faulty memories. Herndon heard often when he asked people about Lincoln, "If I had known he would be so famous, I would have paid more attention." If an incident is shown only in one or two questionable sources, I have given a reference. Most sources of information are multiple, undisputed, and therefore not footnoted.

All of the Lincolns were very private about their feelings. It is interesting to speculate how much more we would know about the man and family if Mary, Robert, or even Tad had kept a diary, preserved personal letters, or had written as profusely as the Jefferson Davises.

I have generally relied on the recent and highly respected *Lincoln* by David H. Donald for date and site locations when in conflict with other sources, and have pointed out disagreements with that outstanding source. Most spelling relies on Mark Neely's *Abraham Lincoln Encyclopedia*. *Lincoln Day by Day* is generally used to settle the staggering number of date conflicts, but this is not infallible or entirely complete. Otherwise I have generally used the latest authorities and majority of sources in relating most of the facts. No doubt some stories are legends only, and I have indicated which ones may be questionable. Other improbable incidents, such as locations of Lincoln's alleged drinking, or his seeking out of Confederate General George Pickett's wife in Richmond are not shown, as they are thought to be unreliable. Some significant places related to other historical personalities are too close and easily accessible to Lincoln sites not to mention.

Probably a study like this will never be complete, as evidence and new sites will be disputed and discovered, and the descriptions will evolve. I can annotate every fact and statement, but feel that it would be too cumbersome to do so except as shown. Therefore the bibliography shows source titles first so that area references are easier to identify. It is hoped that knowledgeable readers will supplement this book with documented information of their own. Readers who wish to provide me with information that may be included in subsequent editions of the book may contact me care of the publisher.

Ralph Gary
July 2001

Arkansas

braham Lincoln made a trip down the Mississippi River from Indiana with Jefferson Ray in 1826 to sell his father's produce, at least according to some accounts. He sold to buyers along the river-bank near Memphis, and got a job on a plantation in Crittenden County (adjacent to Wappahocca Lake) owned by Colonel William D. Ferguson where he worked beside slaves. This would have preceded the 1828 trip with Allen Gentry. (*Lincoln Day by Day* does not mention this trip, and Louis Warren says this did not take place, which is probably correct. The William Dean Howells biography, reviewed and unchallenged by Lincoln, says his first trip to New Orleans was in 1828. Of course it is possible that a trip was made to Tennessee and Arkansas in 1826, so that statements about "the first trip to New Orleans" later would be accurate.) Ferguson told a story that Lincoln worked for him several weeks in his woodyard in Greencock on his way back about 1828 (1826?) to pay his way. Greencock has since washed away in the river. He claimed to have renewed his acquaintance with Lincoln in the White House and discussed the trip. If 1828 is the accurate date, it is more probably true. Otherwise, if Lincoln ever set foot in Arkansas, it would have been during the later New Orleans trips when he camped on the banks and may have drifted into nearby towns.

Connecticut

Lincoln made several speeches in Connecticut after his New York Cooper Union Address in February 1860. Officially, he went to Exeter College in New Hampshire to visit his son who was there preparing to repeat his Harvard entrance exams that he had failed. This gave the little-known political aspirant an opportunity to be seen and heard in the important eastern states before the Republican convention. He had been through the state in September 1848 on the way to Massachusetts, but made no appearances then in Connecticut.

BRIDGEPORT: In his last speech on his New England tour, Lincoln spoke at **CITY HALL OR WASHINGTON HALL** on March 10, 1860, filled to capacity. This is marked with a tablet at the **NORTHEAST CORNER OF STATE AND BROAD**. He was entertained at the home of **CHARLES F. WOOD** at **67 WASHINGTON STREET** where he first ate New England fried oysters.

HARTFORD: Lincoln spoke at the overcrowded **OLD CITY HALL** then at **85 MARKET STREET**, March 5, 1860, after being introduced by Governor Buckingham. He first apologized for his "slovenly appearance" due to his just having arrived from New Hampshire. He then stated: "One sixth of the population of the United States are slaves, looked upon as property, as nothing but property. The cash value of these slaves, at a moderate estimate, is $2 million. This amount of property value has a vast influence on the minds of its owners, very naturally. The same amount of property would have an equal influence upon us if owned in the North . . . Public opinion is found, to a great extent, on a property basis . . . The love of property and a consciousness of right and wrong have conflicting places in our organization which might often make a man's course seem crooked, his conduct seems a riddle." The *Hartford Courant* commented that this was "the most convincing and clearest speech we have ever heard made."

Lincoln's future secretary of the navy, Gideon Welles, was on the dais during the speech that Welles realized was a summary of his recent Cooper Union Address. The site is now a parking lot near the OLD STATE CAPITOL, on the west side of MARKET BETWEEN CENTRAL ROW AND TALCOTT STREETS. He spent the night with MAYOR T. M. ALLYN AT 81 TRUMBULL STREET, in the middle of the block on the west side of the street BETWEEN PEARL AND JEWELL STREETS. This is also a parking lot. Neither site is marked.

Welles later met Lincoln at BROWN AND GROSS BOOKSTORE AT MAIN AND ASYLUM STREETS and had a long talk while many gawked. They met again at the office of the *Hartford Press*. The State Archives has in storage a desk given by President Cleveland's secretary of the treasury upon which it is claimed Lincoln signed the Emancipation Proclamation. But, even the Archives personnel doubt this. The claim of having the chair used on the White House veranda to listen to band music is more probable since this was given by the Gideon Welles estate.

A bloodstained regimental flag that hung in Lincoln's box in Ford's Theater when he was assassinated is on display at the Connecticut Historical Society at 1 Elizabeth St. off I-84, exit 46. It may also be the banner that snagged John Wilkes Booth's spur when he leaped from the box. It is believed Lincoln may have clutched the flag after being shot and that it was placed under his head.

MERIDIAN: Lincoln spoke two hours at OLD TOWN HALL on March 7, 1860, where, "his side-splitting humor well entertained even those who hated his doctrines." The hall was located on a triangular plot between MAIN, LIBERTY, AND CATLIN STREETS. A special train of three hundred supporters arrived with the speaker, including a Yale professor who was so impressed in New Haven that he came to hear the speech again. A tradition that Lincoln stayed at a tavern at Broad and East Main is believed to be in error, as the *New Haven Palladium* reported he went back to New Haven after the speech. It is also claimed that he visited some of the local factories.

NEW HAVEN: Lincoln arrived at the CHAPEL STREET STATION on February 28, 1860, on the way to Providence. The station was two blocks east of the Public Square at FLEET, CHAPEL, CROWN, AND UNION STREETS. He spoke a block away at UNION HALL at 75 UNION STREET, March 6, 1860, producing, "the wildest scene of enthusiasm and excitement that has been in New Haven for years." He was entertained at the home of J. F. BABCOCK, 92 OLIVE, after the Meridian speech, who spoke highly of Gideon Welles for the cabinet. A parade of one thousand headed by the New Haven Band escorted the speaker from Babcock's home to Union Hall. The newspaper lamented, "It is a shame to New Haven that we have, as yet, no Hall that can accommodate a tithe of those who would attend"... to hear "the eloquent champion of Freedom."

His hour-and-a-half speech held the audience completely in his hand. He related several times in other speeches that he met Senator Cassius Clay of Kentucky on the train here and commented to Clay that a man they saw nearby was like the slavery question. The man had a sore on his neck, which Lincoln said was a danger to be cut out as he may bleed to death. But if he did not have it removed, it would shorten his life.

NEW LONDON: Lincoln had a layover for three hours on March 8, 1860, traveling from New Haven to Providence. The chairman of the Republican Town Committee, Julius W. Eggleston, heard he was due in town. After missing Lincoln at the station, he was found walking on Main Street and taken to eat at the CITY HOTEL. While Lincoln ate, Eggleston went out and rounded up some prominent Republicans who came to the hotel to hear Lincoln describe himself as a plain, logical speaker. He also signed an autograph book at the station where he changed trains again on March 10.

NORWICH: Lincoln probably came on the way to Massachusetts about September 11, 1848, on the Norwich Line Steamer, and then the Norwich and Worcester Railroad. He came back for a speech at the TOWN HALL on March 9, 1860, and "was listened to with unflagging attention." The excitement was increased due to a hot rivalry between two political clubs who wanted Lincoln's support and the fact that a delegation was brought in from another town to hear the westerner. Also this was the home city of the governor, and the Republicans wanted a big event. While Lincoln stayed at the WAUREGAN HOTEL AT MAIN, UNION, AND BROADWAY, he received many visitors and had political discussions with the rival factions.

Delaware

WILMINGTON: On June 10, 1848, Lincoln addressed a Whig meeting. The press dubbed him the "Lone Star of Illinois" and called his speech eloquent and patriotic. The president-elect was invited to speak here on the way to Washington in 1861, but time and circumstances did not permit a stop.

Illinois

Cousin John Hanks moved to Illinois and wrote back to his family in Indiana about the opportunities and fertile soil. Squire Hall and Dennis Hanks, both married to Lincoln's half sisters, became enthusiastic and decided to move. Lincoln's stepmother could not stand the thought of being far away from her daughters and their families and urged her husband, Tom, to follow. Abraham had turned twenty-one and was now free of legal obligations to his father, but decided to help and follow his close-knit family group of thirteen in March 1830.

The Lincoln National Memorial Highway was routed by a commission appointed to determine the much-disputed path from the old home to the new home near Decatur, Illinois. It attempts to follow the route as they crossed the Wabash River at Vincennes, Indiana, and probably followed a path leading through **LAWRENCEVILLE, PALESTINE, AND DARWIN, NEAR WESTFIELD, AND CHARLESTON** to a spot west of **DECATUR**, chosen by John Hanks. It is possible they turned north just across the Wabash and went through **RUSSELVILLE** on the way to **PALESTINE**.

Abe lived rather aimlessly near Decatur for about a year. After the bitter winter of 1831, he made a second river trip to New Orleans where he was delayed in New Salem. When he returned, he spent a brief time with his family, who had moved to Coles County, and then set out on his own to New Salem where he had been offered a job. Here he lived while serving in the Black Hawk War, probably courted and fell in love with Ann Rutledge, and had some kind of relationship with Mary Owens. He ran for the Illinois legislature, lost, and then won four straight elections, followed by another win several years later that he did not serve. In the legislature he worked with attorney John T. Stuart and began to study law more earnestly. This led to a move to Springfield after admission to the Illinois Bar. He was active in politics, married into a prominent family, served one term in Congress, lost two bids for the U.S. Senate, and practiced law until moving to Washington as president-elect in 1861.

He was absent from home for several months each year handling cases in other counties, mostly on the Eighth Judicial Circuit. It was a colorful way of life affording Lincoln his most pleasurable years of swapping stories and gaining influence. Travel was arduous, monotonous, and primitive, with only a few occasional, crowded, and dirty inns or houses to stay in and eat at while his family at home was lonely. But Judge David Davis said, "In my opinion Lincoln was as happy as he could be on this circuit and happy in no other place."

Lincoln rode this circuit even after Lincoln's own Sangamon County switched to another jurisdiction. Many of the other lawyers came home on weekends or other convenient times, but Lincoln did not, adding speculation about his home life and domestic unhappiness. Author David H. Donald believes that these long stays away from Springfield were professionally necessary for his sole income from legal practice. Ward Hill Lamon stated, "Mr. Lincoln was, from the beginning of his circuit riding, the light and life of the court . . . he loved (circuit) life, and never went home without reluctance. Here he forgot the past, with all its cruelties and mortifications; here were no domestic afflictions to vex his weary spirit and try his magnanimous heart."

Tavern food was plentiful, but often poorly cooked with poor sanitary conditions. Biographer William Herndon quoted one circuit rider: "No human being would endure what we used to on the circuit. I have slept with 20 men in the same room—some on bed ropes, some on quilts, some on sheets—a straw or two under them. And oh—such victuals—good God! Excuse me from a detail of such meals."

The judge, attorneys, prisoners, parties to cases, travelers, and host family ate at the same table. The lawyers generally slept two to a bed, which must have been a challenge considering Lincoln's long legs. Fellow circuit rider Henry Whitney wrote that "Lincoln's endless yarns were irresistibly funny, but the pity is that his funniest stories don't circulate in polite society or get embalmed in type." Lincoln was the best storyteller anyone could remember. He told "perfect" dialect jokes and stories in Irish, German, Negro, Scottish, and other accents. He did not use tobacco or alcohol, and when offered he simply said that he had no vices. Once he was told that it was the experience of his fellow traveler that a man with no vices generally had few virtues. (Contrary to other biographers, Dr. Wayne Temple has recently suggested that Lincoln may have drunk "upon occasion.")

After Lincoln served one term in Congress, most of his attention went to a growing legal practice until the Kansas-Nebraska Act rekindled a fire leading him back into the political arena. This legislation ended a prior settlement of the slavery expansion question. Now the institution was opened up into the territories. Lincoln abhorred this thought, and began to speak and almost crusade for containment. His fame and political maturity continued through the 1850s until he was elected president in 1860 and left Illinois.

ALBANY (LOGAN COUNTY): Lincoln plotted this town as a surveyor on June 16, 1836. It is a few miles west of the present town of Lincoln. He often traveled on the major east-west route by Rankin's Mill on Salt Creek at Rocky Ford, about a block from the business district. Actually the business of Albany was the mill, before the railroad. The town no longer exists, but the site is on Illinois Highway 22 at Salt Creek, about three miles due west of Interstate 55, exit 123.

ALBION: Lincoln first came to GENERAL WILLIAM PICKERING'S OAK GROVE on October 21, 1840, in support of the Harrison-Tyler presidential ticket, and again in 1856 to speak at a Republican rally for Frémont. Before the 1840 speech, Lincoln went to the town's log schoolhouse to borrow a copy of Byron's works, stimulating the interest of all the students who then attended that evening. The Democrat opposing speaker had lived in the town, and Lincoln wanted to offset the hometown connections. During the debate, he quoted a dark poem embarrassing the Democrat, asking "why he came not before," implying that the Democrat was a prodigal who should have returned home earlier.

After that speech or debate, Lincoln spent the night at the HOME OF WILLIAM VERDEN, in the southeast corner of Wayne County, five miles west of Albion. Verden's daughter later wrote that they talked about the War of 1812 and Black Hawk War until midnight. Lincoln was campaigning for the Whig ticket in the hopes of gaining some federal appointment, such as the Chargé d'affaires at Bogotá, Columbia. Harrison was elected but died shortly after being sworn in, so that a chance of a political reward or appointment was ended under the Democratic vice president, John Tyler, who assumed the presidency. This was one of the several appointments Lincoln failed to get or refused.

ALTON: On April 9, 1840, Lincoln as presidential elector addressed citizens in the courtroom in **CALVIN RILEY'S BUILDING AT MARKET AND BROADWAY**, then Second Street and the Public Landing.

On September 22, 1842, Lincoln was in town to fight a duel with the state auditor of Illinois, James Shields. Someone had written several satirical letters in the Springfield newspaper ridiculing Shields and signed "Rebecca." Lincoln probably wrote the first. Mary Todd, soon to become Mrs. Lincoln, may have written the second, at least in part. Lincoln claimed authorship and apologized, but Shields, a crack shot, demanded satisfaction. To avoid dueling, Lincoln offered to fight with cow pies. But Shields would not be put off. When Lincoln could not back down, he offered to duel with cavalry broadswords, across a plank, ten feet long and nine to twelve inches wide, within three miles of Alton, on the Missouri side of the river.

Dueling was illegal in Illinois, so to avoid being arrested the two men agreed to fight across the Mississippi River. They rowed to **SUNFLOWER ISLAND** (also known as Tow Head or Bloody Island). Asked to choose weapons, Lincoln, who was much taller with longer arms, picked a broadsword and then hacked at branches out of Shields's reach. Apologies were renewed and the duel was called off at the last minute, although the circumstances are not known. The party then rowed back to Alton where those awaiting the outcome had no idea what had transpired. As the boat carrying the parties returned to the landing, many anxious spectators gathered to see a "bloody corpse" on the floor of the boat. Some women fainted, but Lincoln, Shields, and the others burst out in laughter. The "corpse" was a log covered with a red shirt. Regardless of the levity at this ending, both parties to the affair were deadly serious and willing to give up their lives to uphold their honor. The animosity continued between the participants, including the seconds, who continued threats and challenges for some time afterward.

After the duel, the parties were hosted at the **OLD '76 TAVERN at FRONT AND MARKET STREETS** (adjacent to the 1858 Lincoln-Douglas debate site). Sunflower Island is now mostly under water, and it is speculative as to exactly where the site of the duel was. A ring of trees can be seen at low water, probably remnants of the trees there at the time. The ferry to St. Charles then went near the island to the west of the present Clark Bridge, Route 67. The Lincoln-Shields Recreation

Area is near, although there is no monument or marker. A marker might be put there by officials if the site can be identified with greater accuracy. During the Civil War a Confederate prison hospital was located on the island, and many who died were buried there, maybe as many as 300 Confederates plus many civilians and Union guards. Altogether 1,641 Confederate soldiers, Union convicts, and civilians are said to have died in the Alton prison and on Sunflower Island. The island then became known as Smallpox Island. Many graves were relocated after the war, but many bodies are still at the site.

If the duel had proceeded, as had many others in our history, two promising political careers would have ended. Shields later became a brigadier general in the Mexican and Civil Wars and U.S. senator from Illinois, Minnesota, and Missouri. In 1855, Lincoln was the favorite to unseat him in Illinois, but Lyman Trumbull defeated both.

The Lincoln family passed through Alton on the way to Washington, D.C., in late October 1847. On March 27, 1849, he passed through on the way back from his congressional session and on August 5, 1856, on the way to Terre Haute. He was back the next October 2 to make a speech in front of the **PRESBYTERIAN CHURCH** while the state fair was in progress at the present site of the **URSULINE CONVENT ON DANFORTH STREET**. The Alton *Weekly Courier* reported on October 10 that Lincoln was one of the most popular speakers at the fair. It stated: "The demonstration last night far surpassed the anticipation of the most ardent friends of freedom. . . . Hon. A. Lincoln, finding it necessary to return by the evening train, spoke in the afternoon to a large audience in front of the **PRESBYTERIAN CHURCH**. He made, as he always does, an earnest, patriotic and exceedingly able speech." The church was then on **BROADWAY AND MARKET**, directly east across from the City Hall.

Lincoln and many others were outraged at the shooting of abolitionist Elijah P. Lovejoy on November 7, 1837. Lovejoy and nineteen citizens protecting him in the interest of public order were at the foot of Williams Street and Broadway in Mayor Gilman's warehouse to defend themselves and a newly arrived press. Three prior presses of the abolitionist newspaper publisher had been destroyed in this town close to the slave states of Missouri and Kentucky. Lovejoy had claimed the right of free speech guaranteed by the Constitution and a number of men and boys from the town gathered to protect this right. Only three or four were abolitionists. They could not prevent the shot fired from ambush. Hundreds of newspaper editorials led to further attacks on antislavery papers elsewhere that fanned the slavery controversy leading to the Civil War.

The site of the last **LINCOLN-DOUGLAS DEBATE** is on **BROADWAY AT THE END OF MARKET STREET** and north of the prominent casino on the river. A platform was erected by a window at the east side of the **CITY HALL**, and is now marked by a platform with two bronze figures representing the speakers. The old building burned down in the 1920s. Lincoln and Douglas traveled on the same steamer from Quincy and arrived together. This was the last of the great debates and occurred on October 15, 1858. Thousands had come by boat from St. Louis and by the Alton and Sangamon Railroad. Alton was the southern point on the railway connection between Chicago and St. Louis. Lincoln had owned stock in this company, the only corporate stock he ever owned.

Both Lincoln and Douglas went first to the **ALTON HOUSE**, Douglas's headquarters, located a block south of **CITY HALL** at **FRONT AND ALBY STREETS**. The boat landing, City Hall, and railroad depot were at the same general location. A committee of Republicans then escorted Lincoln to the **FRANKLIN HOUSE**, a few blocks away at **208 STATE STREET**, just north of Broadway. Mary and Robert soon joined them, and the family ate dinner and spent the night. Lincoln and Douglas had both attended a reception there in 1841. This is now a restaurant, and the restored bedroom where Lincoln stayed can be seen on the second floor facing State Street.

During the campaign, Lincoln had followed Douglas in speaking on twenty-three of eighty days, and there were seven days of debates. During the last hundred days, Douglas had traveled 5,277 miles of primitive roads and made 130 speeches. Lincoln had traveled 4,350 miles and made 63 addresses. Douglas was worn down and his voice was failing. Lincoln's harsh tenor was clearer and stronger than ever. Lincoln argued, before a crowd estimated at between five thousand and ten thousand, that the fundamental difference between his followers and those who followed Douglas was whether or not slavery was wrong. "That is the issue that will continue in this country when these poor tongues of Judge Douglas and myself shall be silent." Douglas, his voice worn out by continual public speaking, maintained, as he had in the previous debates, that each state should decide the slavery question for itself. He told the crowd that Lincoln believed that a Negro was as good as a white. Lincoln repeated his prior statements and belief that a house divided against itself could not stand, and that the states must be all slave or all free. He believed that a crisis was approaching that would make the country move in one direction or the other. The arguments setting out their basic disagreements gradually evolved through the first six debates. Douglas tried to make voters believe that Lincoln was an abolitionist.

Lincoln carried Douglas's home county of Cook (Chicago), and Douglas carried Lincoln's home county. Lincoln won more votes to elect state representatives, but the Democrats elected more representatives, who then elected the U.S. Senator. The obsolete apportionment, in effect, made it necessary for a thousand Northern voters to offset 750 Southern ones. Thus Douglas returned to the senate and retained his dominance in the Democratic Party long enough to secure the 1860 presidential nomination, but not before splitting the party and the normally dominant Democratic majority in the country.

Lincoln's friend **LYMAN TRUMBULL** lived at **1105 HENRY STREET**. The house was built in 1820 and purchased by Trumbull in 1849. There is no record that Lincoln was a guest, but surely he must have been. Local tradition says that Lincoln visited, but did not spend the night. Trumbull served in the senate during the Civil War and was an author of the Thirteenth Amendment to the Constitution, freeing the slaves.

During the senate race in 1855, voting began in the legislature with Lincoln having a clear and almost commanding lead. Mary sat with her close friend of many years, Julia Trumbull, in the gallery at the State House to watch her husband's expected election. But Anti-Nebraska Democrat Trumbull was running also, although he could get only five votes to Lincoln's forty-four and Democrat Shields's forty-one on the first ballot. When it became clear that Lincoln could not get a majority and an unacceptable Democrat might win on the next ballot, Lincoln threw his support to Trumbull who was elected.

Just north of town at the **JUNCTION OF HIGHWAYS 267 AND 67** is the pretentious large stone house of a friend, **BENJAMIN GODFREY**, where Lincoln probably stayed and visited. There are also many other houses in the historic town dating before the mid-nineteenth century that Lincoln must have seen. Many are located on William, Belle, and State Streets. The house at **506 STATE STREET** was once the only hotel in town, the **MANSION HOUSE**. The *Alton Evening Telegraph* reports that Lincoln stayed there, but no dates are given. Also, locally it is said that he stayed at **514 STATE STREET**. The old **BUCK INN** was located about two miles north of the business center at **STATE AND DELMAR**, and dated to the mid-1830s. The historical society has a letter relating that the writer saw Lincoln as he was "going to Buck Inn."

Just north of William and Broadway, on the west side, are the remains of a prison built in the early 1830s and used beginning in 1862 as a Confederate prison. The facility contained 256 four-foot-by-seven-foot cells, but many more prisoners were kept here, with six to ten deaths a day.

AMBOY: The **LINCOLN BOULDER**, at 106 Main Street, marks the site of a Lincoln speech on August 26, 1858, the night before his Freeport debate. He spoke from the balcony of **DR. FELKER'S OFFICE** above Vaughn's Funeral Home, and stayed in the **PASSENGER HOUSE**, north of the depot. The barber at Flack's barbershop never used his razor on anyone else after shaving Lincoln. It is possible Lincoln stayed at the **SILAS NOBLE HOME** on that day.

ANNA: Lincoln spent the night of September 14, 1858, with the **D. L. PHILLIPS FAMILY, 511 SOUTH MAIN**, before the Jonesboro debate. After being met at the train station by Phillips and others, he attended a conference at Phillips's office, on the site of the **ANNA NATIONAL BANK, 201 SOUTH MAIN**. Phillips was the local postmaster, later appointed U.S. Marshal of Southern Illinois by President Lincoln.

ATHENS: This small community is located about four miles northwest of Springfield toward New Salem. The successful legislator was honored at a banquet held on August 3, 1837, at **200 SOUTH MAIN** in a building now known as the **ABE LINCOLN LONG NINE MUSEUM**. The toast was given, "Abraham Lincoln: one of Nature's noblemen." The Long Nine were nine tall representatives from Sangamon County who were instrumental in getting the capital of Illinois moved to Springfield.

While here he was the guest of his colleague, Robert L. Wilson, who has left us this description: "He seemed to be a born politician. We followed his lead; but he followed nobody's lead. It may almost be said that he did our thinking for us. He inspired respect, although he was careless and negligent. We would ride while he would walk; but we recognized him as a master of logic. He was poverty itself; but independent. He seemed to glide along in life without any friction or effort." Wilson said Lincoln stayed with him often and generally spent time in the stores with friends telling stories and whittling.

ATLANTA: Samuel Hoblit built the **HALF-WAY HOUSE** on the Kickapoo Creek nearby in 1839 where Lincoln stayed when traveling between Springfield and Bloomington. It was halfway between Postville and Bloomington. He arrived one day in 1849 to find the family temporarily gone except for sixteen-year-old John who was set to cooking fried potatoes and eggs. Lincoln then sat on the porch for hours telling stories. Nine years later Lincoln arrived to spend the night to find that the house had burned down and the family was living in a carriage shed. John offered to find other lodging with a neighbor, but Lincoln replied that he wanted to visit them and said the shed would be just fine. John was expecting his second child at the time, and it was named A. Lincoln Hoblit. The rebuilt Half-Way House was torn down in 1942, but the carriage house survives and is marked.

Lincoln spoke in a Republican rally on October 23, 1856, in UNION HALL, located in the present-day LAURASIAN BUILDING AT ARCH AND RACE STREETS, diagonally across the street from the library and museum. He came to town on August 26, 1858, to transact business for his client Richard T. Gill, and then used a back, upstairs room in a bank then next door to practice in a loud voice for his Freeport debate the next day. On July 4, 1859, he attended a celebration in TURNER'S GROVE, marked about a mile northeast of town center, on RED HAW HILL near the present cemetery. He had been asked to speak, but instead recommended James Matheny. Lincoln was presented an orangewood walking cane—with knots inlaid with silver and inscribed with his name—that he later carried to Washington. The CONGREGATIONAL CHURCH had just been built, and Lincoln went to a festival there with Gill. (The church no longer exists.) A local baker presented a cake to the surprised lawyer who is said to have become so embarrassed that he could not speak. Lincoln finally saved the situation by answering, "Well, I'm not so hungry as I look."

AUGUSTA: Lincoln gave a speech on August 25, 1858, in CATLIN'S GROVE, west of the business district and a little south of town at a site now marked by a boulder. He stayed in the palatial ELDER STARK HOME ON CENTER STREET, Route 61, west of the elementary school. Most of the crowd stayed for the speech even though it started to rain soon after Lincoln started. While here he drove over to Huntsville to call on his old teacher, Azel Dorsey.

AURORA: Lincoln stopped at various hotels several times. In 1851 a ten-year-old girl met him in HOYT'S STORE on the east side of RIVER STREET. Someone remarked that she could sing in French, and Lincoln requested a sample. She performed to his delight. He asked what kind of candy she liked best, and then bought her a pound of horehound.

BANDINSVILLE: Lincoln wrote several letters from here on October 24, 1858 (not on current maps).

BATAVIA: Mary Lincoln was confined to BELLEVUE PLACE in 1875, then an asylum, after having been declared insane in a Chicago court. This was built in the 1850s as a school, but became a rest home and sanitarium in 1867. It is on **UNION AVENUE** off Illinois Highway 31 just west of Chicago, and noted with a historical marker.

BATH: Lincoln, then deputy surveyor of Sangamon County, surveyed the town on November 1, 1836. He stayed in the log cabin of **CHARLES RICHARDSON** now on **GRAND ISLAND STREET** where he drew the plat for the original fifteen blocks. In a speech on August 16, 1858, from a porch of his friend and political ally, **GENERAL JAMES M. RUGGLES**, he recalled that twenty-two years before "he had with his own hands staked out the first plat of this town of Bath, then a wooded wilderness." This was two blocks south of the square at **ELM AND FOURTH**. Several people with Lincoln had been in his company during the Black Hawk War. Ruggles was a member of the General Assembly of Illinois. He was sick when the time came for the assembly to name the next senator when Lincoln was running, so he was carried to the Capitol on a stretcher to vote for his friend. The pretentious mansion is still standing. Lincoln practiced in the Mason Circuit Court in nearby Havana.

BEARDSTOWN: Lincoln and his militia company camped, before pursuing the warrior Black Hawk, at the **NORTH END OF WALL STREET NEAR THE ILLINOIS RIVER**. This is noted with a historical marker in **SCHMOLDT PARK**. He was officially elected and commissioned captain on April 21, 1832, with his friend, Jack Armstrong, as first sergeant, as shown on the marker. To determine which company got the best camp ground, Captain Lincoln wrestled Lorenzo Dow Thompson, who threw him twice. The company drilled for several days and was enrolled into state service before moving out on the twenty-ninth to a camp near Rushville.

Lincoln practiced in the Cass Circuit Court, although it was not on the Eighth Circuit. The old courthouse is now the **CITY HALL**, across from the southeast corner of the square at **THIRD AND STATE STREETS**. Here is the original courtroom on the second floor where Lincoln defended Duff Armstrong in 1858, the son of his former New Salem friends, Jack and "Aunt Hanna." This was the main theme of the Henry Fonda–John Ford movie, *Young Mr. Lincoln*, although reworked as a fictitious family of strangers in an earlier time frame. The legendary case has become known as the Almanac Trial, since Lincoln proved by using an almanac that a state's star witness could not have clearly seen the crime from 150 feet away since the moon was too low. Even more important to the jury was Lincoln's powerful appeal to the emotions. Tears rolled down his cheeks as he pleaded for the boy, picturing the great sorrow of the mother. The gruff, hardened, pioneer jurymen wept with him. Jack had died about a year before, on the day his son was indicted. The historical marker on the front of the building notes that "this was one of the most sensational murder trials in history." One of the best photographs of lawyer Lincoln was taken here by A.M. Byers on the day he cleared Duff.

The CITY SQUARE has granite memorials to mark sites where Lincoln and Douglas spoke. The PARK HOTEL, on the square, claims to have housed Lincoln, Douglas, Jack Dempsey, John Dillinger, and Al Capone. On May 6, 1858, Lincoln was at the DUNBAUGH HOUSE. On August 12, 1858, he was at the NATIONAL HOTEL. About five miles due east is a marker at a place called WALNUT GROVE stating, "Stephen A. Douglas spoke here in this grove on August 12, 1858, and Abraham Lincoln spoke here the following day."

BELLEVILLE: Lincoln spoke at a Whig rally at the courthouse on April 11, 1840, to a reported five thousand to six thousand. He also was evidently here on August 22, 1840. He gave "the speech of the day" on October 18, 1856, for John C. Frémont. Senator Trumbull was the featured orator, but the crowd stayed late to hear Lincoln. A marker in the wall of the JUNIOR HIGH SCHOOL AT LINCOLN AND ILLINOIS STREETS notes that "Lincoln was a guest at the JOHN SCHEEL home on this site and spoke from the balcony." He also spoke at a meeting at the location of the current city hall.

BEMENT: THE BRYANT HOUSE, across the railroad tracks from the business section, may have played a part in the famous debates with Douglas. Francis Bryant was a cousin of poet William Cullen Bryant and a friend of Douglas. Here on July 29, 1858, Lincoln and Douglas reportedly arranged for their debates. Douglas and his wife were houseguests on July 29 and 30, when Douglas spoke at nearby Monticello. Lincoln had written Douglas on the twenty-fourth, formally challenging him to a series of nine debates, one for each congressional district. Douglas had not yet replied when, as he was headed back to Bement, he ran into Lincoln who was headed for Monticello on the current Route 105, about a mile and a half south of Monticello. They stopped and briefly discussed the letter of July 24, and allegedly agreed to meet later in the day to work out details. A plaque marks the spot. Family tradition has long held that they met for a longer conference in the parlor of this house for more detailed discussions. Douglas wrote to Lincoln from Bement on July 30, agreeing to several points about opening and closing, suggesting that their discussion was in more detail than the brief roadside meeting. The house is now at its original site after having been moved about half a block in the late nineteenth century, and is open to the public. (Although this episode is widely reported, some evidence indicates that the debates were arranged solely by correspondence, although an article in the spring 1998 *Lincoln Herald* shows that the meeting is "soundly warranted.")

BLOOMINGTON: Some early legal records still exist from McLean County, but most were destroyed in a 1900 fire. Lincoln first came in April 1837 and attended every court session from the fall of 1849 to spring of 1860, except April 1851 and September 1859. It is said that Lincoln was transformed from a circuit rider to a statesman of national prominence on May 29, 1856, when he made his "Lost Speech" at the Bloomington convention. Maybe he could not have been elected president without the ninety-minute electrifying masterpiece that so hypnotized the approximately twenty newsmen and eleven hundred delegates that few notes were taken.

Several of his longtime friends lived here including Judge David Davis, Jesse Fell, and Leonard Swett, whose homes he frequently visited. He also used their law offices. These influential Republicans were instrumental in securing the 1860 presidential nomination. Danville native Ward Hill Lamon lived in Bloomington from 1857 to 1861. He accompanied the new president to Washington to become Marshal of the District of Columbia and his special bodyguard. Lincoln acquired two lots in 1851 on the NORTHWEST CORNER OF MCLEAN AND JEFFERSON STREETS, and held them for more than four years. It is at least possible that he considered moving here because of the large number of friends in the area, according to local histories.

The DAVID DAVIS MANSION, MONROE AND DAVIS STREET, was the home of U.S. Supreme Court Justice Davis. He began building this home, "CLOVER LAWN," in 1870, eight years after his appointment to the Court by President Lincoln. It was so modern that it had indoor plumbing and a central hot-air furnace. Lincoln was often a guest at a prior home, moved off its foundation to make way for the new one. He stayed with Davis during the eventful May 1856 convention when the Illinois Republican Party was organized, and he made his famous Lost Speech. On September 4, 1858, a crowd escorted Lincoln from here to the town square for a speech.

Davis has been termed "the man who made Lincoln President." He was born in Maryland in 1815 and moved to Bloomington in 1836 where he shortly thereafter struck up a friendship with fellow lawyer Lincoln. The two became good friends and allies. Davis was elected judge on the Eighth Judicial Circuit in 1848. Lincoln practiced before him for the rest of his years on the circuit and substituted for him on the bench when Davis was absent. President Lincoln appointed him to the Supreme Court on October 19, 1862. After resigning from the Court in 1877, he served as senator for one term. He was also the administrator of Lincoln's estate, and guardian of Tad. Robert Lincoln referred to Davis as his second father. Davis died a millionaire after becoming rich due to his business sagacity and investments in real estate, rather than through legal efforts. Early in his legal career he collected a small lot on the edge of Chicago as a claim for a New York client. The client did not want it, so Davis paid $800 and took title. He sold it later for $1 million.

Davis also had the distinction of being able to make a president with his single vote. When the electoral vote dispute between candidates Rutherford B. Hayes and Samuel Tilden was being decided after the 1876 election, an equal number of Democrats and Republicans were named to a commission to decide the validity of the electoral votes of several states. Davis was considered the lone independent, but he resigned from the Supreme Court and the commission. After his replacement the commission voted along party lines to decide the contest by the one vote Republican majority. Davis's vote would have been decisive either way to approve of the disputed electoral votes and thus make either Hayes or Tilden president. Ironically, in that presidential election Robert Lincoln stumped Illinois for the Democratic candidate, and Stephen Douglas's son worked for the Republican.

MAJORS HALL, AT THE SOUTHWEST CORNER OF EAST AND FRONT STREETS, was the site of many Lincoln political addresses including what his law partner Herndon called his greatest, the famous Lost Speech at the first state convention of the Illinois Republican Party. Author Elwell Crissey has studied and written about the event in detail and states, "Many Lincoln authorities agree that his overwhelming eloquence (here) . . . at once vaulted Lincoln into the leadership of the new party," leading to his vision of the presidency and road to the nomination.

The Anti-Nebraska Party convention was being held in 1856, and the State Republican Party was organized from it. At the convention on May 29, 1856, Lincoln "gave what was universally acclaimed as the best speech of his life," according to Professor David H. Donald. This dramatic presentation completely caught up emotionally all in attendance like few reported speeches in history. Many prominent figures in Illinois history and those closely associated with Lincoln were in attendance, including Owen Lovejoy, Leonard Swett, Long John Wentworth, Orville Browning, Norman Judd, Jesse Fell, (later General) John Logan, Judge Davis, William Herndon, John Nicolay, and others.

As the meeting was ending at about 5:30 P.M., there were shouts for Lincoln to speak. Estimates as to the crowd size are from five hundred to two thousand. Based on the size of the hall, author Elwell Crissey estimated eleven hundred, with about 10 percent identified. Lincoln had been repudiated for his stand in Congress several years earlier against many aspects of the Mexican War. He had not been consulted by the convention or officially asked to make a speech. Being late in the day, most reporters thought the session was over and put up their pens. They probably expected jokes anyway. By the time they realized the importance of what was being said, they were caught up in a spell, became enraptured, and could not write.

Lincoln rose to speak without notes and declared that those who deny freedom to others could not hope to retain it for themselves, that the abolitionists would never withdraw from the Union, and that secession by the South would be met by forceful preservation of the Union by the North. The only known quotes assert that "the North will not invade Kansas except by paper bullets in November, and the North won't go out of the Union, and the South san't." Chicago editor Joseph Medill asserted that he prophesied war and said the South was after Nebraska and Kansas. Later and earlier speeches at Peoria, Petersburg, and Springfield were similar and are thought to have contained the same thoughts criticizing slavery on moral grounds. Herndon wrote, "The smoldering flame broke out. Lincoln stood before the throne of Eternal Right, in the presence of his God, and unburdened his penitential and fired soul." The speech made Lincoln a national power, a keynoter of the cause whose popularity swept him toward the presidency.

There is only one published version of the speech, not printed until 1896, by Henry Whitney. He claimed he immediately told Lincoln that the speech was the greatest in Illinois history and would put Lincoln on the track for the presidency. Whitney's earlier book on Lincoln did not mention the speech, and there is a question as to the accuracy of his account, rejected by many, although he was much respected by Lincoln who was his close friend. Ida Tarbell claimed that Whitney had yellowed notes, which he refused to let her examine; so there is a question as to whether they ever existed.

The surviving members of the convention gathered in 1900 and "still considered the speech lost." One author wrote in 1925 that he had interviewed all known survivors, and all denied that Whitney's version was reliable. Another version written at the age of seventy by Judge Cunningham, who had heard the speech at the age of twenty-six, differed greatly from the Whitney version. Other versions have appeared. Medill and others felt that Lincoln purposely did not write down his speech as it was too emotional and dangerous.

Most of Lincoln's speeches before the House Divided Speech in Springfield in June 1858 were lost since they were not recorded or reported. Lincoln may have wished the Lost Speech to be lost as self-imposed censorship. Other theories suggest that reporters sympathetic to Lincoln may not have wanted the speech preserved because of its radical nature, or Lincoln may have just caught the audience up in a hypnotic trance. It may not have read well or made good literature. Whatever the logic, the emotional effect was lasting. Jesse K. Dubois said that "Lincoln's first conception of the Presidency dated from this incident." Shortly thereafter, Lincoln almost received the vice presidential nomination of the new party in Philadelphia. Majors Hall was gutted by fire in 1872, but parts stood until 1959.

THE MCLEAN COUNTY COURTHOUSE MUSEUM, at 200 NORTH MAIN, is a 1903 courthouse on the site of the one used by Lincoln. It is now a museum and research library. Lincoln practiced in a courthouse built in 1836 on the southeast corner of the square, replaced in 1868. That building burned down in 1900, destroying most county records. As a result, Lincoln's court work is mostly known only through newspapers and recollections. He first came to town after being sent by his partner Stuart to represent an Englishman, who was indignant over the appearance of the ungainly, rumpled young lawyer with unpolished, coarse boots and baggy pants too short for his legs. He was quickly dismissed in favor of David Davis. Later, long after Lincoln's reputation and stature increased, he assisted the prosecution in a rare murder case facing his friend Leonard Swett as defense counsel. Swett won, pleading the unique defense of insanity. Several addresses were made to crowds in the square including one on September 4, 1858. Lincoln used Judge Davis's office as his waiting room on the mornings before the court opened. The MCLEAN COUNTY HISTORICAL SOCIETY MUSEUM displays a desk used by Lincoln in KERSEY FELL'S OFFICE.

PHOENIX HALL AND BLOCK were on the south side of the square at 106–112 WEST WASHINGTON. Numbers 106 and 108 are still standing. Lincoln made his last long political speech on April 10, 1860, at Phoenix Hall just west of the current 108 Washington. Above the bank at 106, Jesse W. Fell took him one day to his brother KERSEY'S OFFICE to advise him to declare himself as a candidate for the presidency, and he encouraged Lincoln to write the story of his life so that others around the country might know something of his background. Earlier, on April 8, 1859, Lincoln had been scheduled to deliver his "Inventions" lecture. But only about forty people showed up, and he declined to speak.

Lincoln's friend **LEONARD SWETT** lived at **63 MULBERRY** and had an office in the **DR. CROTHERS BUILDINGS**. Judge Davis told biographer Josiah Holland that Swett and William Herndon were his "intimate personal and political friends" and knew "more detailed information" about Lincoln in his last fifteen years than anyone. Swett acted as Robert Lincoln's attorney during Mary's 1876 insanity trial.

The **HOME OF GENERAL WILLIAM WARD ORME** was located at the corner of **LOCUST AND EAST** in the mid-1850s when Lincoln often visited, and later at **12 LOCUST**.

The **DR. CROTHERS BUILDINGS** were on the corner at **116–118 WEST WASHINGTON STREET AND 111–113 NORTH CENTER STREET**. Lincoln's friends Lamon, Swett, Harvey Hogg, and William Ward Orme had offices on the second floor of the Washington Street buildings. On April 6, 1858, Lincoln was scheduled to give his lecture on "Discoveries, Inventions, and Improvements" in Majors Hall, but this was moved to **CENTRE HALL, AT 113 NORTH CENTRE ON THE SOUTHEAST CORNER OF WASHINGTON AND CENTRE** (now "Center"). After presenting this unsuccessful lecture again in Springfield and Jacksonville, the Ladies' Library Association in Bloomington arranged for him to present it at Phoenix Hall in April 1859, but he declined.

Lincoln stayed at the **PIKE HOUSE, ON THE SOUTHEAST CORNER OF MONROE AND CENTER STREETS**. (The McLean County Historical Society verifies that it was the southeast and not northeast corner shown in some sources.) Earlier, Lincoln had stayed here when it was called the Matteson House. It is claimed that it was in front of the Pike House that Lincoln, on May 28, 1856, said, "You can fool some of the people some of the time, all the people some of the time, but you can not fool all the people, all the time" (see entry on **CLINTON, ILLINOIS**). He spoke to a large crowd in front of the hotel that night. In 1857, he represented the owner in a lawsuit to cancel the sale of the hotel, alleging that the purchaser had committed fraud. Lincoln, Stephen Douglas, and other prominent speakers spoke from the balcony on numerous occasions.

The **JESSIE FELL HOUSE** was on a tract bounded by **BROADWAY, VERNON, AND THE RAILWAY**. Fell was one of Lincoln's closest friends and extended an open invitation to stay with him when in town. Fell had been one of the first lawyers in the area, but he left his practice in 1836 for real estate and railroad investments. He was the first to suggest the idea of a joint discussion between Lincoln and Douglas, urged from

1854 until 1858. It was for Fell and at his urging in the Phoenix Block office that Lincoln wrote a short biography dated December 20, 1859.

The JUDGE REUBEN MOORE BENJAMIN HOUSE, 510 EAST GROVE, was often visited by Lincoln who had signed his law examination certificate. He once recalled that while Lincoln was arguing a case before a jury of farmers, his suspender broke. Lincoln excused himself for a few moments to "mend my tackling," a term used in harnessing and hitching farm animals.

Lincoln stayed at 601 NORTH LEE and the NATIONAL HOTEL AT 105–111 WEST FRONT STREET before the hotel burned in 1855. The current structures, erected in 1857, are the oldest storefront buildings in Illinois that were designed by a professional architect.

THE MILLER-DAVIS BUILDINGS, 101–103 NORTH MAIN AND 102–104 EAST FRONT STREET, are the oldest commercial buildings in Bloomington and were built in 1843. David Davis used the white, one-story building on Front Street for his office until he was elected judge in 1848. The brick building contained law offices of Asahel Gridley, William Hanna, and John W. Scott, who shared their office with Lincoln when he traveled to town. Lincoln also wrote briefs in the office of justice of the peace Zachariah "Squire" Lawrence. Lawrence once asked Lincoln why his legal briefs were so short, and was told that this produced less chance to be proved wrong.

STEPHEN SMITH, the brother of Lincoln's brother-in-law married to Ann Todd, lived at 406 WEST JEFFERSON. Lincoln and Robert are claimed to have visited here. Stephen had stayed with the Lincolns in Springfield, and Lincoln wrote several letters of introduction to Bloomington citizens when the Smiths moved from the capital.

ASAHEL GRIDLEY lived at 301 EAST GROVE STREET. Lincoln won a slander case against Bloomington's first millionaire by arguing that everyone knew the man to be impulsive and to say things he did not mean. Earlier, when the railroad came to town, he had turned over his law practice to Lincoln. When Lincoln saw this new house, he is said to have remarked, "Do you want everybody to hate you, Gridley?"

A plaque at the LINCOLN OAK MEMORIAL, ON THE 700 BLOCK OF EAST JACKSON, attested to by former vice president Adlai Stevenson, states that Stevenson heard Lincoln and Stephen A. Douglas make speeches at the location, although some believe this may not be accurate.

BROOKVILLE: A marker on U.S. Route 52 and Illinois 64, one and a half miles northwest, notes that Lincoln camped nearby on June 8–12, 1832, during the Black Hawk War, and then went to Kellogg's Grove.

CAIRO: The *Chicago Press and Tribune* reported Lincoln was on the way here on July 20, 1859. A town history speculates that he "no doubt landed his well-ladened flatboat here on his two trips down the Sangamon, the Illinois, and Mississippi to New Orleans in 1831." This probably refers also to the 1828 trip from Indiana to New Orleans, which would have come by Cairo, but from the Ohio River joining the Mississippi River here.

CAMDEN: (Name changed from Postville in 1845.) Lincoln practiced law in the Logan Circuit Court.

CANTON: Lincoln spent the night in town on August 17, 1858.

CANTRALL: Lincoln often visited Justice of the Peace George "Squire" Power and is said to have filed his first case in Power's court. The novice lawyer also sought Power's advice when traveling between New Salem and Springfield. It cannot be proved what the case was about, but it probably involved a man who shot a dog, claiming self-defense. The owner claimed that Lincoln's client should have used the other end of the gun, but Lincoln argued that he would have if the dog had come at him with his other end. Lincoln's last case in Sangamon County was also said to have been filed in this court when Power's son was the judge. The old white-frame courthouse is now on the grounds of a later family home built in the 1850s. It is about three miles east of the elementary school. Go east from Illinois 29 on County Road 10N. This road turns north and then east. The Power home is north of the road midway between the eastern curve and Illinois 124.

CARLINVILLE: Lincoln practiced law in the **MACOUPIN CIRCUIT COURT**. On April 6, 1840, he spoke at the courthouse for a Whig rally, "with great power and elegance." The *Democratic Register* called him "the lion of the Tribe of Sangamon . . . and the judgement from outward appearance, originally from Liberia." The courthouse was then on the public square, but has since been moved a block east. Lincoln attended the Whig rally on July 25 of the same year and made a speech in November 1854.

Lincoln was here on August 4, 1858, to discuss with General John M. Palmer, an intimate friend and fellow lawyer, the upcoming senatorial campaign. He spoke at General **PALMER'S HOME** and may have stayed there. Palmer was later governor of Illinois and ran for president in 1896 as a Gold Democrat. Lincoln returned on August 31, when he made a speech at **MORTON GROVE** noted by a marker at **SOUTH**

BROAD AND 1 SOUTH STREETS. This was to a cool audience of about four hundred, whose sympathies were mostly with Douglas rather than the "Black Republicans." Douglas answered the speech on September 8, to a crowd of about eight thousand. Lincoln may have stayed at the **AMERICAN HOUSE ON THE NORTH SIDE OF MAIN STREET** between the public square and the C & A Depot, but there is no guest register to prove it. (Most hotels of the time did not have guest registers.)

CARLYLE: In March 1858 Lincoln was "kidnapped" by newspapermen who were his friends in front of the **TRUES HOTEL** where he was going to stay, put into a wagon, and carried to a Dr. Moore's home for dinner.

CARMI: While Lincoln was campaigning for the Harrison-Tyler presidential ticket in 1840, he stayed in the **RATCLIFF INN**, 206 East Main, a hotel now on the National Register of Historical Places. He spoke in the park known as **STEWART'S GROVE** near **FOURTH AND MAIN** on September 1, and was a guest of Edwin B. Webb, who had courted Mary Todd. Several men rode together in a wagon on the way there. It was noted that all of them got in by stepping on an axle or hub, but Lincoln just swung his long leg over and got in. After the speech Lincoln and Webb rode to Mount Carmel accompanied by Webb's young daughter, who was going to school there; she sat on Lincoln's lap.

CARROLLTON: Lincoln gave a speech on August 28, 1854. He stayed and swapped stories at the **HINTON HOUSE** on the **SOUTHWEST CORNER OF THE COURTHOUSE**.

CARTHAGE: Lincoln made many court appearances and probably stayed in **ARTOIS HAMILTON'S INN**. The site of his October 22, 1858, speech to six thousand is marked at the southern entrance to the courthouse on the square. The *Chicago Tribune* noted that "Mr. Lincoln was in admirable spirits and voice and gave us the best speech ever made in Hancock County." He stayed at the home of **ALEXANDER SYMPSON**.

CENTRALIA: Lincoln and Douglas attended the state fair on September 16, 1858. This date was between the Jonesboro and Charleston debates, and neither spoke on this date. Lincoln wrote three letters from the office of the Illinois Central Superintendent.

CHANDLERVILLE: The town was named after its founder, Dr. Charles Chandler. There was an unwritten agreement in the early days that early settlers left eighty acres on each side of a man's land unclaimed so that an earlier settler could officially claim his land at the land office. If someone violated this custom, he was considered a thief. A man whom Dr. Chandler had befriended told him he did not intend to honor this rule and would enter land that Chandler had settled, telling him, "To hell with customs." Chandler quickly borrowed money to file the claim and started to Springfield in a race to beat his rival to the land office. On the way, as his horse tired at about Salisbury, he ran into two young strangers to whom he confided. One became so indignant that he lent the doctor his fresh horse, and Chandler indeed did beat the rival to Springfield to secure clear title. Later he decided to have his land surveyed and he contacted Lincoln, whom a neighbor had recommended. He was pleased to learn when the young surveyor arrived that this was the man who had lent him the horse.

A marker notes the **CHANDLER HOUSE** where Lincoln stayed while he surveyed the land and later where he and friends stayed on August 13, 1858, while campaigning for senator in nearby Beardstown. This was the main road from Beardstown to New Salem and used many times by Lincoln.

About five miles south of here is **SHICK SHANK HILL** on the Oakford Road. Shick Shank was chief of the Pottawatomies and refused to leave after the 1819 treaty removed his tribe from the area. He persuaded the early settlers to allow him to settle on this hill, which had a spring at the base. James Hickey, a brother of Lincoln's friend Ashly, built a cabin at the base of the hill. Lincoln was here one day when the drunken Ashly challenged him to a fight. Lincoln refused, but Ashly insisted and seized Lincoln, who threw him to the ground and rubbed dog "fennel" into his eyes to prevent further fighting. The two joked about this later. Lincoln got to know Shick Shank and asked him at the tavern why he built his wigwam on the top of the hill. The old chief explained, "Skeeter no bother." Lincoln then asked, "How do you carry your water?" The chief answered, "Humph, squaw do that."

A marker at the hill reads, "Abraham Lincoln met Shick Shank, an Indian Chief in 1831. At the base of Shick Shank Hill in 1833, Lincoln defect ([sic], "defeated") Ashly Hickey, a bully, in a wrestling match by rubbing dog fennel in his eyes."

CHAPIN: It is claimed that Lincoln and Douglas stayed at the home, in the southwest part of town, of **J.D. COOPER**, who was a cousin of Douglas's mother.

CHARLESTON: Lincoln first passed through or nearby, probably deep in mud, in March 1830 on the way to the family's new home during their migration from Indiana. Lincoln later described the trip that pointed to locations nearby. It was a long twenty-eight years until he appeared with Douglas in the fourth of the famous debates in a campaign for the U.S. Senate. In the interim he came back often for his law practice and for political reasons. He occasionally saw his family, who had finally settled nearby in several different locations over the years.

When the Lincolns came to Illinois in 1830, they stopped at Wabash Point, later called **PARADISE**, to see friends and relatives. This is about two miles northeast of the current town of Paradise. They continued to the Decatur area but gave up after the harshest winter in thirty years and little luck on their land. Thomas had become discouraged after a brutal winter of 1830–1831 and decided to return to Indiana. Abraham was ready then to begin an independent life. Thomas and Sarah stopped in Coles County, about sixty-five miles into the journey back, and stayed about two weeks at the John Sawyer home. While here, Thomas helped build the Linder home, and then was persuaded to build a squatter cabin at **BUCK GROVE**. The family then lived on three farms in the area before purchasing the **GOOSENEST PRAIRIE** site.

The first cabin of Thomas Lincoln in the area was located about two and a half miles west and slightly north of Lerna, southeast of Mattoon, about a mile south of the Route 19 junction of Interstate 57. Known as the **BUCK GROVE FARM**, it is located off the road to the east, about a half mile northeast of the ninety-degree turn in Route 19, three miles west of Lerna. They lived here from May 1831 until March 1834, staying on public land and never taking title. Abraham visited after his New Orleans trip for most of July 1831.

One of the local toughs was six-foot-four-inch Daniel Needham. He challenged Lincoln and was defeated in a famous wrestling match held in the area of the Paradise post office at Wabash Point. **WABASH POINT** settlement was about ONE MILE DUE WEST OF EXIT 184 OFF OF INTER-STATE 57 and due east of the northern end of Lake Paradise. Lincoln later stayed many times with Elisha Linder and Aunt Sally. He and Elisha had studied together from the same spelling book in their early Kentucky school days. The Special Commission on the Lincoln Memorial Highway reported that Lincoln stayed more than one hundred times. The house was destroyed by fire in 1930.

The second location of the Lincolns is at the southwestern edge of **LERNA**, now on both sides of the railroad track just beyond the northeast intersection of County Roads 900E and 200N and east of the Routes 673–1667 junction. It is thought that Lincoln visited about December 1, 1835, on the way to a legislative session in Vandalia. The third site is the **PLUMMER PLACE**, about half a mile due south, on the west side of 900E, half a mile north of County Road 100N, where they lived for a short time in 1837. (This is directly south of where Route 673 dead-ends into 1667.) There is no record of Lincoln visiting that location. In August 1837, Thomas and his stepson, John, bought land on **GOOSENEST PRAIRIE**, where they moved with their families. They lived here for three years, until 1840, when they moved, cabin and all, just to the west onto a site where they lived until Lincoln's father died in 1851.

This site is now preserved as **LINCOLN LOG CABIN STATE HISTORIC SITE**, eight miles south of Charleston on the east side of Route 1668, with a replica double house, museum, and visitor's center. The Sargent farm home, built about 1844, and various outbuildings have been moved from about a mile east of the small community of **HUTTON**, approximately **TEN MILES ALMOST DUE EAST AND ABOUT A MILE TO THE NORTH**. Lincoln had visited his friends, the Stephen Sargents, several times at that location. The visitor's center claims that Lincoln visited his father and stepmother sixteen times at Goosenest. (Thomas Lincoln's residences in Coles County are characterized as "log houses" rather than "cabins" as the wood was hewn flat on both sides rather than left round.) As many as eighteen people lived here at one time, including Tom's stepchildren John and Matilda ("Tildy"), with their spouses and eleven children.

The Squire Halls (Tildy's husband) soon moved a mile south on their own farm. John Johnston never made much of himself, was noted as being somewhat lazy, and always had "get-rich-quick" schemes that never worked. But some recollected that Thomas preferred his stepson to his own son. Although Abraham was in Charleston frequently, he rarely visited his family. Sarah said in 1865 that she saw him only "every year or two." Although summoned by his stepbrother, Abraham did not go to see his father when he approached death and did not go to his father's funeral. His father had been sick for some time, and it is possible Abraham visited several times during his last year. He evidently came late in May and June 1849 and delayed his trip to Washington to press his desired Land Office appointment. He also came May 17, 1851, shortly after his father died. It is felt that his father treated him harshly as a youngster, maybe to the extent that Lincoln's hatred of slavery might be related. Several family members have written that he did not love his father, was treated with "great barbarity," and was not shown love or given emotional support as a boy. Dr. Wayne Temple believes that he resented "his father's garnisheeing of his meager pay." Thomas and Sarah never saw their Springfield daughter-in-law or grandchildren, and were evidently not invited to the

Springfield home. David Donald relates that there is no record in all of Lincoln's words that he ever said any favorable word about his father. Possibly he just wanted to turn from his frontier family and their way of life.

Lincoln sold his interest in the cabin to his stepbrother John D. Johnston's family who lived here until it was sold to Johnston's nephew John Hall. He had it dismantled and taken to the Columbian Exposition, then stored with hopes to take it to Washington. It disappeared, and was probably used for firewood. A reconstruction from 1936 is located on the site. The Lincoln and Sargent homes are open daily from nine to five during the summer, and weekends during the spring and fall, complete with living history programs. At both, "it's always 1845."

Lincoln made speeches in Charleston on the north side of the railroad tracks at about Fourteenth Street and Olive in 1840 and 1856. The tracks do not cross here now, but then ran down Railroad and Olive Streets. He stayed at times at the CAPITOL HOUSE OR JOHNSON TAVERN at the northeast corner of Sixth and Monroe, his headquarters during the debate. The COLES COUNTY COURTHOUSE is on the same site now as the one where Lincoln practiced. This is between Sixth, Seventh, Monroe, and Jackson. He also stayed at the UNION HOUSE, across the street on the northwest corner, at various times used as Douglas's headquarters. Charleston was not on the Eighth judicial Circuit, but was adjacent to several counties Lincoln traveled through on his circuit. He also spoke on at least one occasion at MOUNT AND HILL HALL at the SOUTHEAST CORNER OF FIFTH AND MONROE on January 31, 1861.

When Lincoln had law cases in town, he used the OFFICES OF USHER F. LINDER at the northeast corner of the square, at SEVENTH AND MONROE. Linder was sometimes associated politically with Lincoln, but he favored Douglas in 1858 and 1860. His son was later a Confederate soldier who was captured and sent to prison in Maryland. In answer to Linder's plea, Lincoln freed him to the custody of his parents.

One of Lincoln's most famous trials was held here in October 1847, the Matson Slave case. Historian Paul Angle termed this "one of the strangest episodes in Lincoln's career at the bar." It has also been referred to as "one of the oddest anomalies in the life of this man of paradox." John J. Duff, who meticulously studied Lincoln's legal career, deemed this "the most profound mystery ever to confound Lincoln specialists." Lincoln represented a slaveholder trying to get his slaves back. Robert Matson had brought five slaves here, Jane and her four children, in the spring of 1847 to work until the fall. Jane's husband, Bryant, was already in Illinois and free by virtue of the fact that he lived permanently in a free state. When it came time for the family to go back to

Kentucky, Bryant hid them with abolitionists. Matson claimed that since they were there only temporarily, they were still slaves.

There are two accounts as to how Lincoln became involved. In one, Matson went to Springfield to get Lincoln, who he felt was the best lawyer in the state even though he did not like the way Lincoln felt about slavery. Lincoln probably accepted out of professional responsibility and argued technicalities, and not equity or justice. Another account says that Lincoln went to Charleston in hopes of injecting himself into the case, and was approached by Usher F. Linder, Matson's lawyer, as he arrived at the **UNION HOTEL**, a local favorite of visiting lawyers. Lincoln had no other cases here at the time, and was busy preparing to go to Washington to take his seat in Congress.

There is also a disagreement about how diligently Lincoln worked for clients if he did not agree with their position. Some historians believe that if not the best lawyer in the state, he was probably the most conscientious. Thus they believe that it is not true that Lincoln only did his best when he felt he was morally in the right. Here, as always, he held no punches and "labored with indefatigable zeal." His argument in Matson was the opposite of his prior position in *Baily v. Cromwell* before the Illinois Supreme Court, where he reasoned that it was illegal to sell a human being by both the Northwest Ordinance of 1787 and the Illinois Constitution. Some historians report that Lincoln argued weakly, and his speech was fatal to the outcome of Matson's case, but this is disputed, as are many facts and motives in this and other cases involving the future president. He never collected his fee.

The debate with Douglas, held on September 18, 1858, is marked west of **E STREET AT THE EASTERN END** of the **FAIRGROUNDS** on the west side of town, on the south side of State Avenue (State Highway 316). The historical sign says it is about a quarter mile away from the actual site. The two candidates had come from Mattoon that morning along two different roads so that the parade of floats and bands would not conflict. The Republicans used the south road. While going through town, Lincoln reportedly saw his stepmother and stopped to give her a kiss. He then proceeded to his headquarters, the **CAPITOL HOUSE OR JOHNSON TAVERN**. The Democrats had their headquarters at the Union House or Bunnell Tavern. Lincoln and Douglas ate at the hotels, and Lincoln stayed with his friend Marshall, who then lived at **218 JACKSON STREET**, which is still standing (*Pictorial Landscape History of Charleston, Illinois,* page 104, and the commemorative book for the *Lincoln-Douglas Debate Festival,* pages 9 and 17). (*Abraham Lincoln and Coles County* gives two conflicting addresses for this house, Monroe Street between Fourth and Fifth Streets [page 246] and the Richter Block, between

Fifth and Sixth Streets on Monroe Street [pages 177 and 196]. This is
an excellent work on the subject, but is now believed by some local historians to be wrong as to this location.)

A crowd of about twelve thousand packed closely in the stands to
hear Lincoln address the subject of Negro equality and answer Douglas's charges that he advocated racial intermarriage. Charleston was
one of the two moderately Democratic Party–leaning districts among
the seven debate sites that Lincoln had a chance to win over. Here he
made some of his now most disturbing statements on the rights and
abilities of Negroes that disturb modern readers. It must be remembered that the debates were a part of a political process whereby opponents tried to bait and trap each other, and statements were made by
and to people of the times. Although Illinois was a free state, there was
a feeling against Negroes, seen in laws that discriminated, including a
proposed state constitutional amendment to prohibit their settlement
in Illinois.

The SPEAKER'S PLATFORM FACED EAST AND WAS AT THE NORTH END,
WHERE THE EAST GRANDSTAND NOW IS ON THE FAIRGROUNDS. Douglas also
referred to Lincoln's position in the Mexican War, charging that he had
voted against supplies for the army in Mexico. In one dramatic
moment, Lincoln whirled to the back of the platform and, seizing
Orlando B. Ficklin, a former fellow representative and staunch Douglas man, dragged him to the front of the platform before the aston-
ished mass of listeners and forced him to deny the allegations.
Lincoln's friend Ward Hill Lamon thought Ficklin was going to be
injured and grabbed Lincoln's hand to break the grip. One local farmer
commented, "I dont keer fur them great orators. I want to hear just a
plain common feller like the rest of us that, I kin foller an' know where
he's drivin'. Abe Linkern fills the bill."

The next day Lincoln visited his Coles County relatives and spent the
night with Dennis Hanks's son-in-law, Augustus H. Chapman. This
home stood at 400 JACKSON STREET. Lincoln stayed with Chapman frequently. From 1852 to 1857 they lived at the corner of EIGHTH AND
MONROE STREETS.

Lincoln visited Charleston for the last time on January 30, 1861, to
see his stepmother. He arrived at about 6:00 P.M. on a freight caboose
after having missed his connection in Mattoon. He spent the night at
the home of Senator Thomas A. Marshall with whom he had been traveling. In 1861 the home was located on the WEST SIDE OF TENTH
STREET, NORTH OF HARRISON, and set back from both streets. Several
hundred came to see him, and he was serenaded with the town's Brass
and String Band. The next morning he had breakfast at the HOME OF

DENNIS HANKS, then on the **WEST SIDE OF THE SQUARE**. Earlier he had built a house at **218 JACKSON** at the same site as Marshall later had built, and where Lincoln had visited.

The next morning Lincoln and Chapman rode out to see Lincoln's stepmother, who was living with her daughter since the chimney of her own cabin had fallen down the day before. John Hanks may also have gone with them. After Thomas Lincoln died, Mrs. Lincoln lived with various relatives, including her two daughters and the Chapmans. Lincoln's stepsister Matilda's first husband, Squire Hall, had died in 1851, and she had married Ruben or Reuben Moore, who had also died. (Both Hall and Moore are buried in **SHILOH CEMETERY**.) The old **MOORE HOUSE** is reached from **FOURTH STREET OUT HIGHWAY 170** southwest of town and is clearly marked, one mile north of the Lincoln cabin on the Lerna Road. It is open during the summer, and the grounds are always accessible.

When he took his stepmother in his arms, she broke down, telling him that she would never see him again, crying, "Abe, you are too good a man, and they will kill you." He spent most of the day with her, holding her hand and talking about the past. Chapman (and maybe John Hanks, who told Herndon he did) drove the buggy to nearby **SHILOH CEMETERY** and church where Thomas Lincoln is buried, about a mile northwest of the site of the old cabin, clearly marked. A marker in front of the church states that Lincoln visited that day with his stepmother, but it is documented that she did not go then. He had probably visited several times since his father had died ten years before. Many tombstones here now were in place when Lincoln visited, although the stone for Thomas is later. It is also assumed that his stepbrother John D. Johnston is buried here, although, surprisingly, there is no record or tombstone. It is not known how or when he died, but he had passed away prior to this visit. There are no death records for Coles County prior to 1870.

While they were gone, the women received many items of food from neighbors eager to prepare dinner for the president-elect. By the time they returned a great crowd greeted him, including the local children who had been dismissed from school. One of these lived until 1947. One of those present later said that when he left at about three o'clock, his stepmother told him again, "Abe, I'll never see you alive again. They will kill you." When Dennis Hanks told her later of her stepson's death, she lamented, "Yes, I know Denny. I knowed they'd kill him. I've been awaiting fer it." And she never asked questions.

There is a disagreement as to whether Mrs. Lincoln went back to Charleston with her stepson, which is probable in the words of Charles

Coleman in *Abraham Lincoln and Coles County, Illinois*. This would have given them more time as he spent the night with the Chapmans at the address listed above. He met with other members of the Dennis Hanks and Johnston families when he returned to town, and refused an invitation to make a speech at a reception at the Town Hall. He did say that he did not feel that he could make any statement about his policies or administration then, but expressed gratification at the warm feelings expressed on the occasion. The reception was at the **MOUNT AND HILL HALL**, second floor. When he left the next morning, his stepmother again related that she felt that she would never see him again, as his enemies would assassinate him. Lincoln described the event to Joshua F. Speed in 1865, adding credence to the accuracy of this event.

Sarah died here on April 10, 1869, at the age of eighty-one, and is buried next to her husband. William Herndon interviewed her in 1865 after Lincoln had been buried in Springfield. She recalled, "I did not want Abe to run for President and I did not want to see him elected . . . when he came down to see me, after he was elected President . . . my heart told me . . . that I should never see him again."

DENNIS HANKS'S GRAVESITE is in the west end of town in the **OLD CHAMBERS CEMETERY** near the **MADISON AVENUE AND B STREET INTERSECTION** and near the railroad tracks. His tombstone is close to the southeast corner. Hanks makes a claim that he taught Lincoln how to read and write. He had grown up in the same Indiana house with Lincoln and, although about ten years older, had been a constant friend to his younger cousin during those years. He was described as "gay, boisterous, kindly, a skillful hunter, a picturesque talker." He shared many early anecdotes about Lincoln, no doubt somewhat embellished and not always reliable.

CHICAGO: The city of Chicago was chartered in 1837, the year that Abraham Lincoln moved from New Salem to Springfield. It was then about the same size as New Salem, with approximately one hundred inhabitants. By the end of the nineteenth century, Chicago was the sixth largest city in the world. This was the gateway from the west, allowing transportation through the Great Lakes, the world's largest freshwater basin, to the western rivers, over a short portage from the Chicago River. The city had become important enough in 1860 to host a major party presidential-nominating convention, the location maybe decisive in producing the nomination of a favorite son over better-known Republicans.

Lincoln came often, at least 150 total days, for his legal business and political gatherings. His first visit was probably July 5–7, 1847, to attend the Rivers and Harbors Convention. This was the first national convention in what later became known as the Convention City. The *Chicago Journal* reported on July 6, that "This was his first visit to the commercial emporium of the State," and they expected "much" from the only Illinois Whig congressional elect. The convention was called in response to President Polk's veto of a bill for the improvement of rivers and harbors at federal expense. There were no rail connections, and it is unclear how Lincoln came. He returned home by coach along the Illinois and Michigan Canal past Lockport, Joliet, Dresden, Morris, Lasalle, and Peru. He then took a steamboat to Peoria and stagecoach to Tremont.

He gave his first speech on July 6 and made a favorable impression on New York newspaperman Horace Greeley, later a supporter and then critic. The old Fort Dearborn blockhouse still stood at what is now Michigan and Wacker Streets, where in 1812 the inhabitants of the area fled to be massacred by Indians near Stephen A. Douglas's later home (**Site** 52). Lincoln's later visits were generally for his legal practice in one of the two federal courts in Illinois. During the 1860 Republican convention and then during the presidential campaign, the city became his political base.

Lincoln's future visits include the following:

October 5–7, 1848: Lincoln was with his family at the **Sherman House (15)** and spoke two hours for Zachary Taylor at the **Courthouse (16)** to an overflow crowd that only had six hours' notice. Although the text was unreported, the *Daily Journal* noted that this "was one of the very best (speeches) we have heard or read, since the opening of the campaign." Lincoln had stopped returning from service in Congress. They took the canal route to Lasalle on the return home.

July 7–26, 1850: He was trying *Parker v. Hoyt*, an alleged patent infringement of a water wheel, when word reached Chicago on July 9, of the death of President Taylor. A committee asked Lincoln to give a eulogy, but he asked to wait until the trial ended. On July 25, he gave the address to a large crowd at the **City Hall (16)**. (Historian William E. Barton believes that Lincoln visited many times during 1851–1853, but could not document specifics.)

December 8–14, 1852: Lincoln worked in an office **(2)** at Wells and Water as a commissioner to determine compensation for damages in building the Illinois and Michigan Canal. At this time it took him three days to get home.

February 16–18, 1854: Most of the legislature visited as guests of Chicago citizens for an escorted tour of the city. It is "likely" (*Day by Day*) that Lincoln took part, although he was not in the legislature then.

October 27, 1854: After the passage of the Kansas-Nebraska Bill opening the possibility for the extension of slavery, Lincoln's public life took on a renewed fire and determination leading to speaking engagements including an invitation to speak in Chicago. The *Daily Journal* announced: "Hon. Abraham Lincoln, one of the greatest orators and debaters in the country, will address the people of Chicago on the subject of the Nebraska bill, this evening at North Market Hall" **(35)**. Afterward he was described as an honest and powerful speaker.

July 2–18, 1855: Lincoln attended Federal Court in the SALOON BUILDING **(4)**. Congress in 1855 divided the state into two federal court jurisdictions, and Lincoln began making regular appearances in the Chicago court.

July 15–26, 1856: He was involved with court work and made a speech in DEARBORN PARK **(11)**. The *Democratic Press* (a Republican newspaper) reported that "we have never seen an audience held for so long a time in the open air to listen to an argumentative speech. . . . He demonstrated in the strongest manner, that the only issue now before us, is freedom or slavery, that the perpetuity of our institutions is dependent upon maintaining the former against the agressions [*sic*] of the latter, and held up the bugbear of disunion, threatened by the slavery extensionists, to the scorn and contempt it deserves."

August 26–27, 1856: Lincoln came on speaking tour for John C. Frémont and stayed at MATTESON HOUSE **(13)**.

December 9–10, 1856: Lincoln spoke at the TREMONT HOUSE **(7)** at a banquet honoring the election of the state Republican ticket although Democrat James Buchanan had won the national election.

February 21–28, 1857: Federal Court work and speech February 28 in METROPOLITAN HALL **(17)**.

May 21, 1857: The reason for his visit is unknown. The *Daily Journal* announced: "Hon. A. Lincoln, the successor of Stephen A. Douglas in the U.S. Senate, was in town yesterday."

July 7–18, 1857: FEDERAL COURT **(4)** and attended theater twice with Orville H. Browning.

September 1–24, 1857: Court work mainly on the *Effie Afton* case won by Lincoln and others upholding the right of a railroad to build a bridge over a navigable stream. A hung jury was a victory because the case remained unsettled as the westward expansion of the railroads continued uninterrupted.

Late November–Early December 1857, February 18, 1858, and March 11, 1858: Law and politics.

July 9–14, 1858: In town for FEDERAL COURT. Douglas opened his senatorial campaign with a speech at the TREMONT HOUSE with Lincoln seated behind him. Lincoln responded at the same place the next day to a crowd three fourths as large, but with about four times the enthusiasm as reported in the *Press* and *Tribune*. The crowd extended for the whole length of the hotel along Lake Street, and the adjoining buildings were full of spectators leaning out windows and on balconies.

July 21–24, 1858: Conferred with Republicans about debating Douglas, and writes to him with the challenge. Tried to form an alliance with anti-Douglas Democrats.

October 28, 1858: Quick day trip during senate campaign. Stopped at TREMONT HOUSE.

February 27–March 2, 1859: Lincoln visited the city several times during the latter part of 1858, but did not stay long until this FEDERAL COURT session that gave him the opportunity to make a speech March 1, at the Republican Headquarters at MECHANICS INSTITUTE HALL (12). During this visit, Mary sent word that Tad was thought to have pneumonia, and she would be comforted if he would return home.

Early June 1859: With Willie at TREMONT HOUSE.

Mid-July 1859: With family at TREMONT HOUSE.

September 28, October 3, and November 10, 1859: TREMONT HOUSE.

March 23–April 4, 1860: Lincoln had stayed in Chicago before and after his September 30 speech in Milwaukee, and on November 10 and 11. The next lengthy stay was for the Sand Bar case in U.S. DISTRICT COURT involving title to a sandbar that had developed at the mouth of the Chicago River. Lincoln was one of several lawyers for the winning side, and had time to get his bust made by L. W. Volk and speak in Waukegan. The newspapers predicted that this "will of course, bring together one of the largest crowds that Waukegan can furnish."

November 21–26, 1860: The president-elect met with Vice President-elect Hannibal Hamlin at the TREMONT HOUSE in a series of meetings. On the twenty-fourth, Lincoln, Mary, and Hamlin stood side by side at the Dearborn Street front greeting the public for over two hours. Hamlin and Lincoln ate at Lincoln's favorite Chicago restaurant, TOM ANDREWS' HEAD QUARTERS RESTAURANT (8), and Lincoln bought clothes at A. D. TITSWORTH AND BROS. (5).

Chicago was one of the places he may have considered moving to after his presidential administration although the city cannot verify any expressed intent to make Chicago his home. It is claimed that at the time of his death he was making plans to buy a house on South Michigan Avenue. Possibly if he had lived, he would have practiced law here with son Robert who built a very lucrative career throughout most of his later life, much of it in Chicago. It is also claimed that Lincoln accepted an invitation for himself and Mary to attend opening ceremonies of the Northwestern Fair here on May 30, 1865. Mary, in some reports, wanted him buried in Chicago, but gave in to Robert and Judge Davis, who insisted on Springfield. Mary and Tad lived here several years after leaving Washington on May 22, 1865. They moved to Europe in 1868 after Robert's Washington, D.C., wedding and returned in mid-1871. Tad died soon thereafter. Mary was later declared insane in an 1875 trial here and kept in a private sanitarium in nearby Batavia. After several months she was released to Springfield to live with her sister in the house where the Lincolns had married. Robert was a resident of Chicago much of the time from 1865 to 1911, although he had homes and duties elsewhere.

All downtown Chicago structures associated with Lincoln were destroyed in the Great Fire of 1871 except for part of the ST. JAMES CHURCH (40). Robert's house, where Mary was temporarily living, was spared. This and his later home (44) have not survived. Some of their furniture sold before departing Springfield in 1861 was here and was destroyed in the fire. Many other documents related to Lincoln, including many letters, were also lost. Street addresses changed early in the late nineteenth century, and the current locations are shown in this publication. Therefore those addresses not updated in many other sources, even recent ones, are incorrect.

(1) The Republican presidential nominating convention was held in the WIGWAM on the SOUTH SIDE OF LAKE AND MARKET (NOW WACKER), across from the present Merchandise Mart. The city made an extravagant promise: it would erect a special, temporary building if the Republican National Convention were held in Chicago. St. Louis and Indianapolis had tried hard to secure the convention, but it was felt that the latter city would not have enough hotel rooms, and the former was not acceptable, as it was in a slave state. So the party met May 16–18, 1860, to nominate their candidate for the presidency. By this time the Democratic convention had already dismissed without a candidate, indicating a fatal disunity.

The firetrap was 180 by 100 feet long, held the 466 delegates, plus hundreds of newspapermen, something over a thousand in an upstairs gallery, and maybe eight thousand in a series of landings. As an avowed candidate, Lincoln did not consider it proper to attend. He was not as well known or powerful as other leading hopefuls. William H. Seward of New York was the leading candidate. Several others also came with more support than Lincoln had, but they were a long way from home and power bases. Lincoln's backer and campaign organizer, Norman Judd, was on the Republican National Committee and was largely instrumental in getting the convention. He, Judge David Davis, and others organized well.

Lincoln supporter Alexander McClure wrote three decades later: "Had the convention been held in any other place than Chicago, it is quite probable that Seward would have been successful [in getting the nomination]." The leading candidates had problems. Seward and Salmon P. Chase were considered by many as too radical, and Simon Cameron had a reputation for corruption. Edward Bates was too lukewarm. Special trains brought in Lincoln supporters who flooded the halls using bogus tickets that excluded rival delegates. The other candidates underestimated the effect of the convention site and Lincoln ballyhoo barrage on undecided delegates. A political marvel occurred, and the favorite son of Illinois Republicans was nominated. The nominee made no speeches during the presidential campaign and did not leave Springfield after the nomination, until he went to Chicago, met the vice president–elect, and visited the building on November 22, 1860. There is a plaque at 333 West Lake Street.

(2) Lincoln took evidence for several days in December 1852 at the ILLINOIS AND MICHIGAN CANAL OFFICE AT SOUTH WELLS AND WACKER, as a commissioner to determine damages incurred by the construction of the canal.

(3) ROBERT LINCOLN began law practice on LAKE STREET at the Marine Bank, just east of the NORTHEAST CORNER with LASALLE, with Charles T. Scammon. The 1866 city directory shows him to have been a student with Scammon, McCagg, and Fuller in CROSBY'S OPERA HOUSE ON THE SOUTH SIDE OF WASHINGTON BETWEEN STATE AND DEARBORN. He then formed a partnership with Edward Isham in the PORTLAND BLOCK ON WASHINGTON, SOUTHEAST CORNER WITH DEARBORN (21). He also had an office with Isham on the NORTHEAST CORNER OF ADAMS AND CLARK.

(4) The U.S. CIRCUIT COURT was the scene of many cases handled by

Lincoln when it was located in the **SALOON BUILDING** at the **SOUTH-EAST CORNER** of **CLARK AND LAKE**. Lake Street also was the main retail street at the time. Most of Lincoln's legal business in Chicago was here. Friends Norman Judd and Jonathan Young also had offices in the building. In 1848, **GRANT GOODRICH**, one of the most prominent members of the Cook County Bar, may have offered him a partnership then. Lincoln was said to have turned this down as he disliked confinement to the office and preferred life on the circuit. His office was here and later on the **EAST SIDE OF CLARK ACROSS FROM THE COURTHOUSE, BETWEEN MADISON AND MONROE**.

In 1857 Lincoln tried one of his most important cases here, the *Effie Afton* case (*Hurd v. The Rock Island Bridge Co.*). This did more for his reputation than any others he ever tried. It involved a collision of the fastest side-wheeler, the *Effie Afton*, with the first bridge over the Mississippi. Interest ran high as feelings were divided over the rights of river transportation compared to railroads'. The nominal parties to the suit were the owners of the boat and bridge company, but the actual contest was between the river towns including St. Louis and the railway centers including Chicago. After a heated and lengthy trial, there was a hung jury and the case was dismissed, amounting to a victory for the railroad. Lincoln's cocounsel, Norman Judd, later nominated him for president at the Chicago convention and served through the Civil War as minister to Berlin.

(5) On February 28, 1857, Lincoln had his photograph taken at the **ALEXANDER HESLER** studio on the **SOUTH** side of **LAKE ABOUT MIDWAY BETWEEN CLARK AND DEARBORN**. (He also posed at another Hesler studio, **SITE 17**.) He had just left the barber's chair with his hair plastered, so he ran his fingers through his hair saying, "The boys down Sangamon way would never know me this way." Hesler also took several pictures on June 3, 1860, in Springfield. A. D. **TITSWORTH AND BROTHERS** also had its store at this location (**113 LAKE**, old-style number), where Lincoln bought his 1861 inaugural suit.

(6) The **FRINK AND WALKER STAGE LINE**, located on the south side **OF LAKE STREET JUST WEST OF DEARBORN**, was where Lincoln often arrived before the railroads were built.

(7) **THE TREMONT HOUSE** was located on the **SOUTHEAST CORNER OF DEARBORN AND LAKE**. This was a major gathering place for politicians before the Civil War and the hotel in Chicago most closely associated with Lincoln. In April 1854 he attended a meeting of

Whigs and Democrats opposed to Douglas. He spoke on December 10, 1856, to a Republican banquet and responded to a toast with: "The Union—the North will maintain it—the South will not depart therefrom." He stayed in July 1857, attending the U.S. Circuit Court. He listened to Douglas's speech from the balcony facing Lake Street on July 9, 1858, while sitting behind him, and answered him the next day from the same location. This set the pattern for the senatorial campaign for the next six weeks as Lincoln followed Douglas to challenge and announce that he would reply. A meeting on July 24 paved the way for the famous debates.

Willie accompanied his father in June 1859 and wrote to his friend, Henry Remann, on June 6: "This town is a very beautiful place. Me and father have a nice little room to ourselves. We have two little pitchers on a washstand. The smallest one for me and the largest one for father. We have two little towels on a top of both pitchers. The smallest one for me, the largest one for father." Historians believe that Willie was familiar with the *Three Bears* story and patterned his remarks on that theme. The next month, Lincoln came with Mary. During the 1860 Republican convention at the Wigwam, the Lincoln headquarters were here. His campaign chairman, David Davis, and others "wheeled and dealed" until almost dead of fatigue to secure Lincoln's nomination from candidates more popular and better known to most of the country. But in Chicago, Lincoln's home state, a miracle was performed to raise a little-known "westerner" to a position where the nomination propelled Lincoln into immortality.

He then brought Mary in November 1860 and met with vice president–elect Hannibal Hamlin for the first time since the election. Both remembered speeches that the other had made years before when they were in Congress. The two leaders hosted a large reception on the first floor. Lincoln also met with his old friends Joshua and Fanny Speed.

Lincoln and Hamlin had much in common. They were both born in 1809, tall, and had lost a son. Both were athletic and known as "the big bucks" of their "lick." Both began as farmers and became lawyers. Both liked to read, and their favorite book was a life of Washington. Hamlin had been married in Lincoln (Maine). The future vice president had lost his wife; his second wife was his first wife's young stepsister. He would have another son in 1862, when he was fifty-three, the year Lincoln lost his favorite son.

Mary, Robert, and Tad roomed here upon return from Washington in 1865, and Robert lived here alone in 1868. Stephen Douglas died in the hotel on June 3, 1861, after working hard to keep the country unified. He had great strength in the border states and among moderate Southerners. Together he and Lincoln might have helped to shorten the war and ease Reconstruction problems. Prior to 1860, the six-foot-six-inch notorious Republican mayor, Long John Wentworth, lived in the hotel.

(8) TOM ANDREWS' HEAD QUARTERS RESTAURANT, SOUTH OF THE SOUTHWEST CORNER OF LAKE AND STATE STREET, was Lincoln's favorite restaurant in Chicago. He and Hamlin ate here in November 1860 (*Skeptic to Prophet,* page 86).

(9) Lincoln called on General Schenck in March 1860 at the RICHMOND HOUSE, ON THE NORTHWEST CORNER OF MICHIGAN AND WATER.

(10) The ILLINOIS CENTRAL DEPOT was ONE BLOCK EAST OF MICHIGAN ON WATER. This was not the shortest line to Chicago from Lincoln's home, but he had a "chalked hat" or free pass and usually took it after 1854 to Chicago. He frequently represented the company. The Democratic Party nominated General George B. McClellan for the presidency in 1864 at a temporary building at MICHIGAN AND PARK PLACE, near the depot, also called the Wigwam.

(11) On July 19, 1856, Lincoln spoke for presidential candidate Fremont in DEARBORN PARK on the west side of MICHIGAN AVENUE BETWEEN RANDOLPH AND WASHINGTON STREETS.

(12) Lincoln spoke at Republican Headquarters on March 1, 1859, MECHANICS' INSTITUTE HALL, AT THE NORTHWEST CORNER OF RANDOLPH AND STATE.

(13) Lincoln spent the night on August 27, 1856, at the MATTESON HOUSE, AT THE NORTHWEST CORNER OF DEARBORN AND RANDOLPH.

(14) Lincoln visited publisher Joseph Medill and editor Dr. Charles Henry Ray at the *CHICAGO TRIBUNE **Building on the east side of Clark between Randolph and Lake, a little south of midblock***. This was known as Newspaper Row due to the number of newspaper offices there. These men publicized his speeches and dedicated the resources of the paper to his election in 1860. Ray's biography was called *The Man Who Elected Lincoln.* Lincoln climbed to the third-floor office in the mid-1850s to give the men $4 for his subscription. Medill and Ray had just purchased the paper, soon to become one of the most influential in the country. Lincoln told them, "I like your paper. I did not like it before you boys took it over; it was too much of a know-nothing sheet." Lincoln came here before the New York Cooper Union Address to get advice on its content. The two supporters made various suggestions, but evidently none was followed.

Bernhardt Wall's *Following Abraham Lincoln* (page 185) shows that Lincoln visited Medill on July 13, 1858, at another location on Madison Street between Dearborn and State Streets. But this was the location at the time of the Great fire of 1871, after they had moved during the mid-1860s. Other sources also put the office at various locations, but it is clearly shown on contemporary maps and city directories at this location, then 51 Clark, verified in several *Tribune* history books, including *Chicago Tribune* and *History of the Tribune.*

(15) Lincoln is said to have stayed "numerous times" at the SHERMAN HOUSE, AT THE NORTHWEST CORNER OF CLARK AND RANDOLPH, as this was across the street from the courthouse. On July 5, 1847, Elihu B. Washburne (later congressman) recalled: "One afternoon, several of us sat on the sidewalk under the balcony of the Sherman House, and among the number was the accomplished scholar and unrivaled orator, Lisle Smith. He suddenly interrupted the conversation by exclaiming, "There is Lincoln on the other side of the street. Just look at "Old Abe."' And from that time we called him 'Old Abe.' No one who saw him can forget his personal appearance at that time. Tall, angular and awkward, he had on a short-waisted, thin swallow-tail coat, a short vest of the same material, thin pantaloons, scarcely coming to his ankles, a straw hat, and a pair of brogans with woolen socks." The Chicago *Daily Journal* reported that Lincoln stayed with his family on October 6, 1848. Lincoln's friend NORMAN JUDD'S LAW OFFICE was in the same block to the west at then 153 RANDOLPH, BETWEEN CLARK AND LASALLE. He was instrumental in getting the Republican convention to Chicago and in securing the nomination for Lincoln.

(16) The CITY HALL AND COUNTY COURTHOUSE, where Lincoln appeared in court and spoke many times, was at CLARK, RANDOLPH, LASSALLE, AND WASHINGTON. His first public speech in Chicago was here in the public square in July 1847. On October 6, 1848, he was given six hours to prepare for a speech in support of Zachary Taylor. Since the building was crowded to overflowing, the group adjourned to the outside where Lincoln "enchanted the meeting" for two hours. After President Taylor died in the White House, Lincoln returned to deliver a eulogy on July 25, 1850. An estimated 125,000 viewed Lincoln's body in the building on May 1–2, 1865. Mary's insanity trial was here in a later building in 1875, after the Great Fire. A modern building serving the same functions now occupies the site.

(17) The **METROPOLITAN BLOCK** included the **METROPOLITAN HALL** along the north side of **RANDOLPH BETWEEN WELLS AND LASALLE**, and the **METROPOLITAN HOTEL** was on the **SOUTHWEST CORNER OF WELLS**. **PHOTOGRAPHER ALEXANDER HESLER** had a studio in the building where Lincoln sat for portraits. He met here in December 1856, made a speech on February 28, 1857, and attended a minstrel show in March 1860. His friend Robert Blackwell had an office in the building.

(18) The **BRIGGS HOUSE, AT THE NORTHEAST CORNER RANDOLPH AND WELLS**, is where the Lincoln Board of Strategy was lodged during the Republican convention in May 1860 and where Oliver Hickman Browning had his headquarters when Lincoln ran for the senate in 1858. Lincoln was in the city during the earlier race and must have come here. According to *All About Chicago,* Lincoln is said to have "always" stayed here and also "always stayed" in the Tremont.

(19) The site of **FIRST BAPTIST CHURCH** attended by Tad Lincoln was on the **SOUTHEAST CORNER OF WASHINGTON AND LASALLE**.

(20) The **LARMON BLOCK, AT THE NORTHEAST CORNER OF CLARK AND WASHINGTON**, was the scene of the *Sand Bar* case tried by Lincoln and others in March 1860.

(21) The **VOLK STUDIO, AT THE SOUTHEAST CORNER OF WASHINGTON AND DEARBORN**, on the fifth floor, was the site of the studio of Leonard W. Volk when he made a life mask of Abraham Lincoln in March 1860. Two months later, in Springfield, he made casts of Lincoln's hands. These casts preserved features of the physical Lincoln for the future art world. Lincoln's friend, **ISAAC ARNOLD**, had a law office on the **SOUTHWEST CORNER**.

(22) At least one book (*All About Chicago*) claims that Lincoln had stayed at the **CLIFTON HOUSE, AT THE SOUTHEAST CORNER OF WABASH AND MADISON**, but no dates are given or found elsewhere. Mary, Robert, and Tad lived in the "dreary, noisy and public" hotel at various times from 1865 until 1868, when Mary and Tad moved to Europe. When they came back in 1871, they moved here for a short time after leaving Robert's house, and Tad died in the hotel on July 15, 1871.

(23) Lincoln and his wife were entertained in November 1860 at the **WILLIAM H. BROWN MANSION, AT THE SOUTHWEST CORNER OF MONROE AND MICHIGAN**.

(24) Before the war, John Wilkes Booth played at the **MCVICKERS THEATER**, on the south side of **MADISON IN THE MIDDLE OF THE BLOCK WEST OF STATE**. Lincoln is thought to have gone to this theater and the CHICAGO THEATER, also on MADISON, BETWEEN DEARBORN AND STATE.

(25) The POST OFFICE, CUSTOMS HOUSE, AND U.S. COURT BUILDING (now the First National Bank Building) covered the block between CLARK, MADISON, MONROE, AND DEARBORN, and were visited by Lincoln, Mary, and Hamlin on November 23, 1860.

(26) *The Lincolns in Chicago* author believes that Lincoln stayed at the home of ROBERT S. BLACKWELL, AT THE NORTHWEST CORNER OF STATE AND QUINCY STREETS, on July 4, 1855.

(27) Lincoln saw two plays in July 1857 at NORTH'S AMPHITHEATER, at the NORTHWEST CORNER OF WELLS AND MONROE.

(28) The UNION DEPOT on VAN BUREN JUST WEST OF THE CHICAGO RIVER was the scene of Lincoln's arrival on November 22, 1860, and departure five days later. On May 2, 1865, his remains left from here as part of his last journey home. The location in now across the river from the Sears Tower.

(29) CHARLES WILSON'S home at **1145 SOUTH WABASH**, just north of Roosevelt, was the home of the editor of the *Chicago Journal*. Lincoln was said to be a frequent visitor and guest. ROBERT had a LAW OFFICE at **1141 WABASH** (554 under the old numbering system).

(30) The home site of ROBERT LINCOLN is now **1332 SOUTH WABASH** (number 653 under the old numbering system) and is between Thirteenth and Fourteenth Streets on the west side. Mary and Tad stayed a short time after returning from Europe in 1871. After Tad died at the Clifton House, his body was brought here and services were held. Mary also stayed for a while afterward, but soon moved, due partly to conflicts between Robert's wife and her.

(31) Robert was active at the SECOND PRESBYTERIAN CHURCH at **1932 SOUTH MICHIGAN**. Historian Dr. Wayne Temple states that he was not a member, but Goff's biography shows him as "church member, elder and trustee," according to a letter from the church secretary.

(32) In 1874 and 1875, Mary stayed at the GRAND CENTRAL HOTEL, ON MICHIGAN BETWEEN THIRTEENTH AND FOURTEENTH STREETS.

(33) The CHICAGO ACADEMY, on WABASH BETWEEN ADAMS AND JACKSON STREETS, was Tad's school in 1867.

(34) Robert was the president of the PULLMAN COMPANY when their headquarters were on the SOUTHWEST CORNER OF MICHIGAN AND ADAMS, across from the Art Museum.

(35) In spring 1875, Mary stayed at the GRAND PACIFIC HOTEL, BETWEEN THE FOUR BLOCKS OF CLARK, JACKSON, LASALLE, AND QUINCY. Robert failed to get her to stay with him, and got an adjoining room to watch her irrational behavior. She once left the room improperly dressed and was carrying securities worth about $57,000 on her person. She continued to spend large sums of money in a wild manner, leading to an insanity trial.

NORTH OF THE CHICAGO RIVER

(36) During his November 1860 visit, Lincoln surprised the awestruck children meeting in the Moody-Mission Sabbath School founded by Dwight L. Moody. They were meeting at **NORTH MARKET HALL, ON THE NORTHWEST CORNER OF HUBBARD AND DEARBORN STREETS.** This is now Courthouse Plaza and opposite the Hampton Inn, just north of the Chicago River.

(37) The **CHICAGO AND GALENA UNION DEPOT** was between **WELLS AND FRANKLIN**, on the south side of Kinzie. Lincoln used it in 1855 when he went to Rockford, in 1856 to go to Galena, Dixon, and Sterling, and in 1859 and 1860 to go to Wisconsin and northern Illinois.

(38) Lincoln spent the night at the home of **GURDON S. HUBBARD, 916 NORTH LASALLE** (the old number was 302 North Lasalle). *Lincoln in Chicago* lists him having tea with Hubbard at **57 INDIANA STREET** on July 21, 1858. This is just south of the Waterworks.

(39) **THE EBENEZER PECK HOME** at **CLARK AND FULLERTON** hosted Lincoln, Hamlin, and Senator Lyman Trumbull as they discussed cabinet business including the selection for the Cabinet on November 24, 1860. It was not usual for the vice president to be included in the Cabinet selections, but Lincoln needed Hamlin's knowledge of the intricacies of national politics and advice on men who would help the administration. They agreed that they could not afford to let Senator William Seward of New York refuse to accept a cabinet post, as this would be considered a snub by the former Republican front-runner. The strategy of securing his acceptance was discussed. Hamlin was given the right to select an appointee from New England among Charles Frances Adams, Nathaniel Banks, and Gideon Welles.

(40) Lincoln attended services as a guest of I. N. Arnold on November 25, 1860, at the **ST. JAMES CHURCH, ON THE SOUTHWEST CORNER OF HURON AND WABASH**, his last public appearance in Chicago. A remnant of the original walls and most of the tower survived the fire of 1871 and are incorporated into the present building.

(41) Lincoln was in the home of **ISAAC ARNOLD**, his close friend and political associate, at **ERIE AND RUSH STREETS**, many times, including April 1854. The president said that Arnold was the only one who could be relied on during the election of 1864 when it appeared that many were against him. Arnold was instrumental in getting Lincoln to donate the original draft of the Emancipation Proclamation to the Northwestern Sanitary Fair in Chicago in 1863, lost in the Great Fire. He acted as Mary's attorney during her insanity trial at the Cook County Courthouse in 1875, although he did not contest the case and called no witnesses, not even Mary herself.

(42) The **ABRAHAM LINCOLN BOOKSTORE**, now at **357 WEST CHICAGO STREET** near Orleans Street, is a favorite bookstore of Civil War and Lincoln buffs. It has probably the best collection of Lincoln publications for sale anywhere, along with many signatures and other artifacts. It claims to have two thousand Lincoln books for sale and seventy thousand history books. A bed displayed is claimed to be from the Lincoln home in Springfield, which Lincoln's sons may have used. In fact fairly reliable sources claim that his sons may have been born in it. The Civil War Roundtables were first started in the bookstore at a prior location.

(44) **ROBERT TODD LINCOLN LIVED AT 1234 LAKE SHORE DRIVE** at the **SCOTT STREET** intersection. This is described in greater detail below.

(45) The **CHICAGO HISTORICAL SOCIETY, NORTH AND CLARK STREETS**, has furniture from the Springfield home including a desk, sofa, rocker, center table, whatnot shelf, side chairs, candelabra, sewing box, and other items. Also on display is furniture from the Petersen House where Lincoln died, including the deathbed, rocking chair, chest of drawers, and gas jet. Chairs from Ford's Theater are also here. At one time a large amount of Lincoln material was displayed, including furniture from Vandalia and Springfield, Lincoln's coach in Washington—later used by Mary in Chicago—and the table on which the Emancipation Proclamation was drafted. A copy of the Proclamation itself was at the Historical Society and lost when it burned in the Great Fire. Also included in past displays were personal items such as hats, watches, knives, clothes, and the glasses worn in the famous picture with Tad looking at the photo album. These are now mostly in storage; Lincolniana, world history, and U.S. history items have been greatly reduced in favor of local history. Various Civil War exhibits are shown, including a table from the room where Grant and Lee signed the surrender terms at Appomattox Court House.

SOUTH OF SOLDIER FIELD

(43) Lincoln visited JAMES LONG at his home, **2432 COTTAGE GROVE**. Douglas visited also, since this was near his estate. The fireplace where Lincoln told stories was removed to the Chicago Historical Society when the house was torn down in 1929.

(52) THE DOUGLAS MONUMENT, east end of Thirty-fifth Street between Cottage Grove and Ellis, is the tomb of Senator Stephen A. Douglas. It is under a bronze statute by Volk, easily seen from the street. The site is located near the Douglas home site, on his land where the Confederate prisoner-of-war Camp Douglas was located. Robert Lincoln was a trustee on the board to erect the monument. Douglas had maintained a law office in Chicago, although his practice of law was almost nonexistent. He had been Lincoln's opponent: he, too, courted Mary; he opposed Lincoln in the 1858 senate race and debates; and he ran against him in the 1860 presidential election. Although political rivals for most of their professional careers, Douglas and Lincoln remained friends.

In 1860 Douglas was one of the most well known men in the country. He was greatly respected, but also very controversial. He is remembered today mainly for his long association with Lincoln, although his 528-page 1860 biography barely mentions Lincoln. The 1858 debates were mentioned only in passing; only a few pages are devoted to proving that Douglas successfully escaped the Republican trap that Lincoln had attempted to set for him in Freeport, Illinois. Douglas worked hard for the Union after Lincoln's election, and held Lincoln's hat at the inauguration. But he died soon thereafter, in Chicago, in June 1861, at the age of forty-eight. President Lincoln closed government offices on the day of Douglas's funeral. He was a great supporter of the Union, and his loss hurt the country. Stephen Douglas Jr. and Robert Lincoln worked together on many political and civic causes over the years, including the erection of this monument.

(53) The UNIVERSITY OF CHICAGO, at Fifty-eighth and Ellis Avenue, is known for The William Rainey Harper Memorial Library, facing the midway, which has a notable Lincoln collection with manuscripts and portraits. The university was founded by the Baptist denomination. Stephen A. Douglas was an early supporter who aided the beginning of the school, originally proposed to be known as Douglas University.

West Chicago: A monument was erected here many years ago declaring: "During the senatorial contest between Abraham Lincoln and Stephen A. Douglas, a debate was held in this place, August 28, 1858." This was the day after the Freeport Debate and took place in Douglas's home congressional district where the candidates had agreed not to debate. Lincoln missed his train in Turner Junction, now West Chicago, where he had spent the night. He had ridden a hayrack over from Blackberry, now Elburn, with the Lincoln True Hearts, a Republican club who had come to hear the Democratic senator. They persuaded Lincoln to come with them to the Updike Hickory Grove to hear the speech. Douglas invited him to speak, and he stood up in a hayrack and spoke briefly, followed by Douglas's two-hour speech.

Family After April 1865

Much of the life of the president's family centered in Chicago after his death. The following is a brief summary of these three lives.

MARY moved to Chicago on May 24, 1865, with Robert and Tad after the assassination. It would have been economically expedient to move back to Springfield after leaving Washington. No doubt she had many friends and supporters there, including her sisters and their families. But she expressed bitterness toward family members and had too many sad memories of that town. Even though Robert and close friend, Judge David Davis, urged her to return to the family home, she did not want to be reminded of her "idolized husband" and "darling boy lost in Washington." Her brother-in-law had been anti-Republican and there had been bitter feelings about where the president should be buried. Many of Mary's decisions from this time forward cannot be justified logically; she was irrational and could not cope.

Lincoln's estate, worth about $83,000, was to be divided between his two sons and wife equally, since he had no will. This grew to more than $100,000 by the time it was distributed several years later. The amount would be equivalent to more than $1 million in the late twentieth century. However much this may seem, Mary constantly believed she was near poverty, and many decisions for the rest of her life were based on this feeling. (See a more detailed note of Lincoln's finances in the Washington, D.C., chapter, Riggs Bank, number 24.)

The family first lived in the **TREMONT HOUSE (7)**, but Mary felt it was too expensive. They then moved to the **HYDE PARK HOTEL (46)**, seven miles south at **HYDE PARK BOULEVARD AND LAKE PARK AVENUE**, near Fifty-third Street, the railroad tracks, and the lake. The Prince of Wales had stayed there in 1860. Robert and Tad rode into downtown, Robert to work and Tad to go to school for the first time on a regular basis. Mary mostly remained in seclusion. They moved back into central Chicago in November 1865 to the **CLIFTON HOUSE (22)**, which Robert referred to as a very dreary place. On May 22, 1866, she bought a house at 375 (now **1238–40) WEST WASHINGTON (47)**, on the north side of the street between Racine and Elizabeth. A plaque in the wall of the current building marks the spot, the only Lincoln marker in Chicago. Robert was with the family some of the time and lived at this address with them. This was Mary's last home of her own, and she used money received from Congress for Lincoln's remaining 1865 salary to make the purchase.

Mary kept the house for about seven years, but mostly as rental property after moving to the **CLIFTON HOUSE** on May 1, 1867. Beginning October 13, 1867, she and Tad boarded at the **DANIEL COLE HOUSE AT 460 (NOW 1407) WEST WASHINGTON**, on the south side of the street just west of Ada Street **(SITE 48)**. The Washington Street houses were near Union Park, where Tad played and Mary enjoyed spending time. The park is still there and was the center of Chicago's "Kentucky Colony." Mary preferred **THIRD PRESBYTERIAN CHURCH** at **WASHINGTON AND ABERDEEN**, on the north side **(49)**. Tad liked the **FIRST CONGREGATIONAL CHURCH** at **WASHINGTON AND GREEN (50)**, where Mary sometimes visited for his sake.

Here and for the rest of her life Mary suffered physical and emotional disabilities that could not be corrected with the medical knowledge of the day. She frequently petitioned influential people for funds to which she felt she was entitled, citing the resources given to General Grant and the widows of Secretary Stanton, General Rawlings, and others. Judge Davis's slow administration of Lincoln's estate did not help. He and the public generally did not like Mrs. Lincoln, who they felt had squandered too much in clothes, jewelry, and household decorations while living in the White House.

Tad had a tough time in school. He had been allowed to run free, without supervision or schooling, in the White House. He is described in various sources as "mentally retarded," "mildly retarded," "slow," or just having a speech impediment. A more accurate description probably should be that he was undisciplined, hyperactive, and unchallenged, with a speech impediment, but with no mental deficiency or low I.Q. It does appear that he could not read or write when he left Washington at age twelve, in spite of the few scribbles attributed to him from the White House, possibly written by others. He did have a physical disability (cleft palate) and was bound to a sick and an emotionally unstable woman, which was difficult for a young teenager. He is also described as "mentally alert in other respects," but it must have been a trying ordeal to be put in classes with much younger children.

Tad attended school at the CHICAGO ACADEMY on the west side of WABASH BETWEEN ADAMS AND JACKSON (33) while living downtown, and at the BROWN SCHOOL (51), AT THE NORTHEAST CORNER OF WARREN AT WOOD, when living in that area. He was coeditor of the school newspaper. (Lillian Russell, Eddie Foy, Edgar Rice Burroughs, and Florenz Zeigfeld also attended the school before it was torn down in 1956. A newer building, Brown Elementary School, is now on the site.) His speech impairment caused him to be known as "Stuttering Tad." He dated a girl who lived on Washington near State and attended FIRST BAPTIST on the SOUTHEAST CORNER OF WASHINGTON AND LASALLE (19).

Mary and Tad went to Europe in October 1868, thinking that Tad could be educated better and cheaper there. Robert, Tad, and Judge Davis all objected to the move. Now the teenager was the sole companion to the hypochondriac, unstable mother who continued to live below her financial means in cold, damp places, undermining the health of both. They spent two years in Frankfurt am Main, Germany, with Tad in school at Ober Ursel, but they fled to England at the outbreak of the Franco-Prussian War. Prior to that they traveled widely on the Continent, seeing Florence, Paris, Baden-Baden, Wiesbaden, and other places. They then lived in London, across from Russell Square, and in Leamington, England. Mary traveled extensively in Scotland, visiting Edinburgh, Glasgow, and many castles including Balmoral and Glamis.

In July 1870 Mary heard that Congress had approved a $3,000-per-year presidential widow's pension. They then returned to the United States in the late spring of 1871. Tad was described in the *New York Tribune:* "He had grown up a tall fine-looking lad of 18 who bears but a faint resemblance to the tricksy little sprite whom visitors to the White House remember." They returned to Robert's house when they arrived back in Chicago. But Mrs. Lincoln was becoming more difficult to live with. She and Tad moved after a few days to the CLIFTON HOUSE (22), where Tad died on July 15, 1871, after great suffering. He had caught a cold on the way back, causing an intractable pleurisy, possibly from pneumonia or from a primary infection from tuberculosis bacilli in the lining of his lungs. The body was taken to Robert's house, where a service was conducted by a Baptist minister before the Springfield funeral at First Presbyterian.

Before she died, Mary said that Tad's death hurt her even more than the assassination of her husband. She lived with Robert for a time, but a severe conflict between her and Robert's wife caused another move. Mary later stayed at the **GRAND CENTRAL HOTEL (32)** on **MICHIGAN BETWEEN THIRTEENTH AND FOURTEENTH**, west of where the Field Museum now stands. In 1875 Mary was in Florida when she got the feeling, unsupported in fact, that Robert was dying. She wired him to please recover for her sake, and rushed back. She refused to stay with him and took a room in the **GRAND PACIFIC (35)**. She was having hallucinations, had been diagnosed to be a diabetic, and probably suffered from hypoglycemia. The paregoric she took caused tantrums, drug withdrawal, and symptoms of intoxication.

While at the Grand Pacific, Robert took a room next to her to watch her disturbing behavior. On May 21, 1875, without being properly dressed, she went to the drugstore in the hotel to request laudanum and camphor for neuralgia in her arm. The druggist put her off and then followed her to Adams and Clark, where she made the same request at another store. The druggist there also declined when told the circumstances. She went back to the hotel drugstore, where she was given colored water. Later that night she made another request; Robert and others considered it an attempt at suicide by drug overdose.

Taken to court, she was ruled insane in a trial at the **COOK COUNTY COURTHOUSE (16)** before seventeen witnesses. Trials to determine sanity at this time were rare, and she was allowed no witnesses. After spending four months in a sanitarium in nearby Batavia, she was released to the custody of her sister, Elizabeth, in the Edwards home in Springfield. After she was ruled restored to competence, she traveled to New York in 1877, escorted by a teenaged grandnephew, who reminded her of Tad. She then sailed for Europe where she lived for three years in Pau, France, and visited Marseilles, Naples, and Sorrento. During this time she did not communicate with Robert or his family. After a back injury she returned to live with her sister Elizabeth in the house where she had married, and was finally reconciled to Robert in 1881 when he brought her granddaughter and namesake to see her. She died there on July 16, 1882, probably of serial diabetes.

Mary had been constantly worried about her image and financial condition. She could have improved both by writing reminiscences of her life with the sixteenth president, which would have greatly added to the store of knowledge and anecdotes about both lives. This would have enhanced our understanding and provided us with a valuable and comprehensive source of Lincoln material. Regardless of her mental or emotional state between 1865 and 1882, the extent of her contribution, as well as a source of literary profits, could have been tremendous. Such was not her disposition, but it could have happened.

ROBERT moved to Chicago with Mary and Tad in 1865. He lived with them on and off. City directories list him with Mary during the years she lived there prior to going to Europe. He studied law at the offices of J. Young Scammon located in CROSBY'S OPERA HOUSE on WASHINGTON BETWEEN DEARBORN AND STATE. (General Grant was nominated as the Republican nominee for president here in 1868.) Then he began law practice with Charles T. Scammon, on LAKE STREET JUST EAST OF THE NORTHEAST CORNER (3). Sometime in 1872 he established a firm with Edward Swift Isham at the NORTHEAST CORNER OF ADAMS AND CLARK. During 1868 he took a trip to the Rocky Mountains and lived at the TREMONT HOUSE in Chicago. On September 24, 1868, he married at 304 H in Washington, D.C. His home was 653 (now **1332)** WABASH STREET (30) near Isham on Wabash between Twelfth and Harman Court. (This is south of Roosevelt, and not between Congress and Harrison as reported in several sources. This has been verified with the Chicago Historical Society based on conversion tables for Chicago address changes, maps, and post-1880 city directories showing current addresses.)

He was in the city at the time of the Great Fire, but it missed his house and there appears to be no record of his experiences during that event except that his law office was destroyed. Most of Lincoln's papers were in Bloomington with Judge Davis during the fire. Robert's son, Abraham II, called Jack, showed great promise, but died in London while Robert was the U.S. ambassador. The seventeen-year-old had surgery on an abscess or carbuncle that resulted in blood poisoning despite the best doctors in London and Paris. (His address in London was Number Two, Cromwell House, Kensington.) The boy, who resembled his grandfather mentally and physically, probably died as the result of unsanitary surgical procedures common in the day. Jack was buried in Kensal Green Cemetery in London, then moved to Lincoln's tomb in Springfield, and finally moved to Arlington National Cemetery, Virginia, where his father was buried.

After serving as ambassador to Great Britain, Robert built a house in 1893 at **1234** LAKE SHORE DRIVE, at the northwest corner of Scott **(44)** near Lincoln Park. He was president and later chairman of the board of the PULLMAN COMPANY (34) from 1897 until 1922, when the headquarters were located on the southwest corner of Michigan and Adams, opposite the art museum. The home was sold in 1911 when he bought the house at 3014 N Street in Georgetown (Washington, D.C.), where he lived in winter, and "Hildene," near Manchester, Vermont, the rest of the time. He stated that after his father died, everyone he met for the rest of his life commented that they greatly admired the president. Apparently few recognized Robert's accomplishments. He died just before reaching his eighty-third birthday and is buried in Arlington National Cemetery. His estate has been estimated by experts to have been worth about $183 million (relative to the year 2000). His wife suffered from neurasthenia (nervous disability) and lived until 1937.

SUMMARY OF LINCOLN SITES IN CHICAGO

(1) Wigwam, Lake and Wacker: Temporary building site of the 1860 Republican Party nominating convention.

(2) Illinois and Michigan Canal Office, Wells and Wacker: Lincoln worked in December 1852 as a commissioner.

(3) Robert Lincoln law office, mid-1860s, east of the northeast corner, Lasalle and Lake.

(4) U.S. Circuit Court, southeast corner of Clark and Lake.

(5) Hesler Photographic Studio, clothing store that made inaugural suit, south side of Lake between Clark and Dearborn.

(6) Stage Line Office, west of the southwest corner at Lake and Dearborn.

(7) Tremont Hotel: Favorite of Lincoln and family, at the southeast corner of Lake and Dearborn.

(8) Lincoln's favorite restaurant, south of the southwest corner of State and Lake.

(9) Richmond House, northwest corner of Michigan and Wacker: Lincoln called on General Schenck in March 1860. Also site of Fort Dearborn.

(10) Illinois Central Railroad Depot, one block east of Michigan on Water.

(11) Dearborn Park, west side of Michigan between Randolph and Washington: Lincoln spoke for Fremont on July 19, 1856.

(12) Mechanics Institute Hall, Republican Party Headquarters, northwest corner of Randolph and State: Lincoln spoke March 1, 1859.

(13) Matteson House, northwest corner of Dearborn and Randolph: Lincoln stayed August 27, 1856.

(14) Chicago Tribune, north of northeast corner of Randolph and Clark: Lincoln visited editor Joseph Medill.

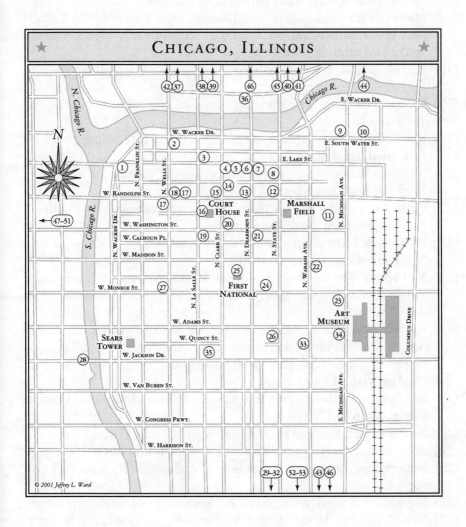

CHICAGO, ILLINOIS

N. Chicago R.

N

N. Chicago R.

S. Chicago R.

Chicago R.

E. WACKER DR.

W. WACKER DR.

E. SOUTH WATER ST.

E. LAKE ST.

W. RANDOLPH ST.

COURT HOUSE

MARSHALL FIELD

W. WASHINGTON ST.

W. CALHOUN PL.

W. MADISON ST.

FIRST NATIONAL

W. MONROE ST.

ART MUSEUM

W. ADAMS ST.

SEARS TOWER

W. QUINCY ST.

W. JACKSON DR.

W. VAN BUREN ST.

W. CONGRESS PKWY.

W. HARRISON ST.

N. FRANKLIN ST.

N. WELLS ST.

N. WACKER DR.

N. LA SALLE ST.

N. CLARK ST.

N. DEARBORN ST.

N. STATE ST.

N. WABASH AVE.

N. MICHIGAN AVE.

S. MICHIGAN AVE.

COLUMBUS DRIVE

42 37 38 39 46 45 40 41 44

36

9 10

1 2 3 4 5 6 7 8

47–51 17 18 17 15 14 13 12 11

16 20 19 21 22

25 24 23

27 34

28 26 33

35

29–32 52–53 43 46

© 2001 Jeffrey L. Ward

(15) Sherman House Hotel, northwest corner of Clark and Randolph: Lincoln stayed "numerous times."

(16) Court House, Clark, Randolph, Lasalle, and Washington: Appeared in court and spoke many times. Body viewed.

(17) Metropolitan Block and Hotel, north side Randolph at Lasalle and Wells with hotel on southwest corner with Wells: Lincoln spoke and attended meetings and shows.

(18) Briggs House Hotel, northeast corner of Randolph and Wells: Lincoln strategy board met.

(19) First Baptist Church, southeast corner of Washington and Lasalle: Tad attended.

(20) Larmon Block, northeast corner of Clark and Washington: Lincoln tried *Sand Bar* case.

(21) Sculptor Volk's studio, southeast corner of Washington and Dearborn: Lincoln sculptured.

(22) Clifton House Hotel, southeast corner of Wabash and Madison: Mary and family lived; Tad died.

(23) William H. Brown mansion, southwest corner of Monroe and Michigan: Lincoln entertained.

(24) McVickers Theater, south side of Madison west of State: John Wilkes Booth played. Lincoln came several times, including July 8, 1857.

(25) Federal Courthouse, Madison, Monroe, Dearborn, and Clark: Visited by the Lincolns and Hannibal Hamlin, November 1860.

(26) Home of Robert S. Blackwell, northwest corner of State and Quincy: Visited by Lincoln.

(27) North's Amphitheater, northwest side Wells and Monroe: Lincoln saw plays in 1857.

(28) Union Depot, Van Buren, west of river: Used by Lincoln.

(29) Charles Wilson House, 1145 South Wabash: Lincoln visited.

(30) Robert Lincoln House, 1332 South Wabash: Mary and Tad also stayed.

(31) Second Presbyterian Church, 1932 South Michigan: Robert active.

(32) Grand Central Hotel, Michigan between Thirteenth and Fourteenth. Mary stayed 1874–1875.

(33) Chicago Academy, Wabash between Adams and Jackson: Tad went to school in 1867.

(34) Pullman Company, southwest corner of Michigan and Adams: Robert was company president.

(35) Grand Pacific Hotel, Jackson, Clark, Lasalle, and Quincy: Mary stayed in 1875 and exhibited irrational behavior.

(36) North Market Hall, northwest corner of Hubbard and Dearborn: Lincoln visited children in Sunday school in November 1860.

(37) Chicago and Galena Railroad Depot, Wells and Fullerton: Used by Lincoln.

(38) Gurdon S. Hubbard home, 916 North Lasalle: Visited by Lincoln.

(39) Ebenezer Peck home, Clark and Fullerton: Lincoln and Hamlin visited November 24, 1860.

(40) St. James Church, southwest corner Huron and Wabash: Lincoln attended November 25, 1860.

(41) Isaac Arnold home, Erie and Rush: Close friend of Lincoln's.

(42) Abraham Lincoln Bookstore, 357 West Chicago: Best-known store for Lincoln material.

(43) James Long house, 2432 Cottage Grove: Visited by Lincoln.

(44) Robert Todd Lincoln's house purchased in 1893, and lived in until 1911, 1234 Lake Shore Drive at northwest corner of Scott. This has been destroyed.

(45) Chicago Historical Society, North and Clark, with Lincoln artifacts including the deathbed.

(46) Hyde Park Hotel, Hyde Park Boulevard and Lake Park: Mary, Robert, and Tad stayed.

(47) Home of Mary Lincoln purchased in May 1866, 1238–40 West Washington.

(48) Rooming house of Mary and Tad in late 1866, 1407 West Washington.

(49) Third Presbyterian Church, Washington and Aberdeen: Mary and Tad attended while living on West Washington Street.

(50) First Congregational Church, Washington and Green: Tad liked to go to this church.

(51) Brown School, northeast corner of Warren and Wood: Tad went in 1866–1867.

(52) Douglas Monument and grave, Thirty-fifth near Cottage Grove and Ellis: near his home site.

(53) University of Chicago, Fifty-eighth and Ellis: Lincoln artifacts and materials.

CLARY'S GROVE: Lincoln had many friends there when he lived at New Salem in the mid-1830s. He stayed with Jack Armstrong and his family here. The community had many cabins and covered a large area near New Salem. It is in the general vicinity of Rock Creek and Five Points Road, on both sides of Route 123, southwest of New Salem. Nothing remains of the town.

CLINTON: On May 22 and May 23, 1840, Lincoln and Stephen A. Douglas worked together to represent Spencer Turner who was charged with murder, the first such case in the county. Lincoln's argument is said to have won the acquittal. Douglas got his fee immediately. Lincoln had to sue for it, and six years later he received payment. He did take possession of Turner's horse, then discovered it to be blind.

Another case of Lincoln's here involved fifteen ladies from nearby Marion, now DeWitt, who were indicted for trespassing. They felt that their husbands and sons had spent too much time drinking at a certain establishment. The ladies banded together and rolled a keg of whiskey from the saloon into the street. Lincoln said if he could change the name of the case he would call it *The People v. Mr. Whiskey.* He compared their spirit to the Boston Tea Party and spoke of the saloon keeper's disregard for God and man. At the conclusion of testimony, the judge told the ladies to go home, and they would be called if found guilty and fined. They were so found, but never called back.

His friend Lawrence Weldon told the story that while Lincoln was here in 1858, he and a company of men heard a small boy tell a friend, "There goes old Mr. Lincoln." Some asked him how long he had been referred to as "old." Lincoln replied, "Oh, they have been at that trick for many years. They commenced it when I was barely thirty." (Elihu Washburne related that he was first referred to as "old" in front of the Sherman House in Chicago in 1847.)

The **DEWITT COUNTY COURTHOUSE** was on the Eighth Judicial Circuit and frequently visited by Lincoln. This was on the **NORTHWEST CORNER OF THE SQUARE**, now a park with no building on the site. Lincoln first met future general George B. McClellan here while McClellan was appearing as a witness opposing Stephen Douglas in a railroad case in 1855. McClellan wrote in his memoirs that he often traveled "with him [Lincoln] in out-of-the-way county seats where some important case was being tried, and, in the lack of sleeping accommodations, have spent the night in front of a stove listening to the unceasing flow of anecdotes from his lips." (Clinton and Mount Vernon are the only references that I have documented of the two together in Illinois.) Of course, Douglas and McClellan were Lincoln's two Democratic opponents in the presidential elections of 1860 and 1864.

A statue on the former courthouse lawn alleges that here Lincoln made his famous remark, "you can fool some of the people all the time, all the people some of the time, but not all of the people all the time." Some, including historian Paul Angle, believe that Lincoln did not say this, but the town library is full of newspaper articles and statements of witnesses who claim otherwise. Angle remarked on February 20,

1964, that Lincoln could have made the statement here, but if it was so good, why did he never repeat it?

Lincoln had been in the audience on July 27, 1858, when Douglas falsely charged him with advocating political equality for Negroes. At the conclusion of the speech, Lincoln rose to announce that he would speak that evening at the courthouse. He only had a moderate crowd when he supposedly made his famous remark.

Lincoln ate with Douglas during this visit, and Douglas gave him a letter that Lincoln did not read until later. In the letter Douglas agreed to debate. (Note that this is one of several stories about the agreement to engage in the famous debates. See entries on Bement, Illinois, and Chicago, Illinois.) Since Lincoln knew he was speaking in Monticello the next day, he took the train to Bement, and then a horse and buggy to meet Douglas on the road, resulting in a meeting in Bement later in the day to work out an understanding for the famous debates.

It is claimed that Lincoln stayed many places including:

1. **BARNETT HOTEL, 201 SOUTH CENTER**, much favored by Lincoln and other notables of the time. It has been moved from the original location and altered at 738 North Grant.
2. **JOHN J. MCGRAW, 223 NORTH CENTER.**
3. **GEORGE L. HILL, 138 SOUTH RAILROAD STREET.**
4. **ANDERSON HOTEL, CENTER AND CLAY.**
5. **ARGO HOMESTEAD, 100 SOUTH RAILROAD.**

DALLAS CITY: Lincoln spoke on October 23, 1858. The site is marked by a plaque at the foot of Oak Street. Steamboats had brought in crowds from Oquawka and Fort Madison, Iowa, although the speech was for Illinois legislature candidates who would select the next senator. When he entered the town, a large banner hung over Main Street showing a Negro with the word "Equality." Stephen Douglas did not plan to come here or nearby Rushville on his senatorial campaign, so that the Democrats could only show support for their party by exhibiting hostility toward the Republican.

DANVILLE: Lincoln practiced law from 1841 until 1859 in Danville and argued at least 209 cases. Only in Springfield did Lincoln argue more cases. The two-story courthouse was fifty feet square and built in 1832–1833 on the same lot as the current courthouse. Most houses were on mud streets within four blocks of the courthouse. The circuit riders came from the Chapaingn Circuit Court in Urbana across the "Grand Prairie" blooming in spring and summer with sunflowers, blue stem, and Indian grass. As in many journeys, they started at dawn and arrived after midnight, depending on weather and road conditions. They ate at the **BUCKHORN TAVERN**, north of Fairmont, and at farmhouses along the way. Leaving town, they crossed the Vermillion River at Gilbert Street and were pulled across on a ferry with horses and ropes. The Wabash train station was just north of Main Street, several blocks east of the courthouse and west of the Harmon House. Lincoln made his final address in Illinois from the train bound for Washington; the train tracks are still there. He stated then, on February 11, 1861, "If I have blessings at my disposal, Old Vermilion (County) will come in for a bountiful share." But Tolono to the east also claims the honor of hearing the last Illinois speech.

A boulder on the lawn marks the spot of an impromptu speech while a guest in 1858 of **DR. WILLIAM FITHIAN, AT 116 GILBERT STREET**. Lincoln arrived after walking from the train depot, with a crowd following, and went upstairs to relax, taking off his boots. Dr. Fithian realized that the crowd would not go away without a speech and told Lincoln that he should go out. He could not get his boots on easily over his swollen feet, so Fithian suggested that he just speak out the window so no one could tell that he didn't have his boots on. This is the southeast, second-story window. This old house also serves as the county museum and has the bed Lincoln slept in and other Lincoln memorabilia, including a handwritten note and several photographs.

Lincoln ate often at the **REASON HOOTON HOUSE, 207 BUCHANAN**. Colonel Hooton was an attorney and friend who had vineyards and crushed his own grapes. This is now the International Nursing Home. Local legend says that Lincoln came close to being tipsy on homemade wine. Given Lincoln's lifelong aversion to drink, this story is probably not true. More accurate may be the account of associate Henry C. Whitney, who says Lincoln took a sip of several homemade wines and comically said, "Fellers, I'm getting drunk." "That was the nearest approach to inebriety as I ever saw him."

The **SITE OF THE LINCOLN-LAMON LAW OFFICE** was the at the **NORTHWEST CORNER OF PUBLIC SQUARE**, called Redden Square after World War I, at **MAIN AND VERMILION**. This was Lincoln's only permanent office on the circuit. It was located in the Barnum Building, above a saloon and next to a house of ill repute. Ward Hill Lamon was a longtime friend of Lincoln's and traveled with him on the Eighth Judicial Circuit. They formed a law arrangement in 1852, the only permanent relationship with Lincoln on the circuit, probably not a partnership as such. An advertisement did appear in the paper that year advertising a copartnership, but Lamon probably placed this. Their legal association lasted for five years. According to Judge Davis, "Abe trusted Lamon more than any other man." He was a hard-drinking, brawling, banjo-playing Virginian who remained a close friend through life. Lamon was a man of great strength and accompanied Lincoln to Washington in 1861, including the secret night ride from Harrisburg, Pennsylvania, to serve as Lincoln's bodyguard and Marshal of the District of Columbia. He introduced Lincoln at Gettysburg on November 19, 1863. His presence in Ford's Theater might have changed history, but he was in Richmond on April 14, 1865. No home of Ward Hill Lamon is in existence, and it is believed that he lived in various rooming houses.

Once Lamon accidentally tore the seat of his trousers. Later in the day he appeared in court with his trousers unmended. Another lawyer began soliciting contributions for Lamon so that he could go to the tailor shop. But Lincoln said he could contribute nothing to the end in view. Another story is told that Lincoln and Lamon were in Judge Davis's court in Danville in 1850 as spectators, when Lincoln leaned over and told Lamon a story, causing his friend to convulse into such loud, disruptive laughter that Davis fined him $5. The judge then turned to Lincoln and asked, "Is this my court or yours?" Later Davis called Lamon to the bench and asked what was so funny. When told, Davis could not help himself and laughed as hard as Lamon, at which time he remitted the fine.

The JOSEPH LAMON HOME stood at 302 WEST NORTH STREET near downtown and was believed to have been visited by Lincoln. It was moved to Lincoln Park in the 1980s. There is no record that Ward Hill Lamon, his cousin, was ever in the house, but it was saved in honor of the law associate of Lincoln. Thought to be the oldest frame residence in the Danville area, this 1840s Greek-Revival cottage is a showcase of mid-1800s furnishings. Joseph Lamon's wife was Melissa Beckwith. The town of Danville was named for her father, Dan Beckwith. Melissa's brother Hiram was also an attorney, and was given his bar exam by Lincoln. He lived at the northeast corner of Robinson and North.

Lincoln is thought to have attended a magic lantern show in the building at 8 PINE STREET, now the VETERANS OF FOREIGN WAR POST. He is also reported to have spoken to a large crowd on the south side of MADISON BETWEEN PINE AND GILBERT, the present site of the WASHINGTON SCHOOL GROUNDS. But the Vermillion Country Museum Society questions this, as they do several other Lincoln sites. One is that he was entertained at Dr. Theodore LAMON'S HOME ON SOUTH HAZEL STREET on the east side near South Street, but the local historical society doubts this, as he was proslavery. Also a 1927 letter from Adois Senor Woodbury in the files of the Lincoln Trail Association claims that Lincoln was "many times" at the **Palmer house** at the southwest corner of **North and Gilbert** and at the **O. L. Davis residence** on the site of the present **Federal Building**.

The **site of Lincoln Hall** is **14 West Main**. This is claimed to be the first building named for him, and he wished it success in 1859. This is also the site of Dr. Woodbury's drug and general merchandise store where Lincoln loafed and told tales. In 1858 he bought a humor book here entitled *Phoenixians*, from which he used quotes in the debates with Douglas.

The **McCormick House at 103 West Main** was used by Lincoln in his visits to Danville. It was in the same block as his law office. In October 1859 Lincoln accepted an invitation to speak at the Cooper Institute in New York City, answering on McCormick House stationery. Fellow attorney Henry Whitney wrote that once he found Lincoln sitting before the fire talking "the wildest and most incoherent nonsense" in his sleep. "A stranger to Lincoln would have supposed he had suddenly gone insane. Of course I knew Lincoln and his idiosyncrasies, and felt no alarm, so I listened and laughed." Here Lincoln was tried before an "Orgmathorial Court" of fellow lawyers on the charge that his fees were too low. Found guilty, he paid his fine with a gallon of whiskey.

Lincoln often attended the social events at the home of **Reverend Enoch Kingsbury, at the northwest corner of Walnut and Water**.

Lincoln "frequently" visited in the home of **Oscar F. Harmon**, until recently the Colonel Harmon Mansion Restaurant at **522 East Main**. Harmon was an attorney and friend. He ate "many times" at the **Amos Williams Home on South Clark Street**, on the bluff overlooking the river, and traded at the Geurdon (sometimes spelled "Gurdon" or "Gordon") S. **Hubbard Trading Post, at the southeast corner of the public square**.

DECATUR: Lincoln's first home in Illinois is located in **Lincoln Homestead State Park**, six miles west and three miles south on the Sangamon River. A direction marker is on Interstate 72 at Niantic. Signs will direct you eastward to near Harristown, where you cross over the interstate highway and travel about five miles south. This is a beautiful spot overlooking the river and has many picnic tables and other facilities.

The Lincoln family reached this small town of a few log houses, a store, tavern, and courthouse on March 14 1830. Their first night in the area they camped on the courthouse square, which Lincoln liked to point out later. Lincoln's cousin, John Hanks, had drifted here earlier and selected a site for the family. After staying at John's house, four miles from town, they built a small cabin with logs from trees Hanks had cut down. Fifteen acres were fenced and planted. Hanks had previously selected the site for himself, but built elsewhere. This was government land that could have been purchased for $1.25 an acre, but the new settlers just became "squatters."

A large boulder and bronze plaque mark the approximate site of the cabin, where a replica burned down in 1990. Some historians believe that the cabin was closer to the river than it is shown now. The original cabin was taken to the Chicago Sanitary Fair in 1865 and exhibited there at Randolph and Wabash, then almost on the lakefront. It next went to Boston Common. Souvenir canes were sold at both places, supposedly made from rails made by Lincoln around Decatur. The cabin was then displayed in the Barnum Museum in New York City, but then disappeared after starting for England.

Hanks and Abe hired themselves out when possible during the summer and made several thousand fence rails for William Warnick. Lincoln had passed his twenty-first birthday and was no longer legally obligated to stay with his family. During these days, a son was obligated and expected to labor for the good of the family until age twenty-one, and his wages were the property of the father. Lincoln no doubt felt an obligation to help his family get settled in this new, raw land. He worked for John Hanks's brothers, William Jr. and Charles, in the Harristown township and in an area now in Decatur between Union, Monroe, Wood, and the railroad tracks. William lived at 452 West Main.

Lincoln pored over books at the home of MAJOR WILLIAM WARNICK, the county's first peace officer, and hired out as a plowboy and railsplitter there and on surrounding farms. He slept in the attic. Lincoln had a narrow escape in trying to wade through the snow to Warnick's house three or four miles away, across the river from his own home. His canoe had overturned and his feet were frozen. Mrs. Warnick cared for him several weeks when he stayed here. The family claimed later that Lincoln's first love was Mary, called Polly, whom he courted in the parlor. If so, she wasn't interested since she married in June 1831. He is claimed to have thrown the bully of the county in a wrestling match in Warnick's harvest field. The home was located on an old circuit road between Decatur and Springfield about two miles west of the junction of Routes 51 and 48, southwest of Decatur on Route 28. It burned down in 1975, on the day its application was filed to go on the National Register for Historic Sites. There was a log schoolhouse in the area where Lincoln attended spelling bees and singing bees. This is near the present Bethlehem Church on the old Springfield Road.

The first fall most of the Lincoln family fell ill to a common fever and ague affecting the area. Thomas got so discouraged that he decided to return to Indiana when the snow cleared the next spring. That winter was known as the "winter of big snows." Heavy snows, freezing rains, vicious winds, and bitter cold lasted for weeks. Livestock froze or were devoured by wolves. Settlers were marooned in their cabins where many starved or died of the cold. Thomas had enough by the thaw. He started back with most of the family, but Abraham stayed and rarely saw his father or stepmother again. The family wound up in Coles County near Charleston, and Lincoln headed for New Orleans where John Hanks had arranged with Dennis Offutt to take a flatboat with produce.

LINCOLN SQUARE in Decatur is where North and South Main crosses East and West Main. A bronze tablet on a building at the southwest corner commemorates the arrival by oxcart and campsite in 1830 of the Lincoln family. This is also the site where Lincoln practiced law and made his first political speech. In the summer of 1830, he was working at the farm of either Mr. Shepard, west of Church Street and north of Main, or for William Hanks Jr., near Main and Union. He heard a commotion in the public square, came to investigate, and heard the last part of a political speech denouncing a candidate for the Whig Party. The young farmhand is said to have hopped up on the stump in front of Harrell's Tavern to speak in defense of the Whig. The splinters hurt his bare feet as he shifted around, but the crowd cheered wildly, and he learned he could speak. A bronze statue stands on the northeast corner and is entitled, "Lincoln's First Political Speech." It depicts Lincoln as barefoot with one foot on the stump.

He is claimed to have made other speeches here. North of the statue are twelve structures dating from 1845 to 1857 that Lincoln would recognize from his days of law practice. He made purchases at the REN- SHAW'S STORE over a period of time, including a tonic made with Peruvian bark containing quinine for the "Illinois shakes." The site is now the Lincoln Theater just south of Prairie Street, about HALF A BLOCK NORTH ON THE WEST SIDE OF NORTH MAIN OR LINCOLN SQUARE. Lincoln became a friend of Uncle Jimmy Renshaw who lived on the NORTHEAST CORNER OF BROADWAY AND CONDIT.

John Hanks helped to build the first courthouse of Macon County in 1829 and was paid $9.87 for "chinking and daubing" the building. It was on the SOUTHWEST CORNER OF THE SQUARE. It is known as the LOG CABIN COURTHOUSE and moved first to FAIRVIEW PARK, MCLELLAND, AND WEST ELDORADO STREETS. Now it is at the Macon County Histori- cal Society Museum at 5580 North Fork Road. This is south of Route

105, east of town off Mount Zion Airport Road. Macon County was on the Eighth Judicial Circuit and saw Lincoln the lawyer many times. A second courthouse was built in 1838 on the SOUTHEAST CORNER OF THE SQUARE. Lincoln practiced law in both. When he came, he stayed with relatives (John Hanks and others) and at public houses including the MACON HOUSE. Virtually all of the Lincoln court documents have missing signatures, lost to researchers and souvenir hunters.

The REVERE HOUSE WAS ON THE SOUTHEAST CORNER OF FRANKLIN AND PRAIRIE. In December 1849 this was called the MACON HOUSE. Lincoln was here then with Leonard Swett when a wagon bearing a piano arrived, but no one would help get it inside. Lincoln insisted that he and Swett could, and they did. The owner then treated him and others to "Old Dan Tucker," "Rocked in the Cradle of the Deep," and other favorites.

The CASSELL HOUSE, LATER THE ST. NICHOLAS HOTEL, was on the west side of SOUTH MAIN MIDWAY BETWEEN WOOD AND WEST MAIN, back from the Southwest corner of the square. On February 22, 1856, there was a meeting of Anti-Nebraska editors of Illinois here. Its purpose was to draft resolutions to organize several disorganized factions and suggest a governor. Lincoln was invited, although he was not an editor, met in conference with the committee drafting the resolutions, and spoke at the closing dinner. He was suggested for governor and was toasted as "our next candidate for the U.S. Senate." He objected to the former and agreed with the latter. This meeting led to calling a state convention in Bloomington to organize the Illinois Republican Party.

Lincoln passed through later, en route to the Bloomington convention on May 27, 1856, and had a layover waiting for the train connection. *Day by Day* shows that he stayed at the Oglesby House, but it was evidently at the Cassell. Lincoln strolled around town and entertained many well-wishers with reminiscences of his early experiences in Macon County. Fellow attorney Henry Clay Whitney tells that they went to the woods south or southwest to the Sangamon bottoms, where they spent most of their time telling stories. He returned to Decatur after the Bloomington meetings and spoke at the courthouse, probably giving some of the same arguments as his famous Bloomington speech. Later in the year he spoke at rallies and mass meetings for the Republican presidential candidate, John C. Frémont. He and Senator Trumbull dined with DR. H. C. JOHNS at his house in the 400 BLOCK OF EAST NORTH STREET after a September meeting.

In 1858, he gave his last speech before the senatorial election at POWERS HALL, 135 EAST MAIN, now a parking lot. It is said that he debated Douglas in IMBODEN'S GROVE and spoke in front of the I. C. Pugh store about two blocks west on Main (*Decatur Business*). A marker in front of the historic but more recent Millikin House on West Main recalls that Lincoln traveled that way on the circuit.

In May 1860 the Illinois Republicans endorsed Lincoln as its candidate for president and gave him the sobriquet of "Rail Splitter" at the **WIGWAM.** The location is marked on **SOUTH PARK STREET, AT THE SOUTHWEST CORNER OF STATE STREET JUST NORTH OF EAST MAIN BETWEEN WATER AND FRANKLIN.** The state convention met to nominate a governor and state officials, but spent most of its time discussing possible presidential candidates. Support was divided, and Lincoln's supporters needed to ensure his unanimous Illinois endorsement. This temporary structure was located a block and a half east of Lincoln Square. The platform was at about the middle of the block on **STATE BETWEEN PARK AND EAST MAIN.** Lincoln could not find accommodations at the Macon House or Cassell House, and stayed at the **JUNCTION HOUSE AT THE DEPOT, ABOUT TWO BLOCKS NORTHEAST OF THE NORTHEAST CORNER OF MARTIN LUTHER KING AND ELDORADO,** where Cerro Gordo and Hinton Streets would cross if they ran that far.

Lincoln's supporters felt that he needed a label like "Old Hickory" or "Tippecanoe," made popular for predecessors. His widely known sobriquets, "Old Abe" and "Honest Abe," were felt to be colorless. A friend of Lincoln's and lawyer from Decatur, Richard J. Ogelsby, who was later governor, arranged for Lincoln's cousin, John Hanks, to bring some of the fence rails made thirty years before. Ogelsby, not a delegate, arose to be allowed, "as an old Democrat, to make a contribution." He proposed that a distinguished citizen, Abraham Lincoln, be invited to sit on the stand. At this time there were three thousand people crowded into the one-hundred-by-seventy-foot structure, with one thousand outside, including Lincoln. He was then "seized and jerked to his feet." An effort was made to jam him to the platform. But this failed due to the packed house, and he was lifted up and passed over the heads of everyone there. After some discussion on the nomination for governor, Ogelsby rose again and said he had another proposal, prompting old John Hanks to come down the isle with two (or more) rails with the sign.

ABRAHAM LINCOLN

The Rail Candidate for President in 1860
Two Rails From A Lot of 3000 made in
1830 by Thos. Hanks and Abe Lincoln—
Whose Father was the First Pioneer of Macon County

The assembly went wild and John M. Palmer jumped up and moved that Lincoln was the first and only choice for president. With little ceremony the convention passed the following resolution:

> *That Abraham Lincoln is the choice of the Republican party of Illinois for the presidency, and the delegates from this state are instructed to use all honorable means to secure his nomination by the Chicago Convention, and to vote for him as a unit.*

Pandemonium broke out and almost wrecked the Wigwam. Of course Thomas Lincoln did not split any rails and was not the first pioneer; Hanks and others had preceded him to a town already established. But this labeled Lincoln's image as the "Rail Splitter." It did not do any harm to Hanks, who then began to sell fence rails for $1 per rail, claiming they were from the old farm. Now Lincoln's supporters had a label, just as Andrew Jackson had been "Old Hickory" and William Henry Harrison had been "Tippecanoe." Lincoln left before the rail demonstration, but he was found in Peake's jewelry store, lying on the couch asleep. He was brought in and gave a short speech.

He passed through Decatur two mores times. Once was on the way to see his stepmother on January 30, 1861. Upon passing near **HARRISTOWN**, just west, he told his companions that he had made enough rails to fence ten acres of ground here. Shortly afterward he passed through on the way to Washington and stopped at the depot to make a short speech. Some thought he seemed to be saying good-bye to his friends, very sorry he had to go.

After attending Lincoln's funeral in 1865, John Hanks displayed many relics associated with Lincoln. Then had a more grandiose idea. He and Dennis bought the old Lincoln cabin and displayed it at various locations. John died in Decatur in 1889, at the age of eighty-seven. He is buried in Boiling Springs Cemetery, north of town. This is a turn off Route 121 to Riedel Avenue and two blocks to Tropicana, where a sign indicates the direction of the cemetery.

DELAVAN: Lincoln spoke on July 25, 1846, during his congressional campaign. He passed through on the way to court in Tremont, and probably stayed at the **DELAVAN HOTEL.**

DIXON: The **LINCOLN MONUMENT STATE MEMORIAL** on the west bank of Rock River marks the site where Lincoln camped for about eighteen days in May and June 1832 during his service in the Black Hawk

War. It is the site of the Dixon blockhouse and ferry on the Galena-Peoria Road.

Lincoln arrived on May 12, 1832, in a volunteer group of about twelve hundred called on to assist removing Chief Black Hawk and his band of Sac and Fox Indians from Illinois. The first battle took place at present-day Stillman Valley on May 14, and Lincoln helped bury the dead there the next day. Lincoln's company then returned for several days, moved north, and returned several times, camping on both sides of the river. General Winfield Scott, Jefferson Davis, and Zachary Taylor were here also, as were future generals Albert Sidney Johnston, Joseph E. Johnston, and Robert Anderson, who was the Union commander at Fort Sumter when the Civil War started. The statue at the memorial of "Lincoln the Soldier" is the only statue depicting him in military uniform. There is no record that he ever saw Davis (evidently Davis did not arrive until after Abe had left), although stories persist that he did. Later, when president, Lincoln asked Anderson if he had remembered meeting him. Before he answered "no," Lincoln said his memory was better than Anderson's, as Anderson had mustered him into service in 1832.

He passed through on the way back home after being mustered out of the army in July. His horse had been stolen or lost, and several lent him the use of theirs, although he and his friend George Harrison had walked much of the way. By the time he got here his shoes were worn out and he was barefoot. One morning here he complained about his feet being cold, and someone told him, "No wonder, there's so much of you on the ground."

There is no evidence that he returned to Dixon until he spoke on the north lawn of the courthouse on July 17, 1856. The newspaper commented that he was "anything but handsome in the face (but), as a close observer and cogent reasoner, he has few equals and perhaps no superior in the world." The speech was said to be "masterful" with "unanswerable arguments." A stone on the courthouse lawn marks this speech at a Frémont rally. One journalist wrote that he and Noah Brooks sat together and "made fun of Lincoln's excessively homely appearance. He was dressed in an awkwardly fitting linen suit evidently bought ready made at a country store, and intended for a man at least five inches less in statue than he was, the vest and trousers not meeting by at least an inch and a half, and the last-named garment being short at the feet."

It is assumed that he spent the night in the **NACHUSA HOTEL,** across the street south of the courthouse, after being entertained during the day in the **JOSEPH CRAWFORD HOME** located on a bend in the river east of town. After the speech he and various political leaders went to a home called **HAZELWOOD,** on the Rock River, and the next day continued to Sterling, Polo, and Oregon on his speaking tour.

The **NACHUSA AT 215 SOUTH GALENA** claims to be the oldest hotel in Illinois. Presidents Lincoln, Grant, Teddy Roosevelt, Taft, and Reagan stayed there at various times. (President Ronald Reagan lived in several houses in Dixon; one is open to the public.) Lincoln was also at **JAMES CHARTER'S HOME AT BRINTON AND EVERETT**. He passed through on the way to the Freeport debate and tradition says he spent the night of August 26, 1858, with Silas Noble, but he probably stayed in Amboy (as per *Day by Day*) and addressed the crowd here at the station the next day.

This was the last documented trip to Dixon, although he may have been there in mid-July 1859 when the family traveled with a group of state officers and appraisal experts who made a nine-day tour of the Illinois Central Railroad. The train traveled only in daylight and stopped at all of the stations along the route. Since the Nachusa House was one of the larger hotels on the route, they may have stayed there, although the hotel had no register to verify this.

DUNLEITH: The Chicago *Press and Tribune* reported that Lincoln had been here on about July 19, 1859.

EDINBURG: Lincoln was conveyed two hundred acres on this town site, to hold in trust for Joshua Speed to secure a note.

EDWARDSVILLE: On the way back from New Orleans in 1831, Lincoln probably walked here from St. Louis with his stepbrother, John D. Johnston. He then went to Coles County where his family had just moved. On later trips, Lincoln often stayed at the **EDWARDSVILLE HOTEL**. He spoke in town on May 18, 1857, and later, on September 11, 1858, at the **COURTHOUSE**. He attempted to explain the differences between the Republican and Democratic Parties by saying, "Republicans see slavery as a moral, social and political wrong and Democrats do not." He would not say they deem it right, but that view had been constant and unmistakable for five years. He felt that Judge Douglas's statement that he did not care whether slavery was voted up or down showed indifference. The marker at the present courthouse refers to this as the "opening speech of the senatorial campaign." Lincoln and

Douglas both stayed at the **OLD WABASH HOTEL** on the WEST SIDE OF MAIN, A FEW DOORS SOUTH OF THE SQUARE.

ELBURN: Lincoln came to Blackberry, now Elburn, on August 27, 1858, after the Freeport Debate with Douglas. He spent the night with a cousin about three miles from town, and then reportedly went to Turner Junction (now West Chicago), where he and Douglas also spoke.

ELKHART: Lincoln stopped at the **LATHAM TAVERN** when he began to ride the First, then Eighth Circuit. He also stayed with Judge Joseph Gillespie with whom he had served in the legislature. It is also claimed that he stayed twice in the **KENTUCKY HOUSE** on the east slope of Elkhart Hill. His funeral train stopped here to pick up water.

ELPASO: Lincoln had an hour's wait at the railroad station on August 28, 1858.

EQUALITY: Lincoln probably spoke in September 1840, campaigning as elector for William Henry Harrison while at Shawneetown.

EUREKA: A marker on the site of the **WALNUT GROVE ACADEMY** states that Lincoln spoke there in 1856.

EVANSTON: Lincoln stayed in April 1860 (dates vary) at the home of the harbormaster of Chicago and a member of the Board of Trade who resigned to raise the Thirty-seventh Illinois Volunteers. The local paper observed that he endeared himself to the house full of children and was serenaded by a quartet. Lincoln is said to have put his hand on the shoulders of the leader and said he "wished he could sing like that, but he only knew two tunes; one is 'Old One Hundred' and the other isn't." (Grant is quoted saying basically the same thing during the Civil War.) He was also entertained at the **JULIUS WHITE HOUSE, 2009 DODGE**, on April 3, which has been moved to the **NORTH-WEST CORNER OF RIDGE AND CHURCH**. He made a public speech at about this time.

FAIRFIELD: Lincoln had at least two cases here, but the courthouse burned down in 1886 and the records were destroyed. He arrived after his Albion speech in September 1840. A marker is at the site of the courthouse.

FORRESTON: Lincoln is claimed to have spent several weekends in the home of **SAMUEL HITT**, ten miles south.

FREEPORT: The site of the second **LINCOLN-DOUGLAS DEBATE, AT NORTH STATE AVENUE AND EAST DOUGLAS STREET**, is marked by a memorial boulder dedicated by President Theodore Roosevelt in 1903 and a life-size statute, "Lincoln and Douglas in Debate." About fifteen thousand swelled the town of seventy-five hundred to hear the "Freeport Doctrine," said to have cost Douglas the presidential election in 1860, or at least the presidential nomination of the full Democratic Party. Southern delegates in 1860 were upset at his statements at Freeport and split the party rather than give him the nomination. After that two other parties were created that nominated their own candidates.

Lincoln and his advisors had felt that he had been too weak and defensive in the first debate. Now he attacked. The "Freeport Doctrine" was Douglas's answer to Lincoln's question whether any territory could exclude slavery against the wishes of any citizen prior to the formation of a state constitution. Lincoln knew the probable answer since Douglas had already the given the answer "yes," which the South considered an insult. In *Freeport's Lincoln*, the future president is quoted telling his advisors: "I do not know how Senator Douglas will answer. If he answers that the people of a territory cannot exclude slavery I will beat him. But if he answers as you all say he will, and as I believe he will, he may beat me for Senator, but he will never be President."

Douglas answered that, yes, local police regulations could keep slavery out of a territory no matter what the Dred Scott decision said about Congress's inability to do so. Slavery could be excluded if unfriendly legislation was enacted or police support was withheld. The stated position outraged President Buchanan and alienated the powerful senator from his party. This answer was expected, and he won the senate. But it cost him the presidency, according to author Shelby Foote and others.

On the front of the book *Freeport's Lincoln* are the words: "The Fate of the Nation Was Decided At Freeport." Other authors have stated that Lincoln expected a "no," implying that slavery could be excluded, whereas the "yes" meant that slavery could not exist unless supported. The answer troubled the South by emphasizing a no-win situation. The South felt that Douglas was robbing the victory of the Dred Scott decision by telling the territories how to prevent the expansion of slavery.

Both Lincoln and Douglas were guests at the **BREWSTER HOUSE**, two blocks from the debate site at the **NORTHWEST CORNER OF STEPHENSON AND MECHANIC**, on August 27, 1858, where they attended a reception and appeared on the balcony together.

FOUNTAIN GREEN: Three first cousins of Lincoln lived in Hancock County, the sons of his uncle Mordecai. All were described as mentally and physically like their famous cousin and afflicted with nervous disorders including "hypos," "Lincoln horrors," melancholia, and depression. They died in 1837, 1852, and 1867. Lincoln visited the younger Mordecai at his home when he came to Knox College for the 1858 debate with Douglas. It is not known if any relatives came to the debate. The son of one, Robert, was invited to accompany Lincoln to his inauguration. All of the family here were Union supporters.

GALENA: Lincoln passed through on June 10, 1832, with his military company during the Black Hawk War after having camped at the nearby **APPLE RIVER FORT**. This is a few miles northeast, now restored and open to the public. The courthouse was located on Main between Perry and Franklin and may have seen lawyer Lincoln. Later he stayed at the **DESOTO HOUSE AT MAIN AND GREEN STREET**, still open for business. He spoke from the balcony on July 23, 1856, "and pointed out, like a true statesman, the consequence of permitting the curse (of slavery) to spread itself over our immense territories." This was said to have done much to change the political complexion of the county. A controversial quotation appearing three days later in the Galena newspaper reported Lincoln as saying they ought to submit to the Supreme Court's Dred Scott decision. Lincoln denied it, and current historians do not believe that these statements are accurate.

ULYSSES S. GRANT'S HOME was here before and after the Civil War. His first home was at **121 SOUTH HIGH**. His family remained here for much of the war, although they did spend time with the general at various locations. After the war the town presented him with a new home on **BOUTHILLIER STREET** on August 19, 1865, at a DeSoto House reception. This is open to the public with period furnishings and Grant trophies, souvenirs, and family heirlooms including china and silver used by them in the White House. The **GRANT STORE** site where he worked for his father is marked at **120 SOUTH MAIN**.

The **JOHN RAWLINS HOME, 515 HILL STREET**, was the home of Grant's head of staff during the Civil War and secretary of war in the Grant administration.

The **ELIHU B. WASHBURNE HOME, 908 THIRD STREET**, was the home of the congressman who sponsored Grant early in the Civil War and was a friend of Lincoln's. It is open for tours. Washburne surprised Lincoln at 6:00 A.M. on February 23, 1861, on his "secret" arrival in Washington at the train station; Washburne had a carriage and drove Lincoln to Willard's Hotel. Lincoln had arrived unannounced to avoid an assassination attempt discovered by Pinkerton detectives.

GALESBURG: The first documented time Lincoln visited was August 24, 1858, where he made a speech at the **BANCROFT HOUSE HOTEL**. This was located south of **BERNEN STREET BETWEEN PRAIRIE AND KELLOGG** just north of the depot and railroad tracks. The depot site is marked at the **END OF DEPOT STREET**. This is about a quarter mile due east of Knox College. The tracks are still in use. Earlier he had been in town and got a haircut on Main Street while waiting for a train.

The fifth Lincoln-Douglas debate was at the east end of **OLD MAIN** on the **KNOX COLLEGE** campus on South Street. This is the only building associated with the debates still standing. The speakers entered the north door and stepped out on the platform through a window since the platform blocked the exit door from the building. Lincoln remarked that now he had gone through college. The window is at the south side of the exit door. A banner had been hung on the south side of the building where the debate was to take place. But, because of high winds, the platform was moved to the east side where it was felt the building would shelter the speakers. The banner was rehung and torn by the wind, so that the lettering was turned inward during the debate, making many drawings of the event inaccurate. Two students, who lived in a dormitory known as East Bricks, had a ton of coal delivered to their door on the morning of the debate. It was so trampled into the ground that "it had to be re-mined." East Bricks was about fifty yards east of Old Main. Various artists' depictions of the event do not include this building, which would have blocked the view from further east. All of the windows and the entire roof were filled with spectators.

Lincoln arrived on October 7, 1858, from nearby Knoxville, where he had spent the previous night. A large procession accompanied him to town, and he was taken to the home of **MAYOR HENRY SANDERSON** at the **SOUTHEAST CORNER OF SIMMONS AND BROAD STREET**. The excellent city library now occupies the site, not marked, although the home was closer to the street. Lincoln was given a bath, with the mayor of the town acting as "Master of the Bath." (This possibly occurred after the debate.) Sanderson told the story often and always ended by remarking that "he was the strongest man I ever looked at." It is thought that Lincoln ate here and later with **MRS. ABRAM S. BERGEN**, who lived on **MAIN STREET** four doors west of **THE NORTH-WEST CORNER WITH CEDAR STREET**. He had been a friend of her husband in Springfield, and she sent her son to bring him to her house for dinner. It is probable that this meal was after the debate, which gave Mrs. Sanderson time to get ready for the long reception in her house, lasting for several hours.

Douglas arrived by train the same day and was received at the Bancroft House. He was then taken to his hotel, the **HASKELL HOUSE ON THE NORTH SIDE OF MAIN BETWEEN CHERRY AND PRAIRIE**. The town was full of people who followed the parade and candidates down **MAIN TO THE SQUARE AND TURNED INTO BROAD STREET TO KNOX COLLEGE**. Douglas rode in a carriage drawn by six white horses. Crowds are estimated at fifteen to twenty thousand. Galesburg only had a population of only fifty-five hundred, so most visitors slept in tents or other shelters that would keep them dry from the unusually cold weather.

Although this was a working day, the crowd may have been the largest of the debates. After an hour-long speech by Douglas, Lincoln reportedly tossed his cloak to Salmon P. Chase and remarked, "Chase, mind my garment while I stone Stephen," an obvious biblical reference to the first Christian martyr. However, it is not believed that Chase was here, and these remarks were reportedly said at various other places also. At least one in the crowd said, "When Douglas finished and Lincoln rose, I felt like crying. I was sorry for him and ashamed of my politics, but he hadn't spoken ten minutes until I was shouting with the rest of them."

On the thirty-eighth anniversary of the debate, Robert Lincoln gave a commemorative address, the only speech he ever gave on the subject of his father. He gave no insights and wondered what his father would think about the multitude who had come together to honor him after all these years. In 1908, Douglas's grandson, Robert, spoke here.

GLADSTONE: Lincoln spoke on October 9, 1858, after resting at the home of **S. S. PHELPS**.

GRANDVIEW: Speech made August 7, 1856, for Fremont.

GRAYVILLE: Lincoln went through as he passed from Olney to Mount Carmel.

GREENUP: During the family migration in 1830 to Macon County, Illinois, the Lincoln family passed through what would become Greenup a few years later. Five miles south along the Palestine road they stayed in a barn at Joseph Gilbert's farm. The National or Cumberland Road came this far, which the Lincolns had followed, but they went to Decatur rather than follow the road to Vandalia.

When they arrived in what would become Greenup, several men were building a structure, the **BARBOUR INN**. Although Lincoln was no doubt tired from the day's journey, he helped cut the wood or build a well, according to differing stories. Lincoln stayed in the hotel on several occasions in later years. It is claimed that he made a campaign speech just south of the hotel that influenced many pro-slavery-minded settlers to adopt the abolitionist's doctrine. The old hotel operated for 141 years before being demolished. It stood on a now vacant lot **ACROSS FROM THE CARNEGIE LIBRARY** at the southern end of the historic downtown, and next to the restored depot that has been moved from a nearby site. A historical marker is on the site. The historical society also shows that Thomas Lincoln and Dennis Hanks came to the town in 1832 to help build the first bridge over the Embarras River at about the spot where they had forded in 1830. They also worked on the well at the hotel site and other structures, as Greenup is near their Coles County homes. Abe also stayed with friends in town and nearby, including the home of **DR. JAMES EWART**, in the historic area.

Between May 17 and May 19, 1847, Lincoln tried and lost the manslaughter case of *The People v. Lester* (sometimes spelled "Lustre," as shown on the historical marker at the site). The trial was held in a little log schoolhouse, two blocks east of the Barbour Inn. The town had no funds for a town hall, so the schoolhouse was used for multiple purposes. A single-story brick residence now occupies the site. Lincoln later got up a petition to have Lester pardoned. Tradition says that during an adjournment in the trial, Lincoln and the lawyers went to the river for a swim like a gang of boys.

GREENVILLE: Lincoln stopped at the **FRANKLIN (EUREKA HOUSE), AT THE NORTHEAST CORNER OF THIRD AND COLLEGE**, on September 12 and 13, 1858, and spoke on the **THIRTEENTH AT COLCORD'S GROVE** west of town, marked by a bronze tablet. This is between **WASHINGTON, WINTER, FOURTH, AND SIXTH**. A town history (*Tales and Breadcrumbs*) lists him here in September 1859 (should probably be 1858) and notes that after his speech he came to an ice-cream social in **SARAH BROWN'S YARD ON SECOND STREET**.

GRIGGSVILLE: Lincoln was hosted in the **AARON TYLER HOUSE**, still at the **SOUTHEAST CORNER OF CONGRESS AND TYLER**, about three blocks east of the city hall. A marker in front notes that Lincoln stopped after stumping against Douglas. The marker also shows that the lumber for the two-story white frame house was shipped here from Maine. In fact many of the homes here are similar to those found in New England. Griggsville was on the stage and mail route from Quincy to Jacksonville. An original stage stop used during Lincoln's day still stands a few miles south at the northwest junction of the Griggsville-Pittsfield Roads.

The home of **CHARLES PHILBRICK** still stands, unmarked, at **113 NORTH COREY AT THE NORTHWEST CORNER WITH LIBERTY**. This is one block north of the business district and two blocks north of the city hall. He is buried in the city cemetery at the northwest edge of town, as are members of the O. M. Hatch family. Hatch, also from Griggsville, was a political associate of Lincoln. Philbrick had been chief clerk and then assistant secretary of state for Illinois when Hatch served as the secretary of state. When the president asked Hatch for a recommendation for an additional secretary, he suggested Philbrick. Hatch also had earlier recommended Lincoln's secretary, John G. Nicolay, and his assistant, John Milton Hay. Philbrick then became the third presidential secretary from Pike County (including Nicolay and Hay), which is remarkable since Lincoln only had five during the war. Philbrick served from September 1864 until he went home for a visit in April 1865. He heard about Lincoln's assassination and never went back to Washington.

HANOVER: Lincoln practiced in the Woodford Circuit Court.

HAVANA: Lincoln appears in the background of Havana history in various roles for a period of twenty-six years: as a returning soldier, surveyor, lawyer, and candidate for the U.S. Senate. On the way back from the Black Hawk War, he sold his canoe here, which he had purchased in Peoria after his horse was stolen. He is described here as having, for his chief amusement, the telling of anecdotes and stories. He usually stayed at the **WALKER HOUSE**, one of the oldest hotels in the state, after 1866 called the Taylor House. This was located at the **SOUTHEAST CORNER OF MAIN AND SCHRADER**. He also was a guest in the **FRANCES LOW HOUSE** for several days, arriving on August 13, 1858. The county history says he stayed with Low many times, but nothing found identifies the location. The house now at **117 WEST WASHINGTON** claims to have hosted Lincoln and Douglas before it was moved from a riverside location. Great crowds would gather around in the evening, laughter filling wherever it was he stayed, said to cure ills. The wharf used in those days is now known as Riverfront Park.

The Mason County COURTHOUSE is a replica of the original burned down in 1882, where Lincoln practiced law. ROCKWELL PARK, several blocks north of the courthouse, has a marker commemorating a Lincoln speech there in August 1858. Douglas also spoke here, at the site of ancient American Indian Rockwell Mound dating to about A.D. 150, the largest of the Western Hopewell or Havana culture.

HENNEPIN: Speech October 31, 1848.

HENRY: Lincoln spoke in a grove nearby on July 20, 1846, on the BONHAM FARM during his congressional campaign and later on, on August 23, 1858.

HIGHLAND: Lincoln spoke on September 11, 1858, and stopped at the JOSEPH UPPIGER HOUSE.

HILLSBORO: BECKEMEYER SCHOOL, once the county fairgrounds, is the site of a speech in September 1858. Lincoln stayed at the BLOCKBURGER INN, ON MAIN AND TILSON STREETS, on trips to Vandalia. He also stayed here just before the Shields duel. Lincoln was often a guest at the JOSEPH T. ECCLES HOME, AT THE CORNER OF BERRY AND WATER. The courthouse was the site of a July 20, 1844, speech, and Lincoln was probably here again for a speech on July 15, 1843.

HINSDALE: Lincoln stayed in a hotel on Ogden Street according to the Chicago *Sun Times,* January 12, 1961. This community is located near Chicago just west of Interstate 294, northwest off the Interstate 55 interchange.

HUNTSVILLE: Lincoln once drove over while staying in Augusta to see his old teacher Azel Dorsey, who lived in a home still standing in the mid-1950s.

HUDSONVILLE: Lincoln spent the night on March 8, 1830, on the way from Indiana to Decatur (not on current map).

HURON: Lincoln surveyed and platted this town northwest of Petersburg on March 21, 1836. This is no longer on the map, but it was on the Sangamon River at Port Huron Ferry, three miles east and one mile north of Oakford. The ferry linked Springfield and New Salem to Fort Clark, now Peoria. Lincoln's friends, the Jack Armstrongs, moved here in 1855. Jack died in 1857, at the time his son was indicted for murder. He is buried near Ann Rutledge's first grave in Old Concord Cemetery near Petersburg. Lincoln came this way to stay with the family while he tried the sensational case in Beardstown involving Duff Armstrong.

JACKSONVILLE: Several documents in the local library outline Lincoln's forty-one known trips to Jacksonville, although others are also documented in various sources. His first strong antislavery speech was claimed to have been made in the **COURTHOUSE SQUARE**. Lincoln was well known and in demand here as a lawyer and speaker. Stephen Douglas arrived in November 1833 but could not find a job. He moved to Winchester where he taught school and then moved back to Jacksonville to begin law practice in 1834. He acquired his sobriquet, "The Little Giant," after making a stirring speech to despondent Democrats here. The **COURTHOUSE** was at the northwest corner of the present square and was the site of many Lincoln and Douglas cases and speeches over the years. The site is now **CENTRAL PARK** at the town center, a block east of the present courthouse built in 1868. No markers recall the events of the Lincoln era. Grant and his forces camped on the way to Missouri as marked on the square and fairgrounds.

  DUNCAN PARK, 4 DUNCAN PLACE AT STATE AND WEBSTER STREETS, was a home where Lincoln, Daniel Webster, and President Martin Van Buren were entertained. This is west of the business district.

  BEECHER HALL AT ILLINOIS COLLEGE, 1101 COLLEGE, is sometimes erroneously identified as the location of a famous Lincoln lecture on February 11, 1859, entitled "Discoveries and Inventions," received with "repeated and hearty bursts of applause." However, this lecture appears to have been given at Union Hall, noted below. Lincoln's partner, Herndon, had gone to school here. According to tradition, Lincoln's possible marriage to Ann Rutledge was delayed when she came to Jacksonville to attend the Female Academy and gave Abe time to begin his legal pursuits. There are some stories that she tried to get him to attend the college during this time.

  On March 16, 1840, Lincoln probably came with Edward D. Baker, who opened a three-day political debate. The next day Josiah Lamborn replied. Lincoln then followed with a speech at **MARKET HOUSE**, but before he finished he asked to continue that evening at the **COURTHOUSE**. He spoke for two hours there, arguing corruption in the Van

Buren administration. He spent the night of September 20, 1842, in order to avoid possible arrest and a potential duel with James Shields.

JOHN J. HARDIN was a cousin of Mary Todd and knew Lincoln in the legislature. He had succeeded Lincoln's law partner, Stuart, in Congress. Author Douglas L. Wilson refers to him as "one of the ablest and most admired men of Lincoln's immediate world." After Edward Baker served a term in Congress, Hardin became Lincoln's rival in the 1846 congressional election. Lincoln came to confer with him in the fall of 1845 about the prospects of running for Congress. Lincoln expected him to abide by an informal agreement to serve only one term. The meeting changed nothing, and it appeared Hardin would run again. After much political maneuvering, Hardin saw that he could not prevail and withdrew. He then joined the army to go to Mexico, where he was killed. His home is marked by a stone at the northeast corner of EAST STATE AND HARDIN, and just east of the Yates House mentioned below. The site is just east of Our Savior Church Rectory at 462 East State and Brown Streets. Hardin sold part of his property to Richard Yates, who gave his eulogy at the Hardin home, and the Catholic church. Part of Hardin's funeral, attended by Lincoln, was held here, after a procession from the square, and a huge lunch was served just to the east.

It is possible that the 1842 reconciliation of Mary and Abraham occurred in Hardin's home, rather than the Frances house in Springfield as generally thought. Hardin had been instrumental in reconciling the Lincoln-Shields rift. It is claimed that James Shields and Lincoln came here five days after their "duel" (see ALTON, Illinois). Wilson's *Honor's Voice*, beginning with page 283, traces facts implying that Abraham and Mary met at a wedding celebration at the Hardin home on September 27. Mary and Abraham then stayed at the house while the rest of the party went for a ride; they settled their differences then, rather than at the Frances house in Springfield as generally supposed. The couple married in November 1842.

Other activity in Jacksonville is as follows:

October 6, 1843: Prior to a recent election, Lincoln had proposed a bet between Sangamon County and Morgan County Whigs about which county could muster more votes. Sangamon won, and Lincoln, with his political cronies and others, came on this day to be hosted with a barbecue. A Chicago Democratic paper characterized the affair as the "most disgraceful affair that ever happened in the state."

March 21, 1854: Lincoln stayed at MANSION HOUSE while trying an important assault case. This was on NORTH MAIN ACROSS FROM THE COURTHOUSE.

August 25–27, 1854: Lincoln stayed then, where he is said to have always been welcome, at the house of future governor **RICHARD YATES** on **EAST STATE STREET**, just west of where Yates Street would dead-end if it ran as far as State. It is just west of the rectory mentioned above. His son, Richard Yates II, also a governor of Illinois, was born here early in the Civil War. A flat monument on the north side of State in front of McMurray College marks the spot.

September 2, 1854: Lincoln went to the state convention in Winchester and spoke in Jacksonville.

September 6, 1856: Lincoln spoke in the **COURTHOUSE YARD** for Frémont and urged antislavery Democrats not to vote for Buchanan. He spoke at another Frémont meeting on November 1.

May 8, 1858: While waiting in the **GREAT WESTERN STATION** for a train to Springfield, stretched out on two seats, a fellow lawyer asked Lincoln for advice on winning a law case. The lawyer followed Lincoln's suggestions and won. The station is just east of the Hardin homesite.

February 11, 1859: Lincoln lectured on "Discoveries and Inventions" at the Congregational Church, then known as **UNION HALL**, that "was received with repeated and hearty bursts of applause." The presentation was a financial disappointment as the promoters lost money. The lecture was given several times and was the only one Lincoln ever gave. This was on the **EAST SIDE OF THE SQUARE ABOUT MIDWAY BETWEEN STATE AND MORGAN**, and set back some from the street. Afterward he was a guest of honor at a tea party given by **DR. OWEN M. LONG** at his home, located a block north at **C ALLEY AND COURT STREET**. Because of the train schedule, he probably spent the night and returned the next day to Springfield.

Lincoln is also reported to have visited several times at the **GRIERSON HOME**, open to the public at **852 EAST STATE**. The famous cavalryman Benjamin H. Grierson lived here.

JAMESTON (RIVERTON): Lincoln canoed into town in March 1831, and then walked the rest of the way to Springfield with John Hanks and John D. Johnston to see Denton Offutt, who had hired them to take a flatboat of produce to New Orleans.

JOLIET: Lincoln spoke for Frémont on October 8, 1856.

JONESBORO: The fairgrounds on **NORTH MAIN**, a quarter mile north of Lincoln Square, was the site of the third **LINCOLN-DOUGLAS DEBATE**,

September 15, 1858, before about fifteen hundred listeners, with estimates ranging from five hundred to two thousand. A parade escorted
the candidates from the courthouse to the site. The COURTHOUSE was
WEST OF THE SQUARE ON MARKET STREET in the same place as now.
There are markers on Lincoln Square and at the park.

This was a Wednesday, a working day for most people, resulting in
the smallest attendance of any of the debates. Also, the event was held
in a sparsely populated area, and a state fair was taking place in nearby
Centralia. Many came from the slave states of Missouri and Kentucky.
This was hostile territory for Lincoln, and Douglas also received only a
moderate reception. Both candidates arrived at the Anna-Jonesboro
train station the day before and stayed in Anna. After a conference with
several party members at the postmaster's office in Anna, the present
site of the ANNA NATIONAL BANK, Lincoln went to DAVID L PHILLIPS'S
HOME AT 511 SOUTH MAIN (see the ANNA Illinois, entry also): Later he
went to the UNION HOUSE in Jonesboro at the SOUTHEAST CORNER OF THE
SQUARE AND ROUTE 146 where he sat outside in front of the building,
greeted visitors, and marveled at Donati's Comet then appearing.

On the morning of the debate, Lincoln accepted the offer of Dr.
McVane and his host, Phillips, to take a ride in the country. Together
with Phillips's eleven-year-old son, they rode toward Willard's Landing
on the Mississippi. The boy later wrote that Lincoln kept everyone
"constantly in an uproar of laughter" during the three-hour ride. He
and Douglas also visited the home of former senator John Hacker's
daughter-in-law. During the debate, Lincoln reminded his audience
that he was raised in nearby Indiana.

KNOXVILLE: Lincoln tried cases at the old KNOX COUNTY COURT-
HOUSE. On October 6, 1858, he arrived in a violent storm and stayed at
the OLD HEBARD HOUSE INN, ON THE NORTH SIDE OF MAIN ABOUT TWO
BLOCKS EAST OF THE COURTHOUSE. A brass band played and a crowd
gathered to hear a speech. When he appeared, someone came up to the
porch and held a lantern close to his face. This prompted Lincoln to
remark, "My friends, the less you see of me the better you will like me."
A procession met him the next day and grew in length as it proceeded
to the debate with Douglas in Galesburg. Farmers in hayracks and
wagons joined the line of buggies and floats carrying banners.

LAWRENCEVILLE: The Lincoln Trail Monument on U.S. 50 nine
miles east of town marks the site where the Lincoln family entered Illinois from Indiana in 1830. It is not definitely known which route the
family followed from Gentryville, Indiana, to Decatur, Illinois. The

Indiana Lincoln Memorial Way Commission chose the Troy-Vincennes trail in Indiana, passing through Polk Patch (now Selvin), Petersburg, and Monroe City. It probably took four or five days to get to Vincennes. The Lincoln family crossed the Wabash at Vincennes on March 6, 1830. Spring rains flooded the river. Lincoln's dog fell into the icy water and was rescued by his master.

From the ferry they probably passed on the old road, mostly under water, to Purgatory Bottom and then ten miles to Lawrenceville. From here they turned northeast to Palestine where the land office was located. Another possibility was that they took an old road that still runs north from about a half mile west of the river.

A plaque on the north side of the courthouse lawn at State and Eleventh Streets commemorates an October 30, 1840 dispute arising while Lincoln was on a campaign trip in Lawrenceville. A local physician, William G. Anderson, accused Lincoln of being an aggressor and of insulting him during a rally at the square. Lincoln wrote a letter denying any aggression or ill feelings.

Lincoln returned several times and made speeches in 1844 and on September 19, 1856.

LACON: Lincoln arrived unannounced during his congressional campaign on July 18, 1846, but a crowd demanded and got a speech. It was announced on October 17, 1854, that Lincoln and Douglas would speak. Both arrived, but Douglas claimed to be hoarse and in ill health, and did not wish to make an address. Lincoln proposed that he also would decline, and this was announced from steps of the hotel. Friends of Lincoln felt this was because Lincoln got the better of him the day before in Peoria, and Douglas was not ready to compete with Lincoln. Douglas did speak the next day in nearby Hennepin. Lincoln spoke in Lacon to twenty thousand on September 30, 1856, for Frémont.

LAHARPE: Lincoln spoke at the **METHODIST CHURCH** on October 23, 1858.

LAMOILLE: On the way to the Freeport debate Lincoln stayed with Dr. John Kendall who operated a hotel on the first floor of his home on Main Street.

LASALLE: At the southern end of the Spippingsport Bridge is the site of **FORT WILBOURN**, which is marked. It was where Lincoln enlisted as a private in Jacob N. Early's company on June 16, 1832, for service in the Illinois Volunteers during the Black Hawk War.

LEBANON: The **MARMAID INN, AT 112 EAST ST. LOUIS STREET**, hosted Lincoln and later author Charles Dickens. There is a story told locally, perhaps apocryphally, that one day when Lincoln was still eating breakfast, he was told to board the coach since it was leaving. He calmly remarked that if it left without him, it would soon return. It did leave without him, and he calmly finished. Soon the proprietor and employees were scurrying around in great excitement. The silver spoons had disappeared from the inn and it was logically reasoned that someone on the stage had stolen them. Officers were summoned; they pursued the coach and brought it back. Lincoln calmly drew the silver from under the table and "leisurely took his seat in the stage and the journey continued." Lincoln scholars would no doubt question the truth of this tale.

LERNA: The Thomas Lincoln family lived in this area for most of their time in Illinois. The sites of the four farms are discussed under the entry on **CHARLESTON**, Illinois, which also discusses nearby **WALNUT POINT OR PARADISE**.

LEWISTOWN: Lincoln tried many cases, and Douglas served as judge in the **COURTHOUSE** on the public square, long since vanished. The pillars standing in Lincoln's day are now a memorial in the Protestant Cemetery. The towns of Lewistown and Canton were engaged in a bitter county-seat war in the mid-1890s when an incendiary fire destroyed the old building that had known both Lincoln and Douglas. Douglas spoke to five thousand on August 16, 1858, in Proctor's Grove, in the southwest part of town. Lincoln answered on the next day at the courthouse, to a crowd of about six thousand.

MAJOR NEWTON WALKER lived at **1127 NORTH MAIN**. Walker served in the legislature with Lincoln and hosted him many times. He died in 1899 and was fond of relating many anecdotes about Lincoln, for whom he often played the fiddle in exchange for stories.

LEXINGTON: Lincoln gave a brief speech on November 21, 1860.

LINCOLN-LOGAN COUNTY: This was the only town named for him with his knowledge and consent. The three town founders met in Lincoln's office so he could to draft legal documents founding the town. They suggested naming the town after their lawyer. Lincoln replied, "You'd better not do that, for I never knew anything named Lincoln that amounted to much." The town is the third seat of Logan County, and all are locations in which Lincoln practiced law. The county was named for a friend of Lincoln's, Dr. John Logan, and grew from an effort of Lincoln's to split Sangamon County into four smaller counties in 1839.

The first courthouse in the county was on the site now known as the **POSTVILLE COURTHOUSE SHRINE AND MUSEUM, AT 915 FIFTH STREET OFF U.S. 66**. Postville is now a part of the town of Lincoln. A fire destroyed the county records in 1857 so that little specifics are known about Lincoln's practice in Postville or Mount Pulaski. There is a story that once Lincoln was absent when due in court. The sheriff was sent to bring him to his duties and found him in adjacent Postville Park "playing townball with the boys." The present structure is a replica of the 1839 structure, the first courthouse in the Eighth Circuit Court District when Lincoln rode the circuit. After 1847 when the seat of Logan County moved to Mount Pulaski, the old courthouse was sold for $300 to a local resident and used for civic and religious purposes, and later for private housing. Henry Ford purchased the old building in 1929 when he was organizing his Greenfield Village in Dearborn, Michigan, with numerous historical buildings forming a heritage park and outdoor museum. The building was dismantled, including stones from the old foundation. The boards were numbered and then reassembled with original nails in Michigan, where it can be visited today. The original Illinois site remained an empty park until 1953, when an exterior replica was completed. The interior was finished three years later. The replica has an exhibit area, an 1840s-style courtroom, and an office, arranged as they might have been when Lincoln practiced law.

The second county seat was at Mount Pulaski, ten miles south on Highway 121, and served from 1847 until 1853. The coming of the railroad brought change to the area, and there was a need to locate the central seat of justice and business on the line and to a more central location. Three partners had acquired land and granted the Chicago and Mississippi Railroad a right-of-way through the potential town side. Lincoln was hired to prepare documents to establish joint ownership of the land, gave power of attorney to promoter, Colonel Latham, and bestowed on the township the name of Lincoln. After the town site had been surveyed, lots were announced for sale. Contracts drawn by Lincoln provided for the release of the purchasers in the event that the county seat was not established on the site within one year. To be on the safe side, Latham deeded to the county the sites for the courthouse and jail, and two tracts for parks. An election soon established the town as seat of the county. It was christened that day, August 29 (*Lincoln Day by Day*), 1853, by Lincoln, who broke open a watermelon and sprinkled the juice into a cup and then on the ground. (Lincoln scholar

James T. Hickey believed that Robert, ten, was then with his father. See *The Lincoln College Story 1865–1995*, for a reference attributed by that author to Dr. Hickey.)

This spot is now marked at the **AMTRAK STATION** at the corner of **SANGAMON AND BROADWAY STREETS** with a marker that reads, "Near this site Abraham Lincoln christened the town with the juice of a watermelon when the first lots were sold on August 27, 1853. Lincoln purchased no lots although he did attend the sale, but did acquire one in 1857 as compensation for a fee." This is the **OLD ALTON DEPOT**, which adjoins the present depot. Douglas spoke here on April 26, 1861, and Lincoln's funeral train stopped briefly on May 3, 1865, under an evergreen arch with the words, "With Malice toward none, with charity for all."

A fire destroyed the courthouse in 1857. Lincoln and other lawyers then used the **CHRISTIAN CHURCH ON PEKIN BETWEEN KICKAPOO AND MCLEAN** as a courtroom. The site is now a parking lot. Lincoln acted as judge here for the absent Judge David Davis. He shared a law office west of the courthouse on Kickapoo Street with Sam C. Parks.

Lincoln arrived unobserved on September 4, 1858, as a tremendous Douglas rally was being held. A circus band led the crowd to a tent where Douglas spoke while Lincoln listened in the rear "almost unnoticed." A marker at the corner of **LOGAN AND FOURTH STREETS** reads, "On this site during the senatorial campaign of 1858, Stephen A. Douglas spoke to a Democratic political rally held in a circus tent on September 4. Douglas' opponent for the senate seat, Abraham Lincoln, was on the train from Bloomington to Springfield and stopped to hear the speech." The tent was toward **DECATUR AND SANGAMON**. President-elect Lincoln spoke on November 21, 1860, while traveling to Chicago.

The **LOGAN COUNTY COURTHOUSE**, at **PULASKI AND MCLEAN** Streets, stands on the site of two buildings where Lincoln once practiced law. The current structure was erected in 1905 and has been the courthouse site since 1853. The first was used from 1854 until it burned to the ground in 1857, destroying most of the records of Lincoln's practice. Much of the early history is therefore missing. The next building was dismantled in 1903. Lincoln spoke here for two hours in support for presidential candidate John C. Frémont on September 3, 1856 and spoke again on October 16, 1858.

Lincoln College, at Ottawa and Keokuk Streets, was founded in 1865 and was the first and only college named for Lincoln in his lifetime. The cornerstone was laid on his last birthday. Two noteworthy museums are located in the McKinstry Library at 300 Keokuk Street. One is the Museum of Presidents, including documents and signatures of all presidents and most first ladies. Only facsimiles are displayed; all original documents are in storage. In an adjoining room is the **LINCOLN COLLEGE MUSEUM**, with dioramas, 1860 campaign material, and two thousand Lincoln artifacts. These include a coal oil lamp and china from the Lincoln home in Springfield; a rocking chair and table that belonged to Tad; a desk Lincoln used while serving in the Illinois legislature; chairs from the Lincoln White House and Diller's Drug Store in Springfield; law books used by Lincoln and Herndon; and a table once owned by Mentor Graham when he helped Lincoln with his studies of grammar and mathematics in New Salem. Many Mary Lincoln monogrammed personal items, jewelry, letters, and artifacts are shown also. The collection also has tassels from the casket and catafalque covering used in Springfield when Lincoln's body lay in state at the Old Capitol. There is also a piece of the dress worn by actress Laura Keene, who starred in the play being presented in Ford's Theater on the night Lincoln was shot. Locks of Mary and Abraham's hair are shown as are many documents with his signature and others of those whom he knew, such as New Salem friends and law partners. A recent gift includes many articles related to the assassination.

Other sites include:

OLD PRIMM STORE and post office, at the **NORTHEAST CORNER OF FIFTH AND WASHINGTON STREET**, which was visited often by Lincoln.

POSTVILLE PARK, AT FIFTH AND WASHINGTON STREET, the town square of Postville. Lincoln engaged in "town ball" (a predecessor of baseball), horseshoe pitching, and throwing the maul (a heavy wooden hammer).

LINCOLN RUSTIC INN, AT 412 PULASKI STREET, where a conspiracy to steal Lincoln's body from its tomb was plotted in 1876 by Terrence Mullins and Jack Hughes. The plot was hatched to hold it for a ransom of $200,000. Although the men broke into the tomb, their scheme failed because of an informant. See entry on Oak Ridge Cemetery in the section on Springfield, Illinois.

ROBERT D. LATHAM HOME, ON THE CORNER OF DELAVAN AND KICKAPOO STREETS at Lathum Place. A marker notes: that, "On this site stood the home of Robert B. Latham who jointed John D. Gillette and Virgil Hickox to found the town of Lincoln in 1853. Abraham Lincoln, judges, and lawyers of the Eighth Judicial Circuit were frequent guests at his home."

DESKINS TAVERN, AT THE CORNER OF FIFTH AND MADISON STREETS, in Postville, part of the town of Lincoln. The marker on the site reads: "On this site Dr. John Deskins erected a tavern in 1836. Abraham Lincoln, David Davis and other lawyers frequently stayed overnight while the Eighth Judicial Circuit Court was in session at the Postville Courthouse. The judges, lawyers, litigants, witnesses, jurors, prisoners often shared the same dinner table." Lincoln frequently told the story of an incident here when a man persisted in trying to get a drink and was refused by the innkeeper. The frustrated guest finally pleaded, "Great Heavens, give me an ear of corn and a tin cup and I'll make it myself."

LINCOLN HOUSE, AT 501 BROADWAY STREET. The marker on the site reads: "On this site the town proprietors erected the original Lincoln House in 1854. Leonard Volk met Abraham Lincoln on the sidewalk in front of the hotel on July 16, 1858, and arranged to make Lincoln's life mask later." Local legend has it that Lincoln made a speech in front of the hotel during the summer of 1858, although it was not recorded.

LINCOLN GALLERY, AT 111 NORTH SANGAMON, has the statue of Lincoln christening the town and Lloyd Ostendorf's oil paintings of Lincoln's life in Logan County, Gettysburg, and Washington, D.C.

A plaque marks the lot at **523 PULASKI**, one of the few pieces of real estate Lincoln ever owned other than his Springfield home. James Primm found Lincoln in New York City in 1857 and got him to guarantee a loan, which he was unable to pay. The lot was in settlement of the debt.

LOVINGTON: The Lincoln family camped in 1830, two and a half miles south of town on State Highway 32, where the road intercepts the Paris-to-Springfield road.

MACKINAW: Lincoln addressed the citizens during his congressional campaign on July 24, 1846.

MACOMB: Lincoln was a frequent visitor and spoke at the MC-DONOUGH COUNTY COURTHOUSE on August 25, 1858. Photographer T. P. Pearson took his picture the next day; some argue it is the best Lincoln photograph of the 1850s. He stayed at the RANDOLPH HOUSE ON THE SOUTHEAST CORNER OF THE SQUARE and wrote out questions for the debate to be held two days later in Freeport. In discussing the second question with Joseph Medill, he was advised not to ask it as it was felt that Douglas would satisfy followers in Illinois and be reelected. Lincoln argued that Douglas may well beat him for senator if he answered, but "if he makes that answer his career in the Democratic Party is ended. He can never be elected president by the Democratic

Party, and a split in that party will be inevitable" (*Chicago Tribune*, August 9, 1891). Republican leaders met at this time and tried to get Lincoln to stop using the phrase, "A house divided against itself." Lincoln held firm and challenged anyone to argue that it was not true. He also stayed at the Randolph on October 12 and 25, 1858, and spoke at the square after a parade and great demonstrations.

MACOUPIN POINT: Lincoln passed through by stagecoach on the way to Vandalia in 1834.

MAGNOLIA: Lincoln gave a speech here on October 31, 1848.

MARSHALL: Tradition says Lincoln made speeches on the south side of the square and at the northeast corner. One was dated September 19, 1840. He also practiced in the **CLARK COUNTY COURTHOUSE**.

MATTOON: Lincoln came here many times. Before the Charleston debate, he stayed at the **PENNSYLVANIA HOUSE** on September 17, 1858, and spent the day in town, as did Douglas. Douglas had his headquarters at the **ESSEX HOUSE** located at the railroad junction. This was the depot at the southwest junction of the tracks, but the site is now the northwest corner of the tracks and the bridge. **THE PENNSYLVANIA HOUSE** was across the street to the south.

Lincoln may have spoken at the Essex on more than the one documented occasion, September 7, 1858, and stopped for a short time there on his way to see his stepmother in 1861. The present depot is on the north side of Broadway, west of Seventeenth Street. The railroad tracks running northeast have been lowered below street level as they pass through town now, and the east-west tracks have been removed. The current depot has a historical marker related to General Grant and there is another Grant marker about a hundred feet to the east. These note that Grant, without uniform or commission, mustered in the Seventh District Regiment on May 15, 1861, nearby and took command of his first Civil War troops on June 15. There are no Lincoln markers.

MAHOMET: Lincoln stayed at the **NINE GAL TAVERN**, one mile east on Route 150 (the owner had nine red-headed daughters) and the **RAE TAVERN** in town.

MECHANICSBURG: While running for Congress in 1834, Lincoln jumped into the crowd and broke up a free-for-all. This won him many admirers.

MEREDOSIA: Lincoln arrived late at the only hotel in town in December 1841, and had to try to sleep on an old settee in the lobby. He spoke here on October 18, 1858.

METAMORA: One of the two original courthouses where Lincoln practiced law is still standing on the original site and is substantially the same as it was when built. The **METAMORA COURTHOUSE STATE HISTORIC SITE** is open daily from nine to five. (The other original courthouse is Mount Pulaski. Lincoln also used the old original Logan County courthouse, now in Greenfield Village, Michigan.) It was completed in 1845, two years after the Woodford county seat was moved from Versailles. From 1841 until 1857, Woodford County was one of the fifteen counties on the Eighth Judicial Circuit in which Lincoln practiced. Stephen Douglas and Adlai E. Stevenson, vice president under President Cleveland, also practiced here with Lincoln.

The judge, district attorney, and lawyers arrived a day or two before each session in the spring and fall to discuss cases with potential clients and other parties. These discussions were carried out at every available meeting place including the courthouse lawn, hallways of buildings, and public dining rooms. In the evening the attorneys, members of the court, and others discussed politics, spun yarns, shared jokes, and engaged in good-natured needling of their associates.

Most of Lincoln's cases here were routine, but two were somewhat notable. In April 1847 Lincoln defended George Kerr and J. Randolph Scott against charges of giving aid to a fugitive slave. Illinois was a free state, but still provided punishment for those who helped slaves escape to freedom. In fact, in 1848 an Illinois constitutional provision banned black immigration. The court dismissed the case according to Lincoln's argument that the state had not proved that the alleged fugitive was ever owned as a slave.

In what was probably his last case here, Lincoln defended Melissa Goings in April 1857, who had struck her husband with a piece of firewood, causing his death. She was rushed to trial and bail was revoked, indicating that the judge had predisposed her guilty. When the case was called, the defendant could not be found. It is not clear exactly what happened, but the bailiff accused Lincoln of suggesting to his client that she flee. When confronted by the bailiff, Lincoln reportedly stated: "I did not run her off. She wanted to know where she could get a good drink of water, and I told her there was mighty good water in Tennessee." Mr. Goings had a reputation of having a bad temper, and the community feeling was with the widow. No serious attempt was made to apprehend her, and the case was later dropped. (Lincoln's secretary, John Hay, tells a similar story in his diary entry for July 19, 1863. He quotes Lincoln describing U. F. Linder telling a client who had stolen a hog to go get a drink, and suggesting that the water was better in Tennessee.)

The county seat remained until 1894 when it was relocated to Eureka. The old courthouse was used for various civic organizations and as an opera house for several years. Later additions to the building have been removed so that it now retains its original appearance. Just south is a locust grove marked as a "Site Where Lincoln Spoke in 1858." Lincoln is said to have stayed in the METAMORA HOUSE.

MIDDLETOWN: Lincoln crossed nearby Musick's Ferry when he made his first survey of Logan County in 1834. Later, on the Eighth Circuit, he stayed at George Dunlap's Tavern, also known as the Stagecoach Inn, and at Musick's home on Salt Creek.

MILAN: A marker south on U.S. 67 at State 92 indicated that Lincoln camped about one mile west on May 8, 1832, where he was mustered into military service.

MONMOUTH: A Lincoln welcoming committee once had to cancel plans to meet him on the Oquawka road because of recent heavy rains. He had to walk through town rather than ride, as the mud was too deep for a wagon. He spoke in 1834 and again immediately following the debate in Galesburg on October 7, 1858. He stayed with the McNeil family, where the Carr mansion was later built.

MONTICELLO: A plaque on the COURTHOUSE LAWN commemorates Lincoln's travels to Piatt County on the old Eighth Judicial Circuit. In the 1850s the town was connected by two railroads and became an important transportation stop for Lincoln in his 1856 and 1858 campaigns. In 1856 he spoke for Frémont at the COURTHOUSE, and stayed with the Guy family. He stayed at the hotel of JOHN TENBROOK on the south side of MAIN ACROSS FROM THE COURTHOUSE. He spoke at the courthouse on September 6, 1858, and to about five thousand at the CITY PARK west of the courthouse. His remarks lasted about three hours "after great excitement, with bands, banners and parades." He chanced to meet Stephen Douglas just south of town, and they agreed to meet later that evening to lay plans for the debates. This site is marked on KRATZ HILL with a stone pyramid, on the west side of Route 105. See also BEMENT, Illinois.

MORRIS: Lincoln spent the night of August 20, 1858.

MOUNT CARMEL: Lincoln spoke twice in 1840 at the COURTHOUSE, located at the same place as the present-day courthouse. He rode here on September 2 in a one-seated buggy from Carmi with Edwin B. Webb, who was also a Whig electoral candidate. Webb's six-year-old daughter, Patty, who was to enter the seminary, sat on Lincoln's lap. Webb was a widower and courted Mary Todd in Springfield, but Mary did not wish to be a stepmother.

MOUNT MORRIS: It is claimed that Lincoln spent many nights in a large stone home just to the northwest belonging to SAMUEL HITT.

MOUNT PULASKI: The Greek Revival courthouse was built in 1847 at the cost of $3,000 when Postville was succeeded as county seat, and remained the seat of justice until 1853 when Lincoln helped persuade voters to move it back to a more central location. *The History of Logan County* comments "Abraham Lincoln was present offener [*sic*] in this building than in any other in the county and during the existence of the county seat in Mount Pulaski, he was on one side or the other of every important case on the docket. Every plank in the structure is therefore sacred with historical significance." This old building then served various public functions until it was acquired by the state in 1936 as a historical monument (see the entry for the TOWN OF LINCOLN, Illinois). The small structure is only thirty by forty feet and two stories high. One of Lincoln's cases involved an alleged patent for a "horological cradle." The invention could be wound to rock a baby. When Judge Davis asked Lincoln "how the thing could be stopped when desirable," Lincoln replied, "It's like some of the glib talkers you and I know, Judge, it won't stop until it runs down."

During court days Lincoln stayed often in private homes, including the THOMAS LUSHBAUGH HOUSE IN THE MIDDLE OF THE 100 BLOCK OF NORTH MARIAN, ON THE WEST SIDE, and with the town founder, JABEZ CAPPS, on the WEST SIDE OF THE SQUARE. He was also at the MOUNT PULASKI HOUSE INN (NORTHWEST CORNER OF THE SQUARE), torn down in 1902. Lincoln's friend SAMUEL C. PARKS lived here, and Lincoln made his legal headquarters in Parks's office and later in the nearby town of Lincoln. In 1860 Parks sent his copy of Howell's campaign biography to Lincoln to read and correct; it is in the Illinois State Historical Library.

MOUNT STERLING: NORTH GRADE SCHOOL is the site of a Lincoln speech on October 19, 1858. Lincoln heard another of the many rumors circulating that Irishmen were being brought in, maybe to work on some new railroad, and to vote Democratic.

MOUNT VERNON: Lincoln met to debate (later general) John A. McClernard in the **METHODIST CHURCH** on Eleventh Street on August 28, 1840, one of several times he spoke in town. Lincoln was the Whig presidential elector candidate and McClernard the Democratic candidate. The church was located **NORTH OF THE PRESENT CITY HALL ON MAIN** and was then the only building large enough to hold the audience. It also was being used as a courthouse. The speakers were to share the noon intermission to make their remarks but McClernard took up the whole time. When Lincoln began, the judge called court into session, forcing Lincoln to stop. The owner of the **KIRBY HOTEL** then announced that he was "for fair play even in a dog fight" and invited the crowd to come to the shade of his hotel around the corner, where the debate could continue. A bronze plaque now marks the spot where Lincoln mounted a box to speak "while the crowd listened, laughed, and swore at him for another hour or so." He stayed at this hotel at **111 NORTH TENTH STREET** numerous times.

At the **APPELLATE COURTHOUSE**, now a museum at **FOURTEENTH AND MAIN**, Lincoln won his largest corporation law case and fees. The case was tried at what was then the Supreme Court House, Southern Division, in November 1859, with nine railroad officials including the future commanding general of the Army of the Potomac, George B. McClellan. Lincoln came on the same stagecoach with McClellan and a twelve-year-old, who later became a Dr. J. Watson. Due to overcrowding on the stagecoach, Watson sat on Lincoln's lap from Ashley and was enthralled with the stories he told. That evening he went to the hotel to hang around the parlor hoping Lincoln would continue the amusement, but was disappointed when he and McClellan stayed in conference in their rooms. The Supreme Court had been held at the **MASONIC HALL AT TENTH AND MAIN** until the building was ready. The new building became the political headquarters of Southern Illinois. It is claimed that Lincoln, Douglas, John Logan (later a Union general), and McClernard met here and at the nearby **MOUNT VERNON INN** for discussions.

NAPLES: Lincoln passed through several times on speaking tours and legal business, including November 3, 1854, August 11, 1858, and October 18, 1858.

NAPERVILLE: According to the *Aurora Beacon News*, dated October 10, 1942, Lincoln stayed in the Pre-Emption House. A boy who was supposed to take bags to the room ran off to tell the townspeople, who demanded and got a speech. Lincoln spoke from the roof of the porch.

NEW BOSTON: Lincoln surveyed the town site in September 1834.

NEW LENOX: Three miles east on U.S. 30, just west of the U.S. 45 intersection (about twelve miles east of Joliet) is the **LINCOLN HOTEL**, built in 1846 and reputedly visited by Lincoln when traveling the old Sauk Trail.

NEW SALEM: Lincoln's New Salem State Park is located about twenty miles northwest of Springfield, just south of Petersburg. Here most of the cabins of Lincoln's friends have been reconstructed as near as possible to the supposed original location. The town existed only about as long as Lincoln lived in it during the 1830s. When he moved to New Salem, it was then about the same size as Chicago. Until 1833 or 1834 it was the trading point for all settlements in the area, really one big community. There were few villages north in Illinois. Chicago had a population of about one hundred, and Springfield's was about five hundred to one thousand, depending on the information source. At the height of prosperity there were about twenty-five families with twenty-five to thirty log or frame structures. Lincoln spent a week or two at many places in and around the community, including the homes of Mentor Graham, Bowling Green, and Jack Armstrong outside the village, and in the village with the Camrons, the Offutt Store, Rutledges, Burners, and others. Thus his presence is felt throughout the community.

Lincoln first came to New Salem in the spring of 1831 accompanied by his half brother and cousin on the way to New Orleans with a load of goods for Denton Offutt. (This is sometimes spelled "Offut," but he and Lincoln spelled it with two *t*'s.) Lincoln had built the flatboat a few miles away at Sangamo Town, about halfway to Springfield. From here they continued on the Sangamon River, joining the Illinois River at Beardstown, and then the Mississippi. While taking the flatboat past New Salem, it got snagged at the milldam. A large crowd gathered to wait for the destruction and loss of the cargo. Lincoln disregarded advice and was able to free the raft after many hours, to the delight of the onlookers. He liked the town and Offutt had promised him a job here after his trip.

Lincoln came to stay in July 1831, uneducated, without any sense of direction, and later described himself as a "piece of floating driftwood." He was for the first time "residing by himself." This was the great turning point in his life. His life could have continued as before, and logically it should have. During this stay of six years, he floated from house to house, clerked, failed in business, lost a love, enlisted in the Black Hawk War, wrote for newspapers, was elected to the General Assembly of Illinois, and gained the self-confidence to begin a professional career leading to the presidency.

Lincoln arrived back from New Orleans before Offutt came to start his store, and boarded in the CABIN OF JOHN CAMRON. (This was located southeast of the Rutledge Tavern where the museum is now and not reconstructed in the present village.) He may have lived with Camron (also spelled "Camron") while working at Offutt's store, when not sleeping in the store loft. He cast his first ballot here on August 1, 1831, as the polls were in Cameron's home. The road from Springfield to Havana ran between Camron's cabin and the Rutledge Tavern, just to the west of OFFUTT'S TAVERN. When the store opened in September, he bunked there with William Greene Jr., who was a few years younger. Business was generally slow, giving Lincoln time to borrow and study books available in the area. When he found out where Kirkham's Grammar was, he walked seven or eight miles to borrow it and consumed the lessons. Greene was later introduced to Secretary of State William Seward in the White House. The president told Seward that this was the man who taught him grammar. When the perplexed Greene asked what he meant, Lincoln explained, "Don't you remember living in Offutt's store and how I read and you held the book to see if I could give the correct definitions and answers? That's all the teaching of grammar I ever got."

Samuel Hill and John McNeil had started a store in 1829, and this was still the center of activity and called "headquarters for all political discussions." Lincoln worked here in addition to Offutt's store. The latter was located on the bluff above the mill about fifty feet from Bill Clary's store or tavern serving mainly liquor to a crowd of local toughs from nearby CLARY'S GROVE, the Clary's Grove Boys. That community was located in a general area between Tallula and New Salem, in the vicinity of ROUTE 123 AND ROCK CREEK ROAD. Loudmouth Offutt spent much of his time in Clary's and proclaimed the physical prowess of his new clerk. The boys had to test him with a challenge from their leader, Jack Armstrong. A wrestling match ensued near the two stores with Lincoln either winning or holding his own with the rowdy, and a mutual respect and friendship began. (A stone once marked the spot of the encounter, but there is none as of the late 1990s.) This event is deemed important in establishing Lincoln as a popular member of the community, and with it was the start of his political career.

As always, Lincoln was to retain his popularity and goodwill with men although not joining in on the drinking bouts and carousals. His friendships with the rough-and-ready pioneers earned him the captainship of the local militia unit and resulting leadership experience. He did not change the entry in Howell's biography stating that his election to the legislature was "through the influence of the famous wrestling match."

Sangamon River navigation was always a pet issue with Lincoln, who had time on his hands before Offutt arrived. Because of his trips with Offutt's flatboat and helping a family headed for Texas from New Salem to Beardstown, he was somewhat familiar with the stream's course, which had more water then than now. When the steamer *Talesman* from Cincinnati attempted to prove that the river could be navigable, Lincoln went to Beardstown to watch the boat come upstream. The river was low, so the young giant organized a body of axmen to clear some of the logs and limbs from the stream. He piloted, guided, or helped (depending on the source) the boat from Beardstown past New Salem to **PORTLAND LANDING, SIX MILES FROM BOTH NEW SALEM AND SPRINGFIELD.** This accomplishment caused an influx of new settlement as it was expected that New Salem would become a river town. It also gave him great notoriety and $40. However, he became liable for debts of about $100 when the promoter went broke, since he and his friend, Rowen Herndon, had agreed to financially back the venture.

Offutt's store failed within a year, and Lincoln worked at odd jobs at a sawmill, splitting rails, and clerking in the several stores in town. He sometimes stayed with Jack and Hannah Armstrong at Clary's Grove. The local schoolteacher, Mentor Graham, helped him develop speaking skills, and he ran for the legislature after announcing his candidacy on March 9, 1832.

Shortly thereafter the Black Hawk War broke out, in April 1832, and Lincoln joined up at nearby Richland. The militia recruits, including the Clary's Grove Boys, met at the **FARM OF DALLIS OR "DALLAS" SCOTT ON RICHLAND CREEK**, nine miles southwest, and elected Lincoln captain. Lincoln said that gave him as much satisfaction as anything that ever happened. This was about **TWO MILES EAST OF PLEASANT PLAINS**, and north of **ROUTE 125**. It is just northeast of Claysville, west of County Road 11W, with County Road 6AN running through it with the northeast curve in the road forming part of the eastern boundary. They then marched to Beardstown and were mustered into the state militia. This turned out to be a "holiday affair and chicken-stealing expedition." In a speech in Congress, he said he didn't see any Indians, but that he had "a good many bloody struggles with the mosquitoes."

The force organized in Beardstown and marched to Black Hawk's village near Rock Island on the Mississippi, where they were mustered into federal service, and then to Dixon's Ferry. Later they went south to Ottawa where they disbanded and reenlisted, being mustered in by Robert Anderson, later the commander at Fort Sumter at the start of the Civil War. They marched north again and at Stillman's Valley buried five men who had been killed and scalped by Indians the day before. They were mustered out at Whitewater River, Wisconsin, four miles above its junction with the Rock River. This taught Lincoln about soldiers' life, the necessity of discipline and morale, and the value and difficulties of leadership; it provided him with useful skills and a store of anecdotes.

On the way back home in Wisconsin, someone stole his horse, and he had to walk or share a ride. This cut his legislative campaign short. He was only able to campaign about a week, during the last week of July and early August. The top four candidates were elected to the legislature or state assembly in August 1832. Although in the area only a few months, he got all but three votes from his precinct and came in eighth out of thirteen in the county. He commented later that this was the only time he was defeated by a vote of the people. (In his defeats for the U.S. Senate in 1855 and 1858, the election was by the state legislature.) He made several speeches, including one at Pappsville, considered his first political endeavor. He was elected every time he ran in 1834, 1836, 1838, 1840, and 1854, although he did not serve the last term. Two speeches made in 1834 included one at **ANDREW HEREDITH'S MILL** at the **HEAD OF LICK CREEK**, ten miles northwest of Springfield, and at **HILL'S MILL** on nearby **SUGAR CREEK**. In 1834 he also decided to read law and to go into that profession.

One of the clerks at the store was **DANIEL GREEN BURNER**, the son of Isaac. In the 1890s, and in his eighties, Daniel wrote reminiscences of Lincoln and described how Lincoln had lived with the family for a time in their double cabin. This is thought to be reliable, but the site of the cabin is in some question (although it has been reconstructed at the New Salem Village). Abe grew to like **JACK KELSO**, who was generally considered a failure, but a dreamer. Lincoln boarded with Kelso and his wife, and enjoyed listening to poetry, particularly Shakespeare. From Kelso he began a lifelong appreciation of Shakespeare, Robert Burns, and the symphonies that could be played with language. He learned that neither Shakespeare nor Burns had much schooling and that he too could aspire to greater things. In the days before Lincoln was assassinated, he had read *Macbeth* aloud for two hours to a circle of friends.

After Offutt failed, Abe considered being a blacksmith, studied with Josh Miller, and went into business with a preacher's drunkard son,

William Berry. In the summer of 1832, they bought out the **HERNDON BROTHERS STORE**, and then later bought out Reuben Radford's store inventory, Lincoln using his $125 compensation from his Black Hawk War service. President Andrew Jackson awarded him the local postmaster's job, allowing him to read newspapers as they were sent and to get mail free. Lincoln was not a supporter of Jackson, but wrote, "He was appointed . . . the office being too insignificant, to make his politics an objection." Jackson was probably also impressed by the fact that Lincoln had been a captain in the militia. Lincoln said later that this gave him more happiness than the presidency, and earned him about $25 to $50 a year, based on the volume of mail received. Lincoln would normally take the letters in the crown of his hat from house to house as he moved around during the day, although delivery was not required. He served from April 7, 1833, until the office moved to Petersburg on May 30, 1836. Accounts differ as to whether he performed this job at his store or at the Hill Store. Hill had been the postmaster before Lincoln. On one occasion Lincoln accidentally overcharged a customer several cents and walked six miles round-trip to return the overcharge. This home, the **HORNBUCKLE HOUSE**, was located southeast of New Salem, just **SOUTHWEST OF THE INTERSECTION OF CLEMENS AND HARRIS ROADS, ABOUT ONE AND A HALF MILES WEST OF ATHENS**.

There are two versions of how Lincoln came across his copies of Blackstone's *Commentaries*. The more popular and interesting story tells about a family that sold a barrel of junk in preparation for moving west. Lincoln bought it to help lessen the horse's load and found that it contained four volumes of Blackstone's *Commentaries on Law*. The more likely version is that he bought them in an auction in Springfield. (Lincoln did not correct the Howells biography, which he reviewed, that stated the latter version, although the former is generally given.) Getting the books renewed his interest in the law, and he went to John T. Stuart's office in Springfield to borrow other books. Stuart was a major in Lincoln's company and was the son of his future father-in-law's sister. Mentor Graham convinced him that he also should know grammar, so he borrowed books on that subject, too. Graham was the schoolteacher who charged five cents a day per pupil, or thirty cents to eighty-five cents per month depending on the age. He first conducted a school in the Baptist Church near Bowling Green's home, to the west of New Salem, although there is some question as to how much of a scholar Graham was. Lincoln always spoke with the highest respect for "my old teacher," who sat on the platform when his onetime pupil was inaugurated president.

The store failed as the town population dwindled. Lincoln gave too much credit to friends and was too much absorbed in his books. Berry was too much absorbed in his drinking. Lincoln did not disagree with Howell's written descriptions of Lincoln being absorbed in study for days on a knoll near New Salem. Berry died and left Lincoln with debts of about $500 that took him years to pay off, although he married and was raising a family while doing so. Graham also claimed to help Lincoln with Flint and Gibson's treatise of surveying, including the trigonometry and logarithms, preparing him to be a surveyor. Lincoln stayed with Graham about six months, according to Graham, who claims to have taught the young scholar trigonometry, geometry, and other surveying skills. Lincoln then got a job as deputy surveyor and surveyed many farms and towns in the area including Petersburg, which became the county seat. A stage route was established through the town in 1834, but Lincoln was too poor to afford the $1.50 fare to Springfield except on rare occasions. GRAHAM'S HOME is not marked. It was located about half a MILE SOUTH OF LAKE PETERSBURG AT A PRIVATE DRIVE ON THE EAST SIDE OF SOUTH SHORE ROAD AND SOUTH OF ILLINOIS 550. A large, lone tree is about one hundred feet west of the site. This is due west of the New Salem Village Park.

The town founder and keeper of another tavern was JAMES RUTLEDGE, the father of nineteen-year-old Ann. Lincoln slept in his attic, clerked in his store, and boarded for a while in 1832 or 1833, probably after returning from the Black Hawk War. In the Rutledge Tavern a "literary society" or debating club met, which Lincoln entertained with stories, original verses, and debates on local issues. Ann was to be married in the fall of 1832, but the family objected because of her age and because they wanted her to get an education. She had promised to be the wife of John McNeil, but he had left town about the time Lincoln came back from the Black Hawk War in the summer of 1832, saying that he was going to New York to bring his parents to Illinois. Lincoln knew John and did not interfere with that relationship while John was in town. But John did not write for three months, said he had been sick, and then did not communicate for another three months, saying his father was sick. As Ann came to inquire about letters at Abe's post office and expressed her anxiety, she and Lincoln probably grew closer.

Rutledge by this time had gone bankrupt and moved most of the family in late 1832 or 1833 to a farm they had previously occupied at Sand Ridge, about seven miles north of New Salem. Then Ann confided to her father that John had confessed before leaving that he had been there under an assumed name to get away from his family, who would want him to support them. His real name was McNamar. Now that he had accumulated property, he was ready to reveal himself to his parents and bring them to live with him. He seemed to have operated the only successful store in the town. When this became known, it created a sensation and controversy as to its truth. Samuel Hill had also been a suitor of Ann and got very upset. He broke up the partnership before McNeil left. Then a tragedy occurred, which might have brought Abe and Ann closer together. In January 1833 Lincoln's friend Rowen Herndon was preparing to go hunting. In taking his gun from the mantle, it discharged, killing his wife who was also a close friend of Lincoln's. Young Sarah Rutledge was there and ran to tell Abe and her sister, Ann, who was evidently managing the tavern or hotel after her parents moved. Lincoln was probably then boarding at the tavern.

More months passed, and Ann began to wonder if McNeil had ever really loved her. By then she had moved to her parents' farm at **SAND RIDGE (OR SANDRIDGE)**. Many believe that Lincoln fell deeply in love, courted, and then proposed to her before going to the legislature in Vandalia in late 1834. She may have been engaged to Lincoln to be married in the fall of 1835.

Lincoln's last law partner, William Herndon, began lecturing after Lincoln's death that Ann was Lincoln's only love, that his marriage to Mary was "hell," and that "he had no joy for twenty-three years." There has been speculation since then as to the relationship between Lincoln and Ann. Certainly two young people in a small community would have been drawn together. There are no details of the courtship. Lincoln scholar John Y. Simon believes Herndon speculated, surmised, and mishandled the story so that neither his nor Ann's reputation ever recovered (quoted in *Honor's Voice*).

When Lincoln visited her at **SAND RIDGE**, he generally stayed with "Uncle Jimmy" Short who lived nearby, west of the Rutledge property and about three miles south of Oakford on the Barker Hill and Bobtown Roads. When Lincoln's store went bankrupt and he had to sell his surveying instruments and other belongings at an auction, Short bought them and gave them back to Lincoln. Lincoln did not forget this, and gave him a federal job when he became president. Short is buried in **CONCORD CEMETERY**.

When Lincoln returned from the legislative session at Vandalia, he was still poor, and it was decided that Ann would live with her brother in Jacksonville and go to school there while Lincoln studied the law. Soon she was to finish school, and he would be admitted to the bar. In early August 1835, she became ill, probably from typhoid, and lingered until she died on August 25. It is said she cried for Lincoln during her last hours, and he alone was at her bedside when she died. Then he went through a terrible period, threatening to kill himself. He is quoted saying, "I can never be reconciled to have the snow and rains and storms beat upon her grave. My heart is buried there."

He walked many times to her grave at the **OLD CONCORD CEMETERY** (see entry on **PETERSBURG, ILLINOIS**, for location of the cemeteries and Sand Ridge). **BOWLING GREEN**, a sort of father figure, took him into his home a short distance north of New Salem, where he and his wife kept him busy. But Lincoln's melancholia remained and deepened throughout his life. Their home was located across the road north of the east end of the camping ground at New Salem. It is now a depression or gully on the **NORTH SIDE OF ILLINOIS 550 (SOUTH SHORE DRIVE), AT THE TOP OF THE HILL WEST OF ILLINOIS 97**. It is just northwest of a private park road to the maintenance area on the south side of the road and due north of the village park.

McNeil (McNamar) did return with his family shortly after Ann's death and started another store in the fall of 1836, maybe operated out of the Lincoln Berry Store. James Rutledge died shortly thereafter, and the family was greatly surprised that McNamar had obtained title to the land. Mrs. Rutledge was dispossessed. McNamar took up residence at the Sand Ridge home, married in 1838, and died there in 1879. He is also buried at the **CONCORD CEMETERY**.

The Ann Rutledge story did not appear in print until 1862, and was written by McNamar's partner's son, who was only three years old when Ann died. Herndon interviewed many later, but the story is based on hearsay and selected remembrances. Some argue that Lincoln's melancholia was brief, nonexistent, or caused by his debt problems.

No written words or other spoken words about her from Lincoln can be proven, although two questionable sources later in life quote him to have said that he loved her. One is the recently published purported secondhand reminiscences of Lincoln's housekeeper, Mariah Vance. Historians have questioned the accuracy of specific comments Mariah made many years later. It does not seem likely that Lincoln would have confided in her. Another witness, Isaac Cogdal, quotes Lincoln as president-elect in the Illinois statehouse admitting he "truly loved the girl and think often—often of her now." David Herbert Donald quotes this without question (*Lincoln*), although Don Fehrenbacher disputes the probability that the statement is accurate (*Lincoln in Text and Context*).

Robert and Mary Lincoln discounted these various stories related about Ann, as have other authors who believe that we will never know the truth of their relationship. Recent publishing of *Herndon's Informants*, showing long unavailable source material collected by William Herndon, indicates that these documents are far more important than previously believed. Coeditor Dr. Douglas Wilson pointed out that of the witnesses interviewed by Herndon, nearly all stated that Lincoln loved and courted Ann, grieved at her death, and had an understanding about marriage. These included close personal friends Mentor Graham and Bowling Green. Paul Angel deems the story "one of the great myths in American History." Jean Baker confirms that the relationship was probably more important than previously believed. Before Professor John Simon, only Albert Beveridge had access to the Herndon material. He did not challenge Herndon's conclusions. Seventeen interviewees confirmed that he grieved over her death. Clearly Herndon mingled evidence with speculation and embellishment, but the reality of the story still appears certain.

In 1833, after the Rutledges moved to Sand Ridge, a young woman from Kentucky, Mary Owens, visited her sister in New Salem. She and Lincoln were frequently seen together at the Bennett Abell's. (This site has not been located, but is possibly now in Lake Petersburg near Jack Armstrong's home, according to early maps.) She returned to Kentucky and two years later, after Ann died, her sister offered (maybe jokingly) to bring her back if Lincoln would marry her. He said he would be delighted, and Mary did return. Little about the romance survives, but the relationship continued until after Lincoln moved to Springfield. The two corresponded, and he evidently considered that he had a standing proposal of marriage. He may have proposed as a joke; at best it was halfhearted. He wrote to her that he would stand by the obligation, but she would be the loser. To his chagrin and surprise, Mary turned him down. One of Lincoln's friends, T. G. Onstot, wrote that she weighed the things she liked against what she did not like, and the latter overbalanced. She lived until 1877 and stated that "Mr. Lincoln was deficient in those little links which make up the chain of a woman's happiness." Lincoln is quoted as saying that he had come to the conclusion never to think of marrying for the reason that he could not be satisfied with anyone who would be blockhead enough to have him.

The village reverted back to nature until restored in the early twentieth century. Newspaperman William Randolph Hearst became interested in the site, bought it, and transferred it to Old Salem Chautauqua, which later transferred it to the state of Illinois. The only original building in the park is the **ONSTOT COOPER SHOP**, built in 1835. It was moved to Petersburg when the town withered, as were many of the other cabins, and moved back in 1922. The Lincoln-Berry store was the first reconstructed building, begun in 1932. The restoration now shows the village much as it was in the mid-1830s. Maps are available at the museum and visitor center.

The restoration at New Salem State Park includes twelve timber houses, ten shops, stores, industries, and a school where church services were held. These were furnished with period pieces and many articles used in New Salem. The restorations on the original sites include the first and second Berry-Lincoln stores, Denton Offutt and Samuel Hill's stores and Isaac Burner's house where Lincoln boarded and stayed several months, and the Rutledge Tavern where he worked, lived, and courted Ann for a time. Lincoln probably attended church or Sunday school at the Burners' cabin. All of these mentioned have direct and significant realationships to the future president. The old mill has been rebuilt at the original site, but the river changed course so that it is now several hundred yards from the Sangamon River.

The Mentor Graham Trail begins at the southwest end of the main parking lot and goes to the original site of the second Graham schoolhouse, also used for a church. The school was reconstructed in the 1930s and is now in the historical village rather than on the original site. The old New Salem graveyard is also here, although only six gravestones remain, all after 1844. One of Mentor Graham's children died in the deep snows of 1831 and is buried there in an unknown spot. (He had fifteen children; five died at birth.) Graham is buried with his wife just south of New Salem, on the east side of Route 97, just south of the Route 123 junction, at **FARMERS POINT CEMETERY**. It is five miles south of Petersburg. The grave is beyond the cemetery road, in the back, southeast section.

NORMAL: Lincoln often visited his friend, **JESSE FELL**, at **502 SOUTH FELL AVENUE**. Fell was a founder of the town and one of the three key men who helped to make Lincoln a candidate for president. He saw possibilities in Lincoln's background and kept after him until he got the material he needed for a promotional campaign to sell his candidate to the country at large. One of the notes Lincoln prepared for Fell reads: "There were some schools, so called, but no qualifications were ever required of a teacher beyond 'readin', 'writin', and 'cipherin' 'to the rule of three. . . . There was absolutely nothing to excite ambition for education. Of course, when I came of age I did not know much. Still, somehow, I could read, write, and cipher to the rule of three; but that was all. I have not been to school since. The little advance I now have upon this store of education I have picked up from time to time under the pressure of necessity." The house has been moved from its original site.

OAKFORD: A marker put up in 1935 notes that Lincoln met Ashly Hickey on October 30, 1836, and stayed at the **DEER LICK TAVERN** on the way to survey the town of Bath. This was a notorious place to congregate and swap yarns and stories. Settlers gathered in the evenings to hear guests tell stories and experiences. Lincoln was a favorite storyteller and stopped on many occasions, surveying and riding the circuit. Lincoln came back through and spent the night on the way to Havana to deliver his report.

The **McGINNIS-PURDY FERRY** was about three and a half miles northwest on the Sangamon River near the Cass-Menard County line. Lincoln is believed to have crossed at least fifty times between 1832 and 1858 at this connecting link to the Springfield–New Salem–Bath Trail. He liked to come in the fall to gather hickory nuts and pecans and eat persimmons. He carried a sack filled in equal proportions at both ends to sling over his horse. The town of Huron, about three miles northeast of the ferry, was surveyed by Lincoln. He spent some time there with the Armstrong family during the trial of Duff in Beardstown.

OHIO: On the way to the Freeport debate, Lincoln stayed at the tavern of Dad Joe Smith, just north of here.

OLNEY: A Democratic newspaper reported that Lincoln's speech on September 20, 1856, was to such a small crowd that Lincoln soon gave up. It was reported that he "tried his best to get up steam." About thirty were in the audience, but did not appear attentive. He said if twelve would sit and listen, he would continue. Twelve sat down, but after trying for a few minutes he quit and left in disgust.

OQUAWKA: Lincoln once took a nap at the home of **S.S. PHELPS** before making a speech in the afternoon.

OREGON: Lincoln spent two nights on the east side of the Rock River during the Black Hawk War, May 19 and June 29, 1832. He addressed a "monster meeting" on July 25, 1856, and made a speech on the fairgrounds on August 16, 1856, for John C. Frémont. This is depicted in a large mural on the side of a building at the northeast corner of Fourth and Washington, the site of the Sinnissippi Hotel. A boulder at **505 NORTH FOURTH STREET** marks the spot of the latter speech. He may have used the **ROCK RIVER HOTEL** for a conference, and another account says the speakers were entertained at **MOORE'S HOTEL**, later called the Black Hawk Hotel.

After meeting a number of citizens there on August 16, he went to the office of **HENRY A. MIX** at the corner of **THIRD AND WASHINGTON** and then to **MIX'S HOME** at the end of Washington. By now a large crowd had gathered at the public square and escorted the speakers to the grove where they were to speak before an estimated six to ten thousand. A platform had been built for the speakers, but just before they mounted it, it collapsed in a crash. The other speaker, Long John Wentworth, turned to Lincoln and said, "Abe, if you and I had been on the platform with our great load of sin, there would have been little wonder it went down." Wentworth, at least six feet six inches, was one of the few men around taller than the speaker from Springfield. A farmer brought up a large wagon, and the speakers climbed on and sat on the sideboards. No seats were provided for the audience. Wentworth then made the opening address to the audience. He was well known, and the drawing card. After he finished many started to leave, but the chairman called them back. They paused and watched as a speaker described as "in an ill-fitting dress and awkward manner provoked the mirth of the audience to such an extent that the laughter was audible, but when he had fairly begun the people standing moved forward and sat down to listen." It reminded some of an unbeliever "who came to church to scoff, but remained to pray." It is said that his speech far outshone the more popular orator, and kept the people spellbound for more than two hours. Lincoln had spent the night before and after in Polo. The **PATCHWORK INN**, on the **WEST SIDE OF THIRD STREET IN THE MIDDLE OF THE BLOCK NORTH OF ROUTE 64, WASHINGTON Street**, claims Lincoln also spent the night there.

Reporter Noah Brooks, who wrote accounts of Lincoln's time in Washington during the war, wrote that he met Lincoln here before the meeting. At this time Lincoln expressed disappointment as to Frémont's chances of being elected, but felt that every free state would vote Republican in 1860 unless the candidate was a radical or extremist. He felt that the candidate then should be a "national conservative," "unhackneyed by political tegiversations," and untrammeled by party obligations, "a man of the people."

OTTAWA: Lincoln's association with the town began when he was mustered out of the militia during the Black Hawk War at the location of the sundial at the **OTTAWA BOAT CLUB** for his first enlistment, and at **FORT JOHNSON** for the second. **FORT JOHNSON IS LOCATED ON HIGHWAYS 71 AND 23**. Lincoln's company was mustered out of U.S. service here on May 27, 1832, but Lincoln and seventy-one others were then mustered in by Lieutenant Robert Anderson as mounted volunteers. Lincoln had to supply his own arms and horse.

In June 1851 Lincoln lost to Stephen A. Douglas in a case before the Illinois Supreme Court meeting here. From December 3 to 6, 1852, he took testimony in the sheriff's office at the **COURTHOUSE** as a commissioner to determine compensation for damages resulting from the Illinois and Michigan Canal construction.

WASHINGTON PARK, COLUMBUS, AND LAFAYETTE STREETS has a boulder marking the site where the first senatorial debate with Douglas was held on August 21, 1858. The prize was the U.S. Senate seat, currently held by Douglas. Senators were then chosen by state legislatures, and it was unusual for candidates to be "nominated" and to campaign. No names appeared on any ballot for senator. The only election in which the people voted was for members of the legislature. A senatorial candidate had to hope for a majority of his party to be elected. At this time, Douglas was the most famous politician in America. In debating, Lincoln hoped to share the limelight and crowds that Douglas would attract. The REDDICK MANSION across the street was completed in 1858 in time for onlookers to view the debates.

The city had a population of about nine thousand at the time. At least twice that many flocked to the public square on that important day. The New York *Evening Post* reported that "by wagon, by rail, by canal people poured in, til Ottawa was one mass of active life. Men, women and children, old and young, the dwellers of the broad prairies, had turned their backs on the plough, and had come to listen to these champions of the two parties. Military companies were out; martial music sounded, and salutes of artillery thundered in the air. Eager marshals in partisan sashes rode furiously about the streets. Peddlers were crying their wares at the corners, and excited groups of politicians were canvassing and quarreling everywhere."

Lincoln was the guest of MAYOR GLOVER at his home on August 21 and 22, 1858, and ate in the MANSION HOUSE. Before he began speaking, he told Judge Dicky or Burton Cook, "Hold my coat while I stone Stephen." (Note the same statement in the Galesburg, Illinois, entry.) Lincoln was uncomfortable in the debate format, as he had to speak more extemporaneously to answer questions proposed by his opponent. Douglas had attacked with a ferocity that Lincoln characterized as showing that he was still a lion with a sharp teeth. Lincoln was somewhat defensive, and rushed through his remarks. He was best when he had time to carefully phrase and think through his statements. Most of his advisors thought he had not been sufficiently forceful or aggressive. He therefore planned extensively to be more in control at the next debate in Freeport.

Afterward he was enthusiastically and clumsily carried on the shoulders of supporters to the mayor's house. Both candidates' wives were there also. Mrs. Douglas introduced herself to Mary, and said that she had remembered meeting her at Dolley Madison's home in Washington in 1848.

It is possible he visited his friend, John Hossack, at his home at **210**

WEST PROSPECT. He worshiped on the site of the first Congregational Church (United Church of Christ), just across from Washington Park, and is claimed to have stayed many times while on the circuit at the T. LYLE DICKEY HOME AT 2011 CATON ROAD, now a private residence.

PALESTINE: There are many markers in this old community that claims to be the oldest town in the state, chartered in 1811. The Lincolns registered their land claim in March 1830 in this then-important town of five stores, two taverns, a steam sawmill, gristmill, thirty families, and one of the six land offices in the state. That office site is identified with a marker on the grounds of the grade school at the northeast corner of MAIN AND MARKET STREET. The Lincolns were impressed with the town and its "holy name," and the traveling juggler who happened to be passing through also on the same day. Other markers identify the sites of the JESSIE K. DUBOIS TAVERN AT 309 LINCOLN STREET, on the west side between LaMotte and Harrison Streets, where the Lincolns stopped. Abraham began a friendship with the family, and Jessie Dubois was later a neighbor and political supporter in Springfield.

PAPPSVILLE: This "town" was the site of Lincoln's first political speech in Sangamon County. It was here in July 1832 that he stated, "My politics are short and sweet, like the old woman's dance." The town, no longer in existence, was actually one cabin in an open field. The location is west of Springfield, about a MILE NORTH OF ROUTE 125 AND SOUTH OF RICHLAND CREEK ABOUT MIDWAY BETWEEN THE CREEK AND THE HIGHWAY. It is about two and a half miles east of Pleasant Plains and ten and a half miles from the Capitol Building. It is between County Roads 11W and 10.25W and just north of 4.5N. While here he had to jump in and stop a fight in which his friend, J. Rowan Herndon, was involved. He also spoke at Hill's Mill nearby on Sugar Creek.

PARADISE: The Lincoln family spent the night of March 11, 1830, with the Sawyers and Radleys, who were relatives of Mrs. Lincoln. This was on their migration from Indiana to Decatur (see entries on CHARLESTON, ILLINOIS, AND MATTOON, ILLINOIS).

PARIS: Lincoln practiced in the EDGAR CIRCUIT COURTHOUSE at Court, Main, and Central. A Lincoln marker is on the west side of the lawn. Lincoln stayed in various homes including the GENERAL MILTON ALEXANDER HOME, still at 132 SOUTH CENTRAL AND WASHINGTON. He had known General Alexander during the Black Hawk War. At this house he spoke for presidential candidate John C. Frémont, on August 6, 1856, and for himself for the U.S. Senate on September 17, 1858. (The marker says "September 7.") He stayed many times at the home of "Uncle" **LEANDER MUNSELL**, who was a pioneer citizen and merchant. He also stayed at the **GREEN TREE INN ON EAST COURT STREET**, on the southeast corner of the square.

William Simmons related that when he was nine years old he was playing marbles on the courthouse lawn. Lincoln wanted to join in and did so. Will said that Lincoln looked funny on his knees in the midst of a bunch of boys, and "whenever Lincoln made a good shot he chuckled." Lincoln's cousin, Dennis Hanks, lived here with his daughter. At age ninety Dennis died, a month after being injured by a horse. South of Paris was the **WHITE HORSE INN** where Lincoln stayed.

PEKIN: Lincoln acquired supplies on the way home from the Black Hawk War and made an oar for his canoe. Pekin became the county seat of Tazewell County in 1850 and was one of the many court locations in which Lincoln practiced. A fellow lawyer described how Lincoln once evicted a bat in the **COURTHOUSE**. Various ways to get rid of the bat were tried, including a cattle whip. Lincoln finally got it out using his height with a broom. He was described as a highly comical figure in his bobtail sack coat and jeans sixteen inches from his feet.

Lincoln attended the Whig convention on May 1, 1843, which met to pick a nominee to succeed John Stuart in Congress. This began a precedent of nominating congressional candidates, which Lincoln had supported. The convention nominated John Hardin and informally stipulated that the rotation of office for the next two terms would be filled by Edward D. Baker and Lincoln. In 1854 he defended several vigilantes who raided a place where a large quantity of liquor was destroyed. Lincoln argued that the act was against a disorderly house where "drunkenness, idleness, quarreling, profane swearing, obscenity," and other offences were permitted, and therefore his clients were acting in the public interests. **JOHN ALBERT JONES'S** heirs preserve a table used in his office by Lincoln here and in Tremont. Lincoln also visited Jones's home. A former Springfield neighbor, **G. S. BAILEY**, was pastor of the First Baptist Church. Lincoln looked him up on a visit, pledged $10, and brought the money to his home, situated near Seventh Street.

PEORIA: Lincoln had many cases even though Peoria was not on the Eighth Circuit where he generally practiced. Seventeen visits between 1832 and 1858, are outlined as follows:

(1) His army company broke up here July 15–16, 1832, after coming back from Wisconsin. Lincoln's horse had been stolen in Wisconsin, and he walked most of the way. He purchased a canoe here with a companion in the same predicament, and went by river toward New Salem.

(2) On February 10, 1840, he spoke for William Henry Harrison at the COURTHOUSE. He crossed the ferry at the foot of Franklin Street and ate at FULTON HOUSE AT FULTON AND ADAMS.

(3) On April 6, 1844, he spoke at the COURTHOUSE for two hours for Henry Clay to a half-filled room due to heavy rain. The Democrats soon issued a broadside stating that John Calhoun was sorry he was not present to reply then to Lincoln's speech, but he did answer on April 13.

(4) On April 13, 1844, Lincoln showed up at the courthouse and Calhoun spoke until 11:30 in the evening, which did not stop a call by the Whigs for an answer from Lincoln. The Democrats had issued a broadside inviting the Whigs to respond. Lincoln had been called to come from Hanover since the Whigs did not have anyone of his capacity to speak. At first Calhoun continued to dominate the meeting, but he was shouted down by those who wanted Lincoln to speak. Lincoln first declined, protesting that it was too near Sunday and his old friend and neighbor, Calhoun, evidently did not want him to speak. The excited crowd insisted, and he proceeded to "skin, draw and quarter . . . in good nature, the opposition."

(5–7) Lincoln is listed here "probably" on May 27, June 17, and June 19, 1844.

(8) October 15–16, 1844: Sometime in 1844 there was a heated debate at the MAIN STREET PRESBYTERIAN CHURCH. This was about a block and a half north of the courthouse on the east side of Main, just north of the alley between Jefferson and Madison. Dates have not been determined, but probably it was three days beginning about this date:

(9) July 10, 1847, Lincoln passed through returning from a Chicago convention where he took a steamer.

(10) On October 9, 1848, Lincoln gave a speech on Zachary Taylor at PEORIA HOUSE, EAST SIDE OF ADAMS AT HAMILTON.

(11) On September 17, 1852, Lincoln spoke for Winfield Scott at the COURTHOUSE.

(12) On October 16, 1854, it is said, the race for the presidency started at the COURTHOUSE SQUARE, AT MAIN AND ADAMS. A tablet on the south portico commemorates the site of one of Lincoln's great speeches in which he reportedly denounced slavery for the first time. Historian Albert J. Beveridge considered this to be his first great speech. It is sometimes referred to as a joint discussion between Lincoln and Douglas at a Democratic meeting. Douglas spoke from the steps of the COURTHOUSE, facing Adams Street. He did not have to let Lincoln reply, but did not object when Lincoln told the crowd to go home and eat, then return for his remarks that turned out to be about three hours. This was a longer version of the speech he had made twelve days earlier in Springfield, also in answer to Douglas where both had spoken at the State House. In fact, this was Lincoln's longest political speech, over seventeen hundred words. Douglas responded briefly. A debate was proposed, but a "truce" was called, lasting two years, although both continued to speak. Douglas told Lincoln, "You have made more trouble on this Territorial Question . . . than all the members of the U.S. Senate."

This event was been termed by historian Michael Burlingame as the "emerging like a butterfly from a caterpillar's chrysalis." Lincoln had been on the political sidelines for five years, and now returned to the arena "as a political analyst and debater of surpassing power speaking with a new seriousness, a new explicitness, a new authority, and thus grew into a statesman" (Benjamin Thomas). As Professor Burlingame outlines in his work *The Inner World of Abraham Lincoln,* Lincoln previously had sometimes cruelly belittled and satirized his political opponents. But after reentering public life his words and actions possessed a "psychic radiance" and power leading him to the top leadership position in his party and the country. From this point until 1860 he delivered 175 speeches on the one issue of slavery.

(13) On September 28, 1865, Lincoln passed through to attend a meeting in Lacon.

(14) On October 9, 1856, a Republican rally was held where Lincoln and Trumbull spoke. Trumbull had defeated Lincoln for the U.S. Senate in 1854. It was said that "Mr. Trumbull's speech contrasted very unfavorably with that of Lincoln, and made some of the Republicans regret the bargain, which sent Trumbull to the senate instead of Lincoln."

(15) On March 27, 1857, Lincoln was at the PEORIA HOUSE, AT THE NORTHEAST CORNER OF THE COURTHOUSE SQUARE, HAMILTON AND ADAMS, where he and Douglas are said to have made regular stops.

(16) On August 19, 1858, Lincoln spoke to the Republican Convention in front of the COURTHOUSE. Douglas had spoken there the day before.

(17) On October 5, 1858, Lincoln stayed at the **Clinton House at Fulton and Adams**.

Lincoln is claimed to have stayed "many nights" with **Moses Pellengill at Liberty and Jefferson**, and told stories at the **Market House on Washington between Main and Hamilton**.

PERU: This was a landing on the Illinois River where Lincoln caught boats to Peoria.

PETERSBURG: Founded by Peter Lukins and George Warbuton in 1832, the two men played cards to determine the town's name. The town soon failed and the rights were sold to new owners who hired Lincoln to complete a new survey. His plat was filed in 1836. A plaque set in the pavement at the **southeast corner of Jackson and Seventh Streets, on the southwest corner of the square**, marks the spot where he began the survey. Tradition says that he preserved the house of a widow of a Black Hawk War soldier by running the street crooked. On February 17, 1836, Lincoln certified that the town of "Petersburgh" had been surveyed according to law. He is believed to have spent most of March 1836 finishing the survey and planning the town. In fact, surveying jobs took him all over the area. After Lincoln had platted the town, he surveyed **Bennet's Addition**, running along **Cherry Street between Fourth and Seventh**. He appeared during the 1836 political campaign for the Legislature and no doubt in other years. About four blocks northwest of the courthouse at **313 North Ninth** is the **Bennett House** where Lincoln made a speech on part of the foundation as the house was being built. Lincoln shopped at his friend **John Bennett's store** and stayed with him frequently while in Petersburg. Beginning in 1858, Bennett lived at **Ninth and Taylor**. New Salem friend Mentor Graham lived at 923 North Fifth Street. The original house is now occupied by government offices.

Petersburg became the seat of Menard County and was on the Eighth Judicial Circuit from 1839 until 1847. Lincoln came to the sessions at the **courthouse** during these years and frequently made speeches and appeared for various political candidates. Some of his antislavery speeches drew boos during the 1850s. The Whig convention that nominated Lincoln for Congress met here on May 1, 1846.

In 1846, Lincoln spoke to the local clergy and asked this hypothetical question about Dr. Ross, who owned a slave named Sambo: "Is it the will of God that Sambo shall remain a slave, or be set free? The

Almighty gives no audible answer. . . . So Dr. Ross must decide the question. And while he considers it, he sits in the shade and subsists on the bread that Sambo is earning in the burning sun. If he decides that God wills Sambo to be freed, he thereby has to walk out of the shade and delve for his bread. Will Dr. Ross be actuated by perfect impartiality?"

One of the mysteries of Lincoln's life is his relationship with Ann Rutledge whom he had known in New Salem. After Lincoln's death, when Lincoln's law partner William Herndon gave lectures and wrote of Lincoln, he insisted that Ann was Lincoln's lost love (see entry on New Salem, Illinois). The grave of Ann is located in the OAKWOOD CEMETERY in the southwest section of town, south of Washington and Oakland. The "body" was moved from here in May 1890, maybe partly to help sales in a new cemetery and partly to provide for perpetual care of her memory and plot. According to Dale Carnegie in his biography *Lincoln the Unknown,* the only trace of her body found was four pearl buttons scooped up with some dirt and inserted in the new cemetery in town. It is generally believed that more of the body was found, as shown in an affidavit by a man who was nine years old when he witnessed the transfer; he states that several bones where found. But the major part of her dust may still be in Old Concord, as believed by some locally. Lincoln's New Salem friends Hannah Armstrong and Bowling Green are also buried here. Ann's headstone bears the lines written by Edgar Lee Master, who is buried just to the north of Ann:

> *Out of me unworthy and unknown*
> *The vibrations of deathless music:*
> *'With malice toward none, with*
> *charity for all . . . '*

Ann's first burial site in the OLD CONCORD CEMETERY is about four miles away. This was the cemetery where Lincoln went to grieve over her grave, then located along the mail road from Springfield to Havana. No trace of the road exists now. A marker there notes that "Abraham Lincoln made many pilgrimages alone to this sacred spot. He often said, 'My heart is buried there with Ann Rutledge.'" Other markers note, "Where Lincoln wept," and quotes Lincoln, "I can not bear to think of her out there alone."

The cemetery can be reached by driving north on Route 97, three miles northwest of the courthouse, to a narrow country road with a street sign, "Lincoln Trail Road." This turnoff is just north of the Worthington Road, running east and west, the only road crossing the highway between Petersburg and Atterbury. Go north on Lincoln Trail about a half mile to a narrow private road to the west. The entrance path to the Old Concord is just north off the Lincoln Trail, toward the east. Since the Lincoln Trail Road is just over one lane wide, there is no place to park except at this little intersection, or you might pull off on the grass at the cemetery "entrance lane," unmarked at the road. The cemetery is reached by going down a path between two cornfields. If the field is cut you might drive to the cemetery about a half mile to the east, but it is an easy walk to the high flagpole and fenced cemetery plot surrounded by fields of corn. Ann was buried with her family in a plot well marked and maintained at the end of the twentieth century, although it was neglected for many years. Lincoln's friend Jack Armstrong is buried near the northwest corner.

Continuing north on the Lincoln Trail for another half mile is the **CONCORD CEMETERY ROAD**, and this graveyard is about a half mile to the east. John McNamar, Ann Rutledge's fiancé, and other former New Salem area residents are here, including various Berrys, Shorts, Clarys, Rutledges, and other familiar New Salem names.

ANN'S HOME was to the northwest and can be reached by following the Lincoln Trail Road (still a narrow dirt road) north from the Concord Cemetery Road junction. Go for about a mile, past the Atterbury Road and several sharp turns, and just north of Concord Creek. At another sharp turn from the west to the north in a front lawn is a sign announcing, "On this very spot stood the log cabin in which Ann Rutledge died, Aug. 25, 1835. On the hillside to the west stood a large oak tree under which Abraham Lincoln wept bitterly after leaving the sick room of Ann Rutledge, where their last communication was held." This is about a half mile south of White Crossing Road on Lincoln Trail Road.

The **COURTHOUSE** on the square at Jackson and Sixth Streets and Routes 97 and 123 is on the site of an earlier building where Lincoln practiced law and made speeches, although it was at the northeast part of the square. After a speech on October 29, 1858, he traveled back to Springfield with reporter Henry Villard. On the way they took refuge from the rain in a boxcar. Lincoln reflected that in his youth his highest political ambition was to be elected to the legislature. Now his wife was insisting that he would be a senator and president. "Just think of such a sucker as me as President!"

The present courthouse has Lincoln papers on display including a will drafted for a friend before he was admitted to the bar and various other legal papers. He often stopped at the **MENARD HOUSE, AT THE NORTHEAST CORNER OF SIXTH AND JACKSON.**

PITTSFIELD: Lincoln was involved in many cases over the years, and a number of original houses from that era still exist. In fact the town claims more homes still in existence with documented Lincoln visits than any other. Lincoln and Trumbull both spoke in "decidedly the largest gathering of people that ever occurred here" on October 27, 1856. CENTRAL PARK (COURTHOUSE) has a boulder marking the site of the Lincoln speech of October 1, 1858. After the two-hour speech a friend asked for a picture, and Lincoln posed for the itinerant ambrotyper, Calvin Jackson. John Milton Hay, Lincoln's secretary and later an ambassador to Great Britain and secretary of state under Presidents McKinley and Theodore Roosevelt, spent two years here as a student in the early 1850s where he met John G. Nicolay, who also lived in Pittsfield. Lincoln met Nicolay here. They were Lincoln's secretaries during his presidency and later wrote a massive ten-volume biography.

The COURTHOUSE AT WASHINGTON, MADISON, MONROE, AND ADAMS STREETS (Washington Street is Route 106) have at least thirteen cases of Lincoln's documented. (*Off the Beaten Path* claims that there is no record that Lincoln "ever served" in Pike County, but that five hundred documents have been found in the courthouse related to his cases.) At one trial, Lincoln asked a witness how much he was getting paid to testify. The audience gasped when this was disclosed. Lincoln won the case with a short jury summation: "Gentlemen of the jury, big fee . . . big swear." A marker on the southwest side commemorates the many appearances of Lincoln and Douglas, including the senatorial campaign on October 1, 1858.

Lincoln met John Nicolay on the east side of the square. He had asked for a recommendation for a good printer, and John Shastid introduced him to the young apprentice at the newspaper office. Nicolay was in Springfield later when asked by Lincoln to be his secretary in Washington. He suggested that Lincoln also hire his friend John Hay. The president-elect at first said he couldn't take everyone in Illinois, but did take the other John, whose name is forever linked with both Lincoln and Nicolay.

REVEREND ZACHARIAH N. GARBUTT lived at **500 EAST WASHINGTON**, and owned the *Whig Free Press* in Pittsfield. A popular story in the town and written local history tells that when Nicolay was a boy, Reverend Z. N. Garbutt observed his stepmother rather "too vigorously punishing him." He found out that the she did not care for him. So Reverend Garbutt, who had no children, offered to take the boy. Nicolay then grew up with Rev. Garbutt and his wife in this home. A marker is in front. John's daughter (*Lincoln's Secretary, A Biography of John G. Nico-*

lay by Helen Nicolay Longman) says that he never had a stepmother so that part of the story is not true, but Pittsfield still believes it. He worked at the age of fifteen in the newspaper office, which he owned at age twenty-two, in 1854, about the time Garbutt died. ("East" Washington is correct, not "West" as per *Off the Beaten Path*.)

MRS. GARBUTT later moved to the NORTHWEST CORNER OF JEFFERSON AND MONROE. She considered her foster son and John Hay as "her boys" and followed their careers from this home.

The old hotel at the NORTHEAST CORNER OF JEFFERSON AND MONROE was operated by the Watson family in Lincoln's time and may have seen Lincoln several times.

Thomas Worthington's home site was at 626 WEST WASHINGTON and hosted Lincoln, Hay, and Nicolay.

The Hodgens migrated from Hodgenville, Kentucky, and entertained Lincoln in 1840. This was on the south side of the street, west of the library, and at about 219 West Adams.

Lincoln ate many times at the home of JOHN GREEN SHASTID, 326 EAST JEFFERSON. One time Shastid told him, when he ate so many quail, that he was nothing but a hog, which made his son break out laughing.

One mile east of the courthouse, on the south side of Washington Street at Washington Court, is the pretentious home of COLONEL WILLIAM ROSS. Lincoln stopped for the night of September 30, 1858, and spoke the next day at the public square for two hours.

Lincoln was a dinner guest on at least one occasion in REUBEN SCAN-LAND'S home, built about 1850. This is located at the NORTHWEST COR-NER OF WEST AND WASHINGTON. A procession took place from here, taking Lincoln to the courthouse with one hundred girls dressed in white.

The William Watson home, at the NORTHEAST CORNER OF WEST AND WASHINGTON, was built in the late 1830s and is one of the oldest, if not the oldest, house in town. The bedrooms upstairs still have the original wooden floors. Lincoln had cases for several days in September 1839, and possibly stayed with MILTON HAY, an attorney who bought the house soon after completion. He had been a clerk in the Stuart and Lincoln law office. Hay's nephew, John Hay, moved there at age twelve from Warsaw, Illinois, and lived there while attending Thomson Academy. At this time John formed a lasting friendship with Nicolay. Milton and John moved to Springfield in 1855, where Milton became a partner with Stephen Logan, who had been Lincoln's partner. John left with Lincoln for Washington in 1861 and kept a diary in Washington as Lincoln's secretary. He and Nicolay lived in the White House and had easy access to the president, who is said to have treated Hay like a son. Professor Michael Burlingame compares the relationship to the earlier wartime father-and-son surrogates, George Washington and Alexander Hamilton.

The home was later the boyhood home of **OLIVER BARRETT**, one of the greatest collectors of Lincolniana. When he was in grade school, he was punished by having to sit next to the only Negro in the class. When he tried to get sympathy from his mother, she explained about Lincoln and the freedom for the slaves, and soon took him to Lincoln's home and tomb. This started the lifelong interest, leading to one of the largest Lincoln collections.

The home of **WILLIAM A. GRIMSHAW** is northwest of the business section at the **NORTHEAST CORNER OF CLINTON AND PERRY**. He was a friend of Lincoln and tried many cases with him. The home dates to 1842. It is believed that Lincoln may have stayed, or surely visited his friend.

PLEASANT PLAINS: **CLAYVILLE TAVERN**, on Highway 125, twelve miles west of Springfield, was a frequent stop for Lincoln and local rallying point for his political supporters. This is open to the public. Lincoln's longtime advisory, Peter Cartwright, is buried in the cemetery under a large, prominent oval stone.

POLO: Lincoln spent two nights just west during the Black Hawk War, June 8 and 12, 1832. On August 15, 1856, he was guest of **SENATOR ZENAS APLINGTON AT LOCUST AND FRANKLIN STREETS**. He traveled to Oregon the next day, and returned to spend that night and part of the seventeenth in Polo. He ate breakfast at the **SANFORD HOUSE ON MASON STREET**.

PONTIAC: Lincoln practiced law here, but most of the records were lost. On January 27, 1860, he stayed with Jason W. Strevell in a house still standing at **401 WEST LIVINGSTON**. Strevell asked Lincoln to stand in his stocking feet next to a door casing where his height was marked, six feet four inches. When son Charles moved to Utah many years later, he took this as a Lincoln memento. During this visit he addressed the Young Men's Literary Association at the Presbyterian Church.

PORTLAND: Lincoln stayed a week in March 1832 before a trip down the Sangamon River as assistant to a boat pilot.

POSTVILLE: See Camden, Illinois, and Lincoln, Illinois, entries.

PRINCETON: Lincoln visited his friends here at the following locations:
Cyrus Bryant, 1110 Main.
John Bryant, 1518 South Main. This was reportedly on the underground railway.
Owen Lovejoy, east side of town. Lovejoy was an abolitionist minister and brother of Elijah, the Alton editor killed by a proslavery mob. Lincoln made a speech to about ten thousand on July 4, 1856, in Bryant's Woods.

QUINCY: Lincoln stayed at the **Quincy House, at the southeast corner Fourth and Maine**, on November 1, 1854, and spoke at **Kendall's Hall on the southwest corner of Maine and Sixth Streets.** Although the address was for his friend Archibald Williams who was running for Congress, Lincoln spoke on the Nebraska Bill. The *Quincy Daily Whig* reported that this "was one of the clearest, most logical, argumentative and convincing discourse on the Nebraska question" they had heard.

The sixth debate with Douglas was held on October 13, 1858, at **Washington Park**, then courthouse square, on the **east side of Fifth Street between Hampshire and Maine (sometimes spelled "Main").** As was customary, Douglas arrived in his lavish railroad car and was paraded with a torchlight parade to the **Quincy House.** Lincoln arrived in a regular car after keeping the occupants of the train entertained with "all sorts of quaint stories." Journalist David R. Locke (Petroleum v. Nashby) first saw Lincoln at the Quincy House on this date. He obtained an interview and wrote that Lincoln sat with his boots, tie, collar, and coat off, and one suspender dropped. Locke said he never saw a more thoughtful, yet dignified and sad face. Lincoln felt that he could beat Douglas in the popular vote, but that Douglas would be elected to the U.S. Senate by the legislature because of "the skillful manner in which the state had been districted in Douglas' favor." Lincoln commented, "You can't overturn a pyramid, but you can undermine it."

The day was sunny and pleasant, but the crowds had to brave hazardous roads soaked with heavy rains. By midday between ten and fifteen thousand, including many taking steamers from Hannibal, Missouri, and Keokuk, Iowa, had gathered "with no end of cheering and shouting and jostling." A railing on the platform erected in front of the **courthouse** gave way just before the proceedings started, sending a dozen dignitaries and a large bench crashing to the ground. Then a bench set up for the benefit of many ladies gave way under the weight and collapsed. When order was restored, Lincoln opened in a shrill voice that "seemed to be heard to the remotest edge of the crowd." He asserted that the Negro was entitled to the rights of the Declaration of Independence, but that the Democrats were conspiring to make slavery national and permanent. Douglas charged that Lincoln changed his views to suit his audience, and refused to debate the right or wrong of slavery.

The *Quincy Daily Whig* reported that "when Douglas concluded, 'Old Abe' mounted the stand and was received with three such tremendous cheers as make the welkin ring. His happy, good-humored countenance—in such contrast with that of Douglas, which is black and repulsive enough to turn all the milk in Egypt sour—at once, cheered and animated the immense crowd." Lincoln divested the slave question of political issues and vigorously observed: "I suggest that the difference of opinion, reduced to its lowest terms, is no other than the difference between the men who think slavery a wrong and those who do not think it wrong." The courthouse is no longer in the Park.

Lincoln stayed at the home of **O. H. BROWNING** on October 13, 1858, on the **SOUTHEAST CORNER OF SEVENTH AND HAMPSHIRE STREETS**, and then left for the debate in Alton. Browning was a frequent guest in the Lincoln home. During this period of few and poor hotels, friends and associates stayed with one another as much as possible. Mrs. Lincoln would have preferred him as her husband's law partner instead of Herndon. After Stephen Douglas died early in the Civil War, Browning was appointed to the Senate to fill his place. He ran again in 1862, but was defeated. He wanted to be appointed to the Supreme Court, but Lincoln felt this would bring criticism. Browning and his wife remained close friends with the Lincolns in Washington. Lincoln asked Browning to review a draft of his First Inaugural Address. He is credited, along with William H. Seward, of making the most vital changes. At their suggestion Lincoln softened his pledge to "hold, occupy, and possess" property from his original "reclaim." He was later secretary of the interior under President Andrew Johnson (see also the entry on Browning in the **WASHINGTON, D.C.**, chapter). The home was destroyed by fire in 1904.

It is believed that Lincoln had been shaved at the **HELLMER BROTHERS' BARBERSHOP, 140 HAMPSHIRE STREET**, before the debate. It is also claimed that he stopped at a saloon on Hampshire between Fifth and Sixth for some refreshment after the debate. During the reception at Browning's home, Lincoln came to the **FARMER'S HOTEL** at the **SOUTHEAST CORNER OF NINTH AND HAMPSHIRE** where he rented a room and rested for an hour. Office seekers and well-wishers had besieged the candidate throughout the trip, and he asked to retire for a short period. He stayed on the second floor at the northwest corner.

THE QUINCY HISTORICAL SOCIETY, AT 425 SOUTH TWELFTH STREET, has items of George Atzerodt and Lewis Paine who were involved with

Booth in the plot to assassinate Lincoln. This was the home of Governor John Wood, a friend of Lincoln and one of the organizers of the Republican Party.

RICHMOND: Lincoln attended a political meeting on April 5, 1834, in this community, located nine miles southwest of New Salem.

ROCHESTER: Lincoln traveled to this small town, five miles east of Springfield, on June 17, 1842, as part of a committee to welcome Ex-President Martin Van Buren. His well-known humor entertained everyone that night in the **DOTY HOUSE**, and Van Buren said his sides were sore from laughter. The tour continued to Springfield the next day for a reception at the American House. The Doty House was located about TWO BLOCKS EAST OF THE CURRENT CITY HALL, just before a dip in the road, near the funeral parlor at 200 East Main. Lincoln spoke later at the top of the hill opposite this site. He also probably spoke here on March 9, 1844, and at least one other time. This was the road from Springfield to Decatur that Lincoln traveled many times, south of the Sangamon River, through Bolivia and Mount Auburn. Along this road, now Routes 556, 2, and 28, Lincoln surveyed several farms and stopped at several taverns (Hinkle, Nickols) and farms (William Furrow, Warnick) (see **DECATUR ILLINOIS**).

The **SOUTH FORK SCHOOL** site is now a church about three and a half miles south, and a little east of Rochester, as the crow flies. The site is marked noting that Lincoln gave a temperance lecture there in 1846. It is south of Illinois 29, on county Routes 7S and 7.5, just west of the 8E intersection.

ROCKFORD: Lincoln visited on July 7, 1855, to study a reaper in preparation for defense in the case of *McCormick v. Manny & Co.* It is claimed that Lincoln spent the night in Manny's home. The suit was tried in Cincinnati, but Lincoln was dismissed from the case due to the objections of his co-counsel, Edwin Stanton, later secretary of war. A settee upon which Lincoln is said to have sat in Manny's home is at the Robert H. Tinker House, 411 Kent Street. The Manny plant was near the railroad bridge.

ROCK ISLAND: This was the site of the first bridge across the Mississippi, extending from Illinois to Iowa with a portion of railroad tract over the island in the river. A steamship, the *Effie Afton*, hit the bridge piers and sank, resulting in a famous suit (see the entry on the U.S. Circuit Court in Chicago). Lincoln visited on September 1, 1857, to study the rebuilt bridge and currents in preparation for the trial between the boat and bridge owners. The bridge engineer, Benjamin Brayton Sr., accompanied him and explained various technical details. Lincoln did not seem satisfied with some of the answers by the bridge master, engineer, and others. Brayton's fifteen-year-old son was there also, and wrote that Lincoln asked him to sit on the bridge with him to answer some questions. Both sat on the bridge with their legs hanging over while Lincoln questioned the youth at length on some of the same questions asked to his father. His answers were apparently to Lincoln's satisfaction. He later spoke at the COURTHOUSE in 1858 and visited nearby Davenport.

ROSSVILLE: Lincoln lodged at the **GEORGE WILLIAM BICKNELL HOME** when it was two miles north, although it has now been moved into Rossville on Route 1.

RUSSELVILLE: This tiny town on the Wabash River was the first town entered in Illinois by Lincoln and his family in their migration in March 1830. Residents maintain that it was here, rather than Vincennes, that Lincoln crossed the river.

RUSHVILLE: During the Black Hawk War, Lincoln and his troops camped nearby. While waiting to move on, a wrestling match was arranged between Lincoln and Dow Thomson, who threw Lincoln twice. (This might have occurred elsewhere or was repeated at other locations.) When his friends claimed a foul, Lincoln declared that both falls were fair and that Thompson "was as strong as a grizzly bear."

Later Lincoln returned many times to practice law in the COURT-HOUSE. On October 20, 1858, Lincoln was entertained at the home of **WILLIAM H. RAY** and spoke at the courthouse. A tablet in the center of town commemorates this event. Democrats welcomed Lincoln by flying a black flag from the top of the courthouse. A gang of boys climbed on the roof and tried to drown him out, yelling for Douglas. Then some ladies in windows of the courthouse began to make loud, offensive remarks until Lincoln had to stop his speech and ask them to quit. When Douglas spoke here for the same senate campaign, his friends wanted to give him a welcome that would be memorable. They borrowed a canon from Beardstown, hauled it to the public square, and loaded it with a heavy charge of powder and wet scraps of leather. When the salute to Douglas was fired, the canon blew into a hundred pieces, but miraculously no one was hurt.

SALISBURY: Lincoln attended a political rally on July 14, 1836, as noted by a marker on the town square. This is on the road between New Salem and Springfield and was the approximate location where Lincoln loaned his fresh horse to Dr. Chandler so that he could beat his rival to Springfield and register his land (see entry on **CHANDLERVILLE, ILLINOIS**).

SALEM: Lincoln made frequent visits from 1840 to 1855, and gave a poorly received speech in 1840 for William Henry Harrison. Original houses in which he stayed are located at **304 WEST SCHWARTZ** and **321 SOUTH FRANKLIN**. He stayed on the way to Washington in June 1849 and at the **SALEM HOUSE** on September 22, 1856.

SANGAMO TOWN: In March and April 1831, after Denton Offutt failed to obtain a flatboat at Beardstown, Lincoln, John Hanks, and John D. Johnston built one here in order to sail produce to New Orleans. This was directly north of where the marker notes that Lindbergh Field was later located. It is seven miles northwest of Springfield on the west side of the river, north of Hazlett Road and west of Winch Road. The logs were cut at Kirkpatrick's mill on Prairie Creek, one and a half miles southwest. While here, Lincoln petitioned the county commissioner's court to fill the office of constable. He became a favorite storyteller with the locals.

SHAWNEETOWN: Lincoln and John A. McClernard debated on September 5, 1840, after a big parade with twenty-six young ladies (one for each state) posed on a canoe. The speeches were near the **RAWLINGS HOTEL** that had welcomed General Lafayette in 1824 or 1825. Lincoln then went to Morganfield, Kentucky, at the request of a delegation from there. Two days later, Lincoln was back to debate another candidate, Josiah Lamborn. He visited the home of **JOHN MARSHALL** when in town for a law case.

SHELBYVILLE: Lincoln practiced law in the **SHELBY CIRCUIT COURTHOUSE** and stayed at **TALLMAN TAVERN**, on the **EAST SIDE OF THE SQUARE, AT THE NORTHEAST CORNER WITH ROUTE 16**. One day in the 1850s he tore his trousers getting out of a cart. He had them repaired at a tailor shop, but they could not be fixed in time for court. He had to borrow another pair from the tailor, said to look like knee pants. He made a speech on June 27, 1840, for Harrison. Most of the people appear to have come to hear General W. L. D. Ewing and left when he finished, before Lincoln spoke. The courthouse has several historic paintings including Robert Root's depiction of the Lincoln-Thornton debate, claimed to have launched Lincoln's national political career. This is in the upstairs courtroom.

The June 15, 1856, appearance with Anthony Thornton occurred when Lincoln was asked to repeat his Lost Speech made in Blooming- ton about three weeks before. At the time he was in Shelbyville run- ning as a presidential elector for Frémont. He spoke for three hours after which Thornton made some derogatory comments about him dominating the meeting, and then spoke only a short time. He said later, "Lincoln cut him down like a file cuts soft soap." One spectator said, "That was no debate! Abe Lincoln made a speech." The speech or debate was not well known until the 1903 painting.

SPRINGFIELD: Lincoln came to Springfield for the first time in March 1831, to find Denton Offutt at Elliott's Tavern, for whom he was to take a flatboat to New Orleans. Springfield had a population then of less than one thousand. A few months later he acted as assistant pilot for the steamer *Talesman*, attempting to prove that the Sangamon River was navigable, and landed near here at Portland, halfway between the present Alton and Illinois Central bridges, west of town. Then he attended a ball at the courthouse on March 26, 1832. He also served on juries, which rekindled his fascination with the law begun earlier in Indiana. Later the same year he made a political speech in the same building on the public square, later the site of the Old State House.

Lincoln moved to Springfield at the age of twenty-eight on April 15, 1837, to share a room with Joshua Speed and form a law partnership with John Todd Stuart, one of Mary Todd's many cousins. He would die twenty-eight years later to the day. By now he had been elected to the General Assembly of Illinois or state legislature twice and would serve twice again. The Democratic Party controlled the state, and he saw little future in seeking state advancement as a Whig. His future and income seemed to be in the law. By the early 1840s his reputation as an attorney was growing. Few could equal his ability to argue before a jury or prepare a case on appeal. He had assured his future by help- ing secure the location of the new state capital in Springfield in 1839.

Mary Ann Todd came to Springfield in May 1837 to stay with her sis- ter, Elizabeth, and her sister's husband, Ninian Edwards. The younger Todd sisters made their way here from Kentucky, one by one, hoping to find a suitable spouse. But Mary probably soon felt that her presence was too much of an economic strain since Frances was already living in the home. Therefore Mary returned to Lexington the same year to become a schoolteacher so she could pay her own way. Frances married William Wallace in May 1839 and moved to the **GLOBE TAVERN**. Mary then returned, probably late in 1839, and sister Ann followed later as all four sisters made their home in Springfield.

Stephen A. Douglas was a frequent guest at the Edwards' home while he was registrar of the Land Office and later secretary of state. He was Mary's frequent companion, among other suitors. At twenty-six he was already known as "the Little Giant," and was destined to become one of the mightiest political forces in the United States many years before Lincoln was known. Historians are in a disagreement as to whether he ever proposed marriage to Mary, or how close they were. Springfield remembered the two as having a special relationship. Later she confided that she could have never married a Democrat. Maybe Douglas was just more convenient as an escort than the much-absent Lincoln. After Mary became first lady, she revealed to a confidant that she had turned Douglas down because she wanted to become Mrs. President, and felt it could not be as Mrs. Douglas. She claimed to have felt Lincoln's chances for president were better, although during the 1830s and 1840s, this appeared not to be the case. One of Mary's sisters stated she would have married Douglas if she had not pledged to Lincoln. Thus she is said to be the only woman in our history courted, and maybe proposed to, by two future opposing presidential candidates. As it turned out, she was escorted to the 1861 Inaugural Ball in Washington as first lady, by Douglas.

Sometime in 1839 she became aware of Abraham Lincoln, and the relationship moved from friendship to courtship sometime in 1840, maybe to make Douglas jealous. Very little is known about the details of the relationship with Lincoln or who pursued whom, but something was going on between the two. Lincoln was heavily involved in court and political campaigning during 1840, and Mary spent several months in Columbia, Missouri, visiting friends. Lincoln was now past thirty, awkward, unschooled, and socially deficient. Mary was well born, well educated for the times, witty, flirtatious, vivacious, spoiled, and an accomplished conversationalist. Her brother-in-law, Ninian, said she could make a bishop forget his vows. The awkward Lincoln was not a great catch, as historian Jean Baker states, as he was struggling economically and on a different social plain. Lincoln was seen with her more and more, and there were hints of marriage. But as Douglas L. Wilson traces in *Honor's Voice*, little of the "strange courtship" is known.

About January 1, 1841, the courtship abruptly ended; no one knows why. Some have argued that an engagement was broken, but the exact understanding between the two is not known. Mary's niece believes Lincoln was late for a date to escort Mary to a party. When Lincoln arrived at the party to see her flirting with Douglas he left in a huff. Later harsh words over the incident caused Mary to tell him, "Go and never, never, never come back." Some suggest it was because Lincoln fell in love with Matilda Edwards, Ninian's cousin visiting from Alton, also courted by "lady's man" Joshua Speed and Douglas. Possibly Lincoln's rival, Edwin Webb, entered the picture, and maybe Lincoln had committed some slight that Mary could not forgive. David H. Donald suggests that Lincoln did actually propose and gives a variety of reasons for the breakup. A depressed and melancholy Lincoln later referred to the "fatal first of January," but the date may not refer to his relationship with Mary. This is also about the time Joshua Speed sold his interest in the store and prepared to move back to Kentucky.

Speed told William Herndon that Lincoln had written a letter to Mary saying that he did not love her and that Lincoln wanted him to deliver to her. Speed urged Lincoln to say the words to her, which he did. There is a popular story that wedding plans were canceled, but the family claimed there were never definite plans for any wedding, and this seems true. Lincoln sank into a deep melancholic stupor that he called his "discreditable hypochondriaism." Herndon stated that Lincoln went "crazy as a loon," and quoted him saying, "I am now the most miserable man living. If what I feel were equally distributed to the whole human family, there would not be one cheerful face on earth. Whether I shall ever be better, I cannot tell; I awfully forbode I shall not. To remain as I am is impossible; I must die or be better." While the town gossiped, Lincoln went to Louisville, Kentucky, to stay several weeks with Speed in his family home.

There is much speculation about the relationship and true feelings, before and after marriage, between the two who did not speak of their relationship. He may have courted and even proposed to Sarah Rickard, the teenaged half sister of Mrs. Butler where he boarded. The Butler family had taken Lincoln in while he was in the depths of despondency in January 1841. Orville Browning, who was living with the Butlers at the time, told Herndon later that Lincoln had proposed to Mary but was in love with Matilda Edwards (*Honor's Voice*, page 242). Or there may have been just a mild relationship. Sometime in 1842, mutual friends Simeon Frances and his wife got Mary and Abraham together in their parlor. Thereafter their courtship was renewed and continued in secret. Lincoln, and then Mary, began a series of anonymous published poems and letters, known as the Rebecca letters, lampooning and ridiculing Democrat officeholder James Shields to the extent that he challenged Lincoln to a duel, after Lincoln took the blame.

The challenge progressed to an island in the Mississippi, where cooler heads prevailed (see Alton, Illinois). Lincoln might have lost some face in this embarrassing episode and refused to discuss it as long as he lived, but his relationship with Mary was strengthened. Elizabeth, who considered him plain, again tried to break up the match before marriage by pointing out the different social background and nature. Sister Frances agreed and considered him the ugliest man in town. Many felt they were opposites. The Edwards family felt that Mary liked Douglas better, and encouraged that relationship.

Somewhat suddenly and surprisingly, on November 4, 1842, Lincoln and Mary hastily rounded up their friends James Matheny and Julia Jayne to stand up for them. They might have tried to hide the marriage from Mary's disapproving family. The couple had planned a quiet ceremony at Reverend Dresser's home, but Lincoln met Ninian Edwards on the street and told him about the upcoming event. And Mary told Elizabeth who insisted it be at their house. It was too far to travel to the bride's parents' house in Kentucky as would have been customary, and Mary did not like her stepmother. Dresser was the pastor of the church attended by the Edwards family and by Mary while she was their guest. The Lincolns immediately moved to the **GLOBE TAVERN** where Robert Todd Lincoln was born the next August. They later moved around the corner, but it became apparent that those limited accommodations were insufficient for a growing family. Lincoln purchased **DRESSER'S HOME** at Eighth and Jackson in January 1844, where they remained until after the presidential election of 1860.

In the words of Mary's biographer, Jean Baker, Lincoln was on good terms with almost everyone in Springfield, and Mary was on bad terms with many. She was formally educated for years, while Lincoln received less than a year of formal schooling. She was socially fashionable; he was scruffy in dress and manners. Although an excellent lawyer, he was no more organized in his profession than he was as a man. The Lincolns were political allies and shared common parental ideas. They had different ideas in the handling of money and were different in temperament. Their differences complemented each other's in many ways, and she educated him up to the standards of the day. Her vivacious manner added zest to Lincoln's life of melancholy. Her ambition and political knowledge complemented the ambition of her husband to the highest level. Various stories of her violent temper and vicious treatment of others may be exaggerated.

After Lincoln served four two-year terms in the legislature, he served one term in the U.S. House of Representatives. His political career temporarily ended when he did not run again due to arrangements within his party to share opportunities to the only relatively safe Illinois Whig seat. He had also taken an unpopular position concerning the Mexican War, and felt washed up politically in 1849 when his term in Washington ended. He concentrated on the law until 1854, increasing his income and prominence in the Illinois Bar. He did try, in vain, to get an appointment to the Land Office in Washington and went there in 1849 to press his claim. He also lost his pursuit of a foreign appointment in Bogotá, Columbia. He thought he was due something since he had campaigned hard for President Zachary Taylor. The president offered him the office of governor of Oregon Territory, and later as secretary for the remote western state, but he turned the offers down with strong advice from his astute wife. When someone suggested later that he was fortunate not to have accepted since he probably would have come back senator, but not president, Lincoln agreed he was probably right. "I have all my life been a fatalist. What is to be, will be; or rather I have found all my life, as Hamlet says, 'There's a divinity that shapes our ends, rough hew them how we will.'"

During the early 1850s Lincoln was melancholy and withdrawn, probably thinking he was a failure. Stephen Douglas was emerging as a national leader and looked like the next president in 1852. He was chairman of the Committee on Territories and exhibited strong leadership in averting a conflict by the passage of the Compromise of 1850. Douglas maneuvered through Congress a bill whereby the question of slavery would be determined in new territories by popular vote. This Kansas-Nebraska Act eliminated the slavery limits as set by the Missouri Compromise and reopened this issue in the development of the West.

Lincoln now rose out his political lethargy and began to study the Constitution and law relating to slavery. His political involvement was renewed with answers to Douglas in a State House speech, on October 4, 1854, and an important follow-up in Peoria on October 16. He was elected to the Illinois legislature again in November, but resigned a few weeks later to run for the U.S. Senate. This effort failed the next February, and he lost again in 1858 after his famous debates with Douglas. At that time senators were selected by the legislature. Lincoln's voice and political activity then accelerated within the state through 1859, and then to the country in 1860 when he was elected the sixteenth president.

LINCOLN HOME

(1) LINCOLN HOME, Eighth and Jackson: The one-and-a-half-story home was built in 1839 for Reverend Charles Dresser who mar-

ried the Lincolns in 1842. They bought the house in January 1844 for $1,200 cash and a small lot worth about $300. The family moved during the first week in May to what was the edge of town. This was not the best area of town, but Lincoln could maintain his "log cabin" advantage in politics as he had been accused of joining the rich after his marriage to a Todd. They lived here until 1861 except for a year and a half while Lincoln was in Washington beginning in late 1847, when they rented the home to Cornelious Ludlum and Mason Brayman, although the latter's name is generally not mentioned in the history of the home.

The home is displayed as it was in 1860. The handrail on the stairs is the only part of the original structure that the average visitor can legally touch, although most of the interior and exterior are original. As the diorama across the street in the Dean House shows, the layout inside and the number of outside buildings changed from time to time. There were three major periods as the house changed in about 1846 and again in 1856, although they remodeled seven times. The personal use and arrangement of the interior are not really known before the enlargement in 1856, or even before Lincoln became the 1860 nominee for president when the house was sketched. Different authors, historians, and park rangers here have different theories as to which room was used for what. Probably the master bedroom when the family moved in is where the sitting room on the Jackson Street side now is. But it may have been upstairs. There was no rear parlor on the north side then as later.

The interior was changed beginning in 1846 with the north porch being removed and a back bedroom added that is thought to have been the Lincolns' bedroom where the rear of the double parlor is now. It is possible that Eddie, Willie, and Tad were born and Eddie died in that bedroom, although opinions differ. The front parlor, separated by a wall and door from 1846 to 1856, was where the Lincolns received guests and clients. The children were not allowed there, as this was kept formal for guests. As Robert grew older, he probably slept in one of the bedrooms upstairs. The sitting room on the right when entering the house was where the family spent evenings after 1846. Lincoln's favorite position for reading was to turn up a chair to prop a pillow along the back side and lean against it on the floor. Here and in the hall he would lay for hours and read out loud.

From the beginning there was room for bedrooms upstairs in front on the north and south sides, although the ceiling was somewhat lower. A servant or hired girl would have slept in the large room in the rear on the second floor before the 1856 change, when she would have had only a small bedroom in the rear. Gas lighting and indoor plumbing came after the Lincolns left. The wall and fence in the front on Eighth Street were built in 1850, and then extended along Jackson Street in 1855.

The structure was enlarged to include two full stories in 1856 at the cost of $1,300. The first floor was rearranged also because all bedrooms were now upstairs, and a dining room was created. This was thought to have been paid for by the 1854 $1,200 sale of Mary's land southeast of Springfield, which had been given to her by her father, although Lincoln's yearly income had grown from about $1,500 in 1845 to $3,000. The formal parlor was still to the left and was divided from the rear room by a door. This could be made into a large room for parties, but was normally kept a library and study.

After the enlargement, the marital bedrooms were separated. This arrangement was not unusual at the time. Separate bedrooms were considered a sign of success, and recommended by fashionable interior decorators for well-to-do couples. Mary could retreat here to relative quiet and darkness during her migraine headaches. (Her sister Elizabeth's home also had separate marital bedrooms.) Lincoln's faced the front of the home on the northwest corner. This may have been the master bedroom before the enlargement, although the ceiling would have been lower. He retreated here with political friends, and used his bedroom as a home office. His writing desk and shaving mirror are still here. The mirror is hung on the wall so that he could look straight into it at his six-foot-four-inch height. He used it every morning to shave and straighten his unruly hair. Some believe it was possibly here that he saw a double image, which unnerved the president-elect and his wife. Mary felt that this was a sign that he would survive a first term as president, but not a second. He told the story to Ward Hill Lamon and Noah Brooks, and described it as a swinging glass on a bureau in his "chamber." No one knows which mirror it was, and it could be one now in the parlor.

Mary's bedroom adjoined, believed to have been half of a master suite. The wallpaper probably matched Lincoln's bedroom, as it does now, and is a pattern known to have been in the house. Her nine-foot ceiling is two feet lower than her husband's. The loud carpet pattern is of the period, but it is not known what was there at the time. The younger boys evidently stayed with her until Robert left for school. Now the front room across the hall in the front is designated as the guest bedroom, although the boys probably used it also as it was so shown by guides for years. As Lincoln traveled, he stayed with many friends and then paid them back when they came to Springfield.

The south porch along Jackson Street was a favorite place to read the paper while watching the boys. Part of the ironwork on the second floor is missing, as it was during Lincoln's residency. The children, Tad especially, would like to run off, dressed or not, causing his father to yell and chase. Lincoln generally did his own milking and wood cutting. The cow was kept in the open field to the east. A horse was kept in the stable or barn with a pet crow, named Jim Crow, various cats, and probably their dog, Fido. Lincoln was not a gardener, and sister-in-law Frances claimed that she and Mary accounted for the only greenery. He evidently planted a few rose bushes that died for want of attention.

There were sidewalks in 1860, but not long before that, and the dirt streets alternated between being a morass of sticky mud and the source of dust that filled houses and eyes. There were no street numbers, so most houses had a nameplate as seen here today. Livestock roamed the streets for much of the time the Lincolns lived here, cleaning the streets of grass and creating their own problems. To save on costly friction matches, Lincoln often got a shovel of hot coals from a neighbor to start his own fire, which had to be stoked and tended to constantly.

At the beginning there was no money for servants as there had been in Mary's fancy Kentucky home and in the home with her sister. Mary had to learn and practice many new skills including constant attention to the kitchen fires, cooking, hauling water from the backyard pump, making butter and cheese, preserving fruit and other food without refrigeration, cleaning, sewing, and many other duties that women of the day struggled to fulfill. Lincoln's cousin, Harriet Hanks, lived with them for about a year while she was in school. She helped Mary with housework and with Robert from October 1844 until after Eddie was born. Servants were hired from time to time, generally battling Mrs. Lincoln as well as the housework. The 1860 census showed a fourteen-year-old boy, Philip Dinkell, and hired girl living with the Lincolns who helped with chores. (Extensive research by the Park Service has not revealed exactly who they were.) There were no screens on the windows to keep out insects. In the winter, wood stoves could maybe get the temperature of the house up to fifty degrees. Social customs of the day dictated that men were not to answer the door if a servant or child could do it. If the man of the house performed this duty, he certainly was not to do it without his coat or shoes. Mr. Lincoln broke all of the rules, to his wife's constant dismay and embarrassment.

Lincoln's legal work kept him on the road for long periods, generally well over one hundred days every year. Legal work was his only means of support as he did not have a business, speculate in land, or run a farm, as many other lawyers did. So unlike others, he attended every session at every court site from beginning to end in his Eighth Circuit, plus some other counties. Friends felt that he was happiest at these times; he would spin yarns, tell stories, and establish political and personal relationships, which later aided him in his political bids. For a while a twelve-year-old neighbor, Howard M. Powell, was hired for five cents a night to stay with Mrs. Lincoln, help with the chores, and watch after young Robert. He would go over after supper and read Lincoln's books. He wrote that this lasted from June 1851 until the fall of 1853. He also described how Lincoln acted like a schoolboy when he took Robert and him out to the country to pick blackberries. Evidently other boys were also hired to stay with Mary. Close friend David Davis felt that Lincoln should have stayed home more, but that he preferred compatible males rather than wife and children. Early in his marriage he was seldom away more than two weeks at a time, but the time away gradually increased. By 1854 he was so involved with legal and political work that he stayed away as long as six weeks at a time and was absent twenty weeks that year.

Edward Baker Lincoln was born in the home on March 10, 1846, and named after the man who had just beaten his father in the congressional election. Both parents generally spelled the name "Eddy" although the family also uses "Eddie." During the winter of 1849–1850 he became very sick from what was thought to be diphtheria, but probably was pulmonary tuberculosis. There is evidence that he was chronically ill all his life. His parents suffered with him for fifty-two days until he died on February 1. Reverend Dresser was out of town, so the new rector at the First Presbyterian Church, Dr. James Smith, performed the funeral service in the home. This left a deep mark on both parents, especially on Mary's emotional and physical health. She spent weeks weeping in the bedroom. Her emotions and personality worsened with severe headaches and sudden explosions against family and friends. The death also began a period of worldly and religious reflection for the parents.

William Wallace was born here on December 21, 1850. He is generally considered the favorite son. Another son followed on April 4, 1853, finally named after Lincoln's father, Thomas. But he was called "Tad" as he looked like a tadpole with a large head and wiggled a lot. He probably suffered from what we now call hyperactivity since he could not sit still and did not learn to read until age twelve. He also suffered from a speech impediment so severe that outsiders found it hard to understand him.

The boys loved mischief and enjoyed disrupting the law office. Partner and biographer William Herndon said he wanted to wring their necks. The Lincolns would not discipline their children, and they let them run more or less wild, to the dismay of neighbors and professional colleagues. Although Mary was stricter than her husband, they were both much more indulgent than the average parent of the day. Lincoln clearly spoiled his children here and in Washington. The Lincoln sons were paraded out before guests to recite Robert Burns and Shakespeare and read school compositions, which everyone thought was ridiculous.

On February 5, 1857, five hundred were invited to a party, although only three hundred attended due to rain and a bridal party going to Jacksonville on the same evening. Parties were more like an "open house" as guests were expected to only stay twenty minutes. In an era when birthday parties were not common, the Lincoln boys had theirs, with large numbers of children in attendance. In fact, many parties were held at the home, including large children's parties for Willie's birthdays in 1859 and 1860.

Herndon did not like Mrs. Lincoln and was not a welcome guest of hers, although he was in often the Lincolns' home (contrary to what is sometimes implied). His descriptions of her and the martial relationship were colored by his extreme dislike for Mary on one side and his admiration for the memory of his partner on the other. Other stories are told by those who lived there (Harriet Hanks) or worked there (Mariah Vance), plus other servants, neighbors, and visiting legal associates who stayed in the home. Clearly Mary was subject to headaches and other physical problems. She took drugs, generally paregoric, which has an opium base, now known to cause negative emotional side effects. This caused her to lose control. There are stories of Lincoln being chased from the house, sometimes with various objects flying after him. Throughout Mary's life she suffered great personal tragedies from which she never recovered, especially the loss of her children, who died after prolonged suffering. However accurate the various stories and quotes of Lincoln about his suffering and putting up with her, there must have been love and intellectual compatibility. It is too bad that correspondence between the two has not survived, as it would no doubt reveal a close intellectual and personal partnership. The point is well taken, as many believe, that Lincoln could not have been president if he had married someone less politically astute, educated, socially conscious, and intelligent than Mary Todd.

A ten-member committee came to the home on May 19, 1860, to officially inform Lincoln of his nomination by the Republican Party for the presidency. The first Lincoln encountered was Willie who, at the front gate, announced when asked, that he indeed was Lincoln's son. Tad ran up to also inform the committee that he too was a Lincoln. The committee then proceeded to the rear parlor to greet Lincoln with the official announcement. Teetotaler Lincoln served his guests cold water. He asked about the height of Judge William Kelley of Pennsylvania who admitted that he was six feet three inches, an inch shorter than Lincoln. The judge stated that he was glad the party had a presidential candidate to whom they could look up, for he had heard there were only little giants in Illinois.

After the election the house was flooded with well-wishers and office seekers. On their last day here, they held a grand public levee from 7:00 P.M. to midnight. A newspaper reported that thousands thronged to be greeted by Lincoln near the center of the parlor. When the family moved to Washington in 1861, the house was rented to the head of the Great Western Railroad until he moved to Chicago in 1869. They had also purchased some Lincoln furnishings, lost in the Great Fire of 1871. Several others lived here until 1883, when Osborn H. Oldroyd moved his extensive Civil War and Lincoln museum to the home. He was instrumental in persuading Robert to donate the house to the state of Illinois. Oldroyd stayed as first custodian until moving his collection to Washington in 1893. This collection is now in Ford's Theater Museum and partly in storage at Harpers Ferry, West Virginia. On August 8, 1908, there was a race riot in town and an attempt was made to burn the house down. A torch was said to have been applied but snuffed out, although this is poorly documented. Both floors were not open to the public until 1955. In 1972 the site became the Lincoln

Home National Historic Site as a unit of the National Park Service. It is felt that the house is now seen about as close as possible to what Lincoln would have known.

No one knows how many visitors toured the house before the federal government took over, but the National Park Service counted 10 million between 1972 and 1987 when they started their $2.2 million renovation, structural rehabilitation, and redecoration. For thirteen months the inside of the home was reconstructed using the original materials as much as possible, including original wood and plaster. Steel beams were added to support the heavy visitations of tourists. The house now is furnished with flashy wallpaper and carpet believed by the Park Service to be similar to those that fashion-conscious Mary actually had. About sixty-five pieces of the Lincoln's furniture and accessories are in the home collection. This includes the sofa in the parlor, rocking chair, kitchen stove, dining table, six side chairs in the parlors, hat rack in the entrance way, stereoscope in the sitting room, lap desk he carried in saddlebags while riding the circuit, and Mary's sewing table. I have visited the home often since 1966, and found that opinions change over time as to the use of the rooms at various time periods. At times the guide will point out the original artifacts and will refuse to do so at other times, "for security reasons," as some relics have been stolen. Generally they will confirm that a piece belonged to the Lincoln's if you ask about a specific one.

LINCOLN'S NEIGHBORHOOD

A four-block square area around the Lincoln home has been set aside to preserve fourteen homes to the same size, look, and location that the Lincoln family would recognize. There is no motor traffic or parking within a block of the home. The Lincolns were friends with most of their neighbors and attended large and small social events at these homes. The neighbors shared advice and assistance on child rearing, as well as times of illness, childbirth, and bereavement. The children wandered in and out of the homes, yards, and lives of all those in this close-knit neighborhood. Here Lincoln roamed with his boys and the neighborhood children, pulled them in wagons, went out on walks, and left for expeditions around the countryside. Lincoln was once seen so lost in thought reading a book when pulling his boys in a wagon that he did not realize one had fallen out and was crying. He was known as a great lover of children who would stop and talk and walk along together with many leaving and approaching his home. It was not unusual to see young children catching hold of his long pants and tugging for attention frequently given. He also gave "hossy rides" to the many children who took to him. The occupants of the homes changed from time to time. Some are shown as follows.

EIGHTH STREET BETWEEN JACKSON AND EDWARDS STREETS

(2) The **CHARLES S. CORNEAU HOUSE** was moved in 1998 back to the **SOUTHWEST CORNER OF EIGHTH AND JACKSON** from the north side of the Lincoln Home where it had been moved in 1962. It was built in 1849 and owned by Mr. Corneau, Lincoln's close friend who was a part-owner of Lincoln's drugstore and hangout. His funeral was here in June 1860. Willie and Tad's friend Isaac Diller was Mrs. Corneau's nephew. Even though Isaac only lived about a block away, he liked to stay with his aunt to be close to his friends who were frequent visitors. Isaac is the "smear" in a picture taken of the Lincolns in front of their house in 1860. He told a radio audience about a year before he died in September 1943 that he moved when he heard a wagon go by, and thus missed immortality by not being clearly shown.

(3) **JULIA SPRIGG** purchased this home at **507 EIGHTH STREET** in 1853, about six months after her husband's death. The house has recently been considerably downsized to remove later additions. She was an attractive widow with seven children and became a close friend of Mrs. Lincoln, exchanging letters after the move to Washington. Tad was a frequent visitor and would hide under the furniture when his father came looking for him. Mrs. Sprigg would secretly point to where he was. Then he would squeal with delight when Mr. Lincoln pulled him up. Mrs. Sprigg's daughter helped take care of Willie and Tad and would often stay with Mrs. Lincoln when her husband was out of town. She described Mrs. Lincoln as "the kind of woman whom children liked and would be attracted to her."

(4) The House in the middle of the block at **519 EIGHTH** was the home of **JESSE DUBOIS**, his wife, and their five children. He had become a close friend of Lincoln when both served in the Illinois legislature in the 1830s. His parents were one of the first families to welcome the Lincolns to Illinois as they passed through Palestine. Lincoln helped Dubois find this home after Dubois was elected state auditor in 1856 with Lincoln's support. Dubois was the most important political associate and confidant of Lincoln's living in the immediate neighborhood. He was one of the leaders who organized support for Lincoln's presidential nomination, and he visited Lincoln in the White House several times. Lincoln considered putting him in his presidential cabinet, and may have done so after Secretary of the Interior Usher resigned in May 1865. One of his sons was named for Lincoln. Two other sons were caught with Willie and Tad smoking cigars behind the barn. They were all so sick that the mothers decided not to punish them. The Lincolns reluctantly brought young Willie and Tad once when they insisted on going to a large party. The boys promised to be good if they were allowed to play in the kitchen, but this period of cooperation did not last long. So the children mingled with their parents to the dismay of the hosts and guests who had another story about the overindulgent parents. Dubois accompanied Lincoln's funeral train home.

(5) On the NORTHWEST CORNER OF EDWARDS AND EIGHTH is the home of lawyer GEORGE SHUTT, an outspoken supporter of Stephen Douglas in 1860. Attorney Mason Brayman lived here from 1850 until 1855. He had rented Lincoln's home while Lincoln was in the Congress.

(6) The house of SOLOMON ALLEN, located across the street from Shutt on the northeast corner, is now gone, but the original barn is in the rear of the lot. This is the only such structure of the many existing in the neighborhood of the 1850s. The need for the barns, carriage houses, and privies disappeared long ago, and these have not been reconstructed. A.W. Estabrook lived in the house in 1848. Robert was his pupil between 1850 and 1853 at Seventh and Edwards.

(7) The next lot toward the Lincoln home at **516 EIGHTH** belonged to the JAMESON JENKINS family, although the house is no longer standing. According to tradition, this black man drove Lincoln to the train depot on the morning he left for Washington, and he helped him with his bags. Lincoln's barber and Jenkins's father-in-law was WILLIAM FLORVILLE, known as "Billy the Barber," and lived here and also at SITE 72.

(8) The unnumbered lot in the MIDDLE OF THE BLOCK, TO THE EAST SIDE BETWEEN EDWARDS AND JACKSON AND 508 EIGHTH, was owned by **JOHN ROLL**, who may have lived here with his family. He built and owned the house, but rented it for many years. Roll had helped Lincoln build a flatboat in 1831 at Sangamontown (also "Sangamo Town"). He told the story later that when Lincoln was getting started in Springfield, someone asked him (Roll) why he didn't run for office. Lincoln came along about then, and Roll answered that he would be content to wait for Lincoln to be elected president and give him an office because he helped him build the boat. Lincoln laughed at the joke and so promised. Thus Roll jokingly claimed that he was the first person to whom Lincoln promised an office. Roll lived at a number of places and evidently only occupied this address for a short time. Roll was hired several times to whitewash and repair the Lincoln home. He also lived on the north side of Jefferson between **FIFTH AND SIXTH AND AT THE SOUTHEAST CORNER OF SECOND AND COOK (31)**.

The three Roll boys were friends of Lincoln's sons and took the family dog, Fido, when the Lincolns went to Washington. After Lincoln died, Fido tried to make friends with a drunk and was stabbed to death. It is believed that the large tree in the rear of this lot might date to Lincoln's time. A woman photographer, Sarah Cook, later lived at 508. Her son helped Robert with Lincoln's horse and buggy so they could use them.

(9) On the **SOUTHEAST CORNER OF EIGHTH AND JACKSON** was the home of **FRANCES SPRINGER** who organized the Evangelical Lutheran Congregation in the home in 1841. The present church is now on the site of the Lincoln's in-laws' home at Seventh and Capitol. Springer also had a school in his home, and Robert attended beginning at age eleven. Springer helped start Illinois State University. The house was later owned by **CHARLES ARNOLD** and is now opened for exhibits by the Park Service.

BETWEEN JACKSON AND CAPITOL STREETS

(10) **CHARLES AND HARRIET DALLMAN** are claimed to have lived on the north side of Jackson, a few doors west of Eighth Street. When Charles Jr. was born at about the same time as Tad, Mrs. Dallman could not nurse him, and he became sick. Mary sent Abraham for the baby, and she nursed him back to health. Lincoln rocked the baby to sleep. It is not known exactly where the house was. The National Park Service completed a study to determine the location and concluded that the correct site might have been on the EAST SIDE OF SIXTH BETWEEN JACKSON AND CAPITOL. They later lived on the north side of Monroe Street between Ninth and tenth.

(11) JAMES GOURLEY lived at NINTH AND JACKSON, NEAR THE NORTH-WEST CORNER prior to 1857. His yard backed up to Lincoln's. He remembered "Lincoln would take his children and would walk out on the railway out in the country—would talk to them—explain things carefully—particularly." Lincoln bought milk from Gourley, who had four sons of his own. Later Lincoln bought his own cow, pastured east of the homes with Gurley's. He said that Lincoln would come over to his house in slippers, one suspender, and old pants to milk. The Gourley boys and Robert drove the cows back and forth at milking time, and Lincoln also did this chore on occasion. Gourley lived next to the Lincolns for nineteen years, and Mary would sometimes holler out the back door if she needed him to help her while her husband was gone. Once she asked him to sleep over to protect her while her husband was gone. Gourley quoted her as saying that "if her husband had stayed home as he ought to that she could love him more."

(12) Directly across the street from the Lincolns on the NORTHWEST CORNER lived REVEREND NOYLES W. MINOR, pastor of the First Baptist Church and a "warm personal friend" who visited the president in the White House. When Minor did not have room for his houseguests, some spent the night at the Lincoln's. Lincoln often visited the pastor and his children whom he cuddled and spoiled as if his own. By 1859 Minor was living on the WEST SIDE OF SEVENTH BETWEEN JACKSON AND EDWARDS. Dr. J. Shearer, whose wife was a close friend of Mary's, then occupied the home. The site is now a vacant lot.

(13) The next house on the west side of the block from the corner of EIGHTH AND JACKSON was occupied by the WHEELOCKS (sometimes spelled "Wheeless"), who were close friends. Tad is known to have been watched after by their teenaged daughter while his parents were at the Alton debate with Douglas. This home is no longer standing.

(14) Then the next house toward Capitol Street was built on a lot once owned by Lincoln. Two months after moving to Springfield, Lincoln purchased two lots here for $272. Frederick Dean had sought his fortune in the gold fields in California, and bought half of one lot upon returning for $125 in 1850. Lincoln sold the remaining land in 1853 for $375. HARRIET DEAN taught a school there. In

1860 Mrs. Dean's mind failed, and she was put into an asylum. She committed suicide shortly thereafter. Her house is currently used for exhibits pertaining to the area.

(15) At **413 EIGHTH STREET** is the home of **HENSON LYON**, a farmer, and his nine children. The National Park Service is using this for administrative offices.

(16) The lot north was the home of **MRS. ANN WALTERS** who had borrowed money from Lincoln's friend Joshua Speed to buy the lots and build the house. When she failed to pay, Lincoln had to act to collect the money for Speed.

(17) At the **SOUTHEAST CORNER OF EIGHTH AND CAPITOL** was the **MARY REMANN** home. The Lincolns were especially fond of Mrs. Remann's little girl, Josie, who was treated by Lincoln like the daughter he never had. She later married one of Lincoln's nephews, Ninian Edwards's son, Albert. Their daughter said in *Life* magazine (February 1959) that her grandparents forced Mary to break her engagement to Lincoln, as he was too poor with no prospects. She also told of her aunt Mary buying hundreds of shawls at a time. Once she is described as buying three hundred gloves at one time and two dozen watches. Mary had sixty-four trunks full of things when she died.

Willie's closest friend was Mrs. Remann's son, Henry. Willie wrote to him from Chicago and at least three times from Washington. When Eddie Lincoln died, Mrs. Lincoln would not open his bureau until she watched her friend Mrs. Remann sewing clothes for Henry. She then gave her all of Eddie's. Henry is pictured in several Lincoln books wearing the clothes. His father, also named Henry, had talked Lincoln into studying German before he died of consumption in 1849. Eddie Lincoln got sick with the same symptoms the day after Mr. Remann's December 12 funeral.

(18) Across the street to the north was the home of **S. H. MELVIN** at the **NORTHEAST CORNER OF EIGHTH AND CAPITOL**. This family had five sons and was a popular place for the Lincoln boys. Lincoln would stop on the way home from the office to collect his sons, sometimes with difficulty. Melvin was a druggist who sent Lincoln's pills to the White House.

(19) Near **SOUTHEAST CORNER** of Eighth and Capitol is a reproduction, on a slightly smaller scale, of the center portion of **NINIAN EDWARD'S HOME** where the Lincolns courted and married, and where Mary died in 1882 **(SITE 34)**. It was claimed to have been a "faithful" reproduction, but does not look too much like the pictures of the old home taken late in the nineteenth century. This was constructed as a museum and conference center and opened in 1968, but is no longer used for those purposes. This is on the site of the **JESSE KENT HOME**. His son Joseph would take care of the Lincoln horse when Lincoln was away, and he drove for Mrs. Lincoln. He would sometimes borrow the horse to take the neighbor boys to a creek to swim. He worked up enough nerve once to ask Lincoln to also borrow his carriage, but Lincoln responded, "There are two things I never loan, my carriage or my wife." On the north side of the Lincoln home is now a vacant lot, once the home of Henry Corrigan, his wife, and their two sons, twenty-four and twelve in 1860.

(20) The Lincoln Home **VISITOR'S CENTER** is a block west at the **NORTHEAST CORNER OF JACKSON AND SEVENTH**. A home on this site was rented by the **STEPHEN SMITHS** from 1858 to February 1860. The Lincolns often visited with them and their son, Dudley, born in 1858. Stephen was the brother of Clark Smith who married Mary's sister Ann. They sometimes stayed with Mary when Lincoln was away. Lincoln liked to spoil little Dudley as he would his own sons. Lincoln had a habit of strolling through the neighborhood rehearsing his thoughts and speeches. When practicing out loud his Cooper Union Address, he wandered by, put Dudley on his shoulders, and continued to pace the area, rehearsing the famous speech, with young Dudley the first to hear it. Lincoln escorted Mrs. Smith and Dudley to Philadelphia to visit relatives in February 1860 while he was on the way to deliver the speech.

(21) A block south at the **SOUTHEAST CORNER OF SEVENTH AND CAPITOL** was the home of Mary's sister **FRANCES TODD**, who married **DR. WILLIAM WALLACE**, the namesake of Lincoln's third son. He was always a dedicated small-town doctor, but his life was greatly altered by the Civil War. He accompanied his brother-in-law to Washington in 1861, and was appointed paymaster in Missouri and later Mississippi. He contracted dysentery, and never fully recovered, dying in 1867.

DOWNTOWN AREA (THE STRUCTURES MENTIONED AS FOLLOWS ARE GONE, EXCEPT AS NOTED OTHERWISE)

(22) **THE FIRST PRESBYTERIAN CHURCH** is now at the northwest corner of **SEVENTH AND CAPITOL AVENUE**. Mary joined on April 13, 1852.

The church was attended by the family when it was located at 302 East Washington. Mary's funeral was here in 1882 as she was still a member, although she probably never worshiped at this new location. This building was dedicated in 1868 by the Third Presbyterian Church and sold to the First Presbyterian Church in November 1871. The original pew used by the Lincoln family is now in the present church, although it stayed in the original building until 1912. This had been purchased by Lincoln, not rented as the marker on the front says. (Actually the half used by the Lincolns is here; the other half was sawed off, discarded, and lost. Another half of an original pew was joined to it.) Mary wrote Mrs. S. H. Melvin, whose husband was the church treasurer, "I had intended requesting Mr. Melvin to have given me a promise, that on our return to Springfield we would be able to secure our particular pew, to which I was very much attached, and which we occupied some ten years, may I hope that we will be able to do so." The pew was moved here just in time for Ex-President Theodore Roosevelt to use on Easter Sunday in 1912. Other presidents have also used it.

(23) Robert, Willie, and maybe Tad went to **MISS CORCORAN'S ACADEMY** on the **NORTHEAST CORNER OF EDWARDS AND SEVENTH**. She is also said to have taught Willie in his home (*Willie Lincoln as a Boy of Letters*). A. W. Estabrook had a school here also. Robert attended the **A. W. ESTABROOK ACADEMY** for three years beginning in 1850, and received some discipline for the first time. Willie and Tad followed later. Their former classmate remembered Lincoln coming to play a ball game called "soak 'em." Estabrook also taught at the Springfield Academy on Fifth Street between Monroe and Capitol in the late 1840s and at the Third Ward or Edwards School beginning in 1856 located at the site of the Illinois State Museum.

(24) R. W. **DILLER** lived on the **NORTHWEST CORNER OF SEVENTH AND JACKSON** in 1860. He was Lincoln's friend whose son, Isaac, was a constant visitor at the Lincoln home and had his picture taken with Lincoln in front of the house.

(25) Another friend of Lincoln's and the postmaster, **ISAAC DILLER**, lived on the **EAST SIDE OF SIXTH BETWEEN JACKSON AND EDWARDS**.

(26) JAMES H. **MATHENY** lived on the **SOUTHWEST CORNER OF MASON AND NINTH** before moving to the **SOUTHWEST CORNER OF SIXTH AND SCARRITT** by 1857. He was Lincoln's best man at his wedding, and stated that the groom looked and acted like he was going to a slaughter. He also practiced law in the Tinsley Building **(67)** when Lincoln was there. Before his marriage Lincoln is quoted as telling him that he really loved Matilda Edwards. Evidently she was not interested in any one of her many suitors in Springfield.

(27) Lincoln liked to sit on **RICHARD LATHAM'S** porch and talk on the way home from work. The house was located in 1860 on the **SOUTHWEST CORNER OF SIXTH AND MONROE**. Latham also lived on the west side of **SIXTH BETWEEN EDWARDS AND COOK IN 1857** and at **ADAMS AND SIXTH IN 1855**.

(28) **C.M. SMITH AND MARY'S SISTER ANN** lived at **603 SOUTH FIFTH STREET**, on the corner of Edwards, across the street from the governor's mansion. The Lincolns came here often to visit their family. Mary spent a week here in 1860 helping in the final illness of Ann's son, who had typhoid fever and was the same age as Willie. Willie caught it shortly thereafter, but recovered. It is also claimed that the president-elect began writing his first inaugural speech here to avoid the crowds, and continued at Smith's store. It was later the 1879 birthplace and home of poet Vachel Lindsey, who also died here. The home, open to the public, is one of Springfield's earliest and was built by Reverend Charles Dresser, who sold his later home to the Lincolns.

(29) The **ILLINOIS GOVERNOR'S MANSION** is located between **JACKSON, EDWARDS, FOURTH, AND FIFTH STREETS**. The 1855 section of the mansion is at the north end and was the center of Springfield social life where Lincoln attended many parties. Governor William H. Bissell's daughter wrote that Lincoln came often to the governor's mansion for quiet talks with her father, sometimes bringing Willie and Tad, who apparently always made themselves at home wherever they were. Once they climbed through a window of her room and hung out through a bay window roof on to the roof enjoying the fright of those trying to get them down. Governor Bissell was paralyzed below the waist, and never entered the Capitol Building. He first gained fame, before being paralyzed, by accepting a duel with Jefferson Davis (unfought) in 1850. Lincoln was unofficially a behind-the-scenes strategist and chief legal advisor for the governor. Thus he was here often, and said "good-bye" in an emotional farewell just before Bissell died in March 1860.

(30) Lincoln's trusted friend and first law partner, **JOHN TODD STUART**, lived at **529 SOUTH FOURTH**, the second house north from the corner of Edwards, across from the governor's mansion. The famous, historic mansion was torn down in 1956 to build a motel. Lincoln and other prominent leaders were frequent visitors. Robert stayed here at the time of his father's funeral. Judge Davis credited Stuart with leading Lincoln into the legal profession.

(31) Lincoln's friend, **JOHN ROLL**, lived on the **SOUTHEAST CORNER OF SECOND AND COOK** when Lincoln moved to Washington. The Roll boys, John and Frank, took care of the Lincolns' dog, Fido.

(32) Lincoln's friend and associate, **JUDGE SAMUEL H. TREAT**, lived on the **EAST SIDE OF SIXTH BETWEEN MARKET (CAPITOL) AND MONROE** until about 1857, when he moved to the **NORTHEAST CORNER OF SECOND AND EDWARDS**. Lincoln practiced law in his court when he was on the circuit, before the judge was succeeded by David Davis.

(33) Lincoln's friend and associate, **JOHN G. NICOLAY**, lived on the north side of **JACKSON BETWEEN SECOND AND THIRD**.

(34) The **NINIAN WIRT EDWARDS HOUSE** was located at the south end of the new Capitol Building begun in 1868. Like most large houses, it originally stood on an entire block of ground. Maps show the exact location to be where Jackson and First Streets would have intersected if they had run this far, although it had an address on Second Street. A plaque in the stonework of the Howlett (formerly Centennial) Building says: "Here is the house. . . ." But the actual location is several feet away from where the plaque is located. As seen in old photographs, the site was in the present parking lot between the Howlett and Capitol Buildings.

When built, it was located at the edge of town facing open prairies. Edwards was the son of a governor, and he was in the legislature with Lincoln. The home was a social center and hub of elite society, witnessing many parties, political discussions, and decisions. It was torn down in 1918 "to make way for the Centennial Building," although all or part of the Edwards home appears to be located outside of where this is, and the historic home probably could have been preserved on site. (A smaller replica is now in the same block as Lincoln's home on Eighth Street.) Here Mary stayed when she came to Springfield, and here she courted or was courted by and married Lincoln.

A couch in the drawing room of the Edwards Place on North Fourth Street was in the Ninian Edwards home on which it is claimed that Lincoln proposed. Episcopal minister Reverend Charles Dresser held the marriage in the parlor on November 4, 1842. Neither Abraham nor Mary was of that denomination, but Mary had attended his church with her sister. Of course the Lincolns were here many times during their marriage.

Mary returned to the home late in life, and lived here for a year as the new Capitol was taking shape next door. She had been declared insane in 1875 and stayed with her sister in a probationary period before being declared competent. She was aided then by the first woman lawyer in Illinois, Myra Bradwell, and her lawyer husband. Mrs. Bradwell had passed the bar exam, but the U.S. Supreme Court had ruled, Judge David Davis dissenting, that women were not competent to practice law since the "paramount destiny and mission of women is to fulfill the noble and benign offices of wife and mother." After Mary lived in Europe, she moved back to rent several rooms in her sister's home in late 1880. By then she was in very ill health and almost blind. She stayed here much of the time, arguing with everyone, until her death in 1882, mostly in a dark room as children came by to wonder about the crazy woman upstairs.

The John Owsley house was next door to the south and a social center for the town where Lincoln was a frequent guest. Lincoln went to a wedding here when Owsley's young daughter was in charge of two lively young twin boys who got lost. Several frantically searched around the premises and found them perched on Lincoln's shoulders.

The State Capitol Building was the site of the Mather Estate where the city wanted to place Lincoln's tomb. It was being readied when Lincoln's body returned, but Mary insisted on Oak Ridge Cemetery and threatened to have him buried in Washington's intended tomb in the National Capitol. The Donner Party camped on this site in 1846 on their way to California, where many died in mountain blizzards.

(35) NICHOLAS RIDGELY lived on the SOUTHWEST CORNER OF FOURTH AND MONROE in the mid-1850s. The home of one of the community's leading bankers was the scene of many parties attended by the Lincolns. He also lived on the WEST SIDE OF FIFTH STREET BETWEEN WASHINGTON AND ADAMS in the late 1850s and two blocks west on Jackson on a lot covering the entire block between Sixth and Seventh.

(36) GOVERNOR J.A. MATTESON lived in the new governor's mansion for a very limited time when his term expired, and then built one of the great mansions of the town across the street, back from the SOUTHWEST CORNER OF FOURTH AND EDWARDS. Within the last week of Lincoln's life in April 1865, John Stuart asked Lincoln if he was going to move back to Springfield at the end of his term. The president stated that Mary did not want to, but that he did expect to return to his former hometown. Stuart was planning to organize an Illinois group to buy the Matteson mansion for his former partner. This burned to the ground in 1873.

(37) DR. JOHN TODD, Mary's uncle, lived in the best house in town, built in 1827, on the south side of WASHINGTON IN THE MIDDLE OF THE BLOCK BETWEEN FIRST AND SECOND. Todd was educated at Transylvania University and the University of Pennsylvania Medical School. The Lincolns attended family parties here, including one to honor Mary's father during his 1843 visit. His children included Elizabeth Todd Grimsley, who was close to Mary and stayed several months in the White House when the Lincolns first moved there. Todd's son Lockwood also protected the Lincolns in Washington in 1861.

(38) The HUTCHINSON CEMETERY was located on the SOUTHWEST CORNER OF WASHINGTON AND LEWIS STREETS, where the high school now is, about five blocks west on First Street. This cemetery opened in the mid-1840s and lasted about a decade. Edward Lincoln was buried here. On December 13, 1865, his remains were moved to Oak Ridge Cemetery. His tombstone is in the museum at the State Historical Library in the Old Capitol.

(39) One of the Long Nine in the legislature, and Lincoln's friend ARCHER HERNDON, father of his last law partner, lived and operated a tavern on the NORTHWEST CORNER OF JEFFERSON AND SECOND. Unlike his abolitionist Whig son, he was an avid proslavery Democrat. The town began in this area, and the first courthouse was on this site, as indicated by a marker on the corner. Built in 1821, it was a one-story log house twenty feet long. Archer later lived on the south side of Fourth between Madison and Jefferson.

Lincoln's partner WILLIAM HERNDON also lived here. As David H. Donald says, Lincoln's death was the most important event in Herndon's life. Much of what we know of Lincoln's early life is due to the reminiscence collected by him after his partner's death, which occupied much of the rest of his time and energies. He was devoted to the truth and most of the facts developed are reliable, but he was prone to much speculation, leading to questionable conclusions. He traveled to find facts and badgered friends and family far and wide for reminiscences. The facts gathered were from poor and distant memories by an opinionated fact gatherer. He created enduring but clouded images of Lincoln's home life and relationships. His dislike for Mary probably led to inaccurate conclusions about Lincoln's happiness. His weakness for alcohol, growing dislike for the legal profession, and ill health caused financial chaos that might have been alleviated if he had published his own Lincoln biography in the 1860s.

Most of his material was collected within a few years of Lincoln's death. He wallowed in despair after moving in 1871 to a farm along the Sangamon, six miles north of town, where he tried unsuccessfully to farm. He allowed Ward Hill Lamon to use his collection beginning in 1869 for an unsuccessful biography, and freely gave interviews and a series of lectures that antagonized most of Lincoln's family and friends. He did not publish his own book until 1889 through collaboration with Jesse William Weik. Even though there have been more editions than any other biography, it was not financially successful for him or his family.

(40) On his first trip to Springfield in March 1831, Lincoln found Denton Offutt drunk at **ANDREW ELLIOTT'S TAVERN** near the **SOUTHWEST CORNER OF SECOND AND JEFFERSON**. Offutt was to supply a raft needed to haul his goods to New Orleans. He did not secure a raft or boat, causing Lincoln and friends to have to build one.

(41) **JOHN HAY'S** residence site was at the **SOUTHEAST CORNER OF SECOND AND JEFFERSON**, Lincoln's future secretary and biographer lived here with his uncle, Milton Hay, who practiced law in Springfield after moving from Pittsfield. John was a student at Milton's office on the east side of the public square.

(42) During his single years, Lincoln boarded with **WILLIAM BUTLER** at the **SOUTHWEST CORNER OF MADISON AND THIRD**. Evidently, he paid nothing during these five years, either for food or the clothes that Butler bought for him. He moved here after Joshua Speed **(60)** left Springfield, and lived here from January 1841 to November 1842. Speed and Lincoln may have shared a room here at some time. In fact, according to Butler's statement years later, Lincoln lived here from the time he moved to Springfield until he was married.

Butler was one of the Long Nine with Lincoln in the legislature, and served as a second for Lincoln in the Shields "duel." The home was a large, two-and-a-half-story house with a good-sized yard. The site is not marked but should be because of its close association with the future president. When Lincoln broke up with Mary in 1841, Mrs. Butler cared for him during his emotional breakdown. As he got ready here for his wedding, Butler's little son asked where he was going. "To Hell, I suppose," Lincoln is said to have replied.

(43) **DR. WILLIAM JAYNE**, a political associate of Lincoln's lived on the **SOUTHWEST CORNER OF FOURTH AND MADISON**.

(44) The **SPOTTSWOOD RURAL HOTEL** was on the main street of the early days of Springfield, on the north side of **JEFFERSON, NEAR**

THE NORTHEAST CORNER WITH THIRD Lincoln was included in the group of representatives from the area known as the Long Nine who were instrumental in getting the state capital moved to Springfield. A banquet was held here on July 25, 1837, to celebrate this success. It was the site of an infamous murder in March 1838 where a man shot his unarmed rival. The defendant hired prominent attorney Stephen Logan, and Stephen Douglas was named prosecutor, since the state's attorney was a witness. Logan then retained Stuart and Lincoln. Although Lincoln had only been a member of the bar for a year, he was chosen to give the closing argument. His convincing, conversational closing summation secured an acquittal, although popular sentiment was against the defendant. The case was said to "have made Lincoln," elevated his standing in the community, and resulted in many legal referrals.

(45) The site of the CHICAGO AND ALTON PASSENGER STATION is on the east side of THIRD BETWEEN JEFFERSON AND WASHINGTON, as marked on the current depot. This was the site of the first train to run between Alton and Chicago. Lincoln used this depot many times. On June 14, 1854, he introduced a large crowd to Ex-President Millard Fillmore, who stayed in town all of five minutes. Lincoln had been introduced to Fillmore in 1848 in Albany, New York, on the way home from Congress. William Seward stopped for twenty minutes during the 1860 campaign for a quick conference with the nominee. Lincoln was too busy to stop by to see the Prince of Wales, the future Edward VII, who made a tenminute stop in the fall of 1860. Lincoln's body was received here on his last journey home. President Andrew Johnson, General Grant, and many other dignitaries arrived here in 1866 to pay homage.

(46) ILLINOIS STATE UNIVERSITY WAS NEAR THE SOUTHEAST CORNER OF WASHINGTON AND THIRD STREETS. Robert attended beginning in 1854, at age eleven. The school met in the old buildings of the First Presbyterian Church, which were later sold to the Springfield Mechanics Union. The buildings were just to the south of the newer church attended by the Lincoln family. The Mechanics Union sold these facilities in 1849, and the school began in April 1852 while they waited for their new building to be ready. In spite of its name, this was a private, noncompetitive secondary school, with fairly low requirements. The new building was opened in the northeast part of town in 1854 and dedicated by Lincoln **(85)**. This was located between TWELFTH AND THIRTEENTH where ENOS AND

MOFFAT STREETS would meet if they came through the campus. At
this school Robert became a close friend with John Hay and Clinton Conkling. Robert's father was elected a trustee in 1860. The
education hurt Robert, as he had wanted to go to Harvard University, but failed fifteen of his sixteen examination subjects.

(47) THE FIRST PRESBYTERIAN CHURCH SITE WAS 302 EAST WASHINGTON,
just north of the above. Mary had been raised a Presbyterian, but
joined her sister and family at St. Paul's Episcopal Church until
sometime after her marriage. When Eddie died, the minister of
First Presbyterian was asked to conduct the funeral. He had previously spoken with Abraham and Mary, visited often, and made a
lasting impression. Soon after Eddie's death, the Lincolns became
regular attendants at the eleven o'clock Sunday service. The pastor, Dr. James Smith, had been a doubter earlier in life, but
became a Christian. He wrote a strong defense of his faith, which
Lincoln had read and discussed. (Note the comments about
Smith's book in the entry on Lexington, Kentucky.) Lincoln was
known to attend other meetings and spoke in the church. The
church was dedicated in 1830, but moved to new adjacent buildings in late 1843 where the family attended.

Lincoln bought a pew after Mary joined the church on April 13,
1852. This was the first church she had ever joined. It was common for membership to take place much later in life than today.
The boys attended Sunday school. Lincoln gave to the church and
also gave to other faiths. Tad was baptized on April 4, 1855, his
second birthday, and was eulogized here after his death in 1871.
He was the only Lincoln son to be baptized. Ohio governor
Salmon P. Chase, who was later secretary of the treasury and
Chief Justice of the U.S. Supreme Court, joined Lincoln in his
pew on January 6, 1861. The pew now is at the present church
(SITE 22) as the church congregation moved there in 1872.

(The Lincolns were familiar guests at the homes of the pastors
of this church. Dr. Smith lived in the Manse on JEFFERSON, NEAR
FIFTH. During 1861, he stayed with the Lincolns in the White
House, moved back to Scotland, and later hosted Mary and Tad
there in 1869. Dr. John Howe Brown was called as pastor later, to
begin in January 1857. He lived on the SOUTH SIDE OF JACKSON
NEAR SPRING, and later on at the SOUTHEAST CORNER OF FIFTH AND
CAPITOL at the time of Lincoln's election.)

(48) At 315 EAST ADAMS is the site of the GLOBE TAVERN (or hotel)
where Mary and Abraham moved on their wedding night. This
was probably the nicest place Lincoln had yet lived, but quite a

downward adjustment for Mary from spacious and luxurious mansions. Lincoln had nine cases in Christian County the next week, and promptly left town. Mary was left to adjust from the elegance of the Edwards home to the cramped quarters, said to be eight or twelve feet by fourteen feet, and common meals with other boarders. They occupied the same room previously used by the John Stuarts and later Mary's sister Frances and her husband. Lincoln's first association with the hotel was as vice president of a celebration on October 5, 1836, on the anniversary of the War of 1812 Battle of the Thames.

Robert was born here on August 1, 1843. Since ladies of the time hid their "delicacy," Mary probably spent much of her time in the small $8-a-week room. Lincoln evidently wanted to name the boy after his old friend, Joshua Speed, but Mary would not hear of it. So he was named after her father. Lincoln had to wait until the birth of the fourth son to select his father's name. Little "Bob" had healthy lungs and cried to the displeasure of all other residents. A bell on the roof disturbed the baby, maybe forcing them to move out in about November. This is one of the few Lincoln sites that is marked.

The family also stayed here before leaving for Washington in 1847 and after returning the next year. The economy-wise Lincolns had rented their home for a year while Lincoln served his term in the House of Representatives. The rental contract began November 1, 1847. They returned to Springfield the next October 10 and rented rooms at the Globe until the end of the rental agreement. Since Lincoln had to return for a second session in Washington, it was decided to grant an extension on the lease while the family waited at the Globe. When Lincoln left for Congress in late November 1848, Mary, Robert, and Eddie continued at the hotel until the family was reunited on May 31, 1849. This is generally not stated in biographies, but has been set out works by Lincoln expert Wayne C. Temple. The National Park does have evidence of an extended lease, and relies on Dr. Temple for this information.

(49) THE ST. PAUL'S EPISCOPAL CHURCH was on ADAMS STREET NEAR THE SOUTHEAST CORNER OF THIRD Street. The Illinois Supreme Court met here before the new Capitol was completed in the late 1830s. Lincoln addressed the Young Men's Lyceum on January 27, 1838. Mary attended church with her sister before marriage to hear Reverend Dresser. Robert is reported to have attended Sunday school at the church.

(50) When they left the Globe they moved to **214 SOUTH FOURTH** until May 1844. They were probably here when Mary's father visited around Christmas, although there is also evidence that they were still at the Globe.

(51) When the government of Illinois moved to Springfield in 1839, they found the Statehouse unfinished. Several large churches offered to house state functions. The House of Representatives, of which Lincoln was a member, met in late 1839 in the **SECOND PRESBYTERIAN CHURCH**, located at **217 SOUTH FOURTH**. Lincoln spoke in a Temperance Society meeting here on Washington's birthday in 1842 and told the audience that recent progress on temperance had been made due to reformed drunkards and not to preachers, lawyers, and hired agents. His thinking on slavery is also revealed as he compared it to alcohol dependence. The senate met at **FIRST PRESBYTERIAN** at **302 EAST WASHINGTON (47)**. The Supreme Court convened at the **CHRISTIAN CHURCH** on the **NORTHEAST CORNER OF SIXTH AND JEFFERSON (78)** and later at the **ST. PAUL'S EPISCOPAL CHURCH** on the **SOUTH SIDE OF ADAMS STREET NEAR THIRD STREET (49)**. Lincoln had no case for almost a year after the court moved here, but it is likely that he appeared as a spectator. He addressed the Young Men's Lyceum here on January 27, 1838. He also met at the **CHRISTIAN CHURCH** on April 9, 1842, to nominate candidates for the legislature.

(52) In 1840, the Capitol was still not complete, and the House assembled in the **METHODIST EPISCOPAL CHURCH** at the **SOUTHEAST CORNER OF FIFTH AND MONROE**. While here Lincoln lost a bid for Speaker of the House. One of the last issues argued here was the continuation of the State Bank, which Lincoln favored. On December 5, 1840, the Democrats were trying to kill it by a vote that Lincoln's party hoped to avoid by not appearing and thus preventing a quorum. He and a few Whig friends came in to see what was going on when it appeared that a quorum was present and a vote would be taken. The Illinois State Register reported that when it became clear that they could not get out of the door in time, they jumped out of the window of the church.

This story is said sometimes to have occurred in the new Statehouse or in the old Vandalia Statehouse (Barton's *Life of Abraham Lincoln*). But it could not have been in either, since the windows in both buildings were too high up. In fact, some think it did not take place at all. Judge Joseph Gillespie wrote that it did happen (*Herndon's Informants*, page 187), and it is confirmed in various sources including *Day by Day* and *The Collected Works*. David

Donald in *Lincoln* places the event in the new (now "old") Capitol
(68). Douglas Wilson in *Honor's Voice* and *Lincoln Lore 1376* say
it took place at Second Presbyterian **(51)**. But Wayne Temple's
Illinois' Fifth Capitol and *Day by Day* refer to the Methodist
Church to be where the House was meeting. (In questions of
Springfield history, I believe the best bet is Dr. Temple.) It was a
joke for several days as the reporter said that it was no great feat
since Mr. Lincoln's legs reached almost to the ground anyway. In
jest he suggested that a bill should be introduced to raise the new
building another floor so that members could not jump from the
greater height. During a session in the new Capitol on January 8,
Lincoln remarked that since the "jumping scrape had become so
celebrated it appeared that he should say something about it." He
then stated that he would jump when he pleased.

The pastor of the Methodist Church, Reverend James F.
Jaquess, told the story much later that Lincoln was converted to
Christianity in 1847 in his home after hearing a sermon in his
church. His parsonage was next to the church on one of the two
lots on Monroe Street given by Pascal P. Enos for the church.

(53) The ST. NICHOLAS HOTEL still occupies **400 EAST JEFFERSON AT
FOURTH** in a newer building, now an apartment house. Lincoln
attended many social events here. Douglas stayed in the hotel,
and Lincoln spoke at a dinner for the Pioneer Fire Company on
July 15, 1860. Lincoln's friend, O. M. Hatch, lived here in 1857. In
early 1861, the president-elect sat for a sculpture by Thomas D.
Jones that is now in the **OLD STATE CAPITOL**.

Lincoln's time posing on the fourth floor was also a quiet time
during a hectic schedule to read some of his voluminous mail,
write letters, and exchange stories with Jones. Once a package was
received that he and the artist felt might contain a bomb. They
stuck part of it in clay, hoping this would absorb some of the possible blast, but found that it contained a whistle made from a pig's
tail. Lincoln tried for most the rest of the day to make a sound out
of it but could not. He then gave it to his sons. The next day the
neighbors complained to Mary that her children were disrupting
the neighborhood by making weird sounds from the whistle.

Mary and Tad stayed here in September 1866 when Mary met
with Herndon in the hotel as he researched Lincoln's life. She
later regretted the interview as she felt Herndon distorted her
feelings and statements about their marriage and her husband's
religious faith. No one in town seemed to know they were here,
although the sisters probably did. She described Herndon as his

usual "disagreeable self." He probably had been drinking, and took penciled notes of the "substance" of what she said, which Mary believed to be inaccurate. Later she denied saying the things Herndon attributed to her at this time, and he caused her much anguish.

President Andrew Johnson and a number of generals and cabinet members stayed here when they came to pay homage to Lincoln at his temporary tomb on September 7, 1866. These included Generals Grant, McClernard, and Custer, Secretaries Seward and Welles, and Admiral Farragut. Presidents Kennedy and Truman were here in the twentieth century.

(54) At the **NORTHEAST CORNER OF FOURTH AND WASHINGTON** was the **CHENERY HOUSE** where Lincoln attended a gathering waiting for presidential election returns. Lincoln's friend, O. M. Hatch, lived here in 1860. The Lincoln family moved here after a reception in their home on February 6, 1861, and lived here until February 11. Robert and Mary also stayed a few hours during the day in December 1865 when Lincoln's body was transferred to a new vault. Grant stayed here as the Civil War began as an aide to the governor.

(55) The **NORTHWEST CORNER** of the street is the site of the **JOHNSON BUILDING** that served as Lincoln's office from the end of December 1860 until February 11, 1861. Lincoln used the governor's office when not needed by the governor before the legislature convened. Here Lincoln received many hundreds of office seekers and political leaders until he left for Washington.

(56) The **MELVIN DRUG STORE** at the **NORTHWEST CORNER OF FIFTH AND WASHINGTON** was frequented by Lincoln who liked to play checkers with the owner, a neighbor. He had the largest pharmaceutical business in central Illinois. Beginning December 23, 1860, Lincoln transferred his business here, and Dr. Melvin sent him laxative pills in Washington for his chronic constipation.

(57) At **109 NORTH FIFTH** was the site of **HOFFMAN'S ROW, LINCOLN'S FIRST LAW OFFICE** in 1837, where he began practice with **MAJOR JOHN T. STUART**. Lincoln had met the major in the Black Hawk War. The Springfield lawyer warmed up to Captain Lincoln and encouraged him to consider the law as a profession. Stuart gave him free access to his legal library, and Lincoln wandered into town to borrow and study the books. Stuart and his partner, Henry E. Drummer, had the busiest law firm in town. Drummer described Lincoln as "the most uncouth looking young man I ever saw. He seemed to have little to say; seemed to feel timid, with a tinge of sadness visible in the countenance, but when he did talk all this disappeared for a time and he demonstrated that he was both strong and acute. He surprised us more and more at every visit."

Drummer moved to Beardstown, and Lincoln was offered a junior partnership. This was great good fortune for the young lawyer, and says something about what others saw as potential. Rather than having to scrape for potential business like most young lawyers, Lincoln began with the prominent and successful Stuart's full legal practice while the senior partner campaigned for Congress.

Stuart was well educated, dignified, and an integral part of the cultural and business life of the town. As his partner, Lincoln found easy acceptance socially and professionally. Stuart was elected to Congress in 1838 over Douglas, allowing his partner to handle a full load of cases. But the congressman spent so much time in politics that the two partners ended their relationship after four years, still friends. Stuart refused to join the Republican Party when it formed or to support Lincoln for president. He served in Congress during the Civil War and opposed Lincoln on the Emancipation Proclamation.

Lincoln's friend, Dr. Anson G. Henry, had an office next to Lincoln's, also on the second floor of the building. Dr. William Wallace was on the first floor, with his medical office and also a drug business. He had to take on a partner, J.R. Diller, as two enterprises took too much time. The drugstore here and later on the east side of the square were favorite loafing places for Lincoln.

The Circuit Court of Sangamon County was located on the first floor while Lincoln's second-floor office faced the front and served as a jury room when needed. A trap door was in the ceiling between the two floors, as was the arrangement in the Tinsley Building **(67)**. Once while Lincoln was listening to his friend Edward Baker address a turbulent political meeting downstairs, the speaker was rushed by several of the opposition. Lincoln dropped through the trapdoor to help hold off the surprised attackers. He seized a stone water-jug and shouted: "I'll break it over the head of the first man who lays a hand on Baker!" But then he softened his voice. "Hold on gentlemen, let us not disgrace the age and country in which we live. This is a land where freedom of speech is guaranteed. Mr. Baker has the right to speak and ought to be permitted to do so. I am here to protect him, and no man shall take him from this stand if I can prevent Him." Baker then continued.

In 1840, Judge Jesse B. Thomas attacked the Long Nine in a speech at the courtroom. Lincoln was not there, but was called for and arrived just as the speaker concluded. He rose and made such a "withering and overwhelming reply" that the judge began to blubber like a baby and had to leave.

(58) Across the street at **106 NORTH FIFTH** was the **LINCOLN LAW OFFICE WITH STEPHEN T. LOGAN** that was formed in May 1841. Logan was another of the many cousins of Mary. The firm moved to the Tinsley Building around January 1844. Nine years older than Lincoln and a leading member of the Sangamon Bar, he taught intellectual self-discipline and the value of preparation that Lincoln drew heavily on for the rest of his life. The partnership ended amicably in late 1844 as Logan brought his son into partnership with him. Herndon described him as "a cold, avaricious and little mean man." But this seems overly harsh, as he was also known as an amiable host, urbane and hospitable. Apprenticeships were sought after in Logan's office. Among those receiving training under him were four U.S. senators and three governors.

(59) **LINCOLN OFFICED WITH HERNDON AT 110 NORTH FIFTH** from around 1853 to 1856 (see **64** below).

(60) At the corner of **FIFTH AND WASHINGTON STREETS** facing the square was the **SPEED** store and last law office with **HERNDON**. When Lincoln came to Springfield on April 15, 1837, he asked Speed if he knew where he could stay. He admitted that he had no money to pay rent, and if his experiment in the legal profession were not a success, he would never be able to pay. Speed offered to share his room and bed. Lincoln then proceeded upstairs to the front room, tossed in his few possessions, and came back down to announce, "Well, Speed, I am moved."

Lincoln shared the double bed and his most intimate thoughts, evidently without paying rent, until Speed moved from Springfield in January 1841. This arrangement was not irregular, as it was customary for single or traveling men to share a bed. He remained a lifelong friend, probably the closest Lincoln ever had. He visited Speed in Louisville at a time when he was very depressed after his breakup with Mary Todd. After the 1860 election, the two old friends met in Chicago and again at the White House. Speed's brother was appointed by President Lincoln as U.S. attorney general.

Lincoln continued to trade at the store and bank combination in the building here owned by Irwin and Company. William Herndon lived here shortly with Lincoln and Speed after his father removed him from Illinois College, as he did not approve of the teachers' abolitionist leanings. Herndon called the store "Lincoln's headquarters" in the late 1830s, a sort of informal literary and debating society where men gathered every evening to tell stories, read each other's poems and writings, and debate politics and religion. Included in the discussions were Stephen Douglas, Edward Baker, James Matheny, James Conkling, Milton Hay, and others.

In 1856, Lincoln moved to the same building in a back-room law office on the second floor with Herndon that they occupied until leaving for Washington in 1861. The twenty-by-twenty-two-foot space was about thirty feet from the corner of Washington. Fellow lawyer Henry C. Whitney wrote that this was "the dingiest and most untidy law-office in the United States, without exception." Herndon wrote that Lincoln would frequently bring the "little devils" (Willie and Tad) to the office. "They would take down the books, empty ash buckets, coal ashes, inkstands, papers, gold pens, letters etc. etc. in a pile and then dance on the pile. Lincoln would say nothing, so abstracted was he, and so blinded to his children's faults." Actually Herndon accused him of encouraging the children in their antics. Since the office was generally very untidy anyway, the boys just added to the mess.

It is said that the two partners had no filing system except sometimes Lincoln's hat where he kept important papers. Correspondence and papers were in a perpetual state of chaos, but the firm prospered. Once when Lincoln was engaged in a chess game with Judge Treat, probably Robert (or maybe Tad, in other versions of the famous story) came to get his father for supper. Lincoln, absorbed in the game, did not respond; so whichever child it was kicked the board sending chess pieces in all directions. Lincoln expressed that they would have to finish the game another time. Treat wrote he could never forgive Lincoln for not "chastising that urchin." Herndon told that at times Lincoln would go into a melancholy mood, not speak, and become teary eyed. Not wanting visitors to witness this, Lincoln would retire to a back office, and Herndon would keep everyone away.

Before leaving for Washington, Lincoln told his partner that he should let the Lincoln and Herndon sign remain, and he would come back to resume as if nothing had happened. After 1865, Herndon spent considerable energy and expense to interview those that had known Lincoln and document his partner's life. This effort preserved much of the knowledge that would have been lost otherwise. (Note that across Washington Street, west of the northwest corner, is an original building built prior to the Civil War where the city counsel once met.)

(61) The CHATTERTON BUILDING is an original building on THE WEST SIDE OF THE SQUARE, ONE THIRD OF THE BLOCK NORTH OF ADAMS. Lincoln came to a jewelry store here on his wedding day to buy the ring for Mary that said, "A. L. to Mary, Nov. 4, 1842: Love is Eternal." She wore it always and was buried with it. Lincoln came here to James Conkling's office on May 18, 1860, stretched out on a short settee, and received his firsthand impressions of the Republican convention in Chicago. Conkling was optimistic, but Lincoln stated he felt Chase or Bates would get the nomination, and that he'd better go back to his office and practice law.

(62) The BUNN BANKING HOUSE was on the SOUTHWEST CORNER OF FIFTH AND ADAMS, with a store on the southeast corner. Lincoln was attorney for bankers who helped to finance his presidential campaign. John Bunn was described as one of Lincoln's closest friends.

(63) Lincoln frequented the BUNN STORE also, across the street from the Banking House and on the SOUTHEAST CORNER. On the upper floors was the PRESTON BUTLER PHOTOGRAPHIC AND AMBROTYPE GALLERY where Lincoln was photographed in 1858 and 1860.

(64) About 1850, the Lincoln and Herndon law firm moved to the SOUTH SIDE OF ADAMS STREET MIDWAY BETWEEN FOURTH AND FIFTH. Herndon had been elected city clerk, and the firm then took over that office for their work also. Then about two years later, they occupied an office at **110 NORTH FIFTH STREET (59)** where they remained until 1856, when they moved back to their last office over what had been Speed's store. (The locations of these little-known offices are based on an undated memo by James T. Hickey, curator of the Lincoln collection of the Illinois State Historical Library. It was given to me in 1999 and confirmed by Dr. Wayne T. Temple, a Lincoln scholar and chief deputy director of the Illinois State Archives.)

(65) The WATSON'S SALOON SITE, 514 ADAMS, was an ice-cream and snack parlor frequented by Lincoln, who brought his sons here. He may have been here when he received word that he had carried New York State, assuring him of his presidential election. David H. Donald traces his activity waiting for election reports from the Capitol Building, to here, and then back to the local source, the telegraph office. While waiting for the final results, he had come here as the Republican ladies were serving supper and was first called "Mr. President" by an enthusiastic crowd.

(66) The **C. S. SMITH STORE, BETWEEN** sites 65 and 67, was where Lincoln traded in his brother-in-law's store and used the third-floor office to write much of his inaugural address. Smith's store had been part of the Tinsley Building and was remodeled or extensively reconstructed. Without dismantling, it is impossible to tell how much of the current building dates to the Lincoln era.

(67) The **TINSLEY BUILDING**, now known as the **LINCOLN AND HERNDON LAW OFFICE**, is at the **SOUTHWEST CORNER OF SIXTH AND ADAMS**. Of the seven Lincoln law offices, this is the only remaining original building and contained two offices, one with Stephen Logan and one with William Herndon. It was built in 1840 as a store building, and appears much as it did then. The exterior walls have been sandblasted to restore the original color. Lincoln moved here around the start of 1844 with Logan. The Park Service notes that the dates of his occupancy are hard to determine. The office was in the front of the third floor, next to the jury room, with windows facing north to the Old State Capitol and also to the east. Two chairs from that office were preserved in the room until the year 2000, when they were removed to Illinois State College in Jacksonville. Lincoln continued to occupy the office after the partnership was dissolved, and after his association with William H. Herndon began.

The door from the street leading to Lincoln's office was just north of the restored post office on Sixth Street where he got his mail. Lincoln would generally arrive about nine o'clock and stand on the street to discuss the topics of the day. The stairway up was much narrower then, but at the same location as now. The original wooden floors are still here, as is a trapdoor that opened into the federal court below, allowing Lincoln to listen to the proceedings. This second-floor courtroom was the only federal court in the state until 1848. When Illinois was divided into two federal districts in 1855, Judge Thomas Drummond transferred to Chicago and took the records with him, destroyed in the Great Fire of 1871. Their destruction limits our knowledge of Lincoln's federal court involvement. Mormon leader Joseph Smith was tried here in December 1841 on an attempted assassination charge in the presence of the Lincolns.

When Lincoln went to Congress in 1847, Herndon moved to a smaller area in a back room. The floors, rarely swept, soon became covered with dust, mud, and manure tracked in from the streets. Guides relate that open windows allowed grass seeds to blow in that sometimes sprouted on the floor.

These offices are now restored to their original appearance, as is the U.S. District Court, frequented by Lincoln. Friends and associates James Shields, A. T. Bledsoe, Edward Baker, and James H. Matheny also officed here. Later Matheny moved to an office on the north side of the square over Fisher's Store. It is easy to imagine Lincoln as he read aloud from his newspaper and stretched out on his sofa or chair so low as to sit on his backbone to ponder and discuss cases and politics.

Lincoln's relationship with Herndon began when the then nineteen-year-old clerked at Speed's store **(60)** in 1837 and slept on the floor in the level above, as did Lincoln. When Herndon became a member of the Bar in 1844, he became Lincoln's partner. No one seems to know why he was asked to join Lincoln in legal practice, and Herndon admitted later, "I don't know and no one else does." No doubt Lincoln was tired of being the junior partner, and wanted to be the head of a firm. But with Lincoln's high standing in the bar, he could have gone into partnership with one of the many successful lawyers in town, or could have remained a sole practitioner. They split the fees equally, much to the disgust of Mary who felt her husband should get two thirds, as in most other firms with an older, more experienced partner, as had been Lincoln's prior arrangements. (It is possible Lincoln's percentage during his later years with his prior partners did amount to one half.)

Herndon managed the office and did much research. He had no political ambitions (although he did serve as the mayor of Springfield once), giving him time to earn an income rather than campaign. He did bring in business, and was known as a competent attorney. He also had a drinking problem (as did Douglas and Civil War governor Richard Yates) that got worse later in life.

(68) In the center of the square is the reconstructed **Old State Capitol**. The original was begun in 1837 after the 1831 courthouse here was torn down. It served as State Capitol for about forty years, and was Lincoln's focal point for activities in Springfield. His last session in the legislature was in the building in 1840 and 1841. Gas lamps were in use in the mid-1850s, about as bright as candles.

The House of Representatives hall was the scene of many important speeches, including Lincoln's political rebirth in October 1854. Before a packed house, the powerful "Little Giant" had defended his promotion of the Kansas-Nebraska Bill, reopening the question of slavery extension. As the audience was leaving, Lincoln stood above the crowd on the stairs to gain attention, and then shouted and urged them to return on the next day to hear his answer. He invited Douglas to respond after he finished to ensure a crowd. His address, with Douglas voicing running commentary in the front row, marked the beginning of his political prominence leading to the nation's highest office. On June 26, 1857, he answered Douglas again, who had spoken here about two weeks earlier on the Dred Scott Supreme Court decision. The country was alarmed over the ruling that Negroes could not be citizens of any state and declared that the Missouri Compromise was unconstitutional. Lincoln reasoned that the Supreme Court must be respected, but this decision would be overruled since it was clearly erroneous.

Lincoln was the front-runner for the U.S. Senate election in 1855. The incumbent was Democrat James Shields who had almost fought him in a duel in 1842. On February 8, Ninian Edwards had arranged for a reception to honor the new "Senator Lincoln." Mary sat in the House Gallery here next to her close friend, Julia Jayne Trumbull, where the legislature would elect the next senator. Forty-six votes were needed. In the first vote, Lincoln got forty-four, Shields forty-one, and Lyman Trumbull five. Lincoln could not get the necessary votes as many would not vote for a Whig, although three new people voted for him on the next ballot. But he lost four votes. So a total of forty-seven people voted for him on different ballots that would have made him the next senator if they had all voted for him on the same ballot. A compromise proposed by Lincoln resulted in Democrat Trumbull's election. Lincoln had requested that his votes go to "anti-Nebraska" Trumbull since the Democrats' real candidate, Governor Joel Matteson, was about to gain a majority. Mary turned from Julia in a temper, walked out, and terminated her friendship. Lincoln wondered how his forty-four yielded to Trumbull's five. He also wondered if he had the capacity to be senator. Trumbull had been a Illinois supreme court justice, had quit to practice law, but like Lincoln, reentered politics because of Douglas's Kansas-Nebraska Act. Like Lincoln he had just been elected to the legislature, but resigned to run for the senate. He served until 1873 and was one of the few who voted for the acquittal of President Johnson during his senate trial after impeachment when one more vote would have convicted.

On June 16, 1858, Lincoln delivered his most famous prepresidency speech discussing a "House Divided." This was the last speech at the Republican state convention that nominated Lincoln for the senate, and the first speech of the senatorial campaign that gained him a national reputation. The thoughts of this speech were repeated in many places and argued that the country could not continue forever half slave and half free. It was also here that the president's body was placed on May 3 and 4, 1865, and viewed by an estimated seventy-five thousand.

During the 1860 campaign and after his election to the presidency, the governor allowed him to use his offices and reception room for the never-ending throng. Governor Bissell had died in March. The new governor was from Quincy and rarely came to town. So Lincoln was given the use of the office within a few days of his nomination on May 18, as Lincoln could not see very many in his cramped law office. Throngs of visitors all but ruined the beautiful carpet. A wooden chain carved from one block of wood was given to Lincoln and later stolen, but a replica is hanging on the wall here now. The reconstructed room is believed accurate due to sketches made by *Frank Leslie's Illustrated Newspaper*.

The portraits of Lafayette in the Senate Chamber and Washington in the House were hung in the building in 1841. The basement museum and research library contains many of Lincoln's letters and personal objects. The objects are rotated for exhibition. The original tombstone of Edward Lincoln is there, lost in 1865 when his remains were transferred to Oak Ridge Cemetery. Mary had given it to her sister who had evidently used it as an entrance stone to their burial plot. It was found broken and face down in 1954.

The State Auditor's Office was on the first floor next to the library. Lincoln did business for the state occasionally and wandered in to get his pay warrant. He probably spoke from the steps on the south side of the building for the July 4 celebration in 1845. The office of the secretary of state was here also, and Lincoln met frequently with his friend O. M. Hatch, and his clerk John G. Nicolay. The first secretary of state was Douglas. Nicolay was also a newspaper correspondent, and was extremely disappointed when he found out he was not going to be asked to write Lincoln's campaign biography during the 1860 presidential election. Hatch said, "Never mind. You are to be (Lincoln's) private secretary." Nicolay was Lincoln's only staff until he talked the president-elect into taking John Hay to Washington, although Lincoln said he couldn't take all of Illinois. Hay's family objected as they felt it would interfere with his law studies.

The STATE SUPREME COURT was located on the first floor. It was here that Lincoln made his greatest impact as a lawyer, and maybe his greatest success. He tried more than two hundred cases and spent countless hours in this only full law library on the circuit. Many of his cases were from lawyers in counties outside the Eighth

Circuit, illustrating his importance and reputation in the bar. Always, he had to be meticulously prepared. In most he battled prominent and competent legal opponents. The chamber was also used for banquets and balls, and Mary is believed to have helped serve in at least one sponsored by the First Presbyterian Church.

The SUPREME COURT LAW LIBRARY is also in the building across the central hall from the STATE LIBRARY. The first person to borrow a book from the latter was Lincoln, who made liberal use of both libraries to study and brief cases. His famous Cooper Institute Address and others were researched and prepared here. Lincoln's reputation as a storyteller extended to these halls also. At night the Supreme Court Library was a sort of "men's club," where stories were told until the early morning hours. A fellow lawyer remembered that he never knew a night when Lincoln did not put in an appearance here. He seemed to have an endless supply of new stories and seemed never to tell the same one twice. Lincoln liked to play chess here also.

About two months after Lincoln left for Washington in 1861, Grant arrived and worked in the building for a while before moving his troops off to glory. It would not be until March 1864 that the two Illinoisans would meet in the White House. The building was later remodeled, enlarged, and sold to the county when the new Capitol Building opened. It was almost destroyed in 1899 but preserved due to historical importance. In the mid-1960s it was torn down and reconstructed to its original size with a new interior to match the original appearance and size. All offices and areas mentioned are now open as a museum and memorial.

(69) Across the street on the SOUTHEAST CORNER OF SIXTH was the AMERICAN HOUSE, also directly across from the Tinsley Building. This was built in 1838 and was the largest and finest hotel of the town. The Lincolns attended many social functions here. Lincoln was one of the managers of a "Cotillion Party" held here in late 1839, possibly the party where he first met Mary. Mary told the story that he had blurted out, "Miss Todd, I want to dance with you in the worst way." And she said, "He certainly did!" Exact dates and locations of that event vary and include the Edwards' home. Lincoln was probably here at a reception to honor Ex-President Martin Van Buren on June 17, 1842, since he was on the welcoming committee and assigned to escort him. It is believed that Lincoln introduced his wife here to Joseph Smith, the Mormon church leader, whom he knew. The Chenery House and St. Nicholas later eclipsed the hotel's prominence.

(70) Lincoln would occasionally attend services at the **FIRST BAPTIST CHURCH**, then at the **SOUTHWEST CORNER OF SEVENTH AND ADAMS**, and made a speech here on January 27, 1838. Lincoln allowed the pastor, his friend and neighbor, to use his horse and carriage, which was said "for years aided us in our church work." **BILLY (FLORVILLE) THE BARBER** had his shop between **SIXTH AND SEVENTH ON THE NORTH SIDE OF ADAMS**. The barbershop was another place called a "clubhouse" and "second home" for Lincoln.

(71) Lincoln spoke several times at **COOK'S HALL, 122 SOUTH SIXTH STREET**, including a repetition of his lecture on "Discoveries," April 26, 1860.

(72) **CORNEAU AND DILLER'S DRUG STORE** was located in the middle of **SIXTH STREET** on the east side north of **COOK'S HALL**, just south of an alley then between Adams and Washington. The business was started by Dr. William Wallace in Hoffman's Row and moved here in 1842 to become Corneau and Diller's in 1849. Douglas, Stuart, Logan, Shields, Lincoln, and others loafed, joked, and discussed the issues of the day on the "liar's bench" in front of the store. They also gathered chairs around the big potbellied stove surrounded by a bewildering array of drugs, pills, patent medicine, and other sundries. Lincoln bought castor oil, Pearl Powder, woods restorative, Lubins Extract, sweet oil, cream of tartar, soda water, ox marrow, couch candy, and liniment. Corneau was a neighbor of the Lincolns. The other owner, **R. W. DILLER**, was the father of one of Willie Lincoln's friends. Fire destroyed much of the east side of the square in 1858, but the store was rebuilt quickly.

(73) The **MARINE FIRE AND CASUALTY COMPANY**, Lincoln's bank from 1853 until his death, was located at **104–108 SOUTH SIXTH**. He made a number of withdrawals shortly before leaving for his inauguration, and made deposits as president. This is now Bank One of Springfield. Lincoln's ledger with his account is on display. Despite its name, it was solely a bank. The Greek pillars date to the Lincoln era.

(74) The **COURTHOUSE** was located at **100 SOUTH SIXTH AT THE CORNER OF WASHINGTON** beginning in 1846. Lincoln handled numerous cases until his presidential election. In 1831 a square, two-story brick courthouse was erected in the center of the square, but was razed in 1837 to make way for the new Statehouse. At this time the county leased a space in Hoffman's Row where Lincoln and Stuart had their office. Two court terms were held in the **METHODIST EPISCOPAL CHURCH (52)**, after which the court returned to Hoffman's Row **(57)** until 1846, when it moved to the Sixth Street location. Voting for the 1860 presidential election was on the second floor. From his temporary office in the Governor's Chamber, Lincoln watched voters going and coming all day on November 6, and went to vote himself when he noticed a lull in the crowds. He cut off his own name for the top spot. The courts moved in 1876 to the old Capitol when the new Capitol was completed.

(75) Across the street on the **NORTHEAST OF SIXTH AND WASHINGTON** was the **LOGAN BUILDING** built by Stephen Logan in 1855. Lincoln tried more than ninety cases in the Federal District Court after it moved here from the Tinsley Building on August 17, 1855. The north side of the building was a vacant lot where Lincoln played handball including on the day he was nominated.

(76) North of the center alley on the east side of **SIXTH STREET, BETWEEN WASHINGTON AND JEFFERSON**, was the office of the *OLD ILLINOIS STATE JOURNAL*. Lincoln sometimes wrote editorials and articles for the paper and received their support. Accounts differ as to where Lincoln was when he received word of his Republican Party nomination to the presidency. Most accounts show that he was here, including the William Dean Howells biography that Lincoln read and approved. Dr. Wayne Temple of the Illinois State Archives strongly believes that he was then in a **TELEGRAPH OFFICE IN THE MIDDLE OF THE BLOCK ON THE NORTH SIDE OF THE SQUARE**, where Professor Donald and others locate him when the final word of his election was received in November. On May 18, 1860, Lincoln had stopped here after making numerous trips to the telegraph office to check on the status of the Republican convention in Chicago. He wandered around for several hours in vain trying to find an unoccupied place to play handball or shoot pool. While on the second floor, messenger boy and Robert's friend Clinton Conkling burst in with a telegram, which Lincoln had to stare silently at for three minutes. It announced that "(Votes) Necessary to choice (win) 234—Lincoln 354 . . . nomination made unanimous amid intense enthusiasm." After receiving many congratulations, he hurried home saying, "There's a little woman down the street who would like to know something of this." But she already knew by the time he got there and had started the party to celebrate.

(77) The home of **SIMEON FRANCES** was at the **SOUTHEAST CORNER OF SIXTH AND JEFFERSON**. After Lincoln and Mary broke off their engagement or relationship, probably January 1, 1841, they did not see each other for many months. Sometime in 1842, Simeon invited Lincoln to his home while Mary was invited by Mrs. Frances. Thus, Abraham and Mary were reunited. Frances was the *Sangamo Journal* newspaper publisher, and a friend and supporter of Lincoln. Mary and Abraham continued to meet here, probably so Mary's family would not find out, until they were married on November 4, 1842. Lincoln's close friend and physician **DR. ANSON G. HENRY** lived nearby on **JEFFERSON BETWEEN FIFTH AND SIXTH**. In 1841 when Lincoln broke up with Mary, Henry treated him for his severe depression and was one of Lincoln's few confidants.

(78) Lincoln attended political meetings at the **CHRISTIAN CHURCH**, located on the **NORTHEAST CORNER SIXTH AND JEFFERSON**.

(79) **CONCERT HALL OR MYERS HALL** was located on the top floor of the Henry C. Myers Building on the **NORTH SIDE OF THE SQUARE, MIDWAY BETWEEN FIFTH AND SIXTH**. Here Lincoln gave his lecture, "Discoveries, Inventions, and Improvements," on February 21, 1859. Dr. Temple describes this as "too scholarly and too dull. Lincoln was merely imitating the Eastern lecturers." The first floor contained a "confectionery and fancy establishment" no doubt frequented by the Lincolns. This was also the vicinity of the telegraph office where Lincoln received results of various political races including the Chicago nominating convention and the November presidential election.

The Concert Hall location was also where Lincoln stayed in Springfield when he came to campaign for the legislature or visit before he moved from New Salem. He stayed with his friend Abner Y. Ellis, who lived then on the site. Ellis claimed he introduced the candidate to the leading Whig men in town.

(80) Lincoln frequented the **LEWIS CARRIAGE SHOP** on **MONROE BETWEEN SIXTH AND SEVENTH**.

(81) Lincoln treated his boys and their friends to nuts and candy at the **WEBSTER GROCERY** on the **SOUTH SIDE OF MONROE BETWEEN NINTH AND TENTH**.

(82) The **GREAT WESTERN (LINCOLN) DEPOT** is located at **TENTH AND MONROE**, on the railroad tracks. Lincoln is described as loving to walk with Willie and Tad along these tracks, deep in thought as the "dear little codgers" skipped from tie to tie. He left and returned to Springfield often at this building. Most notable was the last trip beginning February 11, 1861, when he greeted many in the waiting room, left in the rain, and delivered his famous Farewell Address. His trip to the inauguration was long and arduous, but Lincoln, largely unknown, wanted to be seen and heard by the country. He revealed little of the specifics of his intended actions, but left it clear that he intended to preserve the country with God's help.

NORTH OF DOWNTOWN

(83) The ILLINOIS STATE UNIVERSITY site was in the area of TWELFTH, THIRTEENTH, ENOS, AND MOFFAT STREETS. Lincoln dedicated a new building for the school in 1854, attended by his son, Robert.

(84) On December 13, 1860, Lincoln attended the wedding of his friend, Hon. O. M. Hatch, Illinois secretary of state, to Miss Enos at the ENOS HOUSE, AT THE NORTHWEST CORNER OF SEVENTH AND ENTERPRISE.

(85) EDWARDS PLACE at **700 NORTH FOURTH** is just north of downtown, toward the Lincoln tomb. It was the home of Ninian's brother, Benjamin. This is the oldest house in Springfield, on the original foundation, and a showplace from Lincoln's time until now. The Lincolns visited often, and Mary stayed here late in life. It is believed that Mary wanted to buy this home before Benjamin did. The sofa in the drawing room is believed to have been used by Lincoln to court Mary in the Ninian Edwards house. The grounds were used for political rallies, and Lincoln spoke often from the porch balcony.

Lincoln lay on the grass in July 1854, whittling just to the east at about FIFTH AND ENOS while listening to fiery Cassius Clay from Kentucky, who had been barred from speaking in the Capitol Building. Clay had come to speak out on the Kansas-Nebraska Act. Lincoln had been silent on the brewing political storm, and silently listened to and absorbed Clay's arguments. It is presumed that Clay occupied the Lincoln family pew at First Presbyterian and stayed with the Lincolns.

(86) THE LINCOLN TOMB is located in the northern part of the city at OAK RIDGE CEMETERY. The Lincolns had admired the beauty of the cemetery when it was dedicated in 1860. On May 4, 1865, Lincoln's body (with his son, Willie's) was placed in a vault, seen at the bottom of the hill behind the present tomb. City officials wanted to bury him in a large monument to be erected downtown, but Mary threatened to have him buried in Chicago or Washington if he were not laid to rest at the bucolic rural site here. (Lincoln's tomb is shown on the map as **"1."**)

On December 21, 1865, Lincoln's remains were moved to a temporary vault on the hillside northeast of the tomb where Eddie's remains had been placed eight days before. A stone marks this spot halfway up the hill on the northeast side. Construction of the present tomb was begun in 1869 and was dedicated on October

OAK RIDGE CEMETERY: SPRINGFIELD, ILLINOIS

N

SEC. 7

SEC. 12

SEC. 10

SEC. 14

SEC. 32

1	Abraham Lincoln	10	Archer Herndon
2	Governor William Bissell	11	William Herndon
3	William Butler	12	Stephen T. Logan
4	James H. Conkling	13	James Matheny
5	Rev. Charles Dresser	14	General John McClernard
6	Jesse K. Dubois	15	C. M. Smith
7	Edwards family	16	John T. Stuart
8	Nellie Grant (Jones)	17	Dr. John Todd
9	O. M. Hatch	18	Dr. William Wallace

© 2001 Jeffrey L. Ward

15, 1874. Tad was the first one buried, on July 17, 1871, two days after his death. Lincoln's coffin, with those of sons Edward and William, were placed in the crypt on September 19, 1871.

An unsuccessful attempt to steal the body was made on November 7, 1876. The conspirators hoped to hold the body ransom for $200,000 and secure the release of one of their gang members from prison. They were part of a counterfeiting enterprise and were tailed by a Secret Service detective. He did such a good job hanging around the criminals that he was noticed and taken in by them. He revealed the plot to his superiors, who planned to catch them in the act by waiting in the Memorial Hall while the conspirators entered the tomb on the opposite side.

The conspirators broke into the tomb as Secret Servicemen were hiding nearby, and they almost removed the casket from the stone receptacle before the detective could leave to signal for help. He supposedly was leaving to get the wagon to transport the body, but alerted the government men who rushed around to the catacomb chamber. Meanwhile, the grave robbers had left the area in case they were discovered to wait behind a tree for the wagon. They almost approached a Secret Serviceman whom they thought was part of their gang. Then the government men saw some of their own and thought they were the counterfeiters. They fired and missed, but alerted the criminals that they were discovered. They fled, but were arrested a short time later in Chicago and sent to the Joliet Penitentiary for a year.

After this experience, Lincoln's coffin was secreted within the deep recesses of the tomb while countless pilgrims paid homage to an empty sarcophagus. The public was not informed that the body had been removed. Due to uneven settling of the earth under the tomb, a complete reconstruction was begun in 1899 and completed in 1901, with a rededication in 1902. During the fifteen months of reconstruction, the bodies of the president and his family members were secretly buried in a multiple grave away from the monument. The coffins were all returned to the white marble sarcophagus in the spring of 1901, but Robert was not satisfied that they were safe. So his directions were followed to rebury his father ten feet below the floor in solid concrete. This final resting place was dedicated on September 26, 1901. Lincoln's coffin was opened then for the final time to discount persistent rumors that he was not in the inner leaden box. One of the twenty-three persons to see Lincoln then lived until 1963.

Lincoln's coffin now rests about twelve feet under the monu-

ment in solid concrete. The bodies of Edward, William, Thomas
(Tad), and Mary are in the wall facing the tomb. Robert is buried
in Arlington National Cemetery with his wife, Mary Harlan Lincoln, and son Abraham Lincoln II. Lincoln's only grandson had
died in England at age seventeen, and had been buried in the Lincoln tomb in Springfield from 1890 until 1930. Another reconstruction created the marble hallways.

Efforts were made in 1922 to move Lincoln's body to Washington. Robert strongly objected, citing his father's farewell address
to his old friends and neighbors in the little town he had loved.
Robert wrote of the Oak Ridge tomb as follows: "Within it are
entombed the bodies of my father and my mother and my only
son, and it is arranged that my wife and myself shall be entombed
there." It is not clear who made the decision after his death in
1926 for the burial at Arlington, but the body stayed in a receiving
vault for two years before being taken to the National cemetery. It
is thought that his wife wanted Robert to be in a place of honor
separate from his more famous father. Also she is quoted as having said that she "would be damned if she had to live next to her
mother-in-law for eternity."

Many of Lincoln's friends mentioned in this chapter are also
buried in Oak Ridge. In Section 14, across the two nearest east-
west roads directly north of the Lincoln Monument, are the
graves of Union **GENERAL JOHN A. MCCLERNARD (14)** and law
partner **WILLIAM H. HERNDON (11)**. McClernard was a longtime
political opponent of Lincoln's who served with him in the legislature and Congress. Just northwest in Section 7 are the graves of
friends **JAMES H. MATHENY (13)**, **STEPHEN T. LOGAN (12)**, and
WILLIAM BUTLER (3). Butler is at the easternmost point inside the
small circular drive, and Logan is just outside this circle at a location of two o'clock. **JAMES C. CONKLING (4)** is just outside this circle at "five o'clock." Just southwest of these in Section 10 are the
graves of Lincoln's in-laws and extended family, the **EDWARDS (7)**
(Ninian, Benjamin, and so on), the **SMITHS (15)**, **JOHN TODD (17)**,
JOHN STUART (16), and the **WALLACES (18)**. The Edwards family is
west of the road and just north of the center of Section 10. The
others mentioned are just off the road on the eastern edge.

Nellie **GRANT (8)**, the daughter of President Grant, is buried
here also, just west of the road intersection between Sections 8
and 10. **REVEREND DRESSER (5)** is buried in Section 9 west of the
circle, on the southern edge by the road. **JESSIE K. DUBOIS (6)** is
just south of the road curve, at the southeast corner of Section 10.

ARCHER HERNDON (10) and O.M. HATCH (9) are buried near the border of Sections 32 and 34 and inside the large circular drive. This is almost due east and slightly north of the Lincoln tomb. Hatch's monument is the most prominent in the area and next to the Enos tombs. Archer Herndon is at the north edge of the drive, across from a sign marking the grave of Governor Cullom. Author Benjamin Thomas and collector Oliver Barrett are buried down the hill toward the Lincoln monument. GOVERNOR WILLIAM BIS-SELL (2) is buried in the middle of Section 12.

(87) LOGAN PLACE was between NORTH FIRST AND RUTLEDGE STREETS, NORTH OF MILLER. The house was north of where Klein Street intersects with Miller. Lincoln's law partner and friend Stephen Logan lived here from 1836 until his death in 1880. Lincoln visited often and played marbles and games with Logan's four sons and four daughters. The country home was built well north of the city limits in a thirteen-acre forest, since swallowed as the city expanded. His home was a center of entertainment, and strangers were always welcome. He ran for Congress to succeed Lincoln in the only Whig district in Illinois in 1848, but lost to a war hero. In 1860, he was a Republican delegate to the nominating convention that selected Lincoln.

SPRING CREEK MEETINGHOUSE: Lincoln spoke at a Whig Rally here west of Springfield on March 1, 1844.

SUMMARY OF LINCOLN SITES IN SPRINGFIELD

Many of Lincoln's friends are included as it is assumed that he visited them in this small-town atmosphere.

1. Lincoln home 1844–1861, Northeast corner of Eighth and Jackson.

LINCOLN'S NEIGHBORHOOD (EIGHTH STREET)

2. Corneau house: Owned drugstore frequented by Lincoln.
3. Julia Sprigg house: Friend of Mrs. Lincoln.
4. Jesse Dubois house: Political associate.
5. George Shutt house.
6. Solomon Allen house.

7. Jameson Jenkins house site.
8. John Roll house site: Lincoln's close friend lived in the middle of the block before 1850.
9. Charles Arnold house, southeast corner of Jackson and Eighth: Robert attended a school here.
10. Charles Dallman house site, near the Lincoln home: Mary nursed their baby when Mrs. Dallman was unable to do so.
11. James Gourley house site: Backed up to the Lincolns.
12. and 13. Dr. Shearer and Wheeless house sites: Close friends of the Lincolns.
14. Harriet Dean house: Now open with National Park exhibits.
15. Henson Lyon house: National Park administration offices.
16. Walters house site: Lincoln had to sue resident to get money for his friend Joshua Speed.
17. Mary Remann house site: Friend of Mary, and son received several letters from Willie.
18. S. H. Melvin homesite, northeast corner of Eighth and Capitol: Lincoln sometimes stopped here on the way home to collect his sons, with difficulty.
19. Ninian Edwards's home reproduction and Jesse Kent house site: Kent's son Joseph took care of Lincoln's horse.
20. Stephen Smith house site, now Visitor Center.
21. William Wallace house site: Mrs. Wallace was Mary's sister Frances.

OTHER DOWNTOWN SITES

22. First Presbyterian Church (present location after 1871), Northwest corner of Seventh and Capitol: Mary's funeral was here. Contains Lincoln's pew from previous location.
23. Miss Corcoran's Academy, the Smiths, and A. W. Estabrook School sites, Northeast corner of Seventh and Edwards: The Lincoln boys attended school here.
24. Home of R. W. Diller and son Isaac.
25. Home of Isaac Diller.
26. James Matheny house site, southwest corner of Sixth and Scarritt: The best man at Lincoln's wedding lived here after 1856.
27. Richard Latham house site, where Lincoln sat and talked.
28. C. M. Smith home, 603 South Fifth: Lincoln's brother-in-law lived here. Poet Vachel Lindsey was born and died in the house, open to the public.

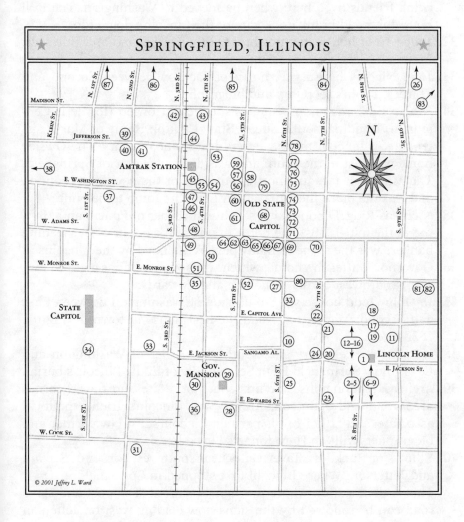

SPRINGFIELD, ILLINOIS

29. Governor's Mansion: Lincoln attended many parties and consulted with the governor.
30. John Todd Stuart house site, 529 South Fourth: First law partner of Lincoln.
31. John Roll house site, southeast corner of Second and Cook: Lincoln's friends lived here when he moved to Washington. The Roll boys, John and Frank, took care of the Lincoln's dog, Fido.
32. Judge Treat house site, northeast corner of Second and Edwards: Lincoln's friend and associate.
33. John Nicolay house site, north of Jackson between Second and Third: Lincoln's secretary and biographer.
34. Ninian Edwards's house site, west edge of Howlett (formerly Centennial) Building, south side of State Capitol: Home of Mary's sister, site of Lincoln marriage, and last home of Mary. The Owsley home was just to the south and was a social center of Springfield. The Mather Estate just north is the site of the new State Capitol, and was the place the city wanted Lincoln's tomb to be built.
35. Nicholas Ridgely house site, southwest corner of Fourth and Monroe in the mid-1850s. The home of one of the community's leading bankers was the scene of many parties attended by the Lincolns.
36. Governor Matteson's home, which was sought after as a gift to Lincoln, Southwest corner of Fourth and Edwards.
37. Dr. John Todd house site, south side of Washington between First and Second: Mary's uncle had the best house in town during the 1830s.
38. Hutchinson Cemetery site, southwest corner of Washington and Lewis, now Springfield High School: Site of Eddie Lincoln's burial.
39. Archer Herndon house and first courthouse sites, northwest corner of Second and Jefferson: Archer was Lincoln's friend, political associate, and father of his partner. Lincoln's last law partner and biographer, William Herndon, also lived here.
40. Elliott's or Buckhorn Tavern site, near southwest corner of Second and Jefferson: Where Lincoln first stopped in Springfield in 1831. This is the location where Springfield started. The post and stage road can be followed by the signs now leading west on Jefferson Street.
41. John Hay's residence site, southeast corner of Second and Jefferson: Lincoln's future secretary and biographer lived here with his uncle, Milton Hay.
42. William Butler house site, southwest corner of Madison and Third: Lincoln boarded from 1837 to 1841, and then lived here until he was married in November 1842.

43. Dr. William Jayne house site, southwest corner of Fourth and Madison: Lincoln's political associate.

44. Spottswood Hotel site, northeast corner of Jefferson and Third: Site where Lincoln and his colleagues celebrated their success in getting the capital of Illinois moved to Springfield.

45. Chicago and Alton Railroad Depot site, slightly north of the present depot on Third between Washington and Jefferson: Lincoln caught trains here, and introduced Ex-President Filmore. His body was received here.

46. Illinois State University, Mechanics Union site, southeast corner of Third and Washington, south of number 48: Robert Lincoln's school in the old church buildings abandoned by First Presbyterian.

47. First Presbyterian Church site, southeast corner of Third and Washington: Site of the church attended by the Lincolns, adjacent to the old church buildings, where Tad was baptized and his funeral was held.

48. Globe Tavern site, 315 Adams: Lincoln and Mary moved here their wedding night on November 4, 1842, and remained until sometime in late 1843. Robert was born in August 1843. During part of the time Lincoln served in Congress in 1848 and 1849, and the family stayed here while his house was rented.

49. St. Paul's Episcopal site, Adams street near the southeast corner with Third Street: The Illinois Supreme Court met here before the new Capitol was completed in the late 1830s. Lincoln addressed the Young Men's Lyceum on January 27, 1838. Mary, before marriage, attended church here with her sister. Robert is reported to have attended Sunday school here.

50. Second Lincoln home site, 214 Fourth Street: The Lincolns lived here from late 1843 until May 1844.

51. Second Presbyterian Church site, 217 South Fourth: Lincoln sat in the House of Representatives, which met here while the Capitol was being completed. He also addressed the Temperance Society in 1842.

52. Methodist Episcopal Church site, southeast corner Fifth and Monroe: Meeting place in November 1840 of the Illinois House of Representatives while Lincoln was a member.

53. St. Nicholas Hotel, 400 East Jefferson: Lincoln attended many social events in an earlier building. Mary was interviewed by William Herndon here after Lincoln's death.

54. Chenery House Hotel site, northeast corner of Fourth and Washington: The Lincoln family stayed here during their last week prior to leaving for Washington in 1861.

55. Johnson Building site, northwest corner of Fourth and Washing-

ton: President-elect Lincoln used this as an office from December 30, 1860, until leaving for Washington.

56. Melvin Drug Store site, northwest corner of Fifth and Washington: Lincoln liked to play checkers with the owner. Beginning December 23, 1860, Lincoln transferred his business here.

57. Law office with Stuart site, 109 North Fifth: Lincoln came to borrow books while living in New Salem, and then practiced law here with his first partner from 1837 until 1841, also a courthouse site.

58. Law office with Logan site, 106 North Fifth: 1841–1843 or 1844.

59. Law office with Herndon site, 110 North Adams:Around 1853 to 1856.

60. Joshua Speed store site: Lincoln came here on April 15, 1837, in the process of moving to Springfield, and lived with Speed until the latter married in 1841. His last law office with Herndon from 1856 until 1861 was in the back of the same building, marked by a plaque. Also site of Williams store where he made purchases. Note the original buildings from Lincoln's time across the street at 425-427 Washington.

61. Chatterton Building, About one third of the block north of Adams on the west side of Fifth: Lincoln called on James Conkling in this old building on May 17, 1860, for a firsthand account of the Republican National Convention. Lincoln bought his wedding ring here.

62. Bunn Banking Building site, southwest corner of Fifth and Adams: Lincoln was attorney for the bankers who helped finance his presidential campaign.

63. Bunn Store site, Southeast corner across from site 62: Frequented by Lincoln. A photographer of Lincoln was in the upper stories.

64. Law office with Herndon site, south side of Adams Street between Fourth and Fifth: Office site in the late 1840s (*Lincoln's Springfield*) or early 1850s (*Lincoln Sites in Springfield*).

65. Watson's Saloon site, 514 Adams: Lincoln first referred to as "Mr. President" after his election in this snack and ice-cream parlor.

66. C.M. Smith Building site, between sites 65 and 67: Lincoln traded in his brother-in-law's store, and used the third floor to write his inaugural address because he could not get peace and quiet anywhere else.

67. Tinsley Building, southwest corner of Sixth and Adams: Lincoln had a law office here with Logan and, later, Herndon. The federal court and post office were also located here. This original building is open to the public.

68. Old State Capitol Building: Reconstructed using the original exterior. Was the scene of famous Lincoln speeches, including the "House Divided" speech, part of Lincoln's term in the General

Assembly, Supreme Court, and libraries frequented by Lincoln. Open to the public.

69. American House site, southeast corner of Sixth and Adams: The Lincolns attended many functions.

70. First Baptist Church and Florville's Barber Shop sites, Adams Street between Sixth and Seventh.

71. Cooks Hall site: Lincoln spoke.

72. Corneau and Diller Drug Store site, middle of block, east side of Sixth between Adams and Washington: Frequented by Lincoln to buy necessities, and also a favorite place to loaf, joke, discuss politics, and tell stories. This was about three doors south of the bank mentioned next.

73. Marine Fire and Casualty Company site 104–108 South Sixth: Lincoln's bank from 1853, and the oldest bank in Illinois. Lincoln's account ledger on display in lobby.

74. Courthouse site, southeast corner of Sixth and Washington: Courthouse where Lincoln tried many cases beginning in 1846 and attended many party caucuses and political rallies.

75. Logan Building site, northeast corner of Washington and Sixth: Lincoln tried at least ninety cases in the federal court after it moved here in 1855.

76. *Illinois State Journal* site, just south of the middle of the block north of the above: Lincoln spent considerable time at this establishment, which favored him. It is generally written that he frequented a telegraph office here on the night of his presidential election, but the office may have been on the north side of the square.

77. Simeon Frances House site, Southeast corner of Sixth and Jefferson: Site of Lincoln and Mary's reconcilement after a year's estrangement.

78. Christian Church site, northeast corner of Sixth and Jefferson: Lincoln attended political meetings.

79. Concert Hall or Myers Hall site, middle of block, north side of Washington between Fifth and Sixth: Lincoln prepared only one lecture in his career, repeated several times including here on February 21, 1859.

80. Lewis Carriage Shop site, Monroe between Sixth and Seventh: Lincoln frequented.

81. Webster Grocery site, south side of Monroe between Ninth and Tenth: Lincoln treated his boys and their friends to nuts and candy.

82. Great Western Railroad Depot, Tenth and Monroe: Lincoln left in 1861 for Washington and gave farewell address on the site.

NORTH OF DOWNTOWN

83. Illinois State University site, in the area of Twelfth, Thirteenth, Enos, and Moffat Streets: Lincoln dedicated a new building for the school in 1854. Robert attended the school.
84. Enos House site, northwest corner of Seventh and Enterprise: Lincoln attended the wedding of O. M. Hatch on December 13, 1860.
85. (Benjamin) Edwards Place, 700 North Fourth: Built in 1833, it is now the oldest home in Springfield and a showplace then and now. The Lincolns visited many times, and Mary stayed in later years. Its fifteen acres were used for political rallies. It is now owned by the Springfield Art Association, and open to the public.
86. Oak Ridge Cemetery: Burial places for the Lincoln family, friends, and relatives.
87. Stephan Logan House site, north of Miller between First and Rutledge: Home of Lincoln's second law partner and friend. Lincoln often visited and played with Logan's eight children.

OTHER SITES

88. Page Eaton House site, west side of Fourth between Wright and Canedy: It is possible that Lincoln approached Eaton at his carpenter's shop on Monroe Street when he was disgusted with his legal career, with the thought of becoming a carpenter. As far-fetched as this sounds, it is believed by some Lincoln students.
89. Ulysses S. Grant House site, 119 South Walnut: Grant lived here for a short time while his headquarters were in Springfield.
90. Clinton Conkling Home site, 802 South Second: Robert stayed in his friend's home while visiting Springfield after his father's death.
91. Camp Butler, six miles east of Springfield: This was the site of the home of Samuel Danley. Lincoln campaigned for the 1834 legislature at Clear Lake, a spring-fed pond (*Oral History of Abraham Lincoln*, pages 11, 134).

STERLING: Lincoln spoke on July 18, 1856, for presidential candidate John C. Fremont. A marker at **607 EAST THIRD STREET** shows where he spent the night as the guest of **WILLIAM MANAHAN**. He was going to stay with Robert L. Wilson, one of the Long Nine he had served with in the General Assembly of Illinois, but Mrs. Wilson was sick. The Manahans were their relatives.

STILLMAN VALLEY: Lincoln helped bury several militiamen who had been killed here May 14, 1835, during the Black Hawk War, at the Battle of Stillman's Run. A monument beside the graves commemorates the battle and is inscribed with the following: "The presence of the soldier, statesman, martyr Abraham Lincoln, assisting in the burial of these honored dead has made this spot more sacred." Lincoln had acted as advance guard of all scouting parties in their advancement north from Beardstown, but was not here at the time of the battle. Evidently, soldiers had encountered Black Hawk's warriors nearby, who waved a flag. Whether it was the white flag for parley or the red for defiance is not known, but the soldiers attacked, maybe under the influence of liquor, without Major Stillman's orders. Then Black Hawk threw in his whole force, causing the raw recruits to flee into a debacle known as Stillman's Run. The warriors went north, and Lincoln arrived the next day. His presence a day earlier might have provided a level, sober head to handle the situation and prevent a premature battle and extended war. It also might have produced one more dead militia captain.

Lincoln spent three nights on the battlefield, May 16, May 20, and June 29, 1832.

SUBLETT: Lincoln was here in 1832.

SULLIVAN: Lincoln is said to have often stayed at the JOE THOMASON HOUSE, and practiced in the MOULTRIE CIRCUIT COURT. Local history says that the circuit riders, including Lincoln and Judge Davis, preferred the JAMES ELDER HOME on the SOUTHWEST CORNER OF MAIN AND HARRISON, across from the courthouse. It is believed that Lincoln visited twice a year for about two days. The courthouse burned down in 1864, destroying most of the records. At one time the prosecuting attorney, David Campbell, got into a fight and tore out the seat of his pants. Other lawyers suggested they buy him new ones, but Lincoln said, "I cannot conscientiously contribute anything to the end in view." (See entry on Danville, Illinois, for a similar story. The many similar stories told about Lincoln could be the results of faulty memory, legend, or repetitions of Lincoln's wit.)

On September 20, 1858, Lincoln and Douglas both spoke, Lincoln in FREELAND'S GROVE, at the site of the entrance to the civic center in WYMAN PARK. This is north of the courthouse where Main and Washington Streets intersect with Scott and Blackwood. At this time, Lincoln stayed at the second ELDER HOME, about a half a mile east of town on Jackson Street, and Douglas stayed with Robert Ginn about five miles east. Lincoln stood on Elder's porch and watched a cheering crowd lead Douglas into town. This was two days after the fourth joint debate at Charleston, Illinois. Their appearance on the same day was a coincidence, although Douglas accused Lincoln of following him around to capitalize on his large crowds. A large crowd had gathered and spent the morning parading Douglas around town and celebrating at the Eagle House, on the northeast corner of Main and Harrison. When Douglas spoke outside at the courthouse, the Republican wagon carrying about a hundred supporters and a band began to proceed around the square. Accounts differ as to exactly what went on, whether the band was playing and whether other attempts were being made to disrupt the Democrats. A riot almost broke out. Lincoln then led his supporters to Freeland Grove, where he spoke.

SYCAMORE: Lincoln camped with his army unit on May 24, 1832, just west of what was later Sycamore.

TAYLORVILLE: Lincoln stayed many times at the **LONG TAVERN** and with Judge H. M. Vandeveer on the north side of the square while practicing law in the **CHRISTIAN COUNTY CIRCUIT COURTHOUSE**.

THEBES: Lincoln practiced in the **COURTHOUSE** from 1854 to 1858.

TOLONO: A boulder in the **VILLAGE PARK** marks the spot where Lincoln last spoke to the people of Illinois as he left the state for Washington, D.C.

TOULON: Lincoln spent the night at the **VIRGINIA HOTEL**, on the south side of the square, on October 8, 1858. He switched trains in town during his January 1861 trip to see his stepmother in Charleston.

TREMONT: Lincoln tried many cases before the county seat moved to Pekin. He spoke at the courthouse on May 2, 1840, for the Whig candidate for president. At that time he "exposed" the Democratic president, Van Buren, of the political sin of advocating Negro suffrage. In April 1850 when the attorneys tried cases for the last time before the removal of the court, Lincoln and others attended a dinner on the grounds of Colonel **PIERRE MENARD'S HOME**, about two miles southwest. Lincoln apologized for coming in his shabby coat, but explained that "traveling is very laborious." Lincoln was attending court when Shields sent him a challenge for a duel (see entry on Alton, Illinois). He was a frequent guest in the **MENARD HOUSE**. It is claimed that David Davis, Lyman Trumbull, and Lincoln came after the 1856 "lost" Bloomington speech to discuss the speech and the organization of the Republican Party.

He probably spoke on October 4, 1856, for Fremont. A marker on the square says he gave a speech on August 30, 1858.

URBANA: A Lincoln Trail memorial on the north side of the **COURT-HOUSE, AT MAIN AND BROADWAY**, marks the place of Lincoln's speeches and court appearances. He argued for the Illinois Central Railroad in 1853. On October 24, 1854, he assailed Douglas and the Kansas-Nebraska Act at the courthouse in what Henry C. Whitney declared was his greatest speech. On June 3, 1855, he stayed at the **PENNSYLVA-NIA HOUSE, ON THE SITE OF THE CHAMPAIGN COUNTY JAIL**. While here on June 20, 1856, he was shown a Chicago newspaper saying he had gotten 110 votes for the Republican Party nomination for vice president.

On April 25, 1858, he had an ambrotype taken in the studio of **SAMUEL G. ALSCHULER, ON MAIN** west of the courthouse. He arrived while Douglas was speaking on September 23, 1858, and went to Mr. Bailey's residence to receive visitors. He also received friends at the **DOANE HOUSE**. The next day, he explained his "House Undivided" speech at the **EVART HOUSE** for about twenty minutes and spoke at the **FAIRGROUNDS**.

VANDALIA: Vandalia was the second capital of Illinois and the terminus of the Cumberland Road, completed at this location in 1838. The first U.S. national highway was started in 1811 in Cumberland, Maryland, and ran 591 miles, connecting the "west" to the center of the young country. The capital of Illinois was moved here in 1820, one year after the founding of the town. All historical sites are easily located south of exit 63 on I-70, down Kennedy Boulevard, which is Route 51. This becomes Third Street at Gallatin Street, the site of the restored Old Capitol.

The small village of Kaskaskia, eighty-five miles below St. Louis on the Mississippi, had been the frontier capital of the new state from 1818, but the population was moving north and the new state needed a central location. The site of the **FIRST CAPITOL BUILDING** located in Vandalia was located on the **NORTHWEST CORNER OF FIFTH AND JOHNSON**. After it burned down on December 9, 1823, another site was chosen for the new building, completed the next year on the west side of **FOURTH STREET JUST NORTH OF GALLATIN**. Here is where Lincoln began his political career when he arrived with his tailor-made, $60 suit in late November 1834 and took his seat on December 1. He shared a room with John Stuart, was considered Stuart's protégé, and was shown around by his future law partner. This capitol was in a state of collapse by the time Lincoln arrived, and members of the legislature almost refused to enter, fearing it was unsafe.

It was razed, and construction began for a new two-story brick building, seen today at **THIRD AND GALLATIN**, across the street from its prede-cessor. This third capitol, or **OLD STATEHOUSE**, was restored beginning in 1933, when it ceased to serve as the courthouse for Fayette County. It housed all three branches of government and was the scene of Lincoln's service in three sessions from December 3, 1836, until 1839.

To win a seat in the legislature, a candidate from Lincoln's county, Sangamon, had to be among the top four vote-getters. Although Lin-coln was a Whig, the Democrats offered to support him in order to elect three Democrats and Lincoln rather than the experienced Whig, Stuart. Lincoln discussed the proposal with Stuart, who thought he could win anyway, and did with Lincoln and two Democrats. At the end of his first term, Lincoln was paid $258 for services and expenses and traveled back to New Salem in subzero weather by stagecoach.

His second term began in December 1836 in the present **OLD STATE-HOUSE**. During this time he worked for passage of an ambitious inter-nal improvements bill and made a long speech in the House on January 11, 1837, opposing a resolution to investigate the state bank. This would have damaged the state's ability to finance improvement proj-ects. In his first published speech, Lincoln announced that he would oppose any move to injure the bank's credit. During this time he also worked in earnest to become a lawyer. Following the legislative session ending in March 1837, he was enrolled as an attorney in the building before the Supreme Court. It was not customary for lawyers to attend law school, but to study with an established attorney who would certify as to his legal knowledge before the court. The last session of the Gen-eral Assembly of Illinois to meet in the statehouse closed on March 4, 1839. The legislature gave the building to the county and the city, and it was used both as a county courthouse and school. The state purchased the building in 1918 to insure its preservation.

Lincoln and his Long Nine friends were largely instrumental in removing the capital to Springfield in 1839. Charges of corruption came almost immediately from the foes of relocation. Many claimed that Springfield-area legislators, Lincoln included, had supported pub-lic works projects throughout Illinois in return for votes to make Springfield the new capital, which was hotly denied. The colleagues celebrated their victory in **EBENEZER CAPP'S TAVERN AND STORE, AT FOURTH AND MAIN**, where Lincoln was toasted: "He fulfilled the expec-tations of his friends, and disappointed the hopes of his enemies." Lin-coln responded: "All our friends: they are too numerous to mention now individually, while there is not one of them who is not too dear to be forgotten or neglected." This site is a block north of the Statehouse, and was the largest retail and wholesale store in southern Illinois.

Several generations have heard the story still told here of how Lincoln jumped out the front window to avoid being counted in a quorum call; however, this story is not documented and probably never happened (see a similar story attributed to the Methodist Church in Springfield, Illinois). During the last session, Lincoln's horse was stolen, and he had to walk home with the other members of the Long Nine. When he complained about being cold, one of them replied, "No wonder, there is so much of you on the ground!" (see a similar story in the comments for Dixon, Illinois). When he got back to New Salem, he borrowed a horse from Bowling Green and rode this horse when he moved to Springfield.

Lincoln rented a room at **615 WEST JOHNSON** and also at **419 GALLATIN**. He stayed in **CHARTER'S HOTEL** then located on the **NORTHWEST CORNER OF FOURTH AND GALLATIN AND FLACKS HOTEL ON THE SOUTHEAST CORNER**. Other historic sites around the present Capitol Square are noted in maps and guides readily available in the area. No original buildings remain except the Statehouse, open as a museum. This is fully restored, showing the House and Senate Chambers, Supreme Court where Lincoln was sworn as a member of the bar, and other state offices. A good map and guidebook is available at the old Statehouse showing other historic sites. The Evans Public Library at 215 South Fifth has an excellent collection of Lincoln books and material, including the Henry B. Rankin collection.

Lincoln returned to speak September 23, 1856, at a Frémont meeting in the **OLD STATEHOUSE** and was guest of Mayor Glover at his home on August 21 and 22, 1858.

VERMONT: On October 27, 1858, Lincoln stayed at the residence of **COLONEL THOMAS HAMER**. He ate and spoke in town. He stood under an umbrella to speak to a crowd of over one thousand. Evidently he was a frequent guest. A marker at **VILLAGE PARK** on Main Street notes his visit.

VERSAILLES: Lincoln practiced law in the **WOODFORD CIRCUIT COURT** in 1841, which was held in a schoolhouse before the county seat was set up in Metamora.

VIRGINIA: Lincoln attended a Whig meeting for the Cass County Clay Club in the **COURTHOUSE**, at Main and Springfield, on February 22, 1844. He spoke on banking and currency issues during the afternoon, and evidently spoke in the evening and next day. The *Sangamo Journal* reported: "'Aunt Becky' [Lincoln's 1842 nom de plume] felt it her duty to deliver herself of a soul stirring harangue. She opened her wise head—'broke up the fountains of the great deep' of natal depravity; and rained 'a horrible tempest' of billingsgate, and vulgar party vitupera-tion on the devoted head of Van Buren."

WATERLOO: Lincoln spent several days in late August 1840, and spoke at the **COURTHOUSE** on August 25. One newspaper commented that he "seemed like a man traveling over unknown ground."

WAUKEGAN: Lincoln spoke in **DICKINSON HALL** on April 2, 1860, and started what is called the only speech that he did not finish, although there were others. He was addressing about four hundred when he was interrupted by a fire alarm outside. One of the listeners arose to state his belief that the alarm was a Democratic plot to break up the meeting. But the audience was uneasy. Lincoln finally stopped and said, "Well gentlemen, lets us all go, as there really seems to be a fire, and help to put it out." Prior to the speech he was a guest of **MAYOR ELISH P. FERRY.**

WINCHESTER: The **SCOTT COUNTY COURTHOUSE** is at the northeast corner of the square on a spot formerly occupied by the **AKIN TAVERN** where Lincoln stayed in 1854. The old courthouse was where the Dou-glas statue is now on the square. A boulder adjacent to the statue marks the site of Lincoln's first speech, August 1854, in which he referred to the Kansas-Nebraska issue. He had been quiet up to now about the issue creating a political storm throughout the nation, the passage of the Kansas-Nebraska Act. The Scott County Whig conven-tion gave him a forum to restart his political voice, leading to the nation's highest office.

Much controversy was created when it was proposed to tear down the hotel and old courthouse so that a park could be created in the cen-ter of the square. Another marker on the square notes that Douglas moved here from the state of Vermont in 1833, where he taught school and began his law practice. The schoolhouse is marked just to the north of the public square on the east side of Main Street. He arrived with thirty-seven and a half half cents in his pockets and taught from November 1833 until the next March.

On September 28, 1858, Lincoln spoke at a meeting west of town and spent the next day at the office of John Moses, on the south side of the courthouse square. He went over various issues of the *Congres-sional Globe* that Moses had indexed, and then spoke at the courthouse in the evening.

Indiana

L incoln lived fourteen of his fifty-six years, from 1816 to 1830, on a tract of land in what is now Spencer County, Indiana. The family arrived on about December 11, 1816, the day the state was admitted to the Union. Now they could expect land with a clear title rather than the confusion of titles in Kentucky. Most early biographers show that the family is believed to have come in the ferry operated by Hugh Thompson from the Kentucky side of the Ohio River, opposite the mouth of the Anderson, to the mouth of the Anderson River just west of Troy, Indiana. This would have been the closest point to their land. However, the Lincoln Memorial Highway Commission says the family crossed at Hawkesville and landed at Cannelton, eight miles south, downriver from the Anderson. Others put the arrival at Bates Landing in Troy. From the north side of the Ohio they made their way up a primitive road or trace to their land, which Lincoln later described as about as hard a time as he ever had. The condition and even existence of a road is questionable. At least four miles were cut through thick underbrush and grapevine-invested virgin forest.

The family lived here until 1830, during which time Lincoln's mother died and Thomas remarried, to probably the "greatest stepmother in history." Lincoln acquired the traits that would see him become what some considered our "greatest statesman and humanitarian." The farm is now part of the Lincoln Boyhood National Memorial that contains the homesite, Memorial Visitor's Center, and Nancy Lincoln grave. A state park nearby contains the sites of many boyhood scenes including the Little Pigeon Church, grave of his sister, school sites, and cabins of friends. Lincoln helped with the family farm to produce food and helped his father in the carpentry business. The boy also hired out as a ferryman and laborer in the area. He went to New Orleans in 1828 to carry a load of goods for his friend James Gentry, and is claimed to have worked in Louisville, Kentucky. Although he reached his twenty-first year and was then free from parental obligation, he accompanied his family to Illinois in 1830 to make a new life there.

He did not return to the state until 1844. Lincoln wrote in 1848, "In the Fall of 1844 thinking I might aid in carrying the state of Indiana for Mr. Clay, I went into the neighborhood in that state in which I was raised, where my mother and only sister were buried and from which I had been absent about fifteen years." Lincoln evidently made many speeches on this trip. Only one (Rockport) was recorded, and many are unknown. He later passed through the state several times for legal work, political speeches, and to assume the presidency in February 1861.

Many stories and incidents related to Lincoln's early life rely on the memory of people who recorded their versions of events many years after their experiences. These stories may be based on faulty reminiscences and conjecture. Therefore several versions may exist, and many beliefs and "facts" set out in any study of Lincoln's early life are questionable and vary from source to source. Huck Finn would have called some of the stories "stretchers." I have generally followed Dr. Louis Warren's *Lincoln's Youth* where the facts in other accounts differ, although varying stories are sometimes mentioned. National Park Rangers in Indiana and Kentucky as well as local historians in both areas believe Warren's work is the most accurate, although there are many unknowns and conflicts with other more recent authors.

BATTLE GROUND: The funeral train passed by on May 1, 1865, at 3:55 A.M., as three hundred people slowly waved flags.

BOONVILLE: As a teenager, Lincoln came to hear cases being tried in the courthouse. He got the first glimpse of circuit practice that later occupied many years of his life and is now a long-vanished institution. He may have borrowed books from attorney **JOHN BRACKENRIDGE**, discussed law, and heard him try cases in the courthouse. When the old lawyer called on President Lincoln in the White House, Lincoln recalled Brackenridge's argument in a murder trial and remarked, "If I could . . . have made as good a speech as that, my soul would have been satisfied; for it was up to that time the best speech I ever heard."

The family stopped in town on the way to Illinois in 1830, and Lincoln bought articles to sell on the road. He returned in October 1844 on his speech-making tour for Henry Clay's presidential campaign and visited with Brackenridge, also an elector for Clay. A correspondent at Boonville on June 5, 1860, wrote to the Evansville *Daily Journal* that "Mr. Lincoln passed through the town some years ago and made a speech in our courthouse. All who heard him (without distinction of party) concur in saying he made one of the best speeches ever heard in this place. His speech was mainly on the tariff question."

BRUCEVILLE: The Lincoln family passed through on their 1830 migration to Illinois and stopped to water their horses at the public well. Lincoln spoke for Henry Clay at the **OLD SCHOOLHOUSE** in late October 1844 in a grove of walnut trees opposite the later Christian Church. This is now **WASHINGTON STREET**, the north side of Route 550, just west of the post office, a block north of the **BRUCE HOUSE**. The place was packed, evidencing the fact that widespread publicity in advance had excited great interest in this forceful speaker. After speaking about five minutes, an alarm was sounded that a huge gang of Democrats was sweeping into town to break up the meeting. Lincoln sat quietly as the audience filed out to confront the situation. It seemed that bloodshed was unavoidable as a Democrat was attempting to speak in an open buggy above the roar of both factions. Cooler heads prevailed, the crowd faded, and Lincoln's audience returned to find him calmly waiting to finish his speech.

Afterward he spent the night at the home of **MAJOR WILLIAM BRUCE** on the southeast corner of **WASHINGTON AND FRONT STREETS**. The home was razed in 1940. (Most references to the site give an erroneous location. Even locals are not aware of it, but a marker noting the site is across the street, covered in brush.) It is not known how many of Bruce's twenty-five children were home at the time.

CAMBRIDGE CITY: Lincoln's funeral train passed at 4:15 A.M., "received with a salvo of artillery and a very tasty arch . . . across the tracks."

CENTERVILLE: Lincoln's funeral train passed through the depot at 3:24 A.M. on April 30, 1865, with about two thousand people formed on both sides of the track.

CHARLOTTVILLE: Lincoln's funeral train passed by at 5:40 A.M. on April 30, 1865, with "many colored people at the depot."

CLARK'S HILL: A congregation at the depot at 2:40 A.M. on May 1, 1865, met the funeral train.

COVINGTON: Some believe Lincoln may have handled cases here, as it is near Danville, Illinois, where he had a substantial practice and time between court sessions. He also was a friend of local attorney Daniel Voorhees, and came in 1844 to the **HIIGLE HOTEL** on the Danville Road. He met that night with several visitors at his hotel including the Honorable Edward Hannegan. On the following day he went to Hannegan's law office, from which both went to THE COURT-HOUSE where Lincoln was introduced to the court. Since he represented an estate from Springfield, he needed to be admitted to the local bar. Hannegan stressed that the applicant was "twenty-one years of age, good looking, and fine moral character" and the best storyteller he ever heard.

DUBLIN: The funeral train passed under an arch at 4:27 A.M. on April 30, 1865.

EVANSVILLE: The *Evening Journal* of Evansville on October 31, 1844, advertised a meeting of the Clay Whig Club at the COURTHOUSE Friday, November 1. The announcement stated that several speeches would be made and that the public was invited to attend. Inasmuch as Lincoln was apparently in the community, it is very likely he addressed the group, although his name does not appear in the newspapers.

FRANCESVILLE: Crowds flocked the funeral train at 5:45 A.M. on May 1, 1865.

FORT WAYNE: The Lincoln Museum and Library have the largest private collection of organized information on Lincoln. Lincoln's only direct connection was that he got off the train at 1:00 A.M. on February 23, 1860, for a short time to change trains on the way to give his Cooper Union Address in New York City. He changed trains again March 13, on the way back.

GRANDVIEW: A marker erected in the 1930s claimed Lincoln visited a tannery there. Locals claimed he worked here and danced at the **LYNN HOUSE**, built for Peter Lahue by Tom Lincoln. This is two miles south on Highway 66. A marker in front of the library notes that Lincoln traveled this way with an ox team hauling barrel hoop poles to the river for shipment.

GREENSBURG: Lincoln's inaugural train stopped, and the president-elect was presented with a large red apple before a speech to about two thousand.

INDIANAPOLIS: It is unknown when Lincoln first visited the state capital. There are stories about traveling with Colonel Tom Nelson and Bayless Hanna in a stagecoach from Terre Haute to Indianapolis in 1847 as Lincoln went to take his seat in Congress. However, it is generally believed that Lincoln and his family went by boat from St. Louis to Louisville and did not pass through Indiana. It is possible that this trip with Nelson and Hanna occurred in 1855 when Lincoln went to Cincinnati in his involvement in the *McCormick Reaper* case, but no evidence verifies this. *Lincoln Day by Day* shows that he came on June 13, 1849, on the way to Washington to seek an appointment as Commissioner for the Land Office with Nelson and Abram Hammond, later governor of Indiana, and stayed in **BROWNINGS HOTEL**.

He did speak on September 19, 1859, evidently his first public appearance. Mary and Tad accompanied him on a trip to Ohio where he had made arrangements for several speeches and passed through Indiana en route. He was persuaded at that time or by correspondence received at his destination to appear in Indianapolis. Returning from Cincinnati in the afternoon, he was entertained at the **AMERICAN HOUSE AT 18 LOUISIANA STREET** where Union Terminal is now located. In the evening, he spoke at the **MASONIC HALL** then on the **SOUTHEAST CORNER OF WASHINGTON AND CAPITAL** at the present site of the Hyatt Hotel. One of the newspapers commented that this was the first time he had appeared before a large audience in Indiana. He told them that he had been brought to Indiana in his eighth year and "grew up to his present enormous height in our own good soil of Indiana." He recalled the "unbroken wilderness there then, and an ax was put in his hand and with the trees and logs and grubs he fought until he reached his twentieth year." According to the *Illinois State Journal*, he made two other speeches in the state, but there is no record where. This first recorded speech in Indianapolis was all but forgotten until an inquiring reporter turned up the fact in 1907. The speech itself was not in the papers then and not found until 1927.

Lincoln arrived February 11, 1861, on his inauguration trip at the railroad siding at **MISSOURI AND WASHINGTON STREETS** near the Capitol at about 5:00 P.M. A state office building stands there now. There is a marker on the north side of Washington between West and Senate Streets noting his movements. After a brief welcoming and remarks, a parade was held **EAST ALONG WASHINGTON, NORTH ALONG PENNSYLVANIA,**

WEST ALONG OHIO, AND SOUTH ON ILLINOIS STREET TO THE BATES HOUSE at the NORTHWEST CORNER OF ILLINOIS AND WASHINGTON. There was no room for Robert in the carriage, and he had to walk. Later the Claypool Hotel was here for many years, and the site is now Claypool Court. Two small boys each handed him a packet containing twenty-five calling cards and asked him to sign one. He signed all fifty.

He appeared on the south hotel balcony three different times. Members of the legislature were received at 7:00 P.M. and the public at 8:00. In responding to the greeting by the governor, he stated, "If the Union of these States and the liberties of the people be lost, it is but little to any one man of fifty-two years of age, but a great deal to the thirty millions of people who inhabit these United States and to their posterity in all coming time." For years a plaque on the Claypool Hotel quoted part of Lincoln's appeal as follows: "I appeal to you again to constantly bear in mind that not with politicians, not with presidents, not with office seekers but with you is the question, Shall the Union and the liberties of this country be preserved to the latest generation."

The next morning the party including Robert, Colonel Elmer Ellsworth, and others walked to the GOVERNOR'S MANSION for breakfast, a block north at the NORTHWEST CORNER OF ILLINOIS AND MARKET. Afterward he addressed the legislature at the Capitol located on the southern half of the current location on the NORTHWEST CORNER OF WASHINGTON AND CAPITOL. The building was in a state of advanced deterioration by the 1870s and was replaced with a much larger one now occupying an area two blocks long. Mary and the younger boys arrived from Springfield that morning and the party proceeded toward Washington.

Several sources report that Robert lost the only copy of his father's inaugural address here, although the city may have been somewhere else. He was told to be careful with the package, but not told what it was, and left it with a desk clerk. When he realized what he had done, he ran to the desk, scared and out of breath, and found it in a pile of luggage. His father did not scold him, but handed it back and just told him, "Now you keep it." This story is sometimes told as happening in other cities. Most sources, including John Nicolay's daughter, Robert's biographer, and *Journey to Greatness*, place it in Indianapolis. Biographer David H. Donald believes Lincoln did then show anger at one of his children for perhaps the only time in his life. Ward Hill Lamon says he never saw Lincoln more angry.

The funeral train carrying Lincoln's remains passed through the city on April 30, 1865, where a hundred thousand viewed them at the Statehouse from 9:00 A.M. to 11:00 P.M.

JASPER: At the eastern edge at the Patoka River is **ENLOW'S MILL**, where the Lincoln family often came to have their grain ground. Thomas once brought a desk here that he had made and traded it for meal. The Lincolns lived about halfway between here and **HOFFMAN'S MILL** on Anderson Creek and divided their trade among the two places. Lincoln is said to have come to Hoffman's often to see his friend, Hoffman's son. The mill was on the Spencer-Perry County line east of New Boston. The story of Abe's kick in the head by a mule is sometimes told as happening here, but it is generally believed to have been at Gorden's Mill close to their home.

LACROSS: The funeral train passed by at 7:50 A.M. on May 1, 1865, where there "was a nice demonstration."

LAFAYETTE: On the way to Washington, D.C., on February 11, 1861, Lincoln spoke at length about the great changes that had taken place since his boyhood. He recognized that "while some of us may differ in political opinion, still we are all united in one feeling for the Union." His funeral train passed by at 3:35 A.M. on May 1, 1865. A large band played "appropriate airs."

LAWRENCEBURG: Lincoln's inaugural train was greeted by an immense crowd. Lincoln said he hoped that all were Union men and friendly with their neighbors across the river. A marker on the crest of the Ohio River levee notes the event.

LEBANON: Lincoln's inaugural train passed through, but since the town was very unfriendly to him and the paper suggested that they had "seen enough of him," it is not clear whether he made a public address or not. The funeral train came this way at 1:30 A.M. on May 1, 1865, under "a beautiful arch of evergreen and roses . . . fested with velvet rosettes, miniature banners, etc."

LEWISVILLE: (HENRY COUNTY): The funeral train passed through on April 30, 1865.

LINCOLN CITY AND GENTRYVILLE: Lincoln City was laid out in 1872 on ground that was once part of the Lincoln farm. The homesite and the cemetery containing the grave of Lincoln's mother are now in the **LINCOLN BOYHOOD NATIONAL MEMORIAL**. The cabin was about a mile and a half east of Gentryville, although that town was not platted until 1854. The last Lincoln home site is marked by a low rectangular wall containing the fireplace, made of stones sometimes said to be original (but now replaced with replicas) and set in its proper position. This may have been a fireplace Thomas was working on when the family left for Illinois or was possibly where the cabin was located before moving. Nearby is a cabin believed to be a close reproduction built from parts of several period cabins.

The Lincoln family settled in the area in 1816 and lived possibly on various sites until 1830. Park Rangers mention several possible places, but no one knows for sure. Some of the old settlers met at the cabin that was here in 1865 after the president died. This was later moved and transported off as a tourist attraction and then lost. A school was built just southeast and the trees were completely cleared. The cabin site was home base for the ball field. A movement started during World War I, and a group of elderly residents met in 1917 to determine the correct site of the cabin. It was dug up, and the stones were found indicating the location of the fireplace at the spot now preserved.

This was virgin forest when the family arrived, and it required hard work to clear the area of the large trees that had grown undisturbed for eons. Thomas Lincoln brought his family here with the promise of good soil free from disputed titles that had disrupted his life in Kentucky. A lean-to may have been ready when they arrived, or in a few days. Thomas had claimed the land shortly before moving by cutting trees to mark a boundary, and he had started a shelter. It is not known how or exactly where the family lived for the first few months. They survived for a undetermined period in the lean-to or half-faced camp, a simple shelter of three sides and an open side where the fire burned continually in the bitter winter. The floor was simply leaves, replaced from time to time. Later, maybe days, weeks, or several months, they moved into a cabin probably eighteen by twenty feet. (Nicolay and Hay wrote that they lived in the lean-to for a "whole year.") Reason would hold that carpenter Thomas would have built a cabin in a few days during the bitter winter with logs previously cut by those who knew of his arrival, probably with the help from neighbors.

Food the first year was almost all game from the woods consisting of bear, turkeys, deer, squirrels, and rabbits. No one bathed until spring warmed the waters, and then infrequently. Much of the first year was spent girdling the large trees, letting them die, and felling others and setting fire to them. In this way the land was cleared for a few acres of crops. More and more trees were cleared each year until the total area farmed was about forty acres. Eventually, Tom would grow enough wheat for the luxury of a cake and would acquire a cow, sheep, and hogs. It is possible that Nancy taught Abe some book learning, and cousin Dennis Hanks, who had been to a Baptist meetinghouse school, taught him further. Nancy probably could read some, but may not have been able to write. She was later described as very intelligent, as was her son who could write at an early age, and wrote letters for his neighbors.

In 1818 the site was on the Corydon-Evansville Road, now Route 162. Two or three years later a road was laid out from Rockport to Bloomington, now Route 231. **JAMES GENTRY** started a TRADING POST at his home a few hundred yards east of the crossroads at Gentryville, and later at the crossroads. The historical marker on the north side of Route 162, the road to the National Memorial Park, says, "On this spot . . ." was the Gentry home. But the exact site is down a trail several hundred yards to the north and easily accessible. Another store was then established about half a mile north of where Route 162 is now and a quarter mile east of Route 62. This is not marked and is about midway between the Gentry home site and Route 62 to the northwest.

Nancy Hanks Lincoln Gravesite: Lincoln's mother is buried beside her aunt and uncle who are said to have raised her, although this even is in question. In 1818, Lincoln's mother, Nancy, and several other members of the extended family and circle of friends became sick with a mysterious illness with no known cure and causing quick death. No doctor at the time could provide any relief. It was not discovered until many decades later that the cause of the problem was the poisonous white snakeroot plant that retained water and was sought after by cows. The milk carries the poison to humans. The only thing known at the time was that when the cows got sick humans soon followed. Betsy and Thomas Sparrow had followed the Lincolns to Indiana and died of the disease in the fall of 1818, in spite of Nancy's care. Their foster son, Dennis Hanks, ten years older than Abe, moved in with the Lincolns, as did Dennis's half-brothers, Squire and William Hall. (Another Nancy Hanks was their mother. One source says Dennis moved to Indiana when the Lincolns did, but this is unsupported. Also, some accounts mention Sophia Hanks as living with the Sparrows when they died, and then moving in with the Lincolns for a short time. The relationship with Nancy Lincoln and the Sparrows is shown differently in various sources. In some they raised Nancy, and she knew them as mother and father. In other sources she was raised by the Richard Berrys, and the Sparrows are not mentioned.)

Nancy was taken ill and died on October 5, 1818. She was buried in a rough coffin made by her husband with little pegs carved by her son. The grave was located next to the Sparrows' burial spot, about a quar-

ter mile from the home cabin, and remained unmarked during the lifetime of her son. It cannot be certain as to the exact location even now,
but the approximate spot is marked in the cemetery. Old neighbors got
together in 1879 to try to identify the spot. The small cemetery became
covered with weeds, and was not marked until a South Bend industri-
alist had a stone placed in the late 1870s. The stone gives her age at
death as thirty-five years, but no one seems to know where that fact
came from or if it is accurate. No doubt Lincoln visited the site many
times as a boy. It is thought that he revisited the graves of his mother
and sister in October 1844 when he returned to make political
speeches in the area. Probably Lincoln never recovered from the death
of his mother; much of his melancholia and near-suicidal depressions
throughout his life relate to the early loss of this lonely nine-year-old.
William Herndon wrote that he stood by her grave longing, no doubt
like many others since then, to be able to whisper into her ear, "Your
son was President."

The Hall brothers soon left the picture, and Abe lived with his father,
sister, and Dennis until his father remarried. About a year after his wife
died, Thomas Lincoln went back to Elizabethtown, Kentucky, and
brought a new wife, Sarah Bush Johnston, with her three children.
There is speculation that Tom had been in love with Sarah Bush in earlier years, but he was ten or twelve years older. When he took a flatboat
to New Orleans with one of her brothers, she married Daniel Johnston,
who had died in 1816. Tom looked up Sarah, or Sally (also "Sallie") as
she was known, and proposed that since both were widowed, they
might as well get hitched. She hesitated because of several debts, but
Tom paid them off and moved the brood of three children back to Indiana in December 1819. It is not known what Tom told his family before
leaving for Kentucky, but it is supposed that the arrival of a new family
surprised them. Dennis later said that they "knowed what he went fur,
but we didn't think he'd have any luck, bein pore as he was, and with
two children to raise." Sally's children were John, probably aged ten
(four, five, seven, eight, or nine given in various sources); Matilda,
about five or eight; and Elizabeth, age nine, twelve, or thirteen,
depending on the source.

No one knows exactly where the cabin was when Tom returned from
Kentucky with his new wife and Lincoln's new brother and sisters. Historian Louis Warren believes there were three structures: (1) half-face
camp built to show possession where they lived upon arrival; (2) one
cabin they lived in for fourteen years; and (3) a new cabin started in
1829 and never completed. The latter is now shown as "the home," but
may never have been lived in. Only the latter site is marked at the park.

There is some speculation that the other cabin was either about fifty feet west of the marked site or about three hundred yards east in what is now a cornfield along the first road to the east. There is also conjecture that Thomas made a new cabin for his new wife after she arrived or that the previous cabin was expanded upon Sarah's arrival or just before moving to Illinois. Old settlers' memories and statements of what happened to the structure or structures and where they were have differed widely.

Many pioneers remembered Abe for his storytelling, pranks, and being involved in barn raisings all over the area. The storytelling ability must have come from his father, who Dennis Hanks claimed "could beat his son telling a story, cracking a joke." It was probably at their last cabin that Lincoln played one of his jokes on his stepmother. After the interior of the cabin had been newly whitewashed, he picked up a youngster who had been walking in the mud and lifted him so that his muddy footprints appeared on the ceiling as if he had walked across.

The number of people in the cabin constantly changed. Abe's half sister Elizabeth married Dennis in June 1821, when she was about fourteen, and they soon moved about a mile east to their own cabin. This site is now just east of a Buffalo Burger restaurant on the road to Santa Claus and just east of Heritage Hills High School. Matilda, about fifteen, married in the home cabin later on September 14, 1826, to Squire Hall. Church weddings were rare, and marriages generally occurred in the home. It is presumed that the two couples lived together temporarily after the marriage. Their children wandered in and out of the Lincoln cabin and sometimes lived there. Cousin John Hanks moved up from Kentucky and moved in with the family. Later he led the family to Illinois.

LINCOLN STATE PARK, south of the Lincoln Boyhood Home National Memorial on State Route 162, contains many sites of these boyhood years. The present LITTLE PIGEON PRIMITIVE BAPTIST CHURCH stands about ninety feet to the northwest of where the original church stood when attended by Lincoln and his family. It contains the original cornerstone incorporated into the foundation. Guide maps to the area erroneously state that this is the same site William Herndon visited after Lincoln's death. He said that the main church door faced east, and you could walk 150 feet east from there to SARAH LINCOLN GRIGSBY'S GRAVE. This would place the original church at a spot now in the middle of the graveyard, a little south of the present, larger structure. Lincoln's sister's grave was one of the first ones here. Her death had a profound affect on her sensitive brother.

The church was located near a spring where, Herndon wrote, "Abe had kneeled and drank a thousand times." The site was near **SAMUEL HOWELL'S CABIN**, about a hundred yards west down the present park trail by the church. Lincoln worked to remember sermons to quote to his stepmother when she could not attend church. At age twelve he helped his father and others build the small church and make the pews. At fourteen, he was the church sexton in charge of keeping the facilities in order and supplying firewood and candles. His parents were members, and his father was trustee for several years. Youngsters could not join until of age, and generally not before they married. Lincoln listened to the sermons well, and would stand on a stump and recite them from start to finish to his friends and family, mimicking the gestures and voices of the preachers.

The **GORDEN MILL** and home sites are marked on Trail 5 in the state park, south of the church, and east of the amphitheater. The mill is where ten-year-old Abe was kicked by a horse he had hit because he thought it was too slow. Later he told the story that "he was believed killed." Thomas was summoned and carried his unconscious boy home. He was thought to be dying, and neighbors gathered by the bed during the night, expecting the worst. He recovered in the morning, much to everyone's surprise. When he came to, he said, "You old hussy." He felt that he had thought that before being kicked, but did not have time to speak it. He then carried the thought in his mind and spoke it when he woke up. The boy probably suffered a concussion. At least one historian has suggested that this caused "petit mal" and possibly brought on attacks of transient aphasia, where Lincoln would drift off into another world or be asleep momentarily while apparently awake.

The "pretend sermons" he practiced gave him a start in a career dependent upon speaking ability and holding crowds with oratory and clear reasoning ability, although some neighbors were upset at his supposed mocking of their preachers. After his Cooper Union Address in 1860, someone asked him how he gained such knowledge of the English language. Lincoln replied, "If I have a power that way, I will tell you how I suppose I came to get it. You see, when I was a boy over in Indiana, all the local politicians used to come to our cabin to discuss politics with my father. After they left, I'd lay awake for hours just a-puttin' their idea into words so that the boys around our way could understand."

Lincoln was especially close to his sister who was quiet, but laughed the hardest at his jokes. Sarah married at age eighteen to Aaron Grigsby. The wedding probably took place at the Lincoln cabin on August 2, 1826. Reuben Grigsby, Aaron's father, and his family lived about a mile to the south of Noah Gorden over the ridge. She died at age twenty during childbirth. Lincoln always blamed his in-laws for calling a doctor too late, and her death had a profound effect on him. During a raw January winter in 1828, Sarah was experiencing severe labor problems, but no doctor or midwife was called until her husband ran for help from his parents who lived about three quarters of a mile southwest. Abe was there doing carpentry work in the smokehouse. Sarah was then loaded into a sled box and slithered across rough hillsides and valleys to the Grigsby house when a doctor was called. He was too drunk to do any good and had to be put to bed himself. Several women experienced as midwife came, and finally another doctor was summoned who lived a considerable distance away. But no one could help. Another version of the story puts Abe at Reuben's in a smokehouse doing carpentry work when Aaron ran up to say Sarah and her baby had just died. Abe sat in the doorway and buried his face in his hands, crying. Sarah and her stillborn child's grave is prominently marked in the churchyard.

Lincoln's sister's house was about two miles south of the Lincoln cabin, and is south of the southeast edge of the **NOAH GORDEN TRAIL** or Trail 3 in the Sarah Lincoln Woods Nature Preserve, part of the state park. It is not marked, but must have been about the spot of a long-standing fenced foliage test site enclosure about two hundred yards south of the trail.

About a half mile to the east of Sarah's cabin was the home of **JOSIAH CRAWFORD**, a site inaccessible now. Tom Lincoln was hired to build the cabin, and his son helped. Later Abe heard that Crawford had a copy of Ramsay's *Life of Washington* that he had heard was much better than *Weems's Life of Washington,* which he had devoured repeatedly. Lincoln was able to borrow it, but it was damaged in a rainstorm during Abe's possession. To make amends with Crawford, he was able to work three days in Crawford's cornfield, which also allowed him to keep the book, probably worth only about seventy-five cents. In other versions of the story, this was Weems's book. Crawford also hired Lincoln to make fence rails, later identified in 1860 by their notches, length, and size to be used for his 1860 political campaign and for souvenirs.

COLONEL WILLIAM JONES STATE HISTORIC SITE was located on the crossroads of the old Boonville-Corydon Road with the Rockport-Bloomington Road. It is now on a back road west of U.S. 231 and well marked. This is the home of an Indiana politician and Union Army soldier who once employed Lincoln in his store. Jones, probably one of Lincoln's earliest political influences, was a Whig representative in the state legislature. Abe got along well with him even though he openly sold slaves, violating the Indiana Constitution. Jones took the Louisville newspaper, which made the store a gathering place to find out the news and discuss politics and events. Lincoln became known for his stories and talk, as a kind of backwoods orator. He became an avid reader of any newspaper he could get, and he soon became a self-appointed news commentator for the entire village. Very few settlers could read and write. Thus, Lincoln was the main source of all the information coming from the outside world. James Gentry opened a rival store, which did not do too well, so he bought out Jones and kept Lincoln in the trade (the Gentry-Romine store was at the southeast corner of the crossroads). The family passed the Jones store on the way to Illinois, and Lincoln bought goods, which were sold on the way, doubling his $30 investment. The house, open to the public, dates from 1834, several years after Lincoln's time, although he probably saw it on his trip back in 1844.

At age seventeen, Abe lived at the home of James Taylor near Troy. Several girls are mentioned linked to him, but nothing serious resulted. Some accounts tell of a trip at this age with his friend Jefferson Ray in 1826. They were said to have taken a flatboat of produce down the Ohio and Mississippi to Memphis to sell on the Tennessee and Arkansas shores. He then worked in the cottonfields beside slaves on Sheriff William D. Ferguson's plantation in Crittenden County, Arkansas, adjacent to Wappanocca Lake, to earn money to return home. The truth of this is questionable, but some trip may have been taken with Ray. Lincoln reviewed and did not change a biography he read in 1860, relating that his first trip to New Orleans was in 1828, implying that there were no other river trips, including one to Memphis. This trip is not reported in Louis Warren's or Ida Tarbell's works after their exhaustive research. It is not mentioned in Herndon's interviews of the neighbors in the area. (Warren does relate that Ferguson claimed Lincoln worked for him in 1828.)

Lincoln spent much of his time with the Gentrys and worked for about nine months at their store. In 1828, James Gentry hired him to go with his son, Allen, on a flatboat loaded with produce to New Orleans. Allen had been there once before and was a year or two older than Abe. The trip lasted about three months, and Abe made $24. They spent three days in New Orleans, saw slaves being sold, and took a steamer back to Rockport. There is also a story told that he worked in Louisville, but had to flee after defending a slave against his master (see entry on Louisville, Kentucky).

Lincoln attended three schools nearby. In 1820 he went several months to the school of **ANDREW CRAWFORD**, two hundred yards east of the church. This was the first time he had been to school in about four years. In 1822, he irregularly attended the James Sweeny or **"SWANEY" SCHOOL** that was probably located just southeast of the current lake in the park (Warren shows this about three miles southwest of the church). Swaney was twenty-one and could barely read and write himself. Later, in 1823, he attended the school run by **AZEL DORSEY** for about six months. This school was near the church, and may have been in the church building before his building was completed. Dorsey was a prominent citizen and well educated. (Herndon and others show different time periods. For a list of possible schools he was said to have attended, see Louis Warren's *Lincoln's Youth*, page 234.)

David Turnham lived in Gentryville. According to legend, Lincoln borrowed his copy of the *Revised Statutes of Indiana*, containing the Declaration of Independence, Constitution, and other significant laws. When Turnham was interviewed by Herndon, he still had what he believed was the first law book Lincoln had ever seen. Lincoln then went to Rockport, Boonville, Troy, Princeton, and maybe New Harmony to get books. He also "studied" *Robinson Crusoe, Aesop's Fables, Watts Hymns,* and *Pilgrim's Progress*.

In 1830 the family moved to Illinois with the families of the two married daughters of Mrs. Lincoln. They feared that the "milk sickness" had returned, and the soil promised to be better in Illinois. Abraham at twenty-one was no longer legally bound to his father, but he decided to help with the move. Thomas and Sarah spent the winter preparing for the journey by selling their livestock and buying two yoke of oxen and a wagon.

In 1844 Lincoln visited his old boyhood community to campaign for Henry Clay as president. He spoke extemporaneously to an audience, including Josiah Crawford and other old friends, at the community center located about two miles west of the boyhood home. When he finished an old farmer asked, "Where's your books, Abe?" He was not used to seeing him without a book or two. He spent a day in Gentryville as a guest in the home of his old employer, William Jones, and visited the area around the church and cemeteries, surely those of his mother and sister. He called at James Gentry's home, but little detail is known of his movements. This was the last time he was in southern Indiana.

Captain J. W. LaMar claimed that he heard Lincoln make a political address in a little log schoolhouse standing in Carter Township at the crossroads between Barker's and Lincoln's old home. This would be about a half mile east of the original cabin site. LaMar quoted Lincoln's closing remarks: "I may not live to see it but give us a protective tariff and we will have the greatest county the sun ever shown upon" (*Lincoln Lore*, page 272). *Lincoln Day by Day* mentions a speech at Carlin Township on November 2, 1844. A boyhood friend, Nat Grigsby, told Herndon in 1865 that he heard Lincoln speak there, about three quarters of a mile from the home farm.

His return to the scenes of his childhood, described in a letter to a friend as being "as unpoetical as any spot of the earth," inspired him to write a poem.

> *My childhood home I see again,*
> *And saddened with the view:*
> *And still, as memory crowds my brain,*
> *There's pleasure in it too.*

Visiting the graves of his mother and sister and their old friends, the Sparrows, put Lincoln in a melancholy mood. All of the ten verses of his poem are in this mood, the last four lines ending:

> *I range the fields with pensive tread.*
> *And pace the hollow rooms,*
> *And feel (companion of the dead)*
> *I'm living in a tomb.*

The National Park Service has an interpretive center with a bookstore and knowledgeable rangers at a visitor's center on Route 162. A trail leads to Nancy Hanks's gravesite about three hundred yards away. From there it is about six hundred yards to the cabin site or a little longer to the Trail of Stones. This has stones from various sites associated with Lincoln's life including home sites, Washington, and Gettysburg. Adjacent is a cabin mostly dating to the 1840s or before, similar to what the Lincolns would have had. The exact spot where they lived during their fourteen years is not known, but it could have been at the present cabin. A marker at the nearby spring west of the cabin by the railroad tracks notes that the family got water there from 1816 until 1830. Assuming this is the spring known to have been on the property, and the original cabin was located on a high spot close by, the marked homestead site appears to be accurate.

LUCERNE: Lincoln's funeral train passed by at 6:25 A.M. on May 1, 1865, and was seen by a "large number in waiting to gratify their uppermost wish of getting a look at the funeral cortege."

MEDARYVILLE: Many people wearing mourning badges met the funeral train in the early morning hours of May 1, 1865, "with drooping flags."

MICHIGAN CITY: The funeral train passed under an arch on May 1, 1865. The site is opposite the present station on North Franklin.

PETERSBURG: Lincoln is believed to have visited here while a teenager.

PORTERVILLE: Lincoln was here in 1824.

PRINCETON: Lincoln at fifteen brought a load of wood to sell in about 1824. He told friends he saw a "very beautiful girl (who made his) heart flutter" when she nodded, resulting in him "falling in love." He was told that she was Julie Evans, but historians can find no trace of her. The son of the boy with whom Lincoln stayed while in town told the story. He slept in the MILL, A BLOCK WEST OF THE COURTHOUSE ON WEST STREET, now a city parking lot. The owner of the mill, MR. EVANS, owned the largest house in town at the corner of BROADWAY (ROUTE 64) AND WEST Street. The tradition that Lincoln stayed at the home is questionable. It is assumed that the girl mentioned above was Evans's daughter. Abe said then and later that he was greatly impressed with the town of about eighty log cabins and an assortment of stores and taverns. In 1861 on the way to his inauguration, he met a man named Stockwell in Lafayette and asked if he was related to the Stockwell who had an impressive store sign in Princeton that he had seen at age fifteen. He answered, "I am the man." Stockwell visited Lincoln later in the White House. The sign was located on BROADWAY STREET, ACROSS FROM THE COURTHOUSE, MIDWAY BETWEEN HART AND MAIN.

REYNOLDS: Farmers and their families met the funeral train at 4:55 A.M. on May 1, 1865, coming from twenty miles away.

RICHMOND: Lincoln's funeral train passed through at 2:00 A.M. on April 30, 1865. It passed under a "beautiful arch which was a tableau of the Genius of Liberty weeping over the coffin of Lincoln."

ROCKPORT: This was the county seat of Spencer County where Lincoln lived. As a youth he listened to lawyers in the courthouse located at the present site. In 1828, he built a boat to go to New Orleans for James Gentry. Gentry's son, Allen, lived near the RIVER LANDING and left his newborn son to go. The landing is below the bluff on the river south of the courthouse, accessible by the road at the tavern site and clearly marked. While building the flatboat, he lived with **ALFRED GRASS** close by the Gentry home. His son wrote later that Abe read by firelight until midnight lying on his back with his head toward the fireplace. Among his friends was **JOHN PITCHER**, the first attorney of Rockport, who had a large library for that time where Lincoln avidly read law, history, and fiction. People described the future president as an odd-looking boy who liked to steal off to a quiet spot where he could meditate or read. He had a great shock of black hair, apparently never combed, patched blue shirt, and buckskin breeches too tight and too short.

Lincoln spoke for Henry Clay on October 30, 1844, and slept in the old **ROCKPORT TAVERN**. The site is marked across from the courthouse. The *Rockport Herald* dated November 1, carried the news item: "Mr. Lincoln of Springfield, llinois, addressed a large and respectable audience at the courthouse Wednesday evening last upon Whig policy . . . pointing out the advantages of the Protective Tariff." His friend, John Pitcher, followed him.

The Lincoln Pioneer Village, located north of the courthouse, contains several cabin replicas; some may have some original logs. These include the John Pitcher Law Office and the Azel Dorsey House. Dorsey taught school near Pigeon Creek and was a fluent speaker from whom Lincoln received his liking for oratory. Next to these is the Daniel Grass House. Grass was one of the first settlers and by far the largest landholder and wealthiest man in Spencer County. Lincoln was a friend of the Grass children and once visited them for several weeks. The courthouse with plats and records burned down in 1833, making it difficult or impossible to locate many of the sites mentioned. The Pigeon Creek Baptist Church, where the Lincolns worshiped, is reproduced, also as is the first home of Josiah Crawford who lived in the Pigeon Creek neighborhood. Lincoln and his father worked at odd jobs for Crawford. The Jones Store is little more than a shack where Lincoln clerked for his friend while he told stories. Even though descriptions of the structures here are variously described as if original, evidently all are replicas. The movie *The Kentuckian* with Burt Lancaster was filmed here.

SAN PIERRE: Two thousand people assembled to view Lincoln's funeral train as it passed by on May 1, 1865.

SHELBYVILLE: Lincoln's inaugural train stopped for Lincoln to make a brief speech from the rear platform.

SOUTHBEND: The Studebaker National Museum, at 525 South Main Street, has the carriage in which Lincoln rode to Ford's Theater on the night he was assassinated.

STATELINE: A marker memorializes the spot where Lincoln spoke on February 11, 1861, on the way to his inauguration. He ate at the STATE LINE HOTEL. This was where the Great Western Railroad ended, and the party transferred to the Toledo and Wabash.

STOCKWELL: Lincoln's funeral train passed many bonfires and lighted lamps at 3:30 A.M. on May 1, 1865.

TERRE HAUTE: There are two traditions about Lincoln and Terre Haute. In 1829 he supposedly worked in Louisville, Kentucky, where he defended a slave being flogged for knocking down a water pitcher that a white boy had actually broken. The owner of the warehouse lashed Lincoln, who then knocked him down, but had to flee the wrath of men who could not allow a white man to side with a Negro. Lincoln skulked through the Indiana wilderness living on roots, nuts, berries, and wild honey to get to Terre Haute. There is another tradition that he brought his son Robert here to be treated for a dog bite, possibly in September 1859, by a lady with a curative "mad stone."

THORNTOWN: Lincoln's train stopped briefly on February 11, 1861, for Lincoln to make brief remarks. The funeral train passed through at 2:10 A.M. on May 1, 1865.

TROY: The Lincoln family crossed the Ohio River probably here in the fall of 1816 to enter Indiana. It is generally believed they landed at THOMSON'S FERRY AT THE MOUTH OF THE ANDERSON RIVER. Abe may have made the trip with his father many times back to the gristmill. Troy was the county seat of Perry County until 1818 when the court-house moved, so Lincoln could not have come here to listen to lawyers argue, as sometimes stated. Later, he came to the post office and was able to read undelivered newspapers. He is said to have loafed at the BATES STORE AT BATES LANDING below TROY AND WILLIAMS TAVERN. He is known to have worked for several around town, and once spent the night with the postmaster on the east side of MAIN STREET, SOUTH OF THE RAILROAD TRACKS AND FRANKLIN STREET (HIGHWAY 66) near the river. Some claim that he briefly attended a school under Adam Shoe-maker in Troy.

In August 1826 Dennis Hanks, Squire Hall, and Lincoln cut and sold firewood at **POSEY'S LANDING** to passing steamers. Lincoln got to know James Taylor who had a ferry and occasionally operated it across the Anderson River, about three hundred yards from the Ohio River. He lived with Taylor at his home about a quarter mile north of the river's mouth, just north of the present highway. A historical marker on the west side of the river is **LINCOLN FERRY PARK**, three acres of the Taylor farm just west of town, although the home was on the east side of the river. Abe got the job of ferryman for $6 a month. The ferry was a sort of flatboat used to carry a wagon and team. It was pulled by some pulleys tied to trees on the banks. Lincoln also worked as Taylor's hired hand and shared a loft with young Green Taylor who remembered Lincoln reading "til near midnight." Here the young ferryman could hear slaves across the river and saw the great commerce of the Mississippi Valley bound for Cincinnati, Pittsburgh, St. Louis, and New Orleans. Sometimes Abe would saunter up to Troy, crowded with boatmen, river pirates, slaves, prostitutes, gamblers, and planters. It is said he tried to imitate the Negro dancers in clog dancing in the street to the amusement of all.

He was remembered for telling a wealth of stories to his passengers. Two Lincoln scholars of the past tell different accounts of Green Taylor being taunted by Lincoln over a girl. Louis Warren related that Green told the story that when he was twelve and Abe about sixteen, he got mad at the hired boy and threw an ear of corn at Abe, resulting in a scar that Lincoln carried to his grave. (Green wrote to Herndon that he was ten years younger than Lincoln.) This is the usual version. Ida Tarbell describes Taylor as "about Abraham's own age," and that Lincoln threw the corn at him, causing Taylor to receive the scar.

In his spare time, Lincoln built a scow to take passengers to steamers on the Ohio River. Once he was taken to court on the complaint that he was operating without a license "to set passengers over the river." He successfully argued that he was only taking them out to the middle of the river, not "across" (see Hawkesville, Kentucky). On one occasion his two passengers each tossed him a half-dollar upon reaching their steamship in the middle of the river. He told Secretary of State William Seward years later that "he was amazed that a poor boy could earn a dollar in less than a day." He commented to Seward, "You may think it was a little thing, but it was a most important thing in my life."

VINCENNES: Lincoln is thought to have visited at least once in the 1820s with his friend Henry Boomer. He may also have come with his father who entered his land claims and payments. The Lincoln family traveled this way in 1830 when migrating to Illinois and stayed a day to see the largest town in Indiana. There is no distinct proof of the route followed on their 225-mile journey from Gentryville to Decatur, Illinois, except passing through Vincennes. The Indiana Lincoln Memorial Way Commission presumed that they followed the Troy-Vincennes trail, passing through Polk Patch (now Selvin), Petersburg, and Monroe City. The trip to Vincennes was about seventy-five miles and would have taken four or five days, probably up the present route of Highway 61.

They saw the site of George Rogers Clark's important victory over the English in the Revolutionary War. Here he captured **FORT SACKVILLE**, of decisive importance to the colonial cause and the winning of the West. Following Clark's victory, Virginia claimed all the lands northwest of the Ohio and the County of Illinois was organized. The fort was just south of the current Lincoln Memorial Bridge that marks the family's Wabash River crossing point. President Franklin Roosevelt dedicated the **CLARK MEMORIAL BUILDING** now on the site. The adjacent **OLD CATHEDRAL** was built in 1826 on the site of the first church probably built about 1732. This church must have been a unique and grand site for the farm boy. Lincoln had enjoyed reading the *Western Sun* and made a point to visit the editor, where he saw his first printing press at **ELIHU STOUT'S PRINTING OFFICE**. A replica of the office is open near the still prominent 1804 **WILLIAM HENRY HARRISON MANSION**, surely the grandest home Lincoln had yet seen. The original printing press was on **FIRST STREET BETWEEN PERRY AND BUNTIN STREETS**. William Henry Harrison brought Stout to publish the legislative laws when this was the territorial capital of Indiana. The future president's impressive mansion is also open to the public. This **"RED HOUSE"** had served as the **TERRITORIAL CAPITOL**.

Lincoln was said to have been often entertained at the home of his friend, **JUDGE ABNER T. ELLIS**, although this is only documented in 1844, located at **111 NORTH SECOND STREET** just east of Busseron. He also stayed at the home of attorney and friend **COLONEL CYRUS M. ALLEN AT 505 MAIN STREET**, now a funeral home. A bronze plaque marks the second-floor bedroom. Allen was the Speaker of the Legislature in 1860 and proposed Lincoln's name for the presidency on April 14, 1860, in the Vincennes *Gazette*. A local tradition says that when Lincoln slept in the house, he jokingly said that he slept just fine except that the bed was too short. (The dates are not documented.) Allen promised to correct the situation and had a local cabinetmaker design an eight-foot-long walnut bed, used by Lincoln on his next visit. It is suggested that the visit occurred about the time of the national convention in Chicago in 1860 where Allen, according to a letter written on May 1, assured him that the entire Indiana delegation would vote for him.

WASHINGTON: A tradition exists that Lincoln spoke at Third and Main in 1844. There is some evidence that Lincoln's decision to make the Indiana trip, aside from political interests, was due to his engagement as a lawyer in a suit tried in the Daviess County Courthouse, and some recalled seeing his name in the records at one time. He is said to have visited the home of COLONEL CYRUS M. ALLEN and the VAN TREES MANSION, AT THE NORTHEAST CORNER OF MAIN AND SIXTH STREETS. Van Trees was county clerk for thirty-seven years and administered the oath to Lincoln when he appeared in court here.

WHITESTOWN: The funeral train passed by at 1:07 A.M., May 1, 1865, illuminated by a large bonfire.

ZIONSVILLE: Lincoln's inaugural train had to stop here outside of Indianapolis for water on February 11, 1861. A stone marker in DEPOT PARK BETWEEN FIRST AND SECOND STREETS, NEAR CEDAR, marks the site where Lincoln spoke from the rear platform of his special train. He reportedly mentioned that there was an event in Washington that could not take place until he arrived. On May 1, 1865, the funeral train passed before a large assembly of people with lighted lamps and torches.

Iowa

BURLINGTON: Lincoln spoke on October 9, 1858, at **GRIMES HALL,** at the **NORTHEAST CORNER OF VALLEY AND MAIN STREETS.** He spent the next day at the **HOME OF JAMES W. GRIMES** and borrowed writing materials to outline his October 13 Quincy, Illinois, speech as part of the debates with Douglas and stayed at the **HUDSON HOUSE, AT THE NORTHWEST CORNER OF COLUMBIA AND FIFTH STREETS.**

COUNCIL BLUFFS: Lincoln came with O. M. Hatch, on August 12, 1859, by steamer from St. Joseph, up to the Missouri River to examine some land proposed to be conveyed to him for a debt. He stayed at the **PACIFIC HOUSE** until August 15, located on the **NORTH SIDE OF BROADWAY BETWEEN MAIN AND PEARL.** He went sightseeing around the area, and viewed the countryside from **CEMETERY HILL,** north of town. When he learned that Grenville Dodge, railway construction engineer, was registered at the Pacific, he returned and spent two hours talking with him about western railroads. Reportedly, Lincoln asked Dodge what the best route was to the Pacific, and Dodge said, "From this town out the Platt Valley." Later, when president, Lincoln selected the city as the eastern terminus of the Union Pacific Railroad.

He accepted an invitation and spoke the next night at **CONCERT HALL,** and attended a reception at the **HOME OF W. H. M. PUSEY, ON THE SOUTHEAST CORNER OF WILLOW AND SIXTH STREETS.** On the fourteenth he attended **FIRST PRESBYTERIAN CHURCH** services held in **CONCERT HALL** located on the **NORTHEAST CORNER OF BROADWAY AND SIXTH STREETS.** He dined at the **HOME OF THOMAS OFFICER, 533 WILLOW.**

While here he showed an old land warrant issued for his services as a captain in the Black Hawk War and voiced his regret that he had never filed it for a record so that his sons might have tangible proof that their father was a soldier. He had neglected to file the warrant because he felt he was "so poor that I was afraid I could not pay the taxes upon the land if I got it." A second warrant, signed by President Buchanan in 1860, was recorded in Crawford County, near Denison, on December 12, 1867. The title of the land passed through a deed signed by Robert Lincoln and his wife dated March 22, 1892. The parcel is located near Schleswig on U.S. 59. (The legal description of Lincoln's Crawford County land is Goodrich [T84N], northeast part of Section 18, Range XXXIXW. This earlier Tama County land is Howard [T84N], western part of Section 20, Range XVW. Maps are shown on page 7 of *Lincoln Herald*, winter 1954.)

There is a Lincoln Monument at **POINT LOOKOUT** at the head of **OAKLAND DRIVE AND LAFAYETTE**, near sixth and G Streets, at the point Lincoln looked over the valley to the Missouri River.

DAVENPORT: Lincoln is claimed to have visited here after an 1858 speech in Rock Island, Illinois.

Kansas

Lincoln made only one trip to Kansas, and stayed about a week in December 1859. This gave him a chance to try out and polish the address he was planning to make in New York City in February, which became known as the Cooper Institute (or Union) Address.

ATCHISON: Lincoln spoke on December 2, 1859, at a site, now the **COURTHOUSE**, where the Methodist church was then located. A plaque at **FIFTH AND PARALLEL STREETS**, north of the business district, marks the location. A band drummed up interest and escorted Lincoln from the **MASSASOIT HOUSE, 210 MAIN STREET**, to the church where there was a full house. The Massasoit was on the **NORTHWEST CORNER OF SECOND AND MAIN STREETS** and is noted in a stone marker at Third and Main. Terrorist John Brown was executed the same day in Virginia, contributing to the atmosphere of the occasion. Lincoln was said to have completely won over his audience in a two-hour-and-twenty-minute presentation. One eyewitness said, "I shall never forget how Lincoln looked . . . with his strange ungraceful gesticulations . . . with his long arms almost as if he could touch his hearers upon the back benches." He spent the night at the Massasoit and may have played billiards there.

DONIPHAN: Lincoln gave a speech on December 2, 1859, at **ABEL LOWE'S HOTEL**, probably to a small crowd, although this was an important Kansas town at the time.

ELWOOD: Lincoln's first stop in Kansas was on December 1, 1859, across the river from St. Joseph, Missouri. There were no plans for a speech here, but the people insisted upon learning of his presence. A crier went up and down the streets shouting: "Abe Lincoln of Illinois will speak at eight o'clock in the dining room of the **GREAT WESTERN HOTEL**. Everybody invited." Because of frequent flooding, the town now is located a short distance to the west from where it was when Lincoln visited, and the old landmarks are gone.

LEAVENWORTH: Lincoln was met on December 3, 1859, at the Fort Leavenworth Military Academy and escorted to the **MANSION HOUSE ON THE SOUTHWEST CORNER OF SHAWNEE AND FIFTH**. The carriage he rode in is now in the Fort Leavenworth Museum. He spoke at the **STOCKTON HALL** (Opera House). A marker on the southwest corner of **FOURTH AND DELAWARE STREETS** notes the site and remarks that this speech was comparable to the Cooper Union Address. He spent the night in a room at the nearby **MANSION HOUSE**, staying up late swapping stories with local men and guests who were mostly Seward advocates. The night was very cold, and as the wood died in the stove, some government patent office reports were used to fuel the fire. Someone asked, "Mr. Lincoln, when you become president will you sanction the burning of government reports by cold men in Kansas?" "Not only will I not sanction it, but I will cause legal action to be brought against the offenders," Lincoln remarked, smiling. This was the only reference to the presidency during the trip.

He spoke to "an immense audience" on December 5, and he stayed in the area until December 7. While here he visited Mark Delahay and his wife at **THIRD AND KIOWA**. The house has been destroyed. They had known each another in Springfield, where Delahay was an attorney, and largely responsible in getting Lincoln to Kansas. His wife was a Hanks. The families were intimate, and he called her "cousin," although probably both knew there was no blood relationship. (Lincoln promised to pay Delahay's expenses to the Chicago Republican nominating convention, even though he did not get an appointment as an official delegate.)

People heard of the speech and prevailed upon him to address the town again. There was no hall large enough so they gathered in front of the **PLANTERS HOTEL**, and he gave an "unplanned" but by now well-rehearsed address. Eastern reporter Henry Villard wired his paper that "It was the largest mass meeting ever assembled on Kansas soil and the greatest address ever heard there." The audience is still considered the largest crowd ever gathered in Kansas Territory. He possibly stayed with the Delahays or at the Planters, and returned to Springfield after local elections held on his last day here. The hotel was a landmark in the city for many years. The site is now a parking lot at the foot of Shawnee Street in the same block as the Riverfront Community Center.

TROY: The same Kansas speech was given on December 2, 1859, after a very cold trip in a one-horse buggy from Elwood. He met correspondent Henry Villard on the way, who described him as "blue with cold." Villard lent Lincoln a buffalo robe that he kept until they met again in Leavenworth. The speech was conversational and given to about forty listeners in a little bare-walled **COURTHOUSE**. One eyewitness had about the same reaction as did others who heard him. He stated, "There was none of the magnetism of a multitude to inspire the long angular, ungainly orator, who rose behind a rough table. With little gestation— and that ungraceful—he began . . . to argue the question of slavery in the territories in the language of an average Ohio or New York farmer. I thought, 'If the Illinoisans consider this a great man their ideas must be very peculiar.' But in ten or fifteen minutes I was unconsciously and irresistibly drawn by the clearness and closeness of his argument. Link after link it was forged and welded, like a blacksmith's chain."

Lincoln stated that John Brown, who was hanged that day in Virginia, was wrong because his act was in violation of the law, and it was futile. "We have a means provided for the expression of our beliefs in regard to slavery. It is through the ballot box." In an effort to hear both sides, the "heaviest" slaveholder in the territory was called to respond. He prefaced his remarks: "I have heard, during my life, all the ablest public speakers, all the eminent statesmen of the past and the present generation and while I dissent utterly from the doctrines of this address and shall endeavor to refute some of them, candor compels me to say that it is the most able—the most logical—speech I ever listened to."

The present courthouse is in the center of the square and dates to 1902. The location in Lincoln's day was the northeast corner. An original small, white-frame house across the street to the north is where Lincoln spent some time with friends, and may have spent the night.

Kentucky

T he future president's grandparents, Captain Abraham and Bersheba (sometimes spelled "Bathsheba") Lincoln, migrated from Virginia to Washington County in the fall of 1781 or 1782. The captain had come to the "dark and bloody ground" in 1780, was captured by Indians and made to run the gauntlet before being released. Early dates and locations are disputed. There is a question as to how many times Captain Abraham was married, but this chapter assumes only once (see the entry on Harrisonburg, Virginia).

It is possible that they lived in Lincoln County, now Casey County, when the family first arrived, or possibly Crow's Station near Danville. They were living in Hardin County by 1783, north of Elizabethtown, although this location is generally not mentioned in biographies. By the mid-1780s the family was finally occupying their four hundred acres on Long Run, claimed May 29, 1780, in Jefferson County. They had five children, including three sons: Mordecai, born about 1771; Josiah, born about 1773; and Thomas, born between 1776 and 1778. Indians killed the captain in an ambush, probably at Long Run, between 1784 and 1788, and his family moved to Washington County, north of Springfield. The president always thought this was 1784, but it was probably 1786, the date shown on his grandmother's tombstone. The father of the president, Thomas, reached maturity in Washington County and moved to Hardin County in 1803. In 1806 he married Nancy Hanks whom he had met as they both lived in the Beech Fork settlement. The president once stated, "I don't know who my grandfather was, and I am much more concerned to know what his grandson will be." But he must have listened to his father tell the story many times around the hearth of the captain's death and coming to Kentucky.

The history of the president's mother is more clouded, and several versions of her background and birthplace are given (see the entry on Mineral County, West Virginia). Historian Albert J. Beveridge comments, "Dim as the dream of a shifting mirage . . . her face and figure waver through the mists of time and rumor." There is an unbelievable void in reliable facts about the family of Lincoln's mother. Books and even national historic sites show theories as facts without suggesting alternatives. There are two different histories with variances related to Nancy Hanks's origins. One version or the other is generally given, but not both. Joseph Hanks may have been the father or grandfather of Nancy Hanks. Nancy may have grown up with the Hanks, Sparrows, and Berrys at different times, depending on the source.

Many historians believe that Dr. Louis A. Warren's books on Lincoln's family history as well as his Kentucky and Indiana years are the most reliable sources. However, his statements as to Nancy are probably a minority view. The National Park Service's handout given at the start of the twenty-first century at the Lincoln Birthplace still follows Warren's beliefs that Nancy was the daughter of James Hanks and Lucy (or Lucey) Shipley Hanks. This belief is repeated in the *Lincoln Lore* publications and in *The Lincoln Kinsman*, a monthly publication printed in the late 1930s and '40s. The couple is said to have been legally married in North Carolina or Virginia, but James had died prior to Lucy moving to Kentucky. Relatives, probably grandfather Joseph Hanks, brought Nancy there with her mother. The year was probably 1786, but could have been anytime between 1784 and 1790. They then lived with Lucy's sister Rachel Shipley Berry and her husband, Richard, at Beech Fork in Washington County. Nancy remained with the Berrys when Lucy married Henry Sparrow. (Others claim that Lucy married Richard Berry, but this does not appear to be correct. An earlier tablet at the Lincoln Birthplace Site in Kentucky listed her parents as Joseph and Nancy Shipley Hanks and stated that she was reared by Richard and Lucy Shipley Berry.) Richard died in 1797, and Nancy's marriage bond was signed by her cousin, Richard Berry Jr. She may have lived with the Sparrows in her teenage years.

In other accounts, a somewhat different story is told. Her involvement and relationships with the Berrys and Sparrows are muddled. Lucy's child, Nancy, was illegitimate and the father unknown. Various writers have listed at least fifty-one different fathers. Nancy possibly moved to Kentucky in the spring of 1784 with her unmarried mother, grandparents, and their five sons and three other daughters. Nancy was only a few months old when her mother, Lucy, soon left the family cabin, leaving the baby with the grandparents. Thus, Nancy would have lived with her grandparents Joseph and Ann Hanks until she was nine.

Lucy's baby, if born out of wedlock, was not only a disgrace, but also subjected Lucy to an indictable offense at the time. Some busybody brought charges in 1790, reluctantly pressed in the county seat. A summons was issued. A neighbor, Henry Sparrow, went to Lucy and proposed marriage to save her from further disgrace. *The Lincoln Kinsman* claims that she could show that she was a widow and the charges were dropped. They were then married by a Baptist pastor, and the indictment was dismissed. According to Dennis Hanks, Lucy became "a fine Christian lady in every respect" and had two sons who became preachers and later outspoken Unionists during the Civil War. Lincoln could remember one or two visits to the couple his mother addressed as Uncle Henry and Aunt Lucy. Uncle Henry told Abe stories of the Revolutionary War and of his being at Yorktown and seeing Washington and General Lafayette. Lincoln did not know until later that "Uncle Henry and Aunt Lucy" were his grandparents.

Grandfather Hanks died in 1793, when Nancy was nine. His wife continued to live at the family home for several months, but yearned to return to Virginia. It was decided that the youngest son Joe would go with her back to Virginia, and Nancy would stay with Lucy and Henry and their two younger children in their cabin in Spencer County. When a new baby was on the way, Lucy's sister Elizabeth came to stay a few weeks to help out. During this time Elizabeth met Henry's brother Thomas, and they were married. It was said that she wanted company, so Nancy went to live with them, maybe about 1796. She became known as Nancy Sparrow, either after the mother or the aunt. Thus, Aunt Elizabeth or Betsy became the "mother," and the mother became the "aunt." The Sparrows continued to be childless and raised Nancy as their own. Lucy eventually had other eight children. It is claimed that Nancy continued to call Betsy and Thomas "father and mother," and Abraham later was told they were his grandparents, but this story too is challenged.

When Nancy, Lucy and Elizabeth's sister, later had a son out of wedlock, Dennis Hanks, Thomas and "Betsy" also raised the boy. Or so that story goes. Warren does not believe these basic facts and does not believe Nancy referred to the Sparrows as shown since she would have known better assuming she did not move there until age twelve or so. And to add to the confusion, noted author and researcher Ida Tarbell believes that Joseph Hanks was the father of Nancy, making her the sister of Joseph Jr. But this conclusion is generally refuted as it is believed the "Nancy" in Joseph's will was Lucy's sister and Dennis Hanks's mother. Thus, the time frames and extent of the relationship between Nancy, the Berrys, and the Sparrows are not clear. After several visits to the area, including research and many local interviews, I have not been able to accurately determine the dates of Nancy's residency with any of these families or their exact site locations, other than the Berrys'.

From 1800 to 1802 the Sparrows evidently lived on the South Fork of Nolin Creek in Hardin County. From 1802 to 1805 they lived in Mercer County, but moved back to Nolin Creek in 1805. Some relate that Nancy visited her friend Polly Berry at her home in Washington County, and stayed there to work as a seamstress. Tom's two brothers lived nearby, and he visited Nancy when he came to the area, either when she was staying with Mrs. Richard Berry or Frances Berry. They decided to marry in that community where they both had friends and family.

Richard Berry Jr. rode with Tom to the county seat at Springfield to sign the marriage bond as guardian for Nancy. It was customary for a family member or close friend to sign as guardian, but some believe that Richard was neither, and signed only as a convenience. Thomas and Betsy Sparrow lived on the way to Elizabethtown, and were probably visited by the Lincolns on the way to their home there. The newlyweds moved from Elizabethtown to live on the Sinking Spring farm bought on December 12, 1808. Although many local historians have tried to find it, it appears impossible today to determine the site of the Sparrow cabin, although it was believed to be about a mile or mile and a half from the Lincolns in 1809.

Abraham was born on February 12, 1809, near Hodgenville on the Sinking Spring farm, and lived there for his first two years. Then the family moved up the road a few miles where a brother was born and died. Then they removed to Indiana in late 1816 because, as Lincoln said later, land titles were confused and the family had a low tolerance for slavery. During their time in these two states, the family name was pronounced "Linkhorn." Abraham returned to his birth state for four major visits in 1841, 1847, 1849, and 1850, to Louisville and Lexington. There is no record of his having visited in later years the places of his Kentucky childhood. In 1860 the native son got less than 1 percent of the presidential vote and about 34 percent in 1864.

BARDSTOWN: The Nelson County Court House is a repository for many court documents relative to the Lincoln and Hanks families, including an appraisement of Captain Abraham Lincoln's estate dated 1789. The **TALBOT TAVERN AT 31 EAST COURT SQUARE** claims that the Lincoln family stayed during a trial over title to their farm. It is also claimed that Andrew Jackson, Henry Clay, Aaron Burr, William Henry Harrison, Zachary Taylor, Stephen Foster, and other prominent Americans were guests. Thomas would occasionally work a day here for unbolted wheat flour.

BIG SPRING: The Lincolns reportedly stopped here, at the junction of Hardin, Meade, and Breckenridge Counties, for several days as an unusually cold winter set in on their way to Indiana in 1816.

CLOVERPORT: As shown on the historical marker on U.S. 60, seven-year-old Abraham and other members of the Thomas Lincoln family (may have) crossed the Ohio River on a log raft ferry near here in 1816 on their move to Indiana. Several decades later a witness to the event remembered that due to the unusual size of the oxen, a crowd gathered. An old slave saw the pitiful condition of the children and ran back to her house to get them bread and butter, eaten on the steps of her house. Several in the crowd helped make a raft to take the wagon across. The Lincolns then came back to swim the two oxen and cow across. This is about fifteen miles east of another crossing spot in Hancock County that may have been used.

CUMBERLAND GAP: The president's parents, Thomas Lincoln (around 1782) and Nancy Hanks (date unknown), passed through as children with their families, as did the Todd ancestors of Mary Todd Lincoln. Markers at this location trace the Lincoln family's route from Virginia to Kentucky as follows: Linville Creek (north of Harrisonburg, Virginia), Staunton, Lexington, Natural Bridge, Ingle's Ferry near Radford, Fort Chiswell near Wytheville, Royal Oak near Marion, Abindon, Bristol, Estelleville (Gate City), and Cumberland Ford in Virginia. Then Logan's Fort near Stanford, Danville, Harrodsburg, and Bardstown in Kentucky.

EASTWOOD (JEFFERSON COUNTY): Nearby is the spot where Lincoln's grandfather was killed in ambush probably in May 1786 at the age of forty-two. This date is found on the tombstone of his widow near Elizabethtown. Captain Abraham Lincoln had moved to Kentucky probably in 1782 with his family, consisting of his wife, two daughters, and sons Mordecai, Josiah, and Thomas. He lived on his own land in Jefferson County and sometimes at Hughes Station, probably just a short distance away, near the cemetery at the head of Floyd's Fork near the Shelby County line. He was working near his home some time between 1784 and 1788 with his sons when he was killed by a single shot. Mordecai ran for a gun, Josiah ran to the station for help, and Thomas stayed with his father. The youngster was on the point of being seized or tomahawked by an Indian who came to scalp the father when Mordecai fired a shot from the cabin or Hughes Station, killing the Indian. The president's father, Tom was somewhere between six and ten years of age.

LONG RUN BAPTIST CHURCH, on Long Run Creek, marks the traditional site of the grave. It is not marked and has not been found. The body was buried on the farm, and the church was built at the site of the graveyard. Captain Lincoln was said to be a strong Baptist, and had given the land for the church. The cabin is believed to have been just north and up to two hundred yards from the present church site. This is located about THREE MILES NORTH OF INTERSTATE 64 in the NORTH-EAST CORNER OF JEFFERSON COUNTY AT THE SHELBY COUNTY LINE about fifteen miles east of Louisville and two miles northeast of Eastwood. Ancestors of President Harry Truman are also buried here.

The time and spot of Captain Lincoln's death are in question, but the above account is believed correct. The administrator of the estate was named in Nelson County in 1788. Some argue that the captain was wounded in Jefferson County and moved to Nelson County, where he died later. Kentucky travel guides and historical markers now in Washington County near the Lincoln Homestead Park north of Springfield confuse the question (see SPRINGFIELD, Kentucky, entry). To add to the confusion, several sources state that Bersheba Lincoln killed the attacking Indian.

ELIZABETHTOWN (HARDIN COUNTY): A number of sources show that Captain Abraham Lincoln lived north of town with his family in 1783 prior to moving to Jefferson County. He helped build the Old Baptist Church of Mill Creek, the third church west of the Alleghenies. This was where the LINCOLN MEMORIAL CEMETERY is now. The family then moved to Jefferson County where Indians killed Captain Lincoln. The widow relocated to Washington County, north of Springfield. In 1803, the president's father, Thomas, purchased a 238-acre tract of land EAST OF MILL CREEK in Hardin County, a few miles north of Elizabethtown on present ROUTE 434, ABOUT A MILE AND A HALF EAST OF THE DIXIE HIGHWAY, ROUTE 31 W. He lived there off and on from 1803 until about two years after he was married. He worked as a carpenter and cabinetmaker. He divided his time between here and his Marrowbone

Creek land, purchased on November 28, 1801, in Cumberland County. His mother, sister Nancy, and her husband came to live with him in 1803, and it is supposed that the cabin was built for his mother. Joseph Hanks lived in town with his family and was a carpenter and cabinet-maker who taught Thomas that trade. Earlier Joseph (Nancy's brother or uncle) had moved back to Kentucky after the death of his mother in Virginia.

Thomas and Nancy Hanks were married on June 12, 1806, at the Berry Home north of Springfield. They moved back to the **MILL CREEK FARM**, and then built a cabin in Elizabethtown where their first child, Sarah, was born in 1808. This exact site is not known. He worked on various houses in town and in the area. The courthouse occasionally displays exhibits of the family history. Various writers and historians have listed numerous sites as possible locations in the area as the future president's birthplace. These include the Mill Creek farm and Elizabethtown cabin owned by Thomas.

A few blocks southeast of the courthouse on the Hodgenville Road or Dixie Highway is a marker at the **BRIDGE** showing the site of a mill raceway built in 1796 along **SEVERN'S VALLEY CREEK**. The marker says that Thomas was employed in building it and received his first monetary wages when about twenty-one years old. It also notes that Abraham crossed here with his family when they migrated to Indiana in 1816. This area is the best guess as to the location of the Lincoln cabin in town where Abraham's sister was born.

Young Abe is said to have been brought into town often prior to moving to Indiana and had friends in town. There is a popular story that he sat on a nail keg in the **BEN HELM AND DUFF GREEN STORE**, on the **SOUTHEAST CORNER OF MAIN** at the **CORNER OF THE SQUARE**, to eat lumps of sugar that the clerk gave him. Later, the clerk became a prominent man in Missouri. Lincoln remembered him as the only man he knew who wore "store Clothes" all week, or so the story goes. In 1859 Lincoln visited the clerk, Honorable J.B. Helm, in his home in Hannibal where Helm claimed they both remembered the incidents with the sugar (see entry on **HANNIBAL**, Missouri). Or at least that is Helm's story, maybe embellished. (Helm was only about ten or twelve years older than Lincoln.) Or Lincoln may have pretended to remember. The boy Helm remembered could possibly have been Lincoln's half brother, John Johnston.

When the Lincoln family moved to Indiana, they probably crossed Mill Creek about here, as shown in the above-mentioned marker. It is not known whether seven-year-old Abe saw his grandmother at the time of this move or at other times, but surely he did since she lived just north of town. Probably the Lincolns spent the night with her on the way to Indiana. Grandmother Lincoln lived to about ninety years of age and is buried in the LINCOLN MEMORIAL CEMETERY, twelve miles north of town off U.S. 31W, now inside Fort Knox. This would have been on the way to Vine Grove and Big Spring. The fort holds the U.S. government's gold reserves. During World War II it held various valuable historical documents including the Declaration of Independence, autographed copies of Lincoln's Gettysburg Address and Second Inaugural Address, and the U.S. Constitution.

The future president's mother died in Indiana in 1818. It is probable that Thomas had courted Sarah Bush earlier in life, and returned to get her at Elizabethtown in 1819, after spending a year as a widower. It is also possible that Sarah and Nancy Hanks were close friends and that Nancy's daughter was named after her. Sarah Bush Johnston then lived on the corner of POPLAR AND QUINCE ALLEY, in back of the house at 117 North Main. Her cabin was claimed to have been shipped away for exhibition and lost. Tom proposed marriage, since they had known each other for many years, were without spouses, and their children needed a father and mother. Sarah pleaded that she had debts, so Tom paid them off. Maybe she counseled her brothers, who knew him. In fact, one had gone down the Mississippi to New Orleans with him. They married on December 2, 1819, at **117 NORTH MAIN**, next to her cabin and just off the square. A plaque on the current building marks the site. Sarah continued to own a parcel of land until September 1829, when she sold it before moving to Illinois. The historic Brown-Pusey House on the opposite side corner, is the home of the local historical society and contains a cupboard made by Thomas Lincoln shown in *Lincoln Lore 1476*.

Lincoln's brother-in-law, Confederate general Ben Hardin Helm, was born in town and is buried at the family homestead about one mile north of town on Highway 31W at Route 421. He had stayed with the Lincolns in Illinois and was deeply mourned by them at his death in the Civil War. Duff Green, a close friend and political associate of President Andrew Jackson, also lived in the house at 117 North Main prior to 1819. He knew the Lincolns when they lived here. While the president was at City Point, Virginia, in April 1865, Green demanded to see him, but was turned away because of his slovenly and offensive appearance. Lincoln discovered that he was there, said that Green was an old friend, and allowed him to come in. Green then insulted the president for his role in the war and "being guilty of setting the niggers free."

Future president James Buchanan, who preceded Lincoln in office, lived in Elizabethtown in 1813, a few miles away from the Lincolns who were then at Knob Creek. Buchanan had come here to look after his family's land interests. It is also noted that the year of the Lincolns' move to Illinois was known as "the year without a summer." There was frost and ice from July to September 1816, and the temperature in October never got above thirty. The winter of the move was also much colder than normal.

LINCOLN HERITAGE PARK is two miles northwest on U.S. 31W at FREEMAN LAKE. Tom Lincoln helped to build one of the 1805 cabins here. His work includes cabinetwork, the mantle, baseboards, stairway, doors, and windows. When the family moved to Indiana in 1816, they probably passed by with Thomas pointing with pride to the roll he played in the prominent home. The Sarah Bush Johnston Lincoln Memorial is located in a memorial cabin built in 1902, also located at the park.

HARDINSBURG: On the east side of Kentucky 261 at the south city limits is a historical marker at the spot of a cabin that sheltered the Lincoln family migrating to Indiana in late 1816. The family rested and recuperated here for about three weeks after having traveled through ELIZABETHTOWN, VINE GROVE (marker on Kentucky 144), and HARNED on the way to the CLOVERPORT river ferry, according to some sources. According to tradition, local residents gave them food.

HARRODSBURG: On the grounds next to Old Fort Harrod is the LINCOLN MARRIAGE TEMPLE. This red brick building was suggested by an old Baptist church in the neighborhood where the pulpit was in the center of the church. The LINCOLN MARRIAGE CABIN stands where the pulpit would ordinarily be. The cabin was removed from the Richard Berry farm at Beech Fork or Beechland Settlement where Thomas and Nancy were married on June 12, 1806. It resembles the one where Lincoln was born and, like his birthplace cabin, it has been reduced in size. The replica of Fort Harrod is across the street and just south of the original site. Lincoln's grandmother, Lucy Hanks, may have met and courted her husband Henry Sparrow in the fort.

HAWKESVILLE: The HOME OF SAMUEL PATE, who was a justice of the peace and held court here, overlooks the Ohio River and is about thirteen miles west of Hawkesville north of U.S. 60 and four miles northeast of Lewisport.

Turn north on Kentucky 1605 for about four miles to a dead end into Kentucky 334. Then turn left (west) and go about a half mile to the historical marker.

Lincoln won his first law case here in 1827, getting himself acquitted from a charge of "ferrying passengers across a stream without a license." He successfully argued that he was not ferrying them "over," but only to midstream to catch a boat going downriver. Pate took a liking to Lincoln, may have lent him law books, and talked with him on his porch about the law. Lincoln rowed back across the river several times to hear other cases argued. Pate is buried near the house, along with a rumored early sweetheart of Lincoln's, Ann (Caroline) Meeker.

The home is two miles southwest of **THOMPSON'S LANDING**, at the northernmost point of Kentucky 334 and the Ohio River. The Lincoln family may have crossed over the Ohio River here when they moved to Indiana.

HODGENVILLE: Lincoln's birthplace is about three miles south in the **ABRAHAM LINCOLN BIRTHPLACE NATIONAL HISTORIC PARK**. The cabin was on the main highway of travel into the south from Kentucky, known as the Cumberland Road. The small town contained a store and mill used by the Lincolns. Here now is the Lincoln Museum with artwork, artifacts, and scenic representations of Lincoln's life.

The family moved from Elizabethtown in December 1808, possibly to be near Nancy's relatives. Little is known about the birthplace cabin, which may have been on the land before the purchase. The tract was known as the Sinking Spring farm due to the spring at the base of the hill where the cabin stands that still produces water. A large oak tree nearby was thought to be three hundred years old when Lincoln was born. It died in the 1970s and was measured to be only 195 years old then, about as old as the Declaration of Independence. The tree site is marked, and a cut-out section is now in the museum.

The first direct mention of the cabin was in 1852 when a deed referred to it. Between this time and the Lincolns' ownership, eight different owners had been in possession. Union troops sought out the presumed birthplace during the Civil War, but found no visible evidence of the exact spot. The first person to take an interest in the cabin was Dr. George Rodman who owned property a mile away. Soon after he visited Lincoln in Washington, he purchased the cabin and had it moved to his farm, probably from the site where it is now. It is not known conclusively that it was at that spot in 1809. The cabin was dismantled and traveled extensively to such places as the Nashville Centennial in 1894 and the Buffalo Exposition in 1901. It originally is thought to have been eighteen by sixteen feet, but now is seventeen by thirteen feet. There is no way of knowing if this was the birthplace cabin or what alterations and reconstruction may have taken place.

(See *Lincoln Lore,* December 16, 1935, and *Number 369* for further history.) Rangers here tell the story that Jefferson Davis's birthplace cabin and Lincoln's were dismantled and stored in the same place. When they were reassembled, some of the logs of Davis's may have been included in Lincoln's. This has not been confirmed in any other source.

Nancy may have earlier lived a mile or two away, where Thomas and Betsy Sparrow continued to live, although this site cannot be identified now. Her cousin Dennis Hanks had rushed to the cabin when he heard she had a new baby. After briefly holding his cousin, he announced, "He'll never mount to much."

Efforts to preserve the site began in earnest in 1906 when several prominent Americans including Mark Twain and William Jennings Bryan formed the Lincoln Farm Association. The cabin was placed inside a marble and granite memorial. The cornerstone was placed by President Theodore Roosevelt in 1909. The National Park Museum contains the Lincoln family Bible, in possession of the Johnston family until 1893. There are many discredited claims of other sites as the president's birthplace.

The Nancy Lincoln Inn is located adjacent to the National Park and is privately owned. Many historic relics are contained inside the building no longer more than a store. For years it contained the "T. L." tombstone found at the **REDMOND BURIAL GROUND** near the Knob Creek cabin in 1933. This is believed to be the marker for Lincoln's brother's grave. The marker is now (1999) under the care of its owner, a local attorney and historian.

About six miles north on the Cumberland Road, now U.S. 31E, is the **KNOB CREEK CABIN** on the Lincoln's 228-acre farm site from 1811 to 1816. The current highway traces what was the main route from Nashville to Louisville at the time of the Lincolns' residency. The cabin, called Lincoln's Boyhood Home, is on what is believed to be the site, but the original cabin has long since vanished. The logs of the replica are from the cabin of Lincoln's boyhood friend Austin Gollaher. This was rebuilt in 1931 with the logs cut down to the original dimensions according to the son of an old schoolmate of Lincolns, Steve Thompson. The son, Robert, had helped his father tear down the original in 1870, used as a corncrib, and returned in the early 1930s to locate the correct site. The National Park Service hopes to acquire the site and make further determinations as to the accuracy of the cabin site, which may correctly be across the road. The family well is said to have been at a location now in the highway.

Abe's earliest recollections are of this place and his younger brother. The boy was born here, and is buried a short distance from the home.

The general location is seen from the front of the reconstructed cabin, across the road at the top of a knob hill. George Redman, Thomas's closest neighbor and friend, allowed the use of his family cemetery. The site was not generally known until WPA workers in 1933 clearing the old pioneer burying ground found a small stone believed to be the gravestone. The dates of Lincoln's brother's birth and death are not known, and listed variously in different sources. There is also a question of his name, presumed to be "Thomas." The boy's age at death is variously listed up to about three years. Abraham and his mother visited the grave for the last time just before they left to go to Indiana. A grown-over Boy Scout trail across the road and creek just south of the home leads to the cemetery on private land. It can also be reached by turning north on the Joe Brown Road just east of the Pleasant Grove Baptist Church, listed below, and going to the end. Permission from the owner should be obtained to cross over private land.

Lincoln remembered helping his father plant one of their three fields between the hills and knobs, composing their farm. These hills funneled the rainwater through their land that at times washed away their growing crops. The last thing he remembered doing here was dropping pumpkinseed in the cornfield behind the cabin that was being planted. The next morning a big rain came in the hills although not a drop fell in the valley. But, he said, the water coming down through the gorges washed ground, corn, and pumpkinseeds, and all clear off the field. This is believed to be the large area just west of the cabin, now a park and picnic area.

Between here and Hodgenville is an **OLD STONE HOUSE**, clearly visible several hundred yards west of U.S. 31E. This house is the first house still standing that Lincoln could remember seeing. Dr. Jesse (George?) Rodman of Hodgenville visited Lincoln in Washington, D.C., regarding the Larue County 1863 draft quota. During this visit they discussed the Knob Creek area. Lincoln told Rodman that the two objects in the area "which were most impressed upon his memory were a big tree that was somewhere on the South Fork and the 'Stone House.'" The occupant told me in 1992 that he believes the house was built in 1792. He tells the story of the old springhouse also visible from the road that sheltered several settlers during an Indian raid in the early nineteenth century. He also believes Lincoln came here as an adult. This is on Stonehouse Road northwest of the junction of U.S. 31E and Route 1797.

When Abe was just past six years of age, he and his sister walked to the school of **ZACHARIAH RINEY,** marked north of the cabin about two miles on the west side of U.S. 31E in Athertonville. Thomas is believed to have worked at a distillery of Wattie Boone, on the site of the distillery buildings near the school site. Abe is thought to have come to see his father. Later, Caleb Hazel taught in the same schoolhouse. This was known as a "blab" school because the students were required to speak lessons over and over, out loud, to show the teacher they were concentrating. Also there were too few books to use the printed material at home, so they needed to memorize. Lincoln probably acquired the habit of reading aloud from these schools, to the dismay of his law partners and family. He also went to the Little Mount (Baptist) Church, about three miles from their cabin.

AUSTIN GOLLAHER, 1806–1898, is buried at the PLEASANT GROVE BAPTIST CHURCH on Kentucky 84 just east of U.S. 31E, about a mile south of the cabin. To reach the grave, walk through the brick gates east of the front of the church toward the brick outbuilding on the top of the hill. Gollaher is buried about 150 feet from the gate and to the right, about opposite the back door of the church.

Austin was a close friend of Abraham and the source of many stories of his youth. He told about many adventures and says he recognized Lincoln's greatness even as a boy. He tells of stopping with Abe many times at the OLD STONE HOUSE and of Abe's many visits with his hero, John Hodgen, and his mother at HODGEN'S MILL. Abe is said to have spent many days and nights on a trundle bed at their home, A BLOCK NORTH of where the CITY HALL ON WATER STREET in Hodgenville now stands. A picture marker was put here noting the spot showing Abe there bringing corn from home. This cannot be found now, and the historical marker noting the site was almost hidden behind a five-hundred-pound soft drink cooler at the water treatment plant on the site when I visited in late 2000. Mrs. Hodgen told many stories of Washington, Columbus, and Robinson Crusoe and helped Abe with his ABCs and the Ten Commandments.

Historians do not believe many of Austin's detailed stories and conversations, although the most famous is generally accepted: Once when they were crossing a creek on a narrow footlog, Abe fell in. (Gollaher is quoted later in life as saying that there was no footlog involved; Abe fell from the cliff by the creek.) Neither boy could swim, but Austin fished him out with a pole. They dared not tell their mothers, so they had to wait until their clothes dried before going home. (Actually they probably wore only long shirts at this time.) It is believed that the incident took place in front of the bluff or cliffs about a hundred yards from the replica cabin. Louis Warren believed it was about eight-tenths of a mile north of the Lincoln home, and near where Austin lived. At the time, Abe was about three and Austin, eight. Austin also said he had a crush on Abe's sister. Lincoln said while president that he would rather see his old friend than any man living, but Austin was too scared to ride the train to Washington. (*The Boyhood of Abraham Lincoln* relates many of these tales from Gollaher.)

Virginia, the parent state of Kentucky, had required those claiming land to provide surveys and descriptions, which were informal, conflicting, and overlapping. Because of this inefficient method, Tom lost all or part of his land near Mill Creek, Sinking Springs, and Knob Creek. The Lincolns were also disturbed about the bitter controversy raging over slavery. Shortly before Lincoln's birth, the South Fork Baptist church, located two miles from the Sinking Spring farm, was closed over disagreement on slavery. By 1816, the Lincolns had enough, and decided to move to Indiana where land titles were more organized and certain, and slavery had been outlawed. Evidently they were able to retain clear title to some of their farm, and sold it before leaving. It is likely that the Lincolns spent their first night on the road to Indiana at the Sparrow home, and then the next night with Grandmother Bersheba near Elizabethtown. They probably also saw Mordecai and the Berrys.

Before moving to Indiana, Thomas built a boat, probably in Knob Creek near the house, to float downriver to the Ohio by way of Rolling Fork. He took along produce and maybe several hogsheads of whiskey, cloth, honey, skins, and so on. But the boat overturned at the mouth of the Salt River and most of the goods and tools were lost. It is assumed they migrated to Indiana overland rather than by boat, although there are some claims that they did go by boat. Austin Gollaher describes the beginning of the trip as coming by their home and Hodgen's Mill, although these were in opposite directions.

LEWISPORT: See Hawkesville, Kentucky.

LEXINGTON: Lincoln's grandfather, Abraham, was close to his brother, Thomas, who settled on Elkhorn Creek about five miles south of Lexington. This is now on Route 68 in South Elkhorn. Both had sons named after the other. Lincoln's father evidently visited his uncle prior to his marriage.

Mary Todd was born and grew up in Lexington, "The Athens of the West." Her mother died when Mary was only six, and she believed her father abandoned her emotionally to marry a woman who was always at odds with the children of the first marriage. Mary's grandmother Parker is felt to have turned the children of the first marriage against their stepmother. As Mary grew she received an advanced formal education that was superior to that of any other president's wife up to her time. It is generally agreed among historians that the cultural atmosphere she created and nourished in her home contributed greatly to her husband's mental capacity and attainment of the social graces necessary for a successful leader.

Mary's husband came to Lexington four times. His first visit to Lexington was in 1841, to see Joshua Speed's fiancée, while Speed's guest at Louisville. The next three visits were with his wife and family, and included visits to Mary's **MAIN STREET** home and other Todd homes on **SHORT STREET, BUENA VISTA,** and **ELLERSLIE.** On the way to Washington in 1847, the family spent a month with the Todds. Then it was necessary for Lincoln to return in 1849 after the death of his father-in-law and in 1850 after the death of Mary's grandmother to handle legal problems in the two estates.

Mary was born on December 13, 1818, at **501 SHORT STREET** and spent most of her childhood in the home, which was torn down in the 1880s. The gatehouse at the Calvary Cemetery on West Main was constructed with the bricks from the house. Her father had bought this house after he had been married next door. Mary spent much time at the home of her grandmother, **511 SHORT STREET**, especially after her father remarried. Grandmother Parker did not approve of her son-in-law's remarriage, and tried to turn the children of the first marriage against those of the second. She had a tower high on the front where she could sit for hours to watch happenings in town. The rear portion is original. The front is now an Italianate-style brick house built in 1871. It served as an orphanage from 1907 until 1975, and now serves as a conference center known as Parker Place. A cabin of Mary's grandfather Parker has been moved to the rear of the house.

Confederate president **JEFFERSON DAVIS** also has close associations to Lexington. He went to school at Transylvania College at age fourteen and lived from 1823 to 1824 in the building still at the **NORTHWEST CORNER OF LIMESTONE AND HIGH.** (Dates of his attendance vary; I am relying on William C. Davis's biography.) He visited his friend Henry Clay Jr.'s father at **ASHLAND**, the Clay estate, still open to the public on the Richmond Highway. Mary's sister, Elizabeth, met her husband, Ninian Edwards, when he came to the college. He was the son of the governor of Illinois, and moved back to Springfield upon completion of school. He married Elizabeth when she was sixteen, who probably wanted to get away from her stepmother. This started the migration of the Todd sisters to Springfield where all three of Mary's full sisters eventually lived after finding Springfield husbands.

The original 1830 Transylvania College main building, **MORRISON HALL**, is still north of **THIRD STREET BETWEEN MARKET AND MILL**

STREETS, just west of downtown. It was used as a hospital during the Civil War. This was the first college west of the Allegheny Mountains. Its graduates include fifty U.S. senators, 101 representatives, three speakers of the U.S. House, thirty-six governors, and thirty-four ambassadors. Gratz Park, across the street on the south side of Third Street, contains many homes and structures dating to the first quarter of the nineteenth century. These include **MARY'S** school, the **WARD ACADEMY** at the **SOUTHEAST CORNER OF SECOND AND MARKET**. Dr. Ward conducted a shockingly experimental formal school where boys and girls both attended. Mary trudged through all extremes of weather to begin class each morning at 5:00 A.M. He was a mentor as well who tried to aid Mary when she could not get into Transylvania. Mary went to school there from age eight until age fourteen, when she entered the select boarding **SCHOOL OF MADAME VICTORIE LeCLERE MENTELLE** located on the Richmond Pike opposite the entrance to Ashland. While there, she returned home on weekends. Various markers nearby tell where senator and perpetual presidential candidate Henry Clay lived, was married, and practiced law in the business district.

THE TODD HOUSE, 578 WEST MAIN, was the home of Mary Todd Lincoln from 1832 and 1839. This is on the south side, between Jefferson and Paterson Streets. Her father had seven children by his first wife and eight by the second. One child from each marriage died young. The large house was needed not only for his large family but also to serve his needs to entertain for social, business, and political purposes. This 1803 tavern was converted to home use, and the Todds moved in 1832, six years after his remarriage. Part of the reason for moving may have been to get away from Grandmother Parker next door on Short Street. Mary grew up listening to the political conversations of Henry Clay, John J. Crittenden (best man at the second marriage), Robert Jefferson Breckenridge, and other notables.

Now restored, it is open to the public, after being used over the years as a grocery, dry cleaners, plumbing supply warehouse, boarding house, and "notorious house of ill fame." It was almost razed in 1946 for a gas station, as it was not easy to raise interest for a "girlhood" home before the era of women's liberation. It contains many personal articles of the Todd and Lincoln families, although most of the original furnishings were scattered during the administration of Todd's estate. Some pieces are from the Lincoln White House. A cup given to Tad Lincoln by a soldier when his brother Willie died is also shown. It is the first shrine restored to honor a first lady.

In November 1847, Congressman Lincoln and his family spent a month with the Todds on the way to Washington. He probably passed through Frankfort in all visits here. The family, including four-year-old Robert and two-year-old Eddie, took the stage to St. Louis, steamer to Louisville, and then the train to Lexington. Mrs. Todd's nephew rode the train from Frankfort with the family and did not know who they were. When he saw his aunt at the DEPOT AT MILL AND WATER STREETS, he blurted, "Aunt Betsy, I was never so glad to get off a train in my life. There were two lively youngsters on board who kept the whole train in turmoil and their long-legged father, instead of spanking the brats, looked pleased as Punch and sided with and abetted the older one in mischief." Then he saw them coming, and stated, "Good Lord, there they are now." When he found out who they were, he made a hasty exit and was not seen again. (Water Street has generally been built over, but was between Main and Vine.)

Mary was a close friend of Senator Henry Clay, a political associate of her father. She visited his home often as a girl and introduced her husband to the statesman there. As a girl, she was quoted by a member of the family as telling the senator, "Mr. Clay, my father says you will be the next president of the United States. I wish I could go to Washington and live in the White House. I begged my father to be President, but he only laughed and said he would rather see you there than to be President himself." Clay was home at ASHLAND for the entire time the new congressman was in town. Lincoln visited and found him cold and unresponsive, possibly because he was still mourning the death of his talented son and namesake in the Mexican War. He had admired Clay and campaigned for him. He grew to feel later that the famous Great Compromiser sacrificed his party for personal ambition, but delivered his eulogy in Springfield when the leader of his party died in 1852. The home is open to the public, although the original 1806 house was largely destroyed shortly after Clay's death. The restored mansion is still one of the landmark homes of America. It is located about a mile and a half east of the courthouse. The home and grounds are much like they were when Clay lived here for forty years, with many original furnishings.

One of Lincoln's chief diversions was going through Todd's extensive library, which included several hundred books. The library is on the east side in the rear parlor, but he generally read in his frontwest bedroom upstairs. There was no chair that was comfortable for his long legs, and he could lay on the floor upstairs and stretch out there. His favorites were *Messages of the Presidents*, Gibbons's *Decline and Fall of the Roman Empire*, Prentice's *Life of Henry Clay*, and biographies of Burns, Shakespeare, Cromwell, and Napoleon.

In Lexington Lincoln encountered apparently contented slaves, including Mammy Sally who had been close to Mary. He spent many hours with Grandma Parker at her home on Short Street, and could look over into a structure that housed and sold runaway slaves nearby on **MECHANICS ALLEY AND BROADWAY STREET**. He spent time admiring the large homes and lawns of the city. He drove out to the Todd Cotton Mills in Sanderville on the Georgetown Pike with Mary's brother Levi, who observed, "The negroes under no circumstances would have accepted freedom from their beloved White folks." Lincoln also spent time at the home of Levi Todd, Mary's birthplace home. He must have been taken by the old Todd home, **ELLERSLIE**, named after the Todd family's ancestral home in Scotland. Mary's father had been born and grew up in the home, one and a half miles southeast of Lexington's business district on the Richmond Pike. Mary did show it to her nephew decades later. The site is now **ON THE WEST SIDE OF U.S. 25 IN THE LEXINGTON MALL PARKING LOT.** Lincoln joked that God only needed one *d*, but the Todds had to have two. Actually the name was spelled with one before moving to this country.

The area around the courthouse was a public meetingplace since Lexington was born and called "**CHEAPSIDE**." Slaves were sold here almost every day. Lincoln had time to study slavery firsthand and saw slaves being sold, as he had in New Orleans. Mary's father sold slaves on November 15, 1847, at the courthouse steps in an auction to the highest bidder to satisfy a judgment, and it is assumed Lincoln must have witnessed the sale. One notorious location was Short and Limestone, one block from the courthouse, where slaves were sold to the Deep South. A park on the west side of the courthouse now preserves the Cheapside name and site. Lincoln had time on his hands and loafed, swapping stories with lawyers on the east side of the courthouse in Jordan's Row. Two prominent statues of Confederate generals, John Hunt Morgan and John C. Breckenridge, both local sons, now dominate the courthouse lawn.

It is believed that Mary and her husband both heard Henry Clay's three-hour speech on November 13, 1847, on the conduct of the Mexican War when he declared that acquiring Mexico would mean acquiring new territory for slavery. It was supposed to be at the courthouse, but there were so many people that they adjourned nearby to **LOWER MARKET HOUSE** on Water Street where a temporary platform was erected. Mary's father was vice chairman and sat on the platform with Clay.

Mary and her family attended the **SECOND PRESBYTERIAN CHURCH** AT **184 MARKET STREET**. On Thanksgiving morning, Lincoln listened to

Dr. Robert J. Breckenridge, the famous preacher-orator in church. ("Thanksgiving Day" was celebrated at varying times in several states before the Civil War, when President Lincoln declared this a national holiday.) The church is no longer there. They also visited a famous confectionery owned by Monsieur GIRON on the WEST SIDE OF MILL STREET BETWEEN MAIN AND SHORT. Among its previous customers were President James Monroe and General Lafayette. Part of the building still remains.

At the time of Lincoln's visit he must have seen the home of Mary's friend, Cassius Clay, on the northeast corner of Limestone and Fifth, the most elegant mansion in town. Clay's abolitionist newspaper made him nationally famous in 1845, when it had been shut down by threatened mob action, and the press was shipped to Ohio. Lincoln heard him speak later in Springfield, Illinois, and he was probably the houseguest of the Lincoln family. He was Lincoln's minister to Russia during the Civil War. The president evidently felt that this Clay had "a great deal of conceit and very little sense."

It is not known how the Lincolns traveled to Washington when Lincoln entered Congress. They might have gone to MAYSVILLE on a stage, and then transferred to a steamer for Washington. Or they could have gone to FRANKFORT by rail, then to PITTSBURGH, OR BROWNSVILLE, PENNSYLVANIA, by steamer, stage to railhead at CUMBERLAND, MARYLAND, and then by railroad. This would have been easiest with small children. A shorter but more uncomfortable trip would have been by stage via WINCHESTER, VIRGINIA. Mary and the boys returned the next spring to spend time around Lexington while Lincoln stayed in Washington attending Congress.

Much of their time was spent at the summer home, BUENA VISTA, on Leestown Pike, eighteen miles from Lexington toward Frankfort. This home was destroyed in the late 1940s. The site is two miles east of the current intersection of U.S. 421 and U.S. 60 with Route 676. A historical marker on the south side of Route 421 notes that the home was about half a mile south, although it was north of the main road when Mary lived here. The exact location is between the fifth tee and eighth green on the golf course, "Links at Ducker Lake." There is no trace of the home, but the original springhouse is nearby in a gully with a small pond, which dams the spring. The Lincoln boys played in the brook that ran from that pond through the woodland. They especially enjoyed the tall, rambling frame house and surrounding countryside after being cramped in Washington. A large, modern black barn stands on the golf course near the site and marks the vicinity. According to Robert, he spent the winter of 1848 with his grandfather in Lexington, although his statement is the only evidence of this.

In October 1849 the family returned to spend three weeks while Lincoln, as executor, settled Mary's father's estate. Todd's will had only one witness rather than the required two. Mary's brother George filed a protest throwing the estate into intestacy. The will had left Todd's wife the estate for life so that she could care for the six minor children, but now the assets had to be divided among the fourteen living children equally. This required the cotton mills and other assets to be converted into cash. The resulting sale and auction produced only a fraction of their fair market value. Lincoln was selected to represent the first set of children, including the four daughters who lived in Springfield. A lawsuit with others was also involved. George later took silverware belonging to the stepmother that Lincoln and others claimed had been a gift to her. Lincoln advised against filing a suit against George, but George did file against all the children.

At this time Lincoln read *Christian's Defense* by Dr. James Smith in Todd's library. Smith was then the pastor of the First Presbyterian Church in Springfield, Illinois. He had been a scoffer at Christianity and attended camp meetings to make fun of preachers. But then he became a believer and pastor. He engaged in a series of debates with a skeptic in a format later followed by Lincoln and Douglas. Smith's arguments and ideas were published, but Lincoln could not finish the long book before returning home. A friend brought Smith to Lincoln's Springfield office where he received a copy to study further, leading to further discussions. When Eddie Lincoln died, the Lincolns were not attending any church, but Smith preached the funeral and gave comfort to the family. The Todd family treasured this book in their library from that point on, and Robert said his father cherished the book given by Smith.

As in other visits, Lincoln spent time at **BUENA VISTA**, but most of the time was at the Short Street homes, Mary's birthplace and Grandma Parker's house. Brother Levi still lived in the birthplace house, and Lincoln was with him much of the time. He was an invalid during the Civil War, and supported the Union. During the 1849 visit they ate in the **PHOENIX HOTEL**, on the **SOUTHEAST CORNER OF MAIN AND LIMESTONE**, where a park and the Central Library now stand. It became Union army headquarters during the Civil War. The family returned in the spring of 1850, after Eddie died, to conduct business in settlement of Mary's grandmother's estate. Lincoln left Mary and Robert at **BUENA VISTA** and returned to Springfield alone.

All Todd children from the first marriage were loyal to the Union during the Civil War except the youngest son, George, who joined the Confederate army. All from the second were loyal to the South except the youngest daughter. The three sons fought and died for the Confederacy, and the husbands of three daughters were Southern officers.

Many members of the Todd family are buried at **LEXINGTON CEMETERY** a few blocks west of the Todd House on Main Street, as are Henry Clay, Vice President and Confederate general John C. Breckinridge, John Hunt Morgan, and other Civil War notables. The Todd family is buried just north of the center of Section F, north of Henry Clay's prominent monument and grave. Mary's father, mother, stepmother, grandparents, and many brothers and sisters are here. Surely, Lincoln visited the site in his 1849 and 1850 visits to see the new graves of his wife's father and beloved grandmother. Mary visited in 1876 with her great-nephew and saw her stepmother's monument to her sons, which still reads, "In memory of my beloved son's—all Confederate soldiers." Mary's beloved half brothers, Samuel and Alexander, killed as Confederates during the Civil War, are buried in the row with their father.

The Parker grandparents are in Section D near Main Street. Grandma Parker outlived her husband by half a century. Mary's other grandfather, General Levi Todd, is buried in the third row behind her father. He was one of the hunters who named Lexington in 1775. He was an aide to George Rogers Clark and succeeded Daniel Boone in command of the Kentucky militia. Mary's favorite half sister, Emilie Todd Helm, is buried in the row behind Robert Todd. Todd's wives are on either side of his grave.

LOUISVILLE: Lincoln and his stepbrother came as day laborers on the Portland Canal around the Falls of the Ohio in 1827, but there are few details. Later he came this way to Lexington. There is a questionable story in several sources that Lincoln came at age twenty and got a job in a tobacco warehouse at Fifth and Main. While working there a white boy broke a water pitcher, but the owner's son blamed a slave and started to whip him. Lincoln protested that the wrong man was being punished. Nevertheless, the owner's son would not be put off and struck Abe, who defended himself and knocked the white man to the floor. Abe then had to flee, pursued by a white mob, and barely made his way to and across the river where he had to hide out from the wrath directed at a man who would defend a slave. He made his way through the wilderness, avoiding trails and roads, to Terre Haute where he circled back to his home.

In August 1841, Lincoln was a guest for several weeks at **FARMINGTON**, the home of Joshua Speed. This was the nicest house Lincoln had visited up to this point in his life. Joshua was one of ten children born into the family, and had been Lincoln's closest friend in Springfield.

John Speed completed the historic house in 1810, generally stated from the designs of Thomas Jefferson. But there is no known direct connection. The estate is located at **3033 BARDSTOWN ROAD AT EXIT 16 OFF INTERSTATE 264,** and open to the public. The home contains the original floors and much of the original furniture. The stone barn and springhouse are also original.

Upon arrival Lincoln was assigned a servant, one of the seventy slaves on the 554-acre hemp plantation. He experienced luxury for the first time as servants brought coffee in bed and served him peaches and ice cream. The slave cabins were at a site now covered by Interstate 264. He spent his time tramping the fields, woods, and roads here and in Louisville. His room is thought to have been in the corner to the left facing the entrance, probably in the basement, but it could have been on the main floor. He was very close to his friend's half-sister, Mary. Once in a playful mood, he locked her in a room "to keep her from committing assault and battery on me."

In Louisville he spent many long, delightful hours with **JAMES SPEED** who would later become his attorney general. His office was on the **WEST SIDE OF CENTRE**, midway between **JEFFERSON AND GREEN STREETS**. Mrs. Speed was a loving woman and gave Lincoln a Bible to read as "the best cure for the blues." When he became president, he sent her a photograph of himself with the inscription, "For Mrs. Lucy G. Speed from whose pious hands I accepted a present of an Oxford Bible twenty years ago." When she heard in 1865 that the president had been killed, she said that she could not have been more upset than if one of her sons had died.

During some of his time, Speed's future wife, Fanny, was spending time with her uncle, John Williamson, at his nearby farm. Speed complained that he could not get a private moment with her since Williamson, an ardent Whig, was constantly arguing politics. When they visited, Lincoln, a Whig leader in the Illinois legislature, pretended to be a Democrat. He proceeded to create such diversions by engaging the old Whig in heated political discussions that Joshua and Fanny could have private moments together.

He and Speed went back to Springfield on about September 7, 1841, via St. Louis. Lincoln had a tooth extracted in Louisville, causing him much pain throughout the trip as a fragment was left in his jaw. Speed completed business affairs and returned to Kentucky permanently. They kept up correspondence, gave each other personal advice about their love lives, and "forebodings, for which you and I are peculiar" (Lincoln). Speed occasionally called on Lincoln at the White House.

MAMMOTH CAVE: Mary Lincoln toured the cave with her great-nephew in 1876 and stayed at Cave City. There is no record of them touring Abraham's boyhood sites nearby.

MORGANFIELD: On September 8, 1840, Lincoln made his only known political speech in Kentucky (according to tradition). He was campaigning in southern Illinois for William Henry Harrison. George W. Riddell of Morganfield encountered him and brought him to his hometown where he was also entertained at the hotel.

SANDERSON: Lincoln visited the cotton mills of his father-in-law in November 1847.

SPRINGFIELD AND WASHINGTON COUNTY: The Washington County Courthouse at the public square is the oldest Kentucky courthouse still in use. A historical marker on the courthouse lawn notes the fact that the marriage bond of Lincoln's parents is kept inside. This is signed by Thomas Lincoln and Richard Berry Jr. The minister who performed the ceremony, the Reverend Jesse Head, also signed the minister's certificate. In the vault are various documents of Thomas Lincoln that can be seen upon request.

The **LINCOLN HOMESTEAD PARK**, seven miles north, marks the site of the log house where the president's grandmother moved sometime after her husband was killed, sometime between September 6, 1786, and October 14, 1788. It is possible that the family first lived nearby in the cabin of Hannaniah Lincoln, her husband's cousin who owed money to the family. A replica of her cabin is on the same spot as the original, by the spring where they got water. Bersheba Lincoln raised her three sons and two daughters at the site and kept the family together until all of the children except Tom were married. Three were married here in 1801. Tom also served in the militia at age seventeen and was here until he was twenty-five, although he lived some in Tennessee with an uncle. Several pieces of furniture thought to have been made by Tom are here, including a corner cupboard and bed. In 1803, Tom moved to Hardin County after he formed his attachment to Nancy. Mrs. Lincoln is believed to have moved to the Mill Creek farm north of Elizabethtown with Thomas, and her daughter and son-in-law.

Some believe that the death of the president's grandfather occurred nearby rather than in Jefferson County east of Louisville. An "unofficial" historical marker about three-tenths of a miles east on Route 438 states that this is the "site of Captain Abraham Lincoln's massacre in 1788 and pioneer cemetery." The WPA Kentucky Guide mentions this, but notes the Jefferson County site as the probable correct location, which does appear accurate and accepted by most historians. *In Lincoln's Footsteps*, a recent historical guide, lists this as the place of his massacre, and suggests that the grandfather is buried near the cabin. But the great weight of evidence indicates the correct site is in Jefferson County, east of Louisville.

It is probable that the president's grandmother, Lucy Hanks, and her only child had moved nearby to live with Lucy's sister and her husband. When Lucy married Henry Sparrow on April 3, 1791, she moved out, leaving Nancy to live with the Berrys (and/or Sparrows) according to tradition. The Berrys and the Lincolns had been neighbors for about seventeen years. Nancy thus lived in nearby **BEECHLAND** up Beechland Road from the Lincoln cabin, with Richard Berry and his wife, but this may have been several years later, after first living with the Sparrows. The exact site is at the tiny community of **POORTOWN**, on Route 438, two miles northeast on a knoll overlooking Little Beech Creek. When Berry's wife died, Nancy may have moved in with **FRANCES BERRY** where she lived while Tom was courting. Tom is claimed to have proposed in front of the immense fireplace. This cabin has been moved across the lawn from the Lincoln cabin. They were married on June 12, 1806, in **RICHARD BERRY JR.'S CABIN**, now in Harrodsburg. There is also a reproduction of the blacksmith shop where Tom learned the trade of woodworking, maybe with Frances. (Some accounts claim Frances's home was the marriage site, but this is discounted.)

Tom Sparrow was the brother of Lucy's husband, Henry. It is also claimed that Nancy moved in with the Sparrows (maybe) at about age twelve and was known as Nancy Sparrow. Dennis Hanks, who was born out of wedlock to another of Lucy's sisters, also came to live with the Sparrows. Dennis claimed he and Nancy were like brother and sister, although he was about six when she married. Berry's wife's niece, Sarah Mitchell, who had been carried off by Indians at age twelve and released five years later, also lived with the Berrys. The Indians had killed her mother, and her father drowned crossing the Ohio searching for her. She was Nancy's maid of honor, and Tom's brother, Mordecai, was best man. Lincoln's sister was named after Sarah. (There are many conflicting stories and traditions about time spent with the Sparrows, Berrys, and Hanks families.)

Nearby on Kentucky 528, about four miles north of Springfield, is the large house of the president's uncle, Mordecai Lincoln, who was one of the leading citizens of Washington County. It is the only remaining residence in Kentucky known to have been owned and occupied by a member of the president's family, still standing on its original site.

Lincoln stated more than once that the brains and talent of the family went to "Uncle Mord." Thomas is believed to have spent time here.

Jefferson Davis went to a Catholic school at Saint Rose Priory, a few miles west, half a mile north of U.S. 150, from age eight to age ten. It was started in 1806, and still stands. His term began in 1816 when seven-year-old Abraham was growing up about twenty miles west at Knob Creek, attending a school taught by a Catholic. Jeff and Abe both had Baptist fathers. The school trained aristocrats, while Lincoln's was the school of hard knocks in a role that would destroy Southern aristocracy.

VINE GROVE: A marker in this community north of Elizabethtown notes that the Lincoln family used the pioneer trail that came through in 1816 as they were migrating to Indiana.

WASHINGTON COUNTY: See Springfield and Washington County entry.

Louisiana

BATON ROUGE: Lincoln and Allen Gentry were attacked on the river-bank about six miles below Baton Rouge on their 1828 flatboat trip to New Orleans. In Lincoln's words, "One night they were attacked by seven negroes with intent to kill and rob them. They were hurt some in the melee, but succeeded in driving the negroes from the boat, and then 'cut cable' 'weighed anchor' and left."

The Pentagon Barracks were clearly visible as they floated down the river. The buildings are now just southwest of the new Capitol Building near the river bluff. These military buildings completed in 1824 replaced a 1779 star-shaped earthen fort, and housed Zachary Taylor, Robert E. Lee, and many Civil War personalities.

NEW ORLEANS: Lincoln arrived at age nineteen with Allen Gentry in late 1828 and again on a trip lasting from April to July 1831 with his half brother and Denton Offutt. In 1828 he spent several days and rented a room on **ST. ANN STREET**. He saw slaves being sold, supposedly at the **OLD ST. LOUIS HOTEL** near the **CABILDO**, and supposedly vowed "to hit this thing hard if he could." The quote is generally attributed to John Hanks, but he apparently left the group on the second trip at St. Louis. (John Hanks told Herndon that he came here, but Lincoln said he did not in his autobiography.) Some sources attribute the remark to Gentry on the earlier trip. Both could be correct. Regardless of the timing and accuracy of the famous statement, the slave trade no doubt deeply affected the young man who became a lifelong opponent. In the later trip, he came with his stepbrother, John D. Johnston, and

Denton Offutt and stayed about a month. They probably returned by steamer to St. Louis. Little is known about either trip as no diary was kept. Regardless of the unknowns, surely he saw the famous cathedral and French government buildings still on the historic square. It is believed that he saw his first printing press here and went to the American Theater "a number of times" (*Lincoln Herald*, February 1948).

Maryland

ANTIETAM NATIONAL BATTLEFIELD (SHARPSBURG): On September 17, 1862, about forty-one thousand scattered Confederates under Robert E. Lee faced eighty-seven thousand Union soldiers under George McClellan. This was the bloodiest day in U.S. history. Casualties numbered about twenty-six thousand, with about forty-eight hundred killed. Not only was Lee's advance into the North reversed, but the stalemate, which could be called a Union victory, gave Lincoln the opportunity to issue the Emancipation Proclamation. McClellan allowed the Confederate forces to escape across the Potomac River and continue the war, but the proclamation broadened the war's purpose and scope, and ended a threat that France and England might soon recognize the Confederacy.

When a copy of Lee's Special Order Number 191 was found by Union troops near Frederick, Maryland, during the second week of September 1862, McClellan knew the location of the split Confederate troops and what Lee's orders and plans were. Noted authors and historians Bruce Catton and Shelby Foote deemed this the greatest security breach in U.S. history, and the only one affecting the outcome of a war. (The spot where the lost orders were found is noted by a historic marker on Route 355 about a mile north of the Monocacy National Battlefield Visitor's Center, south of Frederick.) McClellan boasted that now he had the information to defeat "Bobby Lee." But he procrastinated and was overcautious, allowing most of Lee's forces to reunite. Finally, he engaged the Confederate army, with most of Lee's forces present and attacked in segments rather than simultaneously.

The president visited General McClellan on October 1–4, 1862, and stayed two nights in a tent next to McClellan's headquarters. Historian William C. Davis deems this the most important army visit as it showed Lincoln that he needed to replace the general. His six-hour train trip passed through ELLIOT CITY, SYKESVILLE, MOUNT AIRY, MONROVIA, MONOCACY JUNCTION, BERLIN, AND HARPERS FERRY, where he spent the first night. During his second day he visited troops near Harpers Ferry and arrived late in the afternoon, probably via WEVERTON, BROWNSVILLE, GAPLAND, ROHERSVILLE BY ROUTE 67, MOUNT BRIAR, AND BURNSIDE BRIDGE, where he was met by the general whose name was given to the bridge.

He was photographed in McClellan's tent and outside with various other generals. The precise location has not been identified as McClellan had left his headquarters at the Pry House north of Sharpsburg and moved to a new site from September 27 until October 8. Civil War photography expert William Frassanito (*Antietam*) believes this site to be slightly less than two miles south of the Sharpsburg center square along the Harpers Ferry Road. Harpers Ferry Road is a continuation of South Mechanic Street in Sharpsburg. The headquarters site is unmarked on the EAST SIDE OF THE ROAD, SOUTHWEST OF BURNSIDE BRIDGE, AND HALF A MILE SOUTH OF THE JUNCTIONS OF BRANCH AVENUE AND MILLER'S SAWMILL ROAD WITH THE HARPERS FERRY ROAD. Antietam guide and author John Schildt agrees and describes it as near the Antietam Furnace on the creek to the east of the road (*Four Days in October* and *Drums Along the Antietam*). It was near the Antietam Furnace that the the president reviewed the Ninth Corps.

Another photograph was taken in front of the GROVE HOUSE, also known as "MOUNT AIRY," General Fitz-John Porter's headquarters, still prominently standing several hundred yards south of the SHEPHERDSTOWN ROAD JUST WEST OF SHARPSBURG. The view of the house in the background allows the exact spot of the picture to be pinpointed. These are the only photos of Lincoln on any battlefield. The president reviewed the Fifth Corps at Mount Airy and the First just across the road northwest.

The president visited wounded soldiers in the mansion and apologized to the owners for the damage caused. A correspondent wrote that Lincoln walked down the big hallway talking to the wounded. He told Confederates he would talk to them if they had no objection and said: "Solemn obligations which we owe to our country and prosperity compel the prosecution of this war, and it followed that many were our enemies through uncontrollable circumstances, and he bore them no malice, and could take them by the hand with sympathy and good feeling." A moving scene then followed where wounded from both sides "fervently" shook his hand with not a dry eye among Union or Confederate.

Lincoln reviewed troops around the battlefield, at **BAKERFIELD**, three miles away, and at **SOUTH MOUNTAIN**. He traveled via the **MIDDLE BRIDGE, BLOODY LANE, AND PRY HOUSE**, all marked on the battlefield. McClellan accompanied him to the summit of **SOUTH MOUNTAIN**. (It is unknown if the party went by Turner's or Crampton's Gap.) General Isreal B. Richardson was dying of wounds at the **PRY HOUSE**, and Lincoln climbed the stairs to comfort him. The family claimed that they received a note from the president thanking them for the breakfast that he ate there. The home is now owned (and open) by the National Park Service.

He visited the **MILLER CORNFIELD** and **DUNKER CHURCH** being used as a hospital. The church was destroyed during a 1921 storm, but reconstructed on the same foundation in 1962 using the same bricks and other materials. This is near the National Park Visitor's Center. Lincoln's only recorded addresses were in Frederick on his route back to the capital. On one trip across the **MIDDLE BRIDGE (ROUTE 34)**, the president got a cool drink from the creek. A modern bridge is at the same site.

Lincoln was outwardly congenial toward McClellan throughout their discussions, but was extremely dissatisfied with the general's reluctance to pursue and engage the enemy, not only here but also all during 1862. (McClellan wrote of the visit in his memoirs that Lincoln was "fully satisfied" and later used "entirely satisfied" with "the general.") But the general was relieved on November 7, 1862, and never served again on any battlefield. He always felt that the Confederates were more numerous and better trained than his own men. Certainly he was an expert in organization and inspiration, but he could not properly and effectively use the army. His failure to act more swiftly with the full utilization of forces probably added to the length and destruction of the war. He was Lincoln's Democratic Party opponent in 1864 for the presidency. The great admiration the general had inspired from the troops did not inspire their vote.

Most sites mentioned above are part of the Antietam National Battlefield Park tour.

BALTIMORE: Lincoln's first trip to Baltimore was on the way to Philadelphia to the Whig National convention in 1848 while he was a congressman. On the way to Washington in 1861, he was hurried through from Philadelphia in the middle of the night to thwart a suspected plot to kidnap or kill the president-elect. **THE PRESIDENT STREET**

Station at President, Canton, and Aliceanna Streets is the remaining part of the station used by Lincoln. It is now the Civil War Museum. Lincoln arrived, incognito, in a sleeping railroad car on February 23, 1861, at 3:30 A.M. The car was pulled by horse down **Pratt Street** to the **Camden Station, Camden and Howard**, now adjacent to the Camden Yards ballpark, and attached to the last train to Washington. (Later the Sixth Massachusetts Infantry had to make the same transfer and were attacked on Pratt Street in what is known as the Baltimore Riot, April 19, 1861.) He was supposed to arrive from Harrisburg at the **Centre Street Railroad Station**, also known as the **Calvert Street Station**, the terminus of the Northern Central Railroad to Harrisburg. This was in a block bounded by Calvert to the west, Orleans to the south, and opposite the Franklin Street intersection with Calvert. Here a Baltimore barber and a few conspirators planned to assassinate Lincoln as he emerged from a narrow vestibule. The Lincoln family arrived on the train with the rest of the party and followed the same route as the president-elect. They were harassed by a mob all the way as their railroad car was drawn to the **Camden Station**.

His second nomination for the presidency took place at the Republican National Convention held in 1864 at the **Front Street Theater** at the **northwest corner of Front and Low Streets**. For this election, the Republican Party was called the Union Party and hoped to unite all supporters of the war effort. Lincoln's first vice president, Hamlin, a northern liberal, was replaced by Andrew Johnson, a conservative Southern Democrat. It is probable Lincoln maneuvered behind the scenes to put him on the ticket, as he knew he had to have the support of Democrats to broaden the appeal of the party. What better way was there to woo this vital faction than to place one of its leaders on the ticket? This move put a nonradical on his ticket as a way to reduce the chances that England or France would recognize the Confederacy.

The Democratic National Convention was held in 1860 at the **Maryland Institute** located at the **southwest corner of Baltimore and Market Place**. The convention had first met in the still standing First Baptist Church in Columbia, South Carolina, and then transferred to St. Andrews Society Hall at 118 Broad Street, Charleston. At Charleston, a rule that a candidate had to have two thirds of the vote prevented any nomination as no one could achieve that. So the convention was rescheduled to Baltimore. The same two-thirds rule prevailed. After dissatisfied Southern Democrats left the convention, Stephen Douglas was nominated for president. The Southern Democrats at the **Front Street Theater** then nominated John C. Breckinridge. Another group nominated John Bell on the new Constitutional Unionist Ticket composed mostly of old-line Whigs and American or Know-Nothing Party members. These events split the national Democratic Party and others, greatly enhancing the chances that the minority, sectional Republican Party would prevail in the presidential election.

The president went to Gettysburg in November 1863 by way of the **B&O CAMDEN STATION** (*Guide to Civil War Sites in Maryland*) (**OR BOLTON STATION**, per *New Birth of Freedom*) **AND CALVERT STREET STATION VIA THE NORTHERN CENTRAL**. Lincoln stayed at **702 CATHEDRAL STREET** on April 18, 1864, when he came to Baltimore to speak at the Sanitary Fair at the **MARYLAND INSTITUTE**. Large crowds greeted him at the station and throughout a long parade. He also spoke at **BARNUM'S HOTEL** at **CALVERT AND FAYETTE**. His reception was one of welcome from the city that had changed since his trip through in February 1861. A little over a year later, on April 21, 1865, he lay in state at the **MERCHANT'S EXCHANGE AT GAY AND WATER STREETS**. Mary and Tad stayed at **BARNUM'S HOTEL** on September 27, 1868, after Robert's wedding in Washington.

Assassin John Wilkes Booth is buried at **GREEN MOUNT CEMETERY at GREENMOUNT AND OLIVER STREETS,** as are many Civil War personalities including General Joseph E. Johnston. Booth's body was transferred in 1869 from Washington, where he was first buried at the Washington Arsenal with the others who were hanged for the assassination conspiracy. Numerous claims have been made through the years that Booth actually escaped so that whoever is buried here is not actually the assassin. Attempts have been made in recent years to exhume the body for tests to confirm that this was Booth's body. However, most knowledgeable historians do not believe that he escaped. A request in the mid-1990s to exhume the body was refused, as the deciding judge could not find credible evidence that the body buried was not Booth's.

The Booth burial plot is directly east of the cemetery gate about halfway to the eastern boundary, in the Dogwood Area, plot 9. A small obelisk marks the Booth family and is near a prominent statue with a broken hand and a broken pillar. The obelisk contains the names of the children, including John Wilkes, but his exact grave spot is not marked. A map is available at the cemetery office. (General Johnston's grave is in section VV, plot 30, and is mismarked on the cemetery map. This grave is where curving Cemetery Avenue reaches its easternmost point going north, just northwest of the northernmost edge of the Heartsease "A" section.)

Four others involved in plots to kidnap or murder Lincoln are buried in Baltimore. **MICHAEL O' LAUGHLEN AND SAMUEL ARNOLD** are also located at **GREEN MOUNT**, although neither is on the map. Arnold is in Section P, lot 49, north of the public mausoleum. O' Laughlen is in Section AA near Mayor Joshua Vansant near the western edge of the cemetery. "O' Laughlen" is the spelling on the tombstone, but spelled in different ways in Civil War literature. Conspirator **GEORGE ATZERODT** is buried in **ST. PAUL'S LUTHERAN CEMETERY IN DRUID HILL PARK** in an unmarked grave in the Gotleib Talbert plot. **JOHN SURRATT JR**. is buried at **NEW CATHEDRAL CEMETERY** near a large cedar tree that can be seen from the main gate.

BEL AIR: John Wilkes Booth was born in 1838 at or near **TUDOR HALL** on **FOUNTAIN GREEN ROAD, ROUTE 22 AND TUDOR LANE**, three miles northeast of Bel Air. The home is reported to have been built at various dates from 1822 to 1852 by Junius Brutus Booth, a prominent Shakespearean actor. John was born in a cabin nearby or on site of this house, and lived in it after it was built. This boyhood home of the assassin was a bed-and-breakfast until late 1999, when it was sold to be restored and used as a residence. It is also regarded as the birthplace of Shakespearean Theater in America as the home of John's famous father, Junius, and his brother, Edwin, sometimes said to be the greatest actor in our country's history. At one time Edwin saved the life of Robert Lincoln, who had slipped onto a train track in Jersey City on the way to Washington, D.C., from New York City. Robert wrote that he fell onto an open space and was helpless until "vigorously seized" by the famous actor and pulled to safety. They recognized one another and called each other by name. (There is a question of the date; 1863, 1864, and 1865 are variously given.)

BRYANTOWN: Dr. Samuel Mudd is buried in the churchyard of the **ST. MARY'S CATHOLIC CHURCH** just south of town on Route 232. His prominent tombstone is north of the front of the church. Convicted conspirator Edman (also "Edward," "Edmond," "Ned," "Edmun," etc.) Spangler is buried at St. Peter's Cemetery, two miles west of the Mudd House on Route 382, near the back of the cemetery. His marker was placed by the Mudd Society and Surratt Society. Mudd and Spangler were convicted in the Lincoln Assassination Conspiracy Trial in 1865. The **BRYANTOWN INN**, where Mudd arranged a meeting between John Wilkes Booth and a Confederate operative, still stands in the center of the town. The meeting was in the downstairs room on the right side facing the house. This is on the one short main street, the second house from the northeast corner of the road to St. Mary's Church. It is now a private residence. The Thirteenth New York Cavalry set up headquarters here on April 15, 1865, in pursuit of Booth and David Herold (see the entry on "Trail of the Assassins").

BURKITTSVILLE: On October 4, 1862, Lincoln and General McClellan visited wounded from the Battle of Antietam in both the Reformed (now UNITED CHURCH OF CHRIST) and ST. PAUL'S LUTHERAN CHURCHES. In the latter the president knelt at the altar and "prayed a beautiful short prayer." Both churches are still standing.

CLINTON: Booth and David Herold stopped in Clinton (formerly Surrattsville) on April 15, 1865, in their flight from Washington, at SURRATT'S TAVERN, operated by John Lloyd and owned by Mrs. Mary Surratt. She and her deceased husband had lived there and operated the tavern before he died. This is at the junction of State Highways 223 and 381. It is now open and is the headquarters of the Surratt Society, which studies events associated with the assassination. Mrs. Surratt's delivery here of field glasses on April 14, 1865, at the request of Booth, was an important fact leading to her conviction as part of the Booth conspiracy in the assassination. Booth came on his escape from Ford's Theater to get guns previously hidden. These were suspended from the attic between floors. Booth was not able to take one of these because of his broken leg, and it was left, where it is displayed in the museum. Visitors can see the place where these were hidden. The rifle taken by Davy Herold is in the museum at Ford's Theater.

FREDERICK: After his visit to Antietam Battlefield, Lincoln visited General George L. Harsuff who was recuperating from a battle wound at the RAMSEY HOUSE, 119 RECORD STREET, facing the courthouse and city hall on the square. The president traveled to this location in a procession down PATRICK STREET TO COURT STREET. He then spoke briefly to a large crowd on the front steps and later at the B and O Station on South Market.

Several historic buildings can be observed from the Ramsey house. The first courthouse was begun in 1752. The construction was interrupted when British general Braddock took available wagons to transport equipment for his troops during the French and Indian War. In 1765 the Stamp Act was repudiated here and in a building across the street where patriots met in a secret session. A second courthouse was erected in 1785. The Maryland General Assembly met here to consider secession, but later moved to the KEMP HALL BUILDING AT THE SOUTHEAST CORNER OF MARKET AND CHURCH, about three blocks away. Also facing the square on the north side is the Ross Home at 105 Council Street where General Lafayette was entertained in 1824. On the east side of the square is the former law office of Frances Scott Key and Roger Brooke Taney. Key wrote the National Anthem near Fort McHenry, and Taney was Chief Justice of the U.S. Supreme Court who swore in Lincoln as president in 1861. His Dred Scott decision on the Court fueled the flames leading to the Civil War. Both are buried in Frederick, Taney at a small cemetery near Third and East Streets, and Key in the much larger Mount Olivet Cemetery at the south end of Market Street. All locations are marked.

There are several churches seen by Lincoln within walking distance of these sites, including the Evangelical Reformed Church at 9 West Church dating to 1848. Stonewall Jackson was in town in September 1862 before the Battle of Antietam when he heard that the pastor intended to pray for the success of Union troops. Fearing that some of his troops might disturb the service, Jackson came to prevent trouble. The preacher did pray as expected, but Jackson (who taught Sunday school for slaves in Lexington, Virginia) did not hear any of it; he slept through most of the service, as was his custom. The Trinity Chapel on Church Street just west of Market was started in 1764. Nearby is the Evangelical Lutheran Church, dating to 1753, with spires added in 1854. Pews were used during the war for sick and wounded soldiers. Markers around the center of downtown denote other historical structures from Lincoln's time and related to Civil War events, including an excellent Civil War Medical Museum.

BARBARA FRITCHIE'S HOME is at **154 WEST PATRICK**, also walking distance from the above-mentioned sites. According to tradition and a John Greenleaf Whittier poem, she defied the Rebel army and Stonewall Jackson by waving a Union flag and yelling, "Shoot if you must this old gray head, but spare your country's flag." True or not, a marker in front notes this and visits by many prominent people including Franklin Roosevelt and Winston Churchill in 1943. Her grave is prominently marked at Mount Olivet Cemetery.

POINT LOOKOUT PRISON: Lincoln visited here on December 27–28, 1863. This is located where the Potomac River in Maryland joins Chesapeake Bay.

ROCKPORT: Lincoln made a speech made August 26, 1848, before a Whig convention in Montgomery County and also at a meeting at the COURTHOUSE of the Rough and Ready Club. He was also here in August 1861 with Seward and McClellan to meet General Banks at his headquarters to discuss his actions in suppressing the secession session of the Maryland legislature in September.

SILVER SPRING: Lincoln visited Frances Preston Blair Sr. at his country estate, "SILVER SPRING," on several occasions, and probably nearby FAWKLAND. This is a few blocks from the District of Columbia border and NORTH OF THE INTERSECTION OF GEORGIA AVENUE AND EAST-WEST HIGHWAY. Initially a summer residence, Blair lived here year-round after 1852. The house was located at the site of the interior driveway and loading dock of the post office on NEWELL AND KENNETH STREETS. The entrance to the estate was just across the Maryland line on the present Georgia Avenue.

Blair had been the editor of the *Globe* and advisor to President Andrew Jackson. He continued to observe and sometimes manipulate politics until after the Civil War. Many prominent leaders of the day visited. Jefferson Davis had been a frequent visitor, but he was not allowed to discuss politics. At Lincoln's instigation, Blair unofficially offered Robert E. Lee the command of the Union army in the Blair town home still across from the White House, the BLAIR HOUSE. Immediately after his disastrous vice presidential inauguration, Andrew Johnson sought solace and recovery with the Blairs.

Confederate generals Jubal Early and John C. Breckinridge, former vice president under Buchanan, made this their headquarters for a short time when they raided Washington, D.C., on July 11, 1864. The house was then abandoned, but the generals sought to protect it from vandalism. Breckinridge was a cousin to the Blairs and said that this was the only place that he felt was a home to him east of Kentucky. Confederate soldiers had, in fact, stopped here and nearby to loot, but Early flew into a rage shouting that this delay cost them the campaign. While here, Early sent out his cavalry to test the defenses at Fort Stevens, about a mile to the south where Lincoln saw some action. Confederate forces were fired upon with little effect except to damage local houses, probably causing the fire that destroyed the adjacent home, known as FAWKLAND. But more likely, this home of Francis Blair's son, Postmaster General Montgomery Blair, not protected by Breckinridge, was intentionally destroyed by Confederate troops.

FAWKLAND was located at the NORTHEAST CORNER OF COLESVILLE AND EAST-WEST HIGHWAY, ROUTE 410, a few city blocks from the current site of Silver Spring House. It had been insured, but not against "a public enemy." This loss produced great sympathy for the cabinet member. General Early denied ordering the burning, but said he approved since Union forces had burned Virginia governor Letcher's home. A small acorn house at Newell and East-West Highway is all that remains now of Silver Spring.

SHARPSBURG: See Antietam National Battlefield (Sharpsburg), Maryland.

SURRATTSVILLE: See Clinton, Maryland.

TRAIL OF THE ASSASSINS: On the evening of April 14, 1865, John Wilkes Booth shot Abraham Lincoln at Ford's Theater in Washington, D.C., and fled through Maryland and Virginia where he had hoped to be hailed as a hero by those who had been oppressed by the "dictator in Washington." It is not known exactly how he escaped through the Federal District. One witness reported that he emerged from the alley behind Ford's Theater at F Street and rode west. This does not seem likely. The shortest and presumed route would have been east on F Street to New Jersey Avenue and around the Capitol Building. Then the presumed route continues down Pennsylvania to Eighth and then M Streets. (This would have taken him past conspirator David Herold's house at 1118 Eighth Street.) We know he crossed into Maryland over the NAVY YARD BRIDGE at about the same location of the present Eleventh Street Bridge east of the Washington Navy Yard. To follow the escape route, cross the bridge and follow GOOD HOPE ROAD to the top of the hill, then turn right onto NAYLOR ROAD for 1.3 miles to BRANCH AVENUE, into Maryland. From the traffic light at Naylor Road and Branch Avenue (Route 5), go 2.8 miles south to Interstate 95, the approximate location of SOPER'S HILL. Booth met fellow conspirator David E. Herold here. Herold had been with Lewis Powell (Payne) who had the assignment of killing Secretary of State William Seward. When Powell was confronted in Seward's House, a loud melee broke out, and Herold fled to join Booth at the predesignated spot. Herold had rented a horse from stableman John Fletcher and was supposed to return it earlier in the day. When Fletcher spotted him during his flight at 10:15, he chased Herold to the bridge but did not follow, as he would not have been permitted to come back into Washington at night. Fletcher, of course, did not know about the assassination.

From SOPER'S HILL continue to the first traffic light, at MANCHESTER AVENUE, and turn right onto OLD BRANCH AVENUE, the original route. Three miles ahead is Clinton, known as Surrattsville during the war. The town had been named for Mary Surratt's husband who had been the postmaster. The SURRATT TAVERN is just past PISCATAWAY ROAD and BRANDYWINE ROAD. This was known as a safe house for Confederate spies operating out of Washington. Booth and Herold arrived just after midnight. Mary Surratt's son, John, had delivered two Spencer carbines, ammunition, and other items earlier to be used in the intended kidnapping of the president. On the day of the assassination, Mary had gone to the tavern, at Booth's request, to deliver the field glasses and supposedly told the innkeeper, John M. Lloyd, "to have the shooting irons ready that evening." Booth now stopped to get what he could carry. He refused one carbine, as he could not carry it with his broken leg. Lloyd's testimony was a key in convicting her in the later trial where she was sentenced to death. The Surratt Society conducts tours of the house and Booth's escape route.

After leaving the tavern, continue down **HIGHWAY 5 TO T. B.**, which got its name from a property marker at the boundary of Thomas Brooke's land. Booth had previously arranged for fresh horses at the tavern to be available after he planned to kidnap the president. The tavern was at a spot in the small triangle in the road at the junction of Brandywine Road (the road from the Surratt Tavern) and Route 301, but has been moved to the southwest corner of the intersection. From here Booth went by an unknown route to the home of **DR. SAMUEL MUDD**, arriving at about 4:00 A.M. One route now is to follow **HIGHWAY 5** for three miles south of T. B. to the **MATTAWOMAN-BEANTOWN ROAD** to the **POPLAR HILL-BEANTOWN ROAD** just east of Beantown, then east on **ROUTE 382 TO ROUTE 232, BRYANTOWN ROAD**.

The **MUDD HOUSE** is less than half a mile south of the intersection of Routes 232 and 382 on the west side of 232. Signs and historical markers clearly show the location, on the west side of the road. Booth had spent the night at the Mudd House, probably on November 13 and December 19, 1864. He had broken his leg either from the fall at Ford's Theater, when his horse fell later, or by both injuries. Booth certainly knew how to find the country house in a fast trip in the dark. Whether Mudd was a coplotter or not, Booth needed medical help, food, and shelter. Mudd paid dearly for his assistance.

The Mudd House is original and open to the public on a limited basis by the Dr. Samuel Mudd Society. Mudd's granddaughter, whose father was a baby in the house at the time of Booth's visit, operates the gift shop, at least through 1999. Booth and Herold entered through the front entrance on the east side of the home facing the road. The assassin was treated in the front parlor at the large window, and then occupied the front bedroom overlooking the east entrance.

There is still a controversy about how much Dr. Mudd knew before the assassination and at the time Booth was in the home on April 15. Booth had met him at **ST. MARY'S CHURCH** south of Bryantown on Sunday, November 13, 1864. Mudd was a member of the closer St. Peters Church, and no one knows why he was at St. Mary's. The Mudd family believes that Booth only told Mudd that he was trying to buy a horse, and Mudd aided in finding a seller. In fact, Booth may have spent the night of November 13 with Mudd at the house and much of the following day when he did buy a horse from a neighbor, **GEORGE GARDINER**, whose home can be seen bordering on the north of Mudd's property. The one-eyed animal was used by assassin Lewis Powell to flee Seward's home on April 14. It seems probable that Mudd knew Booth was plotting a kidnapping of the president and was looking for an escape route and Confederate agents who could aid him. Mudd was known to be a Confederate sympathizer and knew other Confederate operatives in the area.

Later on December 18, Mudd introduced Booth to the chief of the Confederate Secret Service, Thomas Harbin, in the **BRYANTOWN INN**. It is possible that Booth stayed with Mudd at this time also. Later, Mudd accidentally ran into or purposely met Booth in Washington on December 23. The two then met John Surratt Jr. on the street and went to Booth's room at the **NATIONAL HOTEL**. So, clearly Mudd knew Booth, but may or may not have recognized him in the early morning of April 15. His supporters will argue that Mudd had nothing to do with either the conspiracy or escape. And in the early, dark hours of April 15, Mudd did not recognize Booth, who was disguised with a false beard. Others find this hard to believe, especially since there is no other evidence of such a beard being used and none was found. At any rate, there is no evidence to believe that Mudd knew what Booth had done until Mudd heard the news in town.

Mudd went into Bryantown during the midmorning with Herold, although Herold decided not to enter town and went back to the farm. When Mudd heard of the assassination, and pursuit of the two suspects in the area, he returned home and either found the assassins gone, about to leave, or he told them to leave, depending on which story one believes. He told his cousin, Dr. George D. Mudd, in **ST. PETER'S CHURCH** the next day, Sunday, April 16. It was agreed that George would tell authorities, which he did on Monday. St. Peters, northwest on Route 382, had been Mudd's church where he was married and where his children were baptized.

Possibly, Mudd could have claimed the large reward offered for the assassins and been a hero, rather than be put into prison, if he had led authorities to his home while Booth was there on Saturday. But he was probably so deep into the kidnap plans that he would have been tried as an accomplice anyway. His house was searched on April 21, when Booth's boot was found. (This is now in the Ford's Theater Museum.) Later, when questioned by authorities, he downplayed his knowledge of Booth. He claimed he had only met Booth once, but Louis J. Weichmann soon informed Secretary of War Stanton of the Washington visit. Mudd was tried by the military commission and charged with plotting to kill the president. He missed a death sentence by one vote, and was sentenced to hard labor for life. President Andrew Johnson pardoned him in February 1869 after a heroic effort to treat yellow fever victims at his Fort Jefferson, Florida, prison in the Gulf of Mexico.

Since Bryantown was crawling with Union soldiers, Booth went south and east from the Mudd House probably to the present **CRACKLINTOWN ROAD** to the east down present **ROUTES 231 AND 232**. About **A MILE EAST OF THE PRESENT BEVERLY DRIVE AND CRACKLINTOWN ROAD** they enlisted **OSWELL SWANN** at his house, no longer traceable, to serve as a guide to the home of **SAMUEL COX**. Possibly Mudd had told them of soldiers in Bryantown and directed them to the Swann home. They then continued through the difficult **ZEKIAH SWAMP SOUTHWEST OF PRESENT ROUTES 232 AND 6** to the present **BEL ALTON-NEWTOWN ROAD** where he came to the Cox home known as **RICH HILL**, built in the early eighteenth century. The house is clearly visible and marked.

Swann claimed that Cox invited the men in for several hours, but Cox and his servants denied this. Cox may have known who Booth was and refused to help, sending the assassin on his way. During the night he changed his mind, and went out to find Booth, whom he found hiding in a ditch. He supplied food and arranged for Confederate agent Thomas Jones to assist the assassins as they hid out in the nearby woods for several days. Jones also provided newspapers to Booth, who was stunned to learn that the world did not praise his act as he had expected. A marker just east of Bel Alton notes that Booth and Herald remained hidden in the nearby pine thicket while Union troops searched for them. After hiding in the woods for several days, Jones was in Port Tobacco when news came in that Booth had been seen a number of miles to the east, and all of the soldiers headed in that direction. Jones then rushed to move Booth and Herold toward the Potomac River into Virginia.

The three men then went to Jones's home, **HUCKLEBERRY**, off Route 301 on Pope's Creek Road, about a mile east past the large ATT Tower. The home is clearly seen north of the road and is noted with a historical marker now at the entrance to a Loyola retreat. Jones kept his boat in the Potomac River nearby below the bluff at the edge of Dent's Meadow, now occupied by the private retreat facilities a short distance from the house. For a while Booth waited in the yard in front of Huckleberry to get food from the house. He begged to come inside as he had been out in the open since leaving Mudd's. Jones refused, telling Booth, "Oh my friend, it would not be safe. This is your last chance to get away. I have negroes in the house; and if they see you, you are lost and so am I." (Jones was later arrested and held for six weeks, but suffered no punishment for his role in the escape. He later wrote a book of his involvement. He began it with these words: "No act ever committed has called forth such universal execration as the murder of that great and good man, Abraham Lincoln. To-day I speak of the murdered president as 'great and good;' thirty years ago I regarded him only as the enemy of my country.")

From there Booth was taken to the river below the present retreat building and provided a boat that he rowed west on the Potomac by mistake rather than east as intended. Herold knew the junction of Nanjemoy Creek, and they rested for the night at the Hughes Home, now generally inaccessible to the public. Herold knew the area, and both felt that operatives familiar with the kidnapping plot would be of help. Possibly, they spent April 22 in a small cabin at the water's edge as Hughes knew who the men were and would not let them stay in his house. During this time various Confederate operatives were spreading false information and planning to aid Booth who knew only part of the aid being planned for him. The trip up the river the wrong way, in fact, had confused Jones's men waiting to aid him in Virginia. Finally at sunset on the twenty-second, Booth and Herold rowed east on the Potomac, under the present Route 301 bridge, to the **QUESENBERRY HOME** in Virginia, where the trail continues in that chapter. Jones had directed Booth to this place, suggesting that he might find help (see chapter and entry on **"TRAIL OF THE ASSASSINS"** in the chapter on Virginia).

WASHINGTON, D.C., AREA FORTS: Forts Foote and Washington are on the east side of the Potomac River, south of Washington, west of Route 210 via Fort Foote Road and Old Fort Road. These and Fort Lincoln on the Maryland border are described at the end of the Washington, D.C., chapter.

Massachusetts

L incoln's first American ancestors settled in Massachusetts, and Lincoln visited twice. He first came in September 1848, after his first year in the House of Representatives, on a speaking tour for the support of the Whig Party and its presidential candidate, Zachary Taylor. In February 1860 Lincoln returned after his famous Cooper Union Address on a visit to see this son, Robert, in school in Exeter, New Hampshire. A number of speeches were made in New England on this later trip, but not a single one in Massachusetts already supporting for William Seward as the next Republican nominee.

Samuel Lincoln landed in Salem, Massachusetts, in 1637, and built a house in **HINGHAM**, still standing. Another ancestor was Obadiah Holmes, who was a glassmaker in Salem. He was also a Baptist preacher by 1651 when he was tied to a post and whipped on Boston Common for preaching doctrines contrary to the belief of the established church. He later served thirty years as pastor of the First Baptist Church in Newport, Rhode Island. Holmes's daughter married the son of another Salem immigrant, John Bowne, and the two helped establish the first Baptist Church in New Jersey located in Middletown. Bowne was one of the twelve men to sign the famous Monmouth Patent in 1665, one of the earliest declarations of religious tolerance, which declared: "Free liberty of conscience, without molestation or disturbance whatsoever in way of their worship." Their granddaughter married Samuel Lincoln's grandson, Mordecai II, whose son John migrated to Virginia and was known as "Virginia John." He was the president's great-grandfather.

BOSTON: Lincoln made only one trip to Boston. He arrived on September 15, 1848, and traveled around the area until September 23. On the fifteenth, he spoke before the Boston Whig Club for Zachary Taylor's election at **WASHINGTONIAN HALL AT 23 BROMFIELD STREET,** near the hotel. This is characterized as a preliminary speech to his main endeavor at Worcester. (Several sources, including *Following Abraham Lincoln,* show a speech at the **STATEHOUSE**, but this is not verified in *Day by Day, Collected Works,* or in various articles, local contemporary newspaper accounts, and other sources tracing the New England trip.)

He returned later to the **TREMONT TEMPLE** on September 22. This building, located across from the **GRANARY BURIAL GROUND ON TREMONT STREET,** burned down in 1852, but later buildings with the same name have occupied the site. He stayed in the **TREMONT HOUSE,** located adjacent to and on the north side of the Granary Burial Ground where Paul Revere, Samuel Adams, John Hancock, and others of the Revolutionary War period are buried, on the route of the famous Freedom Trail.

If Mary, Robert (aged five), and Eddie (aged two) came at this time, they stayed in the Tremont when Lincoln traveled to make his presentations. There is a question as to whether he came with his family, but *Day by Day* and David Donald's biography indicate that he did bring them. Other sources (Baker, Turner, Holmes) indicate the family joined him afterward in New York on the way home, and others (Townsend, Oates) that Mary and the boys went directly back to Springfield from their stay in Lexington.

The program at Tremont Temple included William A. Seward, later Lincoln's secretary of state. This was generally said to be their first meeting. (But see the entry on Worcester, Massachusetts. Numerous Boston newspaper stories through the years mention this as their first meeting.) Seward spoke first and his speech appeared in full in the Boston papers. He told his audience that their first duty was to preserve the Union as a voluntary organization, for "a Union upheld by force would be despotism." Lincoln had no manuscript, and thus no words were printed. He commented to Seward, "I have been thinking about what you said in your speech. I reckon you are right. We have got to deal with this slavery question and got to give much more attention to it hereafter than we have been doing." Seward referred to Lincoln's speech as "a rambling story-telling speech, putting the audience in good humor, but avoiding any extended discussion of the slavery question."

It appears that William Schouler was indirectly responsible for Lincoln's visit. The two had been in contact in the Whig National Convention in Philadelphia earlier, and had been in correspondence. The state Whig convention was being held in Worcester, and Lincoln could conveniently pass through on the way back from Washington to Springfield. Lincoln did not speak at the convention, but did at a mass meeting. In 1864 Schouler was adjutant general of Massachusetts and pushed for recognition of the Widow Bixby by the president. It was claimed that she lost five sons in the war. The famous Bixby Letter was written on November 21, 1864, and probably delivered to her by Schouler. He also gave the text of the letter to the Boston newspapers and a copy of the letter to the *Army and Navy Journal* of New York, published on December 3, 1864. There is no trace of the letter now, and it is arguable that Lincoln did not write it. Author James G. Randall compared it to the Gettysburg Address as a "masterpiece of the English language." Carl Sandburg felt it was "a piece of the American Bible." But Mrs. Bixby, who ran a house of ill repute, lost only two sons and was a Southern sympathizer. She is said to have resented the letter and Lincoln and possibly destroyed it. The text was prominently used in the popular movie, *Saving Private Ryan*.

(Professor Michael Burlingame makes strong arguments that John Hay wrote the letter based on Hay's use of language, his own suggestions, and responsibilities in handling the president's mail. He has authored articles in *American Heritage* [July/August 1999] and in the *Journal of the Abraham Lincoln Association* which set forth his reasoning. But this conclusion is disputed by other historians, who believe that it was indeed written by the president. *Abraham Lincoln and the Widow Bixby* and articles in the *Lincoln Herald* [Winter 1989, February 1943, December 1946, etc.] conclude that "the cumulative evidence clearly restores the pen to the great President's hand." Roy Basler also stresses that Lincoln was the author in a December 1943 *Lincoln Herald* article. The subject has been analyzed many times; see the references shown in the articles mentioned.)

Lincoln passed through Boston on February 29, 1860, on the way to Exeter, New Hampshire. He arrived at the **PLEASANT STREET STATION**, which he had used in 1848 also. He left from the **BOSTON AND MAINE DEPOT ON HAYMARKET SQUARE** and was back here on the return, March 2. On the return he probably used the New York Express via Springfield at the **BOSTON AND WORCESTER DEPOT ON BEACH STREET**, probably used also on the way to Albany in 1848. Since Robert was in Harvard for most of the war, Mary came several times to stay in the **PARKER HOUSE AT 60 SCHOOL STREET.**

CAMBRIDGE: Lincoln gave a speech on the evening of September 20, 1848, at the **CITY HALL**, then at the **NORTHEAST CORNER OF HARVARD AND NORFOLK.** The *Boston Atlas* reported that "Mr. Lincoln . . . is a capital specimen of a 'Sucker' Whig, six feet at least in his stockings, and every way worthy to represent that Spartan band of the only Whig district in poor benighted Illinois."

Robert attended Harvard University in Cambridge throughout most of the Civil War. Senator Stephen A. Douglas had written the letter of introduction to the president of the school. Mary visited him here. Robert came in the fall of 1859, failed his entrance exams, and wound up in Exeter, New Hampshire, to prepare again to seek admission to Harvard, then as now one of the top-rated schools in the country. During his freshman year, 1861, he lived at Pasco's on the corner of Main and Linden. Then he spent two years in room 22 of Stoughton Dorm and his senior year in Hollis Dorm. He endeared himself to his fellow students by describing his father, when asked as "the queerest old cuss you ever saw." Robert had been dubbed "Prince of Rails" during the 1860 presidential election. His father was known as "the Rail-splitter," and the Prince of Wales (later Edward VII of England) had just toured the country. He graduated tied for thirty-second out of ninety-nine in July 1864, and returned to law school until he entered the army the next January.

CHELSEA: Lincoln spoke on September 19, 1848, at **GERRISH HALL.** The *Boston Atlas* described the speech, which "for aptness of illustration, solidity of argument, and genuine eloquence, is hard to beat."

DEDHAM: Lincoln made a speech in the afternoon of September 20, 1848, at **TEMPERANCE HALL**, near the train station. He was escorted by a newspaperman who described him as awkward and ill at ease on the train ride and at the brief reception at the **HAVEN HOUSE.** But when he was introduced, Lincoln instantly changed his demeanor and expression to "bubble out humor and charm." When the train bell began to sound signaling that his train was leaving, Lincoln announced that he had to go. The crowd yelled and urged that he continue, but he ran saying that he was committed to speak in Cambridge.

DORCHESTER: Lincoln gave a speech at **RICHMOND HALL ON WASHINGTON AND SANFORD STREETS**, on September 18, 1848, and spent the night at the home of Nathaniel Safford, a local Whig leader. Here and in other towns, the papers referred to "Abram" Lincoln.

HINGHAM: The **SAMUEL LINCOLN HOUSE**, noted with a historical marker, is where Lincoln's great-great-great-great-grandfather lived and died in 1690. This was Lincoln's first ancestor to set foot in America, coming to America in 1637 at the age of eighteen. He was apprenticed or indentured to a weaver named Frances Lewis in Salem, Massachusetts. Eventually he wound up in Hingham, and worshiped in the nearby Old Ship Church, one of the oldest churches still standing in America. Relative General Benjamin Lincoln is buried here. During the Revolutionary War, he received the sword of British general Lord Cornwallis in surrender at Yorktown, Virginia, by order of General George Washington.

Samuel's son Mordecai's gristmill still stands and is the "**LINCOLN MILL ANTIQUE SHOP**." His home is also here and is a private residence. His wife named a son "Abraham" after her father, and introduced the prolific name to the Lincoln line. Mordecai was the first of Samuel's eleven children to leave; this began the western migration of Lincolns. He settled in Scituate from where his sons went to New Jersey, Pennsylvania, and then Virginia. Lincoln tried to find out something about his family at which time there were at least twenty-nine Abrahams, nineteen Mordecais, and thirty-six Thomases throughout New England, Pennsylvania, Virginia, and Kentucky descended from Samuel.

LOWELL: On September 16, 1848, the *Boston Atlas* reported that "The Whigs of Lowell had one of the tallest meetings on Saturday night that they have yet had . . . addressed by Hon. Abraham Lincoln." The speech was made at **CITY HALL AT MERRIMACK AND SHATTUCK**. It is not known where he stayed, but tradition has it that he was the guest of a reputed cousin of Nancy, wife of **REVEREND STEDMAN HANKS ON KIRK STREET**.

NEW BEDFORD: Lincoln spoke at **LIBERTY HALL (NORTHWEST CORNER OF WILLIAM AND FOURTH)** on September 14, 1848, for Zachary Taylor, and stayed at **41 HAWTHORNE** in the stone mansion of **JOSEPH GRINNELL**, a fellow congressman. The newspapers said, "We have rarely seen a more attentive or interested audience."

SCITUATE: Lincoln's great-great-great-grandfather Mordecai lived here and attended the old church. His seventeenth-century home burned down in 1919, but his 1717 home and gristmill (1691, now the "**LINCOLN**

MILL ANTIQUE SHOP") still stand. He is buried in Groveland Cemetery. His son, Abraham, continued the migration into Pennsylvania.

TAUNTON: Lincoln arrived just after noon on September 21, 1848, and first spoke in a building in the North End. His main address was that evening at **UNION HALL**, close to the center of town. The press did not cover the first speech, but the latter received the most extensive coverage of his entire tour. The *Taunton Daily Gazette* described the presentation as "full of humor and mainly devoted to the political course of Mr. Van Buren and the Free Soil Party." He spent the night at the home of a party member.

WORCESTER: Lincoln attended the state Whig convention and made several speeches in the **FOSTER STREET STATION** (marked by a plaque on **FOSTER STREET**), **OLD SOUTH CHURCH**, and **TOWN HALL, AT THE SOUTH-EAST CORNER OF FRONT AND MAIN**, on September 12 and 13, 1848. The **TOWN HALL** was on the **WEST SIDE OF THE COMMON AT THE SITE OF THE PRESENT TOWN HALL**. The **CHURCH** was at the **SOUTH SIDE OF THE COMMON**. He was entertained at the **HOME OF LEVI LINCOLN JR**. at **25 ELM STREET**, now the offices of the Diocese of Worcester. It was on the **NORTH SIDE OF THE STREET BETWEEN LINDON AND ASHLAND**. The house has been moved to Old Sturbridge Village in Sturbridge, Massachusetts. The ex-governor was also descended from Samuel Lincoln. When they met in Worcester, Lincoln said, "I hope we both belong, as the Scotch say, to the same clan; but I know one thing, and that is, that we are both good Whigs." During the Civil War, the president received a visit from Levi and remembered his meal in Worcester as the best dinner of his life.

According to *William Henry Seward, Lincoln's Right Hand*, Lincoln and his future secretary of state, William H. Seward, shared a hotel room at the **LINCOLN HOUSE** for the night. Seward is quoted as saying, "We spent the greater part of the night talking, I insisting that the time had come for sharp definitions of opinions and boldness of utterance. Before we went to sleep Mr. Lincoln admitted that I was right in my anti-slavery position and principles." (I can confirm this in no other source, including other Seward biographies and the extensive newspaper file at the Lincoln Museum in Fort Wayne, covering Worcester and many other Massachusetts towns.) The hotel was on the west side of **MAIN STREET** with wings extending back to Elm and Maple. This was also known as the Worcester House, and had been the home of Levi Lincoln before he moved in 1835. It was also about a block west of the train station mentioned above.

Michigan

DEARBORN: At the HENRY FORD MUSEUM is the blood-covered chair that Lincoln was sitting in at Ford's Theater when he was assassinated on April 14, 1865. This belonged to theater owner John Ford, and was confiscated by the government. Lincoln's shawl carried that night and part of actress Laura Keene's bloodstained dress are also here. (Also the museum contains the car John F. Kennedy rode in in Dallas at his assassination.) In the adjacent Greenfield Village is the original Logan County, Illinois, courthouse, transported, from Postville where Lincoln practiced law.

DETROIT: Lincoln and his family came through Detroit in early October 1848 on the way back from New England. They took the steamer *Globe* from Buffalo, and then proceeded to Chicago. It is not known whether he took the steamer all the way, as is generally believed, or went by stagecoach and railroad from Detroit to Chicago. At some point, probably on the Detroit River, he saw a steamer piled up on an island or, according to another story, maybe his boat got stuck on a sandbar in Lake Erie. Lincoln got the idea for "expandsible [*sic*] buoyant chambers placed at the sides" that would ease itself off a bar. This was made later into a model, and a patent was granted in May 1849. The model can be seen at the Patent Office in Washington. This was the only patent ever received by a president, called by many a perfect failure as no practical use was ever made of it.

KALAMAZOO: Lincoln gave a speech on August 27, 1856, at BRONSON PARK (then City Park) on South Street between Park and Rose Streets.

His law partner, Herndon, considered the speech to be his best ever. The text was not recorded, and is sometimes referred to as the Lost Speech. (Many of Lincoln's early speeches were not preserved and can also be referred to as "lost." See the entry on Bloomington, Illinois.) He was a guest at the home of **HEZEKIAH G. WELLS**, who had organized the rally and invited Lincoln. Wells's home was in Schoolcraft, thirteen miles south and two blocks west of U.S. Highway 131. He was here campaigning for Republican presidential candidate John C. Frémont. The rally was a huge success; Wells had arranged for special trains to bring participants from other cities. There were dozens of bands, banners, floats, and a huge parade. Estimates of the crowd ranged between ten thousand and thirty thousand, although the population of Kalamazoo was only about ten thousand.

Mississippi

NATCHEZ: Lincoln and Allen Gentry stopped here on November 24, 1828, en route to New Orleans. This was probably the largest town Abe had seen. He probably stopped in 1831 also.

VICKSBURG: Biographer William Herndon believed that Lincoln stopped briefly during the 1831 boat trip. It is possible a stop was made also in 1828. The Mississippi River now bypasses the town, but flowed by it until after the Civil War at the spot now occupied by the Yazoo River diversion.

Missouri

COLUMBIA: Lincoln is sometimes reported to have come here after a political speech in **ROCHEPORT**, Missouri, in 1840 during the presidential campaign. He may have come to court his future wife when she visited relatives. Mary's niece, Katherine Helm, wrote in her biography that Lincoln came here to meet Mary in her uncle's home and attended the Presbyterian Church in the Todd pew. However most historians dispute this, and I can find no support for placing Lincoln in either town. *Day by Day* does not include any reference, but there are some unknown dates during this period.

HANNIBAL: Lincoln first came through here on his way to and from Iowa in August 1859. On that trip he could go by train to Quincy, Illinois, and then downriver to catch the new Hannibal and St. Joseph Railroad without staying in Hannibal for the night. The route went through Palmyra, Ely, Monroe, Hunnewell, Lakeman, Shelbina, Clarence, Carbon, Hudson (Macon), Bevier, Callao, Stockton (New Cambria), St. Catherine, Laclede, Chillecothe, Utica, Breckenridge, Hamilton, Cameron, Osborn, Stewartsville, and Easton. He probably spent the night in town upon return, August 17.

He came through again to and from his Kansas speaking trip in late 1859. He got his hair cut here on the way. A marker notes that he stayed at the **PLANTER'S HOTEL** then located on the **WEST SIDE OF MAIN BETWEEN BIRD AND HILL STREETS**. Upon his arrival he went immediately to the office of **JUDGE JOHN B. HELM** located where the drivethrough of the Hannibal National Bank is now on **MAIN JUST NORTH OF**

BROADWAY. A plaque on a building marked the spot before it was torn down. It is claimed that Lincoln stayed at the judge's home at the NORTHWEST CORNER OF SIXTH AND NORTH STREETS, but it cannot be proven where he stayed. Lincoln commented to the huge crowd following him to the office, that he had known the judge as a boy in Kentucky. His mother brought him to Helm's store in Elizabethtown. He stated, "This man was the first man I ever knew who wore store clothes all week. My ambition when I was a boy, was to reach his position in society" (*History of Marion County, Missouri*, by R. I. Holcombe, 1884, and *The Story of Hannibal* by J. Hurley Hagood and Roberta [Roland] Hagood, 1976. See also the entry on Elizabethtown, Kentucky, which questions this).

Lincoln's funeral train came here after his burial in Springfield, and a mock funeral with an empty coffin was held.

NEW MADRID: It is believed that Lincoln, in one or more of his trips down the river, came into the town "like a seaport" with one hundred boats arriving every day.

ST. JOSEPH: On the way to examine some land in Council Bluffs, Iowa, Lincoln came this way to catch the steamer. He stayed at the PLANTERS HOTEL at MAIN AND 101 FRANCES STREETS on August 16, 1859, coming back and probably August 10 on the way. Lincoln visited the editor of the *St. Joseph Journal* on the latter date. He journeyed here again on November 30 on the way to make a series of speeches in Kansas, and came to the same hotel. The site is now a paper and office supply company near Riverside Park. The hotel is also referred to as the Edgar House.

ST. LOUIS: THE NATIONAL HOTEL, also called Scott's, at the SOUTHWEST CORNER OF THIRD AND MARKET, was the site where Lincoln and his family stayed on the way to Washington in 1847. He met his friend, Joshua Speed, then, and they traveled together to Louisville. The site is now in the widened street across from KMOX-CBS. This is a block from the old courthouse, now a museum, where the slave Dred Scott began a legal action to gain his freedom. It is also across the street from the famous Old Cathedral, still standing. He also passed through several other times, including on his trip to Louisville in 1841, on his return trips alone from Washington in 1849, and probably on his trip to Lexington in the fall of 1849 with the family.

Within walking distance are several other Civil War–related sites. Robert E. Lee stayed in the Old National also, and lived with his family in 1838 at the southeast corner of Vine and Main, about four blocks north of the National. Neither street runs to this location now, currently at the eastern edge of the Arch parking garage roof. Ulysses S. Grant was married in a home then at the northeast corner of Fourth and Caerre Streets about four blocks south of the National site, now a vacant lot adjacent to the exit ramp of Interstate 55 and Interstate 44. Future Confederate general James Longstreet was his best man. Grant had an office before the Civil War at Pine and Memorial Drive and lived at 209 South Pine, 1008 Burton, and 632 Lynch at Seventh Street, all downtown. William Tecumseh Sherman lived at Twelfth Street and Chouteau, at the Planters Hotel on Fourth Street between Pine and Chestnut, and at Sixth and Washington. No original buildings remain although Grant's original home, cabin, and family structures are still in the suburbs. Sherman is buried in Calvary Cemetery north of downtown.

New Hampshire

CONCORD: Lincoln was first introduced as "The Next President" before a speech on March 1, 1860, in **PHENIX HALL** (also spelled "Phoenix"). Lincoln was so surprised that he made no comment, but then later asked if the speaker really meant it. The *Concord Statesman* declared, "A political speech of greater power has rarely if ever been uttered in the capital of New Hampshire." He stayed in the Phenix Hotel.

DOVER: Lincoln spoke at the **CITY HALL** at the **NORTHEAST CORNER OF CENTRAL AND HALE**, on March 2, 1860, and slept in the northeast bedroom at the **GEORGE MATHESON HOME AT 107 LOCUST**. This is now called the **LINCOLN HOUSE**. He visited the **NEW HAMPSHIRE HOTEL ON THIRD STREET**, and got a shave at a barbershop on the corner of **CENTRAL AND ORCHARD**. He also visited **J. FRANK SEARVEY ON CENTRAL AVENUE**.

EXETER: Robert had failed his Harvard entrance exams, and was studying at Exeter Academy to get the foundation he would need to reapply. Lincoln visited his son at the boarding house of **MRS. J.B. CLARK** located at **HIGH AND PLEASANT**. He probably stayed there at least one night, February 29, 1860, and maybe March 3. For a short time, father and son were very close, largely because Willie and Tad were not around. Robert stayed on the second floor of this building dating to 1816. Lincoln spoke at the **TOWN HALL** at **7 FRONT STREET** on March 3, 1860. He spent at least one night at the home of his congressional colleague, **AMOS TUCK,** at **89 FRONT STREET**. Tuck was one of the founders of the Republican Party. Robert and his father also attended the **SECOND CHURCH OF THE NEW PARISH**.

The sculptor Daniel Chester French, whose work includes the Lincoln figure in the Lincoln Memorial in Washington, was born at 34 Court Street and grew up at 5 Nelson Drive. All structures mentioned are original. General Grant sent his son, Ulysses Jr., to Exeter Academy also.

FRANCONIA NOTCH: Mary, Robert, and Tad traveled around New England after Mary's carriage accident in July 1863. There is a picture of them at **THE FLUME**, still a popular attraction.

MANCHESTER: On March 1, 1860, Lincoln and Robert stayed at the **CITY HOTEL, NORTHEAST CORNER OF ELM AND LOWELL**, after Lincoln spoke at **SMYTH HALL** before an "immense gathering." The latter was in the Smyth Block on **ELM BETWEEN WATER AND SPRING STREETS**. He went to the **AMOSKEAG MILLS ON THE MERRIMACK RIVER AT CANAL STREET**. There a machinist hesitated to use his dirty hands to shake Lincoln's, who is reported to have said, "Young man, the hand of honest toil is never too grimy for Abe Lincoln to clasp."

New Jersey

CAPE MAY: The Lincoln family is claimed to have visited here twice, although neither date appears sufficiently supported. Lincoln is claimed to have spent a day or two at this famous resort during an 1857 combination business and pleasure trip, which included Niagara Falls. There is evidence from a guest register that "A. Lincoln and wife" were at the **MANSION HOUSE** on July 31, 1849. *Lincoln Day by Day* shows him in Springfield on that date, and his "signature" is generally considered spurious. The reference also shows that he was back in Springfield by July 4, 1849, and that his trip to Washington was unaccompanied. Ruth Painter Randall's *Biography of a Marriage* claims that Mary was never in Cape May.

FREEHOLD: Lincoln's great-grandfather, John, was born here in 1716. The family later moved to Pennsylvania and then to Virginia where he was known as "Virginia John." Ironworks located in **CLARKSBURG**, Freehold township, were believed to have been built by his father, Mordecai Lincoln Jr.

JERSEY CITY: Lincoln passed through the railroad station on the site of Pennsylvania Station, several times going to and from New York City, including his inaugural trip. He passed through in his journey to West Point in 1862, when he made a brief speech. Robert Lincoln was saved from potential death at the station by actor Edwin Booth, sometime prior to the president's death (see entry on Bel Air, Maryland).

NEWARK: Two thirds of Newark's seventy thousand lined the streets when Lincoln passed through en route to his inauguration on February 21, 1861. His train from New York brought him to the "lower depot," and he rode in an open carriage for one and a half miles to the "upper" depot. He made speeches at both. The route was along CHESTNUT STREET, PAST THE NINTH WARD SCHOOL TO THE CHESTNUT STREET STATION.

INAUGURAL TRIP, FEBRUARY 21, 1861: Short speeches were made at JERSEY CITY, NEWARK, ELIZABETH, NEW BRUNSWICK, RAHWAY, AND PRINCETON on the way to TRENTON.

LONG BRANCH: Mary, Willie, and Tad stayed at the MANSION HOUSE on August 16, 1861.

TRENTON: The president-elect rode in an open barouche west on State Street and spoke at the STATE HOUSE on February 21, 1861. He first spoke to the senate in their chamber where he told them: "In my childhood . . . I got hold of a small book, 'Weems life of Washington.' I remember all the accounts there given of the battlefields and struggles for the liberties of the country, and none fixed themselves upon my imagination so deeply as the struggle here at Trenton. . . . I am exceedingly anxious that . . . this Union, the Constitution, and the liberties of the people shall be perpetuated in accordance with the original idea for which that struggle was made." He said that no one was more devoted to peace than he was or would do more to maintain peace, but at times it must be necessary to put the foot down firmly. He called for assistance to the other house, the General Assembly of New Jersey, in piloting the ship of state through the perils, because if it suffered a wreck now, there would be no pilot needed for another voyage.

After the speeches he ate lunch at the TRENTON HOUSE on the SOUTHEAST CORNER OF NORTH WARREN AND EAST HANOVER Streets. He stayed in room 100 on the second floor facing Warren Street and spoke from the balcony to a large crowd. The 1824 hotel had hosted Lafayette and survived until 1987. The barouche or coach used is now in a glass-enclosed summer alcove of Buckelew House on Buckelew Avenue in Jamesburg, New Jersey. (The founder of the town and owner of the coach was James Buckelew.) Lincoln's funeral train stopped in town on April 24, 1865.

New York

ALBANY: It is believed that Lincoln first came to the capital of New York on September 26, 1848, where he met with influential Whig editor Thurlow Weed, maybe in his Green Street home, and the Whig candidate for vice president, Millard Fillmore.

He visited again on February 18, 1861, on the way to Washington, and spoke briefly from the train platform. He was in a railway car, previously used by the Prince of Wales. At first he was not recognized at the **BROADWAY RAILROAD CROSSING WITH LUMBER (NOW LIVINGSTON) STREET**. His arrival was early and a large crowd had gathered to see the largely unknown westerner. Onlookers went out of control and flooded the area when the train pulled in, with children climbing all over the engine. When order was restored, Lincoln was led to a special speaker's platform, but was greeted with perplexed stares and a faint cheer rather than the expected excited enthusiasm. He did not look like the clean-shaven, rawboned rail-splitter in circulated images. During the election he had grown a beard, and was looking very tired by this time. He then rode to the Capitol in a carriage to address a joint meeting of the legislature, where he told them: "It is true that while I hold myself without mock modesty, the humblest of all individuals that have ever been elevated to the presidency, I have a more difficult task to perform than any one of them. . . . I still have confidence that the Almighty, the maker of the Universe will . . . bring us through this as He has through all other difficulties of our country." The speech clearly revealed his state of mind, as he was about to take over a great burden. The **OLD CAPITOL** was at the **HEAD OF STATE STREET ON CAPITOL HILL** at a spot now in the front lawn facing the southeast corner of the new building built after the Civil War.

He then rode through the crowds **DOWN BROADWAY AND UP STATE STREET**. John Wilkes Booth was playing at Stanwix Hall on Broadway about three blocks from the **DELAVAN HOUSE (BROADWAY AT STEUBEN)** and was seen muttering defiance at Lincoln as he passed. The actor later played his last acting performance on March 15, 1865, in Albany.

The party stayed at the **DELAVAN** where Lincoln received Thurlow Weed and many others before dining at the governor's mansion **(144 STATE)** with Governor Edwin D. Morgan. That evening he greeted about one thousand people and attended a levee held for the ladies. Jefferson Davis was inaugurated president of the Confederacy on the same day in Montgomery, Alabama. (That spot is marked on the steps of the Alabama State Capitol.) There were only seven states in the Confederacy then, including Texas, which had voted for secession on February 1. Some of the eight other slave states seemed certain to follow. Rivalry between the governor and legislature hampered the Albany visit, and the Lincolns vowed never to return.

The president's body was viewed by fifty-five thousand in the **ASSEMBLY CHAMBER OF THE "OLD" CAPITOL** on April 26, 1865. Many were turned away at the doors after the time came to close the viewing. The funeral procession passed **STATE, DOVE, WASHINGTON, AND BROADWAY TO THE DEPOT ON BROADWAY**.

BUFFALO: Lincoln traveled through in late September 1848 on his way home from Washington via New England and Niagara Falls. The family caught the *Globe* steamer for Chicago. After Mary's shopping trip in January 1861 to New York City, she returned through Buffalo, but due to a confusion of trip provisions, she had no ticket or pass to Springfield. Seventeen-year-old Robert went to the superintendent of the State Line Railroad and warned, "My name is Bob Lincoln; I am the son of Old Abe—the old woman is in the cars raising h-ll about her passes." This got her a free ride home.

On his way to Washington, February 16, 1861, a crowd of ten thousand including former president Millard Fillmore greeted the president-elect. He used the **EXCHANGE STREET DEPOT**. Guards of soldiers and police were unable to prevent a disorderly jam, and many in the party were jostled and separated. Major (later General) David Hunter's arm was dislocated. Lincoln rode to the **AMERICAN HOUSE HOTEL** on the west side of **MAIN STREET ABOVE EAGLE AND BELOW COURT STREET**. Here he spoke from the balcony asking that the people maintain their composure. He saw the banner at the YMCA across the street displaying WE ARE PRAYING FOR YOU. He stated that he could not speak more about the present crisis until he waited for further developments. A public reception followed with serenades by singing groups.

The next morning, Fillmore called on Lincoln and they attended a service at the **FIRST UNITARIAN CHURCH AT EAGLE AND FRANKLIN STREETS**. Afterward they returned to the hotel for Mrs. Lincoln and then dined at the home of the ex-president on **NIAGARA SQUARE AT THE NORTHEAST CORNER OF DELAWARE, BETWEEN DELAWARE AND GENESEE**. The square is where the major streets of Niagara, Delaware, and Genesee meet. After lunch with Fillmore, the party went into seclusion at the American House. Willie and Tad had the run of the hotel with the proprietor's son. They got up a game of leapfrog that the president-elect happily joined. Afterward he received friends, ate with the family, and attended a service at **ST. JAMES HALL** led by an Indian preacher. They left the next morning at 5:45 A.M. Fillmore was not a Republican supporter and voted for McClellan in 1864.

On April 27, 1865, the president's body was viewed in **ST. JAMES HALL, ON THE SOUTH SIDE OF EAGLE, EAST OF MAIN**.

DUNKIRK: Lincoln's inaugural train stopped so he could address fifteen thousand from a trackside platform. He stated: "Standing as I do, with my hand upon this staff, and under the folds of the American flag, I ask you to stand by me so long as I stand by it."

INAUGURAL TRIP: On the way to Washington the president made an arduous, circuitous campaignlike excursion to show himself to the people. The trip included brief addresses at **WESTFIELD, DUNKIRK**, and **SILVER CREEK** before arriving for the stayover at **BUFFALO**, February 16–17, 1861. After leaving Buffalo, they stopped at **BATAVIA, ROCHESTER, CLYDE, SYRACUSE, UTICA (BAGG'S SQUARE AND CENTRAL RAILROAD TRACKS), LITTLE FALLS, FONDA, AMSTERDAM, AND SCHENECTADY** on the way to **ALBANY** on February 18. In **ROCHESTER**, he was supposed to appear at the Waverly House, but officials did not delay because of limited time. So he spoke from the back of the train platform on tracks extending into Mill Street. On the way to New York City, February 19, they stopped in **TROY, RHINEBECK, HUDSON, POUGHKEEPSIE, FISHKILL, TARRYTOWN, AND PEEKSKILL**.

LAKE GEORGE: Mary and her sons stayed at the **ASTOR HOUSE HOTEL** on August 15, 1864

NEW YORK CITY: Lincoln passed through on the way to New England in 1848. It is believed he left by train at the NEW HAVEN DEPOT AT FOURTH AVENUE AND TWENTY-SEVENTH STREET, the site of Old Madison Square Garden. He came again in 1857 with his family to collect a court-ordered fee from the Illinois Central Railroad. Little is known about the details of these visits to the nation's largest city. In 1857, they evidently stayed in the ASTOR HOTEL and toured CENTRAL AND BATTERY PARKS. Central Park was the ugliest part of Manhattan prior to becoming the first planned urban park in the country at about this time. Mary wrote her half sister, Emilie, that she had seen the large steamers in New York ready for leaving to Europe, and she longed to go.

When the largely unknown westerner came to speak at the Cooper Institute in February 1860, he was just a favorite son of a faraway state. When he left a few days later, he was nationally known. The end of the train line from Illinois was in Jersey City. No one greeted him as he got off the COURTLAND STREET FERRY, and he walked by himself to the ASTOR HOUSE on February 25. The hotel was called "sensational" when built a few years earlier with interior plumbing. Its top price was $2 per night. He stayed until the twenty-seventh and probably March 10–11 headed back home. It was located at **217 BROADWAY**, on the west side between VESEY AND BARCLAY STREETS, across from CITY HALL. Much earlier the site was the home of John Jacob Astor from 1792 to 1795 and then Vice President Aaron Burr's, listed as "Official Residence of the Vice President," although the capital was in Washington by his term. The site is now almost next to the Woolworth Building, once the tallest building in the world. Although not verified, there is a story that Lincoln was then offered a tempting $10,000 per year retainer at the Astor to serve as General Counsel to the New York Central Railroad, due to his success in representing the Illinois Central.

Lincoln had been invited to lecture or speak at Henry Ward Beecher's PLYMOUTH CHURCH in Brooklyn. He accepted provided he could make a political speech. Shortly after arrival he went to see HENRY C. BOWEN, the publisher of the *New York Independent*, at **4 BEEKMAN STREET**, two blocks from his hotel. There he learned that it was rescheduled for COOPER INSTITUTE. A group of Republicans ostensibly were promoting a series of political lectures, but actually trying to thwart powerful New York senator William Seward's aspirations for the presidency. The original COOPER INSTITUTE or UNION building still stands at COOPER SQUARE, AT THE CONVERGENCE OF THIRD AND FOURTH AVENUES AND SEVENTH STREET. Some considered it the most elegant auditorium in the world.

Lincoln was tired from a two-day trip, and nervous about how his Western mannerisms and quaint rural accent would be accepted in sophisticated New York. February 26 was a Sunday, and he paid two cents to take the Fulton Street Ferry to Brooklyn to hear Beecher at the **PLYMOUTH CHURCH**. He sat in pew number 89, left side of the center section, four rows from the front. Afterward he ate at the **BOWEN HOUSE, AT CLARK AND WILLOW**. That afternoon he met an Illinois friend, Elihu B. Washburne, at his hotel and was shown around the sites of New York. Surely he must have visited **ST. PAUL'S**, the church of George Washington, across the street to the south from his hotel. Then as now it is the oldest church in town, dating to 1764. He would have noticed and maybe visited **TRINITY CHURCH** down Broadway at the head of Wall Street, then the tallest building in town. He probably also saw the nearby 1719 Fraunces Tavern where Washington bade farewell to his senior officers on December 4, 1783, at the end of the American Revolution. This landmark, 54 Pearl Street at Broad Street, is open to the public.

We know he saw the squalor of **FIVE POINTS**, the area where **DIVISION AND BOWERY STREETS** meet. Here, in the city's worst slum, he delivered an impromptu address to a Sunday school class of the **FIVE POINTS HOUSE OF INDUSTRY CHARITY SCHOOL** at **155 WORTH STREET**. The teacher reported that Lincoln was noticed listening to the children's exercises with such genuine interest that he was asked to speak. The talk stirred "the little faces around him" and "hushed the room to silence" because of Lincoln's "convictions and cheerful words of promise." Lincoln became emotional seeing the poor children and could not continue.

The next morning he spent time with Mason Brayman, toured Broadway, bought a hat at the **KNOX GREAT HAT AND CAP ESTABLISHMENT AT 212 BROADWAY AND FULTON**, and was photographed at **BRADY'S**. **MATTHEW BRADY'S STUDIO AND GALLERY** was at several locations over the years. In 1844, the studio was at **BROADWAY and FULTON** photographing some of the most famous men in the world. In 1853 Brady moved to **359 BROADWAY** and then later to **643 BROADWAY** where he now photographed Lincoln. He had another studio at 205 Broadway.

Brady is recognized as the best-known photographer of the Civil War although eye problems probably prevented much direct active photography. Later when Ward Hill Lamon introduced Brady to Lincoln at the White House, Lincoln gladly said, "Brady and the Cooper Institute made me President." Walking down Broadway on the way, Lincoln met an old friend and asked him how he was doing. When the man confessed to have lost $100,000, Lincoln grinned. He pronounced, "Well, I have eight thousand in the bank, the Springfield cottage, and if they make me Vice President with Seward I'll increase it to twenty thousand and that is as much as any man ought to ask."

Lincoln's speech on February 27, 1860, is said to have contributed more than any other single event to his nomination for president. He was not well known outside of Illinois before the speech, but appeared before the "pick and flower of New York." Even though there was a heavy snowstorm in the city that night, about fifteen hundred paid twenty-five cents to hear the man who had rivaled the great Stephen Douglas out west. His first impression and words failed. His new $100 suit was ill fitting, and his appearance was awkward and uncultivated. When the audience heard, "Mr. Cheerman," in his high falsetto, many shook their heads in disappointment and laughed. Some shouted for him to speak louder, and a Springfield friend sat in the back to raise his hat on a cane when he needed to speak up. Lawyer and diplomat Joseph R. Choate wrote that "as he spoke he was transformed; his eyes kindled, his voice rang, and his face shone and seemed to light up the whole assembly. For an hour and a half, he held the audience in the hollow of his hand."

After this night and his follow-up trip through New England, he became a major political figure. Newspaperman Horace Greeley was impressed. He was instrumental in promoting Lincoln over then frontrunner Seward. Lincoln's lectern is still in use. Other notable speakers have included Ulysses S. Grant, William Lloyd Garrison, Henry Ward Beecher, Harriet Beecher Stowe, Woodrow Wilson, and Mark Twain.

After the speech he ate at **108 FIFTH AVENUE**, about ten blocks away. He then went to the *Tribune* **OFFICE AT NASSAU AND SPRUCE** to have the speech published, and left the blue foolscap manuscript after proofreading the copy. Here thus the manuscript representing a labor of months, painstakingly written with great thought in Lincoln's own hand, was unceremoniously tossed in a trash can, never to be seen again.

While in the East, Lincoln went to New Hampshire to see his son in school, and also to let himself be seen and heard by potential voters. Going and coming he used the depot of **FOURTH AVENUE AND TWENTY-SEVENTH STREET**, also used in 1848.

Lincoln and family arrived on the Hudson River Railroad on his inaugural trip on February 19, 1861, going from the **THIRTIETH STREET STATION AT NINTH AVENUE** to the **HUDSON STREET DEPOT AT CHAMBERS AND BROADWAY**. (Mary had come to New York to shop on January 10, and stayed at the Astor.) An estimated 250,000 people watched as he rode in an open carriage sixty blocks to the **ASTOR HOUSE**, where he acknowledged the crowd at about 4:00 in the afternoon. Poet Walt Whitman wrote of seeing him step out of a carriage looking composed and cool, but tall and awkward, with a dark brown complexion, and a "seam'd and wrinkled face" on top of a "disproportionately long neck." Lincoln spoke briefly to the crowd of about five thousand from the balcony. Although the mayor, Fernando Wood, was a Southern sympathizer, he gave Lincoln a warm welcome. The president-elect commented that this made his reception even more pleasing since many in the crowd had voted against him.

He dined with the family at the hotel and then received numerous delegations while Mrs. Lincoln attended a reception. The next morning he ate at the home of former congressman **MOSES H. GRINNELL, AT FIFTH AVENUE AND FOURTEENTH STREET**. Later he met with the mayor and council in the **GOVERNOR'S ROOM** at **CITY HALL**, on Broadway. The building was completed in 1811 at the then northern boundary of the city, one mile north of the southern tip of Manhattan. The room was designed as the New York City office of the state governors and is still used as such. An 1817 guidebook of New York called City Hall "the handsomest structure in the United States; perhaps of its size, in the world."

Lincoln stood beside Washington's writing desk to greet dignitaries and shake hands for about two hours. He emphasized his determination to preserve the Union when he stated: "There is nothing that can ever bring me willingly to consent to the destruction of this Union, under which . . . the whole country has acquired its greatness, unless it were to be that thing for which the Union itself was made." Afterward he spoke from the balcony.

The mayor emphasized that New York, "sorely afflicted, her commercial greatness endangered," looked to the new president to restore friendly relations between the North and South. Lincoln, remaining noncommittal, thanked him, adding that he agreed with Wood's sentiments.

During the afternoon, he spent another two hours shaking hands. **P. T. BARNUM** invited him to his **AMERICAN MUSEUM** at the corner of **ANN STREET AND BROADWAY**, across from and prominently visible from their hotel. He refused although Mary and the boys went. The museum was across from **ST. PAUL'S CHURCH**. Surely, Mary took the boys to see the pew, still here, where Washington worshiped along with both houses of Congress after his inauguration a few blocks away on April 30, 1789. (The Washington inaugural site was nearby Federal Hall, open at 26 Wall Street, across from the New York Stock Exchange.) Photographer

Mathew Brady was now at **TENTH STREET AND BROADWAY**, having moved during the summer of 1860. The president-elect was now photographed again.

The vice president–elect, Hannibal Hamlin, and his wife met the Lincolns at the **ASTOR**. The couples dined in the Lincoln suite and then attended the **ACADEMY OF MUSIC** presentation of a Verdi opera. This was located at **FOURTEENTH STREET AND FIFTH AVENUE**. The president-elect shocked the city's elite by wearing black rather than white kid gloves on his oversized hands, duly noted in the press the next day. This site is **4 IRVING PLACE** on the northeast corner where the Con Ed building now stands. After the first act the audience and cast sang "The Star-Spangled Banner."

Lincoln was a customer of **BROOKS BROTHERS CLOTHING STORE LOCATED AT 462 BROADWAY AT GRAND**. He was wearing their suits at his second inaugural and at Ford's Theater when assassinated. He may have visited the store in 1861 or before. He went again to the **HOUSE OF INDUSTRY AT FIVE POINTS**, and the home of **HIRAM BARNEY**. Even author Charles Dickens claimed the slums in the Five Points District were worse than he had described in London for *Oliver Twist*. The party left the next morning via the **CORTLANDT STREET FERRY** to **POWLES HOOK IN JERSEY CITY AT EXCHANGE PLACE**.

The president passed through New York City on the way to and from West Point on June 24 and 25, 1862. Mary came back to New York several times during the war. She and her sons stayed at the **METROPOLITAN HOTEL** at **578 BROADWAY,** on May 20, August 13, and September 4, 1861. She was with Robert and Tad here in July and August 1862. She liked to shop for shoes at **EDWIN BROOK'S SHOP** for shoes and boots at **575 BROADWAY**.

She was staying at the **FIFTH AVENUE HOTEL ON MADISON SQUARE AT THE NORTHWEST CORNER OF BROADWAY AND TWENTY-THIRD STREETS** when she received word from her husband that their brother-in-law, General Ben Helm, of the Confederate army, had been killed in 1863. They both loved him as a brother. Lincoln had handed him a commission in the Union army on the same day Robert E. Lee pondered his offer from Lincoln to lead the Union army. Helm and Lee had conferred together, and both rejected the president's offer.

The president's body lay in state on April 24–25, 1865, in the **GOVERNOR'S ROOM OF CITY HALL** where more than 120,000 paid their respects for almost twenty-four hours. The room is on the second floor, just inside the balcony. Afterward, the body was moved up Broadway to the **HUDSON RIVER RAILROAD DEPOT**. As the funeral cortege passed **UNION SQUARE**, a photograph was taken of it showing two small boys in the window of their grandfather's house at Broadway and Fourteenth, Union Square. These were future president Theodore Roosevelt, and his brother Elliot, the father of Eleanor Roosevelt, wife of President Franklin D. Roosevelt.

Mary returned several times. In September and October 1867, she and Tad were at the UNION SQUARE HOTEL on Union Square. She moved to the ST. DENIS HOTEL at 799 BROADWAY (west side of the street at Eleventh Street) as "Mrs. Clark," and then moved to the BRANDRETH HOTEL at 415 BROADWAY as "Mrs. Morris." At this time she was trying to sell her old clothes at W. H. BRADY'S AT 609 BROADWAY. After she arrived back from Europe with Tad in 1871, they stayed briefly at the EVERETT HOUSE NEAR UNION SQUARE AT SEVENTEENTH STREET AND 212 FOURTH AVENUE. This had been named for the famous speaker who shared the platform at Gettysburg with Lincoln. In 1881 she came here to get treatment by Dr. Lewis A. Sayre who visited her at her room in MILLER'S HOTEL, 37–41 WEST TWENTY-SIXTH STREET, AT MADISON SQUARE. She felt overcharged and did not like the place, so she moved to the GRAND CENTRAL HOTEL. Robert and his wife spent their honeymoon at the HOFFMAN HOUSE ON MADISON SQUARE AND TWENTY-THIRD, FACING THE WORTH MONUMENT.

Brooklyn: Now part of New York City, it was the third largest city in the country during the Civil War. When Lincoln came to New York to deliver his address in February 1860, he thought it was to be given at the PLYMOUTH CHURCH IN BROOKLYN, the church of famous preacher Henry Ward Beecher. He came on February 26 to hear Beecher. After the speech at the Cooper Union, and his two-week trip through New England, he returned to New York and attended Plymouth to hear Beecher again on March 11, 1860. This church dates to 1829 and is located at 69 ORANGE STREET BETWEEN HENRY AND HICKS STREETS. Lincoln sat in pew 89 on his first visit and in the balcony in the latter service. Mary attended services on May 12, 1861.

NIAGARA FALLS: Lincoln visited the Falls in September 1848 with the family (Mary, Robert, and Eddie) on the way back from a New England speaking tour and again on July 24, 1857, when he signed, "A. Lincoln and Family, Springfield, Illinois." The family then consisted of Robert, age fourteen, Willie, six, and Tad, four. Mary found this very pleasurable as she revealed in her letter to her half sister. They stayed on the American side at the CATARACT HOUSE, which has been destroyed. THE NIAGARA FALLS MUSEUM has a register to show that Lincoln visited there when the museum was near the river bluff on the Canadian side, down from the Horseshoe Falls. Lincoln jokingly said he wondered where all the water came from. Mary and sons visited again in late August 1861.

POUGHKEEPSIE: On February 19, 1861, the inaugural train stopped for one of the many brief addresses to large crowds. Mrs. Lincoln was watching out the window when the crowd shouted to see the children. She called Robert over, and he received a large cheer. "Have you any more on board?" yelled the crowd. Mrs. Lincoln yelled back, "Yes, here's another," and motioned for Tad to come show himself. Tad refused and made himself flat on the floor, laughing at attempts to get him up. Mary finally had to inform the crowds that "the pet of the family" objected to being put on exhibition. Newspapers also reported that along the way to Washington one of the boys, probably Tad, delighted in asking strangers "if they wanted to See Old Abe?" and then pointed out someone else.

SARATOGA: Mary and sons visited in August 1864. She had also been here during the summer of 1861.

SCHENECTADY: Lincoln spoke briefly at the train depot on February 17, 1861, after being introduced by Supreme Court Justice Platt Potter.

SYRACUSE: On February 17, 1861, a large platform was put up in front of the **GLOBE HOTEL** on **SALINA STREET** for Lincoln to address a crowd of ten thousand. The crowd was disappointed when he spoke from the rear of the train instead.

WESTFIELD: On February 16, 1861, Lincoln's inaugural train stopped, and he sought out eleven-year-old Grace Bedell. She had written him to say: "I have got four brothers and part of them will vote for you anyway and if you let your whiskers grow I will try and get the rest of them to vote for you; you would look a great deal better for your face is so thin."

He had begun his beard about the time he left Illinois. On the way he asked George W. Patterson, who had lived in Westfield, if he knew the Bedell family. He did and felt they would be in the crowd. When the train stopped, Lincoln said he had a friend here, and the crowd demanded to know who it was. Grace was then called for and greeted by the president, who "shook hands and kissed her and asked how she liked the improvements she advised him to make." She lived until 1936 and always stated this was her life's greatest thrill. Her letter is now in the Detroit Public Library. Lincoln's letter sold for $20,000 in the 1960s and was offered for sale for $65,000 in 1976.

WEST POINT: The president made a "mysterious" last-minute trip to see General Winfield Scott on June 24, 1862. Scott had been general-in-chief of the U.S. Army at the beginning of the Civil War, but had been shelved in favor of McClellan who could not tolerate anyone above him. Lincoln now sought Scott's advice from his retirement summer home. The press and general were somewhat alarmed and thought that some crisis must be looming, but Lincoln quickly announced that this was just for military advice from the experienced old warrior. He arrived by train, passing to and from New York City. The president was ferried back and forth from Jersey City to New York, and from **DOCK STREET FERRY AT GARRISON** across from West Point. While here, he stayed at the **COZZENS HOTEL** where Scott was living. This was on the hill behind the new West Point Museum near the main street in **HIGHLAND FALLS**. A historical marker at the Abrams Gate from the town to West Point states, "This is the site. . . ." But the site is now a parking lot for the Five Star Hotel, up the hill from the marker, near the bluff overlooking the Hudson River. The site more recently was Ladycliff Academy.

Lincoln inspected guns at Storm King Mountain on the Hudson River near West Point. The inventor Colonel Robert P. Parrott fired across the river. Lincoln was not impressed and said, "I'm confident you can hit that mountain over there, so suppose we get something to eat. I'm hungry." He also visited cadets at **FORT CLINTON**, and met with ten whom he had appointed after becoming president.

The conference with Scott lasted about five hours, after which Lincoln inspected the apartments, barracks, and West Point foundry opposite the academy. A dinner party was held at the hotel in the afternoon. The president charmed all the ladies with his conversational powers and affability at a reception at the hotel that night. All along the route back to New York City the next day, people gathered to get a glimpse of the president. In spite of pleas for a speech, "the president could not see it." But after he had been ferried to Jersey City for the train back to Washington, the president consented to make a few informal remarks.

Several old buildings remain at West Point that Lincoln must have seen, including the chapel and Superintendent's Quarters where Robert E. Lee had lived with his family when he served in that position. General Scott and many other Civil War generals are buried in West Point Cemetery. These include George Custer, Robert Anderson, and General Fred Grant, the son of Ulysses S. Grant, who had accompanied his father at age twelve during the Vicksburg campaign.

Ohio

ALLIANCE: Lincoln stopped on his inaugural trip, February 15, 1861, and repeated remarks he was routinely saying everywhere: "I appear before you merely to greet you and say farewell. . . . If I should make a speech at every town, I would not get to Washington until some time after the inauguration." He accepted the hospitality of the president of the railroad and had dinner at the **SOURBECK HOTEL** as a band played and guns saluted, sprinkling glass on Mrs. Lincoln.

ASHTABULA: Between three and four thousand greeted Lincoln as his inaugural train stopped for a short greeting on February 16, 1861. An empty cattle train had been pulled to a sidetrack, and was fully loaded with about fifteen hundred greeters. Lincoln thanked the crowd for the enthusiastic reception and greeting, but declined to shake hands when offered, saying his arms were almost shaken from his body. Someone called for Mrs. Lincoln to appear, and he brought laughs replying that "he should hardly hope to induce her to appear, as he had always found it difficult to make her do what she did not want to do."

CADIZ JUNCTION: The inaugural train stopped, and Lincoln dined at the **PARKS HOUSE** on February 14, 1861. This was just a small depot, hotel, and blacksmith. But a large crowd gathered and heard the new president as he remarked to the crowd from the rear platform of the train that he was "too full for utterance."

CINCINNATI: Lincoln first appeared in court in Ohio as evidenced by a letter he wrote from Cincinnati on December 24, 1849, implying he might go to Columbus. In September 1855, he was back as he and his future secretary of war, Edwin M. Stanton, were involved in the case of *McCormick v. Manny*. It was thought that the case would be heard in federal court in Springfield and that Lincoln would be of some use in his home state. But the trial was moved to Cincinnati. After he was retained, Lincoln was completely ignored. He got no instructions, information, or copies and played no part in the planning or conduct of the case. In fact he learned of the trial's transfer to Cincinnati through the newspapers, and just showed up.

When he found his way to the **BURNET HOUSE** at the **NORTHWEST CORNER OF THIRD AND VINE** to meet his notable eastern cocounsels, Stanton and the others were unimpressed with Lincoln, mostly because of his appearance. Stanton reportedly exclaimed, "If that giraffe appears in the case, I will throw up my brief and leave." As a result, Lincoln was ignored or dismissed. His brief was thrown in the trash, and he did not sit with the lawyers or speak during the trial. Lincoln clearly felt rebuffed, but how much of an insult he suffered is questionable. He was greatly impressed with the eastern attorneys, and considered his trip a great educational experience. Later as president when he was searching for a secretary of war, he was told that the best man would not be recommended because of the dishonorable way that he had treated Lincoln during the trial. Lincoln acknowledged that this was Stanton, and said that he just wanted the best man.

He stayed with **MR. AND MRS. WILLIAM M. DICKSON**, a cousin of Mary's. On the day that he left (probably September 26), he told his hostess: "You have made my stay most agreeable, and I am a thousand times obligated to you; but in reply to your request for me to come again I must say to you I never expect to be in Cincinnati again. I have nothing against the city, but things have so happened here as to make it undesirable for me ever to return."

Lincoln spent about a week in town and toured various points of interest and suburbs including Walnut Hills, Mount Auburn, and Clifton, and he strolled through Spring Grove Cemetery. He toured the county and city courts, met a number of lawyers (including the father of future president William Howard Taft), and went to the Ladies' Art Museum. On September 22, he visited the estate of **NICHOLAS LONGWORTH AT 316 PIKE AND FOURTH STREETS**, where he became interested in the grounds and conservatories. The home and grounds are just east of downtown between Interstate 71 and Interstate 471. He saw the owner in an old suit, weeding, and remarked that he had heard about the beauty of the grounds and wanted to see them. He then asked, "Does your master allow visitors?" Longworth answered, "My master is a queer duck. He does not allow strangers to come in, but he makes an exception every time someone does come. He would be glad to make an exception in this case." Lincoln then figured out that he was the owner and apologized, but Longworth said he was "quite used to it." He jokingly added that sometimes he got ten cents and sometimes as much as a quarter for showing the grounds. "In fact," he said, "I might say that it's the only really honest money I ever make, having been by profession a lawyer." Lincoln admitted he was a lawyer too, was here on a case, but lost it to Stanton. Longworth replied, "It's an excellent precept, indeed, to retire when a skunk is in the path." The 1820 Longworth home is now the TAFT MUSEUM, after Charles Taft, the brother of the president, who later owned it. There is no record that Lincoln was inside, but there are still gardens at the site.

In Lincoln's 1859 political jaunt, on September 17, he was taken to the BURNET HOUSE upon arrival, and then by open carriage to the FIFTH STREET MARKET PLACE where he spoke from the balcony at the Kinsey Jewelry Store and home on the north side of the square. A marker on the FEDERAL COURTHOUSE, at the NORTHEAST CORNER OF WALNUT AND FIFTH STREETS notes the spot. One of the members of the committee to receive Lincoln was a future president, Rutherford B. Hayes. The family consisting of Mary and Tad also spent part of the eighteenth with Mrs. Dickson. (Willie had stayed with neighbors in Springfield, and Robert was at school in New Hampshire.)

On February 12, 1861, his fifty-second birthday, the president-elect received an immense reception at the train station and rode with the mayor in a two-hour procession to the BURNET HOUSE. Upon arrival he addressed a huge crowd and attended a public reception in the hotel dining room. At 8:00 P.M. he addressed several thousand from the hotel balcony telling them that he felt it was his duty "to wait until the last moment, for a development of the present difficulties, before I express myself decidedly what course I shall pursue. . . . I will simply say that I am for those means which will give the greatest good to the greatest number." After a large reception, Lincoln returned to the room to find a fretful Tad waiting for his father to put him to bed. The boy was then carried to an adjoining room to be tucked in. Tad was not willing to break the custom at home, and it had to be continued in the White House. The bed the Lincolns used is in the Abraham Lincoln Museum at Lincoln Memorial University. He left the next morning from the Little Miami Railroad Depot.

CLEVELAND: On his inaugural trip Lincoln arrived in Cleveland in a snowstorm on February 15, 1861. He detrained two miles from the center of the city at the **EUCLID STREET DEPOT AT EUCLID AND SEVENTY-NINTH STREETS**, to the "deafening shout from tens of thousands (and the) roar of artillery." He spoke from the balcony of the **WEDDELL HOUSE HOTEL**. This was located on the **SOUTHWEST CORNER OF WEST SIXTH ("BANK") AND SUPERIOR**, later occupied by the Rockefeller Building. The Lincoln suites covered the entire block along Superior. (It is sometimes claimed that it was at the Weddell House that Robert lost the inaugural speech. See the entry on Indianapolis, Indiana.) The crowd was addressed from the second-floor balcony and heard, "If all do not join to save the good ship of the Union in this voyage, nobody will have a chance to pilot her on another." That evening he and Mrs. Lincoln attended separate receptions. It is also claimed he stayed in the **KENNARD HOTEL, ST. CLAIR AND WEST SIXTH STREET NW**. The president's body was viewed by 100,000 on April 28, 1865, in a building hastily erected for that purpose in **CITY PARK** at the **PUBLIC SQUARE, AT SUPERIOR AND ONTARIO**.

COLUMBUS: Lincoln spoke from a stand at the east terrace of the **STATEHOUSE** on September 16, 1859. In the evening he addressed the Young Men's Republican Club at the **CITY HALL** located on the second floor of the **CENTRAL MARKET HOUSE, 165 SOUTH FOURTH STREET**. (It was torn down in 1966 to build a bus station). He also attended the Franklin County Fair with Mary and Tad. The family stayed at the **NEIL HOUSE ON HIGH STREET FACING THE CAPITOL**. The first governor in the Statehouse was Salmon P. Chase who became Lincoln's secretary of the treasury.

On the way to Washington he addressed the Ohio legislature at the Capitol as a guest of Governor William Dennison on February 13, 1861. He arrived in Columbus at 2:00 P.M., received a national salute, and got an enthusiastic welcome from a crowd of sixty-thousand as he moved up **HIGH STREET**. At the **CAPITOL** he met with the governor and was introduced to the joint meeting of the legislature by Lieutenant Governor Robert C. Kirk. He remarked at the beautiful building and told them, "We entertain different views upon political questions, but nobody is suffering anything."

The governor's office has been restored to the 1861 appearance, and the desk Lincoln used is still in the office. Afterward, he spoke to the public from the west steps of the Capitol telling the people: "The manifestations of goodwill towards the government, and affection from the Union, which you may exhibit, are of immense value to you and your posterity forever." A great crowd jammed the rotunda to shake his hand, coming through the south door and exiting at the north. Ward Hill Lamon had to use all his considerable strength to force the multitudes back to keep the president-elect from getting crushed, as there was no order. At first Lincoln greeted with his right hand only, then with the right and left. Finally, when exhausted, he mounted the staircase and looked down upon the crowd as it swept past him. He then addressed a great mass of people assembled outside from the west front, and went to an informal reception in the rotunda of the **COURTHOUSE**. This was at **352 SOUTH HIGH AT MOUND STREET**, and torn down in 1884. At 4:30 P.M. he received a telegram informing him that he had been duly elected president by the Electoral College. There was another public reception at the Capitol after supper. That evening he attended a levee in full evening dress at **DESHLER HALL** on the **SOUTHEAST CORNER OF TOWN AND HIGH STREETS** and was received at the **RESIDENCE OF GOVERNOR DENNISON**, at **211 NORTH HIGH**, where the family spent the night.

Lincoln's body lay in the rotunda of the Capitol on April 29, 1865.

DAYTON: Lincoln, Mary, and Tad spent about four hours in town on September 17, 1859. He spoke at the **COURTHOUSE** at the **NORTHWEST CORNER OF THIRD AND MAIN STREETS** for two hours between trains. He arrived at **UNION STATION** and freshened up before the speech at the **PHILLIPS HOUSE** in the center of town near the courthouse. Mary and Tad stayed there during his speech. He stood in front of the courthouse for about two hours shaking the hands of throngs who arrived after having read of his appearance in the morning papers. He gave an autograph to Annie Harries, who was carrying a small Bible. He inscribed it, "Live by the words within these covers and you will (be) forever happy." He had his picture taken at **CRIDLAND'S PHOTOGRAPHIC GALLERY** a few doors to the east of the hotel at **264 THIRD**. He told the photographer, "Keep on. You may make a good one, but never a pretty one."

HAMILTON: On September 17, 1859, en route to Cincinnati, his train stopped for an informal address from an improvised stand near the depot. He told the crowd, "This beautiful and far-famed Miami Valley is the garden spot of the world."

HUDSON: About five thousand people waited for Lincoln as he came through on his way to Washington, D.C., on February 15, 1861, but he did nothing more than appear and bow to the people.

INAUGURAL TRIP, FEBRUARY 1861: The trip to Washington, D.C., was a zigzag, ponderous route and subjected the president-elect to many speeches saying much less than was expected or desired. But the little-known westerner wanted to be seen and tried to calm the nervous nation. Short speeches were made between CINCINNATI and COLUMBUS at MILFORD, LOVELAND, MIAMIVILLE, MORROW, CORWIN, XENIA, AND LONDON on February 13, 1861. On February 14, after spending the night in Columbus, he made short stops for speeches at NEWARK, FRAZEYSBURG, DRESDEN, COSHOCTON, NEWCOMERSTOWN, UHRICHSVILLE, CADIZ JUNCTION, STEUBENVILLE, AND WELLSVILLE before entering Pennsylvania where he stayed in Pittsburgh on February 14. Then he passed back through Ohio, making short speeches at SALINEVILLE, BAYARD, ALLIANCE, HUDSON, AND RAVENNA on the way to CLEVELAND. After leaving Cleveland the train made brief stops in WILLOUGHBY, PAINESVILLE, GENEVA, MADISON, ASHTABULA, AND CONNEAUT. The train passed near President William Henry Harrison's grave in NORTH BEND. The Harrison family gathered by the tracks to watch the train as it slowed while the future president lowered his head in respect.

STEUBENVILLE: On February 14, 1861, the Lincoln inaugural train was greeted by approximately ten thousand people gathered around a carpeted stage near the railroad tracks. Lincoln remarked that the voice of the people determines what the Constitution means.

WELLSVILLE: Lincoln made brief remarks from his railroad car to the waiting crowd on the way to his inauguration, February 14, 1861. A man who said he did not vote for Lincoln asked to shake his hand. Lincoln asked whom he did vote for, and was told, "Misther Dooglas." Lincoln responded that if the ship of the state held together, he could vote for Douglas in four more years. But if the "good ship were broken up, he will never get to be president." The crowd applauded. After leaving Pittsburgh the next day, he passed back through and told the crowd that he would not speak, as he had already done so.

Pennsylvania

BERKS COUNTY: Lincoln's great-great-grandfather, Mordecai, and great-grandfather, John, lived in Berks County. Grandfather Abraham was born here in 1744 and was a boyhood friend of the great pioneer leader, Daniel Boone, although Boone was ten years older. The Lincolns and Boones intermarried. Probably the Boone family convinced the Lincolns to move to Virginia and later to Kentucky. Mordecai's home has been restored in **AMITY**, and he is buried in Exeter Township at the **EXETER FRIENDS MEETINGHOUSE** in an unmarked grave near Boone's grandfather.

ERIE: Lincoln detrained on February 16, 1861, to make a speech in the dining room of the railroad company.

GETTYSBURG: The greatest battle of the Western Hemisphere took place here between July 1 and 3, 1863. It is now the best-marked field and most studied battle in the world. Some feel that the Union's war effort might not have survived if Confederate general Robert E. Lee had prevailed in this campaign in the North. He almost did, and the outcome was not decided until late on July 3, when the Confederate forces were repelled from their assault on Cemetery Hill. Some believe Lee wanted the war to end here at the time of the assault known as Pickett's Charge. He was repulsed, lost only the battle (not the war this day), retreated, but was not pursued with enough vigor to end the war, as Lincoln hoped and expected.

The most famous speech in the history of the United States was made on Cemetery Hill on November 19, 1863. Some historians believe that the address is of greater impact than the battle itself, at least in world opinion, and they call the speech "the defining moment of the War." Recent authors have referred to the address as *The Words That Remade America* and *The New Birth of Freedom*. The address has been memorized by school children ever since, and is carved in bronze on many public buildings in every corner of the United States. The impact and significance seem to be held in higher regard as the years pass.

It was given at a time when the outcome of the war was still in doubt. The South could not conquer the North, but the North was growing ever more weary. Support for continuing the struggle to maintain the Union was eroding. Many questioned the purpose of the war. Were men being killed in vain? Lincoln wanted to define the meaning of the struggles and sacrifices. After the July battle involving as many as 166,829 soldiers and more than 51,000 casualties, attempts were made to identify and ship home as many bodies as practical. It is estimated that 7,610 were killed on the battlefield and 26,358 were wounded, many dying within a few days. (Note the comparison of D-Day, June 6, 1944, when 175,000 American, Canadian, and British invaded Normandy, with 4,900 casualties. Sources vary regarding the statistics for both battles.)

It soon became apparent that a burial site was needed near the town of twenty-five hundred residents where virtually every structure was used as a hospital. Banker and attorney David Wills was made the agent for Pennsylvania governor Andrew Curtin to dispose of the many bodies that had been buried or covered throughout the area. An interstate commission was formed to collect funds and rebury the bodies. Poets Longfellow, Whittier, and Bryant were asked to produce words to properly dedicate the ground, but all declined. Wills then contacted Edward Everett, a scholar, Ivy League diplomat, pastor at nineteen, congressman, governor, minister to England, senator, and secretary of state. At age sixty-nine, Everett was the principal speaker of his time who could enthrall the mass audience expected for the dedication. The date of October 23, 1863, was chosen, but Everett informed Wills that he could not be ready before November 19. This being a state activity, the federal government's participation was not assumed, but the president was officially invited on November 2 to deliver "a few appropriate remarks."

Lincoln knew large crowds and publicity would be expected, along with many state governors and influential people. He also knew the power of his rhetoric and was seeking occasions outside the normal round of proclamations and reports to define war aims. In some accounts it is stated that he did not know that the commission was stunned when he accepted and was almost asked not to speak because they thought he might mar the reverent tone of the day by being clownish (*Lincoln's Failure at Gettysburg, Life* magazine, November 15, 1963). But others, including David H. Donald, believe that the president's acceptance was highly desired.

Mrs. Lincoln did not want her husband to travel away from Washington, and was hysterical about his leaving. Tad was sick when the date arrived, and she was greatly fearful of losing another son. But Lincoln came in spite of strong pleas from his emotionally unbalanced wife, feeling that his duty to the country at this time outweighed his parental responsibility. Lincoln overrode Stanton's plans to take an early morning train on the nineteenth to ensure that no unforeseen difficulty would prevent his arrival. He clearly recognized the importance of his opportunity to be heard, and prepared before leaving, during the trip, and after his arrival to compress his heart into a few short moments.

He probably did not feel well; he returned home two days later with a mild case of small pox, which no doubt weakened him during the trip. (After being quarantined in the White House, he stated that now, at last, he had something he could give everyone.) He had traveled via the **B&O BOLTON STATION IN BALTIMORE** where he was greeted by about two hundred. The cars were then dragged by horses over freight car tracks to the **CALVERT STREET STATION** and then to **HANOVER JUNCTION** where the Governor's Special was to be met. The Pennsylvania governor's train was late, so the presidential party continued to Gettysburg after changing engines, and a short speech was made to the crowds.

Lincoln arrived shortly before dusk at the railroad **DEPOT** still on **CARLISLE STREET** where Everett and Wills met him. He must have clearly seen the large main building of the Pennsylvania College of Gettysburg a few blocks north, still the center of the campus now known as Gettysburg College. This "Old Dorm" was then one of the only three buildings of the college, and served as dormitory, classroom, administration, and faculty quarters. It was a signal station during the battle, and hospital afterward.

The party walked the two blocks to **WILLS HOUSE**, the largest structure on the circle (The Diamond) at the center of town, now **LINCOLN SQUARE**. The building has long since been converted to other uses, but Lincoln's bedroom is open to the public. The first-floor parlor where Lincoln and twenty-one other guests were served and conversed is now accessible as a store featuring historical memorabilia. Lincoln appeared at the door before the crowds but declined to make an impromptu speech saying, he had "no speech to make. In my position it is somewhat important that I should not say foolish things. (Interruption: If you can help it!) It very often happens that the only way to help it is to say nothing at all." The present door on the west side of the building was not there at the time. The remarks were made at a door then on the north side as shown in the photograph on a marker at the site. In response to demands, he also spoke from a window of the house where the above-mentioned words may have been spoken (or repeated).

Everett and other dignitaries also ate and stayed with Wills. Their dinner was constantly interrupted by louder and more frequent calls for the president to appear. Governor Curtin was to stay there also, but did not arrive until 11:00 P.M. after having left Harrisburg, thirty miles away, at 3:00. Wills suggested that he share a bed with Everett, but Curtin took a hint and found arrangements elsewhere, much to Everett's relief, who stated in his diary that "the fear of having the executive of Pennsylvania tumble in upon me kept me awake until one." All together Wills had thirty-eight guests that night.

At 11:00 that evening, Lincoln greeted arriving Governor Curtin and walked through heavy crowds next door to the **HARPER HOUSE** probably to show his speech to Secretary of State Seward, but evidently got no useful suggestions. (This house is no longer standing, and is now the site of Masonic Hall.) Upon leaving he was asked again to make a speech but said, "I can't tonight, gentlemen, I will see you all tomorrow. Good night." Professor Frank L. Klement of Marquette University called this the First Gettysburg Address, "undoubted the poorest (performance/speech) of his life." Seward did appear to give the crowd a rousing, brief but emotional speech in front of the Harper House blaming slavery for the bloodshed and praising those who had fought and died on the nearby battlefield. A telegram was received from Mary at midnight saying that Tad was better and that she would telegram in the morning. Bands and serenaders continued well into the night in the Diamond.

There is speculation whether or not a battlefield tour with Seward, which Lincoln had wanted, took place the next morning. Some think that they took an hour's tour to view the first day's fighting area, toward the seminary, as Seward later claimed. He is said to have seen the spot where General John Reynolds was killed, now marked on the battlefield tour route. This would have taken him past Lee's headquarters site and the stone house where Lee ate. The house is in front of Larson's Quality Inn on U.S. 30, across from the headquarters site. (The historical house is an excellent, small museum.) Whether he did or did not, he must have seen the Lutheran Theological Seminary Building clearly visible on the west edge of the still, small town. Lincoln's secretaries and newspapermen mentioned no tour.

At 9:00 A.M., secretary John Nicolay went to Lincoln's room and waited while the president made a new copy of his address. They left the room a little before ten o'clock and emerged to face a large crowd at the front of the home. One of the first he met was Governor Curtin's twelve-year-old son who received a squeeze on the shoulder. Lincoln mounted a horse too small for him and waited about an hour for the procession to get organized for the parade down Baltimore Street. Chief Marshal Ward Hill Lamon, Lincoln's personal, self-appointed bodyguard and former law associate from Danville, had seventy-two marshals with bright sashes galloping about giving orders and trying to get the four military bands and others to quiet down and get ready. Many original buildings are still in existence along the half-mile parade route down **BALTIMORE STREET TO THE EMMITSBURG ROAD**, turning at the junction where the Holiday Inn is now. Much of the fighting had occurred in this area, and there are now many markers along the street, illustrating the action with personal-interest stories. The route turned again shortly at the **TANEYTOWN ROAD** near where future president Richard Nixon's grandfather had been killed in the battle, about at McDonald's restaurant now. Lincoln seemed lost in thought most of the way to the thousands who strained to see him. When a young girl in her party best was thrust upon him, he gave her a short ride on his horse, kissed her, and handed her back to the pleased parents.

Everett gave his expected two hour address by memory although he had a neatly placed thick text on a table before him. The famous orator worked his familiar magic on those of the fifteen or twenty thousand or so who tried to listen. He already had it printed in Boston and distributed to newspapers to make sure of an accurate rendition. Lincoln had read it prior to this occasion. Those who could not hear were delighted at Everett's animated gestures of emotion and theatrics. He traced the origins of the war, the progress of the battle, and the aftermath. He summarized constitutional and practical arguments, upholding the Union position of the war. The speech truly was a masterpiece. This was the only oration planned, desired, or expected.

Lincoln's "dedicatory remarks" were startlingly brief for what they accomplished, setting the goals of the war into ideological terms rather than military, constitutional, or property arguments. Everett had set out the details of the event; Lincoln gave the war and its aims a holy level to the entire world for all time. His three minutes were interrupted maybe five times by those who could not grasp the significance, still being analyzed. Different reporters reported the crowd response differently. Some reported silence at the conclusion and others reported polite applause. Lincoln's high-pitched, raspy tenor voice was unlike most actors who portray him, but maybe similar to Theodore and Franklin Roosevelt. He was known to be an actor and expert raconteur and mimic who could enchant audiences with Shakespeare, ethnic stories, and cornpone country stories. Years of outdoor speaking to large crowds had perfected his presentation technique and trained his voice for effectiveness at such occasions. Still, it would be difficult to hear. Stories that he was disappointed in his performance are thought to be a myth. There were some unfair and shortsighted newspaper accounts. Some dignitaries are quoted as being "disappointed" although this may not be accurate. Governor Curtin commented that the speech was highly "impressive." Time was needed to reflect upon the words, not so much intended for that audience but the country beyond that day and place.

After the ceremonies, Lincoln returned to the Wills House for lunch and a meeting with local hero John Burns. Burns had fought with Winfield Scott at the Battle of Lundy's Lane in Canada during the War of 1812 and had volunteered to fight rebels at age seventy-three when they invaded his hometown. He had been wounded and left for dead. Lincoln requested to meet him. The two then walked arm in arm to the **PRESBYTERIAN CHURCH** still at the **NORTHEAST CORNER OF BALTIMORE AND HIGH**, and sat side by side on the second row and listened while Ohio's lieutenant governor condemned traitors.

The most often asked question in Gettysburg is: "Where did Lincoln give his address?" The site of the speech was said for many years to be the Soldiers National Monument in the center of the hemispherical rows of graves in the National Cemetery on Cemetery Hill (**SITE 1**). This was pointed out by Park Rangers as the spot, and it is still so noted in tablets in the area and in the minds of many. However, there are other sites, believed by many to have been the correct location. None of these can be supported with certainty. See the map in this chapter for the locations mentioned.

In 1965 a *Parade* magazine article questioned the traditional **SITE (1)**. Louis A. Warren's 1964 book, *Lincoln's Gettysburg Declaration: A New Birth of Freedom*, and *Lincoln Lore Number 1535* (January 1966) discussed this in detail. He concluded that the correct location was **SITE (2)** about 350 feet north of the Soldier's Monument and outside the outer circle of soldiers' graves by 40 feet. Warren also concluded that the platform used by the president faced northwest, as stated by W. Yates Selleck, secretary of the Soldier's National Cemetery Commission at Gettysburg. His copy of the revised report of the commission, in the possession of the Lincoln National Life Foundation, shows his pencil notation of the site outside the outer circle of soldiers' graves near the walk on the north side of the circular arrangement. Certainly his familiarity with the ceremony itself should be conclusive as to the exact spot. But such is not necessarily the case.

Retired Park historian, Frederick Tilberg, in an article published in *Pennsylvania History* challenged this conclusion in April 1973. He questioned Warren's arguments and supported the traditional location (**SITE 1**). Tilberg argued that the route of the procession to the site on November

19, 1863, did not favor the site identified by Selleck and location of graves at the traditional site would have made the Selleck location unacceptable. Tilberg argues that the route was, in fact, logical to the traditional site, and only a few graves would have been present at the time. He also noted that the hills known as the Round Tops and other views described by contemporaries would not have been visible from the Selleck site lower in elevation. And he believed that sufficient people and officials who had been present endeavored to put the monument on the site of the speaker's platform. So the traditional site was now supported again with strong arguments. Tilberg also argues that the platform was on the highest spot in the cemetery that was the monument site. But any personal inspection now will show that this is not so now. Tilberg and Warren supported their positions in a July 1976 article in *Civil War Times Illustrated*.

There was some confusion as late as December 3, 1863, after Lincoln's speech, where the Soldiers Monument should be. But this was decided, and the cornerstone was laid in 1865 and dedicated in 1869 at the present site. Thus, the Lincoln site was associated with this spot. In 1895 Congress provided for a Lincoln Speech Monument to be erected in the cemetery. The committee in charge hoped to erect this at the site where the speech was delivered, but by this time the tradition that this was the Soldiers Monument was well entrenched so that the site was unavailable for the Speech Monument. When this was constructed in 1912, a tablet noted, "The address was delivered about 300 yards from this spot . . . marked by the Soldiers Monument." This is still in place, and the belief in the site survived for many years in all information mediums at the park and elsewhere. But many believe that the official report by the cemetery commission headed by David Wills, as well as other contemporary statements and facts, do not support this. Indeed, analysis of photographs made at the time do not support the Soldiers Monument site, assuming that the flagpole shown in the contemporary pictures and sketch by Joseph Becker is at the present site of the Soldiers Monument.

In 1982 a third site was championed by Kathleen Georg (later Kathleen Harrison), one of Tilberg's successors. No article was published, but Appendix II of Garry Wills's *Lincoln at Gettysburg* discusses the origin of this and other views. Wills concluded that the Harrison site is correct. He agrees with Harrison that the location of the platform where Lincoln sat is located at the Brown Family vault in Evergreen Cemetery based on two key photographs taken of the crowd showing the position of the platform **(SITE 3)**. One of these was taken facing the still-standing Evergreen Cemetery gateway, and the other was taken from the second floor of it. This site seems correct from on-site comparisons of these photos, which show terrain and a flagpole believed to have been on the site now

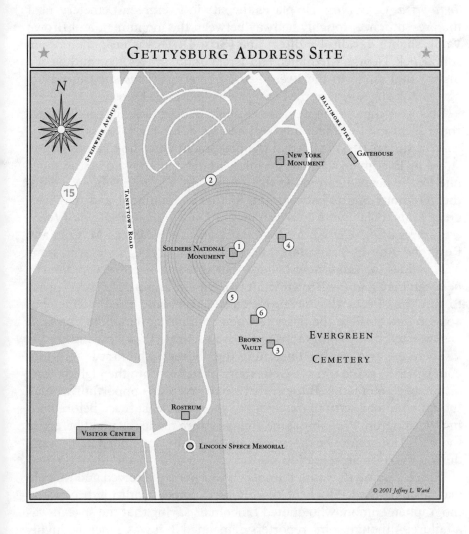

GETTYSBURG ADDRESS SITE

N

STEINWEHR AVENUE

BALTIMORE PIKE

15

TANEYTOWN ROAD

NEW YORK
MONUMENT

GATEHOUSE

②

SOLDIERS NATIONAL
MONUMENT ①

④

⑤

⑥

BROWN
VAULT ③

EVERGREEN

CEMETERY

ROSTRUM

VISITOR CENTER

LINCOLN SPEECE MEMORIAL

© 2001 Jeffrey L. Ward

of the Soldier's Monument. Wills states that this was accepted by most Gettysburg guides and other noted authors including William A. Frassanito, author of photographic studies of Gettysburg and other Civil War sites. But Frassanito did a further study, as shown in his work *Early Photography at Gettysburg*. He places the site in Evergreen Cemetery, near the present fence, roughly halfway between the monument and Brown Vault, slightly north of a direct line **(SITE 4)**. This is near the present John Kock, George Kitzmiller, and Isreal Yount graves. The author of a history and guide to the Evergreen Cemetery (*Beyond the Gatehouse*) agrees, but suggests that the exact site will never be known.

Recent comparisons with the Joseph Becker drawings indicate to some local guides, including author and guide Gary Kross, that the correct site **(SITE 5)** is beyond the prominent Ditterline Family tombstone in Evergreen Cemetery, which would put the site at the fence line by the nearest cannon to the tombstone. The tombstone predates the ceremony and is between the Soldier's Monument and the Evergreen Gate. (The pictures are shown in *Lincoln and the Human Interest Stories of the Gettysburg National Cemetery* by James M. Cole and Reverend Roy E. Frampton, among other sources.) Evidently some park guides, at least, now believe that this site is correct, or maybe between here and the Brown Vault **(6)**. On-site comparisons do appear to put the site at that location, considering only the drawing, but appears too close to the flagpole when comparing the photographs. It is suggested that photographs are more accurate than drawings.

There are two myths concerning the address. The first is that Lincoln wrote it on the train to Gettysburg or in his room the night before, on the back of a letter. But clearly he had given this opportunity much thought and had written much of the speech at least twice before leaving Washington. Probably some changes were made the night before in the Wills House. Maybe the words "under God" were added in his mind during Everett's presentation.

The second myth is that the speech was poorly received and Lincoln was disappointed. Much of this thought comes from his friend and biographer, Lamon, who quoted Lincoln as saying that the speech was a failure. Although some reporters demeaned it, it was generally highly regarded and praised at once. Everett wrote to him requesting a copy, and told him that he had wished he could have come as close to the central topic of the day in two hours as Lincoln had in two minutes.

The excellent museum at the national park contains the saddle from Lincoln's horse used in the parade that day and chairs from the speaker's platform. Ceremonies are held in the cemetery every November 19, with a nationally known speaker to commemorate the address, which is reenacted.

Shortly before his death Lincoln confessed to an Illinois clergyman that when he left Springfield and later went through the "severest trial" of his life, the loss of Willie, he was not a Christian. Then he stated, "But when I went to Gettysburg and saw the graves of thousands of our soldiers, I then and there consecrated myself to Christ" (*Lincoln Herald*, spring 1990).

HANOVER: At Carlisle and Park Streets, a marker notes: "One-half block east of here, on November 18, 1863, Abraham Lincoln spoke briefly to townspeople from his special train. The president was traveling to Gettysburg for the dedication of the National Cemetery." This spot is TWO BLOCKS NORTH OF THE TOWN SQUARE ON ROUTES 94, 116, AND 194, BETWEEN PARK AND RAILROAD STREETS. An old railroad track is still on the side of the street just west of an old depot, but does not extend east.

While waiting for a train going the other direction to pass, the Reverend M.J. Alleman approached the president and said, "Father Abraham, your children want to see you." Lincoln was not fond of being addressed other than just "Lincoln," as friends addressed and referred to him. He did not like "Mr. Lincoln," "Mr. President," and certainly not being called by his first name. The *Philadelphia Inquirer* reported that Lincoln then "delivered one of the brief, quaint, speeches for which he is celebrated."

HANOVER JUNCTION: This still-small town is located about eleven miles east and slightly north of Hanover and fifty miles north of Baltimore. It is west of York and south of U.S. Highway 30, about six miles on State Highway 616. On the way to Gettysburg in November 1863, Lincoln's train changed railroad lines and engines, transferring from the Northern Central to the Hanover Railroad. He was to meet Governor Andrew Curtin's Governor's Special here, containing a host of dignitaries. A brief appearance was made to the crowd. The Special was six hours late, and the president moved west without waiting for its arrival.

HARRISBURG: On February 22, 1861, the president-elect spoke from the portico at the JONES HOUSE on the EAST SIDE OF SOUTH MARKET SQUARE, at the SOUTHEAST CORNER OF MARKET AND SECOND STREETS. Lincoln told the crowd: "It shall be my endeavor to preserve the peace of this country." Members of the legislature and military then escorted him to the STATE-HOUSE where he spoke to the General Assembly. The building is still in use. After a return to the Jones House, he learned of new plans for his trip to Washington, D.C., and had to refuse to stay at Governor Andrew Curtin's home. Evening festivities were planned for the president-elect, but to the embarrassment and outrage of the revelers, Lincoln did not show up at the ball held in his honor. Late in the evening he left the hotel and drove to the outskirts of the city, where he and bodyguard Ward Hill Lamon boarded a special train to Philadelphia in time to catch the special 11:00 P.M. train to Washington. Lincoln was not comfortable to sneak into Washington "like a thief," but he was convinced that plans to do him harm were real. Telegraph lines were cut behind the train to create a "news blackout."

Here Lincoln lost his temper for the only time on the trip to Washington, according to Lamon. He had entrusted a small handbag containing his inaugural address to his seventeen-year-old son, Robert, who then had given it to a waiter, he thought. A careful search was made through the hotel baggage room, and finally the satchel containing the document was found. (This is sometimes said to have happened in Cleveland or Indianapolis.)

Following the assassination, the president's body arrived on April 21, 1865, after passing through Shrewsbury and York to lay in the State House from 8:30 P.M. until midmorning on April 22. Thousands lined the streets to and from the train station.

HONESDALE (WAYNE COUNTY): A marker at 115 Ninth Street in Honesdale, in Wayne County, reads, "In May 1859, Horace Greeley met notable political leaders to create a boom to nominate Abraham Lincoln for president. The events that ensued at the Republican National Convention in Chicago paralleled the strategy planned at the parley held in this building."

INAUGURAL TRIP, FEBRUARY 1861: Lincoln stopped to make brief speeches at ROCHESTER, ALLEGHENY CITY, GIRARD, ERIE, NORTHEAST, BRISTOL, LEAMAN PLACE, AND LANCASTER with longer stays in PITTSBURGH, HARRISBURG, AND PHILADELPHIA.

LANCASTER: On February 22, 1861, Lincoln spoke from the balcony of the CADWELL HOUSE on the SOUTHEAST CORNER OF CHESTNUT AND QUEEN in the hometown of the man Lincoln would replace, President James Buchanan. He spoke little, saying, "I think the more a man speaks in these days, the less he is understood. As Solomon says, there is a time for all things, and I think the present is a time for silence."

Buchanan's home, WHEATLAND, is open to the public. The former president watched Lincoln's funeral train from his buggy.

LEAMAN PLACE: Lincoln's train stopped briefly for a speech on February 22, 1861. Mrs. Lincoln appeared with him, and he told the crowd that this was "the long and short of it." This is now on Route 30 at the point where the Strasburg tourist train turns. It is about six miles east of Lancaster and three miles south of Intercourse.

MILFORD: The Pike County Museum has a flag that is claimed to have been placed under Lincoln's head after he was shot. A group of Lincoln scholars determined in 1996 that the blood on the flag was the sixteenth president's.

PHILADELPHIA: Lincoln first visited June 7–10, 1848, to attend the Whig National Convention held at the CHINESE MUSEUM on the NORTHEAST CORNER OF NINTH AND SANSOM STREETS, although he was not a delegate. It is not known where he stayed but he must have visited INDEPENDENCE HALL and other sites related to the development of our country. CONGRESS HALL is adjacent to Independence Hall, and contains furniture in the building when the U.S. Congress met and where Washington and Adams were inaugurated. This was being used as a courthouse in 1848 and surely interested the Illinois lawyer. After the nominations of Zachary Taylor and Millard Fillmore, the delegates retired to Independence Square where many speeches were made, although a list is not available. It is possible that Lincoln was one of the many speakers who spoke to a large gathering on the grounds. The Liberty Bell was hanging in the belfry, but it had cracked on Washington's birthday two years before, and probably was not used at this time.

The Republican National Convention was held June 1856 in the MUSICAL FUND HALL. Lincoln received 110 votes for the vice presidency. This original building is located on the south side of LOCUST, BETWEEN EIGHTH AND NINTH.

Lincoln changed trains February 25, 1860, on the way to make his Cooper Institute Address in New York. He attempted to meet Simon Cameron and David Wilmot at the GIRARD HOUSE AT THE NORTHWEST CORNER OF NINTH AND CHESTNUT, but missed connections. This was about the time the largest hotel in the city, the Continental House, was opening across the street.

The presidential party arrived on the way to Washington on February 21, 1861, at the KENSINGTON DEPOT and proceeded by carriage through a crowd of 100,000 to the new CONTINENTAL HOTEL at the SOUTHEAST CORNER OF NINTH AND CHESTNUT. The Ben Franklin Hotel now occupies the site, and there is a plaque along the Chestnut Street side. This is in the same block as the Whig convention of 1848. Lincoln used the Ninth Street door and spoke from the balcony, although it was reported that probably not one person heard a single word. After dinner and a reception in the hotel, Lincoln received Frederick W. Seward, the son of the secretary of state nominee, who gave him a letter from his father warning of a possible assassination plot to be executed while passing through Baltimore. The famous detective, Allan Pinkerton, had uncovered the plot.

The next morning Lincoln went to Independence Hall for a flag-raising ceremony. He arrived at the back of Independence Hall on Sixth Street. In a short address to the councils of the city he declared, "I have never had a feeling politically that did not spring from sentiments embodied in the Declaration of Independence. . . . in my view of the present aspect of affairs, there is no need of bloodshed and war. The government will not use force unless force is used against it." He was then taken from Independence Hall to a platform in the front of the building. He told the crowd that "when the flag was originally raised here, it had but thirteen stars . . . under the blessing of God, each additional star added to that flag has given additional prosperity and happiness to the country until it has arrived at its present condition, and its welfare in the future, as well as in the past, is in your hands. . . . I think we may promise ourselves, that not only the new star placed upon that flag shall be permitted to remain there to our permanent prosperity." The photographic image of him then is the first of a president-elect. A marker in front of Independence Hall on Chestnut Street marks the spot where he stood.

Afterward, he left from the hotel by way of the **VINE AND SECOND STREET RAILROAD STATION** for the state capital. Lincoln refused to change travel plans until his obligations in Philadelphia and Harrisburg were completed, except for the ball, which he missed in Harrisburg. After he left Harrisburg, he returned to Philadelphia at the **PENNSYLVANIA RAILROAD DEPOT** on the **NORTH SIDE OF MARKET BETWEEN ELEVENTH AND TWELFTH** with Colonel Lamon, Detective Pinkerton, and the general superintendent of the railroad. They boarded the train to Washington from the **PHILADELPHIA, WILMINGTON, AND BALTIMORE STATION AT BROAD AND WASHINGTON STREETS**, at 11:00 P.M.

Mrs. Lincoln was at the **CONTINENTAL HOTEL** on December 21, 1862, and the president probably traveled through Philadelphia in 1862 on the way to visit General Winfield Scott in New York. The Lincolns, including Tad, attended the Philadelphia Sanitary Fair or Great Central Fair held at **LOGAN SQUARE** on June 16, 1864. The main hall of the fair was located in the center of **BENJAMIN FRANKLIN PARKWAY BETWEEN EIGHTEENTH AND NINETEENTH STREETS**. Sanitary fairs were held in many cities to raise funds to meet needs of soldiers. Crowds gathered around him at all locations to, at, and from the fair so that he had little time to see the exhibits. When he later received an invitation to a fair in Chicago, he said he did not feel he "could stand another big fair."

He stayed at the **CONTINENTAL HOTEL**. Responding to a toast there, he declared: "War, at the best, is terrible. . . . I have never been in the habit of making predictions in regard to the war, but I am almost tempted to make one . . . That Grant is this evening, with General Meade and General Hancock of Pennsylvania, and the brave officers and soldiers with him, in a position from whence he will never be dislodged until Richmond is taken." After speeches by Edward Everett and others, he proceeded back to the hotel where he spoke to a large crowd determined to hear the president. He stated that he had not expected such enthusiastic demonstrations, and was appearing then only to see the crowd and be seen. He then hastened to the UNION LEAGUE CLUB, then at 1118 CHESTNUT. He spoke in the club and on the front steps to the crowds, thanking the crowds again "for this great demonstration, which you have paid me." Getting back to the hotel about midnight, another brief speech was given from the balcony to a still large crowd, which had followed him everywhere. Like Baltimore earlier, the city's enthusiasm for him had changed from 1861.

On April 22–24, 1865, his body lay in INDEPENDENCE HALL near the Liberty Bell, previously moved from the bell tower to the rear of the first floor opposite the front door. After leaving Harrisburg, the funeral train had passed through great crowds at Middletown, Elizabethtown, Lancaster, Parkesburg, Coatesville, Downingtown, West Chester, and Paoli. His remains had arrived at the BROAD STREET RAILROAD DEPOT at BROAD AND PRIME and proceeded over the following route: NORTH TO WALNUT, WEST TO TWENTY-FIRST STREET, NORTH AND THEN EAST ON ARCH TO THIRD, THEN SOUTH TO WALNUT, AND WEST TO THE SOUTH-CENTRAL ENTRANCE OF INDEPENDENCE HALL. The sidewalks were jammed, as were the windows and roofs along the route.

The casket was carried past the Liberty Bell to the middle of the room where the Declaration of Independence was signed in 1776 and the Constitution drafted and signed in 1787. (Many reports are not clear as to the exact locations. Those shown above are believed correct as per officials at Independence National Historical Park and the *Lincoln Herald* [December 1946], diagram on page 15.) Special invitations were extended to a limited number of citizens to view the body on the first evening, and the next morning the public was allowed to pass by in two unbroken streams for twenty hours. Those with special tickets viewed the body from 10:00 P.M. until midnight. By 4:00 the next morning a large crowd had already jammed the front of the building. The doors opened at 6:00 A.M. for an estimated 85,000 to over 300,000 viewers who lined Chestnut Street for many blocks. The funeral train then left at the KENSINGTON DEPOT north of HARRISON BETWEEN FRONT STREET AND FRANKFORT ROAD and headed for New York.

Also of interest is the CIVIL WAR LIBRARY AND MUSEUM at 1805 PINE, which keeps limited hours and, in fact, is scheduled to be closed in 2001. They have a large number of artifacts and research materials. A cane is here said to be found in Lincoln's box at Ford's Theater after he was shot. It was given to the museum years later as Lincoln's, but is probably one carried by someone else and left there inadvertently. General George Meade's stuffed horse and a number of artifacts of his are here. Meade lived and died around the block at the southeast corner of Nineteenth and Delancey. General George B. McClellan was born on the southwest corner of Seventh and Chestnut.

PITTSBURGH: The Free Soil Party met on February 22, 1856, to cement scattered groups in Northern states into a national party. They declared, "Slavery is a sin against God and a crime against man." Then the formal organization took place considered the first Republican national convention. The party agreed to meet later to nominate candidates for a national ticket. This was in LAFAYETTE HALL noted by a historical marker at the SOUTHWEST CORNER OF WOOD AND FOURTH STREETS. Lincoln was a delegate, but did not attend.

On his inaugural trip, Lincoln made short stops in nearby Rochester and Allegheny City and stayed at the MONONGAHELA HOUSE with his party on February 14, 1861. He was greeted by a large crowd standing in the rain along his route to Pittsburgh and through the streets to the hotel. He stood in a chair in the lobby, made a few remarks, and then said he needed to go get some notes to make a longer address. On the fifteenth, he made his longest address of the journey from the balcony of the Monongahela before a multitude of five thousand. This site is at the NORTHWEST CORNER OF FORT PITT AND SMITHFIELD. One of the founders of Goucher College, Rev. John Franklin Goucher, told the story that he, as a young boy, made an effort to "accost" Lincoln here to shake his hand. Lincoln told the lad, "God bless, my son. Love God, obey your parents, and serve your country, and you will give the world cause to remember and honor you."

READING: The LINCOLN HOMESTEAD marker on U.S. 422, 2.6 miles southeast, notes the 1733 stone house of Lincoln's great-great-grandfather, Mordecai. A stone house nearby housed his slaves. Frontiersman and family friend Daniel Boone was born nearby in 1734, marked near Baumstown. Both homes still stand.

WAYNE COUNTY: See Honesdale (Wayne County) entry.

Rhode Island

PROVIDENCE: Lincoln came to give a speech on February 28, 1860, at overflowing **RAILROAD HALL** located on the second floor at the northern end of **UNION STATION ON EXCHANGE PLACE**. He stayed with prominent lawyer **JOHN EDDY AT 265 WASHINGTON STREET**. The speech was said "to show by plain, simple, and cogent reasoning that his positions are impregnable and he carries his audiences with him." The newspapers referred to him as the "great champion of Republicanism in Illinois." He left the next day on the Boston and Providence Railroad. A few weeks later, on March 9, he had a three-hour layover between Woonsocket and Norwich, Connecticut, at the train station.

The Old State House on North Main between North and South Court Streets still stands, which Lincoln must have seen. It was the Capitol Building from 1762 until 1900. Washington, Adams, Jefferson, Lafayette, and many others famous in American history were honored here. The John Hay Library at 20 Prospect Street has one of the most complete Lincoln collections in the world, including the papers of Hay.

WOONSOCKET: Lincoln gave a speech here on March 8, 1860 (*Lincoln Day by Day*), in **HARRIS INSTITUTE HALL** at **157 MAIN STREET**, a few hundred feet from the railroad station. The *Providence Journal* reported, that "The great champion of Illinois has become as much of a favorite in New England as he is in his own state." This is the only building left in the state where Lincoln spoke to the largest crowd ever in the hall. A special train brought Lincoln with a large number of supporters from

Providence. Edward Harris entertained the speaker that night in his home in the northern part of the city. (Note that the *Rhode Island Historical Guide* gives the date as March 6 and address at 169 Main, although a number of sources confirm March 8.)

Tennessee

There is no record that Abraham Lincoln was ever in Tennessee except on the Mississippi River trips to New Orleans in 1828 and 1831. In his sometimes-reported 1826 trip, he is said to have sold produce along the Tennessee banks. However, it seems likely that there was no trip in that year. In 1845 Lincoln was named as a member of a delegation of ten from Illinois to attend the Commercial Convention of Southwestern and Western States in Memphis, but he did not go. Biographer William Herndon believed that Lincoln tied up for a day at Memphis in 1831.

There are several other connections to Tennessee. There were three branches of the Lincoln family in Greene County, the county of President Andrew Johnson. These were descended from "Virginia John," Lincoln's great-grandfather. Lincoln's father, Thomas, had an uncle move east of Elizabethtown on the Watauga River at the base of Lynn Mountain. It is claimed that Thomas worked on his farm for a year in 1797 or 1798, but Uncle Isaac may have gotten disgusted at him for his lack of thrift. He probably traveled over the **Cumberland Gap** then, as he had as a boy migrating to Kentucky. This is at the border with Kentucky and Virginia.

The branches of the Lincoln family were located in **Greeneville** when future president Andrew Johnson settled there. Lincoln's grandfather, Abraham, had another brother whose son, Mordecai, became prominent in the area, and as justice of the peace performed the marriage ceremony for Andrew Johnson. Then slaveholder Mordecai and

Johnson served on the town council and were members of a debating society together. Johnson's youngest daughter married Isaac Lincoln's adopted son. Johnson died at his daughter's house on land that had belonged to Isaac. It is known that this was a source of conversation between the two when Abraham Lincoln and Johnson were in Congress. They both were lonely and liked to read. It is speculated that they met in the old Library of Congress in the Capitol Building. Lincoln related in letters that Johnson had given him information about his kinfolk in several counties around the area. Other descendants of Virginia John fought in the Confederate army.

It might be noted here that Andrew Johnson and his predecessor had many similarities. Johnson was born within six weeks (December 29, 1808) of Lincoln, into poverty in a log cabin now lost. In both cases a replica cabin birthplace is now displayed. Neither had much schooling and lost a parent at an early age. A sister died before both were twenty. Both lost two sons during life, including one during the Civil War, and were survived by a son. Both moved west to a new state, were in the state legislature in the 1830s, Congress in the 1840s, and either served as governor or were offered the governor's office. Both courted and were rejected by a girl named Mary, and married a woman who predicted early on that she would marry the poor prospect. Both wives greatly aided in their husbands' careers. They were in Congress the same time, and each died intestate with an estate worth about $100,000.

HARROGATE: The Abraham Lincoln Museum is on the campus of Lincoln Memorial University located two miles from the Cumberland Gap. This houses one of the largest Lincoln and Civil War collections in the country. It contains various rare items and research materials. Among items included are a silver-topped cane that may have been used the night of his assassination, a lock of Lincoln's hair clipped on his deathbed, Grant's son's autograph book containing the signatures of Lincoln and his cabinet, and the bed he slept in on his birthday in Cincinnati. The college prints the *Lincoln Herald*, used extensively in the preparation of this book.

Vermont

MANCHESTER: On **MAIN STREET, ROUTE 7, AND UNION STREETS** is the **EQUINOX HOTEL** where Robert, Tad, and Mary stayed in 1863 and where Lincoln may have planned to come in 1865. Mary attended the 1830 **FIRST CONGREGATIONAL CHURCH** across the street. Both buildings are still in use. In 1863, Mary stayed in the part of the hotel directly across the street from the 1822 courthouse, on the second floor in the rear away from the street and present gift shop. Her quarters were used as a suite and were refurbished as a presidential suite for the expected visit of Lincoln in 1865. This remains known as the Lincoln suite. The lobby was where the sitting room is now, just south of the gift shop. Union Street came through where now there is an extension of the hotel buildings. In 1864 Mary occupied rooms 50 and 51 on the third floor. Tad was with her, but it is not known if Robert was. The original signed guest register is displayed in the lobby.

Robert Lincoln built his estate, **HILDENE**, two miles south of the junction of Routes 7A, 11, and 30. He visited the area many times and was fond of the nearby summer home of his law partner, Edward Isham. He built his own home in 1904, where he lived much of his time in the mild summer climate until his death in 1926. Long after his death a bundle of records related to Mary's insanity trial was found in the home, revealing what Robert's grandson called "the only definite record of this tragic story." He released the file for scholars, believing Robert had retained it, unlike many other letters and records, so that it could be studied.

Robert was a very private man and hated publicity about himself and family. No doubt a book of his reminiscences about his family would have added many facts and insights into the Lincoln story. He was also a meticulous record keeper. A wealthy golfing crony believed once he observed Robert burning family documents and letters in the fireplace. This alerted President Nicholas Butler of Columbia University and others that valuable insights into Lincoln's life were being lost. Butler rushed here to save "the rest." But he and others were refused any searches. Since Robert had already deposited his father's papers with the Library of Congress, it is questionable if anything of importance was lost. Descendants lived here until 1975 and refused any search of the house for records. But Robert's grandson, Robert Todd Lincoln Beckwith, allowed his friend, James T. Hickey, to search after Beckwith's sister died. Hickey was the curator of the Lincoln Collection at the Illinois State Historical Library. At this time a very private file was found, revealing many details of Mary's insanity proceedings. Since many public and private records of her trial and condition have been destroyed or lost, this file filled a documentary record and missing body of knowledge.

The house is now open to the public and contains original furnishings and personal family effects.

Virginia

ARLINGTON, ALEXANDRIA, FAIRFAX COUNTY: Lincoln often came past Alexandria on the Potomac River south of Washington, just cruising or to review troops. There is no record of his presence at sites in town other than to visit area forts and change boats, but he had good views of the old town on many trips down the river. He boarded a steamer in Alexandria on October 19, 1861, on the way to Fort Washington across the river, and met with McClellan in Alexandria on March 21 and April 1, 1862. A visit was made to **GREAT FALLS ON THE POTOMAC** on May 19, 1861, now accessible as a park. Several reviews were made of the army near Centerville, including one on October 22, 1862. On November 20, 1862, he visited **FORT ALBANY**, a site now on **INTERSTATE 395, ABOUT A MILE FROM THE LONG BRIDGE,** near the present Potomac bridges. The site can be seen from an overlook park at Nash Street and Arlington Ridge Road.

A historical marker notes that Lincoln and his entire cabinet attended a grand review on November 20, 1861, at **BAILEY'S CROSS-ROADS** on **ROUTE 7, 2.48 MILES WEST OF INTERSTATE 395.** The fifty thousand troops involved "the largest and most magnificent military review ever held on this continent" up to that time. This is just west of **FORT MUNSON,** at **MUNSON DRIVE AND APEX CIRCLE,** about five miles due west of Washington's Reagan Airport.

Lincoln visited George Washington's home, **MOUNT VERNON,** in February 1848, and Mary came on March 27, 1861. The popular plantation is just south of Alexandria on George Washington Memorial Parkway and is clearly marked. On April 2, 1862, the president and his wife brought Mary's sister and a party of Springfield friends. There is some question as to whether Lincoln came ashore then, although biographer Benjamin Thomas suggests that he did. *Mount Vernon, The Civil War Years* states that it is uncertain if Lincoln remained on the boat, but suggests it is possible he received inspiration standing by Washington's tomb. It is difficult to believe that he would not have toured the house and grounds of his famous predecessor when given the easy opportunity. The Mount Vernon Association believes that every past president has visited during his term, as of the bicentennial of Washington's death. But the book mentioned in this paragraph says that a visit from Grant is not recorded.

One of the several forts visited nearby was **FORT LYON**, seen with Secretary Stanton the day after a June 9, 1863 explosion. The purpose of this fortification was to hold the heights south of Alexandria from where the town could be shelled. It was located south of **HUNTING CREEK** on **JAMES DRIVE AND NORTH KINGS HIGHWAY**. Another was **FORT CORCORAN** visited several times on **NORTH QUINN BETWEEN KEY BOULEVARD AND EIGHTEENTH STREET, NEAR U.S. ROUTE 29**. This is now in Rosslyn, across Georgetown near the Key Bridge. Tad was held up once here by his father to see a cannon demonstration. The fort protected the Aqueduct Bridge on the C&O Canal. Lincoln had personally settled a complaint of the Sixty-Ninth New York Cavalry, which met him there and cheered when he asked if they would reenlist. Another was **FORT STRONG** (also known as **FORT DEKALB**) on the **LEE HIGHWAY, U.S. ROUTE 29, ON NORTH ADAMS AND NORTH VANCE STREETS**. Nothing remains of any of these. Mrs. Lincoln also visited camps in the area.

In *Lincoln the Unknown*, author Dale Carnegie relates how Washington and General Lafayette came to **CHRIST CHURCH** in November 1781 just after the British surrender at Yorktown. Several young ladies were introduced to the French hero, who stopped to kiss Lucy Hanks. Carnegie writes, "This kiss started a chain of events that did as much to modify the future of the United States as did all the battles LaFayette fought for us. Perhaps more." A rich planter is said to have been impressed with Lafayette's judgment of beautiful women, and then hired Lucy to be his servant. The planter then became the father of Lincoln's mother, and caused Lucy to move in shame to Kentucky. This questionable story is also in other sources.

On May 24, 1861, the day after Virginia seceded from the Union, Lincoln's close friend, Colonel Elmer Ellsworth, led his army unit organized from New York firemen, the Fire Zouaves, into Alexandria to take possession for the Union. A rebel flag over the **MARSHALL HOUSE HOTEL** is always said to have been visible from the White House (although it is probably too far away to have actually been seen), and Ellsworth attempted to remove it. On coming down the stairs, he was shot point blank by the hotel's proprietor, who was then killed by Ellsworth's men. Both became martyrs. Ellsworth had studied law at Lincoln's office, accompanied him to Washington, and was a great favorite with the family. (See the story of his funeral in the White House in the Washington, D.C., chapter.)

There is a plaque at the site, now a Holiday Inn at the **SOUTHEAST CORNER OF KING AND PITT STREETS**, honoring the hotel proprietor for upholding his property rights. The strange marker reads:

THE MARSHALL HOUSE STOOD ON THIS SITE AND WITHIN THE BUILD-ING ON THE EARLY MORNING OF MAY 24, 1861, JAMES W. JACKSON WAS KILLED BY FEDERAL SOLDIERS WHILE DEFENDING HIS PROP-ERTY AND PERSONAL RIGHTS. FIRST MARTYR TO THE CAUSE OF SOUTHERN INDEPENDENCE. THE JUSTICE OF HISTORY DOES NOT PERMIT HIS NAME TO BE FORGOTTEN. NOT IN THE EXCITEMENT OF BATTLE, BUT COOLLY, AND FOR A GREAT PRINCIPLE, HE LAID DOWN HIS LIFE, AN EXAMPLE TO ALL, IN DEFENSE OF HIS HOME AND THE SACRED SOIL OF HIS NATIVE STATE, VIRGINIA.

Lincoln mourned Ellsworth as a son and wept bitterly upon hearing of his death and at his funeral in the East Room of the White House. His uniform is displayed in the New York Capitol Building in Albany, and he is buried in Mechanicville, New York, in the Hudson View Cemetery.

The old colonial town of Alexandria predates the national capital and has many historical structures from colonial America and the Civil War. Some are briefly outlined because they will be of interest to those visiting the Lincoln sites nearby. This hometown of George Washington and Robert E. Lee has three boyhood homes of Lee, several houses of his uncles, and two of his schools still standing. One of the schools, **THE ALEXANDRIA ACADEMY**, founded by George Washington, still sits back of the **SOUTHEAST CORNER OF WASHINGTON AND WOLFE STREETS**. Lee and Washington's church is here, **CHRIST CHURCH**, on **WASHINGTON JUST NORTH OF KING STREET**. You can sit in their pews in this 1773 orig-inal building. The Tomb of the Unknown Soldier of the Revolutionary War is located at the **OLD PRESBYTERIAN MEETINGHOUSE** on **FAIRFAX JUST NORTH OF WOLFE STREET**. The **CARLYLE HOUSE**, torn down and reconstructed in the mid-1970s, is located on **FAIRFAX STREET BETWEEN**

KING AND CAMERON, next to WASHINGTON'S BANK on the SOUTHWEST CORNER OF CAMERON. This was the 1755 meetingplace between English general Braddock and five colonial governors to plan funding and strategy for the French and Indian War. Historical markers in town tell of many events and places in the historic town. Historical maps are readily available at numerous locations.

ROBERT E. LEE'S BOYHOOD HOMES include "The Boyhood Home," AT 607 ORONOCO JUST EAST OF WASHINGTON STREET. It closed to the public in the year 2000 after being opened for decades and is adjacent to the Hallowell School where he went for a short time to prepare for West Point. The home had been the town house of William Henry Fitzhugh, the son of William Fitzhugh of Chatham (see Fredericksburg, Virginia, entry). It was visited by Revolutionary War hero General Lafayette in 1824, who met here the young son (Robert) of his old friend "Light Horse Harry" Lee. Washington visited the home of Lee's future wife's grandfather when Mr. Fitzhugh lived here, and stayed at least two nights. The first president was here also when Fitzhugh's daughter, Mary, married Washington's step-grandson, George Washington Park Custis, on July 7, 1804. Their only daughter later married Robert E. Lee.

Other homes are the "Light Horse Harry Lee" house, the second house from the corner on the north side of Cameron Street, just east of Washington Street and marked by a plaque. Robert moved here with his family at age four. He also lived at a home in the back of 407 NORTH WASHINGTON. Robert frequently visited his uncles at the SOUTHWEST AND SOUTHEAST CORNERS OF WASHINGTON AND ORONOCO STREETS and the SOUTHWEST CORNER OF WASHINGTON AND QUEEN. Another uncle lived at 404 DUKE. All structures mentioned are original.

Arlington Cemetery and the Lee home there are covered in the Washington, D.C., chapter because of the closeness and visibility from the capital.

CITY POINT (HOPEWELL) AND PETERSBURG BATTLEFIELD: The junction of the James and Appomattox Rivers was General Grant's headquarters during the last months of the Civil War. It was then one of the world's largest supply bases, and the largest of the Civil War. The president and Tad visited June 21–22, 1864, and went to the Petersburg front to inspect the lines. A railroad had been constructed from the supply base to forts on the east and south side of Petersburg where the Confederates had been under siege for several weeks. The next day the president and his commanding general steamed up the river as far as it was considered safe and visited **FORT DARLING** at Drewry's Bluff. This is now part of the Richmond Battlefield Park. It can be reached about one mile east of Interstate 95 off Bellwood Road at the junction of Routes 145 and 656 on the James River just south of Richmond. They stopped at **BERMUDA HUNDRED** to pick up General Butler. This is NORTH OF THE APPOMATTOX RIVER JUNCTION WITH ROUTE 10 and is now inaccessible. Lincoln had an upset stomach, was offered champagne, but refused saying too many fellows get "seasick ashore from drinking that very stuff."

Two of Lincoln's last three weeks were spent here. On March 23, 1865, the president, Mary, Tad, and others left from the Seventh Street Wharf in Washington, D.C., aboard the steamer *River Queen,* a sort of floating hotel. Grant's wife, Julia, had suggested that a visit would be a respite from the burdens in the capital. Robert Lincoln, a captain on Grant's staff, was questioned, and he confirmed that surely his father would like to come if he were not intruding. The captain of the vessel entertained the party with tales of pirates and blockade runners, and pointed out many sites along the river where some of the related incidents happened.

On the way down Tad investigated the entire ship and "knew and counted among his friends every man on the crew." Once on land, March 24, Tad became a special pet of the soldiers and was allowed to accompany his father everywhere. That evening, Grant and the president conferred in one cabin while Mrs. Lincoln began a difficult relationship with Mrs. Grant.

A review the next day was postponed when the Confederates attacked **FORT STEDMAN**, a federal position east of Petersburg, now a major stop on the Petersburg Battlefield Tour. The president was at the **JORDON HOUSE**, now a depression in the ground adjacent to the visitor's center, stop 1 on the Battlefield Tour map. The president requested and was taken to the front by a special train to **PATRICK STATION** south of Petersburg. From there the men rode horses while the women rode in an army ambulance. When it was hinted that General Griffin's wife had seen the president to get special permission to remain at the front with her husband, Mary went into an uncontrollable rage, stating that she did not allow the president to see any woman alone. The rage continued until she met General Meade at his headquarters, who diplomatically convinced Mrs. Lincoln that it was the secretary of war who had issued the pass.

The men rode from there along the **HALIFAX ROAD** past **FORT DUSHANE** and **FORT WADSWORTH** (stop 10 on the Petersburg Battlefield

Tour), where the president, Tad, and General Meade witnessed an attack on the enemy for about two hours. This action occurred north of **PATRICK STATION** over the current National Park Flank Road at **FORTS URMSTON, CONAHEY** (stop 12), and **FISHER** (stop 13) over Virginia Routes 613, 676, and 672. All forts and roads are clearly marked on the Battlefield Tour map, off Route 604. (Note that earlier National Park literature and maps saying that Lincoln was at Meade's Station, stop 3, are incorrect.)

Jesse Grant was seven at the time and staying at City Point with his parents. He claimed to be along, and that the party came under fire. Jessie wrote in his book *In the Days of My Father, General Grant,* that Tad was given a spirited horse, which he was uncomfortable with. So Grant told him to switch with Jesse. The boys then got ahead of their fathers, and the horses broke away with the war's major Union leaders chasing after their young sons. That just excited the horses more, so Grant and Lincoln pulled back, allowing soldiers to form a line driving the horses into a corral. They scurried to a shelter to the disappointment of the boys who begged to remain outside during the fighting.

On March 26 the president and party went to **MALVERN HILL** to review General Ord's Army of the James. This well-marked major battlefield site is on the Richmond Battlefield Tour, Route 156, just north of the Route 5 junction. Grant's steamship docked at **AIKEN'S LANDING** where the men went to the parade ground about two miles ahead on horseback and the women proceeded in an ambulance. Aiken's landing and home, built in 1853, is privately owned, but accessible **FROM KINGSLAND ROAD AND VARINA ROAD OFF ROUTE 5**. Kingsland Road intersects with Route 5 about two miles east of its interchange with Interstate 295. The old home and site can be seen just to the east of the Interstate 295 bridge over the James River.

General Ord's wife was unable to ride in the ambulance since it was full, so she went by horseback, to the extreme displeasure of Mrs. Lincoln. Mrs. Ord thus arrived before Mrs. Lincoln, and the president innocently asked her to ride near him during the review. When Mrs. Lincoln appeared to find that Mrs. Ord had taken a place beside the president in the reviewing column, she became hysterical. This caused probably the most celebrated tirade of Mary Lincoln, to the embarrassment of all, particularly the president. She insulted everyone, attacked her husband for flirting, demanded that General Ord be dismissed from command, and generally made life miserable for all. When Mrs. Grant tried to calm the seething first lady, who appeared about ready to jump out of the ambulance, Mary then proceeded to berate her unmercifully. For most of her time afterward Mary stayed in her *River Queen* cabin.

On March 27, the Lincolns visited **POINT OF ROCKS**, four miles west of City Point where they ate beside the Appomattox River at an army hospital. This is now a state park with trails, just to the **WEST OF THE INTERSTATE 295 BRIDGE** over the Appomattox River. It is **SOUTH OF ROUTE 10 ON ROUTE 746, ENON ROAD, AND ALSO EAST OF INTERSTATE 95.** They then strolled through the woods to see a great oak tree said to mark the spot where Pocahontas saved the life of Captain John Smith. The president and Grant climbed a tall signal tower that gave them a commanding view of the area and Confederate tents two miles away. That evening General Sherman arrived from North Carolina for general discussions the next day with Grant and Admiral David Porter on Lincoln's ship anchored in the James River channel. Lincoln was very concerned that the Union generals might let victory slip through their hands. He also did not want terms of peace to be made so difficult for the rebels that they would practice guerrilla tactics and refuse to live in peace after surrender by their leaders. Lincoln made it clear that he wanted generous surrender terms and for the rebels to go home unpunished so that they would "return their allegiance to the Union and submit to the laws." Sherman later wrote, "Of all the men I ever met, he seemed to possess more of the elements of greatness, combined with goodness, than any other."

Lincoln's spirit was restored on the trip. Once he showed "strong muscles" by picking up a heavy ax, chopping wood for several minutes, and then holding it straight out horizontally, steady without a quiver. After he left, several strong soldiers could not duplicate the feat. Other trips were taken around the area. One day the president and his wife rode to an old graveyard on the banks of the James. As they strolled among the gravestones, Lincoln grew thoughtful. "Mary," he said, "you are younger than I. You will survive me. When I am gone, lay my remains in some quiet place like this." This probably affected the decision of where he was buried a few weeks later as plans were made for him to be buried in the Capitol Building, Chicago, and downtown Springfield, all of which Mary adamantly rejected.

After five days of remaining in her cabin without receiving visitors and seldom coming ashore, Mary returned to Washington on April 1, but left Tad. That night Lincoln was severely troubled by a realistic dream of his assassination. During the first few days of April, Lee evacuated Petersburg and moved west toward Appomattox Court House where he surrendered April 9, as Lincoln was returning to Washington. On the third and fourth, Lincoln and Tad visited Petersburg and Richmond, which had also been evacuated. He left Richmond midday on the fifth to return to City Point. (Entries for those cities describe the sites visited.)

Much of the president's time was spent at Colonel Bowers's cabin, which served as the **TELEGRAPH OFFICE**. This was almost adjacent to the south side of the large home, **APPOMATTOX MANOR**, now the National Park Headquarters for City Point. At this time the house was the quartermaster general's headquarters. Lincoln met his first Confederate general in full uniform at the telegraph office. Captured general Rufus Barringer had been staying in Union garrison commander Collis's tent, and may have requested permission to see Lincoln. Or another version is that an officer asked Lincoln if he would like to see a live rebel general in uniform. Lincoln discovered that Barringer was the brother of an old friend and colleague in Congress, and they talked for some time. Lincoln told many of his anecdotes, and both discussed the merits of various military and civil leaders. Barringer started to leave several times, fearing he had overstayed his welcome, but Lincoln remarked that they were both prisoners and might as well talk to remember times when they were in control of their lives.

Upon leaving, the president asked if he could be of service. Onlookers laughed, but Barringer remarked, "If anybody can be of service to a poor devil in my situation, I presume you are the man." Lincoln wrote a note to Secretary of War Stanton to make the general's detention "as comfortable as possible." Barringer was speechless and could not find words. Once outside, he broke down and sobbed audibly. But the president's note had a negative effect on Barringer's imprisonment, as he was at the dreaded prison Fort Delaware when Lincoln was assassinated. He was held over, questioned about his meeting with the president, and investigated until July 24, in a frenzy to uncover a conspiracy. (The general was the brother-in-law of Confederate generals Stonewall Jackson and D. H. Hill.)

While on board the boat Tad encountered a man who claimed to have urgent business with the president, and twice tried to force himself onto the *River Queen*. Later, some thought he looked like John Surratt who was tried in 1867 for complicity in Lincoln's assassination. Tad was called back to Washington, D.C., from Illinois to identify him, but he could only say that this looked very much like the man he had seen.

Mary Lincoln returned to City Point on April 6, on a troop transport with several friends including Attorney General James Speed, Senator Charles Sumner, Senator James Harlan, and Harlan's daughter, Mary, who would later marry Robert Lincoln. They wanted to go to Richmond, and proceeded there while the president stayed behind. One of Lincoln's reasons for coming was to get away from Washington and his advisors. Thus, according to Porter, he was not happy to see Sumner, Speed, and others who came. Later in the day, Vice President Johnson arrived, and Lincoln became very agitated, telling Porter not to let Johnson near him. The frustrated vice president then proceeded to Richmond. Mary Lincoln and her party, including her mulatto seamstress and friend, Elizabeth Keckley, followed the president's steps in Richmond. Mrs. Keckley especially enjoyed sitting in President Davis's chair in the Statehouse.

Lincoln returned to Petersburg on the seventh and then left for Washington, D.C., on the eighth after visiting many of the ten thousand wounded at the Depot Field Hospital about a mile away to the southwest. The **JOHN RANDOLPH HOSPITAL** is now on the site. This hospital visit lasted five hours in an effort to meet each patient, including Confederates. Before leaving, the president asked the military band to play the "Marseillaise" for a visiting Frenchman, and then asked the surprised director to play "Dixie"as "the tune was now federal property," and it's "good to show the rebels that, with us in power, they will be free to hear it again."

The steamer did not leave until 10:00 P.M., after a party on board. Mrs. Lincoln still was not talking to Mrs. Grant, who had taken Mrs. Ord's defense several days before. Mary was very concerned about the relative positions of the ships at the landing and other subtle supposed ways in which she felt she was not being given the proper respect as the wife of the president. So Mrs. Grant had her own party, band and all. While steaming past the Lincoln boat, she had her band blare out, "Now You'll Remember Me." One does not have to wonder why the Grants turned down the president's invitation to sit with the Lincolns at Ford's Theater a week later in Washington.

This area is now a unit of the Petersburg National Battlefield, which maintains the site of Grant's headquarters, the ship landing sites, Appomattox Manor, and several other historical structures and sites of the period. **APPOMATTOX MANOR** dates from 1763 and is the largest structure still existing in a small town of several pre–Civil War homes. This house must have drawn Lincoln's eye and presence, although there is no record that he went inside. **GRANT'S CABIN** was and is in the yard to the east. It was later moved to Philadelphia's Fairmount Park until 1981, when it was put back at its original site. Most of the original logs have rotted in recent years and have been replaced so that only a few logs on the east side are original. The interior of the cabin is open by the National Park Service.

FREDERICKSBURG, FALMOUTH, STAFFORD: Lincoln made several trips to these areas on or near the Rappahannock River, visiting hospitals, troops, and various army headquarters by way of nearby AQUIA CREEK and BELLE PLAIN. Visits to Falmouth included May 23, 1862, April 4–10, 1863, and May 7, 18, after the Union defeat at Chancellorsville. He was also at Aquia Creek on April 19–20 and November 26–27, 1862, and April 19, 1863. This was the site of the longest encampment in U.S. military history.

When he met General McDowell on May 23, 1862, at Aquia Creek and Potomac Creek, the general pointed out a hundred-foot-high, four-hundred-foot-long bridge being built over a ravine. The site is at the EAST END OF ROUTE 625. The president boyishly suggested that they cross over the single-plank pathway. Despite his rigorous cares of office stress at that time, Lincoln was in excellent physical condition and had no trouble, but Secretary Stanton and Admiral Dahlgren faltered. Later Lincoln told the cabinet about the trains regularly traveling over this marvelous bridge made of beanpoles and cornstalks, and they became known as "Beanpole and Cornstalk" bridges.

Just across the river from Fredericksburg, west of the bridge from downtown, is CHATHAM or the LACY HOUSE, claimed to be the only private house visited by both Lincoln and Washington. (But see BERKELEY in Harrison's Landing, Berkeley, Westover Plantations entry below.) During the winter of 1862–1863, the paneling of the mansion and all but four of the many large trees nearby were used as firewood by Union troops. It now serves as the headquarters of the Fredericksburg-Spotsylvania National Historical Park, and is open to the public. On May 23, 1862, Lincoln and Secretary of War Stanton met at General Irwin McDowell's headquarters here with French minister Mercier and Captain John A. Dahlgren of the navy. The group ate in the dining room east of the center hall with General McDowell, several cabinet members, and other generals, which was one of the largest assemblages of officers in the Civil War.

Chatham dates from 1768. A myth persists that George Washington courted Martha here, although they were married in 1759. The builder, William Fitzhugh, was a close friend of Washington, and they visited each other many times. Thomas Jefferson was probably here also. Robert E. Lee was said to have been here as a child, and played with his future wife, Fitzhugh's granddaughter, but this cannot be confirmed. General Lee is quoted as saying to Major Lacy during the Battle of Fredericksburg: "Major, I do not want to shell your fine old house. Besides, it has tender memories for me. I courted my bride under its trees." A nearby Virginia historical marker just north of the bridge relates that Lee indeed courted his wife here. Authors Shelby Foote and Douglas Southall Freeman have frequently related this story. The source of the claim is not known, although it may come from Lacy, who owned the house during the war. However, Lee's association with the mansion as a suitor or guest is questioned and doubted in National Park research documents, as no hard evidence exists. Fitzhugh sold the house in 1806, before Lee was born in 1807. Lee did write to his daughter, Annie, in 1861 that he had been to Chatham, but does not reveal details.

Before eating on May 23, 1862, the president crossed the Rappahannock River on a canal-boat bridge at the **MIDDLE PONTOON BRIDGE** and rode in a carriage into Fredericksburg. The party visited the headquarters of General Marsena Patrick at the **FARMER'S BANK ON THE NORTHWEST CORNER OF PRINCESS ANN AND GEORGE STREETS**. The mayor declined to meet or correspond with Lincoln because he felt his constituents would not approve. The picture-marker across the street shows that Lincoln made a speech from the front steps of the building, still standing. The president, General McDowell, and secretary of war then took a tour of the town and crossed back to Falmouth at the current site of the U.S. 1 bridge over the river.

The **MIDDLE PONTOON BRIDGE** was about a mile east of Chatham on Route 3 at **WASHINGTON'S BOYHOOD HOME SITE**, where he lived most of the time from age six to adulthood. He inherited the **FERRY FARM** from his father, who died in 1743. His mother stayed until 1772 when Washington bought her a house in town. (This still stands and is on the local historical tour of mostly colonial sites.) If George threw the coin across the river or chopped down a cherry tree, it would have been at the Boyhood Home. The original home burned down when George was eight, and this has been located. It is not known exactly where the later house site was. Probably the second home was located at the same spot, but no structure existed here during the war, and no house is here now. The Washington ferry site on the river was used for pontoon bridges by Union troops until the Overland Campaign of May 1864. The site is open to the public.

Lincoln was familiar with these Washington stories and would have passed by several times, although there is no documentation that Lincoln stood at the homesite. The president must have had an interest to see the boyhood scenes, actual or fictional, as depicted in one of his favorite books, Weems's *Life of Washington,* which created the cherry tree legend and other fables. Lincoln used the pontoon here and thus came down the ferry road that still goes through the forest by the Washington home site. Union soldiers knew the Washington stories also and wrote home that they camped on this site where Washington lived. Note that the river was wider prior to being rechanneled in 1870.

The April 1863 visit was the longest stay with the army until 1865. The president arrived via **AQUIA LANDING**, located at the **END OF VIRGINIA ROUTE 608 ON THE POTOMAC RIVER.** It can be reached by Virginia Route 628 following signs from Interstate 95 south of Stafford. This was the head of the railroad terminus. A marker on U.S. Highway 1 just north of Stafford notes the site of the **UNION DEPOT**.

The president, Mary, and Tad toured the army near **FALMOUTH** beginning on April 4, 1863. The trip was delayed when the steamer ran into a furious snowstorm after leaving the Washington Navy Yard and had to anchor in a cove on the Potomac opposite **INDIAN HEAD**. As accompanying correspondent Noah Brooks pointed out, this was a dangerous situation since a rebel patrol could have "gobbled up the entire party without firing a shot." They made it to Aquia Creek the next morning, connected to Falmouth by railroad. The terminus was at **FALMOUTH STATION**, destroyed by retreating Union forces on June 13–14, 1863. The site now is on **ROUTE 607 (COOL SPRING ROAD) JUST SOUTH OF ROUTE 218 (WHITE OAK ROAD), ABOUT A MILE EAST OF CHATHAM.** They rested at General Hooker's headquarters on a high ridge three miles from the Rappahannock River. At the nearby camp of General Daniel Sickles, the president was kissed by Princess Salm-Salm of Prussia, which caused Mary to give him a severe lecture when Tad snitched.

Hooker's headquarters, known as the **CANNON RIDGE SITE**, was the headquarters of the Union army from January 1863, after the Battle of Fredericksburg, until the eve of the Gettysburg campaign in June 1863. This site is **NORTH OF ROUTE 218 AND WEST OF ROUTE 606 (RINGGOLD ROAD) AT MYERS ROAD AND JENNY LYNN ROAD** in a residential addition. A new historical marker on the south side of Route 218 at Kendalwood Street notes the approximate area, but the marker is located where a car can conveniently pull over rather than the actual site several blocks northeast. The camp was a series of tents, and the Lincolns stayed in one during the cold weather. From here, the president rode out to various Stafford County points to make the most expansive reviews of the Union army ever held in the field. The visit played an important part in restoring morale and public confidence in the army by virtue of the publicity and mutual devotion shown to and from the president.

A historical marker at Chatham describes Lincoln's review of troops in April 1863. However, the Park Service now states that there was no review at that sight, as erroneously shown on the marker. Among the several reviews were the **WESTERN END OF ROUTE 606, BOSCOBEL ROAD**

EAST OF THE JUNCTION OF ROUTE 607 (DEACON ROAD) AND ROUTE 608 (BROOKE ROAD), about two miles northeast. Reviews also included troops close to BROOK STATION at Stafford Court House, near ROUTE 607, BOURNE STREET AND ON ROUTE 608 AT A SOUTHERLY DIP ABOUT THREE MILES DUE NORTH OF THE POINT OF WHERE ROUTES 606 AND 605 MEET 608. Tad tried with varying success to keep up on horseback and once tried to change horses with someone near the latter mentioned site. The president was described as "an awkward figure on horseback with a stovepipe hat and elbows stuck out keeping time to the motion of the horse with his chin almost buried between his knees of his long bony legs."

On April 9, 1863, Lincoln reviewed seventeen thousand troops at BELLE PLAIN at what is the SOUTH SIDE OF POTOMAC CREEK NEAR THE POTOMAC RIVER AT THE EAST END OF VIRGINIA ROUTE 604. Cheers were shouted for "The President," "Mrs. Lincoln," "The boy," and "Tommy [*sic*] Lincoln." Since Lincoln maintained a higher degree of public visibility than any president before him did, the Union soldiers developed closeness and loyalty to a man who inspired them to rally to him and his cause. This visibility and the resulting devotion may have dampened an election coup in November 1864 for Democratic presidential candidate General George B. McClellan. Another review was held ABOUT TWO OR THREE MILES SOUTH OF BELLE PLAIN. Lincoln rode past General Burnsides's old headquarters during the Battle of Fredericksburg, the PHILLIPS HOUSE, which had recently accidentally burned down and went to the LACY HOUSE (Chatham). The Phillips House site is north of Route 218, east of the railroad tracks, on Mountain Avenue.

Reviews were made over the area northeast of Fredericksburg occupied by CAMP STARVATION, renamed CAMP PITCHER, and at CAMP SICKLES. The first mentioned covered an area BETWEEN THE RAILROAD TO THE WEST OF ROUTE 626 AND BROOKE ROAD, ROUTE 608 TO THE EAST. IT WAS SOUTH OF ROUTE 624 AND NORTH OF ROUTE 218. CAMP SICKLES WAS SOUTH OF ROUTE 625 AND NORTH OF BROOKE ROAD AS IT RUNS NORTHEAST. A diary notation puts Lincoln at just east of the intersection now of SLEEPY HOLLOW TRAIL and SANDELWOOD TERRACE. Another review was around the FRIENDSHIP BAPTIST CHURCH (DEACON ROAD) AND AT THE WEST END OF BOSCOBEL ROAD, EAST OF BROOKE ROAD. Another diary places Lincoln at the BOSCOBEL HOUSE, on the EAST SIDE OF BOSCOBEL ROAD (ROUTE 606) JUST NORTH OF ROUTE 608 AND WEST OF THE ROUTE 605 INTERSECTION. Soldiers were struck by the president's "cadaverous and emaciated" appearance. One soldier wrote, "Poor man, I pity him, and almost wonder at his being alive. . . . The gigantic work upon his hands, and the task upon his physical frame must be very great."

The president and ten-year-old Tad noticed a young bugler, Gus Schurmann. The thirteen-year-old aide to General Daniel Sickles was about Tad's size and looked to be about Tad's age. Sickles gave him permission to accompany Tad, who was said to have "made the acquaintance of nearly every tent before the first day was done." Tad wanted to see how the "graybacks" looked, and was allowed to go down to the picket lines opposite the town with his new friend, Gus. They were spotted by Confederates who kidded with them, and an officer bowed in their direction. In another visit to the picket lines, a Confederate staff officer was quoted by a Confederate correspondent as saying he saw his "Gorillaship (Lincoln) riding along the picket line." Lincoln commented about a (then) surviving chimney of the Scott House, located between Sophia Street and the Rappahannock River on the south side of an extension of Hawke Street. (The entry on Grover Theater in the chapter on "Washington" relates the story of Gus's visit to the White House and a meeting between the boys and John Wilkes Booth.)

HAMPTON ROADS, NORFOLK, FORT MONROE: Lincoln, with cabinet secretaries Chase and Stanton, left the Washington Navy Yard in Washington, D.C., on May 5, 1862 and arrived at **FORT MONROE** at about 10:00 P.M. on May 6, after a delay due to darkness on the Potomac. General McClellan was advancing toward Richmond, leaving seventy-eight-year-old General John Wool in charge of the area. The army had been stalled twenty miles away at Yorktown, and could not be supplied by the Union fleet, which would not challenge the Confederate ironclad *Merrimack* (renamed the *Virginia*). The dreaded menace was lurking around **SEWELL'S POINT**, immobilizing Union fleet operations in the area and preventing the use of the James River. (The U.S. Navel Base is at Sewell's Point now, directly south of Fort Monroe and Fort Wool at the **NORTHWEST POINT OF LAND**.) This has been called one of the greatest stalemates in American history.

Immediately upon arrival the party took a tug to Commodore Goldsborough's flagship off Fort Monroe. While here, Lincoln stayed in **QUARTERS NO. 1**, an imposing building still **OPPOSITE THE EAST GATE ON BERNARD ROAD**. The historical marker there shows that Lafayette stayed in the building in 1824, and later Presidents Grant, Hayes, Garfield, and Arthur were entertained.

The first morning of the visit, the president and cabinet secretaries rowed over to a great steam yacht that had been strengthened with heavy timbers plated with iron in order to ram the *Virginia* if she attempted to attack Fort Monroe. The party then landed at Old Point

Comfort Wharf (no longer here) near the lighthouse, in constant use since 1802, east of the fort. (The Jamestown settlers landed here in 1607.)

They then toured **FORT WOOL** and inspected the Sawyer gun. The fort was built on an artificial island after the War of 1812. It is now north of the Interstate 64 tunnel in Chesapeake Bay between Norfolk and Hampton. It is accessible only by water, but easily seen from the ramparts of Fort Monroe. They came back to Fort Monroe, then took a horseback ride through the ruins of Hampton and reviewed troops at **CAMP HAMILTON**. The camp covered a large area north of Fort Monroe in **PHOEBUS**. The only building Lincoln passed still standing in Hampton is **ST. JOHN'S CHURCH**, dating back to 1728, at **100 WEST QUEEN STREET**. Hampton, the oldest English-speaking city in the country, was almost totally destroyed by order of Confederate general John B. Magruder on August 7, 1861, to prevent its reoccupation by Union forces.

Meeting at Quarters No. 1 on May 8, the president decided it was time to liberate Norfolk and deprive the *Virginia* of her base in spite of the fact that the professional soldiers advised that the shoals prevented a landing in the area. It was decided to try to land at Sewell's Point under cover of bombardment. The party then watched the bombardment of Sewell's Point from Fort Wool on May 8. This marked the first time that Lincoln had been under enemy gunfire, and the first time he got to directly exercise his powers as commander in chief. But the *Virginia* would not budge, and it was felt an invasion here was too risky.

It was then decided to find another landing place east of Sewell's Point since it was believed that the ironclad could not safely maneuver past the Union forts and the Rodman (Lincoln) gun at Fort Monroe. Also if the *Virginia* left, Norfolk would be at the mercy of the Union ironclad *Monitor*. Chase, Wool, and others took a tug to examine Ocean View on the east side of Chesapeake Bay. When they got back to Fort Monroe, Lincoln was studying maps and had another suggestion. He used a tugboat cruise around Hampton Roads to search for landing sites. The group inspected a site about a mile below Fort Wool and near **WILLOUGHBY POINT**, where northbound Interstate 95 now enters the bay. The president found a landing spot, got out, inspected it, walked up and down the beach, and proved that a landing was possible. But Wool had not gone on the tour and favored the Ocean View site, which he had seen.

On May 10, Lincoln, Chase, Stanton, and Wool went to Ocean View, dropped off Chase and Wool, and returned to Quarters No. 1. While waiting at Fort Monroe, an invasion was then led by Chase and received the surrender of Norfolk. Earlier Lincoln had become infuriated when he learned that troops were being held back. He angrily bounced his tall hat off the floor and ordered them into battle. When he heard that the mayor had surrendered Norfolk, the crusty secretary Stanton actually hugged the dignified General Wool. On May 11, Lincoln decided to go back to Washington, but Goldsborough rushed into Quarters No. 1 to exclaim the electrifying news that the *Virginia* had been blown up off CRANEY ISLAND. Lincoln sailed up the Elizabeth River to tour Norfolk, and past the point where the first Confederate ironclad was destroyed. This is no longer an island. The site is located at the NORTHWEST ENTRANCE TO THE ELIZABETH RIVER. Chase wrote his daughter that this was a "brilliant week's campaign of the president, for I think it quite certain that if he had not come down, (Norfolk) would still have been in possession of the enemy and the *Merrimack* as grim and defiant and as much a terror as ever."

Lincoln stopped here on the way to HARRISON'S LANDING on July 8, 1862, and came to meet Grant on July 30–31, 1864. On February 3, 1865, Lincoln met three representatives of Confederate President Davis at Fort Monroe aboard the *River Queen* in an effort to establish peace. This Hampton Roads Peace Conference included Secretary Seward and Confederate vice president Alexander H. Stephens, a former friend of Lincoln's. All three Confederate commissioners had opposed secession, but joined their states after they left the Union. No notes were taken, so we have only the recollections of some of the participants to reveal what went on.

Lincoln would make no bargain as long as the war progressed. One of the commissioners responded that Charles I of England had negotiated with those rebelling against his government. Lincoln professed that he knew little about history, but he did remember that Charles lost his head. The president did make a generous offer, or suggestion. He said that he had never intended to interfere with slavery where it existed. He felt that the North and South were both equally responsible for slavery and agreed to work toward compensation of slaveowners to the extent of possibly $400 million. Nothing was accomplished except the president promised to exchange a nephew of Stephens, who was at the federal prison at Johnson's Island, for a Union prisoner of equal rank. (Lincoln ordered that he report to the White House and gave the young man a picture inscribed with: "Don't have these where you're from.") Two days after the peace conference he proposed to his cabinet that slave owners be reimbursed in the amount stated if hostilities ended by April 1. The idea was abandoned when the cabinet rejected the idea.

On the way to City Point on March 24, 1865, Lincoln's steamer stopped here for fresh water. Mary left the boat to anxiously telegraph her housekeeper to check on the White House. Lincoln had dreamed the night before that it had caught fire, but considered this only a meaningless vision. He landed again on April 9, on the way back to Washington, D.C. He did not know until getting to the capital that Lee had surrendered.

Fort Monroe was known as the Gibraltar of Chesapeake Bay. Robert E. Lee was the chief engineer during the construction. His quarters, where his first child was born, is marked across the road from the Casement Museum. Jefferson Davis was imprisoned first here for five months after the war in what is now part of the Museum on Bernard Road on the west side of the interior of the fort. He was later moved a short distance to Carroll Hall, which stood in the Northwest Bastion of the fort, and remained a prisoner at the fort for two more years. The *River Queen* was used after the Civil War as an excursion boat, proud of her Lincoln Room, before being destroyed by fire in Washington, D.C., in 1911.

HARRISONBURG: The home of Lincoln's great-grandfather, John, was north on Linville Creek, near Edom. He had moved here at about age fifty-two in 1767 or 1768. John was reared in Pennsylvania close to the Boone family with whom the families had intermarried. Squire Boone and his sixteen-year-old son Daniel had moved to Virginia in 1750, and their relative Josiah apparently accompanied the Lincolns to Virginia near Linville Creek. (Daniel later became a famous explorer and frontiersman.) John Lincoln's son, Abraham, for whom the president was named, was born in Berks County, Pennsylvania, in 1744, and moved to the Linville Creek area with his parents. He served as judge advocate in court in Rockingham County, captain of the militia, and a member of the Linville Creek Baptist Church committee.

The old log cabin houses of the early Lincolns have long since disappeared, but the main portion of a home built in 1800 by Jacob Lincoln still stands along the east side of Virginia Route 42, six miles north of Harrisonburg and noted by a Virginia historical marker. The builder was the only son of "Virginia John," who remained in Rockingham County after the Revolutionary War. The graves of Virginia John and his wife, Rebecca Flowers Lincoln, are marked in the family cemetery just north of the home, and include sixteen other relatives and two family slaves. This is about two hundred yards east of the short parallel road along the east side of Virginia Route 42, the old highway left as a convenience for those visiting the cemetery, where ceremonies are held on the anniversary of the president's birth. A single tree in an open field marks the site. The road ends just north of the John Lincoln homesite, between the cemetery and the road. The house burned down in 1791. The cemetery is on private land, but the owners seem willing to allow people to view the graves. The gravestones of John and his wife date from the mid twentieth century, but Jacob's stone is original, dating to his death in 1822. He was with the colonial forces at Yorktown at the surrender of British general Cornwallis, and was a cousin of General Benjamin Lincoln, who received the surrender for the commander, George Washington. There is no indication that the Lincolns knew one another. At least three of Jacob's children built homes that still stand in the area. There are still many of his descendants in the Shenandoah Valley. When the Union army during the Civil War burned the valley, one Lincoln reputedly said he'd like to see his "cousin" and shoot him.

Thomas, the father of the president, was born about 1776–1778. It is possible that "Captain" Abraham's first wife died after Thomas was born, and Bathsheba was his second wife. It is not certain who his first wife was or if there was more than one marriage, and therefore the grandmother of the president is unknown. Some believe her name may have been Mary Shipley. It is probable that this Abraham was married only once, and Bathsheba was his only wife.

The birthplace site is believed to be across Route 42 at or near the site of the present white bridge across Linville Creek, across the road and just northwest of the cemetery and John Lincoln homestead site. The log cabin, long since gone, was on the land of his father, Captain Abraham, which ran from a spot on the creek due west of the southern border of the cemetery to a ridge to the west. No trace of the cabin has ever been found.

Probably the frontiersman Daniel Boone had urged the family to seek homes farther west. Abraham and his wife, Bathsheba (also spelled or referred to as "Bersheba"), left in the early 1780s with their five children to follow the trail of his friend Boone to Kentucky to a site Lincoln had previously scouted and selected. (The confusion in various name spellings was due to different spellings by semiliterate frontiersmen. In fact the family name "Lincoln" was occasionally written as Lincon, Linkoln, and Linkhorn and commonly pronounced "Linkhorn.") Boone had entered land for him in Kentucky in 1776. Captain Abraham was captured by Indians on the way back to Virginia in August 1782, made to run the gauntlet, and then released. There is a question as to when Boone was here or where he was, but John W. Wayland in *The Lincolns in Virginia* believes that Boone met and married Rebecca Bryan on Linville Creek.

Other Lincoln homesteads are in the vicinity. The Bryan-Lincoln-Pennybacker House, c. 1825, is just to the west of Virginia Route 42 on Virginia Route 782, across a short bridge about a mile south of the Jacob Lincoln home. Pennybacker married one of Jacob Lincoln's granddaughters. The red brick house on the north side of the road is on the site of the earlier Bryan Cabin, where George Washington mentioned in his diary that he was hosted. This lies on the road from Brock's Gap and the crossing of Linville Creek, used by Washington in 1784 when returning from a trip to the Ohio Valley.

The historical marker on U.S. Highway 11 at Lacey Springs reads:

FOUR MILES WEST, THOMAS LINCOLN, FATHER OF THE PRESIDENT, WAS BORN ABOUT 1778. HIS FATHER ABOUT 1782 TOOK HIM TO KENTUCKY. BESIDE THE ROAD WAS THE LINCOLN INN, LONG KEPT BY A MEMBER OF THE FAMILY.

It is rumored that the future president visited the Linville area on the way to take his seat in Congress in 1847 and stayed in the inn, but there is no proof. If he came by way of Winchester, it is possible that he did come here also. A cemetery full of Lincoln relatives, including David, is located about half a mile west of Lacey Springs on Route 806. David corresponded with his famous cousin about their common ancestry. Grandfather Lincoln's route to Kentucky via the **CUMBERLAND GAP** is shown in the Kentucky chapter.

HARRISON'S LANDING, BERKELEY, WESTOVER PLANTATIONS:
The president visited General McClellan on July 8, 1862, at the plantation and home of the Harrison family on the James River. Union troops were camped here for miles along the river. On the way, his steamer ran aground in the mud. While waiting for it to be pulled free, Lincoln took a swim in the river. He therefore arrived late and reviewed the thousands of waiting troops in the moonlight. The next day Lincoln again reviewed troops in the area and at another nearby colonial mansion, Westover, where the main landing was, since this is on the river and not set back like Berkeley. McClellan claimed that the president was not welcome, and he had to order the troops to cheer. This does not appear to be accurate as they seemed to show spontaneous affection. McClellan gave the president a memorandum suggesting that war be conducted only against the Southern army and not the people or slavery.

The beautiful brick colonial mansion, **BERKELEY**, was the birthplace of President William Henry Harrison and his father, who signed the Declaration of Independence. The first floor was used as a hospital. It is believed by guides there and some books for sale on the site that Lincoln did confer with "Little Mac" in the house and visited those in the hospital. This seems logical since there were extensive discussions, and thus would make this the only other private house (in addition to Chatham at Fredericksburg) visited by both Washington and Lincoln. (In fact the first ten presidents were entertained here.) Lincoln is documented only as conferring with McClellan on his steamer in the river. His headquarters were in the woods near the mansion, not on the second floor, as claimed there. (The author of *The Army of the Potomac at Berkeley Landing*, an expert on the site, can find no documentation that Lincoln was inside Berkeley or Westover mansion.)

The Berkeley grounds where Thanksgiving was first celebrated in 1619 and the 1726 colonial mansion are open to the public. Westover mansion, c. 1730, is open only on limited occasions, but the grounds are open.

HOPEWELL: See City Point (Hopewell) and Petersburg Battlefield entry.

PETERSBURG: The town was the headquarters of Robert E. Lee's army for more than nine months as Grant laid siege, surrounded and cut off the town. Lee evacuated on April 2, 1865. The next day Lincoln, Tad, and their party came by way of **HANCOCK STATION**, the **JERUSALEM PLANK ROAD**, and **FORT MAHONE**, where they stopped and observed many dead bodies on the recent battlefield. Tears were seen in Lincoln's eyes. (This fort is on the Park tour, just southwest of the junction of Routes 301-A and 301, South Boulevard and Sycamore Street.) The flag of the Union was seen on an old **COURTHOUSE** on the way to Grant's temporary headquarters at the **WALLACE HOUSE, 204 SOUTH MARKET STREET, ON THE SOUTHWEST CORNER WITH BROWN STREET.** Both structures are still standing, as are many from the period in the area.

Grant was on the porch waiting for him, and Lincoln acted like he wanted to hug the commander. There is some question as to whether they entered the house. While Grant explained his plans in more detail than he ever had to the president, Tad grew restless and was offered some sandwiches by General Sharpe, who thought he might be hungry. Tad grabbed them, as Admiral Porter said, "as a drowning man might seize a life preserver," and cried out, "Yes, I am, that's what's the matter with me," much to the amusement of the staff. When the owner of the house appeared, Lincoln recognized the man as Thomas Wallace, a political ally when he was in Congress. Although invited inside, Lincoln asked to remain on the porch, and Wallace brought out chairs. Lincoln sat close to the edge where his long legs could dangle off the side. Wallace's fifteen-year-old son was asked to entertain Tad, but defiantly ran off saying, "You are not going to let that man come into the house." Wallace replied, "I think it would not do to try to stop a man from coming in who has fifty thousand men at his back!" Lincoln was greatly amused when Wallace told him the story. The large porch here now is a more recent addition.

Lincoln remained there an hour and a half, and then left with a brief tour of the devastated city. Buildings were still on fire. White residents remained hidden inside their homes, but blacks cheered him everywhere. Before leaving he called on **GENERAL ROGER A. PRYOR**, a Confederate who had been paroled whom he had known in Congress. Pryor was then staying in a rented house on **WASHINGTON STREET**. This is thought to have been on the **NORTH SIDE BETWEEN MARKET AND DAVIS STREETS**. He or his wife refused to allow the president inside, his wife saying that her husband "was a paroled prisoner, that General Lee was still in the field, and that no officer could hold a conference with the head of the opposing army."

He returned on April 7, with Mary and Tad, and stopped at Major General George L. Hartsuff's headquarters at **CENTER HILL**, a brick mansion on the **NORTH SIDE OF FRANKLIN BETWEEN JEFFERSON AND ADAMS**. Lincoln and Hartsuff discussed the temper of the white citizens of the ruined city, and Hartsuff spoke of the government renting the house. Lincoln commented that "General Grant seems to have attended sufficiently to the matter of rent." Again the president toured the ruined city. This old home is open to the public.

The Petersburg National Battlefield surrounds the town on the east and south. All of the forts mentioned above are on the National Park Tour map. Lincoln's presence on the battlefield is mainly described in the entry on nearby **CITY POINT**.

PETERSBURG BATTLEFIELD: See City Point (Hopewell) entry.

RICHMOND: The Union captured the capital of the Confederacy on April 3, 1865. Lincoln was visiting General Grant at his headquarters nearby at City Point, and wanted to see the city. The James River had to be cleared of mines, and this was accomplished so that he could go up the next day. This was Tad's twelfth birthday, and he accompanied his father. At **DREWRY'S BLUFF** below the city, a line of obstructions prevented the passage of their ships. (This is just east of the turnpike and accessible from Routes 1 and 301 via STATE ROUTE 656, BELLWOOD STREET, about four miles south of Route 150.) They then proceeded by a shallow-draft barge pulled by a tug, but soon the tug ran aground at ROCKETTS LANDING, about where Thirty-first Street would meet the river. From there the oars were used to drive the barge, which landed about a hundred yards from LIBBY PRISON. The infamous prison was at the SOUTHEAST CORNER OF CARY AND TWENTIETH. Lincoln would have recognized it from many pictures he had observed. (After the war Libby Prison was torn down and rebuilt for the World Fair in Chicago. A facade is now in the Chicago Historical Society.)

At once the president was recognized as the liberator of the many blacks who crowded and knelt around him. Lincoln told them, "Don't kneel to me. That is not right. You must kneel to God only, and thank him for the liberty you will hereafter enjoy." Porter observed that he "lit up with a divine look" as if in another world. The party moved very slowly through the city being hard-pressed by friendly but potentially dangerous multitudes. Lincoln addressed the crowd who remained motionless and quiet as he requested that they let him pass quickly due to limited time. He was allowed to move slowly past LIBBY PRISON, where he heard someone shout to burn it down. "No!" he cried. "Leave it as a monument."

The crowds became greater as he advanced, as spectators jammed the streets, climbed poles and trees, and peered out from every available window. Lincoln, wearing his tall stovepipe hat that made him look even taller, moved up NINETEENTH STREET, TO MAIN for about two blocks, then up SEVENTEENTH TO BROAD. They were now within a half block of the railroad station, and he rested here before climbing the hill into the main business section. By now he was tired and hot in his overcoat. One white woman in the crowd, at the SPOTSWOOD HOTEL (SOUTHEAST CORNER OF EIGHTH AND MAIN) was draped in an American flag. The Spotswood was Richmond's finest hotel, where Lee and others stayed. Jefferson Davis had rooms when he moved to Richmond as Confederate president, and stayed when he returned for his indictment for treason. Lincoln is also stated to have been by the EXCHANGE HOTEL at the SOUTHEAST CORNER OF FOURTEENTH AND FRANKLIN where Vice President Alexander Stevens lived. He passed by the BALLARD HOUSE ON THE NORTHEAST CORNER, where former president John Tyler died during the war, waiting to take his seat in the Confederate Congress. The Ballard and Exchange Hotels were connected by a second-floor passage over the street. After about an hour of this chaos and potential disaster, a squad of blue horsemen was able to clear the streets, and Lincoln proceeded without the crowds. The party, with Tad clinging to his father, proceeded walking up Twelfth Street, past the Capitol and governor's mansion to Jefferson Davis's home, now occupied by Union general Godfrey Weitzel.

The president entered the front door of the CONFEDERATE WHITE HOUSE and turned right from the hallway into a reception room at the west corner. He probably did not know that the east-side balcony, just around the corner on the left as he entered, was the site of the banister from which Davis's favorite son, Joseph, age five, fell to his death less than a year before. Davis's grief had equaled Lincoln's at the death in 1862 of his favorite, Willie. (Davis and his son are buried in Richmond's Hollywood Cemetery. Both presidents had a son named Willie who died at age eleven.) Davis removed the balcony a few months after the incident.

Lincoln met with federal officers in the far right-hand-corner room and sank down into Davis's armchair, still in the room today. He remarked, correctly, that the chair must have been used by "President Davis," and he asked for a glass of water. This was the only time he referred to Davis as president. A few days later Mary Lincoln and her party toured the residence where her seamstress and friend, Elizabeth Keckley, enjoyed sitting in Mr. Davis's chair. A former slave, she had previously been seamstress for Mrs. Davis. (About 80 percent of the original furniture remains in the house.) The party then toured the house and ate in the reception room. It is not believed that Lincoln went above the first floor, although Davis had an office on the second. The family normally used the upper floors, considered private, but Davis was in poor health and worked at home increasingly as the war progressed. If Lincoln did go to the second-floor office, he would have seen the oval table, still there today, around which Davis met with Robert E. Lee, Stonewall Jackson, and others. Afterward Lincoln received several prominent Confederate leaders, including Judge John A. Campbell, who had served as the Confederate assistant secretary of war. Campbell had appeared dignified and tall when he met with Lincoln a few weeks before at Hampton Roads to discuss a possible end to the conflict. Now he was pale and haggard. Lincoln would not give him specific terms of surrender. (The CONFEDERATE WHITE HOUSE, AT TWELFTH AND CLAY STREETS, is open to the public and is adjacent to the Confederate Museum.)

From there the party rode in an ambulance or army hack through the city again. Tad had finished lunch early and came out to hold "a reception" in the backseat of the hack in front of the house, shaking hands with freedmen and some whites who crowded around. One black woman was heard telling her child that a touch of Lincoln's garment would cure his pain. He rode past the governor's mansion, built in 1813 on the site of the earlier governor's house, which was located behind the Capitol. Lee's father had lived there as governor. The president then moved past ST. PAUL'S EPISCOPAL CHURCH, AT THE SOUTHWEST CORNER OF NINTH AND GRACE STREETS, where Davis and Lee worshiped. Davis had to leave during the middle of the previous Sunday's service upon receiving an urgent message from Lee that he could no longer hold the Union troops out of Petersburg and Richmond. (His pew can still be seen and used.) Lincoln then entered the Capitol grounds opposite the church, and is said to have stopped "long before the bronze EQUESTRIAN STATUTE OF GEORGE WASHINGTON under which Davis had been sworn in as President of the Confederate States." President Zachary Taylor had dedicated this with Ex-President Tyler and Vice President Millard Fillmore present.

The party then toured the abandoned and desecrated STATEHOUSE, also the Confederate Capitol, without any recorded comment. He walked through the hall where Virginia delegates met to consider secession and where Lee received his commission to head Virginia troops. The Confederate Congress then used it. Generals Stonewall Jackson and Jeb Stuart had lain in state there. The legislative chamber then extended into the present hallway since the building had no side wings and no front door or steps. He also visited the OFFICE OF PRESIDENT DAVIS in the government offices on BANK STREET, now the CURRENT FEDERAL COURTHOUSE AND POST OFFICE, ACROSS FROM THE FRONT OF THE CAPITOL. This 1858 structure was one of the few that escaped the Evacuation Fire of 1865, which destroyed over nine hundred buildings in the business district. Davis was later brought back here in 1867 to face charges of treason.

The party then headed back through fashionable residential districts and part of the business section devastated by fire. Few faces were seen behind closed blinds or shades. A man in a Confederate uniform appeared to point a rifle directly at the president from a second-story window, causing a brief panic. The party moved on to CASTLE THUNDER PRISON (ON THE NORTH SIDE OF CARY STREET BETWEEN EIGHTEENTH AND NINETEENTH) and LIBBY PRISON, boarding tugs that carried them to the *Malvern*, Admiral Porter's ship. It had made its way past the obstructions and was now anchored at ROCKETTS, at Thirty-first and Main. After boarding, a man hailed the ship, claiming to have dispatches for the president and refusing to give them to anyone else. Unlike the several other similar incidents during the last few days, the president ordered him let aboard, thinking that they might be from Grant and that he was following strict orders. When he was found to be a civilian, he was put off. Admiral Porter claimed later that he was John Wilkes

Booth, but Booth was in New York City at this time. (Grant did not come to Richmond until 1867.)

Lincoln spent the night at the landing and received Judge Campbell again and others during the next morning. In one source (*Lincoln in the Telegraph Office*), the author related an additional tour of the city on the morning of the fifth, including "headquarters," presumably the president's mansion. At 11:30 A.M. they boarded a barge and were tugged down the river to City Point via the Dutch Gap Canal. According to author William Hanchett, Booth's sister believed that her brother was reconciled to the South's defeat but that Lincoln's "triumphant entry into the fallen city (which was not magnanimous), breathed fresh air upon the fire which consumed him."

(Note that I have found no one source that gives Lincoln's full itinerary in Richmond. The above is based on numerous sources in the bibliography including *General Lee's City, Moore's Complete Civil War Guide to Richmond, Abraham Lincoln at City Point, Lincoln Lore Numbers 469* and *774, Lincoln in Richmond,* and numerous conversations with National Park Rangers here and at Fredericksburg.)

STAFFORD: See Fredericksburg, Falmouth, Stafford entry.

TRAIL OF THE ASSASSIN (Continued from the "Trail in Maryland"): After fleeing Washington on April 14, 1865, John Wilkes Booth and coconspirator David Herold fled through Maryland and Virginia, arriving in DAHLGREN, VIRGINIA, on April 23, at the QUESENBERRY HOME. This is at the END OF ROUTE 614, POTOMAC DRIVE AT ROUTE 683. The house is not marked, but is located in front of a boat ramp and dock area in the rear, accessible to the public. This was a Confederate way station for agents in the area, and has been considerably enlarged since the war. The conspirators missed the correct inlet as they saw activity on the river, and landed at the Gambo Creek inlet about a mile short of the house. Herold walked over, and after first being turned down by Mrs. Quesenberry, got her cooperation. In fact, Confederate agent Thomas Harbin was either in the house or nearby waiting for Booth. He had met with Booth and Dr. Mudd in December 1864, at the Bryantown Inn, to plan a route through Maryland and Virginia, which could be used to carry the kidnapped president in the earlier Booth plans. He and his partner, Joseph N. Baden Jr., were now arranging Booth's escape through Virginia after the assassination. These two men had crossed the Potomac on April 16, probably to see Mrs. Quesenberry and pave the way for Booth's escape. But they had been seen, and reports got back to Washington, D.C., that they were possibly

Booth and Herold. As a result, the Sixteenth New York Cavalry was sent to the area.

The fugitives obtained food from Mrs. Quesenberry, and then went north up Gambo Creek to the **BRYANT HOME**. This was just northeast of the **ROUTES 301 AND 614 INTERSECTION**. They got Bryant's cooperation to take them to the home of **DR. RICHARD STUART** (also spelled "Stewart"), **CLEYDAEL**, down present **ROUTE 206 JUST PAST THE INTERSECTION WITH ROUTE 218**. After briefly eating they were told to leave. Stuart was a cousin of Robert E. Lee and had been arrested several times for little reason. He wanted nothing to do with the known conspirators. Stuart was later arrested with Cox, Jones (see the chapter of **MARYLAND**), Mrs. Quesenberry, and many whom Booth encountered in his escape. The white, two-story Stuart Home is in a modern housing addition named Cleydael in the southern part, set apart south of the main road to the east through the addition. After leaving, Booth had sent Stuart an insulting note offering to pay a small amount for "the food he grudgingly offered." This may have saved the doctor from prosecution. In fact, none of those who helped the conspirators in their escape were prosecuted, except Dr. Mudd.

From there Bryant showed them to the cabin of **WILLIAM LUCAS**, just across the road at the intersection with Stuart Road. Lucas was a black man and also refused to allow Booth to stay. By this time, after being turned out of every house he approached in Virginia, Booth forced the old man and his wife outside, at knifepoint, into the cold and spent the night in the house.

From the Lucas cabin, Booth is thought to have followed present Routes 206, 611, 301, 205, 3, 686, 601, 631, 607, and 301. It was now April 24. Lucas's son drove him after Booth started to steal the horses and wagon. One following the trail in this area might simply follow Route 301 from Dahlgren to Port Conway. (Just before reaching the Rappahannock Bridge on the west side, through an avenue of overhanging trees, is the birthplace of President James Madison, on private property.) On the north side of the Rappahannock, Booth and Herold arrived at the home of William Rollins and his wife. Herold was unable to get the ferry operator to carry them across then, but the ferry operator promised to take them later. While waiting, three former Mosby's Rangers rode up, Privates Willie Jett and Absalom Ruggles Bainbridge, both eighteen, and Lieutenant Mortimer Bainbridge Ruggles, age twenty-one. Herold solicited their help to escape, claiming to be soldiers, and then admitted who they were. Rollins's wife later provided the identification leading to the capture of Booth.

On the Port Royal side of the river, Jett took Booth to the home of

Randolph Peyton and his sister, Sarah Jane Peyton, at the southwest corner of King and Caroline Streets. Randolph was not at home, but Sarah agreed "to entertain a Southern gentleman who had been wounded in the war." When Jett then produced the unwashed and unshaven Booth, Sarah said it would not be proper to allow him to stay since there was no man at home. So Booth and Herold had to leave after spending a short time in the front parlor. The house remains, but the paneling was later removed to the Nelson Gallery of Art in Kansas City. They then went across the street to the home of George Washington Catlett, but he was not at home. Then Sarah suggested they go to the Garrett farm just a few miles toward Bowling Green. (The small village still has several marked colonial-era homes including the Fox Tavern near the northwest corner of Walter and King Streets, where George Washington stayed twice. The town had been earlier considered for the site of the national capital.)

After leaving Port Royal, Booth continued down the present Route 301, for 2.65 miles to the Garrett Farm. Booth and Herold parted, and Jett and Ruggles accompanied Booth to the house. Garrett was told that Booth had been wounded near Petersburg, and he readily agreed to allow him to stay with his family of nine children. The two soldiers rode off to Bowling Green to catch up with Herold and Bainbridge. Jett and Ruggles took a room at the Star Hotel in Bowling Green, about nine miles south, while the other two stayed at a friend of Bainbridge's. Booth was made comfortable at Garrett's.

The next day, one of Garrett's sons rushed in with the news that Lincoln had been shot. Booth, the actor, showed no change of expression. Meanwhile, on April 25, soldiers had obtained an identification of Booth from Mrs. Rollins in Port Conway who knew Willie Jett was probably visiting his girlfriend in Bowling Green. The Union soldiers then headed in that direction as Herold rejoined Booth at the farm. Ruggles and Bainbridge saw the soldiers, rode to the Garretts' to warn Herold and Booth, then fled to the woods. The Garretts' suspicions were now aroused, and a son told them to leave. Since they had no transportation, they were allowed to sleep in the barn that night. Two fearful Garrett sons slept in the nearby shed near corncribs to take turns watching the barn after padlocking Booth and Herold inside.

The army caught up with Willie Jett at 12:30 A.M. in Bowling Green at the Star Hotel, across the street to the left, facing the courthouse on Main Street, at the present real estate office. (Historical markers on the courthouse lawn note various Civil War and Revolutionary War activity at this site, including General Lafayette's campsite.) The troops were now on the way to the farm. The date was April 26. They arrived there at 2:00 A.M., threatened to hang Garrett, shoot a son, and then surrounded the barn, ordering Herold and Booth to give up. Herold did, but Booth refused, whereupon the barn was set afire. Probably, Booth had decided to go out literally with a blaze of glory, a gun in both hands. As the inside of the barn lit up and started to consume everything inside, Sergeant Boston Corbett shot Booth with his pistol through the cracks in the wall. The paralyzed assassin survived for about an hour on the steps of the house.

There is no longer any trace of the house or barn in which Booth was shot. The busy highway is divided by a high median and is difficult to cross. The home stood in what is now the median between the northbound and southbound lanes about fifty yards north of the historical marker on the northbound side of Route 301. This is about one hundred yards north of a turnaround in the road from one side to the other. The barn and shed were just across from the home, just west of the southbound lanes. A clearing can be located in the median at the spot of the steps to the house. This is generally kept mowed, although it is not marked or visible from the highway due to heavy foliage. (You can park north of the marker on the left side of the road in the grass to access this area.)

WESTOVER PLANTATION: See Harrison's Landing, Berkeley, Westover Plantations entry.

YORKTOWN: Lincoln was on a select congressional committee for erection of the marble column to commemorate Cornwallis's surrender.

Washington, D.C.

Lincoln's first trip to Washington City, as the capital was generally called during his lifetime, was as the only Whig congressman from Illinois when he took his seat in the old **HOUSE CHAMBER** on December 6, 1847. He lived with his family near the Capitol Building **(SITE 67)**. After three months Mary, Robert, and Eddie went to stay with the Todd family in Lexington, Kentucky. Lincoln attended concerts on the **WHITE HOUSE LAWN**, studied at the **SUPREME COURT LIBRARY**, and argued one case before the Supreme Court, which met under the **OLD SENATE CHAMBER** in the Capitol. He attended sessions in the **OLD SENATE CHAMBER** to hear the famous orators of the day and made various speeches in the area during and just after his first year in Congress.

After leaving on September 9, 1848, he toured New England and returned to Springfield through Albany, Buffalo, Niagara Falls, over Lake Erie, to probably Detroit, but maybe Toledo, and then to Chicago. He returned to Washington alone for his second session from December 7, 1848, until mid-March 1849. The route coming or returning to Springfield then is not known. His congressional term was not a success due, at least in part, to his opposition of the Mexican War. President Polk had termed Mexico the aggressor. Lincoln challenged this by introducing what became known as his Spot Resolutions, demanding to know the spot where these aggressive actions occurred. This unpopular position lost support for himself and his Whig party. Former law partner Stephen T. Logan ran in the next election on the usually impregnable Whig ticket from Lincoln's district and lost.

In June 1849, Lincoln returned for about a week on a short trip to press an unsuccessful bid to a political appointment as commissioner of the General Land Office and next came on February 23, 1861, as president-elect. He had not received a single vote from nine Southern states, except Virginia, as his name was not on their ballots and received only about 39 percent of the popular votes due to the presence of three other candidates. However, if the popular votes of the other three had been combined, Lincoln would still have won in the electoral college, which actually elects presidents. Many relatives voted against him, and he only got less than 1 percent from his home state of Kentucky.

After staying until his inauguration at **WILLARD'S HOTEL (35)**, he resided either in the **WHITE HOUSE (1)** or at **ANDERSON COTTAGE (75)** at the **SOLDIERS HOME** in a slightly cooler environment with more favorable breezes. His only times away from the city were short trips to Virginia, Pennsylvania, Maryland, and New York. In 1864, he was reelected in what historian David Long calls the most significant political canvass in American history. This ensured that the war would be successfully prosecuted with unification and emancipation as its goals. After his funeral in April 1865, an estimated 7 million saw his funeral train and 25 million attended unofficial funerals at their own churches.

This chapter's list of sites includes those associated directly with Lincoln and significant buildings familiar to him. Note that the word "site" used in this chapter designates locations where the original structure no longer exists. Also included are sites associated with family members and the Booth conspiracy. Many sites are open and special exhibitions—at the Library of Congress, various Smithsonian buildings, the Capitol, and other historical locations in the area—will temporarily display letters and other memorabilia of the president and his times. Some buildings important during the Civil War and now open to the public are also included. (All sites are shown at current addresses and in the northwest section unless stated otherwise.)

(1) The **WHITE HOUSE, 1600 PENNSYLVANIA AVENUE,** the residence of all presidents beginning with John Adams, was Lincoln's permanent residence from March 4, 1861, until his death. It was the people's house as well as the president's residence. In the 1860s it was better known as the President's House or Executive Mansion, but known as the "White House" long before the Civil War. Outgoing president Buchanan told his successor, "If you are as happy, my dear sir, on entering this house as I am on leaving it and returning home, you are the happiest man in the country." At the time of the Civil War it was the largest house in the country, but served several functions so that only part of the second floor was used as living space or "home" for the president's family. Various Todd relatives stayed off and on also.

It was in a shabby state when the Lincolns moved in, and Congress appropriated $20,000 to refurbish what had become "bare, worn and spoiled . . . like a deserted farmstead." Mary was the first presidential wife to be called "first lady." She transformed the house, and personally saw to the scrubbing, cleaning, plastering, and redecoration. The sum appropriated was probably four times the family annual income before 1860. Mary soon overspent her funds by $7,000 making her husband furious enough to fume, "It would stink in the nostrils of the American People to have it said that the President of the United States had approved a bill overrunning an appropriation for flub dubs for this damned old house, when soldiers cannot have blankets." After Willie died, she gave the house little time and concern.

The first floor was the "State Floor" for public rooms. The president's offices were on the second. Lincoln allowed the house to be open to the public so that visitors, cranks, endless office seekers, and those with official business crowded much of the mansion daily. He could have closed the house, but had seen it closed, unfriendly and aloof, when he served in Congress. He wanted the presidency to be accessible, but had to endure unfriendly and endless calls with tourists wandering around early in his term. Security was so loose that when Prince Napoleon of France visited on August 3, 1861, no one greeted him as he entered. A private corridor had to be constructed so that the president could move from the family quarters to his office without being seen by the public. It was soon necessary to secure troops to protect the capital, which began to tax the ability of the city to adequately provide for them. Soon after arriving, troops were quartered in the East Room and were so diligent that the family's privacy was invaded.

The current East and West Wings did not exist, but the house followed the general plan of today. All of the rooms on the main floor were devoted to state purposes except the family dining room. When the Lincoln family moved in, Willie and Tad, ages ten and seven, were the only young children of a president to have ever lived here other than ten-year-old Tazewell Tyler. After a brief stay, seventeen-year-old Robert was off to Harvard, and only rarely visited.

The younger boys were spoiled, adored by their parents, and different in many ways. Precocious Willie is referred to as a clone of his father and known, even then, as the favorite child. He was studious and very bright, but Tad was somewhat backward. Talented and lovable Willie took music lessons while here, and seemed eager to learn. Lincoln said his mind and Willie's ran together. Tad was the hellion who pulled beards, pestered callers, asked endless questions about their business, and sometimes forced visitors to make contributions to his "charities" or buy lemonade in the hall. Several authors describe him as retarded or mildly retarded, but probably "undisciplined and unchallenged" would be more accurate terms. It does not appear that he could read until he was thirteen. But as *Lincoln Lore Number 979* states, "No child of the White House ever became more endeared to the American People."

The two boys played on the grounds, rounded up neighbor boys for drilling and reviews, and rode their ponies in view of many curious onlookers. Shortly after moving in, Mrs. Lincoln asked Mrs. Horatio Taft to bring by her sons, Bud and Holly, for a visit. The boys became instant, inseparable friends and had the run of the house to the dismay of servants, guests, visitors, and government officials. It was not uncommon for the president to join in the games of the youngsters and be entertained with their antics. Julia Taft, the boys' sister, writes of entering a room once to see Willie and Bud holding down Lincoln's arms, Tad and Holly holding down his legs, and Tad yelling for her to sit on his stomach. He read to the four balancing two or more on his knees. Bud was sometimes used as a messenger boy by the president. The roof of the house was often used by the boys as a "fort" or "deck of a man of war." Mary let them borrow her dresses for a circus in the attic for which Lincoln paid the five-cent admission and then enjoyed the boys' antics and singing. Mary took Willie and Tad to the army camps around the city to visit men who were overjoyed to see a woman and children who reminded them of home. William O. Stoddard wrote later that Mrs. Lincoln never took anyone else with her on these unreported trips. If she had, newspapermen would have reported her in a better light.

As ordered by Buchanan, the luxury of running water had been installed during the spring with porcelain sinks in most rooms providing cold, polluted Potomac River water. The house was near the smelly Washington Canal, sewerage outlets, and waste dumps that produced unsanitary and unpleasant smells and conditions. This untreated water possibly caused the boys to sicken in early 1862, probably causing Willie's death, from what is now thought to be typhoid.

DOWNSTAIRS

All visitors entered the President's House through the North Portico facing Pennsylvania Avenue, where most visitors now exit. At the front of the house is a large vestibule leading directly to the Blue Room, also in the center and across the hallway. The vestibule was used for a playroom, music room for receptions, and coatroom where hats and coats were generally scrambled, lost, and stolen. Tad once broke a mirror by kicking a ball into it, only to be scolded by Willie. Tad inquired of visitors here what they wanted and how long they intended to wait. Several visitors got to know the "little tyrant" fairly well, and Tad would also give advice. On at least one occasion he took a five-cent toll for passing the stairs for the benefit of the Sanitary Fair, similar to the Red Cross. Visitors were not unwilling to have a friend in court for such a small fee. On another occasion Tad organized a Sanitary Fair with a table set up in the grand corridor and stocked it with small purchases of odds and ends begged from the pantry. The proceeds were disbursed generously so that no profit was made. On the night of April 14, 1865, Tad met the doorman, Thomas Pendel, in this main vestibule, crying over and over, "Oh, Tom Pen! They have killed papa dead."

THE EAST ROOM was used for large receptions where the president often stood for long hours shaking thousands of hands of those who wanted to meet him. Lincoln was first here during his congressional term for a reception with President Polk. This room was as large as their Springfield house. Soldiers camped here during the early days of the war. Mary was criticized for letting the boys use it as a playground, but it was later so used by Theodore Roosevelt's and Taft's sons. Tad once surprised a group of visitors by driving two goats through here, cracking his whip over them as they pulled him latched to a kitchen chair. Someone gave him a set of tools, and he drove nails in the furniture in this room and several others, including Hay's desk. Lincoln's funeral was here, and he lay in state as thousands filed by the open coffin. The two prior presidents who had died in office, Harrison and Taylor, had also laid here in state. Willie's funeral was here also, as

General McClellan and Secretaries Seward and Chase "struggled with their tears."

THE GREEN ROOM, next to the East Room, was used as the place to embalm the body of Willie. His coffin stayed here during his funeral. Mary refused to enter the room after this time. Robert spent the night before the funeral alone in the room with his brother. At noon on the day of the funeral, the president joined Robert to watch over the body behind locked doors.

The elliptical **BLUE ROOM** was opposite the main entrance, in the center of the first floor on the south side facing the lawn, where the president generally received guests at regular levees, generally Tuesdays and Saturdays. On many occasions the reception line passed through to greet the president, and then on to the larger East Room to mingle. His right hand often became so swollen from the vast crowds that he could not use it for hours afterward. The Blue Room was also used for various other social events and receptions for diplomats. To reach the lawn on the south side, the family would step on the back porch going through a window in this room. The family watched parades from the south portico. Once a visitor told Lincoln here, "Up our way, we believe in God and Abraham Lincoln." Lincoln responded, "My friend, you are more than half right." It was here that he first met General Grant who had just become the third lieutenant general in the country's history. (Washington held the rank permanently and Winfield Scott by brevet.) Mary's niece wrote, "The wife of her old friend Stephen Douglas . . . was frequently asked to receive with Mrs. Lincoln," which caused "great offense to many republican women."

THE RED ROOM, next to the State Dining Room, was used as a drawing room or family room by the family and contained the picture of Washington rescued from the British by Dolley Madison, now hanging in the East Room. This was of special interest to Mary, as Dolley was also a Todd. The room was used as a family parlor and a place where all could be informally entertained after dinner. Willie liked to play the piano in the room, and was once scolded here by one of Mary's cousins for playing on the Sabbath. Lincoln's friend Ward Hill Lamon sometimes gave impromptu singing concerts for the president. Lincoln met President Buchanan on February 24, 1861, in the room, and gathered his cabinet after a dinner on March 28, 1861, to discuss the Fort Sumter crisis. Later that year, on September 10, he had an angry midnight confrontation with the wife of General John Frémont, who persisted in defending her insubordinate husband. Some of Mary's séances were conducted in the room, attempting to contact Willie. Author Arthur Conan Doyle wrote that a spiritualist strengthened the president by relaying a message "from the spirit world," while in a trance in the "Red Parlor." The December 1862 message supposedly told him to free the slaves at once and stand firm in his mission from Providence.

THE FAMILY DINING ROOM was on the north side of the first floor, across from the EXECUTIVE OR STATE DINING ROOM on the southwest corner. Lincoln hosted many state dinners here, including his first state banquet on March 28, 1861. Both dining rooms were used as a makeshift schoolroom for the Lincoln and Taft boys before Willie died. They used the dining table, and Mrs. Lincoln ordered a desk for the tutor, Alexander Williamson. Willie took to schooling, as Dr. Wayne C. Temple says, "like a boy to a cookie jar." Tad, according to correspondent Noah Brooks, "simply abhorred books and learning." Formal schooling attempts to teach Tad evidently ended after Willie's death, and Williamson became more of a companion than teacher who tried to instruct from everyday life. Tad was never disciplined, and possibly had a learning disability. He had a speech impediment so that most had trouble understanding him. When Williamson saw him after Lincoln died, he wrote that twelve-year-old Tad had cried, "Oh, Mister Wimson, pa's stot."

UPSTAIRS

LINCOLN'S OFFICE was above the Green Room, and the second office from the southeast corner. It is now known as the "LINCOLN BEDROOM," but he never slept here unless he slept at his desk. The president called this "the shop." There is no evidence that friends or relatives slept here, although Tad spent many hours at his father's side and feet after his brother died, and would go to sleep on the floor waiting to be carried to bed.

Lincoln worked daily from 7:00 or 8:00 A.M. with short breaks, until 11:00 P.M. for four years with no real vacations or holidays. When he stayed at the Soldier's Home, his day in the office would start later. At 9:00 A.M. every weekday for much of the time, crowds of office seekers, inventors, citizens seeking information about soldiers, and general sightseers crowded into the Executive Mansion to solicit information and requests and to gawk at the president. Citizens believed that the house was their own property and enjoyed roaming around inside, sometimes taking a souvenir. The noise and commotion continued throughout the war in spite of assassination threats, danger, and general disruption of work and life in general. Nicolay estimated he spent three fourths of his waking hours meeting people. The new Republican had to replace fifteen hundred Democratic office holders in this pre–civil service era.

The drudgery was broken at times with a ride in the afternoon with Mary. He answered letters by hand, drafted his own state papers, and reviewed thirty thousand court-martial sentences each year. He was only sick once, for about two weeks, after his Gettysburg speech. It is possible that the famous beard was shaved then due to a rash, and he was beardless for a short time. This normally excellent, robust health gave him an advantage over his adversaries, Stephen Douglas and Jefferson Davis. A disappointed office seeker here once told Lincoln, "Why I am one of those who made you President!" Lincoln responded, "Yes, and it's a pretty mess you got me into!"

The president began the Gettysburg Address and signed the Emancipation Proclamation here. The Trumans converted the room to a bedroom and furnished it with the large "state bed" ordered by Mary Lincoln. Now known as the **LINCOLN BED**, Lincoln himself during life probably did not use it, but it is believed he was embalmed on it when it was in the Prince of Wales Bedroom. Willie Lincoln died in the bed, and his father spent many hours by Willie's side during his last illness. President Truman put his mother in the room to sleep in "Lincoln's bed," but she would have none of it and asked to be moved.

The next office adjacent to Lincoln's toward the center was the **CABINET ROOM**, which is now called the Treaty Room. This is sometimes said to have been combined with Lincoln's office. He had in his cabinet most of his rivals for the 1860 Republican nomination, some of whom wanted the nomination in 1864.

The southeast corner was secretary John Nicolay's office. John Hay's office was across the hall at the northeast corner when he did not share an office with Nicolay. These were farther away from approaching visitors so that people coming to the second floor would have reached the president's office first before the secretaries, who still did a formidable job in screening. (Actually Nicolay was the only official secretary, as this was all provided for in the budget. Hay, and later William Stoddard and Charles

Philbrick, were clerks in the Department of the Interior, assigned to the White House, and they served as secretaries or clerks.) Their bedroom was across from Lincoln's office, and they ate at Willard's Hotel. The president worked closely with these two young men and found, in the words of David Donald, "the sons that Robert could never be." Robert was quiet and awkward around his father, and they never seemed to have anything to say to each other.

The room directly above the Blue Room is now called the **YEL-LOW OVAL ROOM**, the center of the floor. During Lincoln's occupancy, it was a library and was used as a family sitting or private parlor. Actually, it was their only living room. Lincoln liked to read a chapter in the Bible while the family gathered for breakfast. The boys had school here briefly. The president and Mrs. Lincoln slept in the bedrooms immediately to the west. The boys slept across the hall in rooms facing north in one of several guest bedrooms overlooking Pennsylvania Avenue. For a short time, Robert shared a room with family friend Elmer Ellsworth before leaving for Harvard. Mary stayed across the hall several weeks until she moved after the assassination, refusing to go to her own or Lincoln's bedroom.

The largest bedroom was the suite at the northwest end known as the **PRINCE OF WALES BEDROOM**, named after the royal guest here shortly before the Lincoln's arrived. Mary bought ornate furniture for the room, including the famous seven-foot Lincoln Bed and companion center table. Mary's sister and half sister stayed in the room during their visits. The Lincolns may have used the room in October 1861 while theirs were being redecorated.

Willie died in the "great bed" and was the only presidential child to die in the mansion. The much-loved son lingered many days and had asked for Bud Taft, who refused to leave his side, clutching his hand for much of the time. Tad too was almost lost to the same illness. Willie's death devastated the family and almost drove Mary insane. All government offices were closed, the only time this happened for the death of a presidential child. Afterward, the house was rather quiet, at least as to the laughter and frolic of small boys, since Mrs. Lincoln would not permit the friends to return to the house. Willie was clearly his parents' favorite, and the affection was transferred to Tad, who became a constant companion. Some sources say Lincoln never entered this room again, while others claim he spent days alone there. No one grieved more over the death of a son. Later Mary's favorite half sister, Emilie Helm, a recent widow of a Confederate general, and her young daughter stayed here several weeks. During her stay, Mary told her that Willie's spirit came to her every night and stood at the foot of her bed, sometimes with Eddie. In 1865, an autopsy was performed in the room on Lincoln's body, and it was embalmed here. The April 19, 1865, edition of the *New York Herald* referred to "the favorite son (Willie)" whose body was taken to Illinois with his father.

At the northeast corner of the second floor was another bedroom, part of the Prince of Wales Suite, and now is the **PRESIDENT'S DINING ROOM**. (The Clevelands, McKinleys, and Alice Roosevelt slept here.) It is also believed that Lincoln slept in this room with Tad for much or all of the time after Willie died. Two small bedrooms were also located across from the Oval Room.

The north lawn adjacent to Pennsylvania Avenue was enclosed by a fence, appearing about the same as the one now. A similar fence enclosed Lafayette Park across the street and was later moved to be a border between Evergreen and the National Cemetery in Gettysburg, Pennsylvania. The **STATUE OF JEFFERSON**, now in the Capitol rotunda, stood in front of the house and was climbed on by the rambunctious boys. Lincoln sometimes conferred with General Winfield Scott in the driveway to save the gouty Scott from having to climb the stairs. He also reviewed troops on the **PENNSYLVANIA AVENUE SIDEWALK** in front of the house. Marine band concerts were held on the south lawn until Willie died. Mrs. Lincoln put a stop to the public performances for over a year until she was persuaded by Secretary Welles and others to resume them in the summer of 1863. Near the south lawn toward the unfinished Washington Monument was marshland that opened into the Washington Canal where Constitution Avenue is today. The Lincolns hosted traditional egg rollings on the lawn. On Easter Sunday 1862, Tad met a lame boy there who had recently lost his father in battle, and expressed a desire to see the president, which Tad promptly arranged.

Interior paths crisscrossed the grounds, connecting the State Department on the east and the Navy and War Departments on the west. There was no telegraph in the White House, so the president crossed the lawn almost nightly to the War Department to examine and answer telegrams and talk with the operators. It was on these gravel paths that Lincoln and Tad played "Followings," a game where pebbles are thrown at an object.

A stable located about two hundred yards south of the White House caught fire on December 10, 1864, and destroyed Willie's horse. The president raced from his bedroom, jumped over hedges, and tried to save the animal. He, Tad, and Nicolay each lost two horses. Later Lincoln was seen crying in the East Room, looking out at the still-smoldering ashes. Tad explained that it was because Willie's pony was there.

Tad did not like gruff Secretary of War Stanton and once sprayed him up and down with a water hose. Lincoln had recently sent a note to Stanton by Congressman Owen Lovejoy. When he returned, Lovejoy quoted Stanton's answer to Lincoln, Mary, and Tad, "The president is a damned fool!" Lincoln commented, "If Stanton said that, I reckon I must be, for he is nearly always right." The president grinned, but Tad had been upset and retaliated with the hose. When the secretary complained, Lincoln responded, "Stanton, you had better make friends with Tad." The crusty secretary did, and commissioned Tad a lieutenant, complete with uniform and saber, now displayed at **FORD'S THEATER MUSEUM**. Robert once told Nicolay that he "had a great row with the President of the United States" over Tad's actions with his "commission." Tad had ordered a quantity of muskets sent to the White House, dismissed the guards, armed the gardeners and servants, drilled them, and put them on duty around the residence.

When the Lincolns visited the Army of the Potomac in April 1863, Tad made friends with a young aide to General Daniel Sickles. The thirteen-year-old bugler, Gustav Schurmann, was made Tad's orderly and the boys became instant friends. When it came time to leave for Washington, Tad threw a tantrum as he did not want to leave his new friend, and the commander gave the bugler a two-week furlough. Their first night together in the White House was so boisterous that the president had to come to the guest bedroom early in the morning in his night shirt to quiet them. Gus later wrote that Tad slept beside his father's bed in a trundle although he was ten years old.

Gus stayed for two weeks and wrote of several instances of Lincoln's forbearance with his son's mischievousness. On one occasion Tad took a small hatchet, thought to be Washington's, hacked away at several pieces of furniture, and sawed several banisters on the main stairway, trying to imitate the Washington story of the cherry tree. When the servants reported this to the president, the boys were summoned to his office. Gus expected the worst, but the president simply sat them down and told them stories of his Black Hawk War days with no allusion to the vandalism. Later Tad, with Gus, disturbed a cabinet meeting to ask a question of the president, to the annoyance of Secretaries Seward and Stanton. They asked if this was not an annoyance, but the president simply stated that he needed a diversion. A few weeks after returning to his army unit, Gus was sent again to the White House to be with Tad, although this visit only lasted for about a day. Tad had produced a play and wanted his friend there for the opening performance in the White House, but as it started a courier announced that Lee had invaded Pennsylvania. The heavily burdened president, several soldiers, government officials, and society ladies had watched the "diversion," but the play's run ended with the first performance (note the entry on **GROVER'S THEATER, SITE 34**).

When artist Frances B. Carpenter was using a closet as a darkroom for his pictures, made to aid him in painting the heroic representation of the Emancipation Proclamation now at the Capitol, Tad felt that his territorial rights to a certain room were being challenged. He got the photographers to leave and then got the key to lock them out of the room holding their chemicals and plates. After appealing to the president, Lincoln told Carpenter that he told Tad, "Do you know you are making your father a great deal of trouble?" The boy then burst into tears and immediately surrendered the key. (This story is sometimes told as having taken place at Grover's Theater, but Carpenter himself places it in the Executive Mansion.) He wrote that it was an "impressive and affecting sight . . . to see the burdened President lost for the time being in the affectionate parent, as he would take the little fellow in his arms upon the withdrawal of visitors, and caress him with all the fondness of a mother for the babe upon her bosom!"

The president often spoke to the crowds from the **CENTER WINDOW OVERLOOKING THE FRONT** (north) entrance toward Pennsylvania Avenue and at other times standing below on the front steps. When the war ended, he appeared before the joyful crowds at the window to answer their request for a speech. At first he did not respond, but Tad opened the window and waved a Confederate flag. The president would not make a speech, but asked that the band play "Dixie," "one of the best songs I have ever heard" and "a lawful prize since we fairly captured it." Lincoln made his last speech here on April 11, 1865, when he told the crowds, "We meet this evening not in sorrow but in gladness of heart." Tad ran around below catching the pages of the speech as his father dropped them. Someone yelled that the Rebs should be hung, but Tad shouted that we needed to hang on to them. One listener was John Wilkes Booth, who listened to the president's plan to restore the South, including the vote of the freedmen. He urged Lewis Powell, who was with him, to shoot Lincoln on the spot, then swore that was the last speech he would give. And it was. (The window site appears accurate, but some report that this speech was on the porch at the main entrance.)

After the assassination, Mary lay in mourning for five weeks with President Johnson using an office in the Treasury Building. She was the only "unofficial person" to live alone at the White House for any considerable period of time. The house was then unsupervised and in disarray, with vandals helping themselves to the furnishings.

During the late 1940s the White House interior was gutted to reconstruct the sagging old mansion. Several proposals were made to completely reconstruct the entire building, but the more expensive and complex plan was adopted to keep the exterior walls. The current room arrangement is about the same as in Lincoln's day except that the president's offices are now in the West Wing, constructed in the early twentieth century. The west section used by the family now contains various guest bedrooms and sitting areas.

Robert Lincoln lived in Washington later and served as secretary of war. He visited the White House frequently, and his children played here with the children of President Garfield.

(2) The WAR DEPARTMENT site is where the Executive Office Building now stands on the SOUTHEAST CORNER OF G STREET, SEVENTEENTH, AND PENNSYLVANIA AVENUE. The War Department was at the north end of the building with the Navy Department at the south end. It was just west of the White House and parallel in size and location to the Treasury Building to the east. The telegraph office here was the closest one to the president, who came almost daily for the latest news, often hand in hand with Tad. It is claimed that Lincoln spent more time here than any other place in Washington outside the White House.

The Emancipation Proclamation may have had its beginnings in the telegraph office. The president visited here at all hours of the day and seldom failed to come late in the evening. At times he would stay all night. Lincoln's habit, at least at first, was to go to the secretary's or general-in-chief's office rather than send for them to come to him. McClellan believed it best to give Lincoln as little news as possible, as he did not have confidence in Lincoln's military ability or discretion. He felt that the president would let some important fact slip to the press or Congress. Secretary of War Cameron issued orders to telegraph operators to deal only with the commanding general, again forgetting that Lincoln as commander in chief outranked both the cabinet and commanding general.

(3) The NAVY DEPARTMENT SITE is ONE BLOCK SOUTH OF THE WAR DEPARTMENT ON SEVENTEENTH, east of the intersection with F Street, and part of the War Department Building. The Executive Office Building now extends to this site also. Secretary Gideon Welles was loyal to the president and left a diary with a fascinating story of the inner workings of the Lincoln cabinet.

(4) Lincoln called on GENERAL WINFIELD SCOTT at his RESIDENCE (SITE), AT 1732 PENNSYLVANIA AVENUE, the first day he arrived in the capital, although the general was not at home. Scott, the most famous soldier in the country in 1861, recommended Robert E. Lee to the new president as the country's best soldier. Lincoln later visited Scott here often, including a meeting on August 10, 1861, to soothe Scott's feelings toward General McClellan.

(5) The JEFFERSON DAVIS RESIDENCE SITE IS EAST OF THE NORTHEAST CORNER OF EIGHTEENTH AND G STREETS. The future president of the Confederate states lived here from 1853 until 1857 as secretary of war under President Franklin Pierce. At other times, he lived at 609 Fourteenth and 1736 I Streets, where he last lived from 1857 until January 1861.

(6) The Lincolns attended the wedding of Captain Charles Griffin and Sally Carroll at the RESIDENCE OF WILLIAM T. CARROLL (SITE), at the northwest corner of EIGHTEENTH AND F STREETS, on December 10, 1861. Carroll's father had owned the land where Lincoln's boardinghouse had stood in the 1840s across from the Capitol, known as Carroll Row. The bride was given personal permission from the president to remain with her husband at the war front, causing Mary great discomfort. She was there during a presidential review when Mary threw a very public tantrum on March 26, 1865; Mary from then on did not allow the president to see any woman alone (see the entry on City Point, Virginia). Willie Lincoln was temporarily buried in the Carroll vault in Georgetown until his body was returned to Illinois with his father's.

(7) John Wilkes Booth and John Surratt visited Louis J. Weichmann at the OFFICE OF COMMISSARY GENERAL OF PRISONERS, still standing at the NORTHEAST CORNER OF TWENTIETH AND F STREETS, and may have received information from him in their plots against the president. Weichmann roomed at Mrs. Surratt's boardinghouse and may have been involved in the plot to kidnap Lincoln. But his testimony was needed to convict some of those involved in the conspiracies, including Mrs. Surratt, and he was not tried.

(8) General **WINFIELD SCOTT** had an office at the **SOUTHWEST CORNER OF SEVENTEENTH AND F STREETS** in a modest residential building. General Grant set up offices here after Lee's surrender.

(9) The **WINDER BUILDING**, at the **NORTHWEST CORNER OF F** and **SEVENTEENTH STREETS,** served many functions including Army Headquarters. It has now been restored to its Civil War appearance and still functions as a government office building. Its five floors qualified it as a high-rise building of the day, and it was one of the first buildings to use steel beams and central heating. A succession of high Union commanders had offices here, including Generals Winfield Scott, George B. McClellan, Henry Halleck, and Ulysses S. Grant. Lincoln visited here often, as he hated to wait in his office for people to come to him. Sometimes he came alone at night to the dismay of his secretaries. As headquarters for the Bureau of Military Justice, the building served as center of operations during the search for the president's assassins. The president invited General McClellan to attend a cabinet meeting in General Scott's office on September 27, 1861.

(10) THE **OCTAGON HOUSE, 1799 NEW YORK AVENUE, OR NORTHEAST CORNER OF NEW YORK AVENUE AND EIGHTEENTH STREET,** was used as a girl's school during the war. The prominent mansion is one of the oldest in the city and not far from the White House. It is open to the public. President Madison lived here after the White House had been burned by the British. He signed the Treaty of Ghent in the parlor, which ended the War of 1812.

(11) **CHIEF JUSTICE JOHN MARSHALL'S HOUSE** was at **1801 F STREET**, according to a historical marker at the site. Presidents James Madison and James Monroe and General McClellan also lived here at various times.

(12) Behind the White House between **FIFTEENTH AND SEVENTEENTH STREETS** was an area of the **ELLIPSE** known as the White Lot because a white fence enclosed it. E Street passed through in those days and soldiers camped here. Tad's pet turkey, which had been saved from being Thanksgiving dinner thanks to Tad's intercession, wandered among the soldiers as they were casting their votes for president in 1864. Lincoln, walking nearby with Tad, asked him if the turkey was going to vote. "No," Tad replied, "he is not of age." Early in the war, Lincoln could be seen in this area testing new inventions, including a breech-loading rifle, "coffee mill" gun, and a hand-cranked forerunner of the machine gun. He witnessed several ascensions by a gas balloon here. Two small temporary barracks were erected and used as hospitals for soldiers in the city.

(13) The current **RENWICK GALLERY (OLD CORCORAN ART GALLERY) AT THE NORTHEAST CORNER OF PENNSYLVANIA AVENUE AND SEVENTEENTH STREET** was built to house the art collection of financier William Corcoran. It was taken over by the government and became the largest point of issue in the city for uniforms, tents, and equipage as the headquarters of Quartermaster General Montgomery Meigs's department. Lincoln called on Meigs once to slump in front of the fire and seek advice or solace saying, "The bottom is out of the tub."

(14) In the house east of the Renwick Gallery (**THE BLAIR-LEE HOUSE**), Robert E. Lee met on April 18, 1861, with Frances Preston Blair to be offered command of the Union army on behalf of Lincoln. Lee asked for time to consider, and then resigned from the U.S. Army the next day. Lee said even though "opposed to secession, and deprecating war, I could take no part in an invasion of the Southern states." (It is interesting to speculate the number of lives that would have been spared had Lee accepted command of the Union army when offered. Surely the war would have ended sooner, with far less cost under his competent leadership, and might well have resulted in his future election to the presidency. Many authors and scholars feel that the Virginian's service to the Confederacy was inevitable as he did not feel he could desert his family and Virginia heritage. However, other Virginians did serve the Union including the commanding general at the beginning of the war, Winfield Scott, and one of the most competent and successful Union generals, George Thomas.)

President Truman and his family lived in the Blair House from 1948 until 1952 during the extensive reconstruction of the interior of the White House. It was here that an assassination attempt was made on Truman's life in 1950.

(15) **LAFAYETTE PARK, PENNSYLVANIA AVENUE OPPOSITE THE WHITE HOUSE**, was the "President's Park," the center of social life for the city, as many prominent officials and citizens lived in the area around it. Lincoln crisscrossed the park going to McClellan's house and other sites listed. At the beginning of the war, several houses were taken over by the government for military headquarters and offices, including the still standing homes of Stephen Decatur and Dolley Madison. Soldiers guarding the White House camped in the park, trampled the flower beds, and hung their laundry from the statue of Andrew Jackson, dedicated by Stephen Douglas in 1853. Tad called it the "Tippy-toe statue" because it depicts the seventh president on a horse with the front feet off the ground, and Tad liked to climb over it with his brother. After Willie died, Mary's sister Elizabeth visited for about two months. On one occasion she and the president walked to the statue while Lincoln "unburdened himself" there and pleaded here for Elizabeth to stay. On getting back to the Executive Mansion, they found that Tad had locked the gate and was running off with the key, laughing.

(16) MAJOR HENRY RATHBONE LIVED AT (SITE) 712 JACKSON PLACE. He was the guest of the Lincolns in their box at Ford's Theater when the president was assassinated. Rathbone escorted his fiancée, Miss Clara Harris, to the theater with the Lincolns. It is sometimes said that the Lincolns picked them up at this house on April 14, 1865. But they were likely picked up at Senator Harris's house as shown later. Clara probably saved the major's life that night by wrapping her handkerchief around the knife wound inflicted by Booth, and preventing him from bleeding to death. They were later married and moved to Germany. Major Rathbone never recovered from the grief of Ford's Theater, became deranged, and tried to kill his children. He was prevented from doing so, but was able to shoot and kill his wife, then stab himself. He recovered physically and spent the rest of his life in a German insane asylum, dying in 1911.

(17) THE DECATUR HOUSE, 748 JACKSON PLACE NORTHWEST FACING LAFAYETTE PARK, was home to many prominent people before the Civil War, including naval hero Stephen Decatur, Henry Clay, President Martin Van Buren, Vice President George M. Dallas, and Judah P. Benjamin, prominent in the Confederate cabinet. During the war it housed Quartermaster General Montgomery Meigs. It is still within sight of the White House.

(18) SECRETARY OF THE NAVY GIDEON WELLES HOUSE (SITE), LAFAYETTE SQUARE AND SIXTEENTH STREET, is now 1607 H Street, on the northwest corner. Lincoln visited on April 2, 1863, and probably many other times. Robert stayed here when he went back to Washington after his father's death to court his future wife. He and Welles were close, and Robert had become a close friend with the secretary's son, Edgar. The Hay-Adams Hotel is here now, noting that Lincoln's secretary John Hay lived next door at 1603 H

Street later when he was secretary of state from 1898 to 1905. A double house was built here for historian Henry Adams and Hay. They wrote famous works in their homes, including the Lincoln biography written by Hay and Nicolay.

Welles's wife, Mary, became Mrs. Lincoln's closest friend in the capital, partly because both lost sons to disease during the war. Mary Welles moved into the White House when Willie and Tad were sick in 1862, before Willie died. The Welles's three-year-old died about nine months later, bringing the two families closer in their mutual grief. This, no doubt, affected Lincoln's personal relationship with Welles. Mrs. Lincoln sent word for Mrs. Welles to come to her as the president lay dying. Although sick herself, she went to the Petersen House, and then to the White House with the widow, where she stayed for some time. Welles and Seward were the only ones to serve in Lincoln's cabinet for the entire time of Lincoln's administration. Welles's spicy and candid diary is an excellent source of information and private opinion about the war period and Lincoln's actions.

(19) ST. JOHN'S EPISCOPAL CHURCH AND PARISH HOUSE, **1525 H STREET,** is known as the Church of the Presidents. Lincoln walked from Willard's Hotel to worship on February 25, 1861, with his secretary of state, William H. Seward. They sat in Seward's pew, number 1, now number 65. (This is third back from the front on the middle right side.) He went with General Winfield Scott on July 5, 1861, and met Edward Everett, the principal speaker of the time, who gave the main address at Gettysburg on November 19, 1863, before Lincoln's. Legend says that the troubled president often slid unobtrusively into a back pew during afternoon prayer sessions. All presidents beginning with James Madison have worshiped here, and it is unchanged from the Civil War period. The public is still welcome. The adjoining parish house was once the home of British envoy Lord Ashburton, where the treaty setting the borders of the United States and Canada was negotiated with Daniel Webster.

Vermont Street runs into Lafayette Square just to the east. Lincoln generally took that route to his residence in the Soldiers Home.

(20) The CUTTS-MADISON HOUSE, **1520 H STREET, AT THE SOUTHEAST CORNER OF MADISON PLACE,** was General George B. McClellan's headquarters from November 1861 through March 1862. The general wrote in his memoirs that Lincoln had a "very close" association with him, and he "often came to my house, frequently late at night" to confer and get news. This had been the old home of Dolley Madison, President Madison's widow, where she lived until her death in 1849. During the Ottawa, Illinois, debate, Mrs. Stephen Douglas told Mary Lincoln that she remembered meeting her at Aunt Dolley's home in 1848. On November 13, 1861, the president, Seward, and the president's secretary, John Hay, came across Lafayette Park to see the general. When they were informed that he was out, they waited in the parlor. After an hour they heard him return and go directly upstairs. When the president asked if he knew they were there, he was informed that McClellan knew, but had gone to bed and for them to come back another time. (There are at least four such stories, plus the one told in site **33**, maybe the same or another incident. Three others are mentioned in the footnotes of Michael Burlingame's edition of John Hay's diary, *Inside the White House*, pages 288–289. These incidents include a breakfast that the general would not shorten or interrupt when the president was waiting, a time on October 9, 1861, and in September 1862, which would have been at locations mentioned elsewhere.) Hay noted that hereafter Lincoln summoned the general to the White House, although the president came to see him in December 1861 but was not allowed to go in, as McClellan was sick.

The haughty young, thirty-six-year-old general kept staffs hard at work in two other offices, the Winder Building (**SITE 9**) and on the northwest corner of Seventeenth Street and Pennsylvania Avenue. He spent as little time as possible in these places as he liked to gallop around the city on the way to visit forts, camps, and depots. He was a great organizer, but seemed to want the army for parading and maneuvering, rather than fighting. Lincoln once lamented that the army was only McClellan's bodyguard, and if the general were not going to use it, he would like to borrow it for a while. Some have speculated that the general sympathized with the South and wanted to build a large army to awe the Confederate states back to the Union. He is credited with the building of the Army of the Potomac, but his failure to use the overwhelming resources in early 1862 before the emergence of Robert E. Lee possibly added years and thousands of casualties to the cost of the war.

On one occasion a Union officer, William Woods Averell, passed Lincoln coming across Madison Place informally dressed, to see McClellan. When the president went inside, he could clearly be seen inside the window, where he was an easy target from any would-be assassin in Lafayette Park. Averell and another officer then waited at the door to escort Lincoln back to the White House and warned him of the danger. Averell "at once" sought out Marshal Ward Hill Lamon, who stated that "it was no use to speak to Mr. Lincoln about it for he would forget it immediately if he heeded it at all."

(21) GENERAL MCCLELLAN'S HOUSE SITE in September 1862 was at **334 H STREET**, near the northwest corner of Fifteenth and H Streets. Lincoln came here with General Henry Halleck on September 2, to swallow his pride and reinstate McClellan to the command of the Union army, a position lost earlier for what Lincoln called "the slows." The reinstatement caused a tremendous change of moral in the Union army as the common soldier had overwhelming confidence in McClellan. To do him honor, twenty thousand troops marched past his home on September 6, rather than the White House a block away. He rode out the next day to begin a campaign ending with the Battle of Antietam. The street was the most fashionable in the city during the war, with many socially prominent citizens, generals, and cabinet ministers living in mansions, some still here.

(22) Secretary of State **WILLIAM SEWARD'S HOMESITE, ON THE EAST SIDE OF LAFAYETTE PARK**, was two lots (**ABOUT FORTY-FIVE FEET**) **NORTH OF PENNSYLVANIA AVENUE**. He lived here in a four-story house during the war and was often visited by the president. As senator from New York, he had been the front-runner for the Republican nomination for president in 1860. During the first few months of Lincoln's administration he tried to bully everyone, but later came to admit, "The President is the best of us." The president dined in the home after attending church on February 25, 1861, his first Sunday in Washington. He held many meetings with Seward and others here. As stated, it was Lincoln's custom to visit offices of others, and many conferences were held in the offices and homes of generals and cabinet members, many nearby.

Lincoln came here for the last time on April 9, 1865, after having returned from City Point, Virginia, to read dispatches from Grant. Seward had been severely injured in a carriage accident, and Lincoln laid across his bed to read, looking full into his face. On the night that Lincoln was shot, Booth's henchman, Lewis Powell, also tried to kill Seward in his bedroom. The secretary was stabbed and his son was severely injured trying to keep Powell from attacking his father. The thin Seward was in loose bed clothing, and Powell's blows with his large knife failed to sufficiently meet and penetrate the frail body. The weakened secretary was not told of Lincoln's death, but a week or so later he noticed the flag at half-mast over the War Department. He began to cry and remarked, "The President is dead. If he had been alive, he would have been the first to call on me, but he has not been here, nor has he sent to know how I am, and there is the flag at half-mast." The house was located almost adjacent to the street, in the yard of the present structure.

It is not specifically known why Seward was the target of the assassins. He was not next in line for the presidency after the president and vice president. Under the secession law passed in 1792, the president pro tem of the senate would have acted until a new president was chosen. This was an obscure senator from Connecticut, Lafayette S. Foster. At the loss of both the president and vice president, the secretary of state would have to set in motion procedures for presidential electors to be appointed and chosen from each state. If there were no secretary of state, and no president to appoint one, the government would have been in chaos under the weak Foster. Clearly, Seward was seen as a power in the government, and some then felt that he controlled the president.

Seward continued after Lincoln's death to serve President Andrew Johnson in the same position in the cabinet, but he was not successful in giving advice. Democrat Johnson did not heed his advice to court Republican moderates, and Seward went down with the president in the latter's impeachment. His greatest role after the war was the acquisition of territories including Alaska ("Seward's Folly") and the Virgin Islands. After the election of President Grant in 1868, Seward took a forty-four-thousand-mile trip around the world and died in 1872 of what is now thought to have been amyotrophic lateral sclerosis (Lou Gehrig's disease).

Also on Lafayette Square at what is now 722 Jackson Place was the prewar home of Congressman (later General) Daniel E. Sickles, who killed the son of Frances Scott Key (composer of "The Star Spangled Banner") almost at the front of the Seward House. Philip Barton Key did not know that Mrs. Sickles had confessed to her husband of their affair, so when Key gave his usual signal to her across the square from near Seward's house, he was confronted and shot point-blank. Sickles's trial was a national sensation especially when Mrs. Sickles's written confession was made public, with all the racy details. It has been designated by some as the "Trial of the Nineteenth Century" and was the first time a defendant was found "not guilty by reason of insanity." Edwin Stanton, later secretary of war, was Sickles's attorney. Sickles lost a leg at Gettysburg on July 2, 1863, and was visited by the president and Tad on July 4, either at his home or a nearby residence on F Street across near the Ebbitt House at the southeast corner of Fourteenth and E Streets. He knew his movement of troops two days earlier was in violation of his orders from General Meade, and he was subject to court-martial. The meeting began a lifelong campaign to elevate his stature, starting with the willing ear of the president. His false and misleading statements about Meade's perceived deficiencies clouded Lincoln's judgment of his commander then and maybe for the rest of the war. Sickles was one of the last generals of the war to die in 1914.

(23) The **DEFENSES OF WASHINGTON HEADQUARTERS SITE, AT THE NORTH-EAST CORNER OF PENNSYLVANIA AVENUE AND MADISON PLACE**, was chosen by General McClellan when he was named on September 2, 1862, to the command the defenses of the city after the Battles of Second Bull Run and Chantilly.

(24) Lincoln deposited his salary in the **RIGGS BANK SITE, ON THE NORTH-WEST CORNER OF FIFTEENTH STREET AND PENNSYLVANIA AVENUE**, in a checking account. In late 1863, the press reported that the president had not drawn his salary for over a year and was told that if he had he could have earned $12,000 in interest. He was quoted as saying that the United States needed the money quite as much as any person, and he let it remain. (He had four months' salary warrants or checks in his desk when he died.)

It has generally been accepted that after nearly twenty-five years of law practice Lincoln was worth about $15,000 at the time of his presidential election. His salary as president was $25,000 per year, earning him $102,829 plus about $10,000 in interest. At his death, administrator Judge David Davis found the net valuation of his estate to be $83,343.70 plus real estate in Springfield and Lincoln, Illinois, and two hundred acres in Iowa. Davis managed the estate wisely and was able to distribute $110,974.62 on November 13, 1867. Since Lincoln had no will, his wife and sons inherited the property equally.

How much is this worth in today's economic terms? Historian and author David Herbert Donald used a multiple of "at least ten times" in the article "The Lincolns in the White House," printed in 1994. Other historians have suggested a multiple of 100. An article in *American Heritage* magazine (October 1998) estimates the wealth of the hundred richest Americans from Michael Klepper and Robert Gunther's book, *The Wealthy 100*. The authors attempted to adjust past economic value to equal the current day using the gross national product index, which they admit is a crude instrument. A wide range of figures was used for those dying between 1848 and 1882, with multiples ranging from 107 to 417 for the wealth of those involved to adjust to 1994 values. Thus using a multiple of 100 would be low in that study. In fact the index used for 1863 is 411. Using 100 as an index would indicate a 1994 equivalent presidential salary of $2.5 million per year and a net worth of $11,097,462 at distribution of Lincoln's estate. That appears very high considering their lifestyles during that era and other cost considerations of the day. But clearly the cabin-born rail-splitter had achieved economic success, although his widow believed that she lived in near poverty.

(25) The Lincolns attended General Edward D. Baker's funeral in **GENERAL JAMES WATSON WEBB RESIDENCE (SITE), AT FOURTEENTH AND H STREETS**, on October 24, 1861. The funeral would have been in the East Room at the White House, but this was being refurbished. Lincoln had named his second son after his Illinois friend. Baker had introduced Lincoln at his inauguration, and was killed at the Battle of Balls Bluff, Virginia. Willie Lincoln wrote a poem about the martyr.

(26) The **TREASURY BUILDING, SOUTH OF FIFTEENTH STREET AND PENNSYLVANIA AVENUE**, was to be used by the president and cabinet in case Washington was invaded. It had been stocked with food and the doors were sandbagged. Lincoln raised a flag over the south front at Fifteenth Street and Pennsylvania Avenue after reviewing troops there. The building blocks the intended view from the Capitol to the White House. It is said that President Andrew Jackson was tired of wrangling over where the building was to be built. While out walking and listening to the arguments, he struck his cane in the ground and ordered it built there. The suite used by Treasury Secretary Salmon P. Chase during the Civil War has been restored to the time when Lincoln ambled over from the White House to discuss financing. Down the hall from Chase's office is the Andrew Johnson suite, used by him after the assassination until Mary Lincoln moved out of the White House. He held his first cabinet meeting in the office on the afternoon of April 15, 1865.

(27) The **STATE DEPARTMENT SITE, AT THE SOUTHWEST CORNER OF FIFTEENTH STREET AND PENNSYLVANIA AVENUE**, was at the site of an earlier building burned by the British is 1814. Secretary of State Seward was probably Lincoln's closest friend and advisor in the cabinet. The site is now an extension of the Treasury Building.

(28) Lincoln attended the **FOUNDRY METHODIST CHURCH, ON THE NORTH-EAST CORNER OF G AND FOURTEENTH STREETS**, with many of his cabinet members on January 18, 1863. During the service some-one suggested that the president be made a life director of the Missionary Society. The membership cost $150. The collection plates were passed, and $160 was collected.

(29) The **EPIPHANY CHURCH, ON THE NORTH SIDE OF G STREET BETWEEN THIRTEENTH AND FOURTEENTH STREETS**, served as a hospital in 1862 and was visited by Lincoln, who also attended the funeral of his friend General Frederick Lander at the church.

(30) The site of **A. STUNTZ'S FANCY STORE** is **1207 NEW YORK AVENUE**. Lincoln frequented this toy shop with his sons, Willie and Tad. After Willie's death, the president's companionship with his youngest son increased. This was known as their favorite place to come. The shop stayed open in the evening with lamps highlighting the color and glitter of the toys. Lincoln formed a close attachment to the elderly shut-in who carved toys and had two stories of stocked shelves, making Tad's eyes gleam with delight and excitement. Both Lincolns, father and son, enjoyed talking with this old sol-dier for Napoleon. Lincoln came just before his last Christmas and told Stuntz, "I want to give him (Tad) all the toys that I did not have and all the toys that I would have given the boy who went away (Willie)." After Lincoln's death, workers inventorying and packing family belongings from the White House found a room full of unused toys that had been bought for Willie.

(31) The church attended by the Lincoln family throughout the war was the **NEW YORK AVENUE PRESBYTERIAN CHURCH** (reconstructed), at **NEW YORK AVENUE AND H STREET**. Willie enjoyed the learning and religious experience of Sunday school, but Tad generally rebelled. The president rented the same pew used by Buchanan. Presidents John Quincy Adams, Jackson, William Henry Harri-son, Fillmore, Buchanan, and Andrew Johnson also attended the church. Presidents since then have regularly occupied the Lincoln pew. A modern, slightly larger church was begun in 1951 and President Truman laid the cornerstone, with the help of promi-nent former pastor Peter Marshall's son. It retains the original pew at the same position occupied by the Lincolns. The hitching post used for their carriage is still in the south side pavement near the front.

It was the custom of the church to remain seated during prayers, but Lincoln, who felt otherwise, always stood, as did Mathew Brady when he attended. A stained-glass depiction of Lincoln standing is now in a church stained-glass window. In July 1861 Pastor Gurley announced that "religious services would be suspended until further notice as the church was needed as a hospital." Lincoln stood up and interrupted, saying, "Dr. Gurley, this action was taken without my consent, and I hereby countermand the order. The churches are needed as never before for divine services."

Lincoln was relatively close to Dr. Gurley, prayed often with him at the White House, and (according to church history) discussed the phrasing of the Emancipation Proclamation with him. An initial draft of the proclamation, a gift from Lincoln to Gurley, is displayed in the Lincoln Parlor downstairs. The parlor commemorates Lincoln's attendance in midweek prayer services. His presence was somewhat disruptive, so Dr. Gurley suggested he might want to stay in the pastor's study adjacent to the lecture room, with the door slightly open. Here he could inconspicuously share the inspiration, but not be seen. When Willie Lincoln lay dying in the White House, Dr. Gurley visited several times. On his last visit, Willie asked his mother to bring in his iron piggy bank, which he gave to the church for Sunday school mission work.

The church history claims that Lincoln had made all the necessary arrangements to be admitted into the membership of the church on what was the Easter Sunday following his assassination. This would have been Lincoln's only membership in any church. But historians are skeptical of this and similar stories, such as the one about Lincoln being secretly baptized in Illinois. John Quincy Adams was a member of the church and there is a parlor with memorabilia of his here, as well as letters from President and Mrs. Lincoln.

(32) SECRETARY OF WAR EDWIN M. STANTON'S HOME (SITE) WAS 1323 K STREET. Stanton replaced Simon Cameron as war secretary in January 1862. The president visited and ate here and sometimes stopped to confer with Stanton on the way to or from the Soldiers Home. The two men spent a great deal of time together and developed a lasting, mutual trust and respect. They would have been closer but for hostility between their wives. Stanton died here in 1869, after being a center of controversy leading to the impeachment of President Andrew Johnson, and is buried in Georgetown (see SITE 81).

(33) The home of HORATIO NELSON TAFT was a frequent "second home" for Lincoln's sons Willie and Tad, who also explored the neighborhood around the area, according to Julia Taft Bayne. Taft was chief examiner in the Patent Office. The two Taft boys, Bud and Holly, were close friends of Lincoln's sons. The boys' older sister, Julia, was a frequent baby sitter and stayed with all four boys in the White House when Mary went to New York City. They are said to have spent about equal time in both homes and spent Saturdays at the Tafts as they studied their Sunday school lesson. Willie and Tad preferred going to their **FOURTH PRESBYTERIAN CHURCH** on Ninth Street since it was "more lively" than their parents' **NEW YORK AVENUE CHURCH**. Mrs. Taft came home one day to find a Confederate flag flying from her roof. This was discovered to be the flag Colonel Ellsworth had captured in Alexandria at the beginning of the war and given to Tad. He was made to take it down. Then the four boys formed a branch of the Old Capitol Prison in the Taft attic, and kept dog and cat prisoners who howled and screeched to be released. They also dug rifle pits in the backyard.

Julia's observations of the president during the first year in office were recorded later in life in *Tad Lincoln's Father*, a valuable resource into the personal life of the Lincolns. Mary is described as "sweet and tender." It is from Julia that we get the description of the "circus" produced by the boys in the White House with Willie wearing a dress and his father's spectacles. She also gives a story about a visit by the president to McClellan's house with Bud and Willie. There as they sat in the parlor waiting for the general, they heard him come in and be informed that the president was waiting. They then heard footsteps up the stairs, the boots falling to the floor, and the general throwing himself into bed. The president is then quoted as saying, "Come boys, let us go home." (This is basically the same incident described in John Hay's diary on November 13, 1861, as related in the earlier entry of the **CUTTS-MADISON HOUSE**, **[20]**). An older brother, Charles, was one of the doctors who attended Lincoln in Ford's Theater.

This site is difficult to locate as the Tafts reported different addresses each year, and there is no city directory for 1861. The home during the period mentioned above in 1861 was evidently then on L Street near the corner of Twelfth Street, as indicated in Julia's book (page 16). A neighbor listed as (George?) Bartle is listed at 446 L Street, near Thirteenth Street. Later they were living on Ninth Street (page 157), mentioned as a change from the earlier comments in 1861. The 1862 city directory lists them at 346 Ninth Street near L Street. Washington street numbers changed in 1870. There is evidently no way now to look up addresses from 1861, according to the Washington Room at the City Library, the Washington Historical Society, and other sources.

(34) It is claimed that Lincoln attended GROVER'S THEATER (SITE), (NOW THE NATIONAL THEATER), AT 1321 PENNSYLVANIA AVENUE NW (FORMALLY E STREET), at least a hundred times during his presidency. Grover claimed Lincoln was here when he carried the message of his second presidential nomination to him. Lincoln is quoted as remarking, "Well . . . they have nominated me again. . . . I am a bit curious to know what man they are going to harness up with me. Still, I reckon I'll stay a little while longer and look at the play." Grover also claimed that Lincoln was supposed to come to his theater on the night he was killed and that Booth knew it and had reserved the adjoining box (The *Lincoln Newsletter* of Lincoln College Museum, fall 1993).

Tad was here when his father was killed. There are two versions of how Tad heard of the assassination. In one, the manager came onstage and made the announcement, at which Tad bolted from the theater "like a wounded deer." In the other version, his escort was told in a whisper, and the boy left the theater before the announcement was made to the audience.

The present is the latest of five theaters that have stood here; the others burned down. Julia Taft relates how Lincoln liked Grover's and often took Tad. The president's son was a good friend of Bobby Grover, five years younger, and was said to have attended so many rehearsals that he was almost at home. Once the two boys got into some old devil costumes and had to be restrained from parading down Pennsylvania Avenue. Tad made friends with all the ushers and stagehands, who let him help at rehearsals and move props. Once Tad went backstage during a play, dressed in an oversized soldier's uniform, and came out onstage in a file of men singing the "Battle Hymn of the Republic." His father was at first shocked and surprised, then "laughed hardily," as did the audience when they realized what had happened. In another story, he came out in an oversized blouse while the star was singing "The Battle Cry of Freedom." The singer and crowd gradually realized that this was the president's son, and he was handed a flag that he waved triumphantly, to everyone's delight.

The president, vice president, and their wives attended a performance here after the issuance of the Emancipation Proclamation when feelings among many in the city were running against the administration. The owner of the theater, Leonard Grover, was fearful for the president and accompanied the party to their carriage when the play ended at 11:00 in the evening. When they got outside, they found the crowd hostile and the driver drunk. Grover quickly assumed the driver's position and left with his guests as soon as possible. When they reached the White House, Lincoln took Grover's hand and declared, "Mr. Grover, you have done me a great service tonight and one I shall never forget." Grover later said he believed that attending the theater was one of Lincoln's escapes from the pressures of the White House.

In *The Little Bugler*, a story is told, evidently accepted, of a boy who stayed at the White House for a short time with Tad after he had met the president's family in Virginia. Tad and his friend, Gus Schurmann, attended Grover's to see John Wilkes Booth in *The Marble Heart* on April 18, 1863. Between acts, they went backstage to meet the star, who was very hospitable, chatted while he applied stage makeup, and gave the boys some roses that had been sent to him. It is claimed that Booth was known to have loved children, and this would have been in character. They told him what parts of the play they liked, and Booth expressed a desire for the president to see him perform. Lincoln did see the same actor and play the next November.

(35) WILLARD'S HOTEL, AT 1401 PENNSYLVANIA AVENUE, replaces the wartime structure Lincoln and his family stayed in until the inauguration. Soon after he arrived on February 23, 1861, Lincoln had breakfast here with Illinois congressman Washburne and Secretary Seward. Seward rushed to the hotel as soon as he heard Lincoln was in town, apologizing that he would have welcomed Lincoln at the train depot, but he overslept. During this time he took long walks around the area with Robert, John Nicolay, and others. When they arrived in the city, the peace Convention, presided over by Ex-President John Tyler, was in session in the concert hall of the hotel trying to prevent secession, but the meeting was in vain. They called on the president-elect on his first night in his room at the southwest corner, fronting Pennsylvania Avenue.

This was the city's most famous and prominent hotel, frequented by many military and diplomatic leaders. Many presidents before and after Lincoln stayed here, where it is claimed that Martin Luther King Jr. wrote his "I Have a Dream" speech and Julia Ward Howe wrote the words to the "Battle Hymn of the Republic." The hotel almost burned down on May 9, 1861, but was saved by Colonel Elmer Ellsworth's regiment. Later that month Ellsworth, a close friend of Lincoln and his sons, became the first officer killed in the war, beginning a long line of lives lost among friends and Todd family members in the terrible war.

Lincoln received Mayor Berret and municipal authorities in his parlor soon after arrival and thanked them for their friendly greeting. Lincoln then stated, "And as it is the first time in my life, since the present phase of politics has presented itself in this country, that I have said anything publicly within a region of the country where the institution of slavery exists, I will take this occasion to say that I think very much of the ill feeling that has existed, and still exists, between the people in the sections from whence I came and the people here, is dependent upon a misunderstanding of one another. I therefore avail myself of this opportunity to assure you, Mr. Mayor, and all the gentlemen present, that I have not now, and never have had, any other than as kindly feelings toward you as the people of my own section. I have not now, and never have had, any disposition to treat you in any respect otherwise than as my own neighbors. I have not now any purpose to withhold from you any benefits of the Constitution, under any circumstances that I would feel myself constrained to withhold from my own neighbors, and I hope in a word, that when we shall become better acquainted, and I say it with great confidence, we shall like each other the more." Similar statements were used to later address crowds from the window of the hotel.

President Buchanan called on his successor at the hotel to escort him down the same historic route to the inauguration used by most presidents. During the war President and Mrs. Lincoln attended concerts here.

(36) **GAUTIER'S RESTAURANT (SITE), ON THE SOUTH SIDE OF PENNSYLVANIA AVENUE IN THE MIDDLE OF THE BLOCK BETWEEN TWELFTH AND THIRTEENTH STREETS**, held the only meeting with all of the Lincoln conspirators and John Wilkes Booth. This occurred on March 16, 1865. The subject was the kidnapping of the president. Booth explained that they would capture the president in a theater, lower him to the stage, and escape with him to Virginia. Several thought this was ridiculous. Booth, infuriated, banged his hand on the table and exclaimed, "If worse comes to worst, I shall know what to do!" Theatrical friends had told Booth that the president had planned to ride out to Campbell Hospital on Boundary Street to see a play on the next day. Everything was set for the kidnapping then, but instead, the president received a rebel flag and made a speech at Booth's hotel. (The spelling of the Gautier's name and the location given vary, but this is from the 1865 city directory. The Surratt Society also agrees that this address is correct. The difficulty with the address is probably that it is listed as "252 Pennsylvania" and has to be converted to a current number, which is confusing.)

(37) VICE PRESIDENT ANDREW JOHNSON LIVED AT THE KIRKWOOD HOUSE (SITE), AT THE NORTHEAST CORNER OF PENNSYLVANIA AVENUE AND TWELFTH STREET. He was sworn in as president by Chief Justice Chase in his third-floor suite a few hours after Lincoln died. George Atzerodt, one of Booth's fellow conspirators, had taken a room near Johnson. On April 14, 1865, he was supposed to knock on Johnson's door and shoot him when he answered. He went to the hotel to fulfill his agreement with Booth to assassinate the vice president, but did not carry the plan through. He was later hanged anyway. Booth went there on the day of the assassination and left a note for Johnson that read, "Don't wish to disturb you. Are you home?" and signed his correct name. It is possible that Booth distrusted Atzerodt and wanted to tie Johnson to the conspiracy. When officers arrived later to protect Johnson, they were told that a strange man lived near him, Atzerodt. They went to his room and found Booth's bankbook and other incriminating evidence.

Johnson had been invited to Ford's Theater by Leonard J. Farwell on the fateful night, but wanted to go to bed early. After the assassination, Farwell rushed here, shouting frantically for a guard to be put at the front door, and he rushed to Johnson's room. Friends soon arrived and begged Johnson not to go to the side of the dying president. He did go briefly during the night, and returned to wait, with friends, for the official word of Lincoln's death.

(38) Lincoln and his family attended several plays and operas during his congressional term and presidency at the WASHINGTON THEATRE OR CARUSI'S HALL (SITE), AT THE NORTHEAST CORNER OF C AND ELEVENTH STREETS. C Street no longer extends to this location, now north of Constitution Avenue. The Internal Revenue Building occupies the site, just south of Pennsylvania Avenue. Lincoln attended President Taylor's inaugural ball on March 5, 1849. He and friends stayed until between three and four in the morning. Lincoln then was unable to find his hat, and had to leave bareheaded. Inaugural balls for all elected presidents from John Quincy Adams (1825) through Buchanan were held here, except Pierce, who canceled his because of the recent death of his son.

Mr. and Mrs. Lincoln attended the opera *Il Trovatore* here on January 23, 1862.

(39) FORD'S THEATER, AT 511 TENTH STREET, was the site of Lincoln's assassination and has been restored to its appearance on the night of April 14, 1865. The site was used by the First Baptist Church from 1833 until the three Ford brothers began a theater in March 1862. The president was in attendance for the first time a few weeks later, on May 28. The building burnt to the ground in December after it opened, and was completely rebuilt by August 27, 1863, in time for Lincoln to see five plays by the end of the year. The original north, south, and west walls still stand. The west front or Tenth Street side includes the two original casement windows in the south bay, the pilasters, and the five arched doorways. The east wall was rebuilt after the interior partially collapsed on June 9, 1893.

The famous actor John Wilkes Booth had become a fanatic in trying to save the South. His plan was to bring down the government by leaving it leaderless and bewildered. He, like Jefferson Davis, did not see Robert E. Lee's surrender on April 9 as the end of the war. He felt that some dramatic act might bring down the government and give the South a chance to survive. If not, Lincoln's death would be revenge for the ills Booth considered to have been inflicted on the country. Like many in the South and in Europe, Lincoln was thought of in the mid-1860s as Hitler was in the United States in the 1940s, according to historian Don E. Fehrenbacher. What part the Confederate government played in Booth's prior plans to kidnap the president and the final assassination has been argued ever since. It is believed by many that Booth did have Confederate support to kidnap Lincoln.

Late in the war the South was desperate. A captured president might force the North to release prisoners or back off from harsh demands to end the war with emancipation and reunion. In 1863 Lincoln had seen an opportunity to shorten the war when the newly formed Union Cavalry Corps failed to raid Richmond when it was felt to be virtually undefended. Lincoln wrote General Hooker that they could have "burnt everything and brought us Jeff. Davis." Did this sanction kidnapping? Also, Lincoln was thought to have sanctioned the killing or kidnapping of Jefferson Davis, as revealed in captured dispatches made public carried by Colonel Ulric Dahlgren when the son of Lincoln's friend, Admiral John A. Dahlgren, was killed in a failed Union raid on Richmond.

In the minds of many, including Booth, the war and suffering were attributed directly to Lincoln.

The president had attended Ford's at least eleven times. He was in the Presidential Box on February 10, 1865, with Generals Grant and Ambrose Burnside. Lincoln had seen Booth perform there several times, including November 9, 1863, in *The Marble Heart* when he had heartily applauded the actor. When Booth heard this, he said he would rather have had the applause of a Negro and ignored a request from the president to meet him. Lincoln spent much time at another play here with Senator Charles Sumner answering Tad's many questions.

Mrs. Lincoln had a headache on the night of April 14, 1865, and would have preferred to stay home, but she knew how much the president enjoyed the theater. He was tired that night, but hated to disappoint the crowd that was expecting him. After being turned down by General Grant and his wife, and nine or more others, including their son Robert, the president and his party arrived after the play had started. Major Henry R. Rathbone and his fiancée, the daughter of Senator Ira T. Harris, accompanied them. The Lincolns probably picked up the couple at the senator's house on H Street near Fourteenth Street.

Booth arrived at about 10:00, had his horse held by stagehand Edman Spangler, who probably had no idea what he was up to, and then gave it to a young black helper, Peanuts Burroughs. (Spangler's first name is spelled various ways, but this spelling is on his tombstone in Virginia.) Booth arrived at the rear of the theater in the alley still known as Baptist Alley, so named when the building was used as a Baptist church. The alley can be entered from F Street between Ninth and Tenth Streets. The back door of Ford's was then about where the drainpipe is now.

Booth crossed under the stage, left out a side door, and went to an adjoining saloon on Tenth Street for a whiskey. He then entered Lincoln's box at about 10:15 and shot him in the back of the head as the president held his wife's hand. Rathbone grabbed him and was slashed. As Booth attempted to jump to the stage twelve feet below, Rathbone grabbed him again, distracting Booth so that his fall was broken and his spur caught one of the flags draped on the box. The Treasury Guard flag that probably caught Booth's spur can be seen in the downstairs museum. Most historians feel that Booth broke his leg at this point, although there is some evidence and argument that it may have been broken when his horse fell crossing into Maryland. (Both injuries could have occurred.) The broken leg caused him to have to seek the services of Dr. Mudd in Maryland, slowing his escape. Pandemonium broke out in the theater. Several doctors quickly discovered that Lincoln's wound was mortal, and looked for a more comfortable place to take him. After they carried the dying man outside, a boarder of the house across the street called for them to carry him there.

In February 1869 Booth's body was placed in the stable at the rear of the theater where he had kept his horse on April 14. The body had been removed from its burial place at the arsenal and originally been taken to an undertaker on F Street, but then it was hidden here to get it away from curious crowds (Washington *Evening Star*, February 1869).

The theater was confiscated by the government after the assassination and later used for an office building. The inner floors collapsed in 1893, killing twenty-two and injuring sixty-five to sixty-eight. (As radio commentator Paul Harvey relates in the *Rest of the Story*, this was the day that John Wilkes Booth's famous brother, Edwin, was buried.) The basement was partially restored in 1926 and became Oldroyd's Lincoln Museum. The inside of the building was gutted during the 1960s and reopened in 1969 as a theater and museum. No original plans were found, and the reconstruction was based on Mathew Brady's photographs, a few sketches after the assassination, and oral testimony. It is open to the public when not in use for theatrical performances.

The box where the president sat contains the original couch used by Major Rathbone, but the president's chair is in the Henry Ford Museum in Dearborn, Michigan. The picture of George Washington in front of the box is original. (Booth's spur is in the Naval Academy Museum in Annapolis, Maryland, at Preeble Hall, inside Gate 3 on Maryland Avenue.) The museum in the basement contains many artifacts from the assassination including the guns used by Booth, knife used by Powell (also "Payne" or "Paine"), Booth's knife used to slash Rathbone, Booth's diary with pages mysteriously ripped out, and clothes worn by Lincoln that night. Some buildings across the street date to this time period. The door to the box is also here with the hole Booth may have enlarged to see inside, although Henry Clay Ford's son claimed that his father ordered it made so that the president's guard could see in without opening the door. Other Lincoln artifacts are also in the museum, although many shown here in prior years are in storage at Harpers Ferry.

As with the assassination of John Kennedy, there are many theories about conspiracies and involvement of others in the crime. Even after one hundred years there are books still being written about possible links between Booth and both the Confederate and U.S. governments. It is very possible that Booth and John Surratt were involved with the spy network of the southern states in some way to secure some negotiated settlement of the war. Since the assassination itself was evidently not planned for more time than it took Booth to discover the planned attendance of the president on the same day, it seems probable that this act was his responsibility alone. As in the later death of Kennedy, many rumors spread for years that Booth either escaped or was killed to prevent his revealing others involved, including those in the Union government. These rumors seem unreliable although believed by many.

The Maryland and Virginia chapters cover the escape route of Booth.

(40) After being shot Lincoln was carried to the **PETERSEN HOUSE, AT 516 TENTH STREET,** a rooming house across the street. It was felt that the ride to the White House would be too dangerous for his condition. Mary waited in the front parlor, sobbing hysterically most of the time. From that moment she formally mourned for the rest of her life. She wanted Tad summoned, saying that her husband would respond to the beloved son, but most historians agree that he was not allowed to come. Her closest friend, Lizzie Keckley, did not arrive as a carriage sent to get her went to the wrong address. Stanton began his investigation and supervision of the pursuit of the assassins from one of the adjoining rooms, and had to exclude the hysterical Mrs. Lincoln from disturbing the dying president. The three now open rooms are restored to their condition that night. Possibly sixty-five people were in and out of the bedroom during the night, but it is unknown exactly how many were present when he died at 7:22 A.M. on April 15, 1865. The only one who took notes was Corporal James Tanner, who wrote, "A more agonized expression I never saw on a human countenance as he (Stanton) sobbed out the words, 'He belongs to the ages now.' . . . Dr. Gourley lifted his hands and began, Our Father and our God . . ." but Tanner's pencil broke and he could not get another in time to record the rest. There are many pictorial re-creations of the deathbed scene with many more individuals shown as could fit into the existing space, called the "rubber room" as artists seem to expand it to fit in those depicted. The house is open by the National Park Service.

The Petersen House immediately became a popular tourist site, but unpopular boardinghouse. Petersen fell on hard times and committed suicide in 1871. His children auctioned the contents of the house, which were acquired in 1920 by the Chicago Historical Society where they can be seen now, depending on what is displayed at any given time. The building adjacent to the north side also dates to this period.

(41) John Wilkes Booth and his fellow conspirators met in the HERNDON HOUSE (SITE), AT THE SOUTHWEST CORNER OF NINTH AND F STREETS, the residence of conspirator Lewis Powell (Payne), at about 8:00 on the evening of April 14, 1865, to finalize assassination plans. George Atzerodt claimed that Booth then mentioned assassination for the first time, rather than kidnapping. He was given the assignment to kill Vice President Johnson, Powell assigned to Secretary of State Seward, and Herold was sent to guide Powell, who had no sense of direction. A meeting place and timetable were selected.

(42) The NATIONAL PORTRAIT GALLERY, AT F AND G STREETS BETWEEN SEVENTH AND NINTH STREETS, NW, was the PATENT OFFICE during the Civil War. It is the oldest government building in Washington after the Capitol, White House, and Marine Commandant's House. Begun in 1836, its south portico is a copy of the Parthenon in Athens, Greece. Lincoln visited the Patent Office on April 10, 1848, and again on February 19, 1849, to inquire about an application from a constituent. Robert said his father brought him here on Sundays while he was a congressman in 1848. This was a favorite place for the president to bring Tad also, second only to Stuntz's Toy Shop. The president was caught off guard by the crowd's insistence for a speech while visiting on February 22, 1864. Returning to the White House in the carriage, Mary so severely criticized his reluctant effort that all conversation between the Lincolns and their guest ended.

Troops were quartered for a short time inside, and it also served as a hospital where poet Walt Whitman read to patients. Lincoln raised a flag over the building on May 2, 1861. Several inaugural balls were held here, including Lincoln's on March 5, 1865, attended by, according to the *New York Times*, "5000 people in space prepared for 300." The ball and banquet were on the second floor overlooking Seventh Street in a room now known as the Lincoln Gallery, reached by a narrow hall now called the Civil War Gallery. The Lincoln Gallery was the largest room in America. The Declaration of Independence was displayed on the third floor from 1841 to 1871. President Eisenhower saved it from becoming a parking lot in 1953.

(43) THE POST OFFICE (NOW TARIFF COMMISSION), ON THE WEST SIDE OF SEVENTH STREET BETWEEN E AND F STREETS, is still an impressive building. It was erected before Lincoln's congressional term and was used also as a commissary depot. The first government building of marble is on the site of Blodget's Hotel, built in 1793 and housing the Patent Office in 1814, when the British arrived to burn it down. Patent Superintendent William Thornton persuaded the British to halt when he asked, "Are you Englishmen or Goths or Vandals; this is the Patent Office, the depository of the ingenuity of the American nation, in which the whole civilized world is interested. Would you destroy it?" The building did burn down accidentally on December 15, 1836, destroying seven thousand patent models.

(44) THE FOURTH PRESBYTERIAN CHURCH SITE, ON THE WEST SIDE OF NINTH STREET BETWEEN G AND H STREETS, was the church of the Taft family who were friends of Lincoln's sons. Willie and Tad attended this church on several occasions. The site is now south of Grant Place, midway between G and H Streets at the southern end of the Martin Luther King, Jr. City Library. Tad would generally sit on the floor within the pew and play with whatever he could carry in. He cut himself with a knife during one sermon, and Julia Taft swore she'd never take him to church again. One Sunday the president was admonishing the boys for skipping church services at the New York Avenue Church when they explained they had gone to Fourth Presbyterian. They explained that it was more fun. Lincoln inquired, "But I didn't know you went to church for fun." Tad explained, "Oh yes, Papa! You just ought to see those rebels slam their pew doors and stamp out when the minister prays for the President of the United States." The pastor of the church spoke at Willie's funeral in the White House after Dr. Gurley of the New York Avenue Church. (The Library on this site now has an excellent collection of maps and historical references in the Washington Room on the third floor.)

(45) Lincoln frequented ALEXANDER GARDNER'S PHOTOGRAPHIC STUDIO (SITE) AT 511 SEVENTH STREET, AT THE NORTHEAST CORNER OF SEVENTH AND D STREETS. His last picture was made here four days before his death. Gardner's forty photographs of Lincoln are the most of any of the thirty-one cameramen who captured him on sixty-one occasions.

(46) The BOARDINGHOUSE OF MARY SURRATT, 604 H STREET, was claimed to have been used by the conspirators to plot the kidnapping and assassination of the president. President Johnson called this "the nest that hatched the egg." Mary's son, John, was very much involved in the kidnapping plot leading to the assassination. He was probably out of town at the time of the assassination and escaped to Europe. At the time of his capture in 1867, he was serving as a papal guard in the Vatican. Although he had a long trial, he was never convicted of any crime. His mother was convicted and became the first woman hanged in this country. There is much controversy about her role, if any, in any plot. Indeed her guilt was generally based on statements attributed to her and her supposed knowledge since the conspirators met in her house. Also, she delivered guns and a pair of field glasses to her tavern in nearby Maryland, later used by Booth in his escape. Conspirator Lewis Powell was captured here as he appeared when authorities were arresting others. This has been a Chinese restaurant for several years.

(47) SECRETARY OF THE TREASURY SALMON CHASE'S HOUSE was on the NORTHWEST CORNER OF SIXTH AND E STREETS. The president paid his respects here to the body of his friend, General Frederick W. Lander, on March 5, 1862, and came other times to visit his secretary. Chase had been senator and governor of Ohio before the war, and had lost three wives and four of six children. He had been a rival for the presidency during the 1860 election, and felt, as did his strong-willed daughter, that he would make a better president than Lincoln. Certainly, he never stopped seeking the office. The possibilities of the 1864 presidential opportunities for himself were not lost on him, and he felt that the 1860 political mistake could be remedied in 1864 by his nomination. He resigned at least four times in his continuing power plays with the president. To Chase's surprise, Lincoln accepted the last in 1864. When Chief Justice Roger Taney finally died later in the year, Lincoln appointed Chase as his successor, in time to be sworn in by him in March 1865.

Daughter Kate was the hostess of many prominent parties in the home, to the open disgust of Mrs. Lincoln, who felt that she should be the social leader in Washington, to the embarrassment of the president. Mary did not like the younger, prettier, and slimmer rival for the social leadership of the capital and rightly suspected that she was promoting her father's presidential prospects,

according to David H. Donald. Lincoln attended Kate's wedding
here on November 12, 1863, but Mary refused to go, pleading that
she was still in mourning for Willie. The president stayed for an
unusually long time of over two hours to compensate for his
wife's absence, but dared not dance with any of the pretty young
ladies, fearing his wife's jealousy. Author John Waugh says, "That
ambition, amounting to longing, smoldered sleepless in Chase's
breast, like a glowing ember in an undying fire." Chase's close
friend and later president, James A. Garfield, lived here during the
fall of 1862. Kate, and not Mary, was one of the few women who
attended Lincoln's funeral in the White House.

(48) Lincoln was often at the studio and gallery of the world's first
noted war photographer, MATHEW BRADY, AT 633 PENNSYLVANIA
AVENUE. (The studio is often currently listed at 352 Pennsylvania
Avenue, but this wartime address was renumbered.) This was a
branch of his famous New York gallery. In fact, Lincoln came here
his first day in town as president-elect after visiting President
Buchanan in the White House. This original building probably
saw more famous Americans than any other in the city, other than
the White House and Capitol Building. The second floor over
Thompson's Saloon was a reception room and gallery. The devel-
oping and process room was on the third floor, and the photographs were done on the top floor under a skylight. The president,
his cabinet members, and other famous people of the time had to
climb three steep flights to be immortalized. This was also on or
near the site of portrait painter Gilbert Stuart's studio in the early
1800s. Unfortunately, the building is not open to the public.

As famous as Brady was then and is now, there is some question as to whether he ever took any Civil War photographs due to
failing eyesight. He is credited with eleven pictures of Lincoln,
and his assistant, Anthony Berger, is credited with thirteen. Available and popular photos were carried by soldiers and placed in
homes around the country, making the president well known and
referred to as the world's first photographic celebrity. Brady sent
out teams of photographers, and his appearances on the battlefields may have been supervisory. But there is no question that
the rich heritage we now possess from photographic coverage of
the war was largely due to his leadership and organization on a
grand scale.

(49) Lincoln was often at the Saturday breakfasts at DANIEL WEB-
STER'S HOUSE (SITE) in 1848 where slaves served food. According
to *Following Abraham Lincoln* the location was at the northeast

corner of Connecticut Avenue and H Street, now the U.S. Chamber of Commerce. The 1822 Corcoran House there was presented to Webster in 1841, but he found the house too expensive to maintain and sold it to the founder of the Corcoran Art Gallery. Since he moved prior to Lincoln's congressional term these breakfasts had to have been at his new residence. The city directory of 1846 and a biography lists his residence on the NORTH SIDE OF D STREET BETWEEN FIFTH AND SIXTH STREETS. The 1850 directory describes the same location as "Louisiana Street," but the location is now Indiana Street south across the street, as it angles at the intersection. Thus the addresses appear the same. An article by a local historian in the 1940 *Washington Star* shows a picture of the Webster home here, which was torn down when the police court was built. Therefore I conclude that the site shown in the 1846 directory is the site associated with Lincoln.

(50) Lincoln and his family stayed at BROWN'S HOTEL, AT THE NORTH-WEST CORNER OF PENNSYLVANIA AVENUE AND SIXTH STREET, beginning December 2, 1847, as he began his term in Congress. The family arrived at the OLD TRAIN SHED ON THE NORTH SIDE OF PENN-SYLVANIA AVENUE BETWEEN FIRST AND SECOND STREETS. Later they took up rooms at Mrs. Sprigg's **(SITE 67)**. The Lincolns had leased their Springfield house for a year. John Tyler was living here when he was sworn in as president in one of the parlors after President Harrison's death. This was known as Brown's Marble Hotel or Indian Queen, so named for the swinging sign that bore a likeness to Pocahontas. Grant, Lee, Custer, Andrew Johnson, Sam Houston, and others also stayed in prior years. This was located just east of Brady's studio on Pennsylvania.

(51) Lincoln attended a public dinner on June 13, 1848, at the NATIONAL HOTEL (ALSO KNOWN AS GADSBY'S) (SITE), AT THE NORTH-EAST CORNER OF PENNSYLVANIA AVENUE AND SIXTH STREET. Later his political hero, Henry Clay, died there in 1852. Presidents Jackson and Buchanan also had lived in the hotel, as did Jefferson Davis. On February 28, 1861, the president-elect was honored with a private dinner. John Wilkes Booth lived here and met in his room with Dr. Mudd and John Surratt in December 1864. The plot to kidnap and then murder Lincoln may have been planned and developed in the hotel. It is believed that the plot to kidnap Lincoln was planned for March 17, 1865, but failed as Lincoln had come here, Booth's residence, to make a speech rather than be where the kidnappers had expected him to be. The president spoke from a balcony then and told the crowd that the end of the war was near, as "we can see the bottom of the enemy's resources." While speaking "a genuine Secesh," Lizzie Murty tried to spit on the president. She was arrested and taken into custody after his death. Booth was able to mingle in the crowd by the carriage and was noticed giving a demoniacal expression of hatred toward the president.

(52) PUMPHREY'S STABLE WAS EAST OF THE NORTHEAST CORNER OF SEV-ENTH AND C STREETS. This is where Booth got his horses, including the one he rode to Ford's Theater on April 14 and used to escape from Washington. When he wanted a horse, he whistled out his second-floor window at the National Hotel.

(53) Conspirators Mike O' Laughlen and Sam Arnold roomed and boarded at TYNE'S BOARDING HOUSE SITE, ON THE NORTH SIDE OF D STREET, EAST OF SEVENTH STREET.

(54) GENERAL GRANT lived at **205 I STREET N.W.** much of the time from 1865 until 1869. General William T. SHERMAN lived in number **203**. Admirers gave both to the generals and their families. Before the war STEPHEN DOUGLAS lived in such elegant style at number **201** that his house was known as Mount Julep because he was well known as a host. All three connecting houses were hospitals during the war. The site is now part of Interstate 395.

(55) CITY HOSPITAL, ON THE NORTH SIDE OF E STREET BETWEEN FOURTH AND FIFTH STREETS AT JUDICIARY SQUARE, was used by the military during the war until it burned to the ground on November 4, 1861. All but one of the patients was saved, although it took an hour for the first fire engine to arrive. The new Judiciary Hospital was built in its place and was often visited by the Lincolns.

(56) OLD CITY HALL is located at FOURTH AND D STREETS. The grounds in those days, as now, were known as Judiciary Square. Its architect also designed Arlington House where Robert E. Lee lived. Lincoln's first inaugural ball was held in a temporary structure north of the building. The president and Mayor Barret led the Grand March. (His name is shown spelled various ways, including "Berrett" and "Berret.") Etiquette required that the president's wife not promenade with her husband, so Senator Stephen A. Douglas escorted Mrs. Lincoln, and they danced a quadrille. Coats, shawls, and cloaks were left in the courtroom and council chamber, only to be stolen before the end of festivities.

It had been a slave market before 1850 and served briefly as a fort and then hospital during the war. The mayor was arrested here on August 24, 1861, for refusing to take the loyalty oath to the Union. He was sent to prison in New York where he stayed three weeks before he consented to take the oath and step down as mayor. On April 26, 1862, Lincoln signed an act prohibiting slavery in the national capital, and the city hall was flooded with former slaveholders seeking compensation of about $300 each. After the war, conspirator John Surratt Jr. was tried here in the District of Columbia Court with Tad and Robert as witnesses.

(57) JOHN MARSHAL PARK, AT THE NORTHWEST CORNER OF FOURTH STREET AND PENNSYLVANIA AVENUE, is the site of Chief Justice John Marshall's rooming house (marked by a plaque on Pennsylvania), and residences of Presidents John Quincy Adams and Franklin Pierce. Also near this location on FOURTH AND A HALF STREET BETWEEN C AND LOUISIANA AVENUE was FIRST PRESBYTERIAN CHURCH, attended by Presidents Jackson, Polk, Pierce, and Cleveland, and FREEMASON'S HALL, where inaugural balls for Jackson and William Henry Harrison were held. Frederick Douglass spoke in a lecture to benefit black women and children. Lincoln came here with John Hay on August 6, 1863, but found out the pastor was away. So they continued to the New York Presbyterian Church. JACKSON HALL AT 339 PENNSYLVANIA AVENUE was the site where Lincoln attended an inaugural ball for Zachary Taylor in 1849, held to benefit the poor. Note that various sources relate that Taylor had balls both here and at Carusi's **(38)**.

(58) Lincoln attended a wedding on May 16, 1861, at the TRINITY EPISCOPAL CHURCH (SITE) AT THE NORTHEAST CORNER OF THIRD AND C STREETS.

(59) The ST. CHARLES HOTEL SITE is on the NORTHWEST CORNER OF THIRD STREET AND CONSTITUTION AVENUE, the present site of the U.S. Courthouse. Lincoln's first vice president, Hannibal Hamlin, lived at this location. After he was dumped in 1864, he enlisted and served as a private in the Maine Coast Guard for two months as a cook. He was later senator again from Maine, from 1869 to 1881.

Slave pens were under the sidewalk facing B Street, now Constitution Avenue. The hotel posted in the corridors a notice that "the Proprietor of this hotel has roomy underground cells for confining slaves for safekeeping, and patrons are notified that their slaves will be well cared for. In case of escape, full value of the negro will be paid by the Proprietor."

(60) The WASHINGTON MONUMENT was only partially completed to about 154 feet (figures vary). The stone used to finish the monument after the war did not quite match the prewar stone, as can be noticed when it is viewed closely. Freshman congressman Lincoln took part in the dedication ceremonies on July 4, 1848. His sons later played at the base and in the area while living at the White House. In mid-1861 Lincoln was riding in a carriage with his brother-in-law, C.M. Smith, near the Monument. Smith told the interviewer, John Nicolay, that the president asked him to guess the width of the structure. Lincoln then climbed down to pace off the dimensions, and sat down by the monument to continue their conversation. During the summer of 1863, the president and his oldest son tested a new repeating gun near the base.

Cattle were kept around the area and created a nuisance for the residents of the city. Mounted and infantry troops conducted training around the area, and Lincoln sometimes attended the testing of experimental and new weapons. The Potomac flowed just west of the monument site, separated from the White House area by a foul-smelling and dirty canal where Constitution Avenue is today. The canal widened into the Potomac at about Seventeenth Street, and President John Quincy Adams went skinny dipping there. This was the place where a woman reporter, possibly Anne Royall, stood over his clothes while he, at last, granted a long-sought-after interview while submerged in the water.

(61) The original **SMITHSONIAN** Building **(THE CASTLE)** was completed in 1856 and dominated the Mall. Lincoln was on the platform in front on January 3, 1862, when Horace Greeley faced the president and proposed the end of slavery as "the one sole purpose for the War." Lincoln sat "with an impassive face" as the crowd rose cheering. The president handed out awards here on July 24, 1862, at a school program. In early 1862, an army officer stormed into Lincoln's office with the head officer of the Smithsonian as prisoner and announced that he had proof that the learned and respected professor Joseph Henry was a Confederate spy. He had seen "red lights flashing from the roof at midnight signaling to the Secesh." Lincoln rose and said, "Now you're caught! What have you to say, Professor Henry, why sentence of death should not be immediately pronounced upon you?" Then the president smiled and explained that he himself had been with Henry "experimenting with army signals."

The **SMITHSONIAN HISTORY MUSEUM** is across the Mall. It contains various artifacts of President Lincoln and his family. Mary's dress is on permanent display in the First Lady's Gallery, and other Lincoln artifacts are exhibited on a temporary basis as the museum only keeps about 1 percent of its holdings on display at any one time. The dress Mary wore to Ford's Theater on April 14, 1865, may be seen with special permission.

(62) PENNSYLVANIA AVENUE was the city's main thoroughfare, then and now the ceremonial avenue of the nation. The city's business center was generally dusty or muddy. The streets were partially and badly paved with rough cobblestones and were gas-lit at night. Lincoln used this traditional presidential parade route to and from the Capitol in 1861 and 1865 for his inaugural parades, other trips to the Capitol, Navy Yard, and so on. Stephen Douglas rode with the president-elect during the 1861 parade to the Capitol. Riflemen stood guard on top of buildings on both sides of the street during the inaugural parades. Many regiments made a march down the avenue past the White House their first order of business. Lincoln reviewed them on the sidewalk in front of the Executive Mansion. Lincoln took many walks around the area covering the Avenue. Once someone thrust an armload of documents on the weary president as he was strolling here. He thrust them back, saying that this was no place to set up shop. On February 9, 1864, he gave up waiting for his carriage to go to Mathew Brady's, and walked with Tad from the Executive Mansion. This was the day he had images made, years later put on the copper penny, and the old and new $5 bill. The famous picture of him showing the large book to Tad was also taken then. As he walked he got tired of being called "Mr. President" and told people on the way to call him "Lincoln." Lincoln's funeral procession, composed of thirty thousand men, proceeded slowly down the avenue on April 19, 1865.

(63) The U.S. CAPITOL BUILDING is now much the same inside as it was then. During the war, it was still being renovated and the massive dome was still under construction. The old House of Representatives, now STATUARY HALL, was the site of Lincoln's service as a congressman from Illinois. He was elected in August 1846, but did not take his seat until December 6, 1847. This was the same day freshman senator Jefferson Davis took his seat in the senate. Lincoln drew one of the worst desk locations. Markers in the floor note the spot of the presidents who served in the room. Lincoln's desk was located toward the rear at the statue of Junipero Serra, depicted in priestly robes. Then the floors and ceilings were made of wood, and the "whisper effect" was common in various locations around the room. This is now pointed out by guides and demonstrated at John Quincy Adams's desk site, whereby sound bounces off the ceiling and is carried to another part of the room.

Lincoln was present when the respected ex-president suffered a stroke on February 21, 1848. Their desks were about twenty feet apart, but there is no record of any conversation between the two. The "Liberty" statue overlooking the front of the room and figure of Muse Clio in the chariot at the rear are original. The House used this hall from 1807 until moving to their present chambers in 1857.

One of Lincoln's frequent haunts was the nearby **HOUSE POST OFFICE**, a favorite place to gather and tell stories. A newspaperman wrote that Lincoln was the "the champion story-teller of the capitol." Like his reputation in Illinois, "he never told the same story twice, and seemed to have an endless repertoire always ready, like the successive charges of a magazine gun."

While serving as congressman, Lincoln sometimes listened to debates in the **OLD SENATE CHAMBER**, which served in that capacity from 1810 until 1859. The current picture of Washington, vice president's desk, shield, and eagle were in the chamber at the time. Mary sometimes listened to speeches in both chambers from the visitor's galleries. It is known that Lincoln heard Hannibal Hamlin and William Seward speak against slavery in the Old Senate Chamber. The Supreme Court met here for three quarters of a century beginning in 1860.

The **OLD SUPREME COURT CHAMBER** where the Court met from 1810 until 1860 is restored and open to the public. This was the scene of Lincoln's admission to practice before the court, and his losing argument of a case he had tried earlier in Springfield and appealed. This March 7, 1849, appearance before the Court was his only one (although he was involved in other appeals there) and was just after his congressional term ended. The figures representing Justice carved into the back wall are among the oldest in the Capitol. They were placed prior to the reopening of the building in 1819 after the British set fire to it during the War of 1812. Thomas Jefferson was sworn in as president in 1801 and 1805 in the room, and Chief Justice Roger B. Taney read his *Dred Scott* decision, fanning political fires leading to the Civil War.

While in Congress, the lonely representative frequented the Library of Congress and Supreme Court Library, both then in the Capitol. The **LIBRARY OF CONGRESS** was across from the Senate chamber until destroyed by fire in 1851. The current site is room S-230, the Howard H. Baker Jr. Room, not open to the public. Lincoln is described as carrying his borrowed books to and from the building by placing them on a bandana handkerchief, tying a knot, placing a stick through the knot, and then carrying the load with the stick on his shoulder. He reportedly struck up a friendship with another lonely House member who liked to read, his future vice president, Andrew Johnson.

When the new president arrived in Washington City in 1861, the Capitol was still being remodeled and enlarged from work begun a decade before. Secretary of war, Jefferson Davis had been in charge of the new construction. New CHAMBERS OF CONGRESS had been built since Lincoln's congressional service and are still in use. The president had several occasions to go to both Houses. He passed through the ROTUNDA often as president and congressman and visited soldiers quartered here during the Civil War and in both Houses. The statue of Jefferson now in the ROTUNDA was on the White House front lawn during his residency. The current large paintings and some of the other artwork were here at the time.

On the third day after arrival before his inauguration Lincoln went to both Houses of Congress and the Supreme Court. From the SENATE he heard Senator Crittenden of Kentucky give his farewell speech on March 3, 1861. Also here he witnessed the swearing in of Vice President Hamlin on March 4 with outgoing President Buchanan as they occupied seats in front of the secretary's desk. On December 11, 1861, he was formally introduced in the Senate and escorted to the vice president's chair for a memorial honoring Colonel Edward Baker, killed at the Battle of Ball's Bluff. Baker had introduced him at his inauguration. The president was jolted when Senator Charles Sumner looked directly at him during his eulogy and cried that slavery had murdered Lincoln's close friend. Lincoln and Mary heard readings in the chamber on January 18, 1863. The president was in the chamber just before his own second inauguration as Andrew Johnson was sworn in as vice president. Johnson had arrived unwell from Tennessee and, to steady himself, had drunk several glasses of whiskey offered by outgoing vice president Hamlin. Hamlin may have been hurt to have been dumped, and probably did not prevent his sick successor from leaving the vice president's office drunk. As Mary watched from the gallery, Johnson made a rambling, somewhat incoherent speech before he took Hamlin's nudging to quit.

On January 16, 1864, Lincoln heard popular lecturer Anna Elizabeth Dickinson in the HOUSE CHAMBER. He arrived as she was denouncing his liberal Reconstruction policies, sat opposite the platform, and then heard her endorse his reelection. Lincoln's face is said to have dropped even further, but no one could tell whether this was from the thought of four more years or from the controversial speaker's endorsement itself. He and his wife also attended a meeting of the U.S. Christian Commission in the House Chamber on February 2, 1864, and January 19, 1865, and came for other noncongressional meetings. He and the vice president stood to sing the "Battle Hymn of the Republic" in the chamber at a meeting of the U.S. Sanitary Commission on January 29, 1865.

The opulent **PRESIDENT'S ROOM** was designed for the use of visiting presidents, and first used to sign a bill into law by Lincoln. This is off the private lobby, on the north outside wall behind the northwest corner of the Senate Chamber. The mahogany table he used is still in the room.

Lincoln was inaugurated on March 4, 1861, before thirty thousand, at the east entrance facing the large, white, seated statue of Washington, now prominent in the Smithsonian's Museum of American History. The impressive dome was under construction and caused the building to resemble a Roman ruin. The president insisted that the work continue so that the people would know "we intend the Union to go on." Longtime rival Stephen Douglas held Lincoln's hat during the address. The Bible used is kept in the Rare Book and Special Collections Divisions of the Library of Congress. Outgoing president Buchanan was probably the most prepared man ever elected president. He had served the country for forty years; he was in both houses of Congress, was minister to Russia and Great Britain, and served in the cabinet as secretary of state. Lincoln was one of the most inexperienced men ever elected president. But Lincoln is considered our best president, and Buchanan one of the worst.

The president spoke in front of the building on August 6, 1862, to a large meeting. The 1865 inauguration took place on March 4, 1865, at the east front. Lincoln came early with Tad and spent the morning at the Capitol. Vice President Hamlin escorted him to the Senate Chamber, where he witnessed the swearing in of Andrew Johnson and his embarrassing behavior. John Wilkes Booth said that he passed near the president coming through the **ROTUNDA**, and professed that he had an excellent chance to shoot him then. Booth then stood above Lincoln to his left as he spoke, and can be seen there in a photograph during the Inaugural Address. He was there as a guest of Senator John P. Hale of New Hampshire, the father of his fiancée. He told a friend, "I was so close to the President that I could have shot him, had I wished to." The Second Inaugural Address is one of Lincoln's greatest literary works and carved on the wall of the Lincoln Memorial, as is the Gettysburg Address. A day later, the president and Mrs. Lincoln attended religious services and heard a sermon in the Capitol. A few weeks afterward Lincoln's coffin rested in the center of the rotunda, the first person to be so honored. Two companies of soldiers encircled it while the family funeral service was held with Robert, Tad, and members of the cabinet within the circle. The paneled pictures and statuary were covered with mourning cloth, except for the statue of Washington, which had a black sash. An observer wrote in 1911, "It is doubtful if the rotunda will ever again present so impressive a spectacle or one so deeply touching to the hearts of the American people."

Tad and his friend Holly Taft once got lost in the basement for several hours before they screamed for help. Also in the basement is a tomb site built for George Washington, although he was buried at Mount Vernon. The black-draped bier or catafalque can be seen, built to hold Lincoln's coffin. All of the coffins of the men who have lain in state in the Rotunda since Lincoln have also rested upon it, including the three other murdered presidents.

Lincoln's lifelike statue by Vinnie Ream at the west entrance was created in half-hour sessions during the president's last five months. The seventeen-year-old had been allowed to make sketches in the White House when Lincoln heard that she was poor and young. The statue of President Andrew Jackson at the Rotunda exit leading to the old senate chamber was the approximate location of an attempt to assassinate Jackson in 1835. Two pistols were fired point blank; both misfired but were later determined to be in perfect working order. During the beginning of the war, troops were quartered inside the building. Two thousand cots for wounded were set up in the congressional chambers, corridors, and rotunda after the Battle of Bull Run.

(64) The **OLD CAPITOL PRISON** was on the southeast corner of First Street and Maryland Avenue N.E., in front of the present **SUPREME COURT** Building. It was also the **"OLD BRICK CAPITOL,"** built in 1815 for the temporary home of Congress after the British had burned government buildings during the War of 1812. President James Monroe was inaugurated at the site. After serving in this capacity for four years it became a boarding-house for many prominent members of Congress, including John C. Calhoun who died there. During the war it was called the Old Capitol Prison, where various spies, including Rose O'Neal Greenhow and Belle Boyd, were kept. The commandant of infamous Andersonville Prison, Henry Wirz, was hanged in the yard.

(65) The home of **SENATOR O.H. BROWNING** from Illinois was on **A STREET (FORMALLY 4 A NORTH NEAR THE SUPREME COURT BUILDING,** where it was visited by the Lincolns. The Brownings were frequent White House visitors, and Lincoln sent a carriage for them to stay at the White House when Willie died. The couples made many visits and spent much time together. Sometimes the Lincolns would bring their carriage here to take Browning to or from the New York Avenue Church. Browning had been appointed to fill out Douglas's senatorial term in 1861. He was probably too close a friend and evidently never felt Lincoln was "big enough for his position," as stated several times in his diary and to others. He became increasingly opposed to Lincoln's administration, but remained a close friend. He was one of Lincoln's pallbearers at the White House funeral and served President Johnson as secretary of the interior.

(66) The **BALTIMORE AND OHIO TRAIN STATION** was on the **NORTHEAST CORNER OF NEW JERSEY BETWEEN D AND C STREETS, AT THE LOUISIANA STREET JUNCTION.** Because of probable assassination plots revealed by Detective Allan Pinkerton, President-elect Lincoln arrived here secretly on February 23, 1861, after leaving his official party and family. Congressman Washburne surprised him at 6:00 A.M. and drove him to Willard's Hotel. Whether the plot was real or not, Lincoln always regretted his mode of arrival into the capital. He used the station several times during the presidency. His funeral train to Illinois left from here in April 1865. A corner of the present Union Terminal touches the site, now vacant. The depot was north of the Taft Memorial.

(67) The Lincolns lived in a boardinghouse run by **MRS. SPRIGG** during his congressional term, at the present site of the **LIBRARY OF CONGRESS, JEFFERSON BUILDING,** at the **SOUTHEAST CORNER OF EAST CAPITOL AND FIRST STREETS S.E.** Illinois congressional predecessors John Stuart and Edward Baker also used this boardinghouse. The family moved here probably in late 1847. Lincoln stayed during the rest of his first and second sessions, until the end of his term in 1849. The site is now at the main or Jefferson Building of the Library of Congress. (Lincoln was so poor when he came to Congress that he had to borrow $167 from rival Stephen Douglas.) Mary, Robert, and Eddie left in the spring to go to Mary's family in Lexington, Kentucky. The two boys were the only children there at the time and Mary had been unable to break into Washington society as she wished. Also living here were prominent senator Thomas Hart Benton and his family, including daughter Jessie with husband John C. Frémont. He had just returned from California under court-martial. In 1856, Frémont became the first presidential nominee of the Republican Party. During the Civil War, the buildings were used as a prison. There is some evidence that Lincoln changed his residence sometime in 1849, but the location is unknown. While here he frequented nearby Caspari's bowling alley.

East Capitol Street between First and Second Streets was an open market in the middle of the street, which could be seen by Lincoln from the windows of his boardinghouse and from the Capitol. He called these "a sort of Negro Livery Stable." Slave trading was not abolished in the District until 1850. One of the black servants at his boardinghouse was seized and carried to the slave pen, and then to the auction block in New Orleans. The poor man had paid all but $60 of his $300 price. Lincoln and others tried in vain to help him.

The exact site of Lincoln's boardinghouse is near the street just north of the northern steps of the Jefferson Building. As seen from old photographs, Pennsylvania Avenue intersected First Street where the Neptune Statue and fountain are now. From this point, Mrs. Sprigg's can be seen in pictures about a third of a block north toward East Capitol Street, now part of the lawn in front of the present Library.

(68) FREDERICK DOUGLASS lived at **316–318 A STREET, S.E.** from 1871 to 1877, then moved to **1411 WEST STREET, S.E.** It is now the Douglass **RESIDENCE AND MEMORIAL HOUSE**, and was built about 1855. These were the homes of the man who escaped slavery and met with Lincoln in the White House at least three times to discuss race problems. He stated that Lincoln treated him very courteously without regard to his race. He felt that this was because of their common status as poor boys who had made good. He remarked, "I was impressed with his entire freedom from popular prejudice against the colored race. He was the first great man that I talked with in the Unites States freely, who in no single instance reminded me of the difference between myself, of the difference of color, and I thought that all the more remarkable because he came from a State where there were black laws (forbidding blacks to migrate into the state)." After hearing Lincoln's Second Inaugural Address, he surprisingly made an appearance at a postinauguration reception at the White House where no blacks had ever been allowed. He was barred until Lincoln heard he was there and sent word to allow "his friend Douglass" to enter.

(69) The SIXTH STREET WHARVES, at SIXTH STREET, S.E., SOUTH OF THE CAPITOL AT THE RIVER, NORTH OF FORT MCNAIR, was a busy port during the war where many troops and wounded arrived. The wounded would lie in a large area to be taken to the city's hospitals. On July 11, 1864, with Confederate general Early attacking the northern edge of the city, Lincoln, munching a piece of hardtack for lunch, rode down to the docks to watch the arrival of Union infantrymen who would save the capital.

(70) The WASHINGTON ARSENAL AT FORT MCNAIR, AT FOURTH AND P STREETS, S.W., was the site of the U.S. Arsenal—burned by the British in 1814—and the Washington Penitentiary. In 1864 twenty-four women were killed by an explosion while working here. Lincoln attended the funeral here and led the procession to the CONGRESSIONAL CEMETERY **(74)**, where they were buried. A constant stream of munitions, cannons, rifles, wagons, ambulances, ammunition, shells, cannon balls, etc., were sent from this area. The penitentiary was built in 1820 and closed during the war. On June 24, 1861, Lincoln observed a demonstration of a "Coffee Mill" gun on the grounds with several cabinet members and five generals.

John Wilkes Booth was secretly buried on April 27, 1865, in the floor of the jailer's quarters, now at about the front yard of Quarters 14 on Second Avenue. Two days later the assassination conspirators were moved to a jail here from the Navy Yard.

Their trial was in a building now used as apartments for young army officers and their families on Second Avenue. The defendants included the four who were hanged here, Lewis Powell, David Herold, Mary Surratt, and George Atzerodt, and four others sentenced to prison. The government made no distinction between those involved in the conspiracy to kidnap the president and those involved in the violence of April 14. It was all considered one plot. Boston and New York newspapers reported that Tad was present on the first day of the trial, May 18. Over three hundred witnesses were called, but the defendants were not allowed to testify, as was customary at this time. Some of the government witnesses were proved to be liars later.

Michael O' Laughlen and Samuel Arnold had dissociated with Booth several weeks before, arguing that the plot to kidnap had no chance to succeed. (O' Laughlen is also spelled "O' Laughlin."

The spelling used here is from his tombstone in Baltimore.) Both had left town before the crime, but a letter was found in Booth's room from Arnold, mentioning O' Laughlen. Without this they probably would not have been connected with Booth's crime.

Edman Spangler only held Booth's horse for a short time at Ford's Theater. He was accused of aiding Booth in his escape, and possibly in helping prepare the theater and agreeing to turn off the lights. Dr. Mudd had treated Booth's broken leg, lied in various matters, and probably could have revealed to authorities where Booth was in time for him to be apprehended while at his home in Maryland. He had met Booth several times, but lied about his meetings. Mary Surratt ran the boardinghouse where some of the discussions may have been held and delivered packages to a tavern in Maryland where Booth stopped on his escape. The tavern keeper in Maryland, John Lloyd, and her boarder, Weichmann, were instrumental in her conviction by revealing numerous innuendoes about hushed conversations between her and others in the plot. She also lied about knowing Powell when he showed up at her house on April 17. Various statements by these defendants were used to insinuate knowledge of Booth's plans although they could have been interpreted otherwise. All might have revealed their assumed knowledge of either the plot to assassinate before the actual crime or Booth's whereabouts afterward. Booth's diary was not admitted into evidence by the government and not demanded by the defense. This contained statements by Booth that separated the two plots. Those not hung were sent to Fort Jefferson in the Florida Keys.

The site of the hanging is the tennis court marking the general outline of the old prison yard adjacent to the three-story building used as the court and prison. They were buried near the platform. The much-changed court building and yard site are clearly shown in pictures of the hanging. Mrs. Surratt's ghost is said to be lurking about the building. Fortunately, she is said to be gentle with children but has an extreme dislike for high-ranking officers.

When the old penitentiary was torn down in 1867, the bodies of the conspirators and Henry Wirz, the commandant of the notorious Andersonville Prison who was the only person hanged after the Civil War for war crimes, were removed to a warehouse on the east side of the parade grounds. In February 1869, President Johnson released the bodies to their families and pardoned the prisoners at Fort Jefferson. (O' Laughlen had died earlier.) Mrs. Surratt and Wirz were buried at **MOUNT OLIVET CEMETERY**

(BLADENSBURG ROAD OR U.S. HIGHWAY 1 AND OLIVET ROAD). Mrs. Surratt is in the back on the right side.

(71) The COMMANDANT'S HOUSE, MARINE BARRACKS, AT G STREET BETWEEN EIGHTH AND NINTH STREETS, S.E., is said to be the oldest government building in the capital in continuous use and dates to 1801. Lincoln came by or near here on his frequent trips to the Navy Yard.

(72) Lincoln made frequent trips through the LATROBE GATE AT EIGHTH AND M STREETS, S.E. to the NAVY YARD, AT M AND 9TH STREETS, S.E., sometimes with Willie and Tad, or with Secretaries Welles and Stanton. Reviews were made of many new inventions and mechanical devises tested on the grounds. He received a twenty-one gun salute on April 26, 1862, as he boarded a French frigate, the first president to set foot on a French ship. He also attended several funerals during his term and viewed Colonel Ellsworth's body twice on May 24, 1861.

Several Civil War–era structures include Quarters A, built about 1804, adjacent to the Latrobe Gate on the east side, and two structures down Ninth Street on the west side north of N Street The northernmost dates from 1801, and the Marine Corps Historical Center dates to the mid-1800s. A historical marker in front of the commandant's office relates Lincoln's visits here to Admiral John Dahlgren, a special favorite, and others. This is just east of the Naval Museum. Lincoln visited Dahlgren almost every week to escape the pressures of his office.

When the president visited the army in Virginia, he took a steamer from here. When he returned on April 9, 1865, the family was surprised to see crowds of noisy, celebrating people. Tad called to a bystander for an explanation. The man yelled back, "Why, where have you been? Lee has surrendered!" The president drove out here with Mrs. Lincoln late in the afternoon on April 14, 1865, happy that the war was over, and stretched his legs on the deck of the monitor *Montauk* moored at the dock. At the time of his assassination, the *Montauk* was still berthed here, and the suspects in the crime were retained on board. The body of John Wilkes Booth was later placed on the boat, where an autopsy was performed and numerous identifications were made to ensure that the dead man was indeed Booth. He had taken the Navy Yard Bridge in his escape, about where the present Eleventh Street Bridge goes into Maryland. Booth arrived here within minutes of shooting Lincoln. He was questioned by the guard, gave his correct name and destination (Beantown, where Dr. Mudd lived), and was allowed to pass.

(73) The Long Bridge site is about two tenths of a mile downstream frcm the present **FOURTEENTH STREET BRIDGE**, also known as **THE GEORGE MASON OR INTERSTATE 395 BRIDGE**. On June 13, 1861, the president, along with Secretaries Cameron and Chase, drove over the bridge to inspect camps in Virginia, but walked back across because of damaged beams. Lincoln inspected forts and camps on the south side of the Potomac between here and the **CHAIN BRIDGE**, 3.3 miles upriver from the present Key Bridge at **ROUTES 120 AND 123**. The president attended flag-raising ceremonies at the Chain Bridge and visited camps on June 27, 1861. A railroad bridge called the Long Bridge is here now.

(74) Our first national cemetery is the **CONGRESSIONAL CEMETERY, SEVENTEENTH AND G STREETS, S.E.** Lincoln was on a congressional committee that conveyed John Quincy Adam's body here for burial. Later it was removed for burial in Massachusetts. In October 1861 the president accompanied the body of his close friend, Colonel Edward D. Baker, to his temporary burial site. Photographer Mathew Brady is buried at range 72, site 120. Assassin Davy Herold is at range 46, site 44. Conspirator Lewis Powell (Paine) hid in a tomb here after his attempt on the life of Secretary Seward. He was supposed to meet Booth, but got lost and spent three hungry, cold days in a marble vault.

(75) Lincoln used the **ANDERSON COTTAGE AT THE UNITED STATES SOLDIERS AND AIRMEN'S HOME, ROCK CREEK CHURCH ROAD AND UPSHUR STREET, N.W.**, as a summer White House after 1861. He is said to have spent about 30 percent of his presidency living at the cottage. In mid-2000, President Clinton declared the building used by the Lincoln family as the President Lincoln and Soldiers' Home National Monument. The family moved wagon loads of their furniture and belongings to the home preferred over the more public White House. According to the National Trust for Historic Preservation, a copper beech tree still stands in the yard where Lincoln played with Tad, set his desk and chair, read Shakespeare, and relaxed. Several presidents stayed at this dwelling during their terms, beginning with James Buchanan. Secretary of War Edwin Stanton and his family sometimes lived in another cottage, and the two families spent considerable time together. Although only three miles north of the White House, it was in a rural setting and cooler than the city. Mary would stay as the president rode back and forth to the White House along Vermont Street, sometimes with Tad on his pony. At times the president rode with an armed escort that he did not like. He compared the escort to the twirl in a pig's tail: "it apparently had no purpose, but God (like Secretary of War Stanton), who knows all, must have known what he was doing." The second and final draft of the Emancipation Proclamation was drafted in the upper corner room at the left end of the building under the big gray gable. Other important work and government business was done here, and he met with cabinet members, the vice president, and others frequently. Once near the main gate, Lincoln heard a shot and lost his stovepipe hat after riding through the gate at a full gallop. Soldiers went out to investigate, and brought back his hat with a bullet hole through it. The president and his wife also liked to visit military hospitals in the area, generally along Boundary (now Florida) Street. (*Lincoln. Lore 1589*, July 1970, lists dates at the Home.) The cottage and adjacent main building have changed little since the Civil War.

(76) On July 2, 1863, Mrs. Lincoln's horse ran away near **MOUNT PLEAS-ANT HOSPITAL, AT FOURTEENTH STREET AND FLORIDA AVENUE**, as she was in her carriage. Someone, probably trying to injure the president, had unscrewed the bolts to the seat and it came loose, frightening the horses. She jumped or was thrown at high speed, suffering bruises and a large head gash. Doctors were called to come over from the hospital to treat her. She required three weeks of constant nursing, and her headaches increased. Robert felt that she never recovered.

(77) Remains of **FORT STEVENS, AT THIRTEENTH AND QUAKENBOS STREETS**, are on the Seventh Street Pike. This is just south of Walter Reed Hospital off Highway 29 at Georgia Street. In July 1864 Confederates invaded Washington, D.C., from the north. The president and Mrs. Lincoln rode out on July 11 to witness some of the action. The president's position came under fire, and a man nearby was wounded. Solders "roughly ordered" him off the parapet. The next day, the president and his wife again drove out to the fort with Stanton and Seward to watch the attack of Jubal Early's Confederate troops. Eyewitnesses told of Lincoln climbing the bullet-swept parapet, making himself an easy target. A soldier next to him was shot, and Captain Oliver Wendell Holmes, the future Supreme Court justice, reportedly yelled to the president, "Get down you damned fool." After the president finally sat down on an ammunition box, he continued to pop up to see what was going on. Confederate prisoners claimed they recognized the president and shot at him. This was the first time a U.S. president was under fire during battle. Plaques mark the parapet where Lincoln stood and the famous tulip tree used by sharpshooters. The latter is about one hundred yards inside the Georgia Street entrance to Walter Reed Hospital. (See **SILVER SPRING, MARYLAND,** for locations of Lincoln's visits to a nearby home.)

(78) The site of the **LINCOLN MEMORIAL** and an area almost to the Washington Monument was in the Potomac River until the twentieth century, when it was reclaimed. Dry land was created out of Potomac River marshes with landfill and foundations partly with the original columns of the Treasury Building when they were replaced in 1907. It is sometimes said that the sculptor of the seated Lincoln, Daniel Chester French, had a deaf son; so Lincoln's left hand is in the shape of an *A*, and the right forms an *L* in sign language. However, French wrote many letters stating that this was not true. The left hand was modeled after the Volk cast of Lincoln's hand, and a model of French's own right hand was used. Originally Lincoln was to sit with his left leg forward, but when Robert Lincoln saw the model he stated that his father would have sat with the right leg out as now shown. At the dedication on Memorial Day, 1922, blacks were segregated to a position across the road. When installed the statue had a surprising effect. During part of the day a reflection was like a flashlight being held under one's chin. This lighting problem took several years to correct.

(79) Lincoln often visited The **OLD NAVEL OBSERVATORY (SITE), SOUTH OF E STREET BETWEEN TWENTY-THIRD AND TWENTY-FIFTH STREET** and north of the Lincoln Memorial. Mathew Fontaine Maury, the "pathfinder of the seas," made many scientific discoveries here.

(80) The museum at **WALTER REED ARMY MEDICAL CENTER, AT GEORGIA AVENUE AND FOURTEENTH STREET, N.E.**, displays Lincoln assassination artifacts including the bullet that killed him, part of his skull, and hair removed from the wound. (Part of President Garfield's spinal column showing the path of the bullet that killed him is also displayed, as is General Daniel Sickles's leg.)

GEORGETOWN

Up the Potomac from Washington, Georgetown was a thriving port before the national capital site was chosen. Lincoln visited forts and camps in the area near the bridge and college on several occasions. The town was known as "Southern city" in 1861, and not part of Washington until 1871. After the First Battle of Bull Run in July 1861, many town houses and churches were converted into makeshift hospitals.

(81) The **OAK HILL CEMETERY, AT THIRTIETH AND R STREETS IN GEORGETOWN**, contains the **WILLIAM T. CARROLL VAULT** where Willie Lincoln was buried. It is near the northwest corner, down a hill overlooking Rock Creek. Other vaults at the Carroll site and nearby were filled and in place at the time Lincoln visited and revisited. There are disputed claims that Lincoln had the body twice disinterred or opened the lid to view his son. It is also believed that Lincoln drove by here several times and stood at the gate of the tomb to look inside. The funeral was held in the White House on February 23, 1862, and repeated for the president in the **OAK HILL GOTHIC CHAPEL**, still near the entrance. After the death of the president, Willie's body traveled with his father's back to Springfield. Children were admitted to the funeral car to put flowers on Willie's coffin as they "thought he might be lonely."

Secretary of War **EDWIN M. STANTON'S GRAVE** can be seen from the street, through the fence just north of the end of **R STREET AT TWENTY-EIGHT STREET**. **JOHN NICOLAY**, one of Lincoln's private secretaries, and Dr. **JOSEPH BARNES**, who examined the fatally injured president in the Petersen House, are also buried here.

(82) Major General Henry W. **HALLECK** rented the house at **3238 R STREET** when he was general-in-chief of the Union armies. Lincoln and Grant consulted with him here, and Grant used it as a summer White House during his presidency.

(83) The **METHODIST EPISCOPAL CHURCH, AT 3127 DUMBARTON STREET**, N.W., served as an army hospital and was visited by Lincoln to comfort the wounded.

(84) **ROBERT TODD LINCOLN** lived at **3014 N STREET** when not in Vermont after purchasing the home in 1915. This was the former home of James Dunlop who was the chief justice of the Circuit Court of the District of Columbia at the outbreak of the Civil War and a relative of Robert E. Lee through marriage. President Lincoln had removed him from the bench for his Southern sympathies. Robert built a house at 3018 N Street for his daughter, Mrs. Lincoln Isham. Earlier, while secretary of war, he had rented a house on Massachusetts Avenue, just east of Thomas Circle.

(85) Lincoln was very familiar with the sight of Robert E. Lee's beautiful Arlington House overlooking the capital from across the Potomac. It is now known as the **CUSTIS-LEE MANSION IN ARLINGTON**

NATIONAL CEMETERY. Robert Lincoln and his father's young secretaries obtained a pass to visit on May 31, 1861. They went inside when they talked with "an old negro" born at Mount Vernon before Washington died. There is no record that the president ever entered the mansion. He ordered it converted to a hospital on June 16, 1862.

This was the home of Lee's father-in-law, George Washington Parke Custis. Custis was the grandson of Martha Washington from her earlier marriage and was adopted by George Washington. Lee married Custis's only child in the parlor. Custis later died, leaving the house to his daughter for life, and then to his oldest grandchild and namesake, George Washington Custis Lee. When the Lees were forced to move on May 16, 1861, they took as much of the George Washington artifacts as they could. Some others were found and or stored in the Patent Office. Persons unknown carried off the rest. The family lost the house when it became legally necessary to pay the property tax in person during the war, which was impossible for Mrs. Lee. The federal government then confiscated the property and converted it to a cemetery partly to prevent it from ever being inhabited by a Lee, so the story goes. Lincoln and General Meigs were on a routine visit to the army's tent hospital near the mansion when they noticed bodies awaiting delivery to the Soldiers' Home for burial. Knowing that the cemetery there was full and that there would be a need for the many others who were dying, Meigs ordered the bodies buried where they were near ARLINGTON HOUSE. The first body buried was a Confederate.

Robert E. Lee's son, Custis, a general for the Confederacy, reacquired the property in 1882 as the result of a Supreme Court decision. He then sold the property to the government for $150,000. ROBERT TODD LINCOLN AND HIS SON, ABRAHAM LINCOLN II (1873–1890), are buried not far from the Mansion, about one hundred yards down a path to the north. Their graves are prominently marked to the east of the path. Robert's son was the last "Lincoln" heir, although his sisters and their children survived until the last descendant of the president died in 1985.

Robert had two daughters. Daughter Mary had three children who all died childless. Jessie had a daughter who never married. Her son, Lincoln's great-grandson Robert Todd Lincoln Beckwith, married twice. His first wife had children by a prior marriage, but she died without having another, thirty-five years later. Beckwith, at age sixty-three married a twenty-seven-year-old who had a son the next year, evidently conceived two months before the wedding. Beckwith earlier had a vasectomy and claimed to be sterile. Divorce proceedings began and the mother refused to permit blood tests. The court granted the divorce and ruled that the child was the product of an adulterous relationship. Beckwith had no children by his third wife. After he died in 1985 at age eighty-one, his second wife again raised the claim that the boy had been his. The charities that received the estate of Beckwith's mother after the death of all her heirs later settled the child's claim of heirship, for reportedly about $1 million.

(86) FORT LINCOLN was located on FORT LINCOLN DRIVE AND COMMODORE JOSHUA BARNEY DRIVE, just south of U.S. Highway 1, on the grounds of the elementary school with the same name, at the District of Columbia border with Maryland, and just west of the Fort Lincoln Cemetery. Lincoln met the commander under the "Lincoln Oak," overlooking the Bladensburg dueling grounds and 1814 battlefield when the victorious British then advanced into Washington, D.C. President James Madison had witnessed the defeat, allowing the enemy to enter and burn the city.

(87) The remains of the FORT FOOTE, MARYLAND, FORT FOOTE ROAD AND PARK, are some of the best in the area. This is about three miles south of Interstate 95/495, at exit 3 and on the east bank of the Potomac off Oxon Hill Road. Lincoln was here August 20, 1863, with members of the cabinet. The fortification made nearby FORT WASHINGTON obsolete; that old masonry fort could not hold up to the canon fire of the war were it placed under siege. Fort Washington is just to the south on Old Fort Road off Route 210 and still an impressive sight from both sides of the river. Lincoln was there on October 19, 1861.

SUMMARY OF LINCOLN SITES IN WASHINGTON, D.C.

(1) WHITE HOUSE (Sixteenth Street and Pennsylvania Avenue): Home of the presidents. Open on a limited basis.

(2) WAR DEPARTMENT SITE (Seventeenth Street and Pennsylvania Avenue, southeast corner): Telegraph office frequently visited by Lincoln. Now Executive Office Building.

(3) NAVY DEPARTMENT SITE (East side of F and Seventeenth Streets): South side of the above.

(4) **GENERAL WINFIELD SCOTT'S RESIDENCE SITE** (1732 Pennsylvania Avenue).

(5) **JEFFERSON DAVIS RESIDENCE SITE** (north side of G Street between Seventeenth and Eighteenth Streets)

(6) **WILLIAM CARROLL RESIDENCE SITE** (Eighteenth and F Streets): Lincoln attended a wedding on December 10, 1861. Carroll owned the vault where Willie was buried.

(7) **OFFICE OF COMMISSARY GENERAL** (northeast corner of Twentieth and F Streets): John Wilkes Booth sought information from Louis Weichmann who worked in the building.

(8) **GENERAL WINFIELD SCOTT'S OFFICE SITE** (southwest corner of seventeenth and F Streets): Across from the Winder Building.

(9) **WINDER BUILDING** (northwest corner of Seventeenth and F Streets): Many Union general had offices including Scott, McClellan, and Grant.

(10) **OCTAGON HOUSE** (northeast corner of Eighteenth Street and New York Avenue): President Madison's home after the White House was burned down during the War of 1812. Open to the public.

(11) **JUSTICE JOHN MARSHALL RESIDENCE** (1801 F Street): General George McClellan lived there for a time.

(12) **WHITE HOUSE ELLIPSE**: Camp for troops. Lincoln's sons rode horses on the grounds.

(13) **RENWICK ART GALLERY** (northeast corner of Pennsylvania Avenue and Seventeenth Street): Built as an art gallery, but used in war as largest distribution center for quartermaster. Open to the public.

(14) **BLAIR LEE HOUSE** (east of Renwick): Robert E. Lee offered command of Union troops.

(15) **LAFAYETTE PARK**: Playground for Lincoln boys. The president often walked through the park on the way to church and to see McClellan in his residence and headquarters.

(16) **MAJOR HENRY RATHBONE RESIDENCE SITE** (712 Jackson Place): Rathbone was Lincoln's guest at Ford's Theater on April 14, 1865.

(17) **DECATUR HOUSE** (southwest corner of Jackson Place and H Street): Home of naval hero Decatur, Henry Clay, and President Van Buren. Headquarters of the commissary general during the Civil War. Open to the public.

(18) **SECRETARY OF THE NAVY GIDEON WELLES'S RESIDENCE SITE** (1607 H Street at Sixteenth Street): Lincoln visited; Robert stayed after the war.

(19) **ST. JOHN'S CHURCH** (northeast of corner of H and Sixteenth

Streets): Attended by maybe all presidents, except Washington, including Lincoln. Open to the public.

(20) CUTTS-MADISON HOUSE (southeast corner of Madison Avenue and H Street): Residence and headquarters of McClellan from November 1861 through March 1862.

(21) GENERAL MCCLELLAN'S residence SITE in September 1862 (northwest corner of Fifteenth and H Streets): he was here when he was reinstalled as commanding general.

(22) SECRETARY OF STATE WILLIAM SEWARD'S residence SITE: Lincoln was a frequent visitor. Seward was attacked by Payne here.

(23) HEADQUARTERS FOR THEN DEFENSE OF WASHINGTON SITE (northeast corner of Pennsylvania Avenue and Madison Place): McClellan's headquarters in September 1862.

(24) RIGGS BANK SITE (northwest corner of Fifteenth Street and Pennsylvania Avenue): Lincoln's bank.

(25) GENERAL JAMES W. WEBB RESIDENCE SITE (Fourteenth and H Streets): Lincoln attended his friend General Edward Baker's funeral.

(26) TREASURY DEPARTMENT BUILDING (Fifteenth Street and Pennsylvania Avenue): President Andrew Johnson occupied an office before the Lincoln family moved.

(27) STATE DEPARTMENT BUILDING SITE (southwest corner of Fifteenth Street and Pennsylvania Avenue): Lincoln frequently visited Secretary Seward.

(28) FOUNDRY METHODIST CHURCH (Fourteenth and G Streets): Lincoln attended with cabinet.

(29) EPIPHANY CHURCH (north side of G street between Thirteenth and Fourteenth Streets): Visited as a church and hospital by Lincoln.

(30) STUNTZ FANCY OR TOYSHOP SITE (1207 New York Avenue): Lincoln frequently brought his sons to buy toys.

(31) NEW YORK AVENUE PRESBYTERIAN CHURCH (New York Avenue and H Street): Lincoln attended. (Reconstructed) Open to the public.

(32) SECRETARY OF STATE EDWIN M. STANTON RESIDENCE SITE (1323 K Street): Lincoln visited many times. Stanton lived and died in the home.

(33) HORATIO TAFT RESIDENCE SITE (near Twelfth and L Streets): Second home to the Lincoln boys until Willie died.

(34) GROVER'S THEATER (now National Theater) (1322 Pennsylvania Avenue at E Street): Lincoln attended many times. Tad was here when his father was shot. Open for performances.

(35) WILLARD'S HOTEL (northwest corner of Fourteenth Street and Pennsylvania Avenue): Most famous hotel in the city. Lincoln and

his family stayed before the inauguration. (Reconstructed.) Open for business.

(36) **GAUTIER'S RESTAURANT SITE** (south side of Pennsylvania Avenue between Twelfth and Thirteenth Streets): Only meeting of the conspirators with Booth to plan the kidnapping of the president.

(37) **KIRKWOOD HOUSE SITE** (northeast corner of Twelfth Street and Pennsylvania Avenue): Hotel occupied by Vice President Andrew Johnson.

(38) **CARUSI'S HALL SITE** (northeast corner of Eleventh and C Streets, now IRS): Lincoln and family attended plays.

(39) **FORD'S THEATER** (511 Tenth Street): Lincoln was assassinated here. Open to the public.

(40) **PETERSEN HOUSE** (516 Tenth Street): Lincoln died in rear bedroom. Open to the public.

(41) **HERNDON HOUSE SITE** (southwest corner of Ninth and F Streets): Final meeting of assassination conspirators.

(42) **PATENT OFFICE** (between F, G, Seventh, and Ninth Streets): Lincoln visited this 1836 building as a congressman and had his second inaugural ball.

(43) **POST OFFICE BUILDING** (now Tariff Commission): Built before Lincoln's congressional term.

(44) **FOURTH PRESBYTERIAN CHURCH SITE** (west side of Ninth Street between F and G Streets, now Martin Luther King Jr. Library): Attended by Lincoln's younger sons.

(45) **ALEXANDER GARDNER'S PHOTOGRAPHY STUDIO SITE** (northeast corner of Seventh and D Streets): Frequented by Lincoln.

(46) **MARY SURRATT'S BOARDING HOUSE** (604 H Street): Nest where the plot against Lincoln was hatched. Restaurant is open.

(47) **SECRETARY OF THE TREASURY AND SUPREME COURT CHIEF JUSTICE SALMON CHASE RESIDENCE SITE** (northwest corner of Sixth and E Streets): Lincoln entertained many times.

(48) **MATHEW BRADY'S** Photography studio (633 Pennsylvania Avenue): Frequented by Lincoln.

(49) **DANIEL WEBSTER RESIDENCE SITE** (north side D Street between Fifth and Sixth Streets): Lincoln breakfasted here as a congressman.

(50) **BROWN'S HOTEL SITE** (northwest corner of Pennsylvania Avenue and Sixth Street): Lincoln family lived here for a while in 1848.

(51) **NATIONAL HOTEL SITE** (Northeast corner of Pennsylvania Avenue and Sixth Street): Booth lived here: Lincoln made speeches here.

(52) **PUMPHREY'S STABLE SITE** (northeast corner of C and Seventh Streets): Booth rented the horse used to escape.

(53) **TYNE'S BOARDING HOUSE SITE** (east of northeast corner of Seventh and D Streets): Conspirators O' Laughlen and Arnold lived on this site.

(54) **RESIDENCES OF SENATOR STEPHEN DOUGLAS, GENERAL ULYSSES S. GRANT, AND GENERAL WILLIAM T. SHERMAN SITES** (205 I Street, between New Jersey Avenue and First Street, under Interstate 395).

(55) **CITY HOSPITAL SITE** (north side of E Street between Fourth and Fifth Streets): Lincoln visited here.

(56) **OLD CITY HALL** (D and Fourth Streets): Lincoln's first inaugural ball was located just north in a temporary structure.

(57) **JOHN MARSHALL PARK** (northwest corner of Fourth Street and Pennsylvania Avenue): Several presidents' and Chief Justice John Marshall's residence. Also sites of **FIRST PRESBYTERIAN CHURCH** and **JACKSON HALL** where Lincoln attended President Taylor's inaugural ball in 1849.

(58) **TRINITY EPISCOPAL CHURCH SITE**, (Third and C Streets): Lincoln attended a wedding here.

(59) **ST. CHARLES HOTEL SITE** (northwest corner of Constitution Avenue and Third Street): Vice President Hamlin residence.

(60) **WASHINGTON MONUMENT**: Congressman Lincoln attended dedication here on July 4, 1848, and later stepped off dimensions. Open to the public.

(61) **ORIGINAL SMITHSONIAN BUILDINGS** (south side of Mall, across from Natural History Museum): Lincoln spoke and visited many times. Open to the public.

(62) **PENNSYLVANIA AVENUE**: "Avenue of the Presidents."

(63) **UNITED STATED CAPITOL BUILDING**: Lincoln served as congressman here, and later was inaugurated twice from the east steps. He attended ceremonies in old and new chambers. Open to the public.

(64) **OLD CAPITOL PRISON SITE**: Now location of corner in front of Supreme Court Building, building during the war used as Capitol Building in 1815.

(65) **O.H. BROWNING RESIDENCE SITE**: Home of the close friend of the president.

(66) **B & O RAILROAD DEPOT SITE** (northeast corner of New Jersey Avenue between C and D Streets): Where Lincoln first arrived as president and used later.

(67) **LIBRARY OF CONGRESS, SITE OF CARROLL BOARDING HOUSE** (southeast corner of Capitol and First Street): Lincolns lived on site, now on lawn, here in 1848–1849.

(68) **FREDERICK DOUGLASS RESIDENCE** (316 A Street N.E.): 1870.

(69) **SIXTH STREET WHARVES** (near sixth and M Streets, south of Air and Space Museum): Lincoln visited this port.

(70) **FORT MCNAIR** (at junction of Anacostia and Potomac Rivers): U.S. arsenal visited by Lincoln. Conspirators tried and hung. Open with permission at gate.

(71) **COMMANDANT'S HOUSE, MARINE BARRACKS** (G Street between Eighth and Ninth Streets S.E.): Oldest government building in Washington continuously in use.

(72) **NAVY YARD** (eighth and M Streets S.E.): Lincoln frequently visited. Booth used nearby bridge to escape. Open with permission at gate.

(73) **LONG BRIDGE SITE** (near modern bridge into Alexandria south of the Jefferson Memorial): Used by Lincoln.

(74) **CONGRESSIONAL CEMETERY** (Seventeenth and G Streets S.E.): Lincoln came in 1864 and in 1848 accompanied the body of Ex-President John Quincy Adams when buried. Open to the public.

(75) **SOLDIERS HOME** (Rock Creek Church Road and Upshur): Lincoln and family used as summer White House.

(76) **MOUNT PLEASANT HOSPITAL SITE** (Fourteenth Street and Florida Avenue): Visited by Lincoln.

(77) **FORT STEVENS SITE** (Rock Creek Church and Upshur, near Howard and Catholic Universities): Lincoln was under fire here from Jubal Early's troops. Open to the public.

(78) **LINCOLN MEMORIAL**: Open to the public.

(79) **NAVAL OBSERVATORY SITE** (north of Lincoln Memorial): Lincoln frequently visited.

(80) **WALTER REED ARMY MEDICAL CENTER MUSEUM**: Displays bullet that killed Lincoln, parts of skull, and other artifacts of the assassination. Open to the public.

(81) **OAK HILL CEMETERY** (Thirtieth and R Streets): Willie Lincoln was first buried here, as well as Stanton and Nicolay. Open to the public.

(82) **GENERAL HENRY HALLECK HOUSE** (3238 R Street): Lincoln visited. Grant used as summer White House.

(83) **METHODIST EPISCOPAL CHURCH** (3127 Dumbarton): Lincoln visited.

(84) **ROBERT T. LINCOLN HOME** (3014 N Street): Robert's residence after 1915.

(85) **CUSTIS-LEE MANSION**: Lee's home. Open to the public.

(86) **FORT LINCOLN**: Visited by the president.

(87) **FORT FOOTE**: Visited by the president.

Many other original buildings dating to Lincoln's residency are not listed above, although they remain in Washington and nearby Virginia.

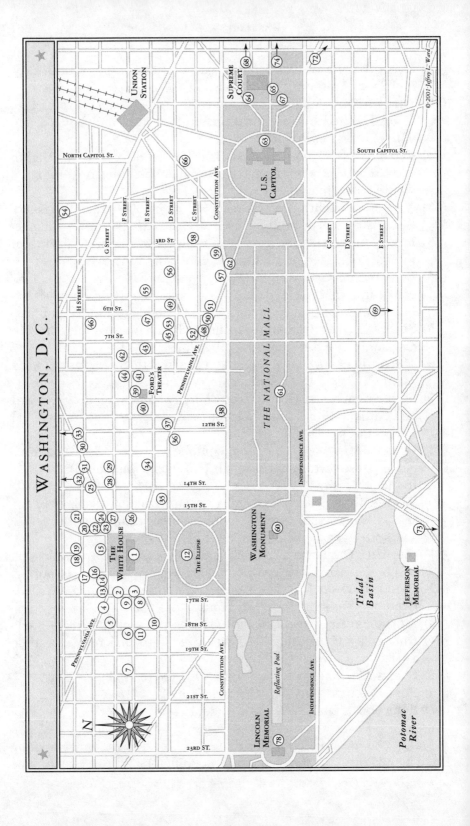

West Virginia

ANTIOCH: Although disputed by the Lincoln National Life Foundation and others, a lonely stone tablet notes the site of the Hanks cabin nearby, claiming to mark the birthplace of Nancy Hanks, Lincoln's mother (see the entry on Mineral County, West Virginia).

HARPERS FERRY: Lincoln visited on October 1, 1862, on the way to see General McClellan at Antietam Battlefield. He arrived by train via the pontoon bridge near the ruined bridge, still visible where the rivers join. The site can be accessed by a path from the railroad tracks and monument marking the original location of Brown's fort, down a steep slope to the river and stone embankments, which anchored the bridge. The president was taken to General Edwin V. Sumner's headquarters. This is now the left side as you face the front of the **MATHER TRAINING CENTER**, prominently located on a hill between **ROUTE 340 AND FILLMORE STREET, BETWEEN JACKSON AND MCDOWELL STREETS** to the east. Lincoln met briefly with McClellan, and then the party traveled to **BOLIVAR HEIGHTS** to review troops. The president then went into town to inspect the ruins of the railroad bridge and see the engine house that John Brown and his men had used for a fort during his 1859 raid. (This had been retaken by U.S. troops under the command of Robert E. Lee. The building has now been relocated a short distance from the original site, as noted in the marker at the new location and obelisk on the original site.) Lincoln then returned to Sumner's headquarters and spent the night. The president also reviewed troops at **LOUDOUN AND MARYLAND HEIGHTS** after spending the night. The Heights are shown on National Park maps available here.

MINERAL COUNTY: The birthplace of Lincoln's mother, Nancy Hanks, is claimed to be here. Her mother, Lucy Hanks, settled at the age of about seventeen on **MIKE'S RUN** on Patterson Creek in 1783. Lucy soon got pregnant, or may have come already pregnant. The father of Lucy's baby remains unknown, but he is believed to have been a Virginia planter. Nancy was born probably during the first part of 1784. This event shamed and embarrassed her family who soon moved to Kentucky. The reconstructed **NANCY HANKS MEMORIAL CABIN** is located on the site thought to have been the cabin of Lucy's grandfather, Joseph Hanks. This is at the Mineral-Grant County boundary on a narrow secondary road southwest of U.S. Highways 50 and 220 at Ridgeway. At the time, this was Hampshire County, Virginia.

Actually, the above is only one of several versions of Nancy's birth and birthplace. Lincoln is surely America's most studied figure, but the birthplace site, date, and circumstances of his mother's birth still elude consensus among historians. As historian Edward Steers comments in his Summer 1998 "Current Status of Research" article in the *Lincoln Herald,* "Of all the mothers of all the presidents none is more shrouded in mystery or controversy than Nancy Hanks Lincoln." (See the article for details into "the mystery," as well as the chapter on Kentucky in this book, giving other versions including beliefs about the background of Lincoln's grandmother and mother.)

A tablet dedicated on May 6, 1933, near **KEYSER**, north of the above-mentioned area, claims Nancy was born at a place called Bare Bones on the Namozine Road between Jennings Ordinary and Fergusonville. Bare Bones Creek is a branch of the Nottoway River.

Wisconsin

BELOIT: Lincoln first entered Wisconsin in June 1832 at age twenty-three near Beloit as a member of a mounted independent spy company when he was in the Black Hawk War. While camped on the Rock River at the confluence of Turtle River here, an old Winnebago chief wandered into camp and may have been killed but for the intervention of Lincoln. (This story is also told as having happened a few days before on Sycamore Creek.) Across the river is Big Hill, a city park, where Black Hawk's scouts kept watch over Lincoln's company.

On October 1, 1859, after the Milwaukee appearance, he was scheduled here for an open-air meeting. He was met at the depot by a crowd of several hundred and introduced by the mayor who suddenly forgot his name. The crowd helped him out. The depot was located SOUTH OF ST. PAUL STREET BETWEEN STATE AND PLEASANT STREETS. He ate in the BUSHELL HOUSE, AT THE NORTHEAST CORNER OF GRAND AND STATE. (Another hotel was here earlier, the Rock River House, and claimed to have entertained Lincoln, Douglas, and President James Buchanan, but there is no documentation for this. Another uncorroborated Lincoln visit was at the CYRUS EAMES HOME ON THE NORTHEAST CORNER OF MILL AND ST. PAUL.)

Lincoln then proceeded to HANCHETT HALL, marked on the NORTHEAST CORNER OF BROAD AND STATE STREETS. The speech was supposed to take place from the iron balcony to a crowd outside, but due to stormy weather he spoke in the corner of the large room on the packed third floor. He spoke somewhat extemporaneously and declared "the fundamental principle of the Republican Party is the hatred of the institution of slavery." He would not interfere with slavery as it existed, but would not allow it to expand. After the presentation, Lincoln consented to go to Janesville, giving him an opportunity to retrace the old war trail, now **PRAIRIE STREET**, and locate familiar landmarks from his 1832 march. It is thought that the historical marker at Riverside and Lawton Streets is wrong claiming that Lincoln camped there. It is now believed that the camp was a little northeast at **PARK AND WHITE STREETS**. **PRAIRIE ROAD** is believed the correct line of march north during the Black Hawk War.

JANESVILLE: Lincoln spoke on October 1, 1859, at the **YOUNG AMERICAN HALL** and attended services the next day at the **CONGREGATIONAL CHURCH, AT THE SOUTHWEST CORNER OF DODGE AND JACKSON**. The hall was at the location of the drive-up teller windows at the Johnson Bank on **MILWAUKEE STREET, EAST OF MAIN**. This was probably the same speech given at Beloit earlier. The church is still located here, but not the building used by Lincoln.

Lincoln stayed at the **TALLMAN HOUSE**, now restored at **440 NORTH JACKSON STREET AT MADISON OFF THE U.S. 14 BUSINESS ROUTE** two blocks northeast of the U.S. 51 junction. The route is well marked and easy to find. The mansion was built in 1855 with such conveniences as running water, a communication system, central heating, plumbing, and gaslights. In 1871 it was called "the finest and most costly residence in Wisconsin." It is said to be the only private residence in the state where Lincoln slept. (The home with Lincoln's bed is open to the public.) After spending two nights, he returned to the Tremont Hotel in Chicago.

MADISON: Lincoln's law partner, John T. Stuart, wrote that he and Lincoln came to Four Lakes (Madison) while serving as privates in the Black Hawk War.

MILWAUKEE: The boat Lincoln's family was on stopped in Milwaukee on the way back from New England on October 4, 1848, and he toured the city with his family. On September 30, 1859, he came to speak at the exhibition of the Wisconsin Agricultural Society, or State Fair. His host had arranged for Lincoln to stay in the best hotel in town, the Newhall House. Lincoln arrived earlier than expected, but at midnight, and found that no rooms were available. After some hesitation, the clerk gave him a cot by the side of the office. This is where his host found him the next morning, after he had gone to the train station to meet his train. After apologizing for the lack of a room, Lincoln stated,

"No apology, if you please. This nice, soft cot was so much better than the trunk of a fallen tree that lets a fellow roll off two or three times in the night, or even the soft side of a flat rock, both of which have served me many a time, that sleepy and a little tired, as I was, I crept with pleasure and slept like a top."

Lincoln spoke to a large group of mostly farmers at the fair. The spot where he stood is marked with a boulder on **WEST THIRTEENTH STREET BETWEEN NORTH WELLS AND WEST KILBOURN**. He toured the grounds and amazed his escorts when he seized and held straight "an enormous sledge with a handle long and strong" used to pound tent stakes. Later in the day friends persuaded him to make an address on current affairs at the **NEWHALL HOUSE** at the **NORTHWEST CORNER OF PRESENT-DAY BROADWAY AND EAST MICHIGAN STREET**. Nothing is known of the latter, although the former speech at the fair was recorded in full. (The claim is unsubstantiated that he stayed in the **COBBLESTONE HOTEL** and the **KIRBY HOUSE**.)

Lincoln was driven to the fairgrounds by the vice president of the State Fair Association, "a dyed-in-the-wool" Democrat who "tried to hold his ground, but Lincoln was too much for him," according to the vice president's son. The then ten-year-old recalled later, "Finally Lincoln put his hand on my head and said: 'My little man, I hope you live long enough to see the day you can vote the Republican ticket.'" After that they had a merry ride, with Lincoln telling funny stories and jokes.

PORT WASHINGTON: Some sources, including the WPA guide for Wisconsin, claim Lincoln stayed for a short time at the **BLONG HOUSE, 317 PIER STREET,** after the death of Ann Rutledge in the fall of 1835. It is possible that he visited Milwaukee and Sheboygan then also, although a visit to Wisconsin at that time appears highly doubtful.

RACINE: Mary came to a spa for her health problems beginning July 1867 while Robert and Tad were in Washington for the John Surratt Trial. She also wanted in investigate putting Tad in a school, what he clearly needed, and he joined her after the trial. But Mary did not like the thought of being away from her "troublesome sunshine," and they both returned to Chicago.

SHEBOYGAN: It is possible Lincoln visited sometime between 1835 and 1840 with the view of opening a law office, although this is not generally accepted.

WHITEWATER: Lincoln was mustered out of service during the Black Hawk War near here on July 10, 1832. His first visit to the state had lasted about two weeks. At the time he was a candidate for the legislature from New Salem and intended to get back in time for some campaigning. But someone stole his horse, and he had to walk the three hundred miles back, or some of it. He shared a ride with friends, and spent some time in a canoe. This so delayed him that he had little opportunity to present himself and his views to the people, with the consequence that he was not elected in his first campaign. (Other sources say he was mustered out at Burnt River, Black River, or Fort Atkinson.)

Appendix I

Mary Lincoln After April 15, 1865

No biography fully traces Mary after 1865, and it is difficult to follow her movements and whereabouts from any one source. This is a summary of various locations and approximate dates related to Mrs. Lincoln after leaving Washington in 1865. Among the sources are historian Wayne Temple's note files (T), Ruth Painter Randall's *Mary Lincoln* (R), Jean Baker's *Mary Todd Lincoln* (B), W. A. Evans's *Mrs. Abraham Lincoln* (E), Linda Turner (LT), and Katherine Helm (H). Well-known dates and places are not annotated.

May 4, 1865: Lincoln buried in Springfield.

May 22, 1865: Leaves White House with Tad. Arrives at TREMONT HOUSE in Chicago traveling through Pittsburgh and Fort Wayne. She lives in Chicago until 1868.

June 8, 1865: Mary, Robert, and Tad move to HYDE PARK HOTEL (R), May 31 (E).

November 1865: Boarding at CLIFTON HOUSE in Chicago (R).

December 22, 1865: Robert and Mary in SPRINGFIELD as Lincoln put into new tomb.

May 22, 1866: Mary buys **375 (now 1238) WEST WASHINGTON, IN CHICAGO**. She continued to own this until sold to Robert in 1874. Attended Third Presbyterian, and Tad went there, to First Congregational, and First Baptist on Wabash. Tad at Brown School (R).

September 6, 1866: Meets with Herndon in the ST. NICHOLAS HOTEL in SPRINGFIELD.

November 1866: Herndon lecture about Lincoln's relationship with Ann Rutledge. (Robert went to Cheyenne, Wyoming, during the fall of this year and also in late 1867.)

May 14, 1867: Mary visits tomb in SPRINGFIELD (E).

Spring 1867: CLIFTON HOUSE (R), WASHINGTON STREET home rented about May 1 (E). Robert is admitted to the Illinois Bar in February.

July 1867: Mary in RACINE while sons are in Washington for John Surratt's trial (T). Trial is from June 10 until August 10 (R). Tad testified on July 5.

September–October 1867: NEW YORK CITY with Tad, UNION SQUARE HOTEL. Then DENIS HOTEL under the name of "Mrs. Clarke," then BRADRETH HOTEL under the name of "Mrs. Morris." Tries to sell clothes at W. H. BRADY'S, 609 BROADWAY.

October 13, 1867: 460 (now 1407) WEST WASHINGTON IN CHICAGO, Tad starts at CHICAGO ACADEMY winter 1867 (R) (E).

January 12, 1868: Mary writes that she is back in the CLIFTON HOUSE (LT) (E).

June 1868: Mary and Tad visited Springfield (R).

July 1868: Summer in ALLEGHENIES, ALTOONA, CRESSON, AND BEDFORD SPRINGS, PENNSYLVANIA. Tad attempted to jump on a passing freight train and his hold slipped. He probably would have been killed under the wheels if a man nearby had not grabbed him (R) (B) (T). Also New England (E).

September 24, 1868: Robert marries at the HARLAN HOUSE, 306 H STREET in WASHINGTON (T). Robert stayed at Welles house during courtship (R).

September 27, 1868: Mary in BALTIMORE at the BARNUM'S HOTEL. Tad stayed in D.C.

October 1, 1868: Mary and Tad sail to EUROPE over Tad's objections. (R).

October 15, 1868: Mary and Tad arrive in SOUTHAMPTON, England, then BREMEN, Germany (LT) (B), then to Hotel d'Angleterre in FRANKFURT, Germany, where she lived for about two years near the Zeil shopping promenade. Tad in school at DR. HOHAGEN'S INSTITUTE NUMBER 17, KETTENHOFSTRASSE, where he learned to speak "German perfectly." Both toured BADEN-BADEN, HEIDELBERG, BLACK FOREST, THE TYROL, AND THE PALATINATE (R).

Summer 1869: Mary and Tad visit SCOTLAND incognito for seven weeks at the invitation of Dr. James Smith, former pastor from Springfield, who had been appointed American Consul at Dundee. He showed them the sites of LONDON for five days and then they visited EDINBURGH, GLASGOW, ABBOTSFORD, DRYBURGH ABBEY, GLENCOE, AND MANY CASTLES INCLUDING GLAMIS AND BALMORAL. (B) (R) (T).

December 3, 1869: LONDON (E).

February 1870: Mary in FLORENCE on February 12, where she saw the PITTI PALACE, then around ITALY, INCLUDING MILAN AND LAKE COMO, AND GENEVA, SWITZERLAND.

Summer 1870: Mary and Tad visit NUREMBERG, HEIDELBERG, THE BLACK FOREST, INNSBRUCK, TYROL, AUSTRIA, and flee Frankfurt due to the Franco-Prussian War (H).

Fall 1870: Mary and Tad settle in LEAMINGTON, England, for nine weeks. They visited KENILWORTH AND WARWICK CASTLES AND STRATFORD-ON-AVON (H), Tad showing signs of tuberculosis. Then moved to LONDON and boarded on WOBURN STREET across from Russell Square and near the British Museum (B) (R).

January 1871: Tad stays in school at OBER URSEL near FRANKFURT, Mary in FLORENCE, ITALY (R).

May 10, 1871: Mary and Tad arrive at the Everett House Hotel in NEW YORK CITY after crossing the Atlantic on the same ship with General Philip Sheridan. The New York *Tribune* reports that Tad has acquired a good knowledge of the French and German languages and had turned into a tall, fine-looking lad unlike the "comic figure" of the White House.

May 1871: After a brief stay at Robert's house in Chicago, Mary and Tad move to CLIFTON HOUSE (R).

July 15, 1871: Tad dies at Clifton House from pleurisy caused by pneumonia or a primary infection from tuberculosis. After a brief service at Robert's house, Tad was taken to the Edwards' home accompanied by Robert in Springfield, then to funeral at First Presbyterian, and the Lincoln tomb.

1871–1873: Mary lives at Robert's house, 1332 WABASH, travels considerably, as does Robert and his family. (Robert's house is spared during the October 1871 fire.) Mary lives in ST. CHARLES OUTSIDE OF CHICAGO, TRAVELS TO BOSTON, WAUKESHA, WISCONSIN, ST. CATHARINES (eight miles from Niagara Falls). (Evans considers these as lost years as very little shows where she was.) Robert travels to Europe with his family for several months in mid-1872.

1874: At GRAND CENTRAL HOTEL in Chicago. Summer in Waukesha, Wisconsin.

Winter 1874: Spends winter in ST. CHARLES AND JACKSONVILLE AND GREEN COVE, FLORIDA.

March 15, 1875: Arrives at the GRAND PACIFIC HOTEL in Chicago (E) (R).

May 19, 1875: Insanity trial at Cook County Courthouse.

May 20, 1875: Arrives at BELLEVUE PLACE, a private sanitarium at Batavia, near Chicago, after being declared insane by a jury in the Chicago courthouse.

September 11, 1875: Robert and Mary arrive at EDWARDS HOME in Springfield where Mary will stay with her sister.

June 17, 1876: Cook County court declares Mary restored and orders restoration of Mary's property.

September 1876: Mary leaves for EUROPE alone, but is accompanied to New York by her seventeen-year-old grandnephew, Lewis Baker. Tours LEXINGTON, Kentucky, with him, which she has not seen for twenty-five years. They also visit the PHILADELPHIA CENTENNIAL EXPOSITION (B).

October 1876: Mary returns to Europe, goes to LE HAVRE AND PAU (GRAND HOTEL DE LA PAIX), FRANCE, NAPLES (HOTEL DE LA RUSSIA, SORRENTO, ROME (HOTEL D'ITALIC), PAU (where it was said "she is driving the British consul nuts"), seaside near SPAIN, four miles from BIARRITZ, MARSEILLES, AVIGNON, AND PARIS (HOTEL AT 10 RUE DE LA PAIX). Pau was headquarters for four years as she speaks French.

April 12, 1877: PAU AND MARSEILLES, FRANCE, AND NAPLES, later in the month to SORRENTO.

July 4, 1878: Pau.

December 1879: Injured in a fall in Europe.

1880: Mary writes at various times from AVIGNON, PAU, MARSEILLES, AND BORDEAUX, FRANCE.

November 1880: Returns from Europe intending on living with sister Elizabeth in Springfield permanently because of deteriorating health (B) (October according to Evans).

Fall 1881–spring 1882: ST. CATHERINES, Canada (near Niagara Falls), and various locations in NEW YORK CITY (Clarendon, Millers [LT], Grand Central [LT]).

January 16, 1882: Congress increases pension to $5,000 and awards a lump sum of $15,000.

March 25, 1882: Rents rooms with sister in SPRINGFIELD. Is suffering from diabetes, arthritis, near blindness from cataracts.

July 16, 1882: Dies at Edwards home in Springfield.

Appendix II

The Ultimate List of Abraham Lincoln–
John Kennedy Coincidences

ASSIGNATION

1. Both were shot in the back of the head,
2. on Friday,
3. in public, before many witnesses
4. from behind,
5. before a holiday (Easter and Thanksgiving),
6. seated beside their wife,
7. who was uninjured,
8. who held his head in her lap until the doctor took over.
9. Both were in the presence of another couple,
10. and the other man was wounded by the assassin,
11. later recovered,
12. and later suffered adversity. (Rathbone murdered his wife; Connally suffered bankruptcy and bribery allegations.)
13. Kennedy's secretary was Mrs. Lincoln and advised him not to go to Dallas. A Lincoln advisor said to be named Kennedy (the former chief of police in New York named John Kennedy?) advised him not to go to the theater according to some questionable sources. (Note that this unverified item is listed only due to the numbers of times it appears in similar lists and therefore is a part of the lore.)
14. Kennedy's secretary's husband was known as Abe Lincoln.
15. A major reason for going to Ford's Theater and Dallas was to be seen by the public.
16. Lincoln was at Ford's Theater and Kennedy rode in a Ford product, a Lincoln.
17. Lincoln sat in box 7 at Ford's, and Kennedy rode in car 7 in the Dallas motorcade.

18. Both had their brain destroyed by the shot, removed during a partial autopsy, and
19. were buried without it.
20. Both had their bodies moved after burial from a temporary site to a permanent memorial, and
21. were laid on the same catafalque
22. in the East Room of the White House,
23. and Capitol Rotunda.
24. Both had artificial respiration and closed-chest cardiac massage and
25. had a leading doctor rushed to his side who could not save the patient since the brain was partially destroyed.
26. Many high government officials were present nearby at both deaths at the Peterson House and Parkland Hospital, including the vice president, although he was not in the room in either case.
27. Both were buried with a predeceased son,
28. after having their journey to the cemetery witnessed by millions in a great outpouring of national grief.
29. In both cases it was claimed and later discredited that shots were fired from another direction.
30. Both had sons who are not now buried with them. (Robert Lincoln is buried in Arlington near Kennedy.)
31. Both exposed themselves to danger to please crowds many times,
32. and had been shot at before—Kennedy was shot in at World War II and Lincoln had a hat shot off on one occasion by an unknown assailant.
33. Both died in a place with the initials P and H (Parkland Hospital and the Petersen House).
34. Mrs. Kennedy insisted that her husband's funeral follow Lincoln's as closely as possible.
35. Both were buried in mahogany caskets.
36. In each case press photographs of the president's body were forbidden by a cabinet member,
37. but photos of the body were published in later years.
38. The chair in which Lincoln was sitting at Ford's and Kennedy's car when shot are now in the same building in Dearborn, Michigan (Ford Museum).

PERSONAL LIFE

39. Both had same number of letters in last name (seven).
40. Lincoln and Kennedy both liked rocking chairs (Kennedy for his back; Lincoln was sitting in one when shot),
41. and had a deviate eye or wandering eye in some portraits.
42. Both had a brother who died before the presidential election,
43. who had been named after his father,
44. neither of whom is buried in a marked grave. (Joe Kennedy was blown up in a plane and his body was never recovered. Thomas Lincoln Jr.'s gravesite is unknown except as to general location.)
45. Both Kennedy and Lincoln had a sister who died before their election to Congress.
46. Both Kennedy and Lincoln were almost drowned earlier in life (Lincoln's life was saved by a playmate from Knob Creek, Kentucky, and Kennedy's boat was sunk by the enemy in World War II).
47. Lincoln and Kennedy were both the second-born child,
48. the older sibling having predeceased at the time of election to the House.
49. Both presidents were named for their grandfathers.
50. Both birthplaces are national monuments.
51. Kennedy and Lincoln both could trace ancestors to suburbs of Boston (Lincoln's were from Hingham)
52. and then to Great Britain.
53. Both were tall,
54. athletic,
55. were known for humor, and
56. had books published relating to their wit.
57. Both, known for their stand on civil rights,
58. were famous for expressing themselves well (Kennedy won a Pulitzer Prize and Lincoln's speeches are literary classics).
59. Both Kennedy and Lincoln are well known for highly quoted speeches.
60. Both were related to a senator (Lincoln to Isaac Barnard, Pennsylvania, 1827),
61. were boat captains (Lincoln was cocaptain of a small Mississippi River boat),
62. and were in the military (Lincoln was a captain in the Black Hawk War).
63. Lincoln had sons named Robert and Edward. Kennedy had brothers by the same name.

64. Both moved a short distance away from their birthplaces in early childhood,
65. had a brother born there,
66. and then moved away from their birth state before age ten.
67. Likenesses of both Kennedy and Lincoln appear on U.S. coins.
68. Both Kennedy and Lincoln liked to quote from the Bible, and are claimed to have
69. suffered from genetic diseases. It is claimed that Lincoln had Marfan's disease and Kennedy suffered from Addison's disease. It has been alleged that both of their life spans would have been limited had they not been shot. (The author is convinced that Lincoln, in fact, did not have Marfan's.)
70. Neither was known to carry money and constantly borrowed from friends.
71. Both showed no fear of death and disdained bodyguards,
72. often stated how easy it would be to shoot a president, and
73. received many death threats. In 1865 Lincoln received over eighty such letters and Kennedy over eight hundred.
74. Both had a son die while he was president.
75. Lincoln had a son graduate from Harvard; Kennedy had a brother who graduated from the same school.
76. Both of the above men were named Robert,
77. served on the cabinets of later presidents, and
78. were supported for president themselves.
79. Both had children ride ponies on the White House grounds,
80. who later became lawyers
81. and worked for the government.
82. Kennedy and Lincoln both had sons who were lawyers who pursued nonlegal careers.
83. Both had relatives who were mayor of Boston (Lincoln's cousin, F. W. Lincoln, and Kennedy's grandfather).
84. Both had close relatives who were ambassador to Great Britain (Lincoln's son, Kennedy's father), and
85. had a relative who graduated from Harvard and became attorney general (Levi Lincoln in Jefferson's cabinet, Robert Kennedy).
86. Both knew a Dr. Charles Taft (one was a son of President Taft and the other was a half brother of Lincoln's son's playmates who was one of the first doctors who reached Lincoln after the shooting.)
87. Kennedy was advised by Dr. Billy Graham, and Lincoln was advised by Billy (Mentor) Graham, both of whom were Baptists.
88. Kennedy and Lincoln were both known for quoting Shakespeare.

89. Kennedy was survived by his mother, and Lincoln was survived by his stepmother who had raised him from the age of nine.
90. Kennedy's sister and Lincoln's wife were held to be mentally incompetent,
91. and confined to an institution for the insane.
92. Both Lincoln and Kennedy were in mid-thirties when married (thirty-three and thirty-six)
93. and had proposed to other women and had been rejected.

POLITICAL LIFE

94. Both entered to Congress in '47, and were
95. elected to president in '60.
96. The '60 election win was at least partly due to a famous debate with the other main candidate,
97. both of whom had been a senator,
98. who was better known at the time of the debate, and
99. who sat near the president-elect at the inauguration.
100. Both won their party's nomination against older, more experienced politicians
101. who were later selected for high places in government (Seward—secretary of state, Stevenson—UN ambassador, Johnson—vice president, etc.).
102. Lincoln shared with his successor vice president (Andrew Johnson) the fact that he had been elected from a state other than his birthplace. Kennedy and his successor were elected from their birth state.
103. Lincoln and Kennedy were both runner-up candidates for vice president in '56, and
104. ran against the incumbent vice president in '60,
105. who later suffered disgrace (Nixon resigned, Breckenridge fled the country to escape capture as a traitor for serving the South).
106. Both Lincoln and Kennedy were much younger than their predecessors who were
107. Buchanan and Eisenhower, whose homes are about sixty miles apart in Pennsylvania, and
108. who were the two oldest presidents prior to Kennedy.
109. Kennedy and Lincoln were both concerned with the rights of blacks,
110. and this work was culminated in '63 (Emancipation Proclamation—1863, and civil rights message to Congress—1963).

111. Both knew a prominent Illinois Democrat named Adlai Stevenson.
112. Both called troops for a war that was unpopular with many, had citizens flee to Canada to avoid the draft, and
113. had a revolution occurring in a neighboring country (Cuba and Mexico),
114. which involved limited U.S. intervention.

VICE PRESIDENTS

115. Lincoln and Kennedy were both succeeded by men who were born in '08.
116. and had successors with the same number of letters in their full names (nineteen).
117. Both vice presidents were from states beginning with the letter T.
118. Both successors profited from having an educated wife who aided them greatly,
119. had two girls,
120. were opposed for reelection by men with names starting with G. (Goldwater and Grant),
121. and choose not to run in '68
122. because they had grown very unpopular.
123. Both succeeding vice presidents had been senators,
124. came from a poor background,
125. were named "Johnson,"
126. survived a sister,
127. had a brother,
128. died at about the same age (sixty-six and sixty five),
129. and lived about the same length of time after leaving office (six years and four years).
130. Both successors were near the president when he was dying (Lyndon Johnson was at the hospital and Andrew Johnson came to the Petersen House).
131. Both of the Johnsons had been officers in the military. Andrew was brigadier general, and Lyndon was a commander in the navy.
132. Both successors were large men and
133. known to be coarse and vulgar.
134. Both succeeding vice presidents were followed in '68 by a Republican successor (Nixon and Grant)
135. who was later reelected,
136. and had the second administration clouded with scandal.

137. The Johnsons were the only presidents known to have urethral stones.

WIVES

138. Lincoln's and Kennedy's wives were within six weeks of their twenty-fourth birthday at marriage.
139. Both had been proposed to by someone else,
140. were from affluent families,
141. were raised with stepbrothers and stepsisters and a stepparent,
142. were well educated and socially prominent,
143. spoke French,
144. had four children,
145. two of whom died before becoming a teen,
146. had three children living in the White House,
147. lost a son while president (Patrick Kennedy, Willie Lincoln),
148. one before the presidential election,
149. and had the care of a minor son after the death of her husband.
150. Both wives lived in Europe after their husbands' deaths,
151. and in a major U.S. city other than where they had lived during marriage (Mrs. Kennedy in New York and Mrs. Lincoln in Chicago).
152. Both wives spent lavishly on the White House decorations
153. and renovated the White House after years of neglect.
154. Both wives were known to spend lavishly on clothes.
155. Both had lived in Washington before the presidential election.
156. Both wives were at least nine years younger than their husbands,
157. survived them by at least seventeen years, and
158. died at about the same age (Mary lived 63 years, 215 days, and Jackie lived 64 years).

ASSASSINS

159. Both assassins were in their mid-twenties,
160. and born in '38–'39.
161. Both were enemy sympathizers,
162. and allegedly were spies for the enemy,
163. had the same number of letters in their full names (fifteen),
164. fled and escaped after the shooting, and

165. were captured later.
166. Both Oswald and Booth adopted nearly identical slings for their carbines.
167. Both were shot
168. and killed within a short time of being discovered,
169. attempted to shoot the captor,
170. were injured prior to being shot
171. in a theater (Booth broke a leg and Oswald had cuts on his head received in a Texas theater), and
172. had it questioned later whether they were in fact killed or even guilty of any crime.
173. Efforts were made in court decades after their crimes to exhume their bodies to determine if they were actually in the graves.
174. Both had attempted to commit a violent political crime (Oswald tried to shoot General Walker and Booth had tried to kidnap Lincoln).
175. Both prior crimes failed. Oswald missed Walker, and Lincoln was not in his carriage when it was seized.
176. Autopsies were performed on both assassins to clarify identity.
177. Both assassinations were carefully planned once the presidents' locations were made known (published shortly before their appearances).
178. Both Booth and Oswald learned of the president's location by reading it at their place of employment, selected that location as the place of the attempt,
179. altered their place of employment to make shooting easier (Booth is thought to have drilled a hole in the door box and Oswald set up boxes to prop his rifle and obscure view of himself),
180. and fired the fatal shots from their workplaces.
181. Oswald's father was named Robert E. Lee and Oswald was named after Lee. Booth admired Robert E. Lee, as did Lincoln, who offered Lee command of the Union army before Lee resigned his commission. Kennedy is buried at the foot of the hill upon which stands Lee's Arlington home.
182. Both were trapped by officers named Baker (barn door was being held by Luther Baker, and Oswald was confronted at the School Book Depository door by Officer Marion Baker).
183. Both workplaces are now museums because of the assassinations and have been restored to look like the site at the time.
184. A woman named Paine got Oswald his job; a man named Paine helped Booth in his crime. Oswald Swan also helped Booth escape.

185. Those associated with the events received financial rewards. (Zupruder sold his movie; Corbett and others received rewards for capture of Booth).

186. Both assassins were overshadowed by two older brothers in a profession they greatly admired (Oswald's brothers were in the military; Booth's were famous actors),

187. and they could not attain the same success.

188. Both assassins used three names: John Wilkes Booth and Lee Harvey Oswald.

189. Both are buried in large cities thirty to forty-five miles from their crime (Baltimore and Fort Worth).

190. Both were in the military (militia and marines).

191. Both used aliases ("J. Wilkes" and "A. Hidell").

192. A part-time concession operator who held Booth's horse at Ford's Theater was Peanuts Burroughs, and the concession operator at the Texas Theater was Butch Burroughs.

193. Both assassins received fame posthumously, unlike other presidential assassins who are now mostly unknown.

194. Both assassins were shot by religious men

195. who had changed their names (Corbett changed his name from Thomas to Boston; Ruby changed his from Jacob Rubinstein).

196. Both kept a diary or journal,

197. which was partly withheld from the public, and

198. were deprived of a father figure (Booth's died when he was thirteen and Oswald's parents were divorced).

199. Both were shot with a single shot from a Colt

200. while being subdued by captures in strong light (fire; TV and camera lights),

201. then lived only a matter of minutes

202. and denied the world father knowledge and insights into their deeds.

203. Formal investigations were held

204. and later reopened (Surratt's trial in 1867 and Andrew Johnson's impeachment in 1868; and 1975, 1978, etc. inquiries).

205. None of the further investigations or inquiries resolved who else may have been involved in the assassination.

206. Many conspiracy theories in both cases still exist today but are unproved,

207. some of which suggest possible involvement by prominent persons.

208. The killers of Booth and Oswald were both volatile, unstable,

209. unmarried,

210. and later declared insane.

211. Both had earlier opportunities to kill (Ruby in a police station and Corbett at closer angles in the barn).

212. Booth shot in a theater and was captured in a warehouse or barn. Oswald shot from a warehouse, and was captured in a theater.

213. Both assassins were stopped by officers and released (Booth at a bridge out of Washington, Oswald at the entrance to the Depository).

214. It was questioned later whether or not Booth and Oswald were really killed and buried in their graves.

215. Of the four presidential assassinations, Robert Lincoln was near all when they were shot except Kennedy's, and he is buried near Kennedy. (After McKinley's death, Robert considered himself a jinx and would not go near a president.)

216. Women affected at the time by the crimes suffered similar fates: Mrs. Kennedy and Fanny Seward, the secretary of state's daughter, both of whom were raised in New York, suffered amnesia of the events following the attempts on the lives of their husband and father. Seward was attacked the same time as Lincoln.)

217. After the assassination Robert Lincoln moved to 3014 N Street, in Georgetown, and John Jr. moved to 3017 N Street.

218. Both presidents were greatly vilified during their terms of office and became very popular and revered after death.

219. More is known today about Lincoln and Kennedy because of their assassinations. They became very popular after death and a number of books were written about them by people who had known them and could detail many personal incidents that would have been otherwise lost to history but for the sudden increase in public interest and fame.

220. In both cases a Robert (son of Lincoln and brother of Kennedy) tried to suppress many of the books.

221. Many books also have been written about possible conspiracies, none of which has been generally accepted.

222. Numerous movies have been produced concerning these assassinations, while the other presidential assassinations have been virtually ignored. These include

223. two recent movies that propose as reality possible conspiracy theories widely disputed and unproved (*JFK* and *The Lincoln Conspiracy*).

224. Both have been portrayed in many movies and TV shows. In fact, Lincoln's total is at least ninety.

225. Of the four presidents assassinated, Lincoln and Kennedy died within hours, although they were for all practical purposes dead when hit. The other two lived for weeks.

226. Lincoln was the first Republican; Kennedy was the first Catholic president.
227. Both presidents may have seen their death coming. Lincoln dreamed about his assassination and informed several around him in April 1865. Kennedy wrote a note on June 5, 1961, found by secretary Evelyn Lincoln: "I know there is a God and I see a storm coming. If he has a place for me, I am ready."

Appendix III

Lincoln Lore

The following issues of the *Bulletin of the Lincoln National Life Foundation* were among those used in the preparation of this book and may be of further reference to those interested. Contact the Lincoln Museum, 200 E. Berry, POB 7838, Fort Wayne, IN, 46801-7838 (219-455-3864). The descriptions set out are not necessarily the titles.

2. Burial procession	171. Grandfather
7. Lincoln caravans	174. Grandmother Lincoln
11. Chronology	193. Tad
15. Biography	197. Respect for father
19. Freeport debate	216. Log cabins
22. Children	218. Mother's grave
24. Tom Lincoln cabins	224. Lincoln in Chicago
28. Nancy Lincoln birthplace theories, parentage	225. Lincoln's Shipley ancestors
29. Nancy Lincoln birthplace theories, parentage	226. Near tragedies
	227. Where Lincoln lived
31. Lexington	238. New Salem restoration
35. Old Virginia	242. Reliance on God
37. Genealogy	244. Brother, sons, grandson
43. Early life	248. Places Lincoln visited
114. Picture, Danville	257. Michigan speech
115. Memorial highway	258. Lincoln relatives
122. Political calendar	263. Ohio
132. Mythical birthplaces	267. Wisconsin
137. Indiana home	271. Indiana
154. Springfield introduction	272. Indiana
155. Mary chronology	298. Springfield home
	309. New England

Appendix IV

Abraham Lincoln–Jefferson Davis Comparisons

BOTH:

1. Were president during the Civil War.
2. Were born within eight months and one hundred miles of each other in Kentucky.
3. Moved twice as young boys to grow up out of their birth state.
4. Lost a parent before age seventeen.
5. Grandfathers were born in Pennsylvania.
6. Had fathers who were Baptists, but
7. sent their sons to a school taught by a Catholic,
8. and generally failed to show much love and affection to them.
9. Had an older sister,
10. and a brother, named after his father.
11. Walked through the woods with an older sister to a log school.
12. Went down the Ohio-Mississippi Rivers at an early age (Davis was eleven and Abe was nineteen).
13. Lost their loved one within twenty-one days of each other and were devastated (Lincoln's sweetheart, Ann Rutledge, died August 25, 1835, and Davis's first wife, Knox, died September 15, 1835.)
14. Were married by an Episcopal priest,
15. to a Kentucky woman,
16. after an earlier breakup,
17. and married against the family's approval,
18. both of whom were daughters of prominent fathers (Davis married the daughter of Zachary Taylor, who became president).
19. Lost his first election for the state legislature.
20. Served in the U.S. House in the mid-1840s.

21. Took their seats in Congress as freshmen on September 6, 1847, Davis as senator and Lincoln as a representative.
22. Served in the Black Hawk War, at Dixon, Illinois, but saw no action.
23. Were supported for governor, but did not serve (Davis lost the Mississippi election, and Lincoln turned down an appointment in Oregon).
24. Married much younger women,
25. who lived at least sixteen years as a widow,
26. and grew up in a house or replica still standing and open to the public.
27. Wives were difficult, intelligent women
28. who outlived all of their children except one child
29. who lived into the twentieth century.
30. Spent much time away from his wife.
31. Wives humiliated their husband by widely publicized fits of jealousy over another woman in an innocent relationship (Mary Lincoln over Kate Chase and Mrs. Ord; Varina Davis over Mrs. Dorsey who let Davis use her house to write his book).
32. Had a wife accompany him to Washington to take a seat in Congress and then left after a few weeks to come home.
33. Were involved in incidents leading to an illegal duel involving James Shields. Shields was Lincoln's opponent and was a second for the challenged Illinois congressman Bissell. Both ended without bloodshed.
34. Were avid readers, moody, subject to melancholia, and ate sparingly.
35. On the other hand, Davis was short-tempered, self-centered, oversensitive, micromanaged, chronically sick, and could not work with those he did not like. Lincoln was the opposite.
36. Wives had the same seamstress, a former slave, Elizabeth Keckley,
37. and both wives liked to tour the White Mountains.
38. Had four sons,
39. three of whom died young,
40. including a Willie
41. who died at eleven.
42. Lost his favorite son during the war.
43. Had a son named after his father.
44. Had a son die within one block of Fifteenth Street in Washington who was buried in a Georgetown cemetery.
45. Had a child attend school in Germany.
46. Loved all children, relished them with attention and affection,
47. and were indulgent with his own children, letting them interrupt important meetings.
48. Lived in a boardinghouse on Capitol Hill, with Senator Thomas

Hart Benton, stayed at Willard's Hotel, and a hotel at Sixth Street and Pennsylvania in Washington (the Lincolns stayed at Brown's at the northwest corner for a short time, and Davis lived at the National, on the northeast corner).

49. Spoke at Independence Hall in Philadelphia.
50. Took a long, roundabout trip to his first inauguration.
51. Were reelected president during the Civil War.
52. Had a close association with Lexington, Kentucky (Lincoln's wife was from there, and he visited her home three times; Davis went to school on Gratz Park there near the Todd homes; Mary Todd Lincoln also went to a school facing the park).
53. Had a close association with Springfield, Kentucky (Davis went to school there at age eight when Abe was living about twenty miles away; Lincoln's parents grew up nearby and their marriage license is in the courthouse).
54. Had a brother-in-law who was a general in the Confederate army.
55. Were in a combat zone during the war with bullets hitting nearby.
56. Were shot at during the war while riding a horse in the capital city, and narrowly missed.
57. Were criticized for excessive pardoning of soldiers condemned to die.
58. Suffered adversity after the war (assassination and poverty).
59. Final homes are open to the public (Springfield and Biloxi).
60. Had a namesake die young, at about the same age (Robert's son Abraham died at seventeen, and Jeff Davis Jr. died at twenty-one).
61. Were much maligned in their lifetimes, but greatly honored after death.
62. Are buried near his wife and some of his children, but not his parents.
63. Are referred to by abbreviations of their given names, which they despised (Abe and Jeff).
64. Have statues almost side by side in the Rotunda of the Kentucky State Capitol
65. and statues in the U.S. Capitol.
66. Were noted for their stubbornness and determination, which prevented an earlier end to the Civil War.
67. Are honored in the two largest mountainside carvings in the country, Mount Rushmore and Stone Mountain.
68. Neither has descendants with his family name. Although they had a total of ten children, only child of each had children. One Davis daughter had descendants, and Lincoln's only grandson died while a boy. Only Davis has living descendants today.

Appendix V

Publications Listing Sites Visited by Lincoln

**This is listed by the title rather than author to make it
easier for the reader to trace sources.**

AAA Guides (all states are contained in this publication), AAA Publishing, various
   years
Abe Goes Down the River, F. Lauriston Bullard, *Lincoln Herald,* February 1948.
Abe Lincoln, An Anthology, Edited by Hilah Paulmier, Knopf, 1953.
Abraham Lincoln, Lord Charnwood, Cardinal Edition, 1952.
Abraham Lincoln, Benjamin P. Thomas, Knopf, 1952 (1994).
Abraham Lincoln, Carl Sandburg, Harcourt, Brace, reprint, 1959.
Abraham Lincoln the Christian, William J. Johnson, Abingdon Press, 1913.
Abraham Lincoln at City Point, Donald Planz, H. E. Howard, Inc., 1989.
Abraham Lincoln and Coles County, Illinois, Charles Hubert Coleman, Scarecrow
   Press, 1955.
Abraham Lincoln: A Document Portrait through His Speeches and Writings, Don E.
   Fehrenbacher, New American Library, 1964.
Abraham Lincoln at the Hampton Roads Peace Conference, Fort Monroe Casement
   Museum, 1968.
Abraham Lincoln and His Ancestors, Ida M. Tarbell, University of Nebraska, 1924
   (reprint 1997).
The Abraham Lincoln Encyclopedia, Mark Neely Jr., McGraw Hill, 1982.
The Abraham Lincoln Encyclopedia, compiled by Archer H. Shaw, Macmillan, 1950.
"Abraham Lincoln and Family," Ralph E. Pearson, *Kentucky Pioneer Genealogy and
   Records,* July 1979.
Abraham Lincoln, From Skeptic to Prophet, Wayne C. Temple, Mayhaven, 1995.
Abraham Lincoln Goes to New York, Andrew A. Freeman, Coward-McCann, 1960.
Abraham Lincoln, His Speeches and Writings, Roy P. Basler, World, 1946.
Abraham Lincoln in Indiana, Roscoe Kiper, *Kiwanis* magazine.
Abraham Lincoln: The Man Behind the Myths, Stephen B. Oates, New American
   Library, 1984.
Abraham Lincoln and Others at the St. Nicholas, Wayne C. Temple, St. Nicholas, 1968.
Abraham Lincoln in Peoria, R. C. Bryner, Edward J. Jacob, 1926.
Abraham Lincoln Sees Peoria, Ernest E. East, Record Publishing, 1939.

Abraham Lincoln, Postmaster, Wayne C. Temple

"Abraham Lincoln, Prairie Lawyer," Stephen B. Oates, *American History Illustrated.*

Abraham Lincoln Quarterly, March 1942, December 1942.

Abraham Lincoln's Religion, George G. Fox, Exposition Press, 1959.

"Abraham Lincoln and the Reverend, Dr. James Smith," Robert J. Havlik, *Journal of Illinois State Historical Society,* Autumn 1999.

Abraham Lincoln Traveled This Way, Fred Holmes, L. C. Page, 1930.

Abraham Lincoln: An Unforgettable American, Mabel Kunkel, Delmar, 1976.

Abraham Lincoln's Visit to Evanston in 1860, J. Seymour Curry, 1914.

"Abraham Lincoln's 1860 Visit to Rhode Island," William F. Hanna III, *Lincoln Herald,* winter 1978.

"Abraham Lincoln: Western Star Over Connecticut," Nelson R. Burr, *Lincoln Herald,* spring 1983.

Abraham Lincoln's World, Genevieve Foster, Charles Scribner's Sons, 1944.

"Afar Off, Lincoln Glimpses the White House," Elwell Crissey, *Lincoln Herald,* winter 1967.

"The Aftermath of the Assassination," Dorothy Meserve Kunhardt, *Life* magazine, April 16, 1965.

Alexander Williamson: Friend of the Lincolns, Wayne C. Temple, The Lincoln Fellowship of Wisconsin, 1997.

All About Chicago, John M. Ashenhurst, Riverside Press, 1933.

Alton—A Pictorial History, Charlotte Stetson.

Alton General City Directory for 1858.

The Amazing Saber Duel of Abraham Lincoln, James E. Myers, Lincoln-Herndon Building, 1968.

American Assassins, James W. Clarke, Princeton University Press, 1982.

"The American Heritage 40," Michael Klepper and Robert Gunther, *American Heritage,* October 1998.

America's Little Giant, Civil War Times Illustrated, Robert W. Johannsen, April 1974.

Anatomy of An Assassination, John Cottrell, Funk and Wagnalls, 1966.

"Ancestry of Abraham Lincoln," Louis A. Warren, in *Lincoln for the Ages,* edited by Ralph G. Newman, Doubleday, 1960.

The Ancestry of Abraham Lincoln, J. Henry Lea and J. R. Hutchinson, Houghton Mifflin, 1909.

"Another Assassination, Another Widow, Another Embattled Book," Marian Wefer, *American Heritage,* August 1967.

Antietam, The Photographic Legacy of America's Bloodiest Day, William A. Frassanito, Charles Scribner's Sons, 1978.

An Autobiography of Abraham Lincoln, compiled by Nathaniel Wright Stephenson, Bobbs-Merrill, 1926.

"Aquia Creek," Harold F. Round, *Virginia Cavalcade,* summer 1963.

The Army of the Potomac at Berkeley Landing, John M. Coski, 1989.

Ashland, Home of Henry Clay, Members of the Board of the Henry Clay Memorial Foundation, undated.

The Assassination, Champ Clark, Time-Life, 1987.

The Assassination of President Lincoln, Harold R. Manakee, Wheeler Leaflet on Maryland History, Number 22, Maryland Historical Society, n.d.

Autobiography of O. O. Howard, Baker and Taylor, 1901.

The Avenue of the Presidents, Mary Cable, Houghton Mifflin, 1969.

"Ballard's Bixby Book," William H. Townsend, *Lincoln Herald,* October 1946.

"Barrister Lincoln: Abraham Lincoln's Practice Before the United States Supreme Court," John A. Lupton, *Lincoln Herold,* summer/winter 1999.

The Beleaguered City, Richmond, 1861–65, Alfred Hoyt Bill, Knopf, 1946.

Beyond the Gatehouse, Brian A. Kemmell, Evergreen Cemetery Association, 2000.

Bicentennial History of Ogle County, Illinois.

The Black Hawk War, Frank E. Stevens, 1903.

"The Bonds of Affection, Abraham Lincoln's Search for His Ancestry," Richard Hanks, *Lincoln Herald,* fall 1997.

"Booth's Escape Route: Lincoln's Assassin on the Run," *Blue and Gray* magazine, Michael W. Kaufman, June 1990.

The Boyhood of Abraham Lincoln, J. Rogers Gore, Standard Printing, 1921.

Brevet's Illinois Historical Markers and Sites, Brevit Press, 1976.

The Budger Collection, David Alan Budger, 1893.

Buffalo, Lake City in Niagara Land, Richard C. Brown, Windsor, 1981.

By Square and Compass: The Building of Lincoln's Home and Its Saga, Wayne C. Temple, Ashlar Press, 1984.

Canals and Railroads of the Mid-Atlantic States 1800–1860, Christopher Baer, Eleutherian Mills-Hagley Foundation, 1981.

"The Case That Made Lincoln," Willard L. King, *Lincoln Herald,* winter 1981.

Cass County Historian, June 1988.

The Centennial History of the Civil War, Bruce Catton, Doubleday, 1961.

Centennial History of Madison County, W. T. Norton, Lewis, 1912.

Century 1, Notes on Sullivan Illinois, Moultrie County Historical Society.

Chatham, The Life of a House, Ralph Happel, Eastern National Park and Monument Association, 1984.

Chatham, Preliminary Historic Resource Study, Fredericksburg and Spotsylvania County Battlefields Memorial, Ronald W. Johnson, U.S. "Department of the Interior,"

Changing the Lincoln Image, Holzer, Boritt, Neely, Louis Warren Lincoln Library, 1985.

Chapin, the First 125 Years, undated (about 1985).

"Charles Henry Philbrick: Private Secretary to President Lincoln, Wayne C. Temple, *Lincoln Herald,* spring 1997.

Chicago, A Pictorial History, Herman Kogan and Lloyd Wendt, Bonanza Books, 1958.

Chicago city directories, 1855–1873.

Chicago's Great Century, 1833–1933, Henry Justin Smith, Consolidated Publishers.

Chronicles of Hardin County, Kentucky, 1776–1974, Mrs. Thomas Winstead, Citizens Bank of Elizabethtown, 1974.

Cincinnati, The Story of the Queen City, Clara (Longworth) De Chambrun, Charles Scribner's Sons, 1939.

Citizen of New Salem, Paul Horgan, Farrar, Straus, and Cudahy, 1961.

City directories for many cities including Albany, Alton, Boston, Buffalo, Chicago, Concord, Dayton, Leavenworth, Lowell, Manchester, New Bedford, New Haven, New London, Norwich, Providence, Springfield, Taunton, Trenton, Worcester, Washington D.C., 1860, 1862–1865.

City of Hartford 1784–1984, Marian Hepburn Grant and Ellsworth Strong Grant, Connecticut Historical Society, 1986.

The Civil War, A Narrative, Shelby Foote, Random House, 1958.

The Civil War Day by Day, E. B. Long, Doubleday, 1971.

The Civil War Dictionary, Mark M. Boatner III, David McKay, 1976.

The Civil War in Maryland, Daniel Carroll Toomey, Toomey Press, 1983.

The Civil War and New York City, Ernest A. McKay, Syracuse University Press, 1990.

Civil War Sites in Virginia, James I. Robinson Jr., University Press of Virginia, 1982.

"The Civil War at West Point," *Blue and Gray* magazine, December 1991.

Clinton 1835–1985

Collected Works of Abraham Lincoln, edited by Roy P. Basler, Rutgers University Press, 1953.

Collections of the Illinois States Historical Library: Vol. III, *Lincoln Series:* Vol. I, *The Lincoln Douglas Debates of 1858.*

Collier's magazine, *Lincoln Centennial Issue*, February 13, 1909 (reprint).

Columbia Historical Portrait of New York, John A. Kouwenhoven, Harper and Row, 1972.

Columbia Historical Society, Reprints from the Records, Vol. 21, Gist Blair, 1921.

"Coming to the Crisis: 1860," Robert W. Johannsen, *American History Illustrated*, June 1973.

Community Guide and Business Directory, Greater Silver Spring Chamber of Commerce, 1998.

A Companion to the Lincoln Douglas Debates, John Splaine, A C-Span Publication.

The Complete Book of Presidents, William A. DeGregorio, Dembner Books, 1984.

Congressman Abraham Lincoln, Donald W. Riddle, University of Illinois Press, 1957.

Conversations With Lincoln, edited by Charles M. Segal, G. P. Putnam and Sons, 1961.

Crooks city Directories (Chicago), Chicago Historical Society, 1855–1875.

Davenport, Iowa, Sunday Times-Democrat, February 10, 1963.

The Day Lincoln Was Shot, Richard Bak, Taylor, 1998.

The Day Lincoln Was Shot, Jim Bishop, Harper, 1963.

Days of Darkness, The Gettysburg Civilians, William G. Williams, Berkeley Books,

Diary of Gideon Welles, Houghton Mifflin, 1911.

Dinwiddie Co., R. L. Long, Board of Surveyors, 1976.

Dixon, A Pictorial History, George Lamb, G. Bradley, 1987.

"Dr. Anson G. Henry," Harry E. Pratt, *Lincoln Herald*, October 1943.

Dr. Samuel A. Mudd and the Lincoln Assassination, John E. Hale Jr., Dillon Press, 1995.

Dorchester . . . Old and New, Dorchester Massachusetts Tercentenary Committee, Chapple, 1930.

Drums Along the Antietam, John W. Schildt, McClain, 1972.

An Early History of Alton, thesis by Alfred Leavell, Jr., Southern Illinois University.

The Early Life of Abraham Lincoln, Ida M. Tarbell, A. S. Barnes, 1974.

Edwards City Directories (Chicago), 1855–1876.

Elizabethtown and Hardin County, Kentucky, Guy Winstead, Donning, 1989.

The Emergence of Lincoln, Allan Nevins, Charles Scribner's Sons, 1950.

The Encyclopedia of Indianapolis, edited by David J. Bodenhamer and Robert G. Barrows, University of Indiana Press, 1994.

The Encyclopedia of New York, edited by Kenneth T. Jackson, Yale University Press, 1995.

The Escape and Capture of John Wilkes Booth, Edward Steers Jr., Thomas, 1992.

The Everyday Life of Abraham Lincoln, Frances F. Brown, 1896.

Facts About the Presidents, Joseph Nathan Kane, H. W. Wilson, 1981.

The Falls, A Stopping Place, A Starting Point, Judy and Bill Munro, Portland Museum, 1979.

Family Encyclopedia of American History, Reader's Digest, 1975.

First Methodist Church (of Springfield), W. G. Piersel, January 1947.

"The Flight of John Wilkes Booth and the Corpse Brought From Garrett's Farm," Mark L. Siegel, *Lincoln Herald*, winter 1982.

Following Abraham Lincoln, Bernardt Wall, Algonquin, 1943.

Footprints of Abraham Lincoln, J. T. Hobson, Otterbein Press, 1909.

"Fort Lesley McNair and the Lincoln Conspirators," Mike Kauffman, *Lincoln Herald*, winter 1978.

Fort Monroe Guide Book, The Casement Museum, Fort Monroe, 1993.

Four Walking Tours of Exeter, New Hampshire, Nancy C. Merrill, Exeter Historical Society, 1980.

Fredericksburg Civil War Sites, vols. 1 and 2, Noel G. Harrison, H. E. Howard, 1995.

Free Lance-Star (Fredericksburg, Va.), February 12, and, June 11, 1999.

Freeport's Lincoln, W. T. Rawleigh (author and publisher), 1930.

The Frontier Years of Abraham Lincoln, Richard Kigel, Walker, 1986.

Gettysburg, A Journey in Time, William A. Frassanito, Charles Scribner's Sons, 1975.

The Gettysburg Soldier's Cemetery and Lincoln's Address, Frank L. Klement, White Maine, 1993.

Gideon Welles, John Nivin, Oxford University Press, 1973.

Gideon Welles, Robert S. West Jr., Bobbs-Merrill, 1943.

Grant and Lee, The Virginia Campaigns, William A. Frassanito, Charles Scribner's Sons, 1983.

"The Graves of Ann Rutledge and the Old Concord Burial Ground," Gary Erickson, *Lincoln Herald*, fall 1969.

The Great Chicago Fire, edited by David Lowe, Dover, 1979.

The Great Chicago Fire 1871, Herman Kogan and Robert Cromie, G. P. Putnum's Sons, 1971.

Greater Chicago Historical Tour Guide, D. Ray Wilson, Crossroads Communications, 1989.

Great Hartford Picture Book, Wilson H. Faule, Donning, 1985.

A Guide to Civil War Washington, Stephen M. Forman, Elliot and Clark, 1995.

Guide to Historic Alton, Illinois on the Mississippi, Alton Area Landmarks Association.

Hannibal Hamlin of Maine, H. Draper Hunt, Syracuse University Press, 1969.

"The Happiest Day of His Life," William Hanchett, *Civil War Times Illustrated,* December 1995.

Hartford city directory, 1860.

Hartford Currant May 31, 1939; May 6, 1860; February 12, 1940.

Hartford Landmarks, Curriculum Research Project, 1966.

"Have We Done Lincoln Justice at Gettysburg?" Louis Warren and Frederick Tilberg, *Civil War Times Illustrated,* July 1976.

Haycroft's History of Elizabethtown, Kentucky, and Its Surroundings, Samuel Haycroft, 1869; reprint 1960.

"Here He First Came to Win Immortality," John Drury, *Chicago Daily News,* February 12, 1859.

Here I Have Lived, Paul M. Angle, Abraham Lincoln Book Shop, 1971.

The Hidden Lincoln, From the Papers of William H. Herndon, Viking Press, 1938.

High on the Okaw's Western Bank—Vandalia, Illinois, 1819–39, Paul E. Stroble Jr., University of Illinois Press, 1992.

His Name Is Still Mudd, Edward Steers, Jr., Thomas, 1997.

His Name Was Mudd, Eden C. Weckesser, McFarland, 1991.

Historic Homes of Lexington, Richard L. Ruehrwein, Creative Company, 1996.

Historic Nelson Co. (Kentucky), Susan B. Smith, Gateway Press, 1971.

Historic Resource Study and Historic Structure Report (Lincoln's neighborhood), Edwin C. Bearss, U.S. Department of the Interior.

Historic Towns of the Middle States, edited by Lymon P. Powell, G.P. Putnam Sons, 1899.

Historical Atlas of New York City, Eric Hamberger, Henry Holt, 1994.

A Historical Guide to the United States, American Association for State and Local History, Penguin Books, 1986.

Historical Sketches of Quincy, Carl A. Landrum, n.d.

"Historians Oppose Opening of Booth Grave," Michael Kaufman, *Civil War Times Illustrated,* June 1995.

Historical and Descriptive Sketches of Edwardsville, Alton Etc., 1866.

Historical Souvenir of Greenville, Illinois, Will C. Carson, LeCrone Press, 1905.

History of Cambridge, Mass., Lucius R. Paige, H.O. Houghton, 1877.

History of the City of Cairo, John M. Landen, Southern Illinois University Press, 1910.

History of Coles County, Illinois, Windmill Publications, 1990 reprint.

History of DeWitt County, Illinois, 1839–1968.

History of Edgar County, William Baron, 1879.

The History of the Equinox Hotel.

A History of Fort Knox, Louisville Corps of Engineers, 1997 and 1998.

History of Jefferson Co. (Illinois), William Henry Perrin, Globe, 1883.

History of Knox and Daviess Counties, Indiana, Vincennes Historical and Antiquarian Society, 1973.

A History of the Lexington Cemetery, Burton Milward, The Lexington Cemetery Company, 1989.

History of the Lincoln Homestead, Frank Darneille, 1938.

History of Logan County, Lawrence B. Stringer, Pioneer, 1911.

History of Macon County, O.T. Banton, Macon County Historical Society, 1976.

History of Macoupin County, Illinois, Charles A. Walker, S.J. Clark, Publishing 1911.

History of Macoupin County, Illinois, Brink, McDonough, 1879.

History of Madison Co., Illinois.

History of the New York Avenue Presbyterian Church, Frank E. Edgington, New York Avenue Presbyterian Church.

History of Sangamon County, Inter-State, Publishing, 1881.

History of Shelby and Moultrie Counties, 1881.

History of Tazewell Co. Illinois, Charles C. Chapman, 1879.

History of Tazewell County, Ben C. Allensworth, 1905.

History of Troy, Indiana, Frank Baertich, 1983.

History of Union Co. (Illinois), George E. Parks.

History of Warrick, Spencer and Perry Counties Indiana, 1885.

History of Worcester and Its People, Charles Nutt, Lewis Historical Publishing, 1919.

Hollywood Cemetery, The History of a Southern Shrine, Mary H. Mitchell, Virginia State Library, 1985.

"The House at Eighth and Jackson," Geoffrey C. Ward, *American Heritage,* April 1989.

"Houses That Lincoln Knew," undated newspaper story.

"How Chicago Influenced the Career of Lincoln," *Chicago Sun Times,* February 6, 1955.

"How Lincoln 'Lost' His Inaugural Address," James T. Sterling, *Lincoln Herald,* December 1943.

Hudson River Guidebook, Arthur G. Adams, Fordham University Press, 1996.

I, Mary, Ruth Painter Randall, Little, Brown, 1959.

In the Days of My Father, General Grant, Jessie R. Grant, Harper and Row, 1925.

"The Illinois Campaign of 1856," Robert P. Howard, *Lincoln Herald,* Summer 1985.

Illinois Department of Conservation Publications.

Illinois' Fifth Capitol, Sunerine (Wilson) Temple and Wayne C. Temple, Philips Brothers, 1988.

Illinois Historical Markers, A Guide, edited by Nancy Hochsteller, Guide Press, 1986.

Illinois History, various issues including February 1961, 1963, 1965, 1966, 1968, 1979, 1987, 1989, 1993, 1995; April 1998; March 1979; October 1987.

Illinois, Off the Beaten Path, Rod Fenson and Julie Foreman, Globe Pequot Press, 1987 and 1999.

Illinois State Historical Library: All file folders pertaining to Lincoln, Lincoln Memorial Highway.

Illustrated Encyclopedia and Atlas of Madison County, Illinois, 1873.

In Lincoln's Footsteps, Don Davenport, Prairie Oak Press, 1991.

In the Footsteps of the Lincolns, Ida Tarbell, Harper and Row, 1924.

In the Lincoln Country, Carl and Rosalie Frazier, Hastings House, 1963.

"Incident of Destiny," Wilson Crady, *Lincoln Herald,* Fall 1981.

Indiana, A New Historical Guide, Robert M. Talor et al., Indiana Historical Society, 1989.

Indianapolis From Our Corner, Charlotte Cathcart, Indiana Historical Society, 1965.

The Insanity File, The Case of Mary Todd Lincoln, Mark E. Neely Jr. and R. Gerald McMurtry, Southern Illinois University Press, 1986.
"Inside History of the White House." Gibson Willets, *The Christian Herald,* 1908.
Inside the White House in War Times, William O. Stoddard, edited by Michael Burlingame, University of Nebraska Press 2000.
"The Intimate Lincoln," Joseph E. Suppiger, *Lincoln Herald,* various issues beginning 1981.
Jefferson County, Facts and Figures, Jefferson County Historical Society, Taylor Publishing, 1978.
Jefferson Davis, Hudson Strode, Harcourt, Brace, 1955.
Jefferson Davis, The Man and His Hour, William C. Davis, Louisiana State University Press, 1996.
The Jewel of Liberty, David E. Long, Stackpole Books, 1994.
"John E. Roll Recalls Lincoln," Garda Ann Turner, *Lincoln Herald,* fall 1960.
J. Wilkes Booth, Thomas A. Jones, Heritage Books, 1990 facsimile reprint.
John Wilkes Booth, Asia Booth Clarke, University of Mississippi Press, 1996.
John Wilkes Booth, Francis Wilson, Houghton Miffin, 1929.
John Wilkes Booth's Escape Route, James O. Hall, Surratt Society, 1984.
"John Wilkes Booth and the Murder of Abraham Lincoln," Michael W. Kauffman, *Blue and Gray* magazine, April 1990 and May 1996.
Kennedy and Lincoln, John K. Lattimer, Harcourt Brace Jovanovich, 1980.
The Kentucky Encyclopedia, edited by John C. Kleber, University of Kentucky Press, 1992.
Kentucky's Abraham Lincoln, John E. Kleber, Kentucky Historical Society, 1997.
"The Land of Lincoln," *Historic Traveler Magazine,* April 1998.
Landmarks of the American Revolution, Mark Boatner III, Stackpole Books, 1973.
Lexington, A Century in Photographs, Bettie L. Kerr and John D. Wright Jr., Lexington-Fayette County Historic Commission, 1984.
Lexington, Heart of the Blue Grass, John D. Wright Jr., Lexington-Fayette County Historic Commission, 1982.
The Lexington, Kentucky Cemetery, Hisle's Headstones, 1986.
The Library of Congress, Gene Gurney and Nick Apple, Crown, 1981.
Life of Lincoln, William Henry Herndon, Da Capo, 1983.
The Life of Abraham Lincoln, William E. Barton, Bobbs Merrill, 1925.
Life of Abraham Lincoln, William Dean Howells, 1860 (original version corrected by Lincoln; reprinted 1938 with Lincoln's notes).
The Life of Dr. Samuel A. Mudd, Nettie Mudd, Dick Wildes, reprinted 1975.
Life of Stephen A. Douglas, James W. Sheahan, Harper, 1860.
Life of Stephen Arnold Douglas, Frank E. Stevens.
Life on the Circuit With Lincoln, Henry Clay Whitney, Caxton Printers, 1940.
Lincoln, David Herbert Donald, Random House, 1995.
Lincoln 1840–1846, Harry E. Pratt, Abraham Lincoln Association, 1939.
"The Lincoln Boyhood National Memorial," David A. Kimball, *Lincoln Herald,* spring 1964.
"Lincoln and Douglas at the Bryant Cottage," Jim Fay, *Lincoln Herald,* winter 1998.

Lincoln and Douglas Debate Festival Booklet, 1994.

Lincoln Finds God, Ralph G. Lindstrom, Longsmans, Green, 1958.

Lincoln, A Pictorial History, Edward Steers Jr., Thomas, 1993.

Lincoln, A Picture Story of His Life, Stefan Lorant, Harper and Brothers, 1957.

Lincoln in American Memory, Merrill D. Peterson, Oxford University Press, 1994.

Lincoln and His America, David Plowden, Viking, 1970.

Lincoln and the Law, Geoffrey C. Ward, Sangamon State University.

Lincoln and the Lincolns, Harvey H. Smith, Lacoste, 1931.

"Lincoln and Macon County, Illinois," Edwin Davis, *Journal of Illinois State Historical Society,* April–July 1932.

"Lincoln and the Music of the Civil War," Kenneth A. Bernard, *Lincoln Herald,* spring 1964.

Lincoln at Gettysburg, William E. Barton, Bobbs-Merrill, 1930.

Lincoln at Gettysburg, Clark E. Carr, A.C. McClurg, 1906.

"Lincoln at The Wisconsin State Fair As Recalled by John W. Hoyt," Henry J. Peterson, *Lincoln Herald,* December 1949.

Lincoln as a Lawyer, John P. Frank, University of Illinois Press, 1961.

Lincoln as a Lecturer, Jacksonville Journal Courier

"Lincoln Assassination," William Hanchett, *Lincoln Herald,* winter 1997.

"Lincoln's Assassination: The 'Forgotten' Investigation," Gary R. Planck, *Lincoln Herald,* winter 1980.

Lincoln's Assassins, Roy Z. Chamlee Jr., McFarland, 1990.

Lincoln As They Saw Him, Herbert Mitgang, Rinehart, 1954.

Lincoln at Gettysburg, Wilson E. Barton, Peter Smith, 1930; reprint 1950.

Lincoln Before Washington, Douglas Wilson, University of Illinois Press, 1997.

Lincoln's Boyhood—A Chronicle of His Indiana Years, Francis Marion Van Natter.

Lincoln in Bloomington—Normal, Donna Reinking, McLean County Historical Society.

Lincoln and the Bluegrass, William L. Townsend, University of Kentucky Press, 1955.

"Lincoln and the Burners at New Salem," Wayne C. Temple, *Lincoln Herald,* summer 1965.

"Lincoln in Champaign County," Daniel Kilham Dodge, *Illinois* magazine.

Lincoln in Chicago, Blain Brooks Gernon, Ancarthe, 1934.

Lincoln in Chicago, Chicago Historical Society, n.d.

The Lincolns in Chicago, Blain Brooks Gernon, Ancarthe, 1934.

Lincoln's Connections with the Illinois and Michigan Canal, Wayne C. Temple, Illinois Bell, 1968.

The Lincoln Country in Pictures, Carl Frazier, Hastings House, 1963.

Lincoln in Danville, supplement to the *Commercial News* of Danville, February 12, 1993.

The Lincolns in Tennessee, Samuel C. Williams, Lincoln Memorial University, 1942.

Lincoln Day by Day, Editor-in-Chief, Earl Schenck Miers, Morningside, 1991.

The Lincoln-Douglas Debates, Harold Holzer, HarperCollins, 1993.

The Lincoln-Douglas Debates, Robert W. Johannsen, Oxford University Press, 1965.

The Lincoln-Douglas Debates, John Splaine, 1994.

"Lincoln's Failure at Gettysburg," Dorothy Meserve Kunhardt, *Life* magazine, November 15, 1963.

"Lincoln Finds a Rebel General," Mary B. Daughtry, *Blue and Gray* magazine, October 1989.

"Lincoln's First Gettysburg Address," Frank L. Klement, *Blue and Gray* magazine, December 1990.

Lincoln's First Love, Carrie Douglas Wright.

Lincoln for the Ages, edited by Ralph G. Newman, Doubleday, 1960.

"Lincoln's Funeral," R. Gerald McMurtry, *Lincoln Herald,* June 1944.

"Lincoln's Funeral Train in Pennsylvania," Charles William Heathcote, *Lincoln Herald,* December 1946.

Lincoln at Gettysburg—The Words That Remade America, Garry Wills, Simon and Schuster, 1992.

"The Lincolns' Globe Tavern," James T. Hickey, *Journal of the Illinois State Historical Society,* winter 1863.

"Lincoln's Step-Brother, John D. Johnston," Marilyn G. Ames, *Lincoln Herald,* spring 1980.

"Lincoln Greets Ashtabula," John H. Cramer, *Lincoln Herald,* June 1944.

Lincoln Herald, 1941 to present, many articles and notes in addition to those listed.

Lincoln Heritage Trail Tour Guide Magazine, various dates.

Lincoln's Herndon, David Donald, Knopf, 1948.

Lincoln Herndon Law Offices Volunteer Manual, Mark Johnson et al., Illinois Historic Preservation Agency, 1986.

"Lincoln History Tour of Chicago," *Chicago Daily News,* February 9, 1957.

Lincoln: His Words and His World, Country Beautiful Foundation, 1965.

Lincoln Highlights in Indiana History, R. Gerald McMurtry, Lincoln National Life Insurance Company.

The Lincoln Home, Hickey and Hostick, King V. Hostick, 1964.

"Lincoln's Bixby Letter: A Study in Authenticity," Joe Nickell, *Lincoln Herald,* winter 1989.

"Lincoln in the Governor's Chambers of the Illinois State House," Wayne C. Temple, *Lincoln Herald,* winter 1982.

"Lincoln's Hoosier Home," Don Davenport, *Lincoln Herald,* summer 1991.

Lincoln in His Wife's Home Town, William H. Townsend, Bobbs-Merrill, 1929.

Lincoln in Illinois, Octavia Roberts, Houghton Mifflin, 1918.

Lincoln's Interests in Jacksonville, thesis by Anita Gady

Lincoln's Journey to Greatness, Victor Searcher, John C. Winston, 1960.

"Lincoln in Massachusetts," *Lincoln Herald,* summer 1978.

"Lincoln in Philadelphia," Charles Williams Heathcote and John H. Cramer, *Lincoln Herald,* December 1944.

"Lincoln's Intimate Friend, Leonard Swett," Robert S. Eckley, *Journal of the Illinois State Historical Society,* autumn 1999 (and similar article in spring 2000).

"The Lincolns in Tennessee," Samuel C. Williams, *Lincoln Herald,* October 1941.

"Lincoln in Trenton, N.J.," Wayne C. Temple, *Lincoln Herald,* fall 1993.

"Lincoln in Trenton, N.J.—A Sequel," Daniel Bassuk, *Lincoln Herald,* spring 1995.

Lincoln Lived Here, Walter H. Miller, (author and publisher), 1971.

"The Lincoln Log Cabins," Adin Baber and Mary E. Lobb, *Lincoln Herald,* spring 1969.

Lincoln Lore, Lincoln National Life (numerous bulletins shown in Appendix 3).

Lincoln's Lost Speech, Elwell Crissey, Hawthorn, 1967.

"Lincoln Made His Mark in Ohio," Lloyd Ostendorf, *Lincoln Herald,* spring 1997.

The Lincoln Marriage, Jean Baker. Two speeches in Gettysburg, Pennsylvania: November 18, 1998, at the Lincoln Forum and November 19, 1999, at Gettysburg College (from notes made by author).

Lincoln's Marriage Ceremony, edited by Wayne C. Temple, Lincoln Memorial Press, 1960.

Lincoln's Mothers, Dorothy Clarke Wilson, Doubleday, 1981.

Lincoln's Men: How President Lincoln Became Father to an Army and a Nation, William C. Davis, Free Press, 1999.

The Lincoln Murder Conspiracies, William Hanchett, University of Illinois Press, 1983.

The Lincoln Murder Plot, Karen Zeinert, Linnet Books, 1999.

Lincoln National Memorial Highway, Hearings before the Special Commission—September 30, 1930, *Report to Governor*—July 7, 1929, *Report of Route Recommended*—August 11, 1932.

"Lincoln's New Home," Harold Holzer, *Americana* magazine, February 1989.

Lincoln's New Salem, Benjamin P. Thomas, Abraham Lincoln Association, 1934.

Lincoln's New Salem, Guidebook of the Record of the Historic Site, Terrance E. O'Brien, New Salem Lincoln League, 1984.

The Lincoln Nobody Knows, Richard N. Current, Hill and Wang, 1958.

The Lincoln No one Knows, Webb Garrison, Rutledge Hill Press, 1993.

"Lincoln's Ohio Tour," Lloyd Ostendorf, *Lincoln Herald,* spring 1960.

Lincoln in Ohio, John A. Lloyd, address to Queen City Optimists Club, February 9, 1980.

"Lincoln on June 3, 1855," Wayne C. Temple, *Lincoln Herald,* spring 1961.

Lincoln's Own Stories, Anthony Gross, Garden City Publishing, 1912.

Lincoln's Parentage and Childhood, Louis Warren, Century Company, 1926.

Lincoln Parks, The Story Behind the Scenery, Larry Waldron, KC Publications, 1986.

Lincoln in Photographs, Charles Hamilton and Lloyd Ostendorf, University of Oklahoma Press, 1963.

Lincoln, A Pictorial History, Paul E. Gleason, G. Bradley, 1998.

Lincoln's Quest for Union, Charles B. Strozier, Basic Books, 1982.

"Lincoln's Quest for Union," Charles B. Strozier, in *The Historian's Lincoln,* edited by Gabor Boritt, University of Illinois Press, 1988.

Lincoln Reader, edited by Paul Angle, Rutgers University Press, 1947.

Lincoln Reconsidered, David Donald, Random House, 1961.

"Lincoln's Religion and the Denominations," Charles L. Woodall, *Lincoln Herald,* fall 1982.

"Lincoln in Richmond," Clifford Dowdey, in Lincoln for the Ages, edited by Ralph G. Newman, Doubleday, 1960.

"Lincoln's Samuel Pate," Harold James Spelman, *Lincoln Herald*, fall 1964.

Lincoln's Secretary, A Biography of John G. Nicolay, Helen Nicolay, Longman, Green, 1949.

Lincoln and Shelbyville, Helen Cox Tregillis, private printing, 1979.

Lincoln Sites in Springfield, James T. Hickey, Illinois State Historical Library, n.d. (probably mid-1960s).

"The Lincolns and Spiritualism," *Civil War Times Illustrated*, August 1976.

Lincoln's Sons, Ruth Painter Randall, Little, Brown, 1955.

"Lincoln's Sons and the Marfan Syndrome," Harriet F. Durham, *Lincoln Herald*, summer 1977.

"The Lincolns and Spiritualism," Peggy Robbins, *Civil War Times Illustrated*, August 1976.

Lincoln's Springfield—A Guidebook and Brief History, Abraham Lincoln Association, 1938.

Lincoln in Springfield, Paul M. Angle, Lincoln Centennial Association, 1925.

Lincoln's Springfield, Harry E. Pratt, Illinois State Historical Society, 1955.

Lincoln Spoke Here, speech by Ely Dickerson Palmer.

Lincoln Talks, Emanuel Hertz, Bramhall House, 1986.

Lincoln in the Telegraph Office, David Homer Bates, Century, 1937.

The Lincolns in Tennessee, Samuel C. Williams, Lincoln Memorial University, 1942.

"Lincoln's Todd In-Laws," J. Duane Squires, *Lincoln Herald*, fall 1967.

Lincoln in Text and Context, Don E. Fehrenbacher, Stanford University Press, 1987.

Lincoln's Third Secretary—Memoirs of William O. Stoddard.

Lincoln Trail Association (files), Illinois State Historical Library.

Lincoln Under Fire, John Henry Cramer, Louisiana State University Press, 1948.

Lincoln the Unknown, Dale Carnegie, Forest Hills, 1932.

Lincoln's Unknown Private Life, Mariah Vance, Hastings House, 1995,

Lincoln's Vandalia, William E. Baringer, Rutgers University Press, 1949.

"Lincoln vs. Douglas, Debate Reenactment," no author listed, *Life* magazine, November 10, 1958.

The Lincolns in Virginia, John W. Wayland, C.J. Carrier, reprinted 1987.

The Lincolns Visit Lexington.

Lincoln in Year 1855, Paul M. Angle, Abraham Lincoln Association 1929.

Lincoln's Youth, Louis A. Warren, Indiana Historical Society, 1991.

Lincoln Visits Beloit and Janesville, Wisconsin, Lincoln Fellowship of Wisconsin, 1949.

Lincoln vs. Douglas, Richard Allen Heckman, Public Affairs Press, 1967.

Lincoln the War President, Gabor S. Boritt, Oxford University Press, 1992.

Lincoln Was Here (For Another Go at Douglas), C.C. Tisler and Aleita G. Tisler, MoCowat-Mercer Press, 1958.

The Lincoln Way, Report of the Board of Trustees of the Illinois State Historical Library, 1913.

"Lincoln's Western Travel, 1859," Waldo W. Braden, *Lincoln Herald*, summer 1988.

The Lineage of Lincoln, William E. Barton, Bobbs-Merrill, 1929.

The Little Bugler, William B. Styple, Belle Grove, 1998.

"The Little Giant," Patricia Denault, *American History Illustrated,* October 1970.

A Little History of a Great City, Fredric William Bond, Book and Print Guild, 1934.

Little Known Facts . . . Abraham Lincoln and the Civil War, George I. Cashman, Lincoln Center, 1963.

"Little Mac's Last Stand, Autumn 1862," Dave Roth, *Blue and Gray* magazine, holiday 1999.

The Living Land of Lincoln, Thomas Fleming, Reader's Digest Press, 1980

The Living Lincoln, Paul Angle and Earl Schenck Miers, Rutgers College, 1955 (1992).

Living with Lincoln, Paul Angle, Barnes and Noble, 1992.

"Loafing with Lincoln," Wayne C. Temple, *Lincoln Herald,* summer 1961.

"Location of the Rural Hotel in Springfield Where Abraham Lincoln Drank a Toast," Wayne C. Temple, *Lincoln Herald,* fall 1979.

Lost New York, Houghton Mifflin, 1968.

Love Is Eternal, Irving Stone, Doubleday, 1954. (I have not relied upon this novel for historical accuracy, but include it here as a favorite Lincoln book.)

Louisville, the Gateway City, Isabel McLennan McMeeklin, Julian Messner, 1946.

Louisville, Kentucky City Directory, 1843, G. Collins.

Louisville Lincoln Loop, Louis A. Warren, Standard Printing, 1922.

Macomb, A Pictorial History, John E. Hallwas, G. Bradley, 1990.

"The Man at the White House Window," Stephen B. Oates, *Civil War Times Illustrated,* December 1995.

The Man Who Elected Lincoln, Jay Monaghan, Bobbs Merrill, 1956.

Marks of Lincoln on Our Land, Maurice W. Redway and Dorothy Kendall Bracken, Hastings House, 1957.

Mary Lincoln, Biography of a Marriage, Ruth Painter Randall, Little, Brown, 1953.

Mary Todd Lincoln, Jean Baker, W.W. Norton, 1987.

"Mary Todd Lincoln," Mary Elizabeth Massey, *American History Illustrated,* May 1975.

Mary Todd Lincoln, Her Life and Letters, Justin Turner and Linda Turner, Knopf, 1972.

"Mary Todd Lincoln's Birthplace," J. Winston Coleman, *Lincoln Herald,* spring, 1963.

Mary, Wife of Lincoln, Katherine Helm, Harper, 1928; reprinted 1999.

Maryland, A New Guide to the Old Line State, Earl Arnett, Johns Hopkins Press, 1999.

Massachusetts, A Pictorial History, Walter M. Whitehill and Norman Kotker, Charles Scribner's Sons, 1976.

Mathew Brady, James D. Horan, Bonanza Books, 1955.

Mathew Brady and His World, Dorothy Meserve Kunhardt and Philip B. Kunhardt Jr., Time-Life Books, 1977.

Mattoon, A Picture History, Jean Johnson et al., G. Bradley, 1988.

McClellan's Own Story, George B. McClellan, Charles L. Webster, 1887.

Meade of Gettysburg, Freeman Cleaves, University of Oklahoma Press, 1960.

Memoirs of Abraham Lincoln in Edgar County, Illinois, Edgar County Historical Society, 1925.

Menard County, Illinois, Taylor, 1988.

Mentor Graham, The Man Who Taught Lincoln, Kunigunde Duncan and D.F. Nickols, University of Chicago Press, 1944.

The Missing Chapter in the Life of Abraham Lincoln, Bess V. Ehrmann, Walter M. Hill, 1938; reprinted 1990.

Montgomery County—Two Centuries of Change, Jane C. Sween, Winder Publications, 1984.

Monticello, A Celebration, Monticello Celebrations, 1987.

Moore's Complete Civil War Guide to Richmond, Samuel J.T. Moore Jr., revised ed. 1978.

Mount Pulaski 1836–1986 edited by Chuck Fricke, S.J. Clarke, 1986.

Mount Vernon, The Civil War Years, Dorothy Troth Muir, Mount Vernon Ladies Association, 1993.

Mr. Lincoln's City, Richard M. Lee, EPM, 1981.

Mr. Lincoln's Forts, A Guide to the Civil War Defenses of Washington, Benjamin F. Cooling III and Walton H. Owen II, White Mane, 1988.

"Mr. Lincoln's Growth in Faith," W. Emerson Reck, *Lincoln Herald,* spring 1990.

"Mr. Lincoln's Light From Under A Bushel-1851–5," Richard Friend Lufkin, *Lincoln Herald,* various issues from 1952 to 1956.

Mr. Lincoln's Neighborhood, George Painter, Eastern National Park and Monument Association, 1985.

Mr. Lincoln's Washington, Stanley Kimmel, Bramhall House, 1957.

Mr. Lincoln's Washington—The Civil War Dispatches of Noah Brooks, P. J. Staudenraus, Thomas Yoseloff, 1967.

Mr. Lincoln's White House, (website:) The Lehrman Institute, 2000.

Mrs. Abraham Lincoln, W.A. Evans, Knopf, 1932.

"Mrs. Lincoln's Visit to Springfield in 1866," Wayne C. Temple, *Lincoln Herald,* winter 1960.

"The Mystery of Little Eddie," Jason Emerson, *Journal of the Illinois State Historical Society,* autumn 1999.

Nancy Hanks, Adin Baber, private printing, 1963.

Nancy Hanks Lincoln, Harold E. Briggs, Bookman Associates, 1952.

"Nancy Hanks. West Virginian?" Edward A. Steers, *Lincoln Herald,* summer 1998.

National Park Service Maps and Guides for Petersburg, Richmond, City Point, Abraham Lincoln Birthplace, Fredericksburg, Gettysburg, Harpers Ferry, Washington, D.C.

"New York City During the Civil War," *Blue and Gray* magazine, December 1996.

New York, Yesterday and Today, Judith H. Browning, Corsair, Publications, 1990.

Niagara, A Brief History of the Falls, Pierce Berton, Kodansha International, 1997.

Niagara, River of Fame, Kiwanis Clubs of Niagara Falls and Stamford, Ontario, Ryerson Press, 1970.

O Albany, William Kennedy, Viking, 1983.

"The Occupation," Thomas Thatcher Graves, in *Battles and Leaders,* vol. 6, edited by Castle Books, 1956.

Off the Beaten Path—Illinois, 5th ed., Bob Puhala, Globe Pequot Press, 1999.

Old Illinois Homes, John Drury, Illinois State Historical Society, 1948.

Old Landmarks and Historic Personages of Boston, rev. ed., Samuel Adams Drake, Charles E. Tuttle, 1975.

Old New York in Early Photographs, Mary Black, Dover, 1973.

Old Philadelphia in Early Photographs 1839–1914, Robert F. Looney, Dover, 1976.

On This Spot: Washington D.C., Douglas E. Evelyn and Paul Dickson, Farragut, 1992.

On Broadway, A Journal Uptown Over Time, David W. Dunlap, Rizzoli, 1988.

An Oral History of Abraham Lincoln, John G. Nicolay's Interviews and Essays, edited by Michael Burlingame, Southern Illinois University Press, 1996.

Our Land Through Lincoln's Eyes, Carolyn Bennett Patterson, National Geographic.

Owen Lovejoy, Abolitionist in Congress, Edward Magdol, Rutgers University Press, 1967.

"The Passing of a Shrine," J. Winston Coleman Jr., *Lincoln Herald,* October 1947.

Peoria, Jerry Klein, Peoria Historical Society, 1985.

Perry County, A History, Thomas James De La Hunt, W.K. Stewart, 1916.

The Personal Finances of Abraham Lincoln, Harry E. Pratt, Lakeside Press, 1943.

Personal Recollections of Early Decatur, Abraham Lincoln, Richard Ogelsby, and the Civil War, Jane Martin Johns, 1912.

Petersburg in the Civil War, William D. Henderson, H.E. Howard, 1998.

Petersburg's Story, Edward A Wyatt, Titmas Optical, 1860.

Philadelphia, A Three Hundred Year History, edited by Russell F. Weigley, W.W. Norton, 1982.

Philadelphia in the Civil War, Frank H. Taylor, City of Philadelphia, 1913.

A Pictorial Guide to West Virginia's Civil War Sites, Stan B. Cohen, Pictorial Histories, 1990.

Pictorial History of Edgar County, Paris Beacon, 1997.

Pictorial Landscape History of Charleston, Illinois, Nancy Easter Shick and Douglas K. Meyer, Raden Graphics.

A Piece of Time, Laura Isabelle Osburn Nance.

Pilgrimage Conducted, Louis A. Warren, 1937.

The Pioneer and the Prairie Lawyer, Willard Mounts, Ginwill, 1994.

Pioneer Kentucky, William R. Jillson, State Journal, 1934.

Pittsburgh, The Story of an American City, 4th ed. Stefan Lorant, Authors Ed., 1988.

"A Pittsburgh Album, 1758–1958," Roy Stoyker and Mel Serdenberg, *Pittsburgh Post Gazette.*

Places and People in Old Decatur, Helen Beeson et al., 1975.

"The Plot to Rob Lincoln's Tomb," John R. Kerwood, *American History Illustrated,* January 1971.

Prairie Progress, Taylor, 1976.

Prairie of Promise, Springfield and Sangamon County, Edward J. Russo,

Prelude to Greatness, Don E. Fehrenbacher, Stanford University Press, 1962.

Prelude to Progress—The History of Macon County, Illinois, Ruth Wallace Lynn, Mason County Board of Supervisors, 1968.

Preservation News, July 1988.

President Lincoln's Third Largest City, Brooklyn and the Civil War, E.A. Livingston, Budd Press, 1994.

Presidential Anecdotes, Paul F. Boller Jr., Penguin, 1981.

The Presidential Families, E.H. Gwynne Thomas, Hippocrene Books, 1989.

Presidential Places, Gary Ferris, John F. Blair, 1999.
The President's House, William Seale, White House Historical Association, 1986.
The President's Wife, Ishbel Ross, G. P. Putnam's Sons, 1973.
Pioneer Days in Troy, John E. Schroeder, 1966.
Pioneers of Menard and Mason County, Illinois, T. G. Onstot, reprinted 1986.
"A Question of Faith," Edward Steers, Jr., *North and South* magazine, September 1999.
"Rally Day in Carmi," *Illinois History* magazine, February 1962.
"'The Real Issue,' An Analysis of the Final Lincoln-Douglas Debate," James W. Anderson, *Lincoln Herald,* spring 1967.
Recollected Words of Abraham Lincoln, Don E. Fehrenbacher, Stanford University Press, 1996.
Recollections of Abraham Lincoln, Ward Hill Lamon, University of Nebraska Press, 1994.
"Rediscovering The Supposed Grave of Lincoln's Brother," R. Gerald McMurtry, *Lincoln Herald,* February 1946.
"Reminiscences of Abraham Lincoln," Thomas J. Pickett, *Lincoln Herald,* December 1943.
Reminiscences of Abraham Lincoln, collected by Allen Thorndike Rice, North American Publishing, 1886.
Reminiscences of General Herman Haupt, files at Fredericksburg National Military Park.
Reminiscences of Peace and War, Mrs. Roger A. Pryor, Macmillan, 1904.
Restoration of Ford's Theatre, George J. Olszewski, National Park Service, 1963.
Restoring Mr. Lincoln's Home, Judith Winkelmann, Taylor, 1989.
Rhode Island, An Historic Guide, Sheila Steinburg and Cathleen McGuigan, Rhode Island Centennial Foundation, 1976.
Robert Todd Lincoln, A Man in His Own Right, John S. Goff, University of Oklahoma Press, 1969.
Rochester Union and Advertiser, several articles by Lieutenant George Breck from the collection at Fredericksburg Battlefield Visitor's Center.
Rock Island Argus and Union, February 11, 1922
Rockford Morning Star, February 10, 1952
Rockport-Spencer County Sesquicentennial, 1968.
St. Louis Post-Dispatch, February 12, 1997.
St. Louis District Historic Properties Management Report No. 36, U.S. Army Corps of Engineers, November 1988.
The Sangamon Country, Helen Van Cleave Blankmeyer, Philips Bros. Inc. 1965.
The Sangamon Saga, Bruce Alexander Campell
Sangamon Valley Library. Various newspaper files on Springfield, Illinois, sites.
The Second Rebellion, James McCague, Dial Press, 1968.
"Seize Mr. Lincoln," Richard Betterly, *Civil War Times Illustrated,* February, 1987
Selected Menard County, Illinois Cemetery Inscriptions, no author, n.d.
A Series of Monographs Concerning the Lincoln's and Hardin County, Kentucky, R. Gerald McMurtry, Enterprise Press, 1938.
Service with the Sixth Wisconsin Volunteers, Rufus Davis, Morningside Press, 1914.

Seventeen Years at 8th and Jackson, Dyba and Painter.

"Shapers of Lincoln's Religious Image," Joseph R. Nightengale, *Journal of the Illinois State Historical Society*, autumn 1999.

Shelbyville Past and Present, Chautauqua History Book Committee, 1991.

Sickles the Incredible, W.A. Swanberg, Scribners, 1956.

Silver Spring Success, Richard C. Jafferson, 1996.

The Site Adrift in the City—The Evolution of the Lincoln Home Neighborhood, thesis by Timothy P. Townsend, historian for the National Park.

Six Months at the White House, F.B. Carpenter, Hurd and Houghton, 1866.

Springfield in 1892.

"Springfield's Public Square in Lincoln's Day," Harry E. Pratt, *Illinois Bar Journal*, May 1952.

Stanton, Benjamin P. Thomas and Harold M. Hyman, Knopf.

Stephen Douglas, The Last Years, 1857–1861, Damon Wells, University of Texas Press, 1971.

The Story of Farmington, Farmington Historic Home, 1997.

The Story of Oregon, Illinois, "Book Committee."

Story of Peoria, Earnest E. East, Record Publishing, 1939.

Story of Peoria's First Presbyterian Church, Frank Stewart, 1967.

"Strange History Brought to Light . . . And His Face Was Chalky White," Dorothy Meserve Kunhardt, *Life* magazine, February 15, 1963.

Surratt Courier, August 2000.

Tad and His Father, F. Lauriston Bullard, Little, Brown, 1915.

Tad Lincoln, John D. Weaver, Dodd, Mead, 1963.

Tad Lincoln's Father, Julia Taft Bayne, 1931.

Tales and Breadcrumbs, Kathryn E. Wilson, NACO, 1993.

Tails and Shrines of Abraham Lincoln, Lincoln Memorial, 1934.

Tanner, Corporal James. Typed notes of the Lincoln deathbed scene at Lincoln College Library.

Taylorville, Illinois newspaper clippings, February 9, 1985.

Ten Years in the Saddle: The Memoir of William Woods Averell, edited by Edward K. Eckert and Nicholas J. Amato, Presidio Press, 1978.

"'Til Death Do Us Part: The Marriage of Abraham Lincoln and Mary Todd," *Lincoln Herald*, spring 1982.

"There I Grew Up," William E. Wilson, *American Heritage*, October 1966.

They Broke the Prairies, Earnest Elmo Calkins, University of Illinois Press, 1937, 1989.

This Damned Old House: The Lincolns in the White House, David Herbert Donald, in *The White House, The First 200 Years*, edited by Frank Freidel and William Pencak, Northeastern University Press, 1994.

"This Side of the Mountains: Abraham Lincoln's 1848 Visit to Massachusetts," *Lincoln Herald*, summer 1978.

"Thomas and Abraham Lincoln as Farmers," Wayne C. Temple, Historical Bulletin No. 53, Lincoln Fellowship of Wisconsin, 1966 (from review in *Lincoln Herald*, fall 1997).

Three Hundred Years of Union Co. Illinois, George Parks, 1984.

Through Lincoln's Door, Virginia Stuart Brown, 1952.

A Tour Guide to Civil War Sites in Maryland, Susan Cooke Soderberg, White Mane Books, 1998.

A Tour Guide to the Civil War, Alice Hamilton Cromie, Quadrangle Books, 1965.

Tour of Historic Springfield, Floyd S. Barringer.

"The Tragedy of Major Rathbone," W. Emerson Reck, *Lincoln Herald*, winter 1984.

Trenton Old and New, Harry J. Promore, revised and edited by Mary J. Messler, MacCrellish and Quigley, 1964.

The Trials of Mrs. Lincoln, Samuel A. Schreiner Jr., Donald I. Fine, 1987.

"The Trouble with the Bixby Letter," Michael Burlingame, *American Heritage*, July/August 1999.

A True History of the Assassination of Abraham Lincoln, Louis J. Weichmann, Knopf, 1975.

Twenty Days, Philip and Dorothy Meserve Kunhardt, Harper and Row, 1965.

Two Centuries in Elizabethtown (Kentucky), Gary Kempf.

Two Centuries in Elizabethtown and Hardin County (Kentucky), Daniel Elmo McClure Jr., 1977.

Two Hundred Years at the Falls, A History of Louisville, George H. Yater, Heritage Corporation, 1979.

"Vacation Tour Through Lincoln Land," Ralph Gray, *National Geographic Magazine*, February 1952.

The Valiant Hours, edited by W. S. Nye, Stackpole, 1961.

Vandalia: Wilderness Capital of Lincoln's Land.

Vincennes, A Pictorial History, Richard Day, G. Bradley, 1994.

A Walk Through Oak Ridge Cemetery, Floyd Barringer, Sangamon County Historical Society, 1967.

Walker's Brief History of Illinois.

A Walking Tour of Historic Georgetown, Foundation for the Preservation of Historic Georgetown, 1971.

A Walking Tour of Virginia's Historic Petersburg, Chamber of Commerce of Petersburg, 1969.

Washington in Lincoln's Time, Noah Brooks, Quadrangle Books, 1871.

We, the People, Unites States Capitol Historical Society, 1976.

We Saw Lincoln Shot, Timothy S. Good, University Press of Mississippi, 1995.

"When Lincoln Left Town with Another Woman," Wayne C. Temple, *Lincoln Herald*, winter 1966.

"When Lincoln Visited New Jersey," Evald Benjamin Lawson, *Contemporary Life*, February 1943.

When Lincoln Went to Egypt

The White House, Kenneth W. Leish, Newsweek Book Division, 1972.

"Who Is Buried in Booth's Tomb?" Joseph George Jr., *Lincoln Herald*, winter 1995.

"Who Wrote the Letter to Mrs. Bixby," Roy P. Basler, *Lincoln Herald*, February 1943.

Wilkes Booth Comes to Washington, Larry Starkey, Random House, 1976.

William H. Seward, Edward Everett Hale Jr., George W. Jacobs, 1910.

William Henry Seward, Thornton Kirkland Lothrop, Houghton Miffin, 1896 (Riverside Press, 1924).

William Henry Seward, Glyndon G. Van Deusen, Oxford University Press, 1967.

William Henry Seward, Lincoln's Right Hand, John M. Taylor, HarperCollins, 1991.

"William Herndon, Memory, and Lincoln Biography," Rodney O. Davis, *Journal of the Illinois Historical Society,* winter 1998.

"Willie Was the Favorite," Dorothy Meserve Kunhardt, *Life* magazine, April 23, 1963.

With Malice Toward None, Stephen B. Oates, Harper and Row, 1977.

The Women Lincoln Loved, William E. Barton, Bobbs Merrill, 1927.

The World of Mathew Brady, Ray Meredith, Brooke House, 1976.

"Why Seward," *Lincoln Herald,* May 1998.

WPA Guidebooks, various states (Connecticut, District of Columbia, Iowa, Kentucky, Illinois, Indiana, Maryland, Massachusetts, Michigan, New Hampshire, New Jersey, New York, Ohio, Pennsylvania, Rhode Island, Virginia, Wisconsin).

Yesterday's Cleveland, George E. Condon, E. A. Seemann, 1976.

Yesterday's Columbus, George E. Condon, E. A. Seemann, 1977.

Yesterday's Philadelphia, George E. Condon, E. A. Seemann, 1976.

Young Abe Lincoln, W. Fred Conway, FBH, 1997.

Appendix VI

Comparisons Between Robert E. Lee and Ulysses S. Grant

1. The two men were the most prominent and famous of all the generals in the Civil War. (They faced each other in battle only less than a year and fought only three major battles against each other. The only clear victory was Lee's at Cold Harbor.)
2. Both have one syllable in their last names, and
3. two in their middle names.
4. Both fathers went bankrupt before the sons were born.
5. Both went to West Point
6. largely because the family could not afford to send them to another school.
7. Both were born in a house, still standing
8. by a major river (Potomac and Ohio).
9. At both birth dates a Virginian was in the White House.
10. Both had at least two brothers and
11. two sisters.
12. Both moved from their birthplaces before age four
13. to a town on the same river as his birthplace.
14. Both had three sons,
15. one named after himself,
16. one with his father's name,
17. and one named after his father-in-law.
18. The latter was the firstborn, who
19. went to West Point like his father and
20. became a general.
21. Both middle sons were known by nicknames bearing no relationship to their given names. William Henry Fitzhugh (Rooney) Lee and Ulysses (Buck) Grant.

22. Both parents moved while their sons were at West Point.
23. Lee's mother to the Georgetown section of Washington, and Grant's parents from Georgetown, Ohio.
24. Both moved very slowly through the military ranks, which strained their finances, family relationships, and careers.
25. Both had at least one daughter.
26. Both had a wife raised on a plantation
27. who was cared for by slaves.
28. Both were married at about the same age (Lee, twenty-three, and Grant, twenty-six)
29. to younger women about the same age (twenty-one and twenty-two)
30. with a two-syllable first name (Mary and Julia)
31. in their (Lee' and Grant's) father-in-law's home
32. overlooking a major river (Arlington House—Potomac River and Dent town house in St. Louis—Mississippi River).
33. Both wives had a physical problem (Grant's wife was cross-eyed and Lee's was confined to a wheelchair with arthritis.)
34. Both lived in New York City for several years.
35. Both were descended from English ancestors, and
36. from Revolutionary War Continental officers.
37. In an age where childhood deaths were common, all eleven of their children survived to adulthood.
38. Both spent 1861 in relatively minor positions
39. but wound up the commanding general of their army,
40. although they served in that capacity a fairly short period (Grant about thirteen months and Lee about two months).
41. Both were expert horseman
42. but were severely injured by a horse before a major battle
43. beginning with the letter S (Shiloh and Sharpsburg).
44. Both were strongly supported by their president when they failed and many in the public turned against them.
45. Both had sons to participate in the Civil War. Lee had two who were generals and one a lieutenant. Young Fred Grant served as an informal aid to his father.
46. Both had a son with him at a major Civil War battle (Grant's twelve-year-old son was with him at Vicksburg, Lee's sons were in various battles with him and all three were in the Appomattox Campaign).
47. Both had sons develop life-threatening conditions in 1863 as a result of their involvement in the war. Rooney Lee was wounded,

and Fred Grant caught a severe fever at Vicksburg, and was also wounded in the leg near there.

48. Their two most famous and capable subordinates were William Tecumseh Sherman and Thomas Jonathan (Stonewall) Jackson. Both have two syllables in their first name,

49. three in their middle, and

50. two in their last, which has

51. seven letters.

52. Both Sherman and Jackson lost their fathers when they were young,

53. and were brought up by other families.

54. Both Sherman & Jackson went to West Point

55. at the same time, and

56. had been college instructors

57. at schools known by three letters (VMI and LSU).

58. Both had a child die young and

59. married a daughter of a prominent public figure (Sherman—senator, Jackson—college president).

60. Both Jackson and Sherman were considered highly eccentric

61. and had as their greatest achievement a campaign through a mountainous area (Shenandoah Valley and march from Chattanooga to Atlanta).

62. Both Lee and Grant had two sons marry two times.

63. Both Lee and Grant served in the Mexican War,

64. under Winfield Scott

65. in Mexico City.

66. Both served in Texas and

67. stayed in the Menger Hotel in San Antonio.

68. Both married into a family much wealthier than their own.

69. Both lived in St. Louis with their family while on military duty.

70. Both were asked by Lincoln to lead the Union army.

71. Both had descendants or close relatives serve the United States as generals after the Civil War (Grant's son, Lee's nephew).

72. Probably Lee and Grant's greatest defeats were very similar charges across open ground at a fortified position, which cost them the battle and thousands of lives wasted (Gettysburg and Cold Harbor).

73. Probably the two most significant events of the Civil War occurred to both within a day of each (defeat at Gettysburg and surrender of Vicksburg, July 3 and 4, 1863, Lee's biggest mistake and Grant's greatest triumph other than the surrender itself).

74. Both were beardless before the war and

75. both wore one for the remainder of their lives after the war started.
76. Both had his oldest son follow his profession (Fred Grant became a general, and Custis Lee followed his father as president of Washington (and Lee) College).
77. Both had a high-ranking subordinate general with a name beginning with "H" who lost an arm during the war (Howard's arm was amputated and Hood's was totally paralyzed).
78. At the end of the war both sides had two main armies with similar commands, Lee versus Grant, Johnston versus Sherman. The Confederate commanders were from Virginia, both retreating from
79. Union commanders who had been born in Ohio,
80. but were living in other states at the start of the war.
81. Johnston and Sherman had the same number of syllables in their first, middle, and last names,
82. lived in Washington after the war, and
83. wrote their memoirs in the mid-1870s.
84. The Confederate armies were fleeing from major Southern capitals, which had been burned (Columbia and Richmond).
85. Both Southern generals (Lee and Johnston) had gone to West Point
86. at the same time and
87. had served in Texas,
88. had been near the top rank of all army officers in the U.S. Army at the start of the War,
89. and were the sons of Revolutionary War heroes who had been friends.
90. Both were still in the army when the war started.
91. Both Union commanders had also gone to West Point,
92. at the same time,
93. had served in California, and
94. were out of the army at the start of the war.
95. Both armies surrendered at about the same time
96. in small, out-of-the-way hamlets.
97. Both Grant and Lee died at age sixty-three,
98. old beyond their years.
99. Both Sherman and Johnston died in 1891 (Johnston as a result of catching pneumonia standing bare-headed in the rain at Sherman's funeral)
100. and are buried in states beginning with "M" (Missouri and Maryland).
101. Neither Grant nor Lee used profanity.
102. Both were known to hate slavery, but
103. Both had wives who had owned slaves.

104. Both were given at least two houses, still standing, to live in after the war that they did not have to purchase. (Grant was given one in Galena, Illinois, by the citizens there, and a second in D.C., and of course the White House was "loaned" to him for eight years. Lee lived in the two houses on the Washington College campus—old president's and new president's houses, as well as Derwent, west of Richmond, for a while).

105. Both served as a president after the war, Lee of Washington College.

106. Both were promoted for president of the United States in 1868.

107. Both died relatively poor,

108. although their descendants gained quick wealth (from a book Grant wrote and recovery of an interest in Arlington Cemetery property by Lee's oldest son and heir of the property's former owner, his grandfather).

109. Both spent the night in the same hotel on consecutive nights in Farmville, Virginia during the march to Appomadox.

110. Lee is considered the last "old-style general" and Grant the first modern general.

111. Both survived two brothers and two sisters.

112. Both died in a mountainous area (Blue Ridge and Adirondacks)

113. from medical conditions caused or aggravated by the war (Lee's heart problems began during the Civil War and were initiated by the stress. Grant started smoking heavily after the newspapers reported that he liked cigars. He got so many from admirers that he began to smoke heavily rather than waste them. This caused the cancer that killed him).

114. Both are buried in a building or mausoleum rather than a cemetery,

115. close to a church (Lee Chapel of Washington and Lee and across from the Riverside Church in New York City),

116. in the state in which they died.

117. Both were survived by their wife,

118. all sons, and

119. had four children survive to the twentieth century (Lee five and all of Grant's).

Appendix VII

The Ultimate List of Comparisons and Similarities between Theodore and Franklin Roosevelt

1. Both had a common ancestor who came to America in the 1640s. Therefore the two men were distant cousins and had many common relatives.
2. Both TR and FDR had eight letters in their first names.
3. Both were from New York State.
4. The families knew each other fairly well and visited back and forth. FDR's wife also visited the homes of both as a child, and Franklin romped with TR's children as a boy. FDR's only recorded act of defiance as an adolescent with his parents was when he was told not to leave school to visit Sagamore Hill but he did anyway.
5. In 1880 TR's mother hosted several parties at their home for TR's fiancée. At one a close friend of his older sister Anna met a man twice her age and then married him in a few months. The friend was Sara Delano, FDR's mother, who told her son that she would have been an old maid if she had not gone to the party at TR's home and then been escorted by TR's mother and sister to James Roosevelt's home to further the relationship.
6. TR's brother was FDR's godfather and father of his wife, Eleanor.
7. TR's sister Anna, known as Bamie or Auntie Bye, was very close to TR, Eleanor, and FDR.
8. She had been proposed to by FDR's father, whom she rejected.
9. Also she wanted to marry FDR's half brother and pursued him to England where he rejected her.
10. When TR came to Washington after being sworn in as president when President McKinley died, he and part of the family lived in Bamie's house at 1733 N Street. Later FDR and his family stayed for several years in the same house when he was assistant secre-

tary of the navy. Therefore it can be said that they both lived in at least three houses, counting the Governor's Mansion in Albany and the White House.

11. Anna also raised TR's first child, Alice, for her first three years after his wife died. She was considered a close confident and advisor to her and to FDR's wife (Anna Eleanor), who was an orphan and was considered to be named partly for her mother and for Anna.

12. Both had fathers who died when they were about 100 days of their nineteenth birthday. Surprisingly FDR's father was born before TR's.

13. The fathers were friends and cousins.

14. Neither father served in the Civil War although they were in their thirties at the time of the war.

15. Both fathers had known a president. TR Sr. met Lincoln, and James Roosevelt knew Arthur and Cleveland well.

16. Both fathers died in New York City,

17. and their last words to their son were "to be a good man."

18. Both of TR's parents died young, in their forties, while both of FDR's died old, at seventy-two and eighty-six.

19. Both TR and FDR were the second child of their family,

20. and named a son after himself.

21. Both suffered from severe physical handicaps requiring years of great physical effort and exercises to try to overcome although neither completely did. (TR had severe asthma as a child and FDR had polio after he ran for vice president. TR also became blind in one eye during his term as president.)

22. Both went to out-of-state locations to improve their health (Georgia and North Dakota).

23. Both have parks created in their honor. (TR National Monument in North Dakota and Warm Springs in Georgia. TR went to North Dakota after his first wife died to restore his mental health and strengthen his body. FDR spent many days at Warm Springs to strengthen his legs in warm waters there.)

24. Both sent their sons out of state to toughen them up.

25. Both wore glasses, and

26. Both preferred pince-nez type.

27. Both were educated by private tutors,

28. except for a short time when they went to school in Europe.

29. Both as young teenagers were amateur photographers,

30. avid readers,

31. liked Mark Twain whom they both met,

32. and shot and stuffed hundreds of birds as amateur naturalists,
33. some of which were sent to the American Museum of Natural History,
34. where they both were members from early childhood.
35. Both graduated from Harvard,
36. with a bachelor of arts degree.
37. Both attended Columbia Law School,
38. but did not graduate. (FDR got his license by passing the Bar exam.)
39. Both became bored with the law after working in a law office. (FDR told his fellow law clerks that he intended to follow a career modeled after TR's by going to New York General Assembly, becoming assistant secretary of the navy, governor of New York, president.)
40. Both were elected to Phi Beta Kappa.
41. Both were married in their early twenties (twenty-two and twenty-three),
42. although both proposed at twenty-one
43. to women about two and a half years younger.
44. (TR gave away Eleanor at FDR's wedding. She was his niece and visited and played with TR's children as a child.)
45. Both had a wife with a first name beginning with "A" (Alice, Anna Eleanor).
46. TR's wife died the same year in which FDR's wife was born to TR's brother, 1884,
47. and both events took place in New York City.
48. Both had a wife with a name beginning with "E" (Edith was TR's second wife),
49. whom they knew as a young child,
50. and who had a brother die in infancy,
51. and named a child after themselves (*Kermit* Roosevelt and *Anna Eleanor*).
52. TR's wife suffered a miscarriage after their first son was born and FDR and his wife lost an infant after their first son.
53. All other children survived childhood, with several close calls from severe illnesses that were nearly fatal.
54. Both had a wife who was an activist and close political advisor, involved in social work, and initially did not like to greet people.
55. Both primarily left the discipline of the children to their wife,
56. although TR and FDR both put so much stress and pressure to succeed on especially the first son that both became ill.
57. Both had a wife who had lived in London (Edith moved there after her father died, and Eleanor went to school in a suburb).
58. Both had a wife who toured Europe extensively as a child.

59. Both lived with his mother in her house with his wife after his marriage.
60. Both were married for over thirty-one years.
61. Both lived next to an adjoining New York identical house owned by a family member (TR's uncle and FDR's mother).
62. TR's brother Elliott and FDR's son Elliott were both second sons (other than FDR's infant who died), were family rebels who did not go to Harvard like all their brothers, lived in Texas, and had severe martial problems, and
63. lived openly with mistresses.
64. Neither branch of the family supported the other politically since TR's family were Republicans and FDR's were Democrats. However, FDR and his father supported TR, whom they admired more than any other living person. TR Jr. was narrowly defeated for governor of New York through the efforts of Eleanor, which indirectly led to FDR's election later.
65. Both honeymooned in Europe for about three months.
66. Both had six children born,
67. Both with about the same number of years between the births.
68. Both had a daughter born first,
69. in New York City,
70. with a name beginning with "A" (Alice, Anna), each named after the mother.
71. Both daughters married a man at least ten years older than she was,
72. were married while her father was president,
73. and had a daughter as her first child.
74. Both TR and FDR had a son born second,
75. with his (TR's and FDR's) father's name,
76. who was an avid football player in spite of numerous health problems,
77. whose first job was a laborer at a mill,
78. and lived in California.
79. Both second sons were regarded as the black sheep of the family,
80. were named for his wife's family,
81. were pets and favorites of their mother,
82. were sent west to toughen them,
83. wrote a book about the family,
84. had notorious extramarital affairs,
85. and served in England during the Second World War.
86. Both had a son born last,
87. in a location far from their permanent New York home (Washington, D.C., and New Brunswick),

88. who was the first son to die (other than FDR's infant who died),
89. and the second, third, fifth, and sixth children were boys.
90. Both took two trips abroad with only his second oldest son,
91. one of which was to Africa.
92. Both had a son die before reaching twenty-one.
93. Both had a seventeen-year-old son when first inaugurated president (TR's oldest; FDR's youngest).
94. Both had children born in at least three different states.
95. Both named a son after himself.
96. Both sent all of their sons to Groton Preparatory School. (Franklin also attended this school founded by a friend of TR's. TR was offered a position on the faculty and was a frequent speaker while FDR was a student.)
97. Both had at least three sons graduate from Harvard. (Only Elliott did not go.)
98. Both had a son "defect to the other side" to the dismay of their family. (Kermit became a yachting buddy with FDR and was nearby when FDR was shot at in 1933, and John became a Republican.)
99. No child of TR was divorced, while FDR's were involved in many divorces and had a total of nineteen marriages. (In fact, no president's child had been divorced before FDR).
100. TR's brother and FDR's brother-in-law were brilliant, talented men whose lives and accomplishments were cut short by alcoholism.
101. Both TR's & FDR's wives toured Europe with their two youngest sons when they were about the same ages (TR's sons: eleven and thirteen; FDR's thirteen and fourteen).
102. Both spoke French and German
103. and had a tenor voice.
104. Both were determined but somewhat unsuccessful athletes in college.
105. Both served in the New York State Assembly,
106. in his twenties.
107. Both served as assistant secretary of the navy,
108. in his thirties,
109. and used the same desk.
109. Both were elected governor of New York,
110. with a plurality of less than 3 percent, (TR Jr. later lost by less than 2 percent)
112. in his forties.
113. Both ran for vice president
114. within two years of age forty.
115. Both were elected president from New York.

116. Both were Masons, in Lodge 806 and 8 (FDR).
117. Both ran against at least six other candidates in a presidential election.
118. Both were involved in a war with Japan.
119. Both took the oath as president at a site other than the U.S. Capitol Building (Buffalo and the White House).
120. Both referred to Washington, Lincoln, and God in an inaugural address.
121. Both visited Europe extensively as children. TR spent a year there with his family at ages eleven and thirteen, and FDR went eight times in his first fourteen years.
122. Both had at least six books published in their lifetimes.
123. Both were nominated for president in Chicago.
124. Both defeated presidential opponents from their same state (Parker, Willkie).
125. Both exercised pocket vetoes.
126. Both lived at several locations in New York City and worked there. Their first homes were fairly close, at Twentieth and Thirty-sixth Streets,
127. and then they both lived fairly close further north, at Fifty-seventh and Sixty-fifth Street.
128. Both TR houses have been destroyed, while both FDR houses still exist. TR's birthplace house has been reconstructed, however.
129. Both were victims of intended assassinations,
130. while neither was the president at the time.
131. Both assassins were immigrants
132. from mid-Europe (Germany and Italy)
133. who lived with his uncle upon arrival in America,
134. were in their thirties,
135. and had unusual, seven-letter names (Schrank, Zangara).
136. Both attempts were in cities beginning with *M* (Milwaukee and Miami).
137. at night
138. in an open car
139. while traveling to make a speech.
140. (Of the eleven presidential assassination attempts, only one was directed at an ex-president—TR, and one at a president elect—FDR.)
141. In both cases people were seriously wounded but survived, TR himself in 1912 and several in the attack on FDR.
142. Both assassins were tried and sentenced within a month. Zangara shot at FDR on February 15, 1933, missed Roosevelt, but struck

four other people. He was tried for attempted murder and found guilty. Then Chicago Mayor Cermack died from his wounds. Zangara was then tried again for murder, sentenced to death, had appeals rejected, and was executed on March 30, 1933, thirty-three days after the attack. Schrank was found insane November 13 after his October 14 attack. Also Czolgosz was executed fifty-three days after his attack on McKinley. The time frames shown are in contrast to those in our current justice system.

143. Both named three executors in his will,
144. none being family members except for the oldest son.
145. Both birthplaces and
146. adult homes are national historic sites and are open to the public.
147. Both adult home settings are rural, parklike,
148. multi-acre, on ancient Indian campgrounds, and
149. have names beginning with S (Sagamore Hill and Springwood).
150. Both homes are near small towns with two words in their names, which give their names to two branches of the Roosevelt family line (Oyster Bay and Hyde Park),
151. located on a body of water (Long Island Sound and Hudson River),
152. were built in the nineteenth century,
153. and had a substantial addition built in the twentieth century.
154. Both homes are next to a home built by the original family owner's oldest son (TR Jr. and James Jr., FDR's half brother).
155. Both had a son named after him serve in a legislature (TR Jr. in the state legislature in New York, FDR Jr. in Congress) (James also served in Congress).
156. Both had his namesake son defeated running for governor of New York. (TR Jr. almost defeated the incumbent Al Smith in 1924. He got 48 percent of the vote and won all the counties in the state except Albany and New York City, controlled and probably stolen by the Tammany Hall machine. If he had been elected governor he might have used this as a stepping stone to the presidency, as FDR did later. If so, we might have never have heard of FDR, who ran for governor to take Smith's place when he ran for president in 1928.)
157. Both liked to ride horses,
158. swim, and
159. roughhouse with the children and numerous cousins in similar outdoor settings at Oyster Bay and Campobello Island where the families spent summers.
160. Both had a parent who played piano.
161. Both liked to read and tell stories to children.

162. Both had four sons serve in the armed forces.

163. Both were great collectors of varied objects.

164. Both had at least three sons serve in WW II (in fact, all seven living sons served) who

165. were decorated in World War I or World War II.

166. Both had a son become a brigadier general in World War II.

167. Both were defeated in a presidential election (TR in 1912 and FDR as a vice presidential candidate in 1920).

168. Both had wealthy parents whose money left them free to pursue interests and political careers without having to earn a living.

169. Both had more than one child write a book on the life of their family.

170. Both fought and were fought by Tammany Hall and Hearst political machines.

171. Both lived and advocated the strenuous life, and were described as overgrown children.

172. Both had been told by doctors to avoid physical exercise and exertion, and both ignored this advice (FDR during his polio recovery and TR, in 1880, who had what was diagnosed as a heart problem).

173. Both had a vice president fifty-two years old when inaugurated (Fairbanks, Wallace).

174. Both ran in a presidential election where the Republican Party candidate received only 8 electoral votes, the two worst defeats for that party (Taft—1912, Landon—1936).

175. Both planned and talked about going to Africa after leaving office.

176. Both had a son or son-in-law commit suicide (Kermit; John Boettiger, ex-husband of Anna). (NOTE: there appears to be conflicting beliefs as to whether Kermit died of natural causes or took his own life.)

177. Both were told by doctors that they might have to spend the rest of their life in a wheelchair (TR—1918; FDR—1921).

178. Both were preceded by a Republican president

179. who had been named after his father,

180. was fifty-four at his inauguration,

181. and died in New York.

182. Both were followed by six similar presidential elections: First election: (1908/48) President of their same party elected with name beginning with *T* (Taft and Truman).

183. Second election: (1912/52) President of opposite party elected, born in a Confederate state, grew up in another state, who had been a college president (Wilson and Ike) and who was

184. Third election: (1916/56) reelected and suffered a stroke in his second term.

185. Fourth election: (1920/60) President of their party elected (Harding and Kennedy), who died suddenly in office and whose memory was later tarnished by sexual scandal, succeeded by a vice president born in a rural frame house now open to the public (Coolidge and Johnson), who had many personal idiosyncrasies, two children, and who was

186. Fifth election: (1924/64) reelected and surprisingly did not run again; then died in the final January of the next administration, in their early sixties (sixty and sixty-four), buried in a rural country cemetery, and survived by their wife for twenty years.

187. Sixth election: (1928/68) Republican president elected who left office tainted after a national tragedy (Great Depression and Watergate) . . . followed by a Democrat elected (FDR and Carter) who had attained prominence as a governor, had an activist wife, meddlesome mother, and served with a vice president who later ran for president (Truman, Wallace, and Mondale).

188. Theodore was fifty and a half years old when he left office, and Franklin was fifty-one years and one month old when he began his presidency.

189. TR instigated the Panama Canal and visited the site during construction. FDR was the first president to go through the canal.

190. The first time a president left the country while in office was in November 1906 when TR went to the Canal. The time both the president and vice president were out of the country at the same time was October 1936 when FDR and Garner left.

191. On both occasions, the president was on U.S. soil out of the forty-eight states. (TR was in a territory owned by the United States and FDR was on board a navy ship, technically U.S. "soil."

192. TR was the first president to fly, and FDR was the first presidential candidate to fly to a convention.

193. Even though there are many similarities, one common thing is different. TR's last name is pronounced "Roo" as in "roof," and the FDR side of the family pronounced the name as in "rose."

194. FDR was the only president to serve more than eight years. TR probably had the best chance of any other to serve more, but he did not run in 1908 when he probably could have won. He had earlier pledged not to run again and felt bound by the pledge despite large sentiment that he run anyway. He ran in 1912, but President Taft controlled the convention and was renominated.

He created a new party, which was considered to be an attempt to destroy the Republican Party. By splitting the Republican vote, he allowed the Democrat Wilson to be elected. Because of the animosity aroused in fellow Republicans, he could not be nominated in 1916. He should have just waited until then when the lackluster Hughes was almost elected. After the nation went to war in 1917, Roosevelt again became very popular, and many believed he would have been a sure nominee in 1920, which was a Republican year, but his health failed quickly in early 1919.

195. Both died, old beyond their years,
196. in their early sixties (sixty and sixty-three) and
197. survived a son and
198. survived a brother or half brother.
199. Both were buried in New York state,
200. about an hour's drive from Manhattan.
201. Both were survived by their wife,
202. who lived at least seventeen additional years,
203. to be at least fifteen years older than their husband,
204. to be at least seventy-eight (eighty-seven and seventy-eight),
205. and died in New York.
206. In a listing of last words both said sentences of five words (TR: "Please put out the lights." FDR: "I have a terrific headache.").
207. In a listing of the wealth of the presidents the two closest to $1 million were the Roosevelts.
208. Even though they were sworn in as president thirty-two years apart, both could say they received advice from former president Cleveland. He met with TR in 1901 and had told FDR as a five-year-old in 1887 that he hoped he would never be president.
209. TR proposed a league of nations to preserve peace. FDR laid the cornerstone during his administration and set into motion the organization of the United Nations.
210. During much of FDR's life, the man he most admired was TR.
211. Both have been portrayed in over twenty movies and TV shows.
212. Both have aircraft carriers named after them.
213. Historians in the top ranking of presidents consistently rate both Roosevelts high, in the top ten. There have been various polls in the past several years rating the presidents of the United States. The *U.S. News and World Report* on November 21, 1983 reported that 864 historians rated Franklin second and Theodore fifth. In a 1982 poll by the *Chicago Tribune* they ranked three and four. In a 1962 poll they were ranked third and sixth. In 1996 they were number 3 (FDR) and 7 (TR), and 3 and 5 in 2000 according to the

Wall Street Journal. The C-Span Television Network survey of fifty-eight presidential historians reported in February 2000 that FDR was rated number 2 and TR was number 4. Lincoln is always at the top with Washington, if not FDR, at number 2.

Index